Film Studies: A Global Introduction reroutes film studies from its Euro-American focus and canon in order to introduce students to a medium that has always been global but has become differently and insistently so in the digital age.

Glyn Davis, Kay Dickinson, Lisa Patti and Amy Villarejo's approach encourages readers to think about film holistically by looking beyond the textual analysis of key films. In contrast it engages with other vital areas, such as financing, labor, marketing, distribution, exhibition, preservation, and politics, reflecting contemporary aspects of cinema production and consumption worldwide.

Key features of the book include:

- clear definitions of the key terms at the foundation of film studies
- coverage of the work of key thinkers, explained in their social and historical context
- a broad range of relevant case studies that reflect the book's approach to global cinema, from Italian "white telephone" films to Mexican wrestling films
- innovative and flexible exercises to help readers enhance their understanding of the histories, theories, and examples introduced in each chapter
- an extensive Interlude introducing readers to formal analysis through the careful explication and application of key terms
- a detailed discussion of strategies for writing about cinema.

Film Studies: A Global Introduction will appeal to students studying film today and aspiring to work in the industry, as well as those eager to understand the world of images and screens in which we all live.

Glyn Davis is Chancellor's Fellow and Reader in the School of Design at the University of Edinburgh, UK. He is the co-editor, with Gary Needham, of *Warhol in Ten Takes* (2013), and the author of monographs on *Superstar: The Karen Carpenter Story* (2009) and *Far from Heaven* (2011).

Kay Dickinson is an Associate Professor of Film Studies at Concordia University, Canada. She is the editor of *Movie Music: A Film Reader* (2002) and the author of *Off Key: When Film and Music Won't Work Together* (2008).

Lisa Patti is an Assistant Professor in the Media and Society Program at Hobart and William Smith Colleges, USA.

Amy Villarejo is Professor in the Department of Performing and Media Arts at Cornell University, USA. Her books include *Ethereal Queer* (2014), *Film Studies: The Basics*, second edition (2013), and *Lesbian Rule: Cultural Criticism and the Value of Desire* (2003).

"Finally, there's a Film Studies text that fills the gaps left by other texts – this work proposes to treat film as an international phenomenon rather than the standard European/American model. It also includes much-needed material relative to film as an industry and an art form. Finally, it contains a discussion of the most pressing problem throughout film history: the deterioration, preservation and restoration of film stock, the delicate physical tools of the genre. It's a must-read for casual moviegoers as well as for serious students of the film as an integral factor in the formation of international cultural identity."

Dennis M. Maher, *University of Texas at Arlington, USA*

"*Film Studies: A Global Introduction* is a refreshingly contemporary approach to the study of film. In its embracing of global cinema as a given, rather than simply a discourse, this volume works to enable students to understand documentary, experimental, orphan and narrative film, from Hollywood, Bollywood, East Asian, Latin American and European cinemas, in terms of their textual characteristics as well as the industrial and experiential issues of production, distribution, marketing and the criticism contexts which condition the ways in which we come to appreciate and understand them. Davis, Dickinson, Patti and Villarejo's book is wonderfully well written and organised, channelling a sound understanding of the concerns of undergraduate students and their teachers, introducing not just the world of cinema but the intriguing and fascinating world of film studies as it expands and accelerates in the new millennium."

Deane Williams, *Monash University, Australia*

"This is the perfect handbook for students eager to discover the world of cinema and film studies. It is an astute introduction that will guide them through the various stages and dimensions of contemporary cinema landscapes and offers them the conceptual and analytic tools to tackle the questions these issues raise. The non-classical and fresh approach to a wide variety of topics in film studies will fascinate young readers. It is not only highly accessible for student audiences but also a good read for wider audiences interested in cinema as a cultural, political, aesthetical, industrial, experiential, phenomenon.

All too often introductory handbooks pretend to be global, but still are very Anglo-American in their paradigms, approaches and cases. With this volume, the authors – all established scholars in the field – manage to avoid that pitfall, delivering an excellent introduction to indeed global film studies.

The scope is wide ranging: documentary, fiction, production, distribution, exhibition, reception, archiving, and all topics are approached with the latest state of the art insights from the field. The book equally covers major recent developments of the medium in the digital age.

The structure is logical and crystal clear, as it should be for an introduction. Each chapter comes with excellent pedagogical features such as introductions, summaries, boxed features, exercises, definitions, key terms, case studies outside of the obvious. And the chapters are at their best when giving detailed description of evolutions, processes and cases. Furthermore, the authors not only analyse and tell, they also teach and show students how to write about film.

In short, a timely handbook, a welcome complement to existing English language introductory handbooks."

Philippe Meers, *University of Antwerp, Belgium*

FILM STUDIES

A Global Introduction

Glyn Davis, Kay Dickinson, Lisa Patti, and Amy Villarejo

Routledge
Taylor & Francis Group

NEW YORK AND LONDON

First published 2015
by Routledge
2 Park Square, Milton Park, Abingdon, Oxon OX14 4RN

and by Routledge
711 Third Avenue, New York, NY 10017

Routledge is an imprint of the Taylor & Francis Group, an informa business

British Library Cataloguing in Publication Data
A catalogue record for this book is available from the British Library

Library of Congress Cataloging in Publication Data
Davis, Glyn (Reader in Screen Studies)
Film studies : a global introduction / Glyn Davis, Kay Dickinson, Lisa Patti, Amy Villarejo.
pages cm
1. Motion pictures. 2. Motion picture industry. I. Dickinson, Kay, 1972- II. Patti, Lisa. III. Villarejo, Amy. IV. Title.
PN1995.D34 2014
791.43--dc23
2014016429

ISBN: 978-0-415-73434-9 (hbk)
ISBN: 978-1-405-85918-9 (pbk)
ISBN: 978-1-315-75419-2 (ebk)

Typeset in Helvetica Neue Lt Std Condensed 10/13 pt
by Fakenham Prepress Solutions, Fakenham, Norfolk NR21 8NN

Printed and bound in the United States of America by Sheridan Books, Inc. (a Sheridan Group Company).

CONTENTS

ILLUSTRATIONS

The images below have been reproduced with kind permission. While every effort has been made to trace copyright holders and obtain permission, this has not been possible in all cases. Any omissions brought to our attention will be remedied in future editions.

SECTION I

WHY ARE MOVIES MADE?

INTRODUCTION

All films are made for a reason, perhaps for many reasons. This is true irrespective of such variables as the running time of the film, where it was made, how much it cost, and how many people were involved in creating it. It is true whether or not the film was completed, or was seen by small or large audiences. If you have made a film yourself, even if just on a mobile phone, your own reasons for doing so will have driven you. Perhaps you wanted to entertain yourself, your family, your friends. Perhaps you had a story that you needed to tell, a message that you desired to get across. From the lowest budget to the highest, the production of all cinema is spurred into action by a range of diverse imperatives. This first section of Film Studies: A Global Introduction introduces five distinct reasons for making films: to entertain, to express yourself, to inform, to put across a political message, and to make money. These reasons for making cinema do not operate independently. They often work together in complex ways, some of which we highlight and explore throughout these five chapters.

The first chapter examines cinema as a form of entertainment. The notion that films often entertain us (or at least attempt to) seems to be a straightforward and obvious one. Filmmakers may specifically desire to create movies in order to entertain: to make us laugh, weep, scream and cower with fear, and so on. However, once we begin to scrutinize it, the concept of entertainment is revealed as complicated, supported by a raft of interlocking ideas that it is valuable to unpack. What exactly is entertainment? Can audiences ever agree on what they find entertaining? How exactly can a filmmaker manage to achieve the goal of entertaining people? How are forms of culture designated as "entertainment" different from instances of "high culture" such as opera? Why is "high culture" often characterized as "difficult" but "enlightening" – and why is much cinema not seen in this way? In addition to addressing these questions, Chapter 1 also explores the association between entertainment and leisure time. If cinema is something that audiences pay money to consume in their "down time," then it necessarily fits into particular understandings of how the working day and week are structured, the ways in which work and leisure are pitted against each other, and the things and experiences that working people should spend their wages on.

Chapter 2 considers a variety of ways in which cinema can serve as a medium of self-expression. Filmmakers may want to make movies in order to transmit their voice, their take on the world, to viewers. (There is no reason, of course, that such films cannot also be entertaining!) This chapter invites you to consider what it means for a film to have an author who wants to express their perspective, and the different modes in which such authorship can operate. In addition to a consideration of auteurism, the approach to cinema which positions the director as the key individual leaving a distinctive mark on all of their work, we introduce alternative frameworks: cinema as a form of artisanal practice; filmmaking as collaborative and politically motivated. We also examine in detail forms of cinema that employ particular technologies and/or draw on distinctive aesthetics, and the forms of self-expression that these enable: the "essay film," amateur films and home movies, first-person digital films.

The production of films may also be driven by the desire to inform, to educate, to raise awareness. Chapter 3 introduces this topic through an extensive exploration of the varieties of nonfiction film and documentary that have been produced across cinema history, up to and including more recent manifestations of "reality" footage online and on television. Attempts to categorize and understand this body of cinema by film scholars Michael Renov and Bill Nichols are introduced. The ethics of making "informative" cinema are examined, as are the possibilities of manipulating, altering and restaging material in order to convey particular messages. In order to provide you with a flavor of the diversity of nonfiction and documentary cinema, you will be introduced, amongst other examples, to figures including Robert Flaherty and Jane Fonda (significant individuals in the history of "informative cinema" for very different reasons), to examples of Third Cinema with clear political intent, and to sex hygiene films which attempted to alter the relationships that viewers had with their bodies.

As the discussion of Third Cinema in Chapter 3 makes clear, political imperatives are a major reason for the making of many movies. Chapter 4 picks up this topic and explores it by adopting a broad perspective on the relationship between cinema and politics: indeed, the chapter opens by asking you to consider whether all films, to some extent, are political. Chapter 3 examines the connections between documentary and propaganda; in Chapter 4, this subject is reframed and expanded via a consideration of the many ways in which film (both fiction and nonfiction) can operate as propaganda, and the forms that propaganda may take. The subtle relationships between entertainment and political messages are also considered. Whereas blatant political messages can often be easily detected – indeed, this may be the intention of the filmmakers – in other cases, messages are more subtly advanced. Chapter 4 addresses this subtlety by introducing the concept of ideology, and the various tactics that filmmakers may employ in order to convey ideological content and arguments. As we identify, this may not operate solely at the level of plot, narrative and character, but through particular aesthetic choices.

Finally, Chapter 5 examines cinema's role as a commodity. Filmmakers, and many others involved in cinema as an industry and a business, may want to create films in order to make money. The fact that films are bought and sold – that audiences exchange their cash for the experience of consuming – reveals cinema's commodity status. But in order to comprehend the significance of this, it is vital to identify the ways in which films operate as goods that are traded internationally. This chapter introduces you to some of the main tenets of capitalism, such as how money and profit work. It also outlines how markets operate, including how they expand and contract, and how privatization works. Organizations that assist with trade, and thus make the existence of certain markets possible (such as the International Monetary Fund, or IMF), are outlined. Over the course of cinema's history, many large companies – some in the form of what are known as conglomerates or multinational corporations – have made a great deal of money out of film as a commodity. Strategies employed by these corporations, including horizontal and vertical integration, are introduced.

By the end of Section I, you will have built up a complex understanding of the various different and interlocking imperatives behind the production of cinema. You will recognize and understand the burning desire a documentary maker has to record a particular topic, what might drive an avant-garde filmmaker to set up an isolated studio, the prospective millions that a major producer hopes a specific movie will reap at the global box office. And yet, despite the introduction and examination in these five chapters of a host of films from countries around the world, a script has not yet been written, a frame of film has not yet been shot. Section II of this book takes you on to the next stage, beyond Section I's spurs to action: the film starts to be assembled.

CHAPTER ONE
CINEMA AS ENTERTAINMENT

Let us assume – you are reading this book after all – that you enjoy cinema. And, moreover, that you find it *entertaining*. For many people, entertainment is an expectation that draws them to new films or brings them back to old favorites. It might help explain why crowds have queued round the block for movies, why there have been stampedes when beloved film stars appear at premieres. Entertainment can come in the form of laughter, tension, empathizing with a victim, even being witlessly scared or inconsolably upset. But why is it that we look to films for entertainment? Should we make this presumption about their content? After all, movies are capable of being many things besides. The next few chapters look into some of those other reasons why films exist, such as their potential to inform us or to function as political tools. But, even from those perspectives, the aim is often to entertain, which suggests that there are reasons we stick so closely to that function.

This chapter argues that we judge something to be entertaining based on certain preconditions, habits and assumptions, and that investigating what those are is an important mission for students of film. We certainly do not want to ruin your fun here by pulling apart the magic cinema weaves. The aim is to arrive at a deeper understanding of the medium in order to empathize with how and why large, diverse groups of people are most definitely entertained by movies. We want to celebrate the complex ways in which films entertain, as well as look into their methods and reasons for doing so. Let us move beyond mere surface reactions. Adding these considerations to your involvement with cinema will help you enjoy it more, rather than less.

WHAT WE WILL DO IN CHAPTER 1

- Appreciate how difficult defining entertainment can be, what a contested terrain entertainment is, and why that is so.
- Interrogate the prejudice that has often accompanied academic research into film entertainment, especially when entertainment is diametrically opposed to "high culture".
- Speculate on whether our need for escapist entertainment is precipitated by our experiences of work.
- Closely analyze what it means that entertainment is largely understood as something that can be bought and sold for profit, as well as explore some alternatives to this model.

BY THE END OF CHAPTER 1 YOU SHOULD BE ABLE TO

- Describe the social status and value of film entertainment, giving accounts of why it is thought about in these ways.
- Recognize how and why film is primarily constructed to be entertaining.
- Understand how dominant film entertainment emerges from particular labor and commercial histories and be aware of various other possible ways of producing and accessing it.

DEFINING ENTERTAINMENT

Here is the first question we run up against in the study of entertainment: what exactly is it? One of the characteristics often attributed to entertainment is that it is a distraction, a setting aside of time. Although not always the case, cinematic variants of entertainment frequently proclaim themselves to function in this way. What we will note as we move through this chapter is that "distraction" takes on both positive and negative connotations. And time is a precious, finite thing to many. So, how we spend it becomes something we debate in earnest as a society.

Cinematic entertainment might also be determined by its effect on us, be it escapism, absorption or amazement, all of which have the capacity to contradict each other. Peruse the selection of posters in Figures 1.1–1.4 for some of Australia's highest-grossing movies. You will soon notice that the promotional language and iconography used to advertise these films leans towards fun, enjoyment and freedom, rather than education, information and enlightenment. Very clearly, the image the advertisers wish to create is one where you can leave your worries at the door and have an uncomplicated good time. This may seem a given for popular cinema, but that supposition actually runs counter to many of the ways culture has functioned around the world. For instance, in a host of African historical contexts, it has been anathema to create "meaningless" culture, something uprooted from everyday practices and value or put together primarily for profit. Popular dance and song do not stand alone, at a distance from social bonding or ritualistic activity. Why would something like cinema want to exist far away from the troubles and concerns found in our daily lives?

1.1, 1.2, 1.3, and 1.4 Posters for some of Australia's best-loved movies: *Happy Feet* (George Miller, 2006, courtesy of Warner Bros./The Kobal Collection), *Muriel's Wedding* (P.J. Hogan, 1994, courtesy of CIBY 2000/The Kobal Collection), *Moulin Rouge* (Baz Luhrman, 2001, courtesy of 20th Century Fox/The Kobal Collection), and *The Adventures Of Priscilla, Queen Of The Desert* (Stephan Elliott, 1994, courtesy of Polygram/Australian Film Finance/The Kobal Collection).

However, even if we side with the multitude of film fans who agree that entertainment should be a prerequisite, we all have different notions of *how entertainment is achieved*. Look again at those posters (or any other similar promotional material for films), and you may well want to contest their claims. Any discussions you will have had with friends about your film tastes over the years will easily confirm the fact that ideas about what we each find entertaining conflict. Part of the fun in talking about movies is trying to convince other people of our own beliefs about what is enjoyable and what is not. But the point still stands that we often do not like the same films as our grandparents, as people of a different gender, or citizens from other countries.

Then we have to weigh up how other experiential factors make it hard to squarely determine whether something is entertaining. For example, would the kind of film integrated into a simulator ride at an amusement arcade or fairground be enjoyable if accessed through Netflix? Would we be less likely to watch *Avatar* (James Cameron, 2009) on a mobile device than in a 3-D-equipped IMAX theatre? The numerous formats and viewing opportunities available to us alter the degree to which a movie is regarded as entertainment too.

Ultimately, as these simple examples suggest, who we are, where we come from and where we happen to be now hold great sway over whether something successfully entertains us. When we bear these factors in mind, we extend film studies into thought-provoking, inter-disciplinary terrains. We cannot isolate a movie from its social context to discern what makes it pleasurable. If we could, genres like Westerns would be as popular today as they were in the 1950s, when scores were made each year to meet audience demand. The very fact that what we deem entertaining changes so dramatically over time and space makes understanding these definitions (as mobile rather than fixed) even more pressing to students of cinema. Discrepancies of opinion reveal how complicated and variable entertainment is. Fluctuating social needs and trends can very much mutate its personality.

Such disparities of opinion are no reason to give up on defining entertainment. On the contrary, the very fact of these disagreements reveals an awful lot and maybe this is where the pleasure of analysis starts. Although it is impossible for all of us to settle on a solid, one-dimensional exemplar of entertainment, there is a lot to be learnt from evaluating the discussions critics and fans have about the matter. These inconsistencies are crucial to the very fabric of entertainment culture.

This is because one central attribute of entertainment, which renders it so hard to define, is that it is usually premised on the idea of *personal choice*. It defeats the purpose if we are being told what is and is not enjoyable. We wield our freedom of choice very decisively during our precious leisure time. If we are bored by a movie, we might leave the theatre or switch it off, perhaps tell a whole host of people why we did not like it. We exercise certain individual rights when we encounter entertainment.

Concurrently, film entertainment is often best appreciated when we share it, when it is a social rather than solitary amusement. Another core implication of the word "entertainment" is something that appeals to large and varied groups of people. The label of entertainment cannot be used in any long-term or meaningful fashion unless numerous fans are involved. Films can bond communities, consolidate identities and also, conversely, divide people. These uses of entertainment undoubtedly pre-date the invention of cinema. For instance, think of the Roman imperial dictum about giving the people at large "bread and circuses". This practice reveals just how long rulers have been factoring entertainment into their management of our communities. Furthermore, there are elements of political

CASE STUDY: IMAX

Virtuosity and wonderment have been central to movie entertainment since the invention of cinema. The earliest filmmakers, such as Auguste and Louis Lumière and Georges Méliès, capitalized upon their audience's astonishment over the capabilities of the medium, whether through its realism or its aptitude for amusing trickery. Scale has also played a major role in how cinema attracts its audiences. Technologies like Cinerama (a precursor to IMAX) increased the screen size and its surrounding arc to draw viewers more convincingly into what was projected up there. Blockbuster movies routinely try to outdo each other by incorporating the biggest and best set pieces and the most up-to-date special effects.

One type of film that trades vociferously on what is often dubbed "spectacle" is IMAX, a format that can be clearly projected at dimensions larger than those available to typical cinemas. An abbreviation of Image Maximum, IMAX evolved through a series of multi-screen, multi-projector displays at various international expos, settling into its first permanent theatre in Toronto in 1971. IMAX movies have less to do with intricate plots, intellectual themes or consummate acting ability than with making us feel closer to the action. The enormous screens in IMAX theatres and their movies' frequent use of technologies like 3D and advanced surround sound aim to boost cinema's visceral potential. Audiences momentarily become more physically involved in the depicted world, sometimes even giddy, while viewing. The impact of IMAX films is something we actually feel through our seats and in our stomachs when a camera suddenly lurches in an unexpected direction.

1.5 An audience in an IMAX theatre. Courtesy of The LIFE Images Collection/Getty Images.

Yet it is not as if we truly believe we are actually situated within the movie for one minute. Much of the entertainment value derives from a careful balance of enjoying the immersive experience corporeally, and marveling, with critical distance, at the technology that can achieve such effects. In this respect (and the same goes for big action movies), we will want to think about these movies' popularity in line with this chapter's upcoming proposals about respect for specialized labor skills.

At the same time, we are somewhat in awe of the technology. Here we encounter a tendency within entertainment, which this chapter will later flesh out: that entertainment situates us within a particular social arrangement. We rarely come close to the majesty that IMAX creates, neither in our regular lives, nor in our everyday film viewing activities. IMAX attendance figures as a special event, especially as so few of us can afford a trip to one of their large city-based theatres. Admiration is pivotal to IMAX's entertainment value, but we have to remember that this technology comes at a high price. So, too, do the subjects that are selected for IMAX films. Along with the expensive upkeep of their cavernous theatres, the hard- and software required is so expensive that IMAX output rarely runs for more than forty minutes. This, along with the company's need for exhibition longevity in order to recoup costs, means that documentaries are often favored because of their potential for expanded shelf lives. IMAX does not waste its effects on any old subject. These movies are shot in the most impossible of locations; IMAX has taken us under water, to the Antarctic and into space. Such choices perpetuate a number of responses. One is a sense of amazement not just at the technology, but also at the extremely out-of-the-ordinary places to which IMAX can transport us. The seating in an IMAX theatre is even arranged so that, wherever we are, we have to look up, intensifying the sense of awe we feel in the presence of these impossible feats of science and travel.

This hierarchical relationship is something we can rewardingly interpret through the ideas presented in cultural activist Guy Debord's 1967 *The Society of the Spectacle*. Debord's notion of spectacle is much more all-encompassing than the one that has just been described. For him, "The spectacle is not a collection of images, but a social relation among people, mediated by images."[1] In this instance, the social relation is one where we pay to be amazed by something that is set up to make us feel inferior. Why is it that we are so thoroughly entertained by something that so obviously refuses to massage our egos? By putting these locations and technologies on a pedestal, we are not drawn, Debord would argue, closer to them; we are alienated from them. The entertainment value of an IMAX movie is how it plays cat and mouse with us. It promises to inform and thus allow us mastery of a topic. But then it sets up a hierarchy, which leaves us at a disadvantage. This liaison, for someone following Debord, might serve as the very embodiment of our relationship to entertainment: always promising to give us something to make us feel better, never really fulfilling this so we repeatedly come back wanting more.

What function, though, does the superiority of the technology play? Given how adept IMAX is at rustling up a sense of wonderment, it is unsurprising that the format found an early home in expos like Osaka's in 1971. One key agenda of expos and world fairs has been to show off a country or a corporation's technological advancement and IMAX excels on this front. Entertainment, therefore, can carry all sorts of political messages. Similarly, uneven power relations and policies of domination can be spotted in other IMAX practices. For example, we need to consider the monopoly status the IMAX Company wields, owning as it does the development, production, post-production, distribution and exhibition facilities for the format.

The IMAX Company has proven adept at spotting gaps in the market that they can exploit, which shows (as the final part of this chapter will) the way the drive for profit helps shape where we find our entertainment – also revealing which audiences it is most eager to impress. A good number of IMAX's theatres are situated in science museums (like those in Suzhou, China or Bogota, Columbia), meaning that they can tap into the large audiences provided by school trips. Association with a museum links IMAX to that rare and desirable entity – entertainment that is also educational – which fits in well with their predilection for documentary. Before IMAX's arrival, films had not really made much money from museums, so this was a new market to conquer. At the same time, IMAX has expanded outwards into big budget feature films, with movies such as *Polar Express: An IMAX 3D Experience* (Robert Zemeckis, 2004) and *Avatar* now being simultaneously released in this format. This, in turn, attracts more customers to the Company's theatres because these types of movie have long been dependable entertainment draws.

control at work here. "Bread and circuses" implies currying political favor and social stability not just by feeding a population, but also by entertaining them. Governments perform different versions of this principle in how they do or do not support entertainment financially. Here they, and the other commercial companies that make our cinema, may be addressing their needs alongside ours, maybe with the accent more on their own interests. As the Cuban filmmaker and theorist Tomás Gutiérrez Alea observes, mainstream cinema is "popular, not in the sense that it was an expression of the *people*, of the sectors most oppressed and most exploited by an alienating system of production. Rather, [movies attract] an undifferentiated public, a majority avid for illusions."[2] It is worth noting here that, in English, the word entertainment derives from the Latin verb *tenere*, which means, amongst other things, "to hold". We can simultaneously read this etymological trace as a restrictive action (holding back or too tightly) or a more positively engaging, even nurturing one (holding one's attention or holding in a protective sense). Is entertainment a civic right or a successful tool of persuasion? The centuries-old tradition of "bread and circuses" suggests entertainment is certainly not unmotivated, pure and unhindered by social messages and ideals. But what else might it be? Answering these questions is all the more crucial because of the wide social reach of cinematic entertainment and will be fleshed out even more fully in Chapter 4 on "Film and politics".

You might imagine that the populist appeal of entertainment has made it ripe for analysis over the years. In actual fact, the very opposite has been the case, with scholars seemingly reluctant to delve into the subject out of a kind of snobbery. Material that fascinates broad cross-sections of society has often been deemed "lowest common denominator" output, unworthy of intellectual attention. It is to these reservations that the chapter now turns.

EXERCISE

Let us test out some of these debates about entertainment in relation to your own feelings about cinema. We are presuming that, by picking up a textbook on the subject, you believe films are worth studying. However, it is just as likely that you have encountered people who think this pursuit is a frivolous waste of time, a "Mickey Mouse" subject (as if Mickey Mouse is not an incredibly influential cultural icon). One of the key reasons why they feel this way is down to cinema's relationship with entertainment. Take some time to lay out your thoughts on the following prompts:

- Has anyone ever belittled your interest in seriously studying film by saying "isn't that just sitting round and watching movies"? How do you respond to that? And why would it seem wrong to just sit around and watch movies as a student?
- What other negative comments have you encountered about film studies? Write a list of these and then generate cogent arguments against them. These answers will help you to make some of the debates about "mere entertainment" seem more personally relevant.
- What subjects do people think are worth studying and why? What do these disciplines have that film does not and are these fair value judgements to make?
- Do you know many people who studied film theory at school, college or university thirty years ago? If not, why do you think that was the case? Are entertainment and education irreconcilable?

"MERE" ENTERTAINMENT

One of the most respected books on cinema and our current topic is film history professor Richard Dyer's *Only Entertainment*, a study whose title invokes the typical denigration of the subject. Although it is a canonical book in the field, it is more an anthology of previously dispersed essays focusing on idiosyncratic examples (like Lana Turner and Elizabeth Taylor) than a sustained discussion of the concept of entertainment as a whole. This fact suggests that entertainment still warrants a lot more sustained attention from film scholars. Why the gap? In his first two introductory chapters, Dyer offers some perspectives on how this has transpired. He observes that entertainment has historically been the victim of attacks from all academic quarters, whether it is the aesthetic conservatives who do not think entertainment merits our efforts, or the leftists who declaim its corrosive and numbing effects on our populations. We will return for more from them in a minute.

Let us first consider the aesthetic conservatives. Their prejudice against entertainment often derives from its supposed opposition to "culture," a stand-off that casts entertainment as somehow inferior. Culture has many meanings, impressively summed up by one of its most perceptive analysts, the British writer Raymond Williams:

> We use the word culture in … two senses: to mean a whole way of life – the common meanings; to mean the arts and learning – the special processes of discovery and creative effort. Some writers reserve the word for one or other of these senses; I insist on both, and on the significance of their conjunction.[3]

While you may be more interested in the interplay between the two definitions, conservatives are often most drawn to the second, which can presume something of an elite status that looks down on easy, uncomplicated "entertainment". This take on culture, often further described as "high culture," comprises a collection of material and practices whose gatekeepers have asserted its meaningfulness and richness at the expense of other variants. They might, for instance, favor classical music over country and western, or Chekhov's plays over *telenovelas*. These selections often shut the door on a particular kind of entertainment. Let us think, for a minute, about poetry, which has featured centrally in school curricula around the world for a very long time. Why is it that the more blatantly populist and commercial culture of cinema is only now beginning to creep into the high school classroom, even though it is over a hundred years old? The distinction suggests that these very qualities of populism and commercialism carry negative connotations, which distance them from educational value. In this book, we argue, like Raymond Williams, that there is an enormous amount to learn by probing the things large cross-sections of society love, that our studies should not be constrained solely to the appreciation of difficult materials.

We would also like to stress that it seems somewhat preposterous to distance entertainment and "high culture" from each other in terms of how they move us. If we follow another definition of culture, the broader one, which insists that culture means any shared attitudes and values, then entertainment is culture too. We do "high culture" a great disservice if we presume that it cannot entertain us. The distinction is perhaps wrought in how the two categories are presented to us, which has much to do with the demographics that typically favor each.

Entertainment has frequently been conflated with the mass or popular media, which has traditionally been understood as both lowbrow and working class. There is more than a tinge of class bigotry to the avoidance of this subject matter, then. Entertainment, while often highly sophisticated, rarely wishes to be elitist. It usually wants a broad consumer base, so is not particularly interested in cultivating exclusive tastes that could ostracize large swathes of potential audiences. If we refuse to uphold these distinctions and launch into a less biased study of entertainment, we gain a fresh picture on what cinema is and does. Theorists of entertainment often deliberately avoid trying to squeeze certain popular texts into the **canons** (accepted catalogues of great works) that have excluded them for so long. They would rather dissolve these hierarchies than try and argue that an Adam Sandler movie should hold a position in "high culture" equal to a painting by Picasso. Instead, many see the study of entertainment as a fascinating insight into the choices people make and, as a consequence, our social priorities and aspirations. The focus falls more on curiosity about why Adam Sandler is well-loved, rather than battling to insist that certain people should love him when they refuse to. At the same time, an investigation of popular entertainment can raise important questions about why particular cultural forms are considered more worthy of serious attention than others. These inquiries might, in turn, expose particular class or gender biases.

As an example, let us take a deeper look into what people write about within film studies. There are definitely more books dedicated to the French activist auteur Jean-Luc Godard (the director of *À Bout de*

Souffle (*Breathless*) (1960) and *Week End* (1967)) than there are to family adventure films, despite the fact that the latter are more widely seen and enjoyed. No one is trying to argue that either of these groups of movies is more meaningful than the other here. The point is to break down why more ink has been spilt on Godard than the family adventure genre. In his contribution to the anthology *High Pop: Making Culture into Popular Entertainment*, humanities academic Jim Collins argues that this kind of pecking order stems from European **Romanticism** and has been kept alive by the advocates of **modernism**. Romanticism was an influential cultural and intellectual movement arising out of mid-nineteenth century Europe. One of its many characteristics is a partiality for personal, emotional response that is often in conflict with dominant customs. Modernism came to prominence later, in the late nineteenth and early twentieth century, stretching, within cinema, well into the 1960s. Godard, who has just been mentioned, is often fitted into this designation. Among other things, modernist thinkers and artists have striven to find new and challenging ways of understanding and representing the world. In Collins' eyes, both movements favor an active, interpretative and philosophical response from consumers above all else. Going to a difficult three-hour opera or art movie might challenge many of us, rather than creating an easy, comfortable experience.

Not all of us will want to spend our time this way or fully understand what is going on. Divisions in audience expectations are drawn and particular hierarchies are created around those who do and those who do not. People who invest in this schematization of culture thus gain a sense of satisfaction and even status from their responses, meaning that they are often happy to perpetuate the value of such forms of distinction. It may well be that you feel similarly: that Godard's oeuvre deserves more respect than family films like *Spy Kids* (Robert Rodriguez, 2001) or *Pirates of the Caribbean* (Gore Verbinski, 2003). That decision might pivot on the very fact that Godard's work refuses to be entertaining in the same way. It deviates from conservative stylistic traditions and tackles controversial political issues. By doing so, its devotees would say that it profoundly shakes up our ways of thinking.

However, entertainment rarely sets these kinds of agenda for itself, aspires to unsettle us or pushes difficult boundaries, so it is unfair to judge family adventure films by these specific standards. It is missing the point to consider whether *Spy Kids* could have been a radical activist movie, if it only knew how. High culture is appreciated because it is professed to be "more" than entertainment. As we have seen, this only works if your checklist contains particular criteria that entertainment does not value so highly. When judged by these standards, entertainment can often fail, eliciting a derisory attitude from certain quarters.

There are important issues at stake when these kinds of decisions are made. To get to the bottom of them we shall survey the historical reasons underpinning why much cinema has been defined as "mere entertainment". Here it pays to look at the American context for a moment, influential for other incarnations of entertainment around the world. In his book *Policing Cinema: Movies and Censorship in Early Twentieth Century America*, film scholar Lee Grieveson astutely points out that entertainment was never a "natural" or "given" mode by which cinema would function. Why, ultimately, should films entertain when they could easily be purely educational or documentary? Grieveson notes that, in the United States in the 1910s, a growing concern arose about the impact of movies, most pointedly with regard to cinema's potential to incite political unrest. To further his argument, he details the substantial moral panic created by "white slave" (forced prostitution) narratives such as *Traffic in Souls* (George Loane Tucker, 1913). Film, after all, was a fairly new medium then, so no one was quite sure of the bearing it would have on its viewers. This anxiety eventually led to comprehensive legislation, including a Supreme Court ruling in 1915, which defined cinema as "harmless entertainment". These decisions to legally classify film as an amusement also excluded it from the right to freedom of speech and, most pointedly, meant it could be censored. While tighter management of a new medium may have been the ultimate aim, one side effect was a particular social classification for film. As "harmless entertainment," movies were gradually marginalized from other "serious" arenas, such as education, and all the state support (and funding) these sectors can rally. When we are exposed to histories like these, we begin to see that the trivialization of cinema is intimately tied to political control. The desire for a regulation of film content led, at this point in history, to a long-standing and limiting assumption about what cinema was best suited for.

Coming at this idea from the opposite direction, we might want to dissect the ways in which the film industry manipulates the classification of "mere entertainment". One of the assumptions we are going to argue for in this book is that all movies are socio-politically motivated in one way or another. Yet very few of them openly admit this. We might then wonder: is entertainment's prevalent claim to be "just good fun" a tactic for conveying all manner of messages to large numbers of us – and when we least expect them? Does a movie that alleges itself to be pure entertainment shirk its potential to be truly life-changing and political? Or is it instead simply hiding the fact that it is? Chapter 4 ("Film and politics") will answer these questions more fully.

Whatever the rationale for ostracizing entertainment from other dimensions of meaningful life, it is crucial, as students of film, that we do not follow this lead. As is obvious when you give it some thought, entertainment cannot dwell at a remove from serious social concerns. On the contrary, as sociologist Chris Rojek argues in his book *Leisure Theory: Principles and Practices*:

> it is in our leisure time that we are most exposed to information and policy options regarding the appropriate rights and responsibilities of active citizenship and also to news about the infringement of these conditions. Both directly and indirectly leisure experience supplies the active citizen with data streams on lifestyle options and risks. Leisure never was "free" time.[4]

Many may think of entertainment as predominantly an end in itself, but this does not disqualify its enormous impact. Entertainment soothes us, cheers us up, allows us to explore and discuss beliefs and ideals; it can motivate us and put a spring in our step. If we are to understand the world in which we live, perhaps even think about improving it, surely these effects are all essential considerations. They are not to be side-lined. Richard Dyer, particularly in his famous essay "Entertainment and Utopia" (anthologized in his book mentioned above), begins to address these issues by highlighting the powerful appeal of escapism and wish fulfilment within cinematic entertainment. One of the primary attractions of mainstream film entertainment is that it promises to take us away from where we are and give us something of what we want. In order to comprehend why this imperative is so alluring, we need to look into what we might be running from.

ENTERTAINMENT, LEISURE … AND WORK

There is a Canadian–US film called *Wavelength* (Michael Snow, 1967), which consists purely of what appears to be a slow, single, 45-minute zoom across an apartment. These images are accompanied by a minimal soundtrack dominated by a constant and barely modulating electronic drone. If you are interested, you can easily find clips from it or a complete version online. It is a classic, well-respected avant-garde film with elements of suspense, comedy and contemplation, although not according to any typical standards. Look at the viewers' commentaries on those video-sharing websites, however, and you will find descriptions like "utterly pointless" and "not here to entertain". What the average criticism of *Wavelength* will assert is that the film has wasted your time by being both boring and hard work. Relaxation and engagement are thus central to most people's understandings of entertainment. We seem to require them as counterpoint to the rest of our lives, the periods that are filled with work of some form or other (be that paid, unpaid, educational or even work on our relationships with other human beings). As a consequence, very few of us want to work at our movies in our spare time. In fact, we might be after the exact opposite. In many ways, films oblige. If we visit an actual cinema, say, there is very little demanded of us. We sit in the dark and are not compelled to contribute in an active physical or social way. The same rules apply to many movie-watching experiences, so it makes sense to find ways of analysing how these conventions affect us. The "bread and circuses" idea is certainly one approach. Does the joy that entertainment provides make the rest of life bearable enough for us not to kick up too much of a political fuss about it? We can see minor versions of this in action every time we watch, for example, an in-flight movie. The entertainment acts as a distraction from our frustrations about being in a confined space or high up in the air, and dramatically diminishes the amount of attention we demand from the on-board crew.

Unless we are airline pilots or flight attendants, we probably do not spend that much of our lives needing to be diverted from the discomforts of plane travel. However, the same logic applies to how we might deal with the ardors of our own jobs, chores and duties (airline pilot or not). Moreover, there are even thinkers who propose that entertainment is not only a strategic distraction from work, but that it also mirrors some of the exact ways in which work grinds us down. The two are linked, so, to appreciate how entertainment functions, we have to understand work too. Let us start with the basics. Firstly, the very notion of "free time" is shaped by workers' needs and bears a long legislative history of struggle towards garnering people the right not to work at certain times. Trade unions, since their inception, have been fighting for what they consider to be a basic human right: time off.

Secondly, money is a key reward, perhaps even the main motive behind why we work, and money is also what allows us to access film culture. Movies are a particularly affordable means of entertainment, in comparison to something like yachting or horse racing. Some of the United States' earliest film exhibition spaces were called nickelodeons, a direct reference to how cheap it was to enter them. Most people in the world have been able to afford a trip to the cinema or a pirated VCD (Video CD) at some point in their lives and, for those many millions of us who own television sets or internet connections, it is easy enough to access movies for free. Consequently, we should assess film entertainment according to its broad global accessibility to people on a variety of salaries.

Films are also very flexible in how they slot into our working days. A standard movie length (90–120 minutes for most western features) moulds neatly around many people's spare time after work, meals, child-care and so on. These days, working hours are even longer than they were forty years ago and often irregular. It might therefore be postulated that this trend has prompted the rise of the shorter film, as exemplified by the YouTube clip. Technologies are built into our home entertainment systems that allow us to pause even "live" films if we are busy so we can return to them later when we do have enough time. In countries such as the United States, well into the 1960s and only phasing out in the 1980s, programmes in movie theatres functioned on continuous loops, meaning that you could arrive whenever you wanted and then watch until you reached your individual starting point. As these

1.6 *Wavelength* (Michael Snow, 1967).

1.7 *Wavelength* (Michael Snow, 1967).

concessions are not available with most live entertainment, we should take note of film's adaptive role in relation to our employment. After all, movies could easily be much longer or shorter, but the feature film format has evidently developed for a reason.

Working conditions also color who has the dominant voice in what film entertainment looks like. For instance, women predominantly work longer hours than men, especially when domestic and child-care tasks are factored in. Women enjoy less free time and, as a consequence, the movie industry frequently has male rather than female viewers in mind as its most lucrative consumer demographic. In the past, this was not the case. During the 1930s and into the 1940s, Hollywood judged one of its principal target audiences to be female, hence the dominance of "the woman's picture" during that period. A single-income household with a male breadwinner was more the norm then, freeing up many women's time during the day to visit the cinema.

Clearly factors like changes in the labor market influence the kinds of movie that are made. When we think about cinematic entertainment in these ways, within the parameters of work, we see how profoundly our tastes are shaped by our non-leisure obligations. The complaint that is so often raised against *Wavelength* is that it robs us of our precious free time. It is our work that dictates how much time we have to spare and it is the effects of work that mean we typically want to be soothed, rather than challenged, when we are not in the thick of it.

At the same time, we take a more active interest in cinematic labor than we might, at first, imagine. How many of us relish going to big fantasy or science fiction movies and wondering, "how did they do that?" Similarly, when we are astounded by how close Sean Penn's performance in *Milk* (Gus Van Sant, 2008) is to the mannerisms of the biopic's subject, what we are doing is appreciating specialized labor. We could never mimic Harvey Milk as effectively, so we respect Sean Penn's expertise when he manages it with such aplomb. At the other end of the spectrum, for those who hate it, *Wavelength* harbors everything about work that we want to run from, and none of the dazzling proficiency. Its soundtrack is tedious, repetitive, even mechanized – exactly the kinds of things we might dislike about our jobs, home duties or studies. Structurally, *Wavelength* looks like one single zoom (although actually it is not); we may feel that there is not much skill involved in such a set-up. We can neither admire nor escape work in a standard fashion when we watch *Wavelength*. For many of its aficionados, the movie is actually a satire of work-related attitudes to art, which it achieves by making us work rather than relax while watching. Ultimately, *Wavelength* refuses to pretend that film and work are not interrelated.

This is an idea that resonates through the thinking of Theodor Adorno (1903–1969). Adorno was a philosopher, sociologist, composer, critic and central member of a group of scholars originally based in Germany known as the Frankfurt School. He is perhaps most respected for his sustained expansion into the cultural sphere of Marxist theories of exploitation and alienation, ideas that will be discussed at length in Chapter 8. To speak in more manageable terms until then, Adorno both looks at the content of popular culture to argue against its detrimental effects and inquires into how it is manufactured. For him, cultural production and consumption are inextricably linked.

He notes just how ironic, even oxymoronic, it is to use a term like "the leisure industry," stating that "free time is nothing more than a shadowy continuation of labour."[5] One of the fundamental principles sustaining Adorno's work is that entertainment, within a capitalist system, is constructed so as to keep the wheels of production turning. Not only is money made from entertainment, but entertainment, at the end of a tiring session of labor, makes work the next day more bearable. Ultimately, we have jobs in order to afford the entertainment that eases us after difficulties at work, setting a vicious circle in motion that makes us both work and relax in ever more driven ways. For Adorno, this equation means that free time is anything but free. The opposition of work to leisure is a false one within the current economies. Both systems strive to generate profit in similar ways, he argues, by exploiting us both as producers and as consumers.

Adorno is also highly critical of what he considers to be the stultifying content of much popular entertainment – but he does volunteer alternatives. He is all for eroding the binary between work and leisure. This would involve making work freer and less coercive and, by the same token, promoting out-of-work activities that are demanding and educational, and that equip us to challenge the injustices of labor. We might, for instance, spend an evening watching a movie that encourages us to criticize why women are typically paid less than men (a confrontational documentary such as *Nightcleaners* (Berwick Street Collective, 1975), say) and then we can begin to better act on this inequality. If our working hours were slashed, we would have the necessary energy, so the argument goes, to appreciate more intellectually challenging material when we stopped work.

With this in mind, we might want to return to a film like *Wavelength*. To a certain extent, *Wavelength* asks us to interrogate the format of more "entertaining" movies and why we seek out that kind of distraction. The movie also makes us think about the labor of filmmaking and why we value certain (much more expensive) skills over others. What is it about *Wavelength* that renders it disagreeable to the average viewer? When we ask a question like that, we begin to notice the limits of entertainment. The fact, perhaps, that its abiding logic of choice is to be understood only within certain socio-cultural constraints.

This is just one take on entertainment, a stance that Richard Dyer both partially adopts and challenges when he says:

> Leisure and entertainment are separate from and in opposition to work and domestic cares. In a functional analysis, leisure can be seen either as a way of compensating for the dreariness of work or else as the passivity attendant on industrial labour. But the richness and variety of the actual forms of leisure suggest that leisure should also be seen as the creation of meaning in a world in which work and the daily round are characterized by drudgery, insistence and meaninglessness.[6]

Here Dyer upholds Adorno's wariness about the applications of entertainment. At the same time, he argues that entertainment, far from being dross, as Adorno sometimes has it, bears significant social value. Dyer, as we can appreciate from the quotation above, talks about "richness and variety" which, far from duping or limiting us, "creates meaning" within exactly those painful confines of work that Adorno finds impossible to bear.

EXERCISE

Pick a popular film that you and many others find entertaining. Once you have done that, see what you can do to read it according to a social relationship with work. Work here can stand for something that earns you a salary, as well as other activities like chores, studying or even maintaining functional bonds with other human beings. We have tried this out on *Wavelength*, so maybe use that analysis as a reference point.

- Does the film aim to relax or distract us? If so, how does it achieve this? Here you might want to analyze its ease of comprehension or whether it has a smooth, uncomplicated delivery.
- When we watch it, are we admiring the craft involved (as audiences might have done when they saw *Milk*)? If this is the case, what might that tell us about how we value skill as a form of specialized work?
- Does the movie encourage us at all to revolutionize our ways of thinking about work and the pain work can often provoke?

SELLING OURSELVES TO BUY ENTERTAINMENT

In *White Collar: The American Middle Classes*, his famous book of more than fifty years ago, sociologist Charles Wright-Mills powerfully articulates some of the cycles Adorno identifies:

> Each day men sell little pieces of themselves in order to try to buy them back each night and week-end with the coin of "fun". With amusement, with love, with movies and with vicarious intimacy, they pull themselves into some sort of whole again.[7]

In sum, workers sell their labor in order to receive money, which they then spend on commodities (which are the fruits of other people's labor). What is of note here is the extent to which we think about all these elements – time, labor, ourselves – as entities, as possessions. Abstract qualities like temporality, fun, dreams and value are recast as more concrete things we can trade or acquire. Can something like time be pinned down in this way? Most people's immediate answer would be: no. However, leisure time feels very strongly like something we own ("it's *my* free time, I can spend it as I choose"). During these periods, we are also offered multiple, more tangible entertainment packages that promise to fulfil our needs. Is fun a thing? Again: no, but we can be sold items that promise to deliver it. It makes sense now to scrutinize in what forms film entertainment has reached us over the years and how these have functioned within broader systems of commerce.

Before the widespread ownership of domestic play-back technologies like video recorders, DVD players or computers, most cinematic experience was fairly ephemeral. It principally took place in a movie theatre with audiences buying more of a there-and-then experience than a take-home product. Movie theatre occasions are still a crucial element of film entertainment, as the IMAX case study points out. At the same time, the "event" of cinema has always been supplemented by numerous other opportunities to spend money, on things from magazines and toys to the expensive hardware it takes to create a "home cinema". The ideal viewer is therefore the one most likely to pay out, despite the dispensability of cinema.

As we have already argued, financial transaction has great bearing on what types of entertainment become prevalent, which is maybe not so much the case when entertainment somehow functions less commercially. Currently, big-budget films often have young, richer males in mind, precisely because their crucial financial outgoings are smaller (for instance, if they do not have a family to support). As a consequence, we should be heedful of *whose* sense of entertainment is structuring what cinema is if it operates according to a market logic.

To make money, you have to be canny in how you spend it (or avoid doing so), but you also need to invest suitably to entice the customer. Where entertainment is concerned, alerting a consumer to a product and economizing at one and the same time are effectively attained through the tactic of what is now called "total entertainment". "Total entertainment" is, amongst other things, an attempt to create as many products as possible out of one idea. So a film not only lives through various incarnations in the cinema, on DVD and on satellite television, but it can also procreate books, computer games and even theme park rides. *E.T. the Extra-Terrestrial* (Steven Spielberg, 1982) is one such example that exists in all these forms. These types of fun, although varied, are also concentrated around a diminished set of leisure activities, ones that yield the highest possible profits. We need to take that condition on board. Think, for instance, of how the prominent computer game industry influences the movies that help promote it and vice versa. Fight sequences, chases and crashes work well in both formats, so there are elements of overlap and cross-promotion in evidence when these narrative motifs appear in either. Conversely, it would be extremely difficult for the people behind *Wavelength* to launch a related theme park ride or spin-off TV show in the way a company like Universal Studios have.

The profit motive for mass-distributed cinema is heavily guided by the principle of "giving people what they want". However, some buyers are definitely preferred over others, as we have observed in the example of young adult males as target consumers. This is noticeable in the way only particular types of test audience are consulted before movies are released. If these viewers are not entertained by a movie, then significant attention is paid to re-editing, maybe even re-shooting certain sections. Take *28 Days Later …* (Danny Boyle, 2002): the original version killed off its lead character, Jim (Cillian Murphy), but the story was subsequently modified to end more happily after these early viewers responded negatively to what they had been shown. Understandably, there has been a lot of critique of pandering to these consumers and the broader impact that has on the available options for our leisure time. For a modernist, for instance, a test

1.8 The E.T. Adventure ride at Universal Studios' Florida theme park. Source: Kay Dickinson.

CASE STUDY: "NOLLYWOOD"

In the last twenty years, a lively and profitable entertainment cinema, widely known as "Nollywood," has sprung up in Nigeria. Material is released straight onto VCD – which is priced lower than DVD and region-free – at the rate of at least one film per day. These films are made cheaply and quickly on location, rather than in studio settings, and usually without foreign investment. They are immensely popular in Nigeria, throughout Africa and anywhere with a sizable West African community. You will not find these titles in large high street or mall outlets because they are not distributed by the companies that supply such shops. Instead, they can be sourced in African corner shops, on market stalls, and via the internet on sites such as: http://www.africamoviestore.com, where you can watch previews. Thematically, they vary depending on where they were made. Hausa-language films from the north are more musically and romantically inclined than the English-language and Yoruba melodramas from the south. Wherever they are from within the country, though, these movies prove that low-cost entertainment can succeed globally outside the major distribution networks. They provide a challenge to the dominance of Hollywood fare in some countries, largely because they offer less alienating storylines which deal with African rather than American preoccupations.

To grasp why Nigerian films are thought to be so entertaining by so many people, we have to look into the context from which they emerged. "Nollywood" VCDs provide a specific type of entertainment, which can only be understood in relation to what they are reacting against. When Nigeria was colonized by the British (1900–1960), cinema came, predominantly, in the form of mobile film units. These traveled the breadth of the country, showing, for the most part, somewhat patronizing public awareness documentaries on subjects such as farming or health. Although the screenings were free, entertainment was not high on their agenda. This atmosphere prevailed when Nigeria won its independence. State-owned television rose to prominence, and continued to deliver educational material alongside messages that unequivocally endorsed the government. In both eras, moving image media was controlled by the ruling forces, but did not strictly function as something for sale. In the meantime, there was little in the way of moviemaking in Nigeria. African cinema in post-colonial times has often been funded by European sources and, with that, come all sorts of stipulations and insistences that the movie complies with overseas aesthetics and fixations. We will be concentrating more fully on what these are in Chapter 6 when we shall investigate co-production. For the moment, it is enough to stress that, typically, overseas funding has resulted in sharply political and intellectual work, such as *Silences of the Palace* (Moufida Tlatli, 1994) and *Moolaadé* (Ousmane Sembene, 2004), which deal with how women are oppressed by their own cultures in, respectively, Tunisia and Senegal. Although well-received overseas, they were not considered broadly entertaining within their countries of origin. By contrast, Nigerian VCDs comply with no such external demands beyond those of their local backers and their audiences. In this sense, they are commercial through and through. Their narratives are entertaining precisely because they tap into concerns that these other movies omit, like the joys of being wealthy.

They follow many of the patterns that have been outlined in this chapter. Examples like *Ultimate Risk* (Adim Williams, 2006) are escapist, whilst perpetuating current patterns of labor and spending for leisure. Not only are the films themselves marketable goods, but they contain a high level of product placement, such as *Ultimate Risk*'s references to Lavantis Car Servicing. This highly entrepreneurial mode of production that looks to local business investors in return for advertising is just one indication that Nigeria can no longer rely on its currently enfeebled public sector for support, even if it should want to – in cinema or in most other arenas. The government's perceived inability to look after its citizens is represented by the way most problems in these narratives are dealt with on the personal rather than the political level. Nigeria has recently experience a widening of the gap between rich and poor, which figures prominently in these movies' escapist elements. One major fascination is the upmarket life-styles of the protagonists, something characteristic to many entertainment films. Interestingly, though, the plots also raise questions about where their money comes from. This echoes the current outcry about dubious income streams in Nigeria from sources like the oil industry.

In films such as *Midnight Tears* (Prince Ameka Ani, 2008), characters get their comeuppance in the end, suggesting traces of the moralistic tone of older Nigerian media, as well as African folk traditions. African folk traditions can also be seen in the recourse to curses and other elements of local religious practice, as witnessed in a movie like *The Mat* (Omogoriola Hassan, 2008). So this material remains in tune with its local context and, furthermore, it does so by involving its audience collectively. Nigerian VCDs are typically watched in groups at home

1.9 *Ultimate Risk* (Adim Williams, 2006).

accompanied by no end of outraged or applauding audience commentary about the ethical issues at stake. Community participation has always been central to a great deal of African culture. Even though cinema is typically consumed in more passive, isolated fashion, it has been adapted here to fit into Nigerian entertainment habits.

It is imperative at this point to acknowledge what it means that these VCDs are largely watched at home. Cinemas in Nigeria are not considered safe or decent places; it would not be fun for a woman to attend a movie on her own in most of them. So, in order to gain the largest possible audiences, Nigerian VCDs are targeted more at families. There is a perfect match between screening space and cheaply reproducible home-viewing commodities. By and large, the VCDs are pirated, barring them from uncomplicated programming in public places. We should contemplate this method of distribution in line with the rise of the shadow economies in Nigeria, by which we mean forms of making money that are illegal like smuggling, drug dealing, or distributing pirated goods. Piracy also carries knock-on effects for spectators. These copies are typically of poor value and it is rare that one will play all the way through to the end.

The fact that people around the world still continue to enjoy Nigerian VCDs regardless is verification of their complex and compelling ways of entertaining us. In essence, these films are affordable as well as relevant. They refuse the po-faced address of earlier African media. Instead they offer escapism alongside the potential for social debate. Issues of wealth distribution, economic instability and crime convene with themes and values that are considered more traditional. It is no wonder that Nigeria's VCDs appeal beyond the country's borders because they discuss anxieties that many of us share, pitched in a fashion that concords with recognizable entertainment conventions.

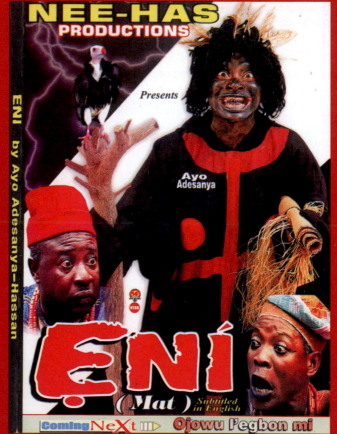

1.10 VCD cover for *The Mat*. Courtesy of Joaquín Serpe.

audience's ability to change the structure of a movie can indicate how banal, repetitive and unwilling to experiment film culture is. To what extent should we all have to accept a particular section of society's notion of reliable relaxation?

In this chapter we have witnessed a few examples of how the need to earn money, both for its consumers and its producers, shapes what is defined and promoted as entertainment. That fun should come with a price tag on it is not, by any means, a natural state of affairs, however. Many cultures and folk traditions do not involve money in the pursuit of enjoyment. We can have fun for free or as part of an exchange that does not present us with a receipt at the end, for instance by having a running race with someone. There are plenty of occasions when entertainment is not fully integrated into consumerism. Most governments fund arts to some degree or other. This might be because they believe that entertainment is a human right of some description, because their support can stimulate the economy, or because movies raise a country's profile internationally. Watch out for how these considerations are treated in detail in various upcoming chapters.

If you look back through history, you will observe that culture has long been subsidized through patronage, for example by rich individuals or religious institutions that have not sought straightforward monetary returns. The pyramids were not originally built so people could be charged entry, although tourists are nowadays. The same is true of the Roman circuses discussed at the beginning of the chapter. We do not wish to claim that these alternative means of funding are any more ethical than those financing commercial films. But the point is: mass production for profit (which is how most movies are currently made) is only one way of perpetuating culture or framing entertainment. Within cinema history, there has been a wealth of attempts to try out alternatives to this model. In the past, countries such as Poland and Syria have figured film as a state-run enterprise not intended to generate profit. Cinema claimed an entirely different social purpose, not wishing to be tied down to how a commercial agenda might shape a movie. Movies made under these conditions are often peppered with overt commentaries on social welfare, challenging political problems and the like. Because of this, they are a far cry from what many of us would consider to be fun. But the point would be to ask: why not? What is it about us that does or does not designate something entertaining? From these variations, we see that entertainment can be shaped not only by work, but also by the different types of financial support in play, what is expected in return and how we are situated within these particular traditions of film funding, making and viewing. All of these concerns will be explored in greater detail throughout this book, starting most pointedly with Chapter 4 on "Film and politics," which considers in detail why governments support filmmaking. For the moment, it is crucial to recognize that cinema has always received less financial help than, say, opera or ballet. This outcome colludes with the rhetoric of "high culture" that was analysed earlier. On balance, film is considered more of a commercial venture, perhaps because, as we have seen, it is thought of as "mere entertainment" without bearing a particular edifying, educational value.

EXERCISE

In many countries, entry to museums is free, while it is rare to be able to catch a movie on a big screen without paying. Why do you think this is the case? Why does cinematic entertainment have to come at a price?

Think through some of the ways in which movies can be seen legally without directly paying, such as on public television or certain free events.

- Does the fact of them being free mean that they are viewed differently? If so, how? Do our expectations vary as a result?
- Does film programming look the same when access is free? Who picks what becomes available in this way and what do you think guides their choices?
- How are such screenings funded and what is the rationale for money other than our own personal resources being spent in this way?

Having heard many perspectives on entertainment, you are now in a position to make more nuanced decisions about what entertainment is, how it functions, the regard in which it is held (or not), and what it has the potential to be. The analysis of entertainment does not stop here; in fact, it has only just begun. For instance, you will be able to develop these ideas still further from more psychological and anthropological perspectives when you have read about "Identification and identity" in Chapter 15.

CHAPTER SUMMARY

We started this chapter with an investigation of how film entertainment is described. It quickly became apparent that our multiple interpretations of what entertainment is open us onto some revealing information about people's mores and ambitions. We also saw that entertainment straddles, on the one hand, individual choice and, on the other, broad social needs. We then moved into an interrogation of the ways in which movie entertainment has, historically, been belittled. From this, we were able to question various forms of snobbery about entertainment, as well as conjecture on whether entertainment could be stretched to encompass more challenging pursuits. By looking into the close relation between entertainment and escapism, we noticed just how closely tied entertainment is to its supposed opposite: hard work. By bringing labor into our understanding of entertainment, we were able to spot the many ways in which entertainment dovetails with the reasons we work and the difficulties they bring. Finally, we focused on the fact that entertainment is predominantly conceived of as a profit-making product and thought about some alternatives to that model.

FURTHER READING

Adorno, Theodor. *The Culture Industry: Selected Essays on Mass Culture*. London: Routledge, 2001.

Often extremely bleak and damning of popular entertainment, this is a collection of some of Adorno's most famous shorter pieces on what he calls the culture industry. Here you will find his elaborations on some of the topics that are central to this chapter, including free time, labor, cinema and commodification.

Debord, Guy. *The Society of the Spectacle*, Detroit MI: Red & Black, (1967) 1977. http://www.marxists.org/reference/archive/debord/society.htm. Accessed 9 October 2013.

Available in many editions but also to be found for free on the internet, this is the work in which Debord extrapolates his theory of the spectacle. It is a complex extended essay, relying on Marxist terminology that will take some time to grasp fully. However, it is broken into short sections that make it more digestible and the ideas are compelling in their expansiveness. Debord's book is invaluable for understanding how things like cinema experiences are rendered as commodities and what the repercussions of this are for how we relate to each other socially.

Dyer, Richard. *Only Entertainment*. London: Routledge, 1992.

Surprisingly, this is one of the few books in English that comprehensively considers cinema through the lens of entertainment. Collecting various important essays by Dyer on the subject, the volume is more balanced in its appreciation of entertainment than the other two books we are recommending. Dyer remains cautious of the palpably damaging effects of mass-produced culture, whilst also thoroughly acknowledging its pleasures and values.

FILMS REFERENCED IN CHAPTER ONE

28 Days Later … (Danny Boyle, 2002)

Avatar (James Cameron, 2009)

À Bout de Souffle (*Breathless*) (Jean-Luc Godard, 1960)

E.T. the Extra-Terrestrial (Steven Spielberg, 1982)

The Mat (Omogoriola Hassan, 2008)

Midnight Tears (Prince Ameka Ani, 2008)

Milk (Gus Van Sant, 2008)

Moolaadé (Ousmane Sembene, 2004)

Nightcleaners (Berwick Street Collective, 1975)

Pirates of the Caribbean (Gore Verbinski, 2003)

Polar Express: An IMAX 3D Experience (Robert Zemeckis, 2004)

Silences of the Palace (Moufida Tlatli, 1994)

Spy Kids (Robert Rodriguez, 2001)

Traffic in Souls (George Loane Tucker, 1913)

Ultimate Risk (Adim Williams, 2006)

Wavelength (Michael Snow, 1967)

Week End (Jean-Luc Godard, 1967)

 **NOTES**

1 Guy Debord, *The Society of the Spectacle* (Detroit, MI: Red & Black, (1967) 1977), http://www.marxists.org/reference/archive/debord/society.htm, point 4, accessed 9 October 2013.

2 Tomás Gutiérrez Alea, "The Viewer's Dialectic," *Jump Cut: A Review of Contemporary Media* 29 (February 1984), http://www.ejumpcut.org/archive/onlinessays/JC29folder/ViewersDialec1.html, accessed 9 October 2013.

3 Raymond Williams, *Resources of Hope: Culture, Democracy, Socialism* (London: Verso, 1989), 4.

4 Chris Rojek, *Leisure Theory: Principles and Practices* (Basingstoke: Palgrave Macmillan, 2005), 4.

5 Theodor Adorno, *The Culture Industry: Selected Essays on Mass Culture* (London: Routledge, 2001), 189, 194.

6 Richard Dyer, *Only Entertainment* (London: Routledge, 1992), 13.

7 Charles Wright-Mills, *White Collar: The American Middle Classes* (New York: Galaxy, 1956), xvii.

CHAPTER TWO
CINEMA AS SELF-EXPRESSION

Cannes Film Festival: Today, everyone is in a lather over *Fahrenheit 9/11*. I've already missed the press screening. This afternoon is the last official screening, but how to get in? I decide to walk over to the Palais and join the pathetic throng of civilians without tickets. I'm thinking: this is probably good for me. Stripped of my press privilege, I have to see how the other half lives, and it's not pretty. Consider the ritual outside the Palais that's rarely reported, since all the press enters by another door and anyone with official tickets gets ceremoniously ushered out of harm's way. The ritual? An unruly crowd of commoners holding up tiny signs begging for tickets, stopping everybody with pleas: "Extra ticket? De plus?" Being homeless at the Cannes Film Festival means being ticketless, and there we are in the Palais version of the street median, holding out signs and hoping for mercy.

Well, not quite. I can't bring myself to hold up a sign. I decide to give it 15 minutes. If I'm meant to see Michael Moore's film, some miracle will intervene; if not, I'll go look for a café. Suddenly, I hear a voice from above: "Ruby, do you need a ticket for this?" Shaking myself out of my reverie, I realize that my personal deus ex machina is actually Tom Bernard, co-exec of Sony Pictures Classics (not this film's distributor), who is casually bicycling by in his shorts, from the back pocket of which he fishes out a crumpled ticket and hands it to me. "Enjoy," he says, and bikes off. Stunned, the envy of all around me, I turn and enter the Palais.[1]

WHAT WE WILL DO IN CHAPTER 2

- Extend our understanding of why people make films by learning about motivations other than entertainment: what senses of the self and forms of privilege underpin self-expression in filmmaking? What ideas of authorship are specific to film as opposed to other arts and industries?

- Become acquainted with the bodies of films known as "art cinema" and "experimental film" or "avant-garde cinema" as strands of creative authorship in film practice.

- Understand how some filmmakers oppose the ideas and practices of self-expression through collective models of filmmaking.

- Learn about alternative modes of self-expression in the essay film and digital platforms.

BY THE END OF CHAPTER 2 YOU SHOULD BE ABLE TO

- Give clear definitions of different film movements motivated by self-expression.

- Provide challenges to the idea of the self that undergirds these movements.

- Make strong connections between your own sense of self and film form.

Ah, what a story! The buzz and frisson of the film festival, the fame of the director, the thrill of joining the select few and the very famous: film scholar and critic Ruby Rich spins an enticing tale of what it is like to be where few of us will ever be — smack in the middle of the most famous film festival in the world, where careers are launched and reputations made. It is the festival that is perhaps most associated with a "director's cinema," with films that are understood as the products of specific individuals' talent, even genius. It is also the festival most responsible for showcasing European cinema to a world market and audience. Films screen in the festival by invitation only, and the prestigious Golden Palm (Palme d'Or) award — awarded to the director of the film selected as the best feature film — has gone to some of the most well-known directors of the art cinema in Europe and beyond. You will recognize some of their names: Marcel Camus, Federico Fellini, Luis Buñuel, Luchino Visconti, Michelangelo Antonioni, Lindsay Anderson, Volker Schlöndorff, Akira Kurosawa, Andrzej Wajda, Wim Wenders, and so on. Oh, and one woman, Jane Campion, the only one so far.

These directors (just part of a much longer list) are those we generally associate with the idea of a director as a film's **author**, much as we think of a novel as emerging from a singular imagination (and, it should be said, many of these directors are in fact also the writers of their films). A particular model of what it means to be an artist underpins this idea of film directors as authors, a model derived from early to mid-nineteenth-century Romanticism (discussed also in Chapter 1). In brief, Romanticism, particularly in Germany, responded to the changes in life wrought by the Industrial Revolution (rationalization, Enlightenment science, urban collectivity, industrialism) by valuing, above all, emotion as the motor of aesthetic experience and expression. Deep emotions catalyzed by nature were the most significant to Romantics, such as the experience of the sublime in response to the precipice of a mountain peak. Heroic individuals confront nature's majesty and seize it through magnificent artistic imagination: Caspar David Friedrich, the German painter most associated with Romanticism, put it succinctly: "the artist's feeling is his law."[2]

2.1 "*Festival de Cannes,*" Cannes International Film Festival logo. Courtesy of Getty Images.

Much of the critical response to film directors as authors similarly highlights the individual genius, intensity, and singularity of emotion in their work. Adjectives like "master" ("undisputed mastery," "cinematic masterpiece") often crop up in assessments of their films, and just as frequently the films are described in the language of art rather than those of commerce, information or even entertainment. As you thought about cinema as entertainment in the previous chapter, you considered a number of motivations for filmmaking practices in particular, and cinema is unusual in focusing on the director as the source of a particular film's vision (as opposed, say, to the focus on the writer in television or literature). There are, however, a number of different traditions and discourses associated with the idea of a cinema of authors, and in what follows in the rest of this chapter, we acquaint you with a number of ways of considering some central questions in film studies: who is really the author of a given film, an art form that is, in many if not most instances, collaborative, industrial and highly mediated? How do we express ourselves in the medium of film? What are the constraints on self-expression, and how does self-expression extend beyond the role of the director as the film's author? By the end of this chapter, you will be able to take a stand in relation to passionate and often competing conceptions of film authorship.

ART CINEMA

Although some scholars allege that art cinema is itself a genre (like the musical or the Western), we treat it here as a more mobile and changing designation that depends upon ideas of a film canon (or group of films considered as the best in quality and essential to know); considerations of exhibition venues ("art house" theatres, film clubs); national cinema traditions and resources, including funding streams; and audiences. Art cinema, we might say, is made through the interaction of these spheres and forces, rather than born naturally from the minds of individual geniuses. We do emphasize its difference from classical narrative cinema in art film's emphasis not only on authorial expressivity but also on strongly character-driven plots and relationship to social realism. Two of the national cinemas most frequently associated with narrative feature-length art cinema, the French and the Swedish, are used here as a laboratory for seeing how art cinema emerges as a form and a discourse. We then turn to shorter, experimental cinema that is similarly authored.

In the early decades of cinema in France, a strong vein of experimental work emerged, and it is useful to consider this body of work as expressive of a particular sense of self that chafed against social order and bourgeois convention. Often associated with broader movements in art such as Dada and surrealism, these films tested the limits of abstraction, meaning, and structure: they wanted to provoke, to titillate, to shock, and to fascinate. A farcical film, René Clair's *Entr'acte* (1924), is a good example. Made to be screened during parts of a ballet performance, the film combines gags, chases, new kinds of perspective (slow motion, a rollercoaster, the undersides of ballet performers), and other tricks with Dada abandon. (Dada was a left-wing art movement that emerged after World War I that embraced irrationality, nonsense, intuition and instantaneity. Many famous artists worked on *Entr'acte*, including Man Ray, Marcel Duchamp, Erik Satie and Francis Picabia.) Films such as this one, and the more famous surrealist experiment by Luis Buñuel and Salvador Dali entitled *Un chien andalou* (1929), challenged many if not all of the conventions of classical narrative cinema: they dispense with causal storytelling, identifiable characters, closure, and even with recognizable images.

These directors tapped their own dreams and interior lives as fuel for their films. Already we can see hallmarks of art cinema in French films in the 1920s and 1930s. Made to be screened in art venues or ciné-clubs, these films appealed to an educated niche audience in tune with the political and aesthetic avant-gardes. Along with Soviet cinema and Italian neo-realist cinema, these films are important precursors to the art cinema that became prominent after World War II, insofar as experimentation with film form, an interest in radical politics and the desire for energetic provocation characterized both cycles of filmmaking. In France, however, the postwar art cinema did not flow directly from these prewar experiments: during the war years of the Vichy occupation, films of the enemy were banned from exhibition, and so the young artists and intellectuals who would become the filmmakers and critics of the postwar period were unable to see classic American films. When the ban was lifted after the war, an enthusiastic group of these young people became associated with the *Cahiers du cinema* ("Notebooks of Cinema" journal), under the influential guidance of the critic André Bazin. Seeing films by Alfred Hitchcock, Orson Welles, William Wyler, Howard Hawkes and John Ford (among other directors) for the first time, these aspiring artists were inspired by the imprint these directors were able to make on their material, the style they could detect even or especially in genre films such as Westerns and biopics. These young French cinephiles, in other words, often saw several films by the same director – all of which had been unavailable – and thereby observed an author's imprint through cumulative exposure. The young filmgoers appreciated how American directors made personal films within impersonal studios. In "A Certain Tendency of the French Cinema" by François Truffaut (one of the young intellectuals who would become a giant of the French art cinema), he dubs this way of watching and identifying true authors of film the "politique des auteurs," or a policy/programme of authors/authorship,

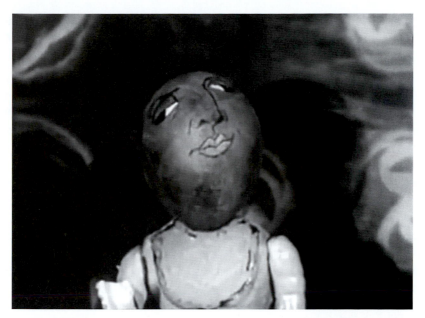

2.2 *Entr'acte* (René Clair, 1924).

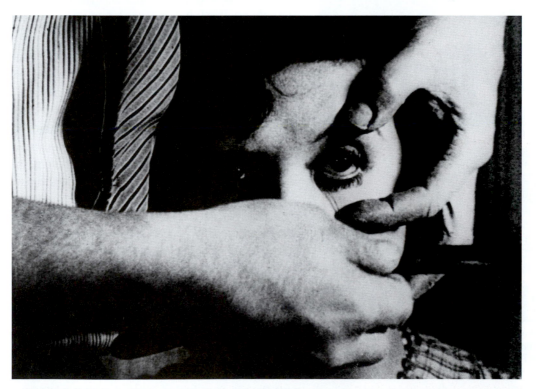

2.3 Simone Mareuil in the opening scene from *Un chien andalou* (Luis Buñuel and Salvador Dali, 1929). Courtesy of Buñuel-Dali/ The Kobal Collection.

which elevated some kinds of writing for the screen and directing for the screen as the work of real film authorship. The key to the "politique des auteurs" is the presence of a visual style that functions as an authorial signature: in any given film by an *auteur*, the astute critic can discern that signature style.

More than just an enthusiasm for the many American films these critics had been unable to see during the war, the "politique des auteurs" endorsed an admiration for serious, personal, deep films. The *Cahiers* group admired Jean Renoir, a director whose work began in the silent era and continued with masterpieces such as *Grand Illusion* (1937) and *The Rules of the Game* (1939). The young filmmaker-critics praised Renoir's contemplative realism, including the use of the long take that allowed spectators to immerse themselves in the complexity of the worlds (often of social conflict) Renoir presented onscreen. Renoir made films, they thought, to invite the truest and most authentic aspects of the *spectator's* self into dialogue with the content of the film. Truffaut, Jean-Luc Godard, Eric Rohmer, Claude Chabrol, Jacques Rivette and others in this *Cahiers* group who are associated with the French New Wave combined an interest in visual/stylistic expressions of a director's personal vision with radical experimentation in film form (and often in political and social life as well). It is this group of films – beginning with Truffaut's semi-autobiographical *The 400 Blows* (1959) and continuing well into the 1970s – we generally associate with French postwar art cinema. They belong to its canon, they were screened at art house cinemas, they were opposed to the French mainstream "literary" tradition of filmmaking, and they captured the aspirations and critical energies of the 1960s generation who were their primary audience (students and members of the counterculture).

2.4 Lobby card/poster for *The Rules of the Game* (Jean Renoir, 1939). Courtesy of Nouvelle Édition Française/The Kobal Collection.

If in the French case art cinema can thus be understood as a long movement of changing forms associated with a large number of filmmakers experimenting with self-expression, in the Swedish case it has only one name: Ingmar Bergman. There were, of course, filmmakers in Sweden before him, including Mauritz Stiller (the director of Swedish film star Greta Garbo) and Alf Sjöberg, for whom Bergman worked, but it is Bergman who is known as the great author of the Swedish screen – actually, of Swedish stages and screens in the plural, since he was an active director of theatre and worked in radio and television alongside the cinema. In each medium, he displayed the kind of consistency lauded by the *Cahiers* group that made a true *auteur*, displaying a strong personal and moral vision, a keen sense of self-discipline, and a sense of pleasure and joy in his work. As scholar Birgitta Steene has noted, much of Bergman's output in all media can be described by what Isaiah Berlin called a kind of "hedgehog" authorship, by which he means an artist focused on a limited range of subject matter and who seldom deviates from that. Steene writes:

After half a century of amazing "hedgehog" production, Bergman has created a cohesive universe of his own making, a personal mythos where his commentators can "feel at home" and can easily identify such central Bergman subjects as: (1) an existential probing manifesting itself in questioning a silent god figure who seems to have withdrawn from human life; (2) an often ruthless unmasking process that discloses the lies and dead conventions that control human beings and relationships and where language can easily be a deceptive tool; (3) a deterministic portrayal of people as helpless and despondent marionettes, yet so full of vitality that most of Bergman's works leave some trace of hope behind; (4) a portrayal of Woman as archetype – as the embodiment of strength and survivability; and (5) an exposure of the modern (usually male) artist as a self-centered and destructive individual, often frustrated in his métier and haunted by demons.[3]

Such themes can make for weighty films as well as wonderful parodies: a 1968 short film called *De Düva* (George Coe and Anthony Lover) is a hilarious send-up of Bergman's films (most notably *The Seventh Seal* (1956) and *Wild Strawberries* (1957)). In one of its best lines, Madeline Kahn (in her first role) holds up a cigar and simply asks, in the fake English/Swedish that is the film's language, "Phallican symbol?"

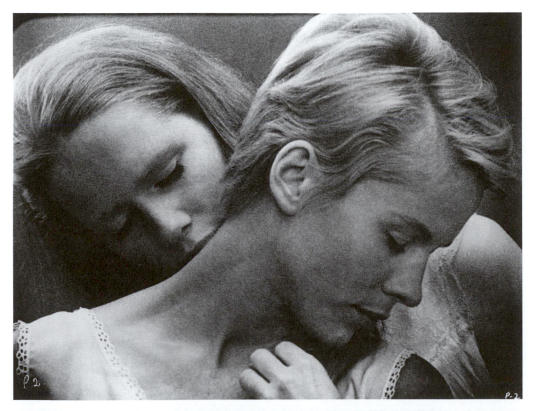

2.5 Bibi Andersson and Liv Ullmann in *Persona* (Ingmar Bergman, 1966). Courtesy of the BFI Stills Collection.

EXERCISE

Mocking Bergman's heavy-handed use of psychoanalytic themes, *De Düva* unwittingly partakes of a kind of *auteur* criticism, that is, the identification of a director's singular vision and style, both visual and narrative. Watch at least three films by a single director, and list those elements that would, in your view, identify him or her as an *auteur*, insofar as they defy convention and establish a unique and personal style. Note: in often shameless acts of self-promotion, directors frequently make available copies of their authored screenplays online. You might wish to *read* three screenplays before watching the films that resulted from them in order to identify just *where* the hallmarks of personal style and vision emerge in the filmmaking process.

If he is trumpeted as a great Swedish *auteur*, however, Bergman never worked alone. Indeed, he maintained life-long working relationships that nourished his output and contributed to the distinct visual style of his films: with cinematographer Sven Nykvist, and with actors including Liv Ullman, Bibi Andersson, Harriett Andersson, Max von Sydow and others. In the next part of the chapter, we present another version of the individual (usually male) artist working in a more artisanal mode, before turning in the following parts to several examples of filmmaking practices that are diametrically opposed to the Romantic idea of personal artistic expression, even if practiced in collaborative environments such as Bergman's. These include forms of collectivity, counterculture, amateurism, commitment and politics.

ART CINEMA REDUX: THE POSTWAR AVANT-GARDE

If the French New Wave and Bergman provide us with vigorous examples of a cinema of European *auteurs* working in feature-length narrative cinema, there are many filmmakers who, by reason of necessity or choice, habit or inclination, tended toward a more artisanal, inexpensive, non-narrative film practice. If Truffaut & Co. might be said to be the novelists of their moment, this second movement – that of the postwar avant-garde, the New York Underground, and the postwar experimental cinema more generally – might be said to be its poets. While the roots of this work snake back to European and American film experiments in the 1920s and 1930s, in which daring amateurs built sets in barns and played with light and shadow, the postwar years brought self-conscious artists, amateurs and dabblers into new configurations. There are many loci of experimental filmmaking in this period – from Vienna to Tokyo – and yet we hone in on the American avant-garde and particularly its practitioners in the United States because it allows us to discuss a specific and rich inflection of "the personal" as it congealed in American cities.

We can trace them geographically and institutionally, thinking about the kinds of resources, audiences and film cultures in which these artists worked. Take Los Angeles, for instance, where experimentation happened within and at the periphery of the commercial film industry. The web project, Alternative Projections (http://www.alternativeprojections.com), compiles three years of research (including the recording of oral histories) into the rich alternative film culture that developed in Southern California, including filmmakers such as Maya Deren (who collaborated with her then-husband Alexander Hammid), Kenneth Anger, Les Blank, Charles and Ray Eames, Hans Fischinger, Robert Florey and Slavko Vorkapich, Russ Tamblyn, James Whitney, and a host of other makers, critics, activists and organizers. These filmmakers (and, later, videomakers) experimented with every possible variable of film form, for example with different gauges (usually 16mm, but also Super-8, 8mm), color, optical effects and multiple exposures, taking whatever resources were at hand for their experiments. In dialogue with both Hollywood and other art movements – such as New York's structural film movement, Conceptual Art, performance art, body art, and California art schools – these makers nonetheless often put a West Coast stamp on their films. Florey and Vorkapich's early expressionist satire film *Life and Death of 9413 – A Hollywood Extra* (1928) gave rise to other wry commentaries on the Hollywood film industry, such as *Even: As You and I* (Harry Hay et al., 1937), a film that also parodies surrealism, and such engagements continued in the postwar years as artists found themselves in dialogue with the commercial film industry and with other artists. A neglected instance of such engagement is the West Coast Black Arts movement, where scholar Daniel Widener identifies "a largely abstract, non-representational, and freeform vision of black art that connected avant-garde jazz, assemblage and 'junk' art, jazz poetry, and experimental neo-realist film."[4] Widener, following other thinkers, reminds us of the importance

2.6 *The Life and Death of 9413 – A Hollywood Extra* (Robert Florey and Slavko Vorkapich, 1928). Courtesy of the BFI Stills Collection.

of art to radical race politics, where art is not an ancillary or secondary domain but instead integral to black politics and struggles: in the decade after World War II, artists had to fight to desegregate the local musicians' unions, for example, since union membership was a prerequisite to finding work in Hollywood. This is an instance where we find almost insurmountable barriers to self-expression due to industry racism and segregation.

The institutional infrastructure in New York was different, insofar as experimental cinema was supported by key arts organizations in the non-profit sector, including the Museum of Modern Art (whose film department opened in 1939), Cinema 16 (a film society founded by Amos Vogel in 1947), Film-Makers Cooperative (created by artists in 1962), and Anthology Film Archives (founded in 1969). Other institutions, such as Andy Warhol's Factory (also founded in 1962), functioned as incubators for artistic experimentation and vibrant filmmaking practices. The 1960s was a particularly important decade for the growth of experimental cinema, with film festivals such as the International Experimental Film Competitions in Brussels nourishing the careers of the group of filmmakers ultimately canonized in P. Adams Sitney's book, *Visionary Film: The American Avant Garde*, begun in 1969 and published in 1974. That book makes explicit the degree to which these filmmakers – among them Stan Brakhage, Jonas Mekas, Peter Kubelka, Gregory Markopoulos, Ken Jacobs, Ron Rice, Jack Smith, George and Mike Kuchar, and Bruce Conner – followed in an explicitly Romantic tradition. And this group soon expanded to include a group of filmmakers associated with structural filmmaking: Hollis Frampton, George Landow, Paul Sharits, Tony Conrad, Michael Snow, Ernie Gehr, Joyce Wieland and Peter Kubelka, among others. While not every single one of these artists lived and worked in New York (Brakhage famously filmed every inch of his Colorado cabin, and Snow is a proud Canadian, just to take two examples), New York's film culture and burgeoning critical discourse fueled the broader experimental film movement with which they are all associated.

Film schools soon began to breed further generations of makers and continue to do so. George Kuchar taught for many years at the San Francisco Art Institute and was beloved by generations of students: in his courses "AC/DC Psychotronic Teleplays" and "Electro-graphic Sinema," Kuchar worked collaboratively with his students to make films on miniscule budgets (with titles like *Hush, Hush Sweet Harlot!* (1999)), making the most of making do. Stan Brakhage returned to Colorado in the early 1960s and taught for more than twenty years at the University of Colorado at Boulder. Bruce Conner hated New York and moved to San Francisco several times, settling there in 1965. In an oral history interview, he describes the university scene that got him into filmmaking:

> Well, I was involved in film societies and [Brakhage] was the first filmmaker I had ever met. When I was at the University of Colorado I started a group called the Experimental Cinema Group. We had ten film programs. Four hundred and fifty people joined the group for three dollars. The films were experimental film, old avant-garde films, historical films, silent films, foreign films, etc. There were a couple of his friends in the group. Brakhage would come from Denver and advise us. He brought his films and showed them. He told me I ought to make movies. But I didn't want to. When I got to San Francisco I knew Larry Jordan, who was sort of a student of his. I mean, he was a friend of Stan's and the films that he was making were very similar to Stan's. We started a film society and I ended up using his film equipment. I was able to get into a position where I would be encouraged and actually have the equipment and learn how to splice film. It depended on me and Stan Brakhage and Larry Jordan.[5]

2.7 Film director Stan Brakhage. Courtesy of The Kobal Collection.

For many filmmakers in this largely male tradition of romantic artisanal cinema, Stan Brakhage is himself an institution. If he was a poet, he was a lyrical one, interested in creating an intensely personal vision through cinema that could touch upon shared human experience; one of the first films of his to be widely circulated, *Window Water Baby Moving* (1959), recorded his then-wife Jane Brakhage giving birth to their first child. What could be more intimate and personal? The Brakhage Center symposium continues to celebrate his legacy by bringing together contemporary experimental filmmakers and scholars, while the Flaherty Seminar, named after Robert Flaherty and founded by his widow Frances in 1955, is the longest continuously running film event in North America and similarly stokes the flames of experimental cinema.

WORKING TOGETHER

Not all experimental filmmakers claim the mantle of individual artistic expression. From the early manifestos of the cinema of national liberation known as Third Cinema, to the activist pamphlets of the Occupy movement, to ongoing experiments in feminist and queer cinema, filmmakers have stressed the collective and shared nature of political artmaking. In Brazil, for example, the Cinema Novo ("New Cinema") movement in the 1960s and 1970s articulated a vision of social equality that had its roots firmly in the experiences of marginalized people. One of its leading intellectuals and artists, Glauber Rocha, coined the term "aesthetic of hunger" to describe that footing. In the essay/manifesto of that title, he writes:

> We [the Cinema Novo] understand this hunger that the majority of Europeans and Brazilians don't understand … They don't know where this hunger comes from. We know – we who make these sad and ugly films, these desperate films where reason doesn't always possess the loudest voice, that hunger will not be cured by the planning of the cabinet [i.e. government] and that the strips of technicolor will not hide but amplify its tumors. That said, only a culture of hunger, looking at its own structure, can rise above itself, qualitatively speaking: it's the noblest manifestation of cultural hunger and violence.[6]

Rather than finding inspiration in individual angst or existential alienation (although there is plenty of both in Latin American cinema!), filmmakers in Brazil turned to the everyday experiences of the working classes and the dark places of Brazilian life: the *favelas* (or urban poor neighborhoods) and the *sertão* (the "backwoods" or "bush" in Brazil's northeast). This is to say that filmmakers of the Cinema Novo movement found collectivity in the *content* of their films, which were nonetheless made by, and signed by, individuals. Such was the case even in Cuba, where the socialized film industry founded by directors such as the great Tomás Gutiérrez Alea produced films under the names of each director; Aléa's own *Memories of Underdevelopment* (1959) was the first post-revolutionary Cuban film to be shown in the US and much of the West. Not so with other movements in the 1960s and 1970s who *produced* films collectively.

2.8 Sergio Corrieri in *Memories of Underdevelopment* (Tomás Gutiérrez Alea, 1959). Courtesy of Cuban State Film/The Kobal Collection.

CASE STUDY: NEWSREEL

One instance of such a collective is the group Newsreel, which was actually a number of decentralized film collectives in US cities during this period. Working anonymously and democratically, Newsreel made politically relevant documentaries. One of the key participants in New York, Roz Payne, remembers the first meetings of the group in 1967–1968:

> About 30 people met weekly to talk about films, equipment, and politics. I think we were great because we came from various political backgrounds and had different interests. We never all agreed on a political line. We broke down into smaller groups to work on the films. The working groups included anti-Vietnam-war, anti-imperialist, high school, students, women, workers, Yippies, Third World, and the infamous sex, drugs and party committee.

> We wanted to make two films a month and get 12 prints of each film out to groups across the country. We wanted to spark the creation of similar news-film groups in other major cities of the United States so that they would distribute our films and would cover and shoot the events in their area.

> The first film I worked on was the 1968 student take-over of Columbia University. The students had taken over 5 buildings. We had a film team in each building. We were shooting from the inside while the rest of the press were outside. We participated in the political negotiations and discussions. Our cameras were used as weapons as well as recording the events. Melvin had a W.W.II cast iron steel Bell and Howell camera that could take the shock of breaking plate glass windows.[7]

The resulting film, *Columbia Revolt*, belongs to an archive of fifty films made by the collective, which extended ultimately to include San Francisco, Detroit, Boston, Los Angeles and other American cities. And the vision of solidarity that Newsreel circulated extended to the world, in a kind of visual internationalism on display in the 1969 film *Amerika*: "against the background of the November 1969 anti Vietnam War demonstration in Washington, DC – footage from all over the world."[8]

Newsreel survives today in two different incarnations: Third World Newsreel (spun from the New York collective) and California Newsreel (spun from the San Francisco group). Working to catalyze new forms of collective filmmaking and to distribute politically relevant cinema to individuals and institutions, these groups retain ties to past collectivities such as the Black Panther Party (with whom they collaborated) while forging new ones.

A lesser-known instance of Newsreel-style radical filmmaking is the body of work by Japanese filmmaker Masao Adachi, who shares with his US counterparts an insistence on non-hierarchical collectives. Active primarily during the 1960s and 1970s, Adachi used cinema to challenge the culture of corporate bureaucracy, conformity and economic aspiration associated with the "miracle" of postwar Japan's ascendency. With collaborators such as the famous director Nagisa Oshima and the obscure artist Koji Wakamatsu, Adachi made films that tested the boundaries of propriety and social mores, such as *AKA Serial Killer* (1969). Putting his beliefs in social action in practice, Adachi traveled to Lebanon in the early 1970s to record, in Newsreel style, the efforts of the Palestinian resistance there, creating a documentary called *Red Army/PLFP: Declaration of World War* (1971). Three years later, he returned to join the resistance as an armed combatant, staying in the Middle East for the next twenty-eight years. Adachi thus shares with his Newsreel compatriots a complicated relationship with the intertwined roles of cameras and guns. As Adachi controversially put it, "instead of replacing the camera with the rifle, why not have one in each hand?"[9]

2.9 *Red Army/PLFP: Declaration of World War* (Masao Adachi and Koji Wakamatsu, 1971).

FEMINIST FILM

Feminist filmmaking is another site where collective production flourished in the 1960s and 1970s, and yet it gave way to another mode of filmmaking, autobiographical film, that bridges the personal vision of the *auteur* cinema with the more social and collective aspirations of political film. This vein of filmmaking itself has diverse genealogies: it was inspired by experimental films in the prewar and postwar periods, such as Germaine Dulac's *The Smiling Madame Beudet/La souriante Madame Beudet* (1923) and Maya Deren's *Meshes of the Afternoon* (1943), by the work of some makers in the French New Wave, such as Agnès Varda and Chantal Akerman, and by filmmakers in the underground and avant-garde scenes such as Carolee Schneemann. These precedents gave us rare, frank glimpses of ordinary women's lives: stories of domestic imprisonment, the expression of women's desire and the countercultural possibilities of the sexual revolution. After a period of time in which feminist filmmaking turned outward towards the urgent issues of the day (abortion, sexual assault, custody battles, the women's movement itself), it turned inward, telling intimate stories of individual lives that nevertheless were meant to stand for larger collectivities. Telling individual stories became a way to tell a much bigger story. Or *stories*.

In German filmmaker Monika Treut's work, for example, the earlier films interweave personal sexual exploration with the documentation of sexual variation, misbehavior, and experimentation. In *Virgin Machine* (1988), and onward in *My Father is Coming* (1991), *Female Misbehavior* (1992) and *Gendernauts* (1999), Treut's characters move through and around striptease, sadomasochism, erotic performance, transgender, lesbian and gay relationships, and so on. In the latter films, personal exploration turns into a post-9/11 quest for a sense of international connection, forged particularly through and among women artists: *Warrior of Light* (2001) in Brazil, *Jump Cut: A Travel Diary* (2004) in Taiwan, and the most recent *Tigerwomen Grow Wings* (2005), in which Treut travels from San Francisco to Rio de Janeiro, from Paris to Jerusalem, and from Toronto to Taipei. Although the stories are Treut's, they are never merely confessions but bridges to other cultures, questions, and imaginations.

2.10 *Meshes of the Afternoon* (Maya Deren, 1943). Courtesy of The Kobal Collection.

Women's experimental cinema flourished in Germany (energized by the journal *Frauen und Film*), in France and elsewhere in Europe, in Canada and the United States. Among the most notable filmmakers are Marie Menken, Joyce Wieland, Gunvor Nelson, Yvonne Rainer, Carolee Schneemann, Barbara Rubin, Amy Greenfield, Marjorie Keller, Barbara Hammer, Chick Strand, Abigail Child, Cheryl Dunye, Peggy Ahwesh, and Leslie Thornton.

The two recent award winners at the London Feminist Film Festival in 2012 stress the importance and impact of non-western subjects and filmmakers and give us a glimpse of a broader film practice. The audience and festival favorite feature-length film, *Ladies' Turn* (Hélène Harder, 2012), focuses on a Senegalese organization of the same name that provides young women with an opportunity to play football (soccer). The winner of the short film competition, *Kung Fu Grandma* (Jeong-One Park, 2012), confronts the rape of elderly women by young men in Korogocho, Kenya, where some of the women are taking a self-defense course. The film celebrates the women's solidarity and self-protection. An Academy Award winning short film, *Saving Face*

Eva Norvind in DIDN'T DO IT FOR LOVE, a film by Monika Treut.

A First Run Features release.

2.11 Promotional image from *Didn't Do It for Love* (Hyena Films, Hamburg, 1997). Courtesy of Hyena Films.

2.12 The Ladies' Turn organization logo. Courtesy of Ladies' Turn.

(Daniel Junge and Sharmeen Obaid-Chinoy, 2011), likewise looks at the victims of brutal attacks, in this case in Pakistan, where women suffer disfigurement through brutal acid attacks; the film tells the story of the plastic surgeon, Dr Mohammad Jawad, who helps to reconstruct their faces and the women who rebuild their lives. The case study on Mona Hatoum and Su Friedrich helps to link the formal practices of two feminist filmmakers from different origins, but we could have selected the work of Deepa Mehta, Aparna Sen, Mira Nair, Pratibha Parmar, Ning Ying, Li Yu, Zero Chou, Lucrecia Martel, Lynne Ramsay, or others we encourage you to seek out.

CASE STUDY: MONA HATOUM AND SU FRIEDRICH

Mona Hatoum is an artist of Palestinian descent who lives and works in Britain. Born in exile from Palestine in Lebanon, she was doubly exiled while visiting London when civil war erupted in Lebanon in 1975. An artist who works in performance and installation modes, she is also the maker of an aesthetically layered 1988 videotape, called *Measures of Distance*, a video held by museums such as the Tate in London and distributed in the United States by Women Make Movies. It is described by the Tate catalog as follows:

> *Measures of Distance* is a video work comprising several layered elements. Letters written by Hatoum's mother in Beirut to her daughter in London appear as Arabic text moving over the screen and are read aloud in English by Hatoum. The background images are slides of Hatoum's mother in the shower, taken by the artist during a visit to Lebanon. Taped conversations in Arabic between mother and daughter, in which her mother speaks openly about her feelings, her sexuality and her husband's objections to Hatoum's intimate observation of her mother's naked body are intercut with Hatoum's voice in English reading the letters.

None of this is immediately clear to an audience. Only gradually does the superimposed script yield to our ability to see the image of Hatoum's mother, coming in and out of focus in different photographs. The script acts both as barrier and as screen through which we perceive. Only gradually do we understand this as an exchange with her mother, and only gradually does the screen also figure for the spectator as a veil or shield, showing us (and especially those of us who neither speak nor read Arabic) the distance the videotape measures in its title (a distance of displacement, exile, diaspora). Hatoum herself has said:

> Although the main thing that comes across is a very close and emotional relationship between mother and daughter, it also speaks of exile, displacement, disorientation and a tremendous sense of loss as a result of the separation caused by war. In this work I was also trying to go against the fixed identity that is usually implied in the stereotype of

2.13 Mona Hatoum in *Measures of Distance* (Mona Hatoum, 1988). Color video with sound. Duration: 15 minutes. A Western Front video production, Vancouver, 1988. © Mona Hatoum. Courtesy of White Cube.

Arab woman as passive, mother as non-sexual being … the work is constructed visually in such a way that every frame speaks of literal closeness and implied distance.[10]

Consistent throughout Hatoum's career are an interest in the body, a strong graphic sensibility, and a feel for layered or multiple planes of action and image (whether on the screen or in performance). In this piece, audiences respond to the intimacy both of Hatoum's voice and of her mother's body, while the graphic presence of the script complicates our access to either or both. In complicating the presumed bond between narrator, subject and audience, *Measures of Distance* distinguishes itself from a body of feminist film and video – more confessional in tone – that sought identification, trust, and collectivity.

Screening this tape alongside another work of feminist experimental filmmaking, Su Friedrich's 1984 film *The Ties That Bind*, reveals valuable connections. Friedrich's film is also about her mother, in this case a German woman named Lori Bucher Friedrich who grew up during Hitler's Third Reich. More conventional, at least in its initial impressions, than *Measures of Distance*, Friedrich's film combines many sources, including images of her mother, footage shot during Friedrich's own travels in Germany, and images of anti-war and anti-nuclear protests. These combine in a genre we might want to call personal documentary. Like *Measures of Distance*, however, Friedrich introduces graphic text: namely, she scratches directly onto the film a running commentary that is her own "voice." Rather than providing voice-over narration, that is, Friedrich's sensibility emerges on the film itself, becomes part of the film's own material, in a gesture that is reminiscent of previous male avant-garde traditions, most notably the signature of filmmaker Stan Brakhage, "by Brakhage," which claimed the artwork as his own in the Romantic tradition we have discussed earlier. Friedrich's aim is different. She is indebted to the avant-garde for its formal experiments with the frame, with rhythm, with text, with layering, and with the surface of the image, but she believes that one must start with one's own stories in order to approach something of a shared human experience. Toward that end, Friedrich creates a layered voice, at times seeming to address or challenge her mother directly (with painful questions about personal responsibility in relation to the Nazi genocide), at times reflecting on her own experience, at times sharing Friedrich's recollections directly with the audience. This voice, like Hatoum's video, ultimately finds intimacy and distance, similarities and differences, between the two generations of mother and daughter.

2.14 Lori Bucher Friedrich and Su Friedrich in *The Ties That Bind* (Su Friedrich, 1985). Courtesy of Su Friedrich.

ESSAY FILM

Friedrich's film practice contains elements of the essay film, which might be defined as a genre that foregrounds the personal or subjective point of view as it organizes its observations and reflections. Essay film entails a more prismatic idea of the personal. This "self-questioning activity" in fact delimits the essay film from other modes of personal filmmaking or other forms of cinematic self-expression. Film scholar Timothy Corrigan calls this type of filmmaking the most vibrant and significant type of filmmaking in the world today, and thus we treat it with equal significance as the experimental and art cinema modes. According to him, there are five prominent sub-genres or modes of the essay film: the portrait or self-portrait, the travelogue, the diary, the editorial and the refractive. In his book *The Essay Film*, he identifies what is distinctive about the "essayistic" as a historical and theoretical genre, and he surveys each of the five modes in a transnational, though mostly western, frame. Since Corrigan offers a comprehensive treatment of the essay film (following scholars such as Laura Rascaroli, whose book *The Personal Camera* treats a similar corpus), we follow his lead in distinguishing the essay film from other self-expressive practices we have already explored, and, later in this section, we elect one example from each of the modes to parse those distinctions even further, asking you, in the spirit of what the word "essay" means, to test your responses to them.

From the French verb "essayer," to try or test or attempt, the essay is organized fundamentally around three interacting registers. Says English writer Aldous Huxley:

> Essays belong to a literary species whose extreme variability can be studied most effectively within a three-poled frame of reference. There is the pole of the personal and the autobiographical; there is the pole of the objective, the factual, the concrete-particular; and there is the pole of the abstract-universal.[11]

For Huxley, the most richly satisfying essays reverberate between all three poles or registers. The first, the personal and autobiographical, means that essay films have a clearly delineated expressive subject, much like the "I" who writes an essay from a personal point of view, whether it is a real or fictional persona whose explorations shape the film (as in Michael Moore's *Roger & Me* (1989)), or a more fragmented and unstable subject (as in Jean-Luc Godard's *2 or 3 Things I Know About Her* (1967)). The second pole – that of the objective and factual – finds the expressive subject venturing into the public sphere or the world of experience. The essay film is not, therefore, simply about an individual consciousness reflecting upon itself but involves an active sense of testing, undoing, recreating and adjusting the self through experience. Powerful changes in the public sphere, such as World War II or the experiences of anti-colonial struggle, make for powerful essay films. Finally, the pole of the "abstract-universal" represents those truths learned in the encounter between the expressive subject and the world around him or her. It is a mode of processing, thinking about, and engaging that experiential and embodied quest so that others may learn from it, too.

The first mode of the essay film, one that stresses the biographical and autobiographical pole of the form, is the portrait film (or self-portrait film). In distinguishing the specifically essayistic qualities of these portraits, Corrigan notes:

> the simultaneous enactment of and representation of a destabilized self as a central focus, topic, and, sometimes, crisis, a self whose place in a public history is at best on its margins or in some cases in an excluded or inverted position.[12]

In these essayistic portraits, the relationship between the self (its face, its voice) and the exterior world becomes a complicated and fractured one, much as the one we have seen in *The Ties That Bind*. To cite some other examples, one could highlight the work of Trinh T. Minh Ha, whose *Surname Viet Given Name Nam* (1989) is a "portrait" not of an individual but of Vietnam and its diaspora; or the work of experimental filmmaker Shirley Clarke, whose film (restored using archival prints) *Portrait of Jason* (1967) presents an intimate study of the life of a young African-American hustler.

The second mode is the essayistic travel film, following the subject as he or she investigates and transforms him- or herself in encounters with the world, in the process of being elsewhere. Chris Marker's *Sans Soleil/Sunless* (1983) may be the most difficult and complex of these journeys, a film that uses the epistolary form (the writing of letters) upon which many travel essays depend. If that film's observations on topics ranging from pet cats (one of Marker's favorite subjects!) to video games illuminate the grand themes of twentieth-century history, we are witnessing the essayistic movement from the personal (in this case a cameraman named Sandor Krasna) to the experiential to the abstract-universal. The French feminist director Chantal Akerman similarly uses letters to narrate *News from Home* (1977), a film Corrigan reads helpfully through the rubric of the essay film, noticing how it highlights the assertion and dispersal of subjectivity in its encounter with the public spaces of an elsewhere, New York.

Third in this taxonomy of modes is the essayistic diary, a form that emphasizes a reflective engagement with daily life and its rhythms. In this movement between the personal/reflective and the shocks and

2.15 Jason Holiday in *Portrait of Jason* (Shirley Clarke, 1967). Courtesy of Shirley Clarke Prod./The Kobal Collection.

aftershocks of public life, the diary film becomes a meditation on cinematic temporality, that is, the multiple times and rhythms we inhabit in modern life and the ways in which cinema can engage those times and rhythms. Some films foreground the experience of speed in the modern city; for instance Italian filmmaker Nanni Moretti's comedic confessional film, *Caro Diario/Dear Diary* (1994). The prolific Lithuanian filmmaker Jonas Mekas has recorded diaries from the 1960s with *Walden* (1969) to the recent film *As I Was Moving Ahead Occasionally I Saw Glimpses of Beauty* (2000); while at this writing Mekas is now 94 years old, he maintains a website of daily digital films, an online diary, called 365 Day Project.

EXERCISE

Compare three films from the 365 Day Project as diary forms of the essay film. Identify the essayistic subject, the experience the film records, and the results of the essay, question, attempt or exploration. Which films do you find powerful and why? What do they ask you to think further about?

The two final modes of essayistic filmmaking are the social/political editorial film (a fairly straightforward category) and what Corrigan calls the refractive mode (a less straightforward type of reflexive cinema). Like many blogs, the editorial essays invite a personal and public reaction to the news of daily life, analyzing not just the news but the subjective agencies involved (that is, the very possibility of taking action or making history in our complex world). Examples include much of the work of French New Wave director Jean-Luc Godard, as well as the films of the German filmmakers Harun Farocki and Alexander Kluge. A controversial and recent example is Zana Briski and Ross Kauffman's *Born into Brothels: Calcutta's Red Light Kids* (2004), a film that may overstate the role of the individual in addressing social problems while ignoring communal solutions and indigenous networks (and, in turn, ignoring the role of the film itself in perpetuating myths about Indian sex workers). In the refractive mode, essay films turn their attention precisely to art or film as a medium, in what Corrigan describes as "reenactments of the cinematic."[13] Rather than an indulgent or hermetic exploration of film as film, however, these films are "anti-aesthetic"[14] in that they always aim to return film to the world, to ideas, and to public experience. Here is a list of some to explore on your own: Alain Resnais' *Van Gogh* (1948), Henri-Georges Cluzot's *The Mystery of Picasso* (1956), Wim Wenders' *Tokyo-Ga* (1985), Sally Potter's *The Tango Lesson* (1997), Alexander Sokurov's *Russian Ark* (2003), Takeshi Kitano's *Glory to the Filmmaker* (2007), and Banksy's *Exit Through the Gift Shop* (2010).

AMATEUR FILM AND HOME MOVIES

Amateur film is usually characterized as a hobby rather than a job, while home movies are more strictly speaking movies emerging from families. Home movies are thus a subset of amateur film, involving the individual and familial practices of recording daily or intimate rituals and events for private viewing.

The making of both amateur film and home movies was made possible by technological innovation and marketing campaigns. As filmmaker and scholar Michelle Citron describes in her book, *Home Movies and Other Necessary Fictions*, with regard to the United States:

> We became a nation of home-movie makers in the first place because of a massive marketing initiative. When Kodak developed 16mm motion picture film in 1921, they asked Marion Norris Gleason, a neighbor of one of the film's inventors, to write a short film to be used to publicize the new technology. The original home movie, *Picnic Party*, was of her son Charles's first birthday celebration. This film promoted the possibilities of the new technology to both company executives and the potential home market.[15]

Citron, and other historians of amateur film including Patricia Zimmermann, highlight the resolutely domestic and familial nature of memory capture through film and, later, video technologies. Historically, the father held the camera and captured images of his wife and children. Historically, too, these images authenticated our experience. Like elements of the diary film we discussed earlier, home movies structure rhythms of daily life, record the growth of children through the years, and serve as evidence for the past we conjure as our own. Further – and cheaper – recording formats made amateur filmmaking accessible for greater numbers of users: Super-8 film was introduced in 1965, a consumer-friendly camera that paved the way for the video revolution that followed in the 1980s, with consumer-level video recorders ("camcorders") appearing in 1983. Today, the capture of moving images has become so ubiquitous that we may not reflect on how recent the phenomenon of cheap amateur filmmaking really is.

An influential academic anthology on amateur film, *Mining the Home Movie*, demonstrates not only its history but its global reach, showing "variegated and multiple practices of popular memory, a concretization of memory into artifacts that can be remobilized, recontextualized, and reanimated."[16] Amateur film helps us expand our sense of visual culture beyond the usual suspects of commercial film and national culture; home movies constitute what Zimmermann calls an "imaginary archive that is never completed, always fragmentary, vast, infinite,"[17] a description that would apply all the more forcefully to an archive such as YouTube. The archive is not static but active, changing all the time, and also crosshatched with power relations.

2.16 Astor Home Movies No. 2. Courtesy of the BFI Stills Collection.

CASE STUDY: ONIR

Onir is an Indian director who makes feature films on the outskirts of the mainstream Bombay film industry known as "Bollywood." Although he uses extremely well-known actors (including the most accomplished figures of twentieth-century Indian cinema, such as Shabana Azmi), his films cost well under half a million dollars to make and often speak to social issues. As we will show in our later discussions of film financing, this is cheap moviemaking compared to the dominant Hindi popular cinema, where budgets can rise above forty or fifty crore Indian rupees (or seven to eight million US dollars). By keeping costs low while speaking to pressing concerns usually excluded from popular cinema, Onir is at once trying to entertain and to educate through film, fighting to have his work distributed widely and ultimately shown on the Indian national television station, Doordarshan. He, like many aspiring filmmakers today, has turned to crowd-sourcing: not just for funds, but for ideas too. This makes him a compelling figure for an expanded version of what "self-expression" might finally mean.

Onir is, therefore, a good example of a filmmaker who is adapting the medium of film to make room for debate over *public* concerns such as AIDS, gay bashing, communal violence, and child abuse. His films are not didactic but use popular forms, including melodrama and song and dance, to convey messages of acceptance and inclusion. For example, Onir's first

2.17 Indian Filmmaker Onir. Courtesy of *Hindustan Times* via Getty Images.

feature, *My Brother… Nikhil* (2005), is the first Indian film to address the AIDS epidemic compassionately. Melodramatic, too, is *Sorry Bhai!* (2008), which pokes fun at every possible cliché of globalization (multilingualism, corporate branch offices in global cities, global brands such as Armani and Pizza Hut, Indian cinema and cinema studies, jazz and its circulation) while enlisting most of them for the production, a sentimental and amusing tale involving two brothers, one girl, and getting true love right.

Onir's *I Am* film had its theatrical release in 2010 and became the first Hindi feature film to be released in India with English subtitles, a testament to its director's hopes that the film find a broad audience beyond India.[18] Immediately, then, we have a category problem: it is an "Indian film," even a Hindi film, that explicitly addresses itself not simply to a diasporic or NRI (non-resident Indian) audience (as many larger films do by setting the action in the UK or US, by stitching themselves to global commodity culture, and by aggressively marketing their address to diasporic communities and their concerns); instead, these English subtitles make available a community of spectators who are potentially just not Indian, who are "beyond India." Like many crowd-sourced films, part of the financing came from a highly networked array of corporate and non-profit partners, donated labor and the contributions of crowd-sourced "co-owners" and co-producers. 400 co-owners donated 1,000 to 25,000 rupees (roughly $25 to $500) and receive listing in the film's end credits. A significant portion, then, of the film's financing derives from individual contributions.

But contributions in the form of stories and simple support/participation (co-producers) sustain the project as well, and here is where the *I Am* project seems to be remaking production cultures. The website for the *I Am* project invites participants to contribute their own stories of social ostracism and belonging, sharing in the world of the film's stories without sacrificing individual voices. Without guarantees, Onir and his star and co-producer Sanjay Suri are betting that they can germinate networks of collaboration, however virtual and however small-scale.

2.18 Director Onir poses after a press conference a few days before the release of his movie *I Am* in New Delhi on April 26, 2011. Courtesy of AFP/Getty Images.

THE CINEMA OF "ME" GOES DIGITAL

In our earlier mention of YouTube, and in our discussion of the repurposing of home movies, we have begun to speak of video and new platforms for self-expression. In this final section, then, we treat first-person media – a new term we introduce here – across platforms that include digital media. "First-person" media, following Alisa Lebow (herself a mediamaker and a scholar), references above all a mode of address: an "I" speaking to spectators and interlocutors, whether through forms we have discussed, such as the essay film, the home movie, or the personal film, or through less tangible forms of personality, autobiography, performance or ethnography. Especially on digital platforms, in fact, one now can find all manner of film and video that lies outside the commercial mainstream: public domain materials; home movies; out-takes; unreleased films; industrial and educational movies; independent documentaries; ethnographic films; newsreels; censored material; underground works; experimental pieces; silent-era productions; stock footage; found footage; medical films; kinescopes; small- and unusual-gauge films; amateur productions; surveillance footage; test reels; government films; advertisements; sponsored films; student works; and sundry other ephemeral pieces of celluloid. (These have tended collectively to be called "orphan film." There are orphan film societies and orphan film festivals, too, the largest and most prominent of which is the annual Orphan Film Symposium.)

This is the extended and open archive we referenced earlier, and you are in the midst of a proliferation of first-person media works that instruct, rant, entertain, confide, interview, stimulate, perform, evaluate, and enlist. The short duration of YouTube videos has stimulated a competitive form, the mobile media mini movie, contests for which have multiplied. One contest (called the M4) limits the length to 120 seconds; another (called "Cellflix") kept it down to 30 seconds. Webcams, by contrast, offer long-duration engagements with other sites (landmarks, beaches, weather, skylines, intersections) and people doing various things, some legal, some not, some free, some for a fee. Social media platforms such as Facebook and Twitter multiply opportunities for short-form expression and create new rhythms of first-person speech; tweets are only the beginning, with Vine and other applications following suit. While some disparage this world of constant self-representation and self-expression as frivolous, we encourage you to test its possibilities for worldmaking.

Even when used in the personal mode, video and digital media can be powerful ethical and political tools for self-representation and witness. Two further examples help broaden our frame of reference. In explaining the Chiapas Media Project, which introduced digital equipment to indigenous autonomous

EXERCISE

Watch YouTube videos by the following superstars of yesterday: Jenna Marbles, Smosh, Ray William Johnson, nigahiga, PewDiePie, Hola Soy German, and Michelle Phan. What defines a YouTube "personality"? How does the form (mode of address, length, framing) of these posts enlist future viewing through subscriptions? Compared to the personal films you have seen (feminist, essay, art), what distinguishes these from those more "serious" idioms?

Zapatista communities in Mexico, bi-national Mexican and North American project leaders make it possible for this movement of primarily indigenous people in southern Mexico to articulate their own positions and politics, testing new forms of democracy and mostly nonviolent action, as a singular movement opposing external control over local resources. The leaders explain their reasoning on the project's digital homepage:

> Why video and internet in the middle of Mexico's southern jungles? The Zapatistas are the most documented indigenous movement in the history of the world, with hundreds of videos, films, books and websites created by people looking in from the outside. Until recently, these temporary visitors have controlled the medium and the message. With the introduction of video cameras and professional training, the communities can tell their own stories from their own perspectives. The impact has been profound.[19]

Through letters, interviews and testimonials (a form of first-person expression crucial to Latin America and indigenous peoples), the videos in the Zapatista catalog demonstrate how speech and silence are already politicized categories, and how choosing silence in the face of military occupation or giving voice to women in the movement can be powerful antidotes to what the Zapatistas see as Mexican politics as usual. Taking advantage of digital environments and multimedia platforms, the Zapatistas have also used radio, rock music (from bands such as Rage Against the Machine), the internet, video news flashes, and other tactical media to make common cause with multiple audiences as agents of social transformation.

A second briefer example helps us to think about the conditions under which first-person films and other media emerge. Under other conditions of media censorship, as in mainland China, underground or independent first-person media help to articulate emergent subjectivities and collectivities. Arising from the emphasis on "individualization" (*gerenhua*) in the New Documentary Movement from the 1990s in China, an increasing number of documentary films shot in digital video (DV) in the early part of the twenty-first century focus on marginalized people in a changing China. To these videos, a new set of questions must be posed, according to scholars in China and in the West who are thinking about their impact:

> can this practice provide an unexpected opportunity for ordinary citizens to make themselves heard? How do these documentarians as well as their subjects grapple with the way power is at once open to contest and resistant to change? How do they articulate in the film- or video-making the production of politics, inequality, difference, and community?[20]

An example discussed in *The New Chinese Documentary Film Movement* is Zhang Hua's film *The Road to Paradise* (2006). Zhang Hua was herself the subject of a documentary by

2.19 Zhang Hua working alongside fellow Chinese documentary maker Li Jinghong. Courtesy of Kerry Seed.

filmmaker Li Jinghong about Zhang Hua's (failed) attempts to run a beauty parlor. "Zhang Hua then took up a DV camera and began to film women like herself, who try to establish their own small businesses, although their failures mean they cannot extricate themselves from the poverty-stricken margins of society."[21] A powerful, observational, realist, common sense aesthetic undergirds these productions, less concerned with *art* than with the inextricable bond between the individual and the social as they are propelled toward witnessing, truth-telling and transformation.

CHAPTER SUMMARY

The conception of a film author is solidified by many institutions and discourses of the world of cinema, from prominent film festivals such as Cannes to critical traditions reaching back to Romanticism. Closely linked with the idea of the *auteur* is art cinema, a domain we surveyed in the first part of this chapter by focusing on France and Sweden, two key national cinemas of the postwar period. Figures in the postwar avant-garde likewise elaborated a personal vision for cinema, often in relation to broader collectivities such as Andy Warhol's Factory or the Black Arts Movement. Counterpoised to the personal vision of the individual artists are models of collective filmmaking, which we surveyed from feminist and other political collectives through to experiments in the essay film and in amateur and home movies. Finally, we brought the discussion round to the digital era in understanding fragmentary film, YouTube, and other experiments in curating ephemera and self-authorship.

FURTHER READING

Blaetz, Robin (ed.). *Women's Experimental Cinema: Critical Frameworks*. Durham: Duke University Press, 2007.

> A lively and wide-ranging collection of essays on the movements associated with feminist and women's experimental cinema.

Corrigan, Timothy. *The Essay Film: From Montaigne, After Marker*. Oxford: Oxford University Press, 2011.

> An award-winning survey of this mode of subjective filmmaking, densely theoretical but also incorporating case studies and close readings amidst broader overviews.

Ishizuka, Karen L. and Zimmermann, Patricia R. *Mining the Home Movie: Excavations in Histories and Memories*. Berkeley: University of California Press, 2008.

> A fascinating subject in the ways it anticipates our current culture of image saturation, the home movie is the core topic of all of the essays in this edited collection.

Lebow, Alisa (ed.). *The Cinema of Me: The Self and Subjectivity in First-Person Documentary Film*. New York: Wallflower Press, 2012.

> A cinema scholar and filmmaker tackles YouTube from the perspective of the very history of personal filmmaking we chart in this chapter.

Zimmermann, Patricia R. *Reel Families: A Social History of Amateur Film*. Bloomington: Indiana University Press, 1995.

The authoritative history of home movies.

FILMS REFERENCED IN CHAPTER TWO

2 or 3 Things I Know About Her (Jean-Luc Godard, 1967)

400 Blows (Francois Truffaut, 1959)

Amerika (Newsreel, 1969)

As I Was Moving Ahead Occasionally I Saw Glimpses of Beauty (Jonas Mekas, 2000)

Born Into Brothels: Calcutta's Red Light Kids (Zana Briski and Ross Kauffman, 2003)

Caro Diario (Nanni Moretti, 1994)

Columbia Revolt (Newsreel, 1968)

De Düva (George Coe and Anthony Lover, 1968)

Entr'acte (René Clair, 1924)

Even, As You and I (Harry Hay et al, 1937)

Exit Through the Gift Shop (Bansky, 2010)

Female Misbehavior (Monika Treut, 1992)

Gendernauts (Monika Treut, 1999)

Glory to the Filmmaker (Takeshi Kitano, 2007)

Hush, Hush, Sweet Harlot (George Kuchar, 1999)

I Am (Onir, 2010)

Jump Cut: A Travel Diary (Monika Treut, 2004)

King Fu Grandma (Jeong-One Park, 2012)

Ladies' Turn (Helene Harder, 2012)

Life and Death of 9413 – A Hollywood Extra (Florey and Vorkapitch, 1927)

Measures of Distance (Mona Hatoum, 1988)

Memories of Underdevelopment (Tomás Gutiérrez Alea, 1959)

Meshes of the Afternoon (Maya Deren, 1943)

My Brother Nikhil (Onir, 2005)

My Father is Coming (Monika Treut, 1991)

The Mystery of Picasso (Henri-Georges Cluzot, 1956)

News From Home (Chantal Akerman, 1977)

The Road to Paradise (Zhang Hua, 2006)

Roger & Me (Michael Moore, 1989)

Russian Ark (Alexander Sokurov, 2003)

Sans Soleil (Chris Marker 1983)

Saving Face (Daniel Junge and Sharmeen Obaid-Chinoy, 2011)

The Seventh Seal (Ingmar Bergman, 1956)

The Smiling Madame Beudet (Germaine Dulac, 1923)

Sorry, Bhai! (Onir, 2008)

Surname Viet, Given Name Nam (Trinh T. Minh-ha, 1989)

The Tango Lesson (Sally Potter, 1997)

The Ties That Bind (Su Friedrich, 1984)

Tigerwomen Grow Wings (Monika Treut, 2005)

Tokyo-Ga (Wim Wenders, 1985)

Un chien andalou (Luis Buñuel and Salvador Dali, 1929)

Van Gogh (Alain Resnais, 1948)

Virgin Machine (Monika Treut, 1988)

Warrior of Light (Monika Treut, 2001)

Window Water Baby Moving (Stan Brakhage, 1959)

 **NOTES**

1 B. Ruby Rich, "Cannes Diary," 2 June 2014, http://www.sfbg.com/38/36/art_film_cannes.html, accessed 5 December 2013.

2 Caspar David Friedrich, "Thoughts on Art," in Richard Friedenthal (ed.), *Letters of the Great Artists: From Blake to Pollock* (London: Thames and Hudson, 1963), 32.

3 Birgitta Steene, *Ingmar Bergman: A Reference Guide* (Amsterdam: Amsterdam University Press, 2005), 21.

4 Daniel Widener, *Black Arts West: Culture and Struggle in Postwar Los Angeles* (Durham: Duke University Press, 2010), 7.

5 Archives of American Art online research collection, http://www.aaa.si.edu/collections/interviews/oral-history-interview-bruce-conner-12017, accessed 30 November 2013.

6 Glauber Rocha, "An Esthetic of Hunger," in *New Latin American Cinema*, Volume 1, edited by Michael T. Martin (Detroit: Wayne State University Press, 1997), 60.

7 Newsreel archives, www.newsreel.us, accessed 30 November 2013.

8 The entry describing the film *Amerika* on the Newsreel archive website: http://www.newsreel.us/rozNR2.htm#1, accessed 6 October 2014.

9 Harvard Film Archive program notes, Masao Adachi, http://hcl.harvard.edu/hfa/films/2013janmar/adachi.html, accessed 30 November 2013.

10 Michael Archer, Guy Brett, Catherine de Zegher and Mona Hatoum, *Mona Hatoum* (London: Phaidon, 1997), 140.

11 Quoted in Timothy Corrigan, *The Essay Film: From Montaigne, After Marker* (New York: Oxford University Press, 2011), 14.

12 Corrigan, 80.

13 Corrigan, 182.

14 Corrigan, 182.

15 Michelle Citron, *Home Movies and Other Necessary Fictions* (Minneapolis: University of Minnesota Press, 1998), 5.

16 Karen Ishizuka and Patricia R. Zimmermann, *Mining the Home Movie: Excavations in Histories and Memories* (Berkeley: University of California Press, 2007), 1.

17 Ishizuka and Zimmermann, 18.

18 http://ibnlive.in.com/generalnewsfeed/news/onirs-i-am-to-release-with-english-subtitles/594717.html, accessed 24 September 2014.

19 Chiapas Media Project statement, http://www.chiapasmediaproject.org/, accessed 30 November 2013.

20 Chris Berry, Lu Xinyu and Lisa Rofel (eds), *The New Chinese Documentary Film Movement* (Hong Kong: Hong Kong University Press, 2010), 11.

21 Berry, Xinyu and Rofel, 25.

CHAPTER THREE
CINEMA AS INFORMATIVE

You have thought now about making movies to entertain or to express a personal vision. In this chapter, we consider the desire to *inform* as that which fuels the filmmaking process. If we had written this book ten or fifteen years ago, we would naturally have had recourse to two terms that generally categorize informational cinema: *nonfiction film* and *documentary*. Of course, we have not jettisoned these, and neither have we abandoned documentary theory, that is, a deep consideration of the modes or tendencies of a large body of canonical cinema. What has changed in these years, in addition to the renewed presence of documentary on large screens and the discovery of how little we really know of the world's variety of informational cinema, is the invention of "reality," as in "reality TV" or "reality competitions". This sense of the term is actually a category of *production*, largely through digital media. "Reality TV" (or those snippets or morsels of reality that circulate on screens such as YouTube and viral video) or "non-scripted television" is the name for a cheap way of making content for digital platforms, and it asks us to recalibrate our assumptions about the relationships among experience, representation and entertainment. You live in the age of "reality" media, and your assumptions about what "reality" therefore means have changed as a result of it.

WHAT WE WILL DO IN CHAPTER 3

- Learn about the history of informational cinema up to "reality" TV.
- Understand the functions and modes of nonfiction filmmaking
- Distinguish the many different reasons for which these movies are made.
- Learn how to respond to documentary arguments and rhetoric.

BY THE END OF CHAPTER 3 YOU SHOULD BE ABLE TO

- Identify a documentary's primary tendency and form.
- Compare different documentary treatments of a single historical event.
- Make your own claims and arguments about what constitutes reality in film.

We begin by assessing the newly configured sense of reality on our screens through a discussion of how the production of informational cinema has been structured historically, and how that structure has shifted over time from some successful centralized systems of **public media** (government owned) to a largely **privatized** (privately owned) and often small-scale artisanal practice. More than with many other cinematic modes, informational work crosses platforms: from film to television, from digital video back to film. This happens through **narrowcasting**: as channels multiply, the numbers of people watching any given program shrink, leading to programming targeted at niche audiences and fierce competition for their attention. Narrowcasting creates **decentralized platforms** for **user-created content**. On the web, you can visit the hits of YouTube like Judson Laipply's "Evolution of Dance," the baby laughs of "Hahaha" and vocalist Tay Zonday's "Chocolate Rain."

Lines between information and entertainment have always been porous, and so we treat these new modes of reality media not so much as mutations necessarily in content or as wholesale shifts in media culture but as effects of the reorganization in the economy and scale of media production for digital platforms.

In discussing these very recent phenomena, we learn that past debates about tendencies in nonfiction form and about modes of documentary cinema have much to teach us. Michael Renov and Bill Nichols, two of the most prominent theorists of documentary, offer models for exploring the concrete processes of composition, function, and effect of documentary cinema. In proposing his "four fundamental tendencies" of documentary, Renov provides us with a framework for testing the primary *goals* of any given work, that is, for understanding what a film seeks to *do*. In offering categories, Renov nonetheless demonstrates through a range of examples how reliant these tendencies are on one another: they are *all* at work in shaping any given nonfiction film to varying degrees. Nichols' classification system likewise proposes six documentary *modes*, by which he means something less to do with goals and more to do with the aesthetic and rhetorical style of any given film. With his scheme, too, Nichols suggests fluid and overlapping ways of categorizing films rather than inert and discrete labels. Nonetheless, both ways of parsing documentary categories help us to characterize what we see and hear in nonfiction cinema.

In seeking, then, to test what these schema enable, we turn to key historical documentary films and film movements, from Robert Flaherty, whose exploration film of Inuit life, *Nanook of the North* (1922), is a requisite touchstone in the documentary canon, to the work of John Grierson and his unit in the UK, to the influence of Grierson and *social documentary* in the United States and Canada throughout the 1930s and early 1940s (in a circle of persuasive cinema that would include figures as diverse as Len Lye, Humphrey Jennings, Paul Strand, Ralph Steiner, Joris Ivens, Willard Van Dyke, Pare Lorentz, Leo Hurwitz, Shirley Clarke, and others). Surveying this range of work, we find, for example in Flaherty, a figure who is rightly heralded for the poetic and expressive power of his record of Arctic exploration. We also find a filmmaker who seized the opportunity to rework that record by supplementing actual events with imaginative dramatizations, and whose romantic conception of First Peoples actively distorts the effects of contact with remote populations. In other words, he made some things up about his encounters with the Inuit people who are the focus of his film. Insofar as power relationships between filmmakers and their subjects continue to haunt documentary work – with the work of Jean Rouch in France and its reworking through a film like *Rouch in Reverse* (1995), for example – we propose a close analysis of Flaherty's work as a prelude for future study. Similarly, the Grierson group is frequently studied in the context of very particular national and imperial projects of Britain in the 1930s, that is, as media produced in the service of imperial citizenship. But that group of films also provides tentacles to progressive media projects both in national contexts where centralized public media followed the British model (Canada, for instance, whose public media were led by the expatriate Grierson himself) and those where such efforts were short-lived and soon privatized (the United States, where Pare Lorentz was but for a brief moment the head of the US Film Office). Our discussion of the New Deal nonfiction films, in other words, emphasizes how they enable us to think about global cinema that followed in their wake. One way to underscore the very different lived experiences of the **nation** that undergirded documentary production following the Grierson experiments comes in comparative study of Nazi-era film: in Germany (with Leni Riefenstahl's *Triumph of the Will*), in Britain (with Jennings' *Listen to Britain*), and in the United States (with Frank Capra's *Why We Fight* series). Wartime documentary similarly remains alive, with pieces on the conflicts in Afghanistan and Iraq competing along ideological, rhetorical and aesthetic grounds depending upon the contexts of their production. A case study on recent testimony in political documentary, arguably an extension of "Third Cinema" but not limited to it, demonstrates yet another genealogical arc of this battle for hearts and minds.

Cinema as information, however, does not restrict itself to the canonical documentaries usually studied in survey courses, and so in the last two sections of this chapter we dwell on perhaps more idiosyncratic objects, but ones which might play a more central role in what French philosopher Michel Foucault would call the "care of the self." From sex education and hygiene films to workout videos, that is from the examples of films as various as *Soapy the Germ Fighter* (1951) to Jane Fonda's workout or the New York Body Plan, informational film helps breed discipline, helps us to regulate and condition our bodies for our labor and leisure lives. Image culture, that is, contributes to self-understanding, whether as a Romantic fantasy of self-expression (such as we detailed in the previous chapter on cinema as self-expression) or as an interrogation of social norms, expectations and behaviors such as we provide in this closing section.

3.1 *Nanook of the North* (Robert J. Flaherty, 1922). Courtesy of Flaherty/The Kobal Collection.

3.2 Film director Jean Rouch, 1961. Courtesy of The Kobal Collection.

DOCUMENTARY PRODUCTION

Documentary impulses were present at cinema's birth: the films of the Lumière brothers (Auguste and Louis), called "actualities" in their time, record the everyday lives and contexts of these earliest French filmmakers. These films were recorded, developed, and screened right away, so that part of their purpose, the reason they were made, was simply to allow people *to see themselves onscreen*, mediated through the new miracle of cinema. In *Workers Leaving the Lumière Factory* (1895), a stationary camera records workers leaving the Lumière family factory, framing their exit with strong diagonals to emphasize the capacity of the new medium to organize movement in depth. Stunning the first spectators who saw it, *The Arrival of a Train at La Ciotat* (1895) enlists speed, perspective (again), and technology as the ingredients of its appeal. This earliest effort at recording everyday sights and sounds was primarily *entrepreneurial* in spirit: the brothers invented a new technology, and hence a whole new way of seeing, and sought to spread its influence and potential throughout the world. Trained cameramen soon ventured across every continent but Antarctica, from Mexico to Russia to Australia; they documented street scenes in Russia, port activity in Liverpool (later explored again in *Of Time and the City* (Terence Davies, 2008)) and the pyramids in Egypt. At its birth, cinema was thus also a global medium, filmed everywhere and screened everywhere to inform audiences about the world. Audiences were therefore thrilled by seeing sights around the world and also excited by the prospect of seeing themselves recorded on film (much as one might look today for the record of one's presence in a crowd of extras, or at an event recorded for television). In some profound way – as has been noted by film theorists from André Bazin onward – film produces a powerful sense of reality, of something or someone *having been there* – really and truly, without magic or illusion: this is one of the most powerful aspects of the cinema's informational role.

The documentary tradition continues through the early decades of the twentieth century with exploration and ethnographic films, genres that find a high degree of Romanticization in Robert Flaherty's *Nanook of the North* (mentioned above and treated later in this chapter). What is important from the point of view of production is that these films, including Flaherty's, were **sponsored** productions, either through philanthropy or industry. It was costly and dangerous to venture into the Arctic (or New Guinea, or the Amazon, or …) in order to make a film, and so many of these films relied on the sponsorship of trading companies or others profiting from the vectors of exchange the films record. This raises questions about the perspective or point of view on offer in these films, made in some measure to promote the sponsors' interests. By the 1930s, when the Scottish filmmaker John Grierson coined the term "documentary," it was the state itself that had become the sponsor of informational cinema, raising similar questions about interests or stakes. State-sponsored cinema is generally known, not pejoratively but descriptively, as **propaganda**, a topic which we will explore further in Chapter 4. In Britain, Grierson's "tyros" (or apprentice filmmakers, a group of politically aware and well-educated young men) were initially organized under the auspices of the Empire Marketing Board (EMB), a unit responsible for promoting trade and a sense of British unity within the context of Empire. There, the group of makers Grierson recruited (who included the leading lights of British documentary, including Harry Watt, Basil Wright, Humphrey Jennings, Edgar Anstey, Alberto Cavalcanti, Stuart Legg, Arthur Elton, and Paul Rotha) made films about, among other topics, herring, butter, and Ceylon tea. As Basil Wright recalled in an interview, these were overtly sociological uses of film, meant to promote the wonders of Empire:

3.3 *The Arrival of a Train at La Ciotat* (Auguste and Louis Lumière, 1895). Courtesy of Lumière/The Kobal Collection.

3.4 Lumière illustration of an itinerant cameraman. Courtesy of The Kobal Collection.

As I remember, at the beginning, we were supposed to educate the British public about the marvels of Empire, because we still had an Empire in those days. We were selling New Zealand butter and Ceylon tea and so on to the British public, in a rather imaginative way. And we were also selling the British to themselves: we were selling the British industrial worker and the British agricultural worker to the British nation as a whole, as people who could be treated with respect. You must remember that in those days they *weren't* treated with respect. They were regarded as the working classes. This was 1930, 1931. Of course Grierson always had a wider point of view, but he had to play his cards very carefully. It was a world in which this use of cinema was very new, after all.[1]

By 1933, the filmmakers moved under the auspices of the General Post Office, charged with glorifying the communications networks as they did in *Night Mail* (Harry Watt and Basil Wright, 1936). Although there were bureaucratic and, as Wright notes, ideological obstacles to producing national culture, Grierson's group persevered with the GPO and also solicited industrial sponsors, such as the gas industry, for informational films. In the late 1930s, Grierson himself was recruited essentially to establish and organize the Canadian national film industry, founding and overseeing what became the National Film Board of Canada (a body that continues to fund and distribute Canadian documentary cinema).

3.5 *Night Mail* (Harry Watt and Basil Wright, 1936). Courtesy of GPO Film Unit/The Kobal Collection.

In the Anglophone British and Canadian cases, highly centralized, non-profit, state-driven television enterprises continued to sponsor informational cinema through the twentieth century. In the United States, however, the system of public broadcasting had a more diffuse history, linked as it was to land grant universities and their radio stations. Major documentary filmmakers in the US *did* work for television for their lifeblood (such as Willard Van Dyke and others associated with political documentary from the 1930s onward), and firms such as Drew Associates (which made some of the most important documentary films in the United States in the 1960s and 1970s) also produced films for industry, such as IBM. Those who worked for Robert Drew and his company – Richard Leacock, the Maysles brothers, D.A. Pennebaker, Anne Drew – became known as the founders of movements known variously as *cinéma verité*, *observational cinema*, and *direct cinema*. (The different names alert us to some contention regarding differences between them.) This style, using sync-sound recording without heavy voice-over narration, relied upon candid footage edited to offer a multifaceted 24/7 story of an event, for example in the award-winning film *Primary* (Robert Drew, 1960) of the battle for the Democratic presidential nomination between John F. Kennedy and Hubert Humphrey. While this style has now become common-place, especially for documentaries of political campaigns (such as *The War Room* (D.A. Pennebaker and Chris Hegedus, 1993) or *Journeys with George* (Alexandra Pelosi and Aaron Lubarsky, 2002)), it was so new and risky that the American television networks declined to broadcast *Primary*. Much of the funding for American documentary therefore came from foundations and a little came from the Corporation for Public Broadcasting, founded in the early 1960s.

As was the case for *Primary*, lightweight 16mm cameras and portable sound recorders, such as a recorder called the Nagra, made possible a whole new style of filmmaking, not quite comparable to what you can do with a mobile device, but still a sea change from the bulky equipment used previously. Still motivated by the desire to be present during a historic process, documentaries in the 1960s got intimate and close to their subjects, with the filmmakers acting as "flies on a wall." The technological revolution continued with video, first analog and now digital recording technologies that democratized image culture (insofar as it proliferated the number of makers) and enabled a number of social movements to capitalize on cheap technology and new structures of dissemination. Although politicized uses of documentary had circulated on film (in Cuba, Brazil, Argentina, Senegal) in the movement known as Third Cinema (discussed in a case study later in this chapter), filmmakers with commitments to social movements found ways to tell stories that enlisted support through the medium of video. Feminist makers embraced the intimacy of video – with its love of the close-up and

3.6 Film portrait of Edie "Little Edie" Beale from *Grey Gardens* (Albert and David Maysles, 1975). The directors of this documentary film, the Maysles brothers, had worked for Robert Drew and his company. Courtesy of Portrait Films/The Kobal Collection.

light – in order to tell stories that were largely absent from commercial and broadcast culture: stories of abuse, of eating disorders, of racial conflict, of coming out, of family life, and of the everyday, to name a few. Feminist video of the 1980s had a confessional feel to it that became its dominant tone, and also made possible work that followed it, such as much queer film around the devastation wrought by AIDS and Todd Haynes' *Superstar: The Karen Carpenter Story* (1987). In that film, Haynes uses a mixture of live action and scenes involving plastic dolls to tell the story of the demise of Karen Carpenter (half of the singing duo The Carpenters) from a lethal eating disorder. The film has been banned from the screen due to its unauthorized use of Carpenters' music but has circulated in bootleg versions – with various degrees of degradation and distortion – since it first made its way to video. As Lucas Hilderbrand has observed, it manages to be timely, poignant, chilling, and disturbing all at once, capturing new modes of connection and allegory (for example, acquiring resonance as a film about AIDS) as it circulates.[2]

Haynes' film is an example of what someone like you, armed with a camera, a good friend (such as Cynthia Schneider, Haynes' college friend who collaborated on *Superstar*), and a good story, can do to document something personally meaningful (the destruction of young lives through illness, music that touches you) in a creative way. Low-cost digital platforms have, in other words, made it possible for millions to make video, bringing us around to the current moment of YouTube. There are certainly cautionary tales: Jonathan Caouette shot his film *Tarnation* (2003) for $218, but the clearance rights for the music he used cost roughly half of the $460,000 invested to clean the film up in post-production for a commercial release.[3] Voracious for cheap content, both digital television and the internet have innovated ways to keep signals flowing. As the television grid expands to include hundreds and hundreds of channels, narrowcasting, as we have said, leads to a demand for lots of different kinds

3.7 *Tarnation* (Jonathan Caouette, 2003). Courtesy of Wellspring Media/The Kobal Collection.

of informational media. The economy of media production has changed the type of content sought by television. Reality television is, therefore, one name for what media costs when it uses non-professionals for its talent and builds much of its content around non-scripted performances, subordinating the work of writers who belong to unions. But reality television has, paradoxically perhaps, been accompanied by a resurgence in documentary work for the large screen, as Michael Chanan notes in *The Politics of Documentary*. He cites filmmaker Morgan Spurlock's claim that "we live in a world where independent documentary film has truly become the last bastion of free speech."[4] As Chanan also acknowledges, not all digital documentaries work in the service of democratic exchange and intellectual provocation: it is a complicated field, regulated as much by economies of production, distribution, and exhibition as the commercial narrative cinema. Even putting aside obvious figures such as Michael Moore and Spurlock himself, documentary film remains one of the most provocative, exciting, daring, and political domains of image culture.

EXERCISE

Choose a nonfiction YouTube video. What can you say about those who made it? How much did it cost to produce, as opposed to its cost to consume? At what audience it is directed? With what equipment was it recorded (audio and visual)? How would you describe its motivation? What does it seek to do? We'll ask you to return to the task of description after providing you with some new vocabulary for documentary rhetoric and poetics.

THEORIZING DOCUMENTARY

In this section, we give you some tools, akin to the forthcoming Interlude, for categorizing and describing nonfiction films. Michael Renov invokes the term "poetics" in his influential article, "Toward A Poetics of Documentary," in order to draw on a tradition begun by Aristotle and continuing through the present moment that involves "the sense of a shared ambition for the building and testing of general theories of textuality which focus on concrete processes of composition, function, and effect."[5] His interest in such a focus is propelled by a strong commitment to creating and sustaining a **documentary film culture**, an "energized climate of ideas and creative activities fueled by debate and public participation."[6]

Debate and participation, the same terrain referenced by Spurlock, require a shared vocabulary, and Renov thus proposes four fundamental tendencies of documentary:

1   To record, reveal or preserve.
2   To persuade or promote.
3   To analyse or interrogate.
4   To express.

All four function as modalities of desire: they are impulsions that drive documentary discourse. In other words, they catalyze exploration. They simply provide the *reasons* for making documentary work.

The first, "to record/reveal/preserve" is, according to Renov, the "most elemental" of documentary functions.[7] Its emphasis is on the replication of the historical real, the creation of a second-order reality cut to the measure of our desire – to cheat death, stop time, restore loss. In recording the world, we stop it from vanishing, decaying: we freeze it or keep it alive for our own purposes. Films hewing to this tendency therefore also provide the opportunity to rework experience: as we will discuss, Flaherty supplements events taking place in his moment of encounter with Inuit life with its imagined counterpart from the past, such as the traditional walrus hunt. In the case of the filmed diary (as pioneered by experimental filmmakers such as Jonas Mekas, the Kuchar brothers or feminist artist Lynn Hershman), the form itself blends recollection with the supplement of enacted experience. In discussing this first tendency, Renov notes that duplication of the world is never unproblematic, that is, "signifying systems bear with them the weight of their own history and materiality."[8] In other words, documentaries never simply reproduce the world; they do so through the kinds of recording, framing and understanding made possible in their historical moments and by their technological capacities.

In addressing the second tendency, "to persuade/promote," Renov insists on the mutability of his four tendencies. One must not, that is, think these are discrete or separable, because, for example, persuasion depends upon what Renov calls the "veridical stamp of documentary's indexical sign-status," part of the first documentary function. By this Renov means that in order to convince you, the spectator, of anything at all, you must believe in the truth of the image, the "having been there" of what you're seeing. If you suspect that it is manufactured, made up, you'll simply choose to opt out of the game of truth. Nonetheless, we can identify some clear examples of persuasion: as in the tradition of Grierson discussed above, in fact, where the screen serves as pulpit, or film becomes a hammer to be used in shaping the destiny of nations. Historically, these films harbor a sense of promotional urgency: something must be done, and now! One can also be persuaded by less direct forms of address. In any case, the persuasive/promotional modality is intrinsic to all documentary forms and demands to be considered in relation to other rhetorical/aesthetic functions.

In the third tendency, Renov understands "to analyze/interrogate" as the "cerebral reflex" of the "record/reveal/preserve" modality: "it is revelation interrogated." This tendency transforms unacknowledged questions that lie beneath all nonfictional forms into potential subject matter:

> that is, on what basis does the spectator invest belief in the representation, what are the codes which ensure that belief, what material processes are involved in the production of this "spectacle of the real" and to what extent are these processes to be rendered visible or knowable to the spectator?[9]

3.8 Film director Jonas Mekas. Courtesy of The Kobal Collection.

Films hewing to this tendency are precisely *about* these questions; they foreground and explore them. Dziga Vertov's *Man with a Movie Camera* (1929) becomes here the ultimate example, serving as a reflexive interrogation of image-making, editing and watching as revolutionary forms of vision. Made in the years just after the Bolshevik Revolution of 1917 in Russia, Vertov's films pursued "Kino-pravda," or "film-truth." He thought this was a truth revealed by the camera and the assembly of images through editing, not visible with the naked eye. In his most famous film, *Man with a Movie Camera*, Vertov fought to establish film as a medium distinct from theatre or literature. He wanted to capture life as it is, without the presence of the camera, as well as life surprised by the camera, provoked by the machine's observation. He thus wanted his audience to reflect on what the camera-machine could make visible for us, could reveal to us, about ourselves. We see this tendency in the films also of Jean-Luc Godard and in films where the sound/image relation is ruptured, such as Alain Resnais' *Night and Fog* (1955) or Chris Marker's *Letter From Siberia* (1957), a film that uses repetition and association (as Marker's films often do) in order to interrogate the world (and not merely to mock it).

> In a culture that values consumption – and the disposable culture responsive to that imperative – it may well be crucial for documentarists to consider the stakes of an intervention: to challenge and activate audiences even in the process of instruction or entertainment. In this regard, analysis remains the documentarist's most crucial support.[10]

The fourth tendency, to express, is, according to Renov, the aesthetic function most undervalued within the nonfiction domain, and this may be because the most frequently used analogy of film's expressivity is to poetry, an analogy difficult to sustain. Think about it for a minute, and you'll see how hard it is to compare a film's language to poetic language and structure. Flaherty, for example, has been called documentary's first poet, but it would be difficult to discern precisely of what his poetry consists. His Romantic conception of the filmmaker? His compositional acuity? The lyrical tone that emerges at times in *Nanook*? An analogy with music sometimes functions more easily to access the expressive dimensions of documentary work, overtly in films such as "city symphonies" (such as *Man with a Movie Camera*) which are structured compositions of daily life but also in films we might take to be "musical." Renov cites the work of Joris Ivens, whose film *Rain* (1929) might stand as a measured, even metered, and abstract study of a storm's coming and passing. The American photographer and filmmaker Paul Strand, too, seems exemplary of a dual emphasis on art/science, experience/experiment, so that the expressive dimensions come to the fore in his work by way of this comparative structure. This tendency can also be understood to expand boundaries of what counts as documentary in order to look at the work of the avant-garde. Ultimately, the question of expressivity is a matter of degree – a film is not disqualified because it documents. Renov says:

> [the] communicative aim is frequently enhanced by attention to the expressive dimension; the artful film or tape can be said to utilize more effectively the potentialities of its chosen medium to convey ideas and feelings. In the end, the aesthetic function can never be wholly divorced from the didactic one insofar as the aim remains "pleasurable learning."[11]

More briefly, Bill Nichols helpfully proposes six documentary modes: the **poetic**, the **expository**, the **observational**, the **participatory**, the **reflexive**, and the **performative**. We can correlate these with the four tendencies proposed by Renov as follows.

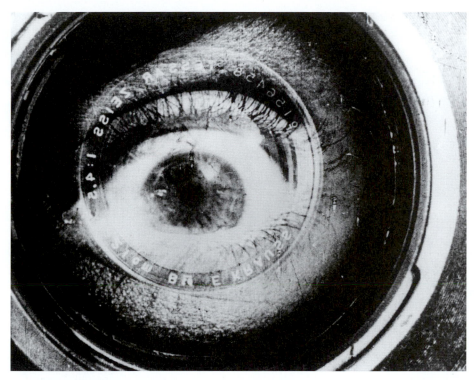

3.9 *The Man with a Movie Camera* (Dziga Vertov, 1929). Courtesy of VUFKU/The Kobal Collection.

3.10 The Holocaust documentary *Night and Fog* (Alain Resnais, 1955). Courtesy of Argos/Como/The Kobal Collection.

3.11 *Rain* (Joris Ivens, 1929). Courtesy of Photofest Inc.

We have encountered the poetic in the expressive. Nichols helpfully identifies internal rhythm, and subjective mood or tone as elements of the poetic mode. In the expository, the emphasis is on rhetorical content. One sees in it film's utility for transferring information. In the observational mode, which we have already mentioned in connection with Drew Associates and direct cinema, the injunction is simply to observe as acutely as possible as many facets of the unfolding event as possible. In the participatory, by contrast, the filmmaker is visible (here we can now include Michael Moore), and here, too, we can delineate the observational from *cinéma verité*, in which the filmmaker's situation and vision is crucial to the film project. In the reflexive we find something akin to analysis and interrogation: Nichols refers to a sophisticated critical attitude and uses the example of Manthia Diawara's film *Rouch in Reverse* (1995), which is itself a critique of visual anthropology. Finally, the performative mode shares with Renov's third tendency a departure from the rhetoric of persuasion to confront problems of aestheticization and authorship; the performative foregrounds the very acts of making documentary and speaking authoritatively.

Both sets of terms are helpful not for putting films into taxonomic baskets but for understanding why documentaries are made and how they approach you as a viewer. We take up these terms in the discussions that follow, suggesting how to extend their own thinking about how documentaries work.

3.12 Promotional image of Manthia Diawara and Jean Rouch for *Rouch in Reverse* (Manthia Diawara, 1995). Diawara's film is a revision of Rouch's ethnographic filmmaking. Courtesy of Manthia Diawara.

EXERCISE

Return to the YouTube video you selected for the first exercise. Using Renov's and Nichols' categories, how would you characterize, first, its strongest tendency? With what other tendencies does it declare its motivations? Using the Interlude to understand these terms, explore which textual features (*mise-en-scène*, cinematography, editing, sound) contribute most prominently to its success. Since many of the films we have mentioned thus far are available in digital domains, try this exercise with one we have aligned with a particular tendency. Were we right, or would you put it elsewhere? Why?

KEY DOCUMENTARISTS

We have suggested that students of documentary are learning about how little they really know of the world's informational cinema and media. In part, this is due to the politics of archives (discussed further in Chapter 13), in part to the ever-changing circuits of digital distribution, and in part to the tendency of educators to repeat canons that are restricted to the West and to key films in them. On the one hand, we take heart that new histories are emerging, such as Chanan's discussion of early Japanese documentary in the study we cite earlier in this chapter and recommend at its end. Other moments in

CASE STUDY: WORLD WAR II

A generative comparison of the aims of three films from three different countries around the period of World War II helps us to understand **propaganda** (which we will explore in more detail in Chapter 4), here defined fairly strictly as films made directly by the government or with state funds in order to promote a specific understanding of a national political position. We can understand that even within a particular tendency ("to persuade or promote") films work very differently from one another. Understanding how they differ not only gives us a lens on one of the most significant moments of recent history, but it also gives us the necessary tools for thinking about crafting arguments and using documentary rhetoric. Taken chronologically, the films are Leni Riefenstahl's German documentary of the Nazi Party rally in Nuremburg in 1934, called *Triumph of the Will* (1936); Humphrey Jennings' British hymn to wartime British life, called *Listen to Britain* (1942); and Frank Capra's American series of films explaining the war to those who will fight it, called *Why We Fight* (1942–1945).

To take the first one: Adolf Hitler rose to power in 1933 and quickly identified film itself as one of the most powerful weapons in winning support for Nazi social and political policy. His propaganda minister, Joseph Goebbels, said: "We are convinced that films constitute one of the most modern and scientific means of influencing the masses."[12] Hitler's concerted attempts to equate "Germany" with "Nazism" with "Hitler" were often accomplished through audio and visual means, generating a sense of his own destiny as a leader of Germany and exchanging symbols of nation with symbols of the Nazi Party to secure authorization for his consolidation of power. He enlisted filmmaker Leni Riefenstahl, famous for starring in "mountain films" that showcased athletic and hearty Germans in the battle with nature. The mountain film Riefenstahl directed, *Das Blaue Licht* (*The Blue Light*, 1932), pleased Hitler, and Riefenstahl was in turn fascinated by the power of Hitler's presence as a leader. Germany = Nazism, to put it baldly, as they did in their films. In Riefenstahl's famous aerial opening sequence to *Triumph*, we see the skyline of the city of Nuremburg through the clouds, medieval spires suggesting Germany's long history and dominion over Europe. In a Lufthansa airplane, Hitler descends to the airfield after a graphic introduction to his predecessors that guarantees him as an inheritor of German power and suggests simultaneously New Testament references to Hitler as Christ in the Second Coming: "Sixteen years after Germany's crucifixion, nineteen months after Germany's rebirth [*Wiedergeburt*] . . ." Here, in this opening, the function of propaganda in building allegiance to state power becomes an explicit act of historiography: writing history from the point of view of its current victors. In other sequences in the thirteen-part film, Riefenstahl visually emphasizes conformity (with bodies arranged in huge formations; what the philosopher Siegfried Kracauer referred to as a "mass ornament"), the subordination of the individual to the crowd, the unity of cities and regions under one Germany, the pleasures of cooperation and labor, the solidity and strength of the Aryan male body and other key facets of Nazi ideology. Long speeches punctuated by cries of "Sieg Heil" and "Heil Hitler" ensure that the major elements of the Nazi Party platform are communicated to the film's audiences across the country, disseminating not

3.13 The opening scene from *Triumph of the Will* (Leni Riefenstahl, 1936).

3.14 The "mass ornament" in *Triumph of the Will* (Leni Riefenstahl, 1936). Courtesy of NSDAP/The Kobal Collection.

only the party line but also the affect and enthusiastic assent expected of the film's viewers. As Tomasulo helpfully suggests, "there is only one role for the individual or collective spectator of these spectacles: as acceptor of the foreordained meanings of their cultural myths."[13]

Jennings' film provides an absolutely different understanding of the nation, recording as he does the calm ability of the British to survive, to "take it," during the Blitz. In contrast to the Nazi values of uniformity, conformity, militarism and symbolic display, *Listen to Britain* showcases British civility, the love of art, individualism, the everyday pleasures of civilian life, and the capacity, as one British war slogan put it, to "keep calm and carry on." He rejects a "voice of God" voice-over in favor of a kind of associational logic that links one image or sequence to the next; many have therefore referred to Jennings as the consummate cinematic poet, or, as filmmaker Lindsay Anderson put it, "the only real poet the British cinema has yet produced." Music is key to the film, from dance songs to radio broadcasts to "Home on the Range" to traditional/folk music. Two quite literal showpieces that foreground the role of audience involve, first, a music hall concert by the team of Flanagan and Allen, performing one of their popular songs, "Underneath the Arches" for an audience of workers. Jennings segues from this popular and working-class form of entertainment to a classical piano concert attended by the queen herself, a performance by Myra Hess (a Jewish artist, in a subtle demonstration of British affection for the Jewish people and inclusion) in the boarded-up National Gallery. Critics debate the juxtaposition of popular with high culture: does Jennings mean to imply that each class has its own music (and that we are therefore somehow one)? Or does he ask us to notice the differences and preserve a sense of class division as an ongoing social concern? In the rest of the film, Jennings does not avert his gaze and ears – for this is importantly a sound film – from the atrocities of war, recording everywhere signs of the blackened windows, of protective sandbags, of shelters and of troops that characterized life in a London under siege. But he is careful at the same time to show that life goes on, especially through these scenes involving music, which are linked, importantly, to both gendered life and to broadcast technologies. Unlike Riefenstahl's rehearsal of the passionate embrace in which audiences are meant to hold their Führer, Jennings asks his viewers to experience the sights and sounds he provides as poetic, lyrical elements of an artwork, open to interpretation and to many different responses.

Finally, Capra's series of seven films addresses an everyman American soldier about to enter the war, providing him with both information and a rallying cry. As many have remarked, following upon Joris Ivens' use of a male voice-over in *The Spanish Earth* (1937) (discussed elsewhere in this chapter), Capra's narrator communicates with a kind of folksy common sense. Indeed, before making the series, Capra thought that "documentary films were ash-can films made by kooks with long hair."[14] (Ash-can refers to an earlier twentieth-century movement in American art that focused on urban realism and gritty poverty.) No kook with long hair Capra: he sought to speak plainly and clearly to the troops about the evils of fascism and the necessary (belated) entrance of the United States into the war. After having seen enemy propaganda in the form of *Triumph of the Will*, he lit upon a strategy for his own series:

3.15 The Queen listening to Myra Hess in *Listen to Britain* (Humphrey Jennings, 1942). Courtesy of Crown Film Unit/ The Kobal Collection.

3.16 Scene still from the series of documentary films titled *Why We Fight* (Frank Capra, 1942–1945). Courtesy of U.S. War Department/The Kobal Collection.

"Use the enemy's own films to expose their enslaving ends. Let our boys hear the Nazis and the Japs shout their own claims of master-race crud—and our fighting men will *know* why they are in uniform."[15] Riefenstahl's own images provide Capra's films with visual evidence of the fascist conception of life and the German will to conquer the world. In the opening moments of the second film in the series, *The Nazis Strike*, after establishing that the German desire for world domination "goes back a long way," Capra unspools the very famous War Memorial march of Hitler, Lutze, and Himmler through an unimaginable mass of followers. The voice-over emphasizes lunacy: Germany's "maniacal will to impose itself on others," and "Germans' insane passion" to rule the world. This fanaticism is, in Capra's logic, simply *visible* in Riefenstahl's film: the task of Capra's film is to expose it and to show the American troops, again plainly and clearly, how the Nazi threat of world domination requires them to fight. Unlike Riefenstahl and Jennings, Capra had the resources of an enormous film industry at his fingertips: in addition to the historical footage and clips of enemy propaganda, Capra relied upon the sound, music, and dubbing departments of 20th Century Fox, Paramount, and MGM, as well as the personal talents of Walt Disney and his studio in creating the films' animation. Like Riefenstahl, Capra was certain of the conclusions his viewers would draw: vanquish the enemy before he rules the world.

Before the war, Capra had been one of the most successful directors in Hollywood, making films that have become synonymous with the uplifting American dream: *It Happened One Night* (1934), *Mr. Deeds Goes to Town* (1936), *Lost Horizon* (1937), *You Can't Take It With You* (1938), *Mr. Smith Goes to Washington* (1939), *Meet John Doe* (1941), and *Arsenic and Old Lace* (1944). After the war, he made what is perhaps his most famous film, *It's a Wonderful Life* (1946), cited frequently as one of the most inspirational films ever made in the United States.

3.17 Promotional poster/lobby card for *It's A Wonderful Life* (Frank Capra, 1946). Courtesy of RKO/The Kobal Collection.

documentary history will prove similarly surprising and interesting: studies of Brazil and Argentina, of contemporary Chinese clandestine documentary, of anti-globalization activism and so on. On the other hand, even while documentary proliferates and we learn more about its specific histories and strains, we are reminded of the power of some much-studied films that are at the heart of the canon. Their power derives as much from their innovations in form as from their staying power. As an example, the Flaherty Seminar, an annual week-long collaboration between documentary filmmakers and scholars, has often screened *Nanook* as its opening film. In what follows, we balance a discussion of some key films in the documentary canon with lesser-known examples, and in the closing sections we discuss two informational arenas you likely won't read about elsewhere.

Flaherty

Robert Flaherty had traveled in the Hudson Bay area of northern Ontario and western Quebec throughout the first decade of the twentieth century for Revillion Frères, a French competitor of the Hudson Bay Company, looking for iron ore and filming in order to recoup the costs of exploration. Tragically, all of the film from his 1914 and 1916 expeditions was destroyed by fire. To film the Inuit people not as they were but as they *had been*, Flaherty returned to make the film *Nanook of the North*, the most prominent historical example of "ethnographic fiction" or "salvage ethnography" or "romantic documentary." It is largely agreed to be the first feature-length documentary film. The central contradiction of this strain of documentary is as follows: even as Flaherty attempts to preserve ("record, reveal," to use Renov's terms) "primitive" or "noble" indigenous culture before its destruction by industrial civilization, Flaherty is himself the advance guard of that culture, of colonizing forces, of the exploitation of their resources and labor.

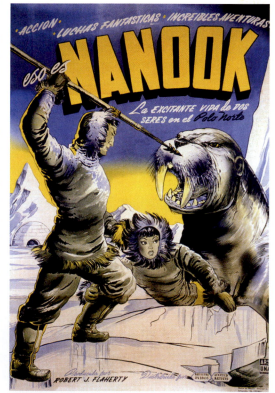

Much of the critical literature on *Nanook* focuses on questions of authenticity and the actual production of the film, thus opening the very questions Renov helps us to understand in his first category. The facts are disparaging, and they tend to instill a sense of let-down in the viewer. Sequences in the interior of the igloos, for example, were shot on igloo "sets" without roofs in order to allow sufficient light for filming. The Inuit had ceased to hunt for walrus by the time of Flaherty's expeditions: the staged walrus hunt actually put the men's lives in jeopardy, and as they called out for Flaherty to shoot the walrus with his rifle, Flaherty pretended not to hear them. The seal hunt was similarly staged: men pulled on the line with which Nanook struggles. In the testimony left by one of the children Flaherty fathered with an Inuit woman, indigenous audiences convulsed with laughter over the seal-hunting scene, and the women in the film were apparently common-law wives of Flaherty. These are damning to the sense of preservation the film imparts, but there are ways to push at the film's critical project further.

3.18 Promotional poster/lobby card for *Nanook of the North* (Robert Flaherty, 1922). Courtesy of Flaherty/The Kobal Collection.

Fatimah Tobing Rony describes *Nanook* as "taxidermy": it seeks to make that which is dead look as though it were still living. It embalms. It is a form of racializing representation that situates indigenous people outside modern history and without intellect. "Nanook," a character played by a man called Allakariallak, feigns ignorance of the gramophone and chomps on a record, this despite the fact that the indigenous Inuit (Quebec Inuit) served as Flaherty's crew and were intimate collaborators in filming, caring for equipment and making repairs. Flaherty produces what Rony suggests is a cinema of arche-typal moments endlessly repeated: the society of man the hunter, man against nature, man as eater of raw flesh (which is what the old term Eskimo is thought actually to mean), and the myth of the authentic first man.

The critical question thus confronts you, and you can look to the film to try to provide an answer: which aspects of the film support this image of the Inuit as animal-like, savage, and cannibalistic? At the same time, which aspects of the film support a reading of this representation of the Inuit as embodying the aspirations of the West: as intrepid and courageous, happy, adaptable, peaceful, hardworking, and independent? Flaherty himself described his subjects as "primitive people whose lives are simply lived and feel strongly."[16] What are the consequences of such a view for his film?

Ethnographic film has lived within these contradictions and has attempted to resolve them largely through reflexive gestures, what Renov would describe as analysis and Nichols as performative but which reflects directly on the tradition of "salvage ethnography" and the legacy of racist vision it supported. Examples in this performative tradition include the film we mentioned at the beginning of this chapter, Manthia Diawara's *Rouch in Reverse*, which provides a critique of visual anthropology by a Malian filmmaker and scholar. Diawara asks how it is possible to forge an African identity that is both African and modern in the wake of representations of Africans as primitive. Using what he calls "reverse anthropology," he re-edits the films of Jean Rouch, the world's most famous ethnographic filmmaker, to make visible new African voices and images. Similarly, Trinh Minh-ha, herself a filmmaker, musical composer, and feminist, post-colonial theorist, innovates new forms to speak back to ethno-graphic projects. In her early film *Reassemblage* (1982), Trinh (who is of Vietnamese origin) meditates on her fieldwork in Senegal by refusing to make an authoritative film on "African culture." Instead, as she continues to do in *Naked Spaces: Living is Round* (1985) and in all of her films that speak to the

3.19 *Reassemblage* (Trinh Minh-ha, 1982). Courtesy of Trinh Minh-ha.

post-colonial condition, she refuses exoticization and mystification in favor of a highly suggestive and oblique style that solicits intellectual reflection. In her writings and other films, she plays with ethnography in that she plays with all of its elements: power inequity, forms of knowledge and revelation, documentary conventions and claims to truth.

SOCIAL DOCUMENTARY

In our earlier section on documentary production, we introduced the work of John Grierson's various filmmakers who worked directly for the British government in various formations: the EMB, the General Post Office, and the Crown Film Unit. As Basil Wright tells us, Grierson's politics were often to the left of the perspectives his films were asked to take, and part of the pleasure of watching them today is to notice how creatively and energetically this group of filmmakers approached topics we would all agree are at least potentially *boring* or at least clearly not the object of the makers' passions. Conditions in the slums, nutrition, mail delivery, radio communications – these do not lend themselves necessarily to dramatic narration, and yet in the hands of these men (for few women worked among them), a mail drop along a rural stretch of railroad becomes a Hitchcockian sequence of suspense (in *Night Mail*, of course).

In the same period in the United States, political filmmaking faced a harder road. There was no state support for social criticism; in fact, many left-wing filmmakers gravitated to the short-lived Film and Photo Leagues under the Communist Party's auspices in order to document the devastating effects of the Depression. Films and photographs of food lines and starvation, what Victor Hugo called "the degradation of man by poverty," served Renov's function of recording the reality of the moment, but they also had a strongly rhetorical function of promoting revolutionary solutions to these problems. In the words of the New York chapter of the Leagues:

> The Film and Photo Leagues were rooted in the intellectual and social basis of the Soviet film … , in the same way as the Soviet cinema began with the kino-eye and grew organically from there on … the Leagues started also with the simple newsreel documents, photographing events as they appeared to the lens, true to the nature of the revolutionary medium.[17]

The Leagues also provided criticism of commercial mainstream cinema (Hollywood and its fantasies) and denounced and picketed Nazi, militaristic and Fascist films. While some had been renowned still photographers (Paul Strand, Margaret Bourke-White, Willard Van Dyke), others sought new roles for cinema aside from its commercial function. Film could explicitly function as a socio-political tool.

A number of different types of filmmaking and filmmakers converged in the 1930s to lend their voices to a period of urgent socio-political confrontation. Several years into the Depression, there were hundreds of thousands of the jobless and the homeless on the streets; labor leaders were kidnapped and murdered; there were hundreds of openly functioning and well-financed fascist, militarist, anti-labor, anti-Semitic, anti-black organizations and media outlets in the United States alone. The world was in crisis, and the filmmakers sought to wield the hammer of cinema alongside their British counterparts in order to address it. Some of them joined forces to collaborate, such as on Leo Hurwitz's peculiar omnibus film, narrated by Paul Robeson, *Native Land* (not released until 1942). State support came for a different group in the form of President Franklin Delano Roosevelt's New Deal, which established federal work projects under the auspices of the Resettlement Administration (later the

3.20 The "Migrant Mother" is a key photograph by Dorothea Lange and much-reproduced. Courtesy of The Library of Congress, Prints & Photographs Division, FSA/OWI Collection.

Farm Security Administration), the unit that housed the photographic section. Their remit? To spread the words of President Roosevelt, who wanted the American people to understand the "one-third of a nation ill-housed, ill-clad, ill-nourished."[18] Great geographic and economic forces became their emphasis, told through images that became iconic, such as Dorothea Lange's photograph, "Migrant Mother." The films that emerged from efforts sponsored by the RA/FSA (and later the US Film Office) have similar iconic force. Among them are the two big films Pare Lorentz oversaw, *The Plow That Broke the Plains* (1936) and *The River* (1938).

As is the case with the Grierson group's work, there is much to admire in the films made collectively by Lorentz, Hurwitz, Strand, Van Dyke, Floyd Crosby, Ralph Steiner and others who worked on them (as there is in the films made by each of them alone). What stands out as their lasting achievement? They realign what "America" and its core ideological ingredients might mean. They write history from the perspective of dignified work and political freedom. They filter the iconography of patriotism through a lens of equality, so that the flag and Abraham Lincoln's memorial become standards testifying to

3.21 *The Plow That Broke the Plains* (Lorentz, 1936). Courtesy of Resettlement Administration/The Kobal Collection.

racial justice. They show the environmental devastation wrought by greed and the bad luck of cycles of drought and flooding, and they argue that federal relief can make ordinary lives better. *The Plow* met with criticism upon its initial release for misstatements and mistakes: Lorentz apparently didn't know much about Texas geography, and he overdraws and magnifies the situation in the western plains. But *The River* was, and is, seen as a magisterial composition, and the flood footage shot by Willard Van Dyke in 1937, when the film was almost completed, is considered among the best footage in the history of documentary film.

CASE STUDY: THE LEGACY OF POLITICAL DOCUMENTARY

In the UK and US contexts of the 1930s, even while most of the filmmakers pledged some version of internationalism (for the brotherhood of workers throughout the world and the interconnected struggle against fascism and capitalist exploitation), the cinemas remained largely national projects of persuasion. They circulated primarily in their home countries, and they were explicitly addressed to the imaginary of citizens who could affect political outcomes at the polls. Like other films we discuss in this chapter, these films toyed with the distinction between make-believe and the real world, between re-enactment and recording.

The movement we call Third Cinema similarly described a national cinema of anti-colonial struggle, from Gillo Pontecorvo's *Battle of Algiers* (1966) chronicling the Algerian revolution, to Ousmane Sembene's films tracing the liberation of Senegal, to Argentinians Octavio Getino and Fernando Solanas' *Hour of the Furnaces* (1968), to Tomás Gutiérrez Alea's *Memories of Underdevelopment* (1959), reflecting upon the early moments of Castro's Cuba. These were films that bore witness, produced testimony, told passionate stories of the downtrodden and hopes for better worlds. Fueled by a concatenation that included, as Roy Armes has noted, "opposition to the Vietnam war, student revolt, a new consciousness on the part of American blacks, the emergence of armed guerilla groups in Latin America, developments within the Communist world opposing China to USSR in terms of revolutionary strategy," filmmakers in the 1960s believed in the political function of cinema within what Armes calls the "euphoria of revolution."[19] In the key theoretical elaborations of Third Cinema in its moment – for example in the now-canonical "For an Imperfect Cinema" by Julio García Espinosa and "Towards a Third Cinema" by Solanas and Getino – we witness an attack upon western formal perfection in works of art, whether demanding, in the former essay, the destruction of the artist's elite isolation (and a film practice which "finds its audience in those who struggle") or, in the latter, a subversive mode of filmmaking dependent upon the destruction of both commercial cinema ("first") and the author's cinema ("second cinema"); finally, it describes innovation and experimentation at the level of form as much as content. In many African instances, for example, "Third Cinema" drew upon folklore, traditional myths and legends to tell stories about the emergent nation and the complexities of post-colonial modernity. Frequently dependent upon allegory, though not all reducible to allegorical structure, the films tend to establish complicated relations to national history.

Even the most prominent discussions of "Third Cinema" undertaken more than twenty years ago suspended the designation as a question precisely to "re-pose the question of the relations between the cultural and the political."[20] Indicting the left's sentimentalism regarding Third Worldist politics, the 1986 Edinburgh International Film Festival conference yielded the book, *Questions of Third Cinema*, which sought to "draw attention to different, non-English approaches to cultural politics."[21] The conference organizers marked the ostensible passing of a moment and of a conceptual frame (both "Third World" and "Third Cinema") that seemed adequate to that moment, which was characterized by the dominance of the national frame, the declaration of a break with the colonial order, and the promise of a national-popular culture articulating the vision and needs of a people newly empowered to shape its image. "Third Cinema," born of Cold War politics, furthermore traveled on a utopian impulse to establish political categories rather than describe them.

The moment has clearly changed, but how exactly? It is not so much that political documentary has all of a sudden shed its ties to nation as it is the case that, within the much broader context of globalization, the politics of the post-industrial landscape urgently require new images and analysis of mobility, survival, migration, and displacement, to name but a few

3.22 Promotional poster/lobby card for *Battle of Algiers* (Gillo Pontecorvo, 1966). Courtesy of Casbah/Igor/The Kobal Collection.

key terms. A recent film about Indonesia, *The Act of Killing* (Joshua Oppenheimer, 2012), sheds light on changes in documentary practices. Oppenheimer revisits the year 1965, a moment when killing squads conducted mass murders of suspected communists (but also ethnic Chinese, intellectuals, and others) in the Cold War panic surrounding Vietnam. Oppenheimer not only interviews men who served on these death squads but *re-enacts* their killings, many of which were inspired by – surprise – the movies. They killed after watching Elvis Presley, and they killed as cowboys attacking Indians. This is re-enactment at its most unsettling, and the film has attracted some controversy as a result, but Oppenheimer remains steadfast in his understanding of the role of the filmmaker. As he remarks on the film's website, "I think it's our obligation as filmmakers, as people investigating the world, to create the reality that is most insightful to the issues at hand."[22] This Indonesian–Japanese film is a provocative, surreal and powerful meditation on action, ethics and responsibility.

3.23 Film portrait from *Hour of the Furnaces* (Octavio Getino and Fernando Solanas, 1968). Courtesy of Grupo Cine Liberacion/The Kobal Collection.

Another place to look for these analyses is in the documentation of the post-industrial landscape and its refuse. In past years, a host of films addressing various practices of gleaning, recycling, trash collection, dumpster diving and the like insist upon showing what otherwise is purposely hidden: the poorest and most vulnerable of the world's people. These include Brazilian documentarian Eduardo Coutinho's short film, *Boca de Lixo* (1993), Marcos Prado's *Estamira* (2004), Agnès Varda's *The Gleaners and I* (2000), and Jardim and Harley's *Waste Land* (2010). Taken together, the films echo the demand to the 1930s documentarians to show the "lower third," or those on the bottom rungs of the social ladder, but less as a showcase of degradation than a dignifying portrait of survival and innovation. They document the movement of food and products through economies of waste and of scarcity, and they follow migrants as well as outcasts who live on heaps of garbage.

Issues regarding the ethical relationship between maker and subject are not restricted to ethnographic cinema as such; indeed, these films foreground the complexity of training the filmmaker's gaze on marginalized and vulnerable subjects. Varda's self-declared inclusion in the practice of gleaning (in her case, largely understood as a gendered history of gathering food crops after harvest) allows her to link her film art – the gleaning of discarded or unpredictable images – to the practices of desperate survival she documents, under the banner largely of feminism. Even if this equation gives us pause, it demonstrates Varda's awareness of the ways in which documentarians can profit from images of despair. More overtly, the artist Vik Muniz, profiled in *Waste Land* as he returns to his native Brazil to make a series of works entitled "Pictures of Garbage Series," actually donates the profits from the sales of the works to the garbage pickers the film profiles. A film by a young Indian filmmaker, Parasher Baruah, entitled *Waste* (2009) was built on months of pre-production participation by Baruah in the lives of the Mumbai pickers he befriended in the immense slum called Dharavi. Part of a larger project by ACORN India, the film is a product of NGO-driven efforts to improve the lives of these pickers, to add, as they put it, another "r" to the recycling process: "reduce, reuse, recycle, and respect." In these latter two cases, we might see all four of Renov's tendencies integrated into ongoing, complicated, pre- and post-cinematic processes of community building.

3.24 Film director Agnès Varda. Courtesy of Cine Tamaris/The Kobal Collection.

SEX HYGIENE AND FITNESS

Lest it appear frivolous to turn from Third Cinema, globalization, slum dwellers, and waste to the topics of sex education and fitness, it is not done simply to end on a relatively light note. All of the examples of informational cinema we cite in this longer section address or contribute to the discourses of morality, discipline, and a vision of what is good. If the scale of such judgments has extended in previous examples to the nation as an entire political entity, or to the world as an international brotherhood, or to cross-cultural contact as a bridge to understanding The Human as such, here it contracts to the self, and to the self as a particular type of entity requiring its own discipline, cultivation, styling, and techniques. The latter terms come from the insights of Michel Foucault, who, late in his career, began a project he never completed to study how it is that we have come to practice ourselves as subjects, that is, as *subject to* a power we imagine as exterior but is rather produced through our practices of subjection. While this may seem an abstract notion, Foucault developed it through his work in prisons, where he observed first-hand how prison inmates become their own wardens: they "internalize," to use a word Foucault would not, their own obeisance. "Internalize" strikes the wrong note in Foucault's understanding, implying an external power then taken inside: we want to reinforce, at the same time using a colloquial term you know, that he means that the practices of self-discipline actually *produce* the power we then believe to exist outside of ourselves. Under Foucault's scrutiny, a whole range of practices of the self came, from antiquity onward, to constitute this disciplinary ensemble of subjection: sex and desire, diet, drink, medicine, dreams, self-knowledge, the centralization of marriage and gendered relations, a relation to civic and political life, and so on. From historical and philosophical documents, he extracts a theoretical framework ranging over centuries. Our aim here is more modest but we imagine it, we hope not immodestly, to extend Foucault's "History of Sexuality" project into the domain of informational cinema.

SEX EDUCATION

If social documentaries were concerned with film as a weapon for political change, sex education and hygiene films undertake social engineering through the language of film. They persuade through pedagogy: they are overtly packaged as "education." More than 3,000 of these films were made since the first decade of the twentieth century, but the peak period of their production followed World War II. (Education films such as *Sex Hygiene* (1942, made 1941) were shown in military sectors, but the focus here is on those films used in schools and colleges aimed at children and teenagers.) Many of these films use the codes and conventions of popular entertainment (Hollywood cinema) as an ideological tool, and they are therefore particularly helpful to study for the way they deploy these codes towards moral ends; the films are used as a kind of inoculation against disease and behavior, and they do this by appealing to convention and codes of popular culture. By such close association with Hollywood, they clothe propaganda and education in the language of entertainment.

Education films and the social and sex hygiene films were used to control or change behavior, discipline the body, and produce and regulate national subjects. Social and sexual health come to be defined through science and technology: technologies of vision, ways of visualizing and seeing via technological means, become the vehicle for self-discipline. By technologies of vision, we mean instruments that can visualize or make visible that which is not seen, especially in the sex hygiene films which seem to be fascinated by the visual and spectacular. They over-invest in the medical gaze, the ability to show us something, either through photography, animation, illustration, the microscope, or x-rays. The films also show us things (body parts especially) we would not ordinarily see, often in the context of a *mise-en-scène* that thematizes looking (the doctor's office, the clinic, the projector, the light box, the microscope). Indeed, the microscope, the camera, and the projector work together in a relay of looks: there is a power involved in the ability to visualize the effects of immoral and undisciplined behavior and, in turn, validating the power and value of medicine in the service of social cleansing. Morality, then, draws on medical discourses that are authorized not only through the figure of the doctor but also through the technology available to him, revealing the horror of disease as the consequence of illicit behavior.

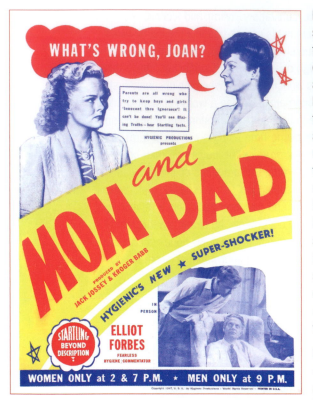

3.25 Promotional poster for *Mom and Dad* (William Beaudine, 1945). Courtesy of the wrongsideoftheart.com.

Education films thereby address their spectators as moral subjects, capable of being shaped and molded according to moral parameters, producing a sense of guilt or lack (not caring properly for your body, for example), in turn creating a self-disciplining relationship to the body. Such morality, however, is achieved now through social-scientific institutions, medicine, and technology because these have the ability to inform and demonstrate, providing us with information packaged as the authority of expertise. Custodians of the child's or teenager's body such as the family and church no longer held as much power in the postwar period, so it became the job of science and government to reveal what happens to a body not sufficiently under control and not sufficiently hewing to social norms (this was, remember, an intensely conservative period). The new figure of the scientist, school nurse or health officer replaces the figure of the father or the priest; an expert takes control of the body. In *Sex Hygiene*, the educator tells us, "Most men know less about their own bodies than they do their automobiles."

Since the films tend to reveal their topics in their titles (*Keep Off the Grass* (1970), *LSD: Trip or Trap?* (1967)), they can be apprehended generically by their specific concerns about behavior and conduct, drugs and alcohol, sex education

3.26 *Teaching with Sound*, 1936. Courtesy of the Prelinger Archives Collection.

and sexually transmitted diseases, manners, driver's education. Some ripe for analysis include the aforementioned *Soapy the Germ Fighter* (1951), *The Outsider* (1951), *Drug Effects* (1959), *Appreciating Our Parents* (1950), and *The Innocent Party* (1959). From ideas about the national body to conceptions of family and "fitting in," these films have the capacity to generate fear and discipline at the same time, and, while historical distance makes them seem fun, even campy, the genre lives in the present moment, as we discuss in our concluding section.

FITNESS

The fitness industry thrives, proving that media retain their capacity to command self-discipline, to produce guilt and a sense of failure, and to circulate what is often misinformation about aerobics, isometrics, and other forms of exercise and their effects. In an article on *Jane Fonda's Workout*, released on home video in 1982, a writer from *Sports Illustrated* diagnoses the workout fever that Fonda's video generated:

> The fervor is sometimes just good technique; after all, exercising is not easy and may require a self-described "ass kicker" like Steinfeld or a relentless get-after-it nagger like Fonda. In other cases the evangelism is the result of an "I found it" conversion, similar, perhaps, to Saint Paul's experience along the road to Damascus. Simmons, for one, loves to talk about his days as a 268-pound fat man and his discovery of the magic elixir of exercise; one of his nicknames is The Weight Saint.[23]

Fonda's video was no mere fad, in other words: it sold seventeen million copies, which makes it the highest selling video in history. Because its rise coincided with the penetration of the VCR into private homes, it actually stimulated sales of the machines: people (women) bought a VCR in order to play and do the workout. Eventually, Fonda made over twenty-three videos.

An American actress from an acting dynasty (her father Henry Fonda, her brother Peter Fonda, her niece Bridget Fonda), Jane Fonda generated a complicated screen persona that mirrored her own complicated life and serial marriages. At the time of the workout videos, Fonda was married to the outspoken activist and politician Tom Hayden, and she was nominally supportive of efforts to organize women clerical workers by an organization called 9to5, the National Association of Working Women. (Fonda had made a movie called *9 to 5* (Colin Higgins) in 1980, a fantasy of women workers' revenge on their sexist boss.) To some degree, the workout videos responded to feminist discourses of the early 1980s: female empowerment through the organization of women workers for collective bargaining (and to address issues of pay inequity, harassment and discrimination, medical care and leave, and childcare), the need for sedentary workers to exercise and move about, dignity in the transition from the language of "secretary" to that of "administrative assistant," and the capacity for ordinary women to exercise vigorously and publicly, prerogatives previously largely restricted to men. Glance just for a moment at a segment of one of the videos, however, and you see a very different picture! Leslie Lilien, a has-been pop artist, sings a blandly inspirational disco-y song called "Do It!" to leotarded cheerful thin people. "There is much more to you than meets the eye" run the lyrics, and the inspiration echoes self-help and personal empowerment banalities that were the currency of the decade. In the chasm between feminist organizing and discourse and the images of sexualized, eroticized, and normatively attractive (thin, stylish, or whatever stylish meant in the world of aerobic wear), we can perceive the contradictory position of this strain of informational media. At once addressing real needs and positive goals and yet replicating a restricted understanding of women's bodies, *Jane Fonda's Workout* engendered often-unattainable routines of self-discipline and self-policing. Many of the videotapes languished unseen. In a footnote to this moment in media history, Fonda re-emerged with the *Workout* brand in 2011, this time with a new set of videos, now on DVD, targeted toward aging baby boomers, the postwar generation, the eldest of whom are now in their mid-60s. Of her own looks, she commented:

> I owe 30 per cent to genes, 30 per cent to good sex, 30 per cent because of sports and healthy lifestyle and for the remaining 10 per cent, I have to thank my plastic surgeon. I'm happier, the sex is better and I understand life better. I don't want to be young again.[24]

Make you want to convert?

Fonda is not alone in her success marketing fitness for home video, and it is not surprising, given the discourse of religious conversion and commitment within the diet and fitness world, that other "gurus" – such as Richard Simmons and David Kirsch, of the Ultimate New York Body Plan – thrive. No source is left unturned for inspiration: Sizzling Salsa and the Brazilian Butt Lift provide "exotic" alternatives to the workouts of Denise Austin or the thousand-calorie burner of Jari Love. While the latter may be effective, it also gestures toward the "quick fix" nature of many of these programs. With a rise in

3.27 *Jane Fonda's Workout.* Courtesy of The Kobal Collection.

3.28 Film portrait of Jane Fonda, Dolly Parton, and Lily Tomlin from *9 to 5* (Colin Higgins, 1980). Courtesy of 20th Century Fox/The Kobal Collection.

popularity of media featuring morbidly obese people, such as the A&E program *Heavy* or the documentary feature *Half Ton Man*, fitness and diet self-help video is located in a wider set of bodily practices seen to be out of control or in "crisis." Foucault shows us that from the Greeks onward, we have been engaged in practices embedded into deep-reaching moral and ethical systems for the management of health and the life of the body. Informational film has done its bit, in the last half-century, to generate ever-new practices of self-discipline.

3.29 Jane Fonda in *Jane Fonda: Prime Time, 2010*. Courtesy of Lionsgate/The Kobal Collection.

CHAPTER SUMMARY

This chapter began with the ideas of reality and information that undergird much of nonfiction filmmaking. We followed with a brief history of documentary, from its beginnings in the actuality films made by the Lumières on to key moments in twentieth-century film history: state-sponsored filmmaking, propaganda film, films of the New Deal in the United States, and obser- vational film and television. We then surveyed two influential theories of documentary, Michael Renov's taxonomy of documentary functions, and Bill Nichols' categories of documentary modes. Finally, we isolated several key documentary figures and movements: ethnographic film, social documentary, political documentary (and questions of ethics), educational film, sex hygiene films, and fitness videos.

FURTHER READING

Barnouw, Erik. *Documentary: A History of the Non-Fiction Film*. Oxford: Oxford University Press, 1974, 1983, 1993.

Although last revised several decades ago, this remains an insightful and passionate overview.

Chanan, Michael. *The Politics of Documentary*. London: British Film Institute, 2008.

Chanan is a filmmaker and scholar, uniquely positioned to understand the complex world of political documentary.

Nichols, Bill. *Introduction to Documentary*. Bloomington: Indiana University Press, 2001.

The new standard introduction, updated and organized to address questions students most often ask about nonfiction film, from ethics to production practices.

Renov, Michael. *The Subject of Documentary*. Minneapolis: University of Minnesota Press, 2004.

By "subject" Renov means the filmmaker him/herself. He studies the making of films for which the filmmaker's own perspective and sensibility are important elements, from political films to YouTube videos.

 FILMS REFERENCED IN CHAPTER THREE

The Act of Killing (Joshua Oppenheimer, 2012)

Appreciating Our Parents (1950)

The Arrival of a Train at La Ciotat (Lumière brothers, 1895)

Battle of Algiers (Gillo Pontecorvo, 1966)

Boca de Lixo (Eduardo Coutinho, 1993)

Drug Effects (1959)

Estamira (Marcos Prado, 2004)

The Gleaners and I (Agnès Varda, 2000)

Hour of the Furnaces (Solanas and Getino, 1968)

The Innocent Party (1959)

Jane Fonda's Workout (1982)

Journeys with George (Alexandra Pelosi and Aaron Lubarsky, 2002)

Keep Off the Grass (1970)

Letters from Siberia (Chris Marker, 1957)

Listen to Britain (Humphrey Jennings, 1942)

LSD: Trip or Trap? (1967)

Man with a Movie Camera (Dziga Vertov, 1929)

Memories of Underdevelopment (Tomás Gutiérrez Alea, 1959)

Naked Spaces, Living is Round (Trinh T. Minh-ha, 1985)

Nanook of the North (Robert Flaherty, 1922)

Native Land (Leo Hurwitz, 1942)

Night and Fog (Alain Resnais, 1955)

Night Mail (Harry Watt and Basil Wright, 1936)

Of Time and the City (Terence Davies, 2008)

The Outsider (1951)

The Plow That Broke the Plains (Pare Lorentz, 1936)

Primary (Robert Drew, 1960)

Rain (Joris Ivens, 1929)

Reassemblage (Trinh T. Minh-ha, 1982)

The River (Pare Lorentz, 1938)

Rouch in Reverse (Manthia Diawara, 1995)

Sex Hygiene (1942)

Soapy the Germ Fighter (1951)

The Spanish Earth (Joris Ivens, 1937)

Superstar: The Karen Carpenter Story (Todd Haynes, 1989)

Tarnation (Jonathan Caouette, 2003)

Triumph of the Will (Leni Riefenstahl, 1936)

The War Room (Chris Hegedus and D.A. Pennebaker, 1993)

Waste (Parasher Baruah, 2009)

Waste Land (Jardim and Harley, 2010)

Why We Fight (Frank Capra, 1942–1945)

Workers Leaving the Lumière Factory (Lumière brothers, 1895)

NOTES

1 James Beveridge, *John Grierson* (New York: Macmillan, 1978), 68–69.

2 See Lucas Hilderbrand, *Inherent Vice: Bootleg Histories of Videotape and Copyright* (Durham, NC: Duke University Press, 2009), 161–190.

3 http://www.nytimes.com/2005/10/16/movies/16rams.html, accessed 27 January 2011.

4 Michael Chanan, *The Politics of Documentary* (London: BFI Publishing, 2007), 15.

5 Michael Renov, "Toward a Poetics of Documentary," *Theorizing Documentary*, edited by Michael Renov (London/New York: Routledge, 1993), 19.

6 Renov, 20.

7 Renov, 25.

8 Renov, 26.

9 Renov, 31.

10 Renov, 32.

11 Renov, 35.

12 Quoted in Frank P. Tomasulo, "The Mass Psychology of Fascist Cinema: Leni Riefenstahl's *Triumph of the Will*," in *Documenting the Documentary: Close Readings of Documentary Film and Video*, edited by Barry Keith Grant and Jeannette Sloniowski (Detroit: Wayne State University Press, 1998), 101.

13 Quoted in Tomasulo, 115.

14 Frank Capra, *The Name Above the Title* (New York: The Macmillan Company, 1971).

15 Capra, 332.

16 Quoted in Fatimah Tobing Rony, *The Third Eye: Race, Cinema, and Ethnographic Spectacle* (Durham, NC: Duke University Press, 1996), 104.

17 Quoted in Erik Barnouw, *Documentary: A History of the Non-Fiction Film*, 2nd rev. edn (New York: Oxford University Press, 1993), 113.

18 Franklin Delano Roosevelt's Second Inaugural Address, available at http://www.bartleby.com/124/pres50.html, l. 28.

19 Roy Armes, *Third World Film Making and the West* (Berkeley: University of California Press, 1987), 88.

20 Jim Pines and Paul Willemen (eds), "The Third Cinema Question: Notes and Reflection," in *Questions of Third Cinema* (London: British Film Institute, 1989), 3.

21 Pines and Willemen, 4.

22 http://theactofkilling.com, accessed 30 November 2013.

23 http://sportsillustrated.cnn.com/vault/article/magazine/MAG1122903/7/index.htm – ixzz1Cj8sbROx, accessed 31 January 2011.

24 http://www.liveleak.com/view?i=8e3_1257846786, accessed 30 November 2013.

CHAPTER FOUR
FILM AND POLITICS

There's something troubling a number of Dr Miles Bennell's patients: they seem to believe that their loved ones have been replaced by imposters, doppelgangers who look as they should but are emotionally distant or cold. When Bennell investigates, he discovers that aliens are growing copies of humans in large pods, and slowly replacing the population of his small town one by one. This is the plot of Don Siegel's film *Invasion of the Body Snatchers*. It was made in 1956, at a time when the United States was embroiled in the Cold War: the threat of atomic bombing by the Soviets, and paranoia relating to infiltration by communists, fed into a palpable sense of hysteria. This reached a particularly public peak with the House Committee on Un-American Activities hearings, overseen by Republican senator Joseph McCarthy, at which hundreds of individuals were interrogated about their affiliations with, or sympathies for, communism.

Invasion of the Body Snatchers, then, seems to be a political allegory about how easily a small community is taken over by outside forces. It suggests that the people you think you know intimately might actually be something other, something threatening. The alien invaders are the Communists, subtly altering people's behavior and beliefs while maintaining an outward appearance of the status quo. Or is the film actually saying the opposite? Perhaps the cold uniformity of the pod people and their mob mentality is a comment on the political conservatism of 1950s North America, with Dr Bennell a lone voice of liberal reason. The ambiguity of the message may in part explain the continued appeal of the Body Snatchers story. It has been re-made by three different directors: Philip Kaufman in 1978, Abel Ferrara in 1993, and Oliver Hirschbiegel in 2007. In each instance, the film's narrative can be read as a commentary on the political situation in the United States at the time of filming.

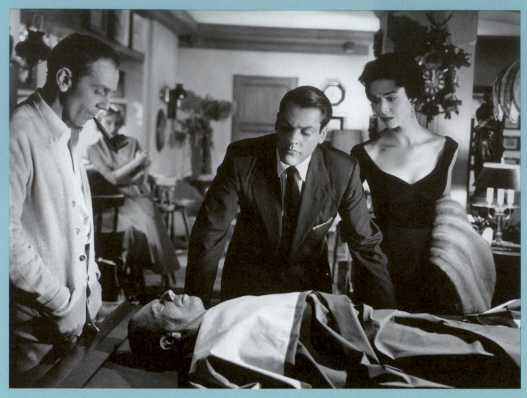

4.1 *Invasion of the Body Snatchers* (Don Siegel, 1956). Courtesy of Allied Artists/The Kobal Collection.

The example of *Invasion of the Body Snatchers* reveals not only that a film sold and consumed as "entertainment" may contain political content, but also that interpreting a film's political messages may not be straightforward. As we noted in the introduction to this book, we do not want to state facilely that all films are political. Rather, it is our intention to highlight some of the complicated ways in which cinema and politics are imbricated with one another. In particular, this chapter will examine how political imperatives and goals can be reasons for a film being made – and the repercussions this may have for the content of such movies.

WHAT WE WILL DO IN CHAPTER 4

This chapter introduces various different relationships between cinema and politics, and highlights that a substantial percentage, if not all, of them are produced for political reasons. Our goal is to provide you with a nuanced and differentiated understanding of politics as it relates to and shapes cinema.

• Following a chart outlining different types of political cinema, our discussion moves to a consideration of propaganda, the most obvious form of cinema produced to political design. We also introduce issue-driven cinema. We examine how both of these types of cinema attempt to influence and/or change beliefs and behaviors.

- In the next section of the chapter, the term "ideology" is introduced and discussed, through a consideration of several key figures: Karl Marx, Antonio Gramsci, and Louis Althusser. Comolli and Narboni's arguments regarding the relationships between cinema and ideology are introduced.

- The chapter concludes with a consideration of cinema and political activism, and an exploration of the notion of cinema as a site of resistance.

BY THE END OF THIS CHAPTER YOU SHOULD BE ABLE TO

- Identify some of the many ways in which cinema can be understood as political.
- Discuss the operations of propaganda.
- Define ideology, and explain the relationship between cinema and ideology.
- Outline how cinema can be used as a tool of political resistance.

VARIETIES OF POLITICAL CINEMA

Consider the following categories or types of political cinema:

1 Films that are directly financed by, and/or express the opinions of, a particular political group. This form of cinema, which may be fictional or nonfictional, is normally a type of **propaganda**. This topic was introduced in the previous chapter, where we looked at examples including Leni Reifenstahl's *Triumph of the Will* (1935), which was commissioned by Adolf Hitler, and the seven documentaries in the *Why We Fight* series, released between 1942 and 1945, which were produced by the US government. Further examples of propaganda would include the 1954 animated adaptation of George Orwell's *Animal Farm*, directed by Joy Batchelor and John Halas, which was financed by the CIA, and *Act of Valor* (Mike McCoy and Scott Waugh, 2012), which was commissioned by the US Navy's Special Warfare Command, with the intention of boosting recruitment.

2 Films that express a clear political argument, or embody an obvious political perspective, but which are not directly financed by a political group or individual. These do not have to be mainstream; indeed, the perspective being put forward may be a minority view. Many of the feminist films and videos that we discussed in Chapter 3 would fit into this category.

3 Movies that covertly support the status quo, the social, political and economic situation as it currently stands within the country of production. An overt example here would be Hollywood films made with the support of the US military, such as *Top Gun* (Tony Scott, 1986). However, many movies do not challenge, directly or indirectly, the current cultural and political state of affairs, either in their country of origin or more globally.

4 Films that have been produced by government-supported (and/or -funded) organizations, which may or may not have their content influenced by these organizations. An example here would be the Canadian National Film Board (NFB), which is an agency of the government of Canada, and

has produced thousands of titles. We will return to the NFB in Chapter 10's examination of film distribution.

5   Movies that are directly about politics. These might include dramas or documentaries about a particular moment in political history, or a key political figure (a prime minister or president, for instance). Although such films may ultimately express preferential treatment for one particular political perspective, they are more likely to be balanced in their approach than the films in category number 2, above. Examples here would include: *Carlos* (Olivier Assayas, 2010); *Lincoln* (Steven Spielberg, 2012); *No* (Pablo Larrain, 2012).

6   Films that are indirectly about politics, and/or which can be read as political allegories. This category would include Don Siegel's *Invasion of the Body Snatchers*, as well as a broad array of other horror and science-fiction films, including *Them!* (Gordon Douglas, 1954), *Godzilla/Gojira* (Ishirô Honda, 1954), and *Night of the Living Dead* (George Romero, 1968).

7   Films that serve a political purpose in their making or consumption. Here, the practices of making, as much as (if not more than) the content, are of major significance. This could include examples of cinema as an inclusive and participatory practice that attempts to level the ground between contributors, such as some of the films of the Cinema Novo movement that we discussed in Chapter 2.

All of the films covered by these categories – which may, in fact, be a significant percentage of all of cinema – are political and ideological. By **ideology**, a subject which we will examine in depth shortly, we mean a system of ideas and ideals which can be used as the basis for shaping policies, actions, beliefs and behaviors. Politics may directly serve as the cause behind the making of individual films: a movie might be funded by a particular political group, or the makers of the film may be driven by the desire to

4.2 *Carlos* (Olivier Assayas, 2010). Courtesy of Films En Stock/Egoli Tossell Film/Canal+Arte France/The Kobal Collection.

get their message and perspective to as wide an audience as possible, or the making of the film itself may serve a specific political purpose. A film's production may be supported and financed because its content bolsters the ideological and political status quo (for instance, in a communist culture, it might support views about appropriate behavior and attitudes). Alternatively, a government may aid the making of a movie because they have a political investment in helping or bolstering arts production, and this particular film is deemed worthy of assistance. Aside from such issues of production, support and financing, other films may be political mainly in terms of their content, whether expressed directly and clearly, or somewhat allegorically.

EXERCISE

Look again at the list above detailing the relationships between film and politics. Think of the last three films that you watched.

- Do all three fall into one or more of the categories outlined? If so, which categories?
- Can you think of films that fall outside of these categories? If so, what is it about these films that removes them from the realm of politics?
- Can you identify other ways in which cinema and politics are connected, not covered by this list? Again, can you name examples which embody these sorts of relationships?

CINEMA AND PROPAGANDA

The most obvious connection between film and politics, one which operates as a reason that a movie would get made, is that it is an instance of propaganda. By "propaganda," we mean that the film puts forward a specific point of view associated with a particular political party or group, and attempts to convince its audience, using a range of techniques, of the correctness of that perspective. In the previous chapter, we considered propaganda from within the framework of informative cinema. Here, we unpack the mechanics of propaganda, the ways in which it works.

The term "propaganda" is usually perceived negatively, and conceptualized as synonymous with lies, distortion, deceit and manipulation. However, the word does not need to be employed pejoratively. The *Oxford English Dictionary* (*OED*) contains this definition of propaganda: "Any association, systematic scheme, or concerted movement for the propagation of a particular doctrine or practice." A propaganda film might, therefore, be used for positive purposes: for instance, to promote awareness of a particular disease or illness, and potential medical treatments that are available. However, theorists of propaganda often identify that World War I is a crucial historical turning point – a time when those with political power mobilized forms of propaganda in order to convince mass audiences of the value of entering into conflict. Throughout the twentieth century, propaganda came to have negative connotations. According to communication theorists Garth Jowett and Victoria O'Donnell, there are two different types of propaganda: agitative and integrative. **Agitative** propaganda tries to rouse individuals toward certain aims and goals, and can result in major changes taking place; **integrative** propaganda, on the other hand, attempts to subdue individuals, making them passive and accepting.

Critical writings on cinema and propaganda largely focus on World War II, and the ways in which particular countries (Germany, Italy, the United Kingdom, the United States) attempted to propagate particular points of view through their cinema. In Germany in the 1930s and 1940s, the National Socialist German Workers Party (the Nazi Party) took a particular interest in cinema. Joseph Goebbels ran the Ministry of Propaganda. He gradually brought the entire film industry within the control of his ministry, and argued that cinema should be the "vanguard of the Nazi military." A school for filmmakers was established. Membership of an official professional organization (the *Reichsfilmkammer*) was made mandatory for all of those working in the film industry. Censorship was increased and film criticism was banned. Goebbels assumed that a national cinema that was entertaining and glamorous would be a more powerful and effective form of propaganda than one that attempted to convince audiences of the worth and significance of the party. The primary goal of the Nazi film policy, then, was to promote escapist cinema that would distract the population and leave viewers in good spirits. Overt propaganda largely took the form of documentaries and newsreels. In other words, most Nazi film propaganda, to use Jowett and O'Donnell's terms, was integrative rather than agitative.

However, some agitative Nazi propaganda films have become infamous. One is *Der Ewige Jude/The Eternal Jew* (1940), directed by Fritz Hippler. It combines feature and documentary elements, including recordings from Polish ghettos, depictions of religious worship, and footage of parading troops. The film's intention is to argue that Jews are soulless criminals, that they are fundamentally different from other people, and that slaughtering them is a logical necessity. Another example is Gustav Ucicky's 1941 anti-Polish film *Heimkehr/Homecoming*. This fictional movie focuses on the experiences of the German minority in Poland, and the prejudice they experience at the hands of the Polish majority. *Heimkehr* can be seen to support Hitler's intention to invade Poland.

4.3 *Der Ewige Jude/The Eternal Jew* (Fritz Hippler, 1940). Courtesy of DFG/The Kobal Collection.

CASE STUDY: CINEMA AND FASCISM – ITALIAN "WHITE TELEPHONE" MOVIES

In Italy in 1922, the Fascist Party under Benito Mussolini's leadership seized control of the Italian government. Their position of power lasted until 1943, when Mussolini was forced from office, the Allies landed in Sicily, and the Partisan movement took hold. Whereas Hitler in Germany and Stalin in Russia managed to take full control of the film industry, harnessing the medium to their political aims, the Fascist Party in Italy was not quite as successful.

However, some effective steps were made. In 1934, Luigi Freddi, supervisor of the Fascist propaganda office, headed the Direzione Generale per la Cinematografia, a state-financed and controlled censorship board that consisted of members of the Fascist Party and War Ministry staff. The Direzione Generale read and altered scripts, and could award money to films with pro-Fascist messages. Its censorship power was substantial: it is alleged that Mussolini himself cut scenes from *Il capello a tre punte* (Mario Camerini, 1935), a film which (in part) depicted corruption within local government. Further steps were taken by the party: the number of foreign films entering the country was regulated; Mussolini opened Italy's first film studio, Cinecitta, in 1937, and set up a film school, the Centro Sperimentale di Cinematografia, in 1938.

According to film academic Mira Liehm in her historical account of Italian cinema:

> The colours of the films made under fascism were "pink" and "black." The pink productions – sentimental comedies and romantic melodramas – far outnumbered the black "truly" fascist films. Of the approximately eighty films produced yearly in the late thirties, some ten openly propagandized fascism.[1]

Here, the colors pink and black were used metaphorically to distinguish between distinct generic forms; in the "soft" pink films, messages were coded, covert, not hammered home. Like Goebbels in Germany, Freddi realized that the best films for the Fascist propaganda office to support were those of an escapist nature. "White telephone" films, or Telefoni Bianchi, were glitzy dramas and comedies produced in Italy in the 1930s and 1940s about the upper classes. A significant number were adaptations of theatrical successes, past and contemporary, including plays by Luigi Pirandello and Alessandro De Stefani. The style and content of these films were influenced by the Hollywood director Cecil B. DeMille's movies, which often featured elegant characters in opulent settings, as well as by 1930s German "UFA films," which combined elements of Hollywood comedy, drawing-room farce, and opera. The Telefoni Bianchi films had glamorous, wealthy settings, typified by the appearance of a white telephone – a symbol of status and money.

Directors associated with white telephone films include Alessandro Blasetti, Carlo Bragaglia, Guido Brignone, Mario Camerini, and Gennaro Righelli. In Blasetti's *La Contessa di Parma* (1938), Marcella (Elisa Cegani) works as a model in a dress store. The owner of the shop, attempting to improve business, requests that his models dress up as ladies of high society and start to frequent elite social gatherings. At one of these, Marcella is mistaken for the Duchess of Parma; whilst trying to manage her mistaken identity, she meets sporting hero Gino Vanni (Antonio Centa). Identity confusion also features in Camerini's *Il Signor Max* (1937). Gianni (played by the future director Vittorio De Sica), who owns a newspaper stand, is given a cruise ticket by an old friend from his school days. Gianni is mistaken for the aristocrat, and spends time entangled with various high society women. At the film's conclusion, however, Gianni ends up marrying Lauretta (Assia Noris), a maid on the ship.

There has been mixed critical commentary regarding Italy's white telephone movies. Some have seen them as pure escapism upholding mainstream political ideology relating to family, religion, and the workings of capitalism; others have derided them as indirect propaganda, films which fail to depict the realities of life in Italy at the time (working-class struggle, social conflicts, and so on). Carlo Lizzani, for instance, sees the white telephone films as hollow spectacle:

> Dutiful camp followers such as Bragaglia, Mattoli, Brignone, Gallone and so on blurred the direct onslaught of out and out propaganda films with a smokescreen of white telephones and mawkish romance … It seems unbelievable that at a time of worldwide suffering there was such a proliferation of films as non-existent, as empty and as alien to the national identity as our "commercial" films of those years … They were full of gesticulating, soulless shadows speaking a language which would be quite incomprehensible today.[2]

And yet the making of these films was supported by the Fascist Party's office of propaganda. White telephone films, then, are a somewhat subtle example of the use of cinema as a tool of propaganda: in putting forth an image of life in Italy as prosperous, wealthy and frivolous, they both distracted audiences from the realities of their everyday existence, and propagated an idealized sense of life under Fascism. These films therefore reveal that entertainment – a subject we explored at length in Chapter 1 – does not operate independently from the machinations of politics; they are not mutually exclusive drivers.

4.4 *Il Signor Max* (Mario Camerini, 1937). Courtesy of the BFI Stills Collection.

Propaganda, then, may be integrative or agitative. There are clear reasons for making both kinds of film: to reassure or distract audiences, or to rouse them in ways which alter their thinking or behavior. Political parties and groups may support – and finance – the making of both types of film. Propaganda may also be categorized as white, black or grey. As with the "pink" and "black" forms of propaganda discussed in the white telephone case study above, these are figurative categories used to distinguish between types of films. The source of **white propaganda** is clearly identifiable, and the information it contains tends to be accurate. As Jowett and O'Donnell note, white propaganda "is presented in a manner that attempts to convince the audience that the sender is the 'good guy' with the best ideas and political ideology."[3] **Black propaganda**, on the other hand, comes from a hidden source or is falsely credited. It takes the form of lies and deceit. In order for black propaganda to be successful, it needs to convince its receiver of its credibility. Black propaganda needs to be carefully assembled, in order for its receivers not to perceive it as suspicious and untrustworthy. Finally, **grey propaganda** falls somewhere between white and black propaganda. The truthfulness of the information is uncertain, and the source may not always be identifiable. According to this tripartite categorization, the Nazi films *Der Ewige Jude* and *Heimkehr* are both "black" propaganda, as they contain false information – about the "natural" state and behavior of Jewish people, and the experience of Germans in Poland – and attempt to convince audiences of their truthfulness.

Beyond World War II examples of film propaganda, there are a wide range of films which can be seen to fit within the *OED* definition of propaganda as "dissemination of a particular doctrine or practice." Here we begin to see an overlap between film as propaganda and film as ideological (the topic of the next section of this chapter). Take, for instance, issue-driven cinema. Some films, fiction and nonfiction, attempt to raise awareness of a particular topic, and perhaps to change opinion and behavior about that topic. The documentary *An Inconvenient Truth* (Davis Guggenheim, 2006) recorded a talk delivered

4.5 *An Inconvenient Truth* (Davis Guggenheim, 2006). Courtesy of Lawrence Bender Prods./The Kobal Collection.

by Democrat politician Al Gore about the impact of climate change on the planet's varied environments. It arguably had two effects: disseminating information about damage being caused to our world, and raising the public profile (and thus, perhaps, degree of political influence) of Gore himself. Morgan Spurlock's documentary *Super Size Me* (2004) – which cost $65,000 to make, and took more than $20 million at the global box office – drew attention to the health risks associated with eating McDonald's food, and significantly contributed to negative criticism of the fast food chain. Hollywood studios regularly produce, support, or distribute issue-driven films – and, arguably, these are the films which then go on to win Academy Awards and other plaudits. *Philadelphia* (Jonathan Demme, 1993) argues for the fair treatment of individuals with HIV/AIDS; *Dead Man Walking* (Tim Robbins, 1995) offers a critique of the death penalty; *Million Dollar Baby* (Clint Eastwood, 2004) suggests that euthanasia may sometimes be an appropriate path of action. All of these films attempt at least to provoke debate, at best to change attitudes and behavior. They are arguably forms of "white" propaganda.

EXERCISE

Both propaganda and issue-driven cinema attempt to influence the beliefs and behaviors of their viewers.

- Can you make a list of films that have influenced your beliefs about particular issues? If so, which aspects of these movies had a specific impact on you? How did the filmmakers convince you of their perspective and arguments?

CINEMA AND IDEOLOGY

Propaganda is (often blatantly) ideological. Arguably, all cinema is ideological in various and complex ways. Ideological intentions – rather than simply propagandist ones – may be the reason that a film is made. But in order to understand how this works, we need to unpack what the term "ideology" means. Writings on ideology regularly accentuate the difficulty of defining the concept: Terry Eagleton begins his book on the subject by outlining sixteen potential uses of the term. However, it is possible to attempt a concise definition. The word **ideology** is used to refer to sets of ideas which give an account of the world, though this account is usually a selective one; these ideas or values are related to the ways in which power is distributed socially; they are usually posed as "natural" and "obvious."

The concept of power is central to any understanding of ideology. It is often assumed that individuals with power have more interest in wielding, and impact in disseminating, ideological influence on or against those without power and status. People without power may in fact willingly collude in this process: ideological messages often pose themselves as "correct," as "common sense," and are thus assimilated by the mass, through a dynamic or process labeled **false consciousness** by the German philosopher and political theorist Friedrich Engels (1820–1895). The problem with this conception, as Eagleton points out, is that not every belief that people might identify as ideological is necessarily associated with those in a position of dominant political power. However, the association of ideology with social and political power persists. This is due in part to the German philosopher and economist Karl Marx (1818–1893), whose foundational writings occupy a crucial position in the history of the concept.

Many of Marx's key ideas about ideology were expressed in an early book he co-authored with Friedrich Engels, *The German Ideology* (*Die Deutsche Ideologie*, 1846). He also discussed ideology in what is often considered his masterwork, *Capital* (*Das Kapital*, 1867). For Marx, capitalist society was primarily a culture of two classes: the elite capitalist class, or **bourgeoisie**, who asserted their power through wealth, and the working class, or **proletariat**, who, Marx believed, had the power to change history through united effort. (You may find it useful to pause at this point and consider whether this model is still applicable today, in your own contemporary context. Who exactly might belong to each of Marx's two classes now?) Marx utilized the concept of ideology to explain how the elite class managed to retain its privileged position; he claimed that the dominant ideas of a society – which may be accepted by that society's citizens as "common sense" – are constructed and disseminated by the capitalist minority in order to maintain their dominant status. Or as Marx and Engels themselves put it in *The German Ideology*:

> The ideas of the ruling class are in every epoch the ruling ideas, i.e. the class which is the ruling material force of society, is at the same time its ruling intellectual force. The class which has the means of material production at its disposal, has control at the same time over the means of mental production, so that thereby, generally speaking, the ideas of those who lack the means of mental production are subject to it. The ruling ideas are nothing more than the ideal expression of the dominant material relationships, the dominant material relationships grasped as ideas …[4]

Of course, Marx's arguments about ideology were put forward before the birth of cinema. Can they be applied to this particular form of culture? According to Marx, dominant ideas are expressed and transmitted via "meaning-making bodies," a raft of diverse institutions that, in our era, would include the mass media of newspapers, television, radio, and cinema. As all major institutions – from government to the press – are owned and/or controlled by members of the elite capitalist class, the messages these individuals (and they are almost always white men) diffuse to the populace through such organizations are their ideas. Members of the proletariat are told what to think and believe by institutions, but also come to believe that those messages and ideas are "true," as they "make sense."

Marx's ideas relating to ideology have been taken up by a host of other thinkers. Arguably, the most noteworthy developments can be found in the writings of the Italian intellectual and agitator Antonio Gramsci (1891–1937). Imprisoned for his involvement in political demonstrations and conflicts – he was the head of the Italian Communist Party – Gramsci examined a broad array of topics in the thirty-three volumes of his *Prison Notebooks*, written between 1929 and 1934. One key subject to which he repeatedly returned was the clash of opposing parties or groups, and their attempts to attain political dominance.

Gramsci argued that, at any one time, a number of groups – all with access to vital economic resources – will vie with each other for social and political power; each group carries, represents and attempts to disseminate specific ideologies. Thus, even at the level of elite political factions, different views or perspectives war with each other to achieve domination, a position of power that Gramsci termed **hegemony**, a dominance achieved by both persuasive and coercive means. This state of affairs – with a range of powerful rival forces battling for the attention and consent of the masses with differing messages – opens up Marx's understanding of ideology to a degree, enabling some space for debate and discussion.

One way in which the workings of hegemony can be observed in cinema is through the various ways in which a particular historical moment or figure is treated across a range of movies. Take, for instance, Elizabeth I (1533–1603), who was queen of England and Ireland from 1558 until her death. Several Hollywood period dramas have been made about parts of her life, including *The Private Lives of Elizabeth and Essex* (Michael Curtiz, 1939), *Young Bess* (George Sidney, 1953), and *The Virgin Queen* (Henry Koster, 1955). More recently, the actress Cate Blanchett has played the monarch in the British film *Elizabeth* (Shekhar Kapur, 1998) and its international co-production sequel, also directed by Kapur, *Elizabeth: The Golden Age* (2007). Although the earlier Hollywood films portray Elizabeth as sometimes manipulative and egotistical, more recent versions of the story accentuate her ruthlessness and violence: *Elizabeth* concludes, for instance, with the Queen authorizing the murder of several figures in her own court, whose bloody deaths the audience witnesses. Which version is more truthful to historical fact – and how does this square with developing perspectives on this period in British history? With this series of films, we can observe hegemony in action: different takes on Elizabeth I's reign are presented, each proposing its own version of events as a valid account. However, all of these films operate within the same ideological parameters: none of them challenge the role or position of the monarchy.

A third crucial figure in the tradition of Marxist writings on ideology is the French philosopher Louis Althusser (1918–1990), who outlined a rather pessimistic model of the system by which ideology is enforced by the dominant ruling body. For Althusser, ideology is not a mass illusion, as Marx suggested, but more the system of cultural representations whereby social groups and classes make their lived

4.6 *Elizabeth* (Shekhar Kapur, 1998). Courtesy of Polygram/The Kobal Collection/Alex Bailey.

experience meaningful. Crucially, Althusser identified two mutually supportive and structurally imbricated forms of control: **repressive state apparatuses** and **ideological state apparatuses**. The former
– which include such institutions as the military, the police force, the prison system, law courts and so
on – attain power through force. The latter – incorporating, among other things, religion, the educational
establishment, the family and the mass media – operate predominantly at the level of ideology. The
all-pervasive nature of this widespread array of intertwined apparatuses causes it constantly to impinge
on the individual subject. Althusser's rather depressing deterministic conceptualization of the workings
of capitalist society suggests that the individual is born into ideology, and that there is no way to escape
its clutches.

Althusser's arguments had a significant impact on the theorization of cinema. One well-known essay
about the relationships between ideology and cinema, Jean-Luc Comolli and Jean Narboni's "Cinema/
Ideology/Criticism" (1969), adopts an Althusserian perspective on film. "*Every film is political*," they
argue, "inasmuch as it is determined by the ideology which produces it (or within which it is produced,
which stems from the same thing)."[5] Cinema, they claim, can never be free from ideology:

> What the camera in fact registers is the vague, unformulated, untheorised, unthought-out world
> of the dominant ideology. Cinema is one of the languages through which the world communi-
> cates to itself. They constitute its ideology for they reproduce the world as it is experienced when
> filtered through the ideology … So, when we set out to make a film, from the very first shot, we
> are encumbered by the necessity of reproducing things not as they really are but as they appear
> when refracted through the ideology. This includes every stage in the process of production:
> subjects, "styles", forms, meanings, narrative traditions; all underline the general ideological
> discourse. The film is ideology presenting itself to itself, talking to itself, learning about itself.[6]

Nearly all films, they state, are "imbued through and through with the dominant ideology in pure and
unadulterated form, and give no indication that their makers were even aware of the fact."[7] Further, any
suggestion that cinema simply provides what audiences desire fails to recognize that what an audience
wants is constructed by the dominant ideology: "Certainly there is such a thing as public demand, but
'what the public wants' means 'what the dominant ideology wants.' The notion of a public and its tastes
was created by the ideology to justify and perpetuate itself."[8] Comolli and Narboni's argument is not
entirely pessimistic: they suggest that there are some cracks in the armor that may enable filmmakers
to disrupt or perhaps even destroy the connections between cinema and the dominant ideology.

Aside from the Marxist approach, psychoanalytic theory provides a second notable tradition in the
literature on ideology. Sigmund Freud, for instance, argued that one of the most significant factors at
work in politics is the erotic relationship between a group and its leader, and that the role of ideology is
to strengthen libidinal bonds between individuals in power and the people that they rule, which results
in a positive perspective towards rulers. Thus, in *Totem and Taboo* (1913), Freud related the origin and
persistence of political power to the Oedipus complex; and in *Group Psychology and the Analysis of the
Ego* (1921), he claimed that "artificial" groups such as armies require single, dominant, charismatic
leaders. As a stark contrast to the Marxist model, Freud's position is an intriguing one – especially in
relation to cinema. To what extent does cinema create a sense of sexual spectacle that holds many
viewers in its thrall? Does the manufactured glamor of film stars, and the industry which raises them
to the position of idealized and idolized figures, construct a particular erotic relationship between

audiences and the movies – one which keeps the average viewer in a position of inferiority? Despite the significance of this second strand of "ideology theory," it is the Marxist approach which is most often adopted in critical writings on the subject.

CASE STUDY: KISSING IN THE MOVIES

In 1963, the artist Andy Warhol began to make a series of silent, short, black-and-white films of couples kissing, each about three minutes in length. These were initially screened as a serial at an experimental venue in downtown New York, appearing as shorts before longer, more feature-length titles by other directors. Shot at twenty-four frames per second, they were projected at the slightly slower speed of sixteen frames per second, giving them a rather dream-like character. In almost all of the *Kiss* films by Warhol, the camera does not move, and it is positioned close to the pair kissing. There is no lead-in or conclusion: the reels start and stop with the couple already in the midst of their physical activity. For those unfamiliar with Warhol's work, the running time – which was dictated by the length of the film reel, and dragged out by the slow projection speed – might seem inordinately long. Having these films screen as "trailers" also seems strange: don't kisses come at the end of movies? These films, then, make us reflect on how kisses normally operate in narrative cinema. Why are kisses in the movies normally brief, and why do narrative films often end with a (heterosexual) kiss?

In Hollywood, even generic narrative films which are not explicitly romantic in content – such as science fiction films or war movies – are likely to end with a heterosexual couple paired off, and locked in an embrace. (You might want to pause and make a list of examples here. Once you start to look for this repetitive element, you will start to see it all over!) Why does this happen? Ideologically, the closing heterosexual kiss connects several powerful messages: that personal satisfaction can be attained in romantic love (aligned here with the pleasures of narrative closure); that the beautiful heterosexual couple, and heterosexuality itself, represent a cultural ideal to which we should aspire; that despite the obstacles that need to be overcome (which might include fighting monsters, enduring combat, or proving one's worth), "true love," itself an ideological construct, will prevail. The roots of this plot element are older than cinema: it can be found in a variety of mythological stories and fairy tales. However, Hollywood cinema and its reliance on repetitive narrative forms has reinforced the mythology of heterosexual romance with a particular force and power throughout its history. From a Freudian perspective on ideology, it is worth asking: why might an audience take pleasure in witnessing this story element over and over again? Why does watching an attractive couple lock lips provide emotional or erotic satisfaction for the viewer?

It is useful to position Warhol's *Kiss* reels in a historical trajectory of kissing in the movies. Linda Williams, in her book *Screening Sex* (2009), traces a lineage from Thomas Edison's fifteen-second film *The Kiss* (1896) to Warhol's assemblage of his *Kiss* reels into a fifty-five-minute compendium in 1964 (the format in which this material is usually now circulated and screened). In both Edison and Warhol's films, Williams notes, the kiss is "radically severed" from any other content or context, "becoming what critics of graphic sex and violence might call gratuitous – a sex act that is there just for sex's sake, with no other narrative or dramatic purpose."[9] Kisses in the cinema, however, normally operate "as textual punctuation – as period, comma, question mark, and, most important, as the dot, dot, dot of ellipsis."[10] Whilst Edison's short film may now seem funny, a brief historical fragment, Warhol's compendium film remains provocative and (for some) uncomfortable to watch: it feels intrusive, salacious, messy. It can remind us, even fifty years after it was made, of the physical and sexual rather than romantic connotations of the kiss – the reason that many moments of kissing-in-the-cinema throughout history, around the world, have been censored.

Indeed, in a global frame, Warhol's *Kiss* invites us to reflect on different national and cultural traditions of including kissing (and other forms of physical or romantic entanglement) in the movies. In Japan during World War II, Occupation forces attempted to "liberalize" cultural values. Previously, even in romantic Japanese films, couples never kissed; all kisses were edited out of imported foreign movies. In 1946, however, under the influence of "liberalization" pressures, Yasushi Yasaki's *Twenty-Year-Old-Youth* and Yasuki Chiba's *Aru Yo no Seppun/A Certain Night's Kiss* gave birth to a new genre: the *seppun eiga* or "kissing film." Historians of Japanese cinema have noted that attempts by the Occupation forces to promote romance, as embodied and symbolized by the screen kiss, were to a significant extent intended to make the private more public, and thereby make the Japanese less "inscrutable" (a pejorative stereotype that still circulates today), and therefore less able to remain unreadable, impenetrable. If a nation's cinema adopts representational strategies familiar from Hollywood, such as the heterosexual kiss, does this entail a broader shift to a more western ideology and system of values? Can including such elements, and exposing audiences to them, produce a change in social and cultural beliefs?

4.7 *The Kiss* (Thomas Edison, 1896). Courtesy of Edison/The Kobal Collection.

CINEMA AND ACTIVISM

Comolli and Narboni concede that it may be possible to produce films that operate outside mainstream ideology, and which challenge the status quo. It might be necessary, they suggest, for such films to adopt a radically different style and form. In this final section of this chapter, we want to consider this type of film: cinema as providing a challenge to mainstream ideologies and messages. For viewers and filmmakers who feel that most cinema supports dominant values and belief systems, how can challenge or opposition be mounted? Is it better to attempt to break into the mainstream, and to subtly shift the types of stories being told and the ways in which they are articulated? Or should resistance be mounted from outside, casting aside the narrative and formal strategies associated with dominant cinema? Whichever strategy is adopted, this cinema is again explicitly political in intent: it is made in order to attempt some sort of rectification of the audio-visual regime to which audiences are regularly submitted. That is, cinema is used as a tool to capture and try to distribute messages and forms of representation that are normally not welcomed – or are purposefully avoided – by the dominant media.

EXERCISE

Mainstream Hollywood cinema regularly employs problematic or degrading stereotypes – of women, of sexual minorities, of particular nations, races and ethnicities – and it has always done so. To give just two examples, *Argo* (Ben Affleck, 2012) puts forward a particular perspective on Iran, and *Taken 2* (Olivier Megaton, 2012) features Albanian villains.

- Identify three examples of films that you think employ prejudicial representations of particular groups or individuals (these examples may not be from Hollywood, of course). How do you think such use of stereotypes might be corrected or omitted?
- Is it possible for cinema to avoid using stereotypes?
- Can more truthful or realistic films about the people stereotyped only be made by people who belong to those groups affected? That is, who has the right to depict certain groups of people, and how is that power attributed?

Most often, films that try to present an alternative perspective to the dominant media are made outside the mainstream industry. They are made by committed individuals with little money on shoestring budgets. They may be made according to more community-centered or collaborative forms of practice than those adopted by the industry, in which roles tend to be clearly demarcated, and lines of power are evidently articulated. They may also be shown in a distinct array of exhibition venues, outside cinemas (in schools, town halls, appropriated spaces, and so on). A valuable example here is the 1978 documentary *Word is Out*, a "talking heads" film which presents around twenty first-person accounts of gay and lesbian life in the United States. The making of the film was driven by ideological imperatives: not only did the filmmakers want to challenge entrenched stereotypes relating to what lesbians and gay men are like, but they were specifically incited by attempts to introduce anti-gay legislation in a number of states across North America. The film was made collaboratively by a group of men and women known as the Mariposa Film Group. All decisions regarding what to film, how to film, and what to include in the final edit were debated at length by the collective. The completed movie was distributed as an educational resource, as well as being shown in some cinemas, in an attempt to reach a broad and diverse public. The format adopted for the film was common and recognizable, but the content was fresh and innovative – and a direct ideological challenge to calcified forms of mainstream representation.

Perhaps the best-known ideological alternative to mainstream film and its associated ideologies is the Latin American film movement known as "Third Cinema." Third Cinema was introduced in the previous chapter's exploration of cinema as an informative medium, but is worth briefly revisiting here, and reframing in relation to this chapter's main concerns. The movement took its name from a manifesto, "Towards a Third Cinema," which was written by the Argentinian filmmakers Fernando Solanas and Octavio Getino and published in 1969 in the film journal *Tricontinental*. The manifesto and subsequent film movement rejected colonialism, capitalism, and Hollywood's approach to cinema as a money-making commodity and distraction. As Solanas and Getino wrote:

> The anti-imperialist struggle of the peoples of the Third World and of their equivalents inside the imperialist countries constitutes today the axis of the world revolution. *Third cinema* is, in our opinion, the cinema that *recognises in that struggle the most gigantic cultural, scientific, and artistic manifestation of our time*, the great possibility of constructing a liberated personality with each people as the starting point – in a word, the *decolonisation of culture*.[11]

4.8 *Word Is Out* (Mariposa Film Group, 1978). Courtesy of Milestone Film & Video.

The manifesto argues in particular for the political power of documentary. It advocates a form of collaborative film practice that avoids the notion of the director as the main figure steering the production and using the work for personal expression. Solanas and Getino also argued against employing traditional exhibition spaces, recognizing that an alternative circuit of screenings could avoid censorship and bypass commercial venues. The Grupo Cine Liberación (The Liberation Film Group) was formed in Argentina by Solanas, Getino, and Gerardo Vallejo; advocates, supporters and practitioners of Third Cinema were also based in Cuba, Brazil, and Bolivia. Key Third Cinema titles made by the Grupo Cine Liberación include Getino and Solanas' *La Hora de los hornos/The Hour of the Furnaces* (1968) and *Ya es tiempo de violencia/Now is the Time for Violence* (Enrique Juárez, 1969).

Not all activist cinema is necessarily left-leaning and liberal in its politics. The mainstream industry and the forms of representation it disseminates also omit far-right and other political perspectives. An example would be the Loose Change collective, which consists of director Dylan Avery and producers Korey Rowe and Matthew Brown. Their film *Loose Change 9/11: An American Coup* (2009), which can be viewed for free online, is a "Truther" documentary: the makers believe that the US government covered up what really happened on 11 September 2001, and they attempt to expose a conspiracy. As filmmaking technologies (cameras, mobile phones, editing software, computers) decrease in price, more and more people around the world are beginning to have access to the means of film production. Similarly, easily accessible forms of distribution such as online platforms (for example, Vimeo or YouTube) make it possible for filmmakers to get their work to audiences for free. (This is not to say that everyone has access to these technologies and means of distribution, of course; many people around the world still lack the financial and cultural means to do so.) This availability provides a challenge to the Marxist conception of "meaning-making" power being located in the hands solely of a minority elite: the proliferation of online DIY films offers up a much more complex and diverse array of stories and forms of representations than the mainstream media could ever imagine or accommodate.

Despite the existence of films such as *Loose Change 9/11*, films that challenge the dominant ideology continue to be associated with left-leaning causes. A valuable example in the use of film technologies for activist political means is Witness, an international non-profit organization that was collaboratively formed in 1992 by the musician Peter Gabriel, Human Rights First, and the Reebok Human Rights Foundation. The main motivation behind the formation of Witness was the Rodney King, Jr. incident in the United States, in which a bystander used video to capture footage of police brutality. The Witness website (www.witness.org) sets out their aims and ethos:

> Witness empowers human rights defenders to use video to fight injustice, and to transform personal stories of abuse into powerful tools that can pressure those in power or with power to act. By bringing often unseen images and seldom heard stories to the attention of key decision makers, the media, and the public, Witness catalyzes grassroots activism, political engagement, and lasting change.

As do many of the other examples that we have been considering in this chapter, Witness uses film specifically in order to attempt to change beliefs and behaviors. Their archive includes over 4,000 hours of footage on such topics as genocide in Guatemala and violence against women in Zimbabwe. This material, they claim, is to be used "in the support of advocacy, prosecution of justice, truth telling, and the historical record."

The films that we have discussed so far in this section on "cinema and activism" have all been documentaries. However, the genre of documentary may carry inherent and unquestioned ideological implications. For instance, how is the authenticity and truthfulness of the documentary image constructed? Perhaps the most politically radical cinema – that which truly challenges mainstream ideologies – needs to be innovative in terms of both its content and its shape. As the experimental filmmaker Barbara Hammer puts it, "radical content deserves radical form."[12] Lav Diaz, a filmmaker from the Philippines, creates very long films with a regular community of collaborators: *Melancholia* (2008) is eight hours in length; *Florentina Hubaldo CTE* (2012) is six hours long. The content of Diaz's films draws attention to the experiences of characters normally marginalized or ignored by mainstream film. *Florentina Hubaldo CTE*, for instance, features a young woman forced into prostitution by her father, whose story intersects with that of two treasure seekers endlessly digging for precious goods, and a farmer whose wife is dying. All of these characters have suffered under colonial rule, at war, or from natural disaster; the duration of shots and of the film itself requires viewers to commit to spending time with these people, and witnessing their suffering and travails. Usually shot in digital black-and-white, employing extremely long static takes, Diaz's films are most often screened at film festivals around the world without intervals. Diaz is allegedly happy for his movies to be illegally distributed on the internet: it is easier (and cheaper) for all parties if those interested in watching his films seek them out through file-sharing sites. In other words, money – a major component of our discussion in the next two chapters – is not the driving force behind Diaz's career; it is more important to him to follow his political imperatives and record on film his particular version of life in the Philippines.

4.9 *Florentina Hubaldo, CTE* (Lav Diaz, 2012).

CASE STUDY: PEDRO COSTA AND LUSOPHONE CINEMA

The Lusophone countries are those in which Portuguese is the main language spoken. The word comes from the name of the ancient Roman province of Lusitania, which once covered an area that today is Portugal and part of Spain. The Lusophone countries include Angola, Brazil, Cape Verde, East Timor, Guinea-Bissau, Mozambique, Portugal, São Tomé and Príncipe and the Chinese Special Administrative Region (SAR) of Macau. Lusophone cinema has often focused on the ordinary and everyday experiences of those living in Lusophone countries, the legacies of colonialism and ownership of land, and the movement of people between these countries and the challenges that those individuals face. In other words, it is often explicitly political, and made in order to disseminate representations of particular places and people. Thus, particular films by Portugese director Francisco Manso – *Napumoceno's Will* (1997), *A Ilha dos Escravos/Slave Island* (2008) – provide an outsider's perspective on life in Cape Verde; titles by Flora Gomes – *Those Whom Death Refused* (1988), *The Blue Eyes of Yonta* (1991), *My Voice* (2002) – reveal the character of Guinea-Bissau. Portuguese director Pedro Costa's films mostly concentrate on life in Portugal – especially the Lisbon slum Fontainas – but have also ventured overseas to other Lusophone countries.

Costa, who was born in 1959, studied at the University of Lisbon before moving to the Lisbon Theatre and Film School. At the latter, he was a student of (amongst others) the director António Reis (1927–1991). Costa's austere style of filmmaking was influenced by Reis; he has been identified as a member of "The School of Reis." Costa's films usually focus on the marginalized and the dispossessed, those barely eking out an existence. A useful sketch of their style and content has been provided by Peter Bradshaw, lead film journalist for the *Guardian* newspaper, who describes them as "severe" and "uncompromisingly difficult":

> He favours interminably long shots, long silences, long aimless semi-audible conversations between semi-comatose drug addicts: like watching a *Big Brother* live feed direct from some of the most poverty-stricken places in Europe … This director increasingly contrives scenes in cramped rooms in semi-darkness, shot from below, with perhaps one light-source in the form of a window in the top right corner of the frame, which glows without illuminating the scene. [His work has evolved] from conventional dramatic movie-making into an experimental docu-installation form, which is something between a real-time "reportage" cinema and an exhibition of animated portrait images.[13]

Indeed, part of the formal challenge of Costa's films is that they trouble at the boundaries between fictional and documentary cinema. Although he has made works that can be relatively straightforwardly categorized as "art films" (*Ossos*, 1997) and documentaries (such as *Ne change rien*, 2009), some of his "fiction" films, such as *In Vanda's Room* (2000) and *Colossal Youth* (2006), adopt a more complex form. *Colossal Youth* was filmed over a fifteen-month period. The director lived with his cast of non-professional actors – drug addicts, immigrants, and poorly paid laborers from the Fontainhas neighborhood of Lisbon – and recorded over

320 hours of material, sometimes shooting particular sequences more than twenty times. The everyday lives of the actors were recreated, performed for the camera, in an attempt to capture an authentic and realistic depiction of their activities and interactions.

But, as the philosopher Jacques Rancière has asked, "How are we to think the politics of Pedro Costa's films?" He depicts the lives of those on the margins, living in slums and scrabbling for labor. However:

> Pedro Costa's camera never once takes the usual path from the places of misery to the places where those in power produce or manage it. We don't see in his films the economic power which exploits and relegates, or the power of administrations and the police, which represses or displaces populations. We never hear any of his characters speaking about the political stakes of the situation, or of rebelling against it … He does not inscribe the slums into the landscape of capitalism in mutation, nor does he design his sets to make them commensurate with collective grandeur.[14]

Thus, in *Down to Earth/Casa de Lava* (1994), migrant worker Leão (Isaach De Bankolé) has a dangerous fall while working on a building site. One of his nurses, Mariana (Inês de Medeiros) escorts him back to his village on Cape Verde. He slowly recovers his health in the local hospital. She struggles to communicate with the locals. The film ends without resolution. Costa's *Colossal Youth*, in contrast, is set entirely in Fontainhas. The film follows Ventura as he wanders the local area, interacting with a variety of its residents. Both films move slowly, featuring numerous lengthy and rather aimless conversations. Protagonists usually walk, accompanied by the camera, rather than using other forms of transport (a comment, perhaps, on the basic forms of mobility available to them). Costa attempts to utilize an appropriate variety of stylistic devices to match and convey the experiences of his characters. Here then, a politics of form and content are combined: Costa uses specific filmmaking strategies to break with accepted conventions, and utilizes these to present stories about individuals who are normally under-represented. The anticipated political content is not present at the level of overt representation, but instead redirected into the deployment of specific formal techniques.

4.10 *Colossal Youth* (Pedro Costa, 2006).

CHAPTER SUMMARY

Politics, this chapter proposes, is one of the main reasons that films get made. Indeed, it is possible that every film has some sort of political aim or intention in operation as part of its fabrication. These political aims are especially evident in relation to propaganda and issue-driven cinema, the focus of the first section of this chapter: with both of these sorts of film, the intention of their filmmakers is to change the thought and behavior patterns of their spectators. More subtle political intentions can be conveyed through the ideological operations of cinema, the focus of the second part of this chapter. Ideology, as was identified, is a complex concept, involving the power relations between different groups and classes of people, and the ways in which that power is exerted and enforced. Cinema, as a widespread mass medium and "apparatus," is regularly deployed to propagate ideological messages. However, this does not mean that alternative messages cannot also be formulated and disseminated, as our third and final section, on cinema and activism, demonstrated. With such films, which offer an alternative to mainstream ideologies, the challenge or provocation may lie not only in a film's overt content, but also in the form it takes, and the aesthetic tools it deploys.

FURTHER READING

Comolli, Jean-Luc and Narboni, Jean. "Cinema/Ideology/Criticism," in Bill Nichols (ed.), *Movies and Methods: An Anthology*. Berkeley: University of California Press, 1976, 22–30.

> This essay was first published in the French film magazine *Cahiers du Cinéma* in 1969. Comolli and Narboni's short, pithy and pessimistic essay, as our discussion in this chapter identifies, is of historical significance as one of the major critiques of the ideological nature of most cinema.

Eagleton, Terry. *Ideology: An Introduction*, 2nd edn. London: Verso, 2007.

> A witty, erudite and entertaining introduction to ideology, and just one of several books by Eagleton on the subjects of politics and ideology (all of which are worth reading). Eagleton offers a historical outline of the operations of ideology, tracing the concept from the Enlightenment to the era of postmodernity.

Jowett, Garth and O'Donnell, Victoria. *Propaganda and Persuasion*, 6th edn. London: Sage, 2014.

> This book offers a rich and thorough framing of the various ways of understanding propaganda. A historical overview of propaganda is presented, and its links with various institutions explored. An array of tools for analyzing propaganda is provided.

Solanas, Fernando and Getino, Octavio. "Towards a Third Cinema," in Bill Nichols, ed., *Movies and Methods: An Anthology*. Berkeley: University of California Press, 1976, 44–64.

> Solanas and Getino's manifesto remains an historically significant piece of writing. It critiques the ideological leanings of most cinema, but suggests potential directions forward, which were subsequently put into practice. Angry, committed, and vital, this should be read by anyone with an interest in the relationships between cinema and politics.

FILMS REFERENCED IN CHAPTER FOUR

Act of Valor (Mike McCoy and Scott Waugh, 2012)

Animal Farm (Joy Batchelor and John Halas, 1954)

Argo (Ben Affleck, 2012)

Aru Yo no Seppun/A Certain Night's Kiss (Yasuki Chiba, 1946)

The Blue Eyes of Yonta (Flora Gomes, 1991)

Body Snatchers (Abel Ferrara, 1993)

Il capello a tre punte (Mario Camerini, 1935)

Carlos (Olivier Assayas, 2010)

Colossal Youth (Pedro Costa, 2006)

La Contessa di Parma (Alessandro Blasetti, 1938)

Dead Man Walking (Tim Robbins, 1995)

Down to Earth/Casa de Lava (Pedro Costa, 1994)

Elizabeth (Shekhar Kapur, 1998)

Elizabeth: The Golden Age (Shekhar Kapur, 2007)

Der Ewige Jude/The Eternal Jew (Fritz Hippler, 1940)

Florentina Hubaldo CTE (Lav Diaz, 2012)

Godzilla/Gojira (Ishirô Honda, 1954)

Heimkehr/Homecoming (Gustav Ucicky, 1941)

La Hora de los hornos/The Hour of the Furnaces (Fernando Solanas and Octavio Getino, 1968)

A Ilha dos Escravos/Slave Island (Francisco Manso, 2008)

In Vanda's Room (Pedro Costa, 2000)

An Inconvenient Truth (Davis Guggenheim, 2006)

The Invasion (Oliver Hirschbiegel, 2007)

Invasion of the Body Snatchers (Don Siegel, 1956)

Invasion of the Body Snatchers (Philip Kaufman, 1978)

Kiss (Andy Warhol, 1964)

The Kiss (Thomas Edison, 1896)

Lincoln (Steven Spielberg, 2012)

Loose Change 9/11: An American Coup (Dylan Avery, 2009)

Melancholia (Lav Diaz, 2008)

Million Dollar Baby (Clint Eastwood, 2004)

My Voice (Flora Gomes, 2002)

Napumoceno's Will (Francisco Manso, 1997)

Ne change rien (Pedro Costa, 2009)

Night of the Living Dead (George Romero, 1968)

No (Pablo Larrain, 2012)

Ossos (Pedro Costa, 1997)

Philadelphia (Jonathan Demme, 1993)

The Private Lives of Elizabeth and Essex (Michael Curtiz, 1939)

Il Signor Max (Mario Camerini, 1937)

Super Size Me (Morgan Spurlock, 2004)

Taken 2 (Olivier Megaton, 2012)

Them! (Gordon Douglas, 1954)

Those Whom Death Refused (Flora Gomes 1988)

Top Gun (Tony Scott, 1986)

Triumph of the Will (Leni Reifenstahl, 1935)

Twenty-Year-Old-Youth (Yasushi Yasaki, 1946)

The Virgin Queen (Henry Koster, 1955)

Word is Out (Mariposa Film Group, 1978)

Ya es tiempo de violencia/Now is the Time for Violence (Enrique Juárez, 1969)

Young Bess (George Sidney, 1953)

NOTES

1 Mira Liehm, *Passion and Defiance: Italian Film from 1942 to the Present* (Los Angeles: University of California Press, 1992), 21.

2 Carlo Lizzani, quoted in Steven Ricci, *Cinema and Fascism: Italian Film and Society* (Berkeley and Los Angeles: University of California Press, 2008), 21.

3 Garth S. Jowett and Victoria J. O'Donnell, *Propaganda and Persuasion*, 6th edition (London: Sage, 2014), 20.

4 Karl Marx and Friedrich Engels, *The German Ideology*, 2nd edn (London: Lawrence and Wishart Limited, 2004), 64.

5 Jean-Luc Comolli and Jean Narboni, "Cinema/Ideology/Criticism," in Bill Nichols (ed.), *Movies and Methods* (Berkeley and Los Angeles: University of California Press, 1976), 24–25.

6 Comolli and Narboni, 25.

7 Comolli and Narboni, 25.

8 Comolli and Narboni, 26.

9 Linda Williams, *Screening Sex* (Durham, NC and London: Duke University Press, 2009), 29.

10 Williams, 26.

11 Fernando Solanas and Octavio Getino, "Towards a Third Cinema," in Bill Nichols (ed.), *Movies and Methods* (Berkeley and Los Angeles: University of California Press, 1976), 47.

12 Barbara Hammer, "The Politics of Abstraction" in Martha Gever, John Greyson and Pratibha Parmar (eds), *Queer Looks: Perspectives on Lesbian and Gay Film and Video* (London: Routledge, 1993), 70.

13 Peter Bradshaw, "Pedro Costa, the Samuel Beckett of Cinema," the *Guardian*, 17 September 2009, http://www.theguardian.com/film/filmblog/2009/sep/17/pedro-costa-tate-retrospective, accessed 5 October 2013.

14 Jacques Rancière, "The Politics of Pedro Costa," booklet with *Colossal Youth* Eureka DVD, 2011, 8–10. (Essay first printed in Tate Modern catalogue for 2009 retrospective of Costa's films.)

CHAPTER FIVE
FILM AS A COMMODITY

Films are many things to many people. But perhaps one of the most abiding roles they play is that of a commodity. A commodity is defined as something that can be bought and sold. When we visit a movie theatre, we typically pay for the experience. Films we watch on television or legally stream have been secured through licence fees, subscriptions or advertising revenues. Granted, not all movies exist for the express purpose of making money. But even that amateur clip of someone's dog performing a somersault that has been uploaded to YouTube cannot stray far from the machinery of commerce. It will certainly have been filmed using commodities, will contain commodities within the frame (including the dog), and the clip will have been surrounded by advertisements for other items we can buy. By becoming YouTube partners, even amateur uploaders can display advertisements within their clips and reap a percentage of the revenues generated by clicks to the product's website. For anyone hoping to work in the film industry, commodification (what we call the transformation of something into a commodity) is crucial. If creative labor is not bought and sold, how is anyone to make a living?

You might think these characteristics almost too obvious to mention. Is it not just common sense that movies are bought and sold? Most people find it next to impossible to imagine films as anything *other* than commodities. Surely something so pervasive and taken for granted is worthy of our critical scrutiny. Commodification's methods are subtle, multifarious and constantly in flux. For anyone hoping to gain a rigorous understanding of cinema – even the world more generally – it is crucial to be analytical, precise and questioning about how commodities come into being and how they distinguish themselves from each other.

To start with, movies exceed the capabilities of many other commodities. As the previous chapter illustrated, films function politically while simultaneously entertaining and educating us (the topics of Chapters 1 and 3 respectively). What does it mean to buy all these things within one package? Should politics, entertainment and education be commercialized in these ways? Then there is the economic bearing of cinema to consider. The world's richest country, the United States, registers entertainment as its number two grossing export commodity. More revenue is generated this way than is earned by many other countries on this planet in total. Enormous wealth is accrued through cinema, so it certainly pays to understand how this is achieved.

WHAT WE WILL DO IN CHAPTER 5

- Work out how films function as commodities by getting to grips with the basics of capitalism and its core doctrines of ownership, profit and money.
- Fathom how the multinational corporations that are now responsible for the bulk of the movies that reach us operate on the global stage.
- Investigate the various national and international bodies that regulate commerce in cinematic trade.

BY THE END OF CHAPTER 5 YOU SHOULD BE ABLE TO

- Confidently use an extensive range of economic terminology to enhance your comprehension of cinema.
- Appreciate how film production and consumption sits within broader economic practices and trends.
- Come to your own conclusions about the merits and shortcomings of film's position within commodity culture.

FILM WITHIN CAPITALISM

Commodification does not happen in a social vacuum. We need to get to grips with the infrastructure that supports and encourages it: **capitalism**. Currently the world's most prevalent political and economic system, capitalism functions according to the conviction that assets can be owned by particular individuals and groups, and then traded by them for profit. Capitalism is so ubiquitous, so embedded in our habits and thoughts that we rarely wonder at its peculiarities, capabilities or limitations. Examining these allows us to comprehend the world, and cinema, more fully.

Let us start by appraising the foundational principle holding capitalism in place that pretty much everything can be privately owned. Again, it may seem straightforward that we possess certain objects. Who out of us could go about our daily business without honestly thinking "such and such is mine, yours or theirs"? Look around the space you are in right now and you will surely be able to label almost every-thing you see in those terms. Think, then, about the political and financial implications of that ownership for you. What rights does it endow you with or restrict you from? How much money has changed hands and to whose benefit? For anti-capitalists, proprietorial claims can, and should, be contested. To what extent do we – or can we – own anything, ranging from our planet's natural resources to our individual ideas? These are profound questions, and both sides' answers to them are deeply ideological. Capitalism pivots upon the premise that, yes, we can own things. Furthermore, its supporters often strive to render ownership small-scale or personal, rather than collective. How many things can you list that are shared by all of us on the planet, as against those which are the preserve of a much more restricted group, if not a single person? This division of the objects and ideas in the world into "ours" and "not ours" is essential to setting the wheels of capitalist commerce in motion, as we will now explore.

5.1 A rare Darth Vader action figure with a telescoping lightsaber. Courtesy of Bill McBride (www.sithtoys.com).

To move on, we need to understand how these convictions about custody knit into the act of commodification. Put another way, commodification is the translation of mere things into commodities and often functions amid a chain of property relations and exchanges. As will become apparent, plotting out these processes reveals the extent of commodification in daily existence (not just when we go shopping) and the ways in which commodification shapes social relations. Let us take a digital camcorder as our example, the kind with which you may be very familiar. A certain group of people will possess land rich in the raw materials necessary for its manufacture (metals, the materials required for plastics and so on). You might want to ask yourselves how or why they have this stake. How did they get to own this land? Whatever the reason, because it is theirs now, they have the potential to make a profit from what it holds. It would be mad not to gain from these resources in some way, but difficult to achieve this singlehandedly. Therefore the landholders typically employ a further raft of people to extract the resources. In turn, the employees, very reasonably, want rewards for their input, input which they feel they own and over which they have autonomy (otherwise they would be slaves). Consequently, their labor comes with a price tag, allowing them to draw a salary – it is commodified too. Once that work has been completed, factory owners will buy the raw materials, hiring other people to move them to a suitable facility and still more to transform them into cameras. If you are interested to know more about this process and its impact on surrounding communities, hunt out *Performing the Border* (Ursula Biemann, 1999), a documentary essay about digital hardware production on the US–Mexico border. When finished, the camcorders are bought, sold and trans-ported any number of times before they reach their new owners: the buyer. At every stage of production, not just at the point of consumer shopping, there is concurrent commodification of resources, labor and so on that is premised on ownership. Successful commodification brings us money, which we can spend on more commodities, thus perpetuating the cycle.

Here we encounter another of capitalism's most appealing facilities – the potential for **profit**. Simply put, profit is a gain that is in excess of input. Who would not want that? The rational questions at this junction would be: how do you fairly measure gain and input in any given situation? The answers, especially with regard to the broader spectrum of commodification, are never simple. For example, there are significant quantities of consumers out there who are willing to pay $6,000 for a 1978 Darth Vader action figure with a telescoping lightsaber. Each one of them will know that it cannot possibly have cost that much to make the figure. So, why are they willing to pay so much?

One reason is that commodities carry much more value than is embodied in the cost of the effort expended to manufacture them as discrete objects. And some of us are happy to forfeit extra for that. What we are often paying for is a different order of labor and investment. We are buying into a stream of cultural and emotional responses to *Star Wars* (George Lucas, 1977), which is the result of many other people's energies (the filmmakers, the advertisers and so on), as well as our own personal investments. For these reasons, cinema reserves for itself a special place within commodification. Films captivate us in ways that extend well beyond the duration of their viewing times. Many of us want to develop those feelings or thoughts further. Look around you and try to account for all the things you have bought because of movies – from direct cinema merchandise, to clothes, drinks and even this textbook. As was stressed earlier, movies are not simply commodities. They powerfully suggest other commodities to us. In fact, it has been argued that cinema emerged at a moment when consumerism was arising as the dominant economic form, and movies helped ease this into place.

Another bastion of capitalism – **money** – functions in a comparably complex and related fashion. Money is always worth more than the sum of its physical parts. A bank note for one hundred Brazilian *reais* will not have cost that much to produce. While thinking about money, another fundamental question arises: why do we buy things anyway? By this, we mean, why do we hand over money, rather than share or trade like for like? One easy answer is because the world is simply too large and diverse for us to exchange what we need by any other means. We require something simple and portable for the task. Something that acts as a token of what things are worth. It is next to impossible, for example, for most of us to trade directly in skills. If a certain amount of human effort goes into making a film, how are any of us going to rightfully compensate those people with our own time and toil? It is not as if we could all go round to the director of photography's house and offer to wash up her dishes for free. This is where money offers a brilliant solution. It allows us to exchange values quickly and easily in a transferrable, often invisible form (if we think about online transactions). It is hard to imagine as effective a substitute.

Because money is not actually the thing (or value) that it represents, it offers plenty of leeway for profit. A conversion into money is an abstraction that opens the doors to negotiation. Value becomes relative and malleable, as became obvious with the Darth Vader action figure. Sellers will evaluate what they think we can all afford, which is why a ticket to a movie in Tanzania costs less than it does in Japan.

Demand is integral to pricing and profit, but so is supply. It is not hard to deduce that the Darth Vader with the telescoping lightsaber fetches a higher price than other *Star Wars* memorabilia because it is rare. The item was poorly designed and swiftly removed from the shops, leaving only a few hundred in existence today. On this occasion, the ratio of demand to supply is lopsided, inflating the profits the figure can accrue far in excess of the time and resources spent on making it. Manufacturers replicate this strategy when they release limited or collectors' editions.

Decreasing output, though, is fairly marginal to cinematic profit-making. After all, movies are mostly mass-produced and hope for as extensive a success as possible at the box office and beyond. They more usually make money by reaching a wide audience with multiples of the same commodity, for example through the distribution of thousands, even millions, of identical DVDs. These themselves replicate the film text that has circulated through theatres; restricted access has not been their marketers' tactic. Scarcity and abundance can be interrelated, of course. *Star Wars* figures mean so much to fans because this blockbuster series is a global phenomenon, the kind that felt it viable to manufacture toys without fear that no one would buy them. In fact, it is one of the most successful films to do so on a large scale and set precedents for selling subsidiary rights for other types of commodities. Demand might also result from geography. The UK distribution company Tartan Films tapped into this with their "Asia Extreme" label. Under this brand, they successfully marketed Asian movies such as *Ring* (Hideo Nakata, 1998), *Battle Royale* (Kinji Fukasaku, 1999) and *Oldboy* (Park Chan-wook, 2003) to western audiences by emphasizing how much more graphically violent these pictures were in comparison to English-language output.

Selling something unusual is not the only tactic vendors use; there are a number of other ways in which mass-produced commodities can augment their profit potential. One of these is by driving down the costs of manufacturing. As will become apparent, the alterable value of money mentioned above (wherein a hundred Brazilian *reais* is not actually worth that value per se) can support this venture. This becomes increasingly possible within the context of **transnational capitalism**, which we will return to later on in this chapter. Just as ticket prices vary between Tanzania and Japan, so do salaries. Money is worth more in some parts of the world than others, so capitalists often do their best to find the places where workers will accept the lowest wages. The people who made the $6,000 action figure most

5.2, 5.3, and 5.4 "Asia Extreme" branding by Tartan Films for the DVD releases of *The Ring* (Hideo Nakata, 1998), *Battle Royale* (Kinji Fukasaku, 2000), and *Oldboy* (Park Chan-wook, 2003). Courtesy of Palisades Tartan.

probably earn less than we would be willing to accept. However, it may have been the best employment option in a limited economic landscape. This takes us back to supply and demand. If lots of people in a certain area are desperate for jobs, they offer themselves up more cheaply than others might.

An obvious argument against this practice is that it is inhuman to exploit workers in this way or even to pay people around the world differently. A pro-capitalist response insists that the wealth that is created even in these circumstances filters down and benefits everyone. Larger numbers of the population gain jobs and therefore access to more commodities. Their lower salaries bring down costs, which benefits the buyer. It therefore makes sense to extend this focus on consumers to our investigation of how profit operates.

EXERCISE

We all make decisions about how and why movies should be commodified on a regular basis. Think through all the films you have seen but *haven't* paid for recently.

- Under what conditions have these movies been free? Were they tied into other commercial processes, like advertising, or an education for which you have paid in some way?
- Should people always pay to watch movies? Plot out some arguments that relate, for example, to how we might provide fair wages for filmmakers or recompense for resources.
- Was a portion of the films under consideration sourced through file sharing? If so, how do the ideas laid out above shape your understanding of what it means to exchange material for free via the internet?
- Can you imagine a world in which films are not commodities? How would they actually get made?
- Do you think there is a way in which private ownership could be evacuated from movie production? How would this impact what films currently are for us? To help with this, it might be worth contemplating other cultural objects that are communally created, such as Wikipedia.
- How would the people involved be compensated for their labor?

MARKET EXPANSION

Profits proliferate when as sizeable a market as possible has been secured. Advertising helps out enormously here and, by the same token, film acts as a seductive carrier of other commodities, as has already been noted. Enlarging the potential market runs deeper than merely making customers aware of commodities – it is a political and ideological endeavor. Later, this chapter will chart out just how dedicated international politics is to the struggle to expand and restrict markets. For example, forty years ago, large tracts of this planet, including China and the former USSR, were much less inclined towards capitalist commodities than they are now. The Cold War (c.1947–c.1991) between the communist-inclined nations and the capitalist ones was, in many ways, a battle over how resources and services should be managed, whether or not profit and commodification was the best way forward. It was also a struggle for geo-political influence, each side seeking to promote their opposing economic doctrines. With the fall of the Berlin Wall in 1989, communism's influence suffered a considerable blow and, as a consequence, populous markets have opened up in formerly communist countries such as Russia. Nation-states that still resolutely stand against capitalism, such as North Korea, severely restrict the movement of cinema from the capitalist countries into their own, not just because films are commodities, but because they often encourage the ideals and practices of commodification. This much you will be able to piece together with the help of the previous chapter's explanations. In turn, non-capitalist nations are duly ostracized and vilified by capitalist ones.

The concept of the commodity therefore plays a crucial part in world politics. This chapter will soon help you make up your mind about who the victors and victims of these struggles are, as well as evaluate how their rules of engagement are set out by international law. But, before that, and now that the basics of capitalism have been mastered, let us deepen our awareness of the tactics the film industry deploys to increase ownership and profit. Markets expand not just territorially, but conceptually, by thinking up or enfranchising new entities to buy and sell.

Part of this opening out of commodification includes the global trend towards **privatization**, which has borne meaningful consequences for cinema. Privatization amounts to the selling off of assets that have previously been considered public. Later on, time will be dedicated to outlining why and how this has happened and who benefits. For the moment, we shall simply examine privatization as a capitalist technique and ponder how its actions determine the social and economic standing of cinema.

Privatization has shaped and changed what film can be enormously, from how it is financed to how we regard its cultural function. In the past, many more countries (from Romania to Cuba) had **nationalized** film industries, meaning, theoretically, that they were collectively owned by all their citizens. If you are hungry for details of how nationalization works on the ground, the section on Czechoslovak animation in Chapter 7 will provide you with a more sustained description. Broadly, though, in a context of nationalization, film is seen more as a *service* than a commodity. And, as such, it takes on a completely different meaning. If we think of cinema as more affiliated to public services (which can include education and libraries) than to non-essential goods (such as chewing gum), then, as a society, we probably would want to fund and nurture it differently. Chapter 3's ruminations on cinema-as-informative presented various debates pertinent to this characterization. Although a government-supported cinema is much more financially secure and does not have to compromise expression to market forces, it can just as easily turn propagandistic. This was witnessed in some of the material treated in the previous chapter. Privatizing public services allows for more competitors to involve themselves in production and, in many ways, this opens out the quantity and choice of films that become available. By the same token, when playing this game of increased profit margins, the onus falls on the commodity to perform well, to be commercially appealing over and above other objectives.

The last fifty years have seen a decrease in the number of services that are protected by policies such as nationalization, including film. In fact, in 1995, the globally authoritative World Trade Organization's (WTO) General Agreement on Trade in Services (GATS) proposed that services too should be treated like other commodities – that they should circulate according to the rubrics of ownership and profit too.

The WTO will feature more prominently later on in this chapter, so central is it to how movies, in fact the majority of things, are commodified. As one of the world's most powerful international bodies, the WTO understands its role to be easing and coordinating the free flow of international trade, promising its member states smoother access to global markets and arbitration during trade disputes. It does so via a number of channels, including through drawing up policies by which its member states are obliged to abide. Of these, the GATS treaty stands as one of many WTO measures which have paved the way for greater privatization, not only of the world's cinema industries, but also of the likes of healthcare, utilities, postal systems and telecommunications. While many countries have run all these as not-for-profit services in the past, such nations are now increasingly pressured into positioning services as for-profit commodities. We shall see how and why presently.

The capitalist inscription of private ownership has also exponentially expanded into the realm of ideas. In the forms of copyrighting, patenting and trademarking, the planet has witnessed rapid growth in what can legally be declared **intellectual property**. The concept of intellectual property presumes that non-tangible things like ideas, inventions and creative manifestations can also be owned. This premise supports and is supported by the idea of self-expression, as delineated in Chapter 2, but, as was noted there, authorial authority is never as simple to attribute as one might at first imagine. The case study on Chinese piracy below presents one of the most prominent divergences on how to conceptualize and register idea ownership (or not) in film history. To fully grasp what is at issue here, the conflicting philosophies that govern intellectual property rights (or their denial) must be acknowledged. Films are full of ideas; this is one of the reasons we love them. Idea commodification has often happened well before a film's inception. Companies within the industry jostle for acquisition rights to storylines (perhaps from novels or comic books) as well as broader, saleable concepts (like video games). Dan Brown received $6 million for the rights to turn his novel, *The Da Vinci Code*, into a film (Ron Howard, 2006). Later on in the production process, music licensing is also big business. The song "Happy Birthday to You" brings in around two million dollars annually for its current owner, the music publisher Warner/Chappell, from its various broadcasts.[1] It may surprise you to hear that, even though "Happy Birthday to You" is practically considered a folk song, placing it in a film could cost anything up to $10,000.[2] You will remember from earlier on in this book how the distribution of films like *Superstar* were rigorously hampered because the makers could not secure music licensing rights.

But, as we can all appreciate, no movie plot or catchy theme song can be entirely new. We probably would not understand or feel comfortable with them if they were. So, where does the novelty of an idea stop and start? If we find it impossible to answer this question, then who should get credit when ideas are bought and sold? Traditionally, things that exist in what is known as the **public domain** cannot be copyrighted. Here dwell the things that no-one owns, whose property rights have, for instance, expired or been deliberately relinquished. Historical events rest in the public domain, yet personal biography can be considered intellectual property. Sometimes public and private prove extremely difficult to disentangle. Creative work is legally deemed intellectual property, but again there are many grey areas in how this can be classified. No one has to pay to reproduce folk tales, for instance, hence, at least partially, their recurrence as the narrative frame for quite a few movies throughout cinema history.

One effort to regularize the attribution of and profit from ideas comes in the form of the Agreement of Trade-Related Aspects of Intellectual Property Rights (commonly abbreviated to TRIPS). Authored in 1994 by the WTO forerunner, the General Agreement on Trade and Tariffs (GATT), this treaty must be ratified if a country wishes to reap the benefits of WTO membership. What is specific to, and contentious about, TRIPS is that it has increased what falls into the remits of property. By incorporating spheres like education and healthcare into its definitions of property, TRIPS has angered the many dissenters who firmly believe that this sort of knowledge should escape the ensuing potential for commodification and be available for free. Here are some of the views on either side of the argument as they apply to cinema, starting with the supporters of profit from ideas.

Simply put, intellectual property makes money and, in the world we live in, we need money to survive. A person who has a talent for innovation, in whatever field, deserves to be credited for what they do and to gain financially. Intellectual property law provides channels through which these income streams can flow.

But do such individuals ever get their just rewards? Not always, by any means. This is one of the many criticisms leveled at current intellectual property legislation. Editing software like Final Cut Pro provides

a good example. The workers who have designed it do not reap the benefits of the sale of each licensed copy – Apple, the corporation that has employed them does. The inventors will have been paid a salary, but their remuneration falls desperately short of the vast sums the software will bring in. In instances like this, the corporation (or a group of corporations) owns the copyright, even though all they have supplied is the backing and infrastructure for its development. To draw a suitable parallel, could we say that, although probably the owner, the patron of a work of art, not the artist themselves, is also its author? That the famous statue of *David* should be credited to Cosimo de' Medici (who commissioned it), rather than to Michelangelo (who won that commission)? Certain creators do own property rights (remember the Dan Brown example) and these vary quite significantly from country to country, as the upcoming case study on Chinese piracy illuminates.

There are also many critics of the very notion of intellectual property. Less concerned with correct attribution, they instead dedicate their energies to fighting the private or corporate ownership of ideas outright. They believe we should share ideas. Inequality of access often drives their campaigning. Licensed editing software (legally sourced, at any rate) is prohibitively expensive. Final Cut Pro X costs $300 and, as a result, reserves moviemaking as the privilege of an unrepresentative global elite. Filmmaking to industry standard is therefore kept as the preserve of relatively rich people.

5.5 Michelangelo's *David*. Courtesy of Mondadori Portfolio/Electa/The Art Archive.

CASE STUDY: CHINESE FILM PIRACY

Each year, the Motion Picture Association of America estimates that Hollywood loses around $170 million of its revenues to Chinese DVD piracy, and $3 billion worldwide. Although it is impossible to truly estimate figures for underground activities, piracy probably accounts for between 80 and 95 per cent of film's market share.

Piracy's networks are as globalized as the big studios are, crossing borders along some of the same trade routes used to traffic both narcotics and undocumented migrant workers. As Pang Laikwan points out, "The so-called tactics involved in piracy are neither humanistic nor democratic in nature but are carried out by their own system of exploitation, through which gangster tycoons earn astronomical profits."[3] Because piracy is so central to how films make their way around the world, this topic will also feature prominently in Chapter 10, which concentrates on distribution.

But piracy also mimics mainstream transnationalized production practices, taking advantage of the differences in employment and copyright legislation around the world. The cheapness of software, hardware and labor in contemporary China, as well as the country's laxer enforcement of intellectual property laws, render it a hub for global piracy. The distributors then take advantage of staggered international releasing patterns. Wherever Hollywood chooses to launch movies later than it does at home becomes fair game for a quick infiltration by unauthorized versions. Piracy of this order (as opposed to, say, internet file sharing) is as capitalist in its make-up as the official channels that supply the planet with movies.

Historically and ideologically, China sits in an advantageous position when it comes to efficient piracy. As was noted above, copyright is premised on the contestable idea that culture can be uniquely authored, owned and commodified. Belief in such characteristics is the fundamental justification for labeling certain acts piracy, rather than simply dissemination. Widespread political doctrine in China has traditionally worked counter to these property claims. China's Communist and Taoist legacies both promote the notion that culture is public, rather than private. Even film viewing practices were, in the past, typically free and communal, rather than domestic and paid-for, activities. As a consequence, the Chinese legal system has not developed a raft of rules for prosecuting copyright violators. China did not have a single copyright law in place until 1990 and, although 2001 saw the establishment of something similar to European IP legislation, it was not effectively implemented.

However, it is increasingly difficult for the Chinese to maintain their political stance on ownership. In 1996, the US Trade Representative threatened China with $2 billion worth of trade sanctions if it failed to tighten up its implementation of copyright law with regard to the profit flows that it felt were due to American corporations. Mindful of this threat, the Chinese Propaganda Department and Press and Publications Administration subsequently clamped down on pirate production. In order to trade on the world stage, China has joined the WTO, which, as was already pointed out, requires ratification of the TRIPS agreement. As such, much more stringent regulations about copying are being actualized. Paradoxically, WTO membership demands a decrease in governments privileging their own products and trading practices, which can weaken internal markets and decrease local wages. Piracy offers one solution for generating profit in this climate, despite the fact it is now more criminalized than ever before.

Such is the current state of play as regards direct product copying. But this is not the only incarnation of intellectual property to enter the debates surrounding Chinese notions of cultural proprietorship. While an industry such as Hollywood may categorically own the copyright on particular films, how are we to treat the host of ideas within them? Here we encounter the tricky unevenness of how intellectual property is framed. In some cases, it could be argued that the qualities that render certain movies so marketable often actually originate from China. Take, for example, the massive sales garnered from the martial arts on screen, which could be claimed to be Chinese intellectual property if genres and fighting techniques happened to fall into copyright's protective ambits. Movies as diverse as *Rush Hour* (Brett Ratner, 1998), *The Matrix* (Andy and Larry/Lana Wachowski, 1999), *Charlie's Angels* (McG, 2000), and *Kung Fu Panda* (Mark Osborne and John Stevenson, 2008) owe an enormous debt to Chinese martial arts culture, but pay very little of this back in actual monetary terms. Moreover, any unofficial Chinese copies of these films would be deemed illegal. The notion of originality is thus both fluid and circumscribed in situations like these.

At the same time, there are certain currents within the industry that are more tolerant of piracy than one might imagine. Piracy often brings material into environments that ban the official product or where distributors do not feel inclined to market their wares. While few financial benefits accrue from the existence of these movies in these spaces, a hunger for the films of this type can develop. This, in turn, can result in increased official sales down the line, including the purchasing of spin-off merchandise. The fights over piracy are extremely complex and fraught because of the substantial financial rewards at stake. As ever, they map out over the principles and practices of capitalism and are rarely in contravention of its core ideals.

5.6 *Kung Fu Panda* (John Stevenson and Mark Osborne, 2008).

These disagreements about availability lead us on to an examination of how film circulates as a commodity, which, ultimately, is the domain of Chapter 10 on the topic of cinematic distribution. However, as a foundation to all this and as a logical intensification of the study of commodities, we need to understand how movies are traded. The rest of this chapter takes on this subject in its manifold forms.

TRADE AND ITS LIMITS

Capitalism, it has been established, helps sustain itself by finding new things to sell. Another of its core objectives is, naturally, greasing the wheels of this trade. The current section investigates the many ways in which capitalists accomplish this. Perhaps the most discussed and contested ethos within contemporary capitalism is that of **trade liberalization**. Its directive is to allow capitalism to function with as few restrictions as possible. None at all, if the purest form of free trade is espoused. Governments, for instance, are discouraged from privileging their own products or taxing those of others. As ever, there are pros and cons.

Advocates of trade liberalization believe that the more we buy and sell, the more we will all benefit. Consequently, curbing the processes of capitalist exchange limits the amount we prosper. These philosophies have been refined and reworked for centuries now, building on the pioneering ideas of British economists such as Adam Smith (1723–1790) and David Ricardo (1772–1823). Here are the advantages claimed by this system. If a greater number of films are churned out, unemployment in the sector decreases. More movies become available, which enriches the choice offered to those of us who love them. We could not be further from the North Korean model described above, whereby the regime strictly controls what comes in and out of the country. Very few of us would welcome that highly constrained access to cinema.

Critics of trade liberalization, from Friedrich List in nineteenth-century Germany to John Maynard Keynes in twentieth-century Britain, put another spin on all this. A good number of them see the benefits of somehow regulating trade, asserting that efficiency and equity do not always align within liberalization. For instance, should corner-cutting in order to keep prices low triumph at the expense of decent salaries for workers? Minimum wage legislation is one such contravention of a purist trade liberalization doctrine.

Most opponents of trade liberalization also argue that the system unfairly favors the rich and powerful, a tendency that regulation could keep in check. A prior history of wealth enables competitive advantage, along with the potential to invest in all the latest technologies and training. Expensive big name stars, impressive visual effects and flashy promotional campaigns, to name but a few costly expenditures, are the sole preserve of movie producers with considerable accumulated capital, allowing for end products that few smaller companies could fruitfully rival.

In an ideal trade liberalized world, unbounded capitalist growth would make space for every investor in the cinematic art. However, its critics stress that there are limited resources over which we fight – a finite number of raw materials, fuels and consumers. Such competition eventually results in winners and losers; big business and the stronger nations end up controlling the majority of market. In order to protect their stakes, these forces often do their best to crush their competitors, instating the sorts of restrictions that come with influence. Hollywood, for instance, maintains costly lobby groups around the world in order to ensure that its products can be made as cheaply and can be distributed as widely as possible.

The trade liberalization response to this is that, while competition is healthy, all such tactics are equally in contravention of their ideals. A truly liberal market is, ultimately, a very difficult thing to achieve. Whatever your opinion on free trade (which is a state that none of us have fully achieved in order to properly test out), you will gain a far more nuanced understanding of cinema by thinking through this paradox within capitalism. On the one hand, there is the allure of choice and profit that comes from commodification and competition. On the other, there is the impact of the struggle for ownership of limited resources that can, ironically, diminish any of the benefits of competition. This interplay provokes resounding repercussions on the types of films available (and unavailable) to us, how we consume them and the lives of the people involved in every stage of their manufacture.

In the most extreme of cases, dominant competitive forces have been known to achieve a **monopoly**, whereby one single enterprise becomes the sole supplier of a particular commodity. IMAX, the company described in a case study in Chapter 1, functioned for many years in something close to this capacity, exclusively providing material in this large, but still densely rich format. Monopolies occur more commonly around the world, however, with utilities such as water or railways, where it is often exorbitantly expensive and impractical to set up a rival system. The same might be said of IMAX, to a lesser extent. Frequently, a monopoly will exploit its exclusive position to charge what it likes. And, when a narrowed-down group of parties controls the industry, they might not only set profit levels as they choose, but also have a freer rein to treat their workers badly. That said, it is often also the case that a monopoly functions beyond the logic of profit to provide a fair working and costing system for all involved. In the end, say the detractors of untrammeled competition, the result is often less choice, rather than more. Think here about the predictability of IMAX fare. It is only since the 2000s that IMAX conceded its theatre spaces to movies on general release, once they have been converted to the correct format at no small expense, or partially shot using costly IMAX stock.

Let us take a closer look at monopoly dynamics in action on a grander scale. Perhaps one of the most written-about incarnations of how competition has resulted in minority control took place in Hollywood in the middle of the twentieth century. This case has occupied film scholars for years, so the current chapter can only really condense a fraction of what has been said on the matter. It makes sense when trying to understand the global trade in films to focus on by far the most profitable industry in movie history, that of Hollywood. As a consequence of its importance and its ground-breaking and successful commercial strategies, Hollywood will logically be the focus of much of the rest of this chapter.

In the period preceding the 1940s, the American movie industry was pretty much stitched up by eight companies. These are known as the "majors," and break down into the "Big Five" (Warner Bros., Loew's MGM, Fox, Paramount and RKO) and the "Little Three" (Columbia, Universal and United Artists). What we have here is known as an **oligopoly** – power is maintained not by one enterprise (as with monopoly), but by a small few nonetheless. Here are a number of suggestions as to why this happened, followed by an analysis of its impact.

Film is an exclusive industry. It has evolved an expensive and convoluted production and distribution process in which hardly anyone can afford to participate. Swathes of the world's population who do not have the necessary capital are excluded from the onset. Furthermore, during the 1940s, a number of regions that were, traditionally, rich enough to take part, such as Europe, were still weathering the economic devastation of two world wars. They therefore chose not to concentrate their investments in non-essential entertainment. Moreover, as this chapter will relate towards its end, the United States offered them aid that was dependent on Europe opening up its market to their products. No wonder American films fared well as export commodities in the immediate postwar period, bringing in record profits from overseas markets of $125 million in 1946, amounting to around 35 per cent of total Hollywood revenues and 45 per cent of its film rental incomes, significantly high percentages at that point in time.[4] In addition, the United States benefits from a large, wealthy domestic market hungry for local product. In 1946, domestic cinema attendance was calculated to lie at between 65 and 100 million people per week.[5] Sheer population allows the US film industry to function according to something smaller nations cannot feasibly muster – an **economy of scale**. This is defined as a reduction in production costs when it is cheaper to manufacture larger quantities of products per unit than smaller ones. Once you have the necessary equipment or skills in place, you no longer have to factor their acquisition into the overall cost. In all sorts of ways, then, the global system presented America with an advantage that it maintains to this day.

From the late 1910s until the late 1940s, the big Hollywood studios used these factors and the resulting revenues to their distinct advantage, widening their command of the market by buying into what is called **vertical integration**. Vertical integration is the term for ownership beyond the means of manufacturing a commodity, reaching out into aspects of product delivery too. Within cinema, this amounts to having a hand not just in filmmaking, but also in disseminating movies and managing cinemas. Each of these three stages – production, distribution and exhibition – consumes a section of this book, so you have plenty of time to get to grips with how they function. In effect, vertical integration meant that studios would make a film, send it around the world via their own distribution channels, and then show it in their own cinemas. There is therefore much more of a guaranteed return on investments. Even if a particular cinema functioned independently, it was still beholden to the dictates of the majors. Big name stars were, as ever, box office draws. In order to screen these highly commercial movies, the studios often insisted that a non-vertically integrated theatre sign up to programming a raft of their other material (including B movies and shorts) without the luxury of assessing it in advance, and sometimes before the movies had even been made. This practice is known as **block booking** and will receive further attention in Chapter 10 ("Distribution"). In short, cinemagoers were at the mercy of whatever the studios wanted to programme, and still are to a large degree.

Clearly, film commerce, at this point, begins to eliminate some of the advantages that free trade upholds, its success stories then pulling away the ladder they used to climb to the top. Such outcomes were duly scrutinized by the American judiciary, which frequently backs liberalization. In 1948, with what came to be known as the Paramount Decree, the US Supreme Court ruled in favor of **divorcement** for the "Big Five". Divorcement was the process of barring these companies from simultaneously owning production, exhibition and distribution wings; in effect, they were denied vertical integration. This chapter's final section will examine in greater detail how legislation of this type operates. While divorcement certainly opened doors for less weighty competitors, it did set in motion a number of bankruptcies and buyouts. Understandably, profits from cinema became less of a safe bet and, as a result, filmmaking grew more expensive and less reliable a revenue generator. Movies had to be made differently, as will be explained in Chapter 7.

THE END OF OLIGOPOLY? NEW PATTERNS OF OWNERSHIP

These legislative developments weakened the industry's financial standing. Here we encounter the rise of **horizontal integration**, whereby studios either scrabbled to make money in other sectors, or, as was more often the case, were bought out by concerns with no prior history in film. As might seem evident, now that you have come to grips with vertical integration, horizontal integration is defined as ownership of interrelated concerns. An example would be how Gulf+Western, originally automotive bumper manufacturers, purchased Paramount Pictures in 1966, following on with acquisitions in companies related to music, sport and zinc, to name just a few. Film is thus linked to a whole range of commodities, with horizontal integration working as a diversification tactic, whereby a company proliferates the products, and therefore the markets, in which it deals. Central to the operations of the contemporary film industry, horizontal integration is closely related to **conglomeration**, the huddling together of various disparate companies under one giant parent corporation. Horizontal integration of this order has allowed for a recalibration of the sorts of ownership and commodification potential that such things as the Paramount Decree had undone.

As the 1960s gave way to the 1970s, the American film industry was in turmoil, partly because of the enforced break-up of vertical integration decades earlier. Increased risks taken in such uncertain times and the ensuing costs (such as those related to advertising competitively in a non-vertically integrated market) put paid to the once comparatively safe venture of major studio production. The era witnessed some telling big budget flops, like *Doctor Dolittle* (Richard Fleischer, 1967) for 20th Century Fox and *Lost Horizon* (Charles Jarrott, 1973) for Columbia Pictures. In addition to the difficulties of predicting and commodifying something as expensive as cinema, there was competition from rival entertainment sectors, particularly television. And, most importantly, all the above took place in an era of more widespread economic downturn. At this point, the majority of the old studios teetered on the verge of bankruptcy and were obliged to go on the market themselves as commodities. In 1969, MGM was taken over by Kirk Kerkorian, and Warner Bros. by Kinney National Services, Inc. In effect, these sections of the film industry were wrapped into **conglomerates**, parent companies with interests that far exceeded moviemaking. Kerkorian, for example, put the MGM brand to good use by adding an MGM-themed casino and hotel to his portfolio of Las Vegas properties.

Conglomeration reformulates how commodities and profits are generated. One of the greatest attractions of the conglomeration model is how it can offset risk. As has already been pointed out, the "Big Five" and "Little Three" flourished because vertical integration provided guaranteed distribution and exhibition for the studios' output. With the Paramount Decree, it became a whole lot harder to insure that an audience would even find out that a film existed, let alone know where to find it. The possibility for making failsafe profit from cinema diminished considerably. It is true to say that the vast majority of the world's films now

5.7 Paramount Pictures' ident (or opening logo) signifying the company's ownership by Gulf+Western.

5.8 The MGM casino, Las Vegas. Courtesy of Getty Images.

play festivals at best and then never secure a theatrical or television distribution deal. Here is where the conglomerate system comes to the rescue. When costs are shared across a broad range of interconnected companies, some of them will be able to cushion financial mistakes or losses, thus keeping the corporation as a whole afloat. If the risks with film production turn into financial errors within a smaller, more freestanding enterprise, they could well ruin it.

Where diversification has not seemed possible or practical through acquisition, joint ventures have thrived. The tactics of the KT Corporation offer a prime exemplar. At one time nationalized (so actually run by the government), this now private company controls the lion's share of telecommunications provision in South Korea. The company makes the majority of its profit through these products. However, it fully understands the growing capacity of the internet and mobile telephony as a means of watching films. Accordingly, it has steadily increased its connections with companies like India's Eros International (a distribution company with whom it forged links in 2011) as a channel for securing cheaper and top quality entertainment products. Eros holds rights for blockbusters like *Kambakkht Ishq* (Sabbir Khan, 2009) and *Housefull* (Sajid Khan, 2010), so receives further attention in Chapter 10 on distribution.

Producing and trading cinematic commodities through conglomerate networks often also streamlines and increases yield. Firstly, wings of a corporation can support one another – a film might advertise a song put out by the same conglomerate, whose video can act as something of a trailer for the movie. Sony, for instance, holds the theatrical and DVD distribution rights for *Country Strong* (Shana Feste, 2010). They also released the soundtrack CD, which showcases tracks by Chris Young and Sara Evans, both of whom are signed to RCA Records Nashville, owned by Sony Music Entertainment. The trailer incorporates various of these songs, particularly the title track "Country Strong" (performed by actor Gwyneth Paltrow), while the official music video meshes fresh performance footage with recycled montages from the movie itself, which, in turn, help promote the film. In this way, the conglomerate internally shares, and thus economizes, on resources. One marketing division will be able to cost-effectively coordinate an interconnected multi-product campaign in a way that is much more ambitious than was conceivable before films were housed within conglomerates (although the big studios of yesteryear did also manage subsidiaries in fields such as music publishing). Similarly, creative ideas, facilities, technologies, and information about markets can rapidly spread through such structures, improving the output of the corporation as a whole. Economies of scale are also achieved because large, successful companies have the money to invest in mass production upfront.

Merging the two characteristics that have just been mentioned (minimizing risk and spreading costs), horizontal integration also helps recoup the sizable expenditure films require. A movie, in and of itself, may not necessarily make back what was spent on its manufacture. However, when such things as

5.9 New performance footage created for the "Country Strong" music video.

5.10 Excerpts from the movie *Country Strong* positioned within the music video for its title track.

merchandising are factored in, then this is much more likely. But this tactic has enormous bearing on the types of films that conglomerates chose to make. After all, who is going to want to buy toys related to a documentary about genocide, or even a video game based on *The King's Speech* (Tom Hooper, 2010)?

Merchandising is not the only means by which conglomerates boost their incomes. As film production scholar John Caldwell points out, "less than 15 percent of feature revenues now comes from theatrical box office income … the electronically mediated home now functions as the most economically strategic site for both television reception *and* film consumption."[6] If we look at what some of the largest conglomerates own, we begin to see a pattern emerging. The following entertainment-invested companies have placed within the top two hundred of the global profit rankings (in this order): General Electric, Time Warner, News Corporation, Walt Disney and Sony.[7] All are extremely diversified and almost all hold assets within hardware production and dissemination (both theatrical and domestic). This renders the film industry a convenient content provider, not just for viewing devices, but also for these companies' interests in the realms of, say, the internet and publishing. And how else will people watch Universal Pictures films on the American Movie Classics channel without paying bills to an energy provider like General Electric, who also owns or holds major stakes in these other companies?

But hang on a minute, this all sounds rather like a revamped version of restricted ownership. What we might call "the film industry" is, as it was in the past, currently owned by a very small number of massive corporations, all of which are invested in distribution, exhibition and a wealth of other financial concerns. The path has been cleared for this by financial legislation, an important dimension of how film is traded which receives its own dedicated discussion below. Different political decisions throughout history have made way for the regrouping of oligopolies. From the last quarter of the twentieth century onwards, and spear-headed by heads of state such as Ronald Reagan in the US, Margaret Thatcher in the UK and Boris Yeltsin in Russia, we have seen a dominant trend in what is termed **deregulation**. Deregulation entails the increased withdrawal of government controls on trading and is one practical dimension of liberalization. In the UK, deregulation was exacted on previously nationalized telecommunications and public transport networks, alongside a reduction in subsidies for cinema, throughout the 1980s and 1990s. Deregulation in the US over the same period included the loosening of restrictions on single corporation ownership of television channels from six to twelve, all within a broader landscape of deregulation of sectors like energy, agriculture, finance, and shipping. For the Russian Federation, this meant a sweeping deregulation of things that had, beforehand, been fixed by the Communist state, including prices. In a famous speech from 1991, Boris Yeltsin outlined his motivations for deregulation, a statement that synopsizes why such measures have been important for trade liberalization's supporters:

> We have defended political freedom. Now we have to give the people economic [freedom], remove all barriers to the freedom of enterprises and entrepreneurship, offer the people possibilities to work and receive as much as they earn, after having relieved them of bureaucratic pressures.[8]

Inevitably, there exists vehement criticism of these policies, including from many ordinary citizens who protested their governments' decisions on the ground. One question skeptics ask is: does deregulation, in the end, curtail the perceived benefits of competition? Along with oligopolistic ownership, contractual relationships between like-minded companies ease away the sorts of rivalries that push producers to strive hard to please their customers through quality and variety of commodities. The tendency to recycle and re-version the intellectual properties that a corporation already owns intensifies. Smaller companies without such a portfolio of media properties find it increasingly hard to get a look in because they cannot run as efficiently. Creating new content is decidedly expensive and, further, more modest enterprises do not have the budgets for flashy international marketing campaigns.

For the critics of deregulation, this new incarnation of oligopoly is distinctly undemocratic. Moreover, as became evident in the previous chapter, media products are persuasive carriers of political messages, many of which perpetuate the agendas of big business. In certain instances, the media and politics intertwine even more tightly, as was the case when media mogul Silvio Berlusconi, who owns a string of TV channels and newspapers, was elected prime minister of Italy (1994–1995, 2001–2006 and 2008–2011).

This is not to say that small film-related businesses have been wiped off the landscape. Far from it. What has changed is the relationship between the minors and majors. Large corporations increasingly set up short-time contracts with these companies, working with, rather than against, them to their advantage. An independent production company might pitch them a film idea, which the conglomerate will agree to back. The production company is then given a fixed sum to realize the movie. If the film runs over budget, it is the production company that has to swallow the unforeseen expenses. The primary benefits for the conglomerate here include, as you can probably guess, the offsetting of risk and the reduction of costs. When film production is both expensive and unpredictable, what better way to shelter a large corporation's assets than to ask a bundle of smaller concerns to shoulder the risks of creativity? Chapter 7 will explore in greater detail how this plays out in relation to movie production processes. To understand how these arrangements can often be exceptionally lucrative, it is necessary to get to grips with how capital functions on the international stage.

FILM AND TRANSNATIONAL CAPITALISM

It has already been established that trade liberalization fights for business to be conducted as effortlessly as possible. This includes across national borders. The current section weighs up some of these contemporary incarnations of trade liberalization, looking first at the composition of the entertainment corporations, then at their impact on workers and customers around the world.

The trends in expanding production, consumption and, more broadly, ownership beyond national boundaries are typically grouped under the terms **transnationalism** or **globalization**. Trade has been international as long as there have been nations, but new developments mark out how goods circulate in the current era. The large corporations examined above are frequently referred to as **multinational corporations** (MNCs) because they function beyond the ambit of one country. Maintaining the basic tenet of capitalist private ownership, MNCs not only conduct business as freely as possible, they also do their best to buy up profitable companies wherever they find them in the world. So, for example, News Corporation owns sizable media properties in Australia, India, the United States and Germany, to name a few, and, of course, sells globally. The final section of this chapter will point out how international legislation has eased this type of acquisition into place when, previously, it might have been exclusively reserved for citizens of the host country.

We shall now examine how various shifts within global capitalism have allowed such coordination to prosper and for diverse products to move quickly and easily from place to place. As was discussed previously, the threat of risk can be significantly decreased when the market is enlarged. If a film can be successfully sold to as much of the world's population as possible, recouping a big budget becomes less of a worry. Once the movie has played the international theatre circuit, there are many television channels that will pay for its rights (or will have paid for them upfront, as the following chapter will elaborate). Transnational commerce concentrates on diminishing the impediments to these sorts of flows and on developing technology to facilitate this.

Think, for example, of how useful digitization has been in this respect. From the producers', distributors' and consumers' perspectives, it is now phenomenally simple to transfer moving images around the world. Film rushes can be delivered speedily to an editing house via the internet, wherever it may be (and perhaps even in an entirely different country to principal photography). Audiences are increasingly invited to watch live theatre, concerts, ballet and opera – from Puccini's *La Bohème* to a David Bowie gig – transmitted in real time to their local cinemas. Known now as "event cinema," this genre is predicted to be worth $1 billion by 2015, with theatres bypassing film studios and liaising directly with film exhibitors.[9] Other innovations in the field of delivery include how companies like Netflix or LoveFilm do away with the time-consuming acts of visiting a DVD rental shop by enabling us to stream from a vast catalogue of material. In his extensive three-volume work, *The Information Age: Economy, Society and Culture*, the social theorist Manuel Castells terms this the "network economy." Crucial to all this is not just the effortlessness with which commodities can reach us, but also how the money we pay for them zooms outwards to its sellers. The abstraction of money, discussed earlier in relation to bank notes, has been renewed. Money travels invisibly through electronic systems and, if we take into account how credit cards work, often without us even owning it.

At this point, it serves to recap on the basic attribute of capital: that money's abstraction allows its value to fluctuate. This becomes all the more apparent when we look at the bigger global picture. You will remember that movie tickets cost more in Japan than in Tanzania. By the same token, movie personnel – from poster printers to actors – are paid less in the latter than the former. The film industry often

EXERCISE

- Take the last piece of hardware through which you watched a film (this may even be a combination of commodities, such as a computer, modem, flat-screen monitor and speakers).
- Work out, to the best of your abilities, where these were manufactured and plot this out on a map of the world. Do you think the necessary components also came from those places?
- Do the same for the movie you watched on these technologies (websites like the Internet Movie Database can help you gain a picture of where the production company hails from, where the shoot took place and so on).
- This will give you a more complete picture of the global spread of commodity production and the resulting divisions of labor that we will analyse further within this chapter. Spend some time thinking about why you think certain commodities are made in particular locations with regards to the capitalist objectives of making profit.

profits from these wage (and thus cost) differentials. Consequently, filmmaking is now global in ways that would have been unimaginable when cinema was first invented. These days, movies are rarely the product of one country, especially when shooting locations and the large-scale manufacturing of all manner of film commodities are taken into consideration. Although industrial centers like Hollywood still exist, it would be foolish to imagine that all the films we think of as from there are actually made in California in their entirety.

The case study below, which explains how animation work is outsourced to South Korea, gives a grounded analysis of globalized production in action. In the meantime, here is a basic example. In China, employees in the factories that make Disney toys work sixteen hour days, seven days a week for salaries that range from $0.135 to $0.36 per hour. This would be deemed untenable, inhumane and, actually, illegal somewhere like Switzerland. But, in China, people are willing to accept these conditions because they would rather have this income than nothing. Chinese employment legislation supports these arrangements. For purchasers of these toys, the cost is distinctly more attractive than it would be if manufacturing took place in Switzerland, where an increased salary would be offset within the price consumers pay.

The ethics of wage differences is one of the most contentious issues within the debates on globalization. The benefits for traders and consumers are crystal clear: greater profits for the former and more affordable commodities for the latter. But worker and other human rights advocates and activists worry about what gets dubbed the "race to the bottom". As was witnessed above, MNCs frequently favor the contracting out of risky investment and manufacturing to smaller companies. This allows them to withdraw quickly without enduring too much damage, to only commit to ownership when it is sure-fire profitable. With global capital so adept at moving to wherever production is cheapest, the actual manufacturers are hamstrung by the principles of competition. If they do not accept disadvantageous terms, they stand to lose everything to whoever out-prices them.

The trade liberal's answer to this is that transnational networks categorically bring wealth, technological innovation and so forth to countries which might not have previously been afforded such opportunities. Chapters 7 and 8, which are dedicated more fully to the labor of moviemaking, will unravel these arguments about the "trickle-down effect." Then there is the unquestionable fact that these working conditions make commodities cheaper, which, in turn, can enhance the quality of life of spenders with low incomes.

But the logic of deflated pricing only goes so far globally. Certainly, an online auction house like eBay will allow us to buy, for instance, a DVD from a country where it costs less than it does at home. However, manufacturers are one step ahead of this game. The DVD will most likely be encoded as specific to a regional zone so that it can only be played on hardware designated for that part of the world, where prices are kept appropriate to the cost of living in those areas. You can find out more about DVD zones in Chapter 10's discussion of distribution. True, globalization lowers costs, but it is not always the consumer who benefits the most. The MNCs are incredibly canny in this respect and trade more freely when it is to their advantage than at others.

How do they handle the market thus? In their famous book, *Empire* (published in 2000), Michael Hardt and Antonio Negri convincingly argue that the MNCs hold the sorts of power that traditionally lay in the hands of state governments. Their sales exceed those of most nations, with ExxonMobil bringing in more than all but two of the twenty-four richest countries.[10] By zipping across borders and taking advantage of the differences in job and consumer markets, MNCs can put enormous pressure on communities by threatening to pull out investment. With this much influence and mobility, they are in a position to shape or shirk delimited local authority. If this is the case, then how are the media and entertainment giants made accountable for their actions? Should they be? The approaching and final section of this chapter lays out some of the attempts to set in place certain global regulations for film trade.

CASE STUDY: FROM AGGLOMERATION TO THE CORE-PERIPHERY MODEL: SOUTH KOREA ANIMATES HOLLYWOOD

How does a particular part of the world come to dominate commodification and profit-making within cinema? Significant portions of this chapter are devoted to unfurling how protectionism (see the last section) and trade liberalization can concentrate and fragment the flows of wealth from the movie business geographically. This case study delineates the circumstances that create centers like Hollywood, as well as disperse the labor that builds those brands around the world.

Throughout the chapter, it has been made clear how the American industry has asserted its dominance through competitive advantage and international economic policy. But the US industry has also created the production conditions necessary for effective profiting in other ways. Hollywood is, at the same time, a finely tuned **agglomeration economy**. This is a term used to describe the close proximity of related enterprises that enable money to be saved on production. Other agglomeration economies within movie manufacturing include Mumbai ("Bollywood") and Hong Kong. From its early days, Hollywood quickly became a geographical center for trade specialization through its concentration of a wealth of different natural and human resources. An appropriate climate for outdoor filming; a wide variety of close-by locations; a cheap, mostly non-unionized labor force; and, at the time, affordable real estate were all favorable conditions to set in motion the development of a smooth filmmaking infrastructure. Once in place, the area became known for producing this particular commodity, which, in turn, attracted migrants eager to work in the industry. There are more aspiring actors in Los Angeles than there are, per capita, in almost any other city in the world. This creates a pool of talent and a competitive employment market, which works to the advantage of the industry, keeping costs low and quality high. In addition, film workers can easily move between the many similar companies that are situated within close proximity, so ideas spread quickly and develop. Agglomeration also lowers things like transportation costs.

However, as has already been stressed, wages are not equal around the world and America has some of the highest. It has therefore proven cost-effective for Hollywood to source cheaper labor from beyond the immediate realms of the agglomeration. The technological developments and trade liberalizing agendas of transnational capitalism facilitate this dispersal of work into what is called the core-periphery model, whereby the center (Hollywood) remains intact, but is sustained by contributions from workers at a much greater remove. This case study analyses how such connections make good business sense, as well as weighing up some of the other non-economic costs incurred by core-periphery filmmaking.

Hollywood has benefited from a long history of what is known as **off-shoring** – the transferral of some of its operations to other parts of the globe. When it comes to animation, the sector that concerns us here, business first flowed to Japan in the early 1960s. However, Japan is now considered too expensive in comparison to other competitors. In the meantime, South Korea has picked up a large portion of this work, including from animation giants like Disney. The year 1979 marks a pivotal moment in this practice. This was the year when American trade unions tried to institute rules to insist that animation contracts should first be offered to indigenous companies. A strike of US animators was held to hammer home this demand. The studios responded by ignoring their actions and taking some of their business elsewhere, happy to pay the accruing fines that were levied. It was still cheaper to settle this bill and recruit lower waged workers in Asia, a fact that made South Korea the world's third largest producer of animation by the 1990s.[11] At present, most cartoons are storyboarded in the United States, sent to countries like South Korea for the bulk of the animation, and then returned back for dialogue and music overlays. *The Simpsons Movie* (David Silverman, 2007) and films 2 to 6 of the popular *The Land Before Time* (various directors, 1988–2007) direct-to-video series were the partial responsibility of the AKOM studio, while *The King and I* (Richard Rich, 1999) was worked on by Hanho Heung-Up. These movies not only attract international audiences, they are also the products of a globalized economy. How, then, did South Korea come to play such a crucial role in films that are generally considered to be "from Hollywood"?

South Korea has traditionally fostered a protective, closed-circuit environment for its movie industry, so it might initially seem surprising that it also looks overseas for work. After the Korean War (1950–1953), the government imposed a 115 per cent admission tax on all foreign films and instigated a quota that demanded large numbers of local films in cinemas. South Korea has witnessed many instances of extreme nationalism amongst film fans. In 1988, anti-American agitation led to death threats, arson and snakes being released in theatres when Hollywood's *Fatal Attraction* (Adrian Lyne, 1987) hit the screens there. South Korean governments have consistently sought to strengthen their cinema as an export commodity through building infrastructure and providing financial aid. In 2006, they allocated around $130 million to this endeavor. There are state-funded programmes to train animators and they have been rewarded with tax breaks of up to 20 per cent. The South Korean private sector, including giants like Samsung, Hyundai, Daewoo and LG, has also invested heavily in cinema, as was observed earlier.

At the same time, America has fought hard to gain traction in the South Korean market. The years 1998–1999 saw the Bilateral Investment Treaty between the two countries, which compelled South Korea to ease off its preferential quotas. The United Sates has also used its influence at the WTO, of which South Korea is a member, to dispute South Korea's protectionist policies. See the section below to understand how these tactics work more generally.

By 1997–1998, South Korea found itself in the grips of the Asian financial crisis. With a highly trained film workforce, but fewer local corporations in the position to employ them, globalized capital began to step in. It was later assisted by South Korea's well-maintained and speedy internet infrastructures and dedicated satellite links that equip the nation to receive and send film data quickly without real loss of time to transportation.

Economic crisis achieved what it typically does: higher unemployment and thus lower wages because of the competition for those jobs that did exist. The attractiveness of this situation to Hollywood is straightforward – the buck goes further in South Korea. Korean animators were obliged to accept wages of around a third lower than their American counterparts and to work longer hours with fewer holidays. In the early 2000s, Phil Roman, owner of the US animation studio Film Roman, estimated that what costs a million dollars to produce in America, Korean animation companies will charge around $100,000 to $150,000 for.[12]

The advantages to Hollywood are clear, but South Koreans have gained too. A typical animator's salary of $1,000 per month amounts to good money in the country, on a par with what university graduates earn. The situation to be wary of here is global competition. South Korea became a favorite for American animation companies because its animators were willing to work fast, to put in the hours in a short space of time – in effect, to produce under near-sweatshop conditions. But it is not the only country with its eyes on American contracts. Thailand, China, Vietnam, India and Indonesia now have a cadre of trained animators who are amenable to even lower salaries. In the Philippines, it is not unknown for animation workshops to locate beds or dorms alongside studios to help augment the hours employees can work. South Korea itself is wise to this and in fact often subcontracts its own American contracts to these countries rather than lose the trade. In effect, what we are witnessing here is a "race to the bottom" with newly skilled workforces vying against each other and therefore driving down the cost for large corporations who are at liberty to relocate their production wherever garners them the most profit. When you next watch a film "from Hollywood," try and gain a sense of how it is actually a global composite commodity, dependent for its profit margins on precisely these sorts of fluctuations in the labor market.

REGULATING FILM TRADE

The transnational scope of these corporations is matched by the global reach of the organizations that set and stretch the parameters of their trading. The most influential of these run as follows: the **World Trade Organization**, mentioned above, which aims to ease international trade, often, as we shall see, by pushing to reduce import taxes and other tariffs; the **World Bank**, which loans struggling nations money; and the **International Monetary Fund**, or IMF, which regulates currencies with the aim of stabilizing local economies (encouraging the value of money to decrease in countries like Tanzania, to return to our earlier example, so that they can competitively offer cheap labor and products to richer ones, such as Japan). Most nations around the world are heavily reliant on these organizations for their economic wellbeing. As a consequence, member states are obliged to conform to various ideological prerogatives by which these institutions stand.

All three organizations believe themselves to be fostering ameliorated international relations, smoother trading and thus prosperity, and pathways towards greater economic stability. They do so according to specific terms. Compliance with or membership of the WTO, IMF and World Bank consistently demands augmented marketization and privatization. If a nation is struggling and hopes to secure their aid for recovery, the World Bank and the IMF will strenuously insist that it reduces public sector spending and open up its markets to international trade and investment. In practical terms, the following measures are regularly imposed upon cinema: the privatization of a nationalized film industry (if one exists); the reduction of subsidies for local production (often making it harder for it to compete and profit globally); and the deregulation of television stations (so there is no guaranteed national market for movies from the region). Many of these measures were enacted on the Nigerian industry, as Chapter 1 witnessed. If media outlets become MNC properties, which is highly likely once foreign ownership is sanctioned, these companies are more inclined to work with their own catalogue of content. Why commission ground-breaking new material from the country in question when re-runs of *Harry Potter and the Sorcerer's Stone* (Chris Columbus, 2001) will undoubtedly bring in the ratings? There are usually advertisers to consider within this model too, which can lead to conservative programming. Sellers do not typically enjoy seeing their commodities placed next to disturbing or controversial material. On the other hand, deregulation may provide welcome breaks from stifling government control. There may be more choice available. The Nigerian video-film industry is a good example of how a deregulated and privatized market can flourish, even when in competition with the MNCs.

The salient point to remember here is that, through these actions, the IMF and the World Bank doggedly insist on film as a commodity. The WTO is even more focused on this agenda and, as such, brings with it all the benefits and disadvantages associated with trade liberalization. Commodities, as became clear earlier, do not thrive exclusively because of canny marketing or their quality. Political pressure is exerted to secure their dissemination and profitability. The WTO has been highly instrumental in establishing market advantage. As such, we should take the time to return to it to investigate its history and motives.

The progenitor of the WTO, GATT, was created almost simultaneously with the Paramount Decree, in 1947. Disbanded in 1993, it was reborn as the WTO two years later. As a multilateral, international agreement, it carries immeasurable influence on global commerce, including that of cinema. Arising from the context of a planet devastated by World War II, GATT devoted itself to principles of accountability and cooperation. It inaugurated a series of meetings and institutions dedicated to resolving disputes between countries. To further the objectives of mutual support and coordination, and to lessen the potential for conflict, it proposed decreases in trade barriers between member states.

Yet, as the opponents of trade liberalization point out, there is the potential, when restrictions are diminished, for the rich to get richer at the expense of the poor. All the more so when a country in a frail economic position is strong-armed into opening up its market without as many viable commodities to ply overseas, or even within its borders. Cinema analysts the world over bemoan how a weak home market cannot compete with the glitz and technological supremacy of Hollywood or Bollywood. The marginalization, sometimes decimation, of a local industry often follows in the wake of an open market. The Mauritanian film director Med Hondo lays out what typically happens in the baldest of terms:

Each year millions of dollars are harvested from our continents, taken back to the original countries, then used to produce new films which are again sent out onto our screens. Fifty per cent of the profits of multinational film companies accrue from the screens of the Third World. Thus each of our countries unknowingly contributes substantial finance to the production of films distributed in Paris, New York, London, Rome or Hong Kong. They have no control over them, and reap no financial or moral benefit, being involved in neither the production nor the distribution. In reality, however, they are coerced into being "co-producers". Their resources are plundered. The United States permits a penetration of foreign films in its domestic market of less than 13 per cent – and most of these are produced by European subsidiaries controlled by the US majors. They exercise an absolute protectionism.[13]

Organizations like the WTO ease these relationships into being, certainly, by maintaining a particular set of biases. Although the WTO presumes to be democratic, it has never actually held a vote between members on how to proceed with policy. Most of its documents and agreements are drafted first by big business and thus bear the imprint of their priorities. But, as Med Hondo alludes in his final two sentences, governments also push hard to gain and maintain preferential positions in the global market. As this is certainly the case with regard to cinema, we should spend time studying how American film commodities came to dominate our screens.

While Hollywood cinema has sold well globally since its inception, the post-World War II period, so central to this chapter, offers clues as to how global and state governance coalesce to further commercial supremacy. Europe, it has been noted, was economically devastated at this point, with the United States appreciably more robust. As such, after the end of the war, in 1948, the US was in a position to launch an economic programme called the **Marshall Plan**. The aim of the Marshall Plan was to help Europe back on its feet. However, in order to secure the funds to rebuild their industries, agriculture, infrastructure and so on, the European countries who signed up were obliged to welcome a substantial proportion of American imports, including movies. In turn, the films came loaded with American values (as Chapter 4 made apparent) and American aesthetics, which subtly shaped local tastes and expectations. The fact that Hollywood still maintains around a 70 per cent share of the European market is a legacy of this history.

At the same time, when it came to film, GATT also provided sturdy ballast against total market infiltration. One of its significant rulings on cinema was that it should be treated as a service, not a commodity. We dealt with that distinction earlier on in the chapter. This definition, for a while, exempted cinema from some of the more extensive liberalization endeavors upheld by GATT members. Most particularly, GATT allowed countries to limit film imports in a variety of ways so that local industries could develop and, it could be argued, best serve up indigenous cultural material. It is one thing for a country to voluntarily sign up to something like the Marshall Plan. It is quite another to forbid nation-states to limit the amount of foreign films they allow in. However, in 1986, during GATT's Uruguay Round of multilateral negotiations, these earlier possibilities for local support were drastically reduced. Subsidies from governments to boost export trade were all but abolished.

A fourth international body, **UNESCO** (the United Nations Educational, Scientific and Cultural Organization), often works to counter these aims. Founded in 1945 under the auspices of the United Nations, UNESCO's aspiration is to promote peaceful global interaction through such things as culture, education and heritage – entities whose best interests are not always served by commodification. UNESCO's priority is to uphold diversity, which, in contradistinction to the advocates of trade liberalization, it does not believe springs so spontaneously from unregulated markets. At the 2005 UNESCO General Conference, all but two member states (the United States and Israel) voted to support trade barriers that would protect local cultural production from the more destructive activities of liberal trading. However, it has to be highlighted that UNESCO rulings exert meagre influence in comparison to those of the WTO.

All the same, at the national level, there are still plenty of ways to try and provide support for a local industry. Governments are adept at raising trade barriers in a number of guises against the tides of globalization and liberalization. Strategies include preferential pricing for home products or heavy taxation of foreign imports so competitiveness is skewed. Collectively, these activities cluster under the banner of **protectionism** (a term referred to in the Hollywood–South Korea case study and in Med Hondo's critique of US trade practices). Protectionism involves limiting the entry of goods into a country or region in order to support local production. At the same time, incentives are offered for those making and buying commodities within particular borders.

To take one example, France spends around 770 million Euros ($1 billion) per year on film subsidies to keep its film industry buoyant.[14] It partially pays for this by levying taxes on ticket receipts. The country has a long tradition of insisting on high quotas of French films on its screens, while limiting the number of American ones. India's film history has run in a similar fashion. A succession of high duties on imports in the 1960s and 1970s, followed by US retaliations in the form of boycotts, successfully (and accidentally, on America's part) reinforced a massive regional market that prefers Indian to American fare. Argentina has also instituted a quota system and, in parallel, offers state funding to its Instituto Nacional de Cine y Artes Audiovisuales to boost film expertise.

Such tactics are routinely extended across borders. They form the foundations of regional trade blocs like the North American Free Trade Agreement (NAFTA), the Mercado Común del Sur (Mercosur, which is a Latin American grouping), or the Asia-Pacific Trade Agreement, many of which have treaties which apply to cinema. The European Union (or EU) houses an initiative called Eurimages which supports film production, distribution, exhibition and digital equipment acquisition amongst EU participants via a €25-million-per year fund raised through member country contributions.[15] In extreme conditions, a constellation like NAFTA or the EU may impose sanctions or an embargo on a country, as many did on Iraq during the regime of Saddam Hussein. Ordinarily, the reining in of commerce stems less from political or ethical imperatives than from cultural or economic ones like the ones that will now be outlined.

EXERCISE

Imagine you have control of how cinematic trade is conducted in your country.

- Would you encourage a protectionist model or open out to trade liberalization?
- Do you think movie production should be supported by the public or private sector? Why have you reached your conclusions?
- Would you welcome foreign commodities and investment, or do you believe in taxing and restricting imported movies? What do you envision to be the repercussions of your decisions?
- What would the cinematic landscape in your country look like under your policies?

Perhaps the most successful manipulation of trade policy, both at home and overseas, has been carried out by the United States. Think back to Med Hondo's statement on strategies used by this industry. The United States takes advantage of trade liberalization in order to boost its own sales internationally, while making it difficult for foreign interests to penetrate its home market. Despite its support of globalized marketization, it would be wrong to assume this country's film industry is entirely supported by the private sector. At home, for example, there are regional and city film commissions, funded by the state to encourage cost-effective location shooting. More broadly, it has to be stressed that the US government expends considerable energy and influence safeguarding the country's trade supremacy, aggressively fighting foreign protectionism while maintaining its own. It has done this for around a hundred years now. Hefty tariffs are imposed on imported films while domestic distribution companies are under no obligation to sell overseas merchandise.

Various trade associations dedicate their energies to maintaining these rights. The Motion Picture Association of America, or MPAA (formed in 1922 and previously known as the Motion Picture Producers and Distributors of America/MPPDA), works to advance the business interests of Hollywood through political and legal channels. There is also its sister institution, the Motion Picture Association (MPA), formerly the Motion Picture Export Association (MPEA), which is dedicated more particularly to international relations. Both bodies have long been allowed to function transnationally in ways that would be deemed illegal within the boundaries of US law. In effect, they have set up trading cartels overseas. They aggressively leverage differential pricing (as evidenced by the DVD region codes), preferential trade barriers like import taxes and payback for US copyright infringement through piracy legislation.

The US government stalwartly supports them and they, in turn, spend significant money on lobbying. Hollywood simultaneously donates large sums to political campaigns and the White House listens carefully to what the MPAA has to say.[16] After all, the government is very much in Hollywood's debt for successfully propounding core US political values globally (something the previous chapter exposed). As one-time MPAA president Jack Valenti declared in 1968, "To my knowledge, the motion picture is the only US enterprise that negotiates on its own with foreign governments."[17] The MPAA is even jokingly referred to as the "little state department" because of the power it wields within the United States. These days, it is similarly influential in forums like the WTO and has offices in strategic locations all around the world.

With knowledge of these negotiations, we can begin to understand how global trade advantages are secured. The previous chapter revealed the extent to which the media and political bodies work hand-in-glove ideologically. Through the content of this chapter, it is easier to see how all these alliances work for economic advantage. The complex weave of trade policy and cinema now gives us a much clearer picture of why certain films might be more popular and more commercially successful than others. Or at least why some reach us more readily. With entertainment products standing as some of the most lucrative commodities on our planet, it has been all but essential to consider how their financial positioning shapes myriad factors within our lives.

CHAPTER SUMMARY

This chapter commenced by building a foundation in how capitalism works, concentrating on its framing of private ownership, profit and money. Understanding core economic vocabulary like this, and the logics that underpin it, opens out a more complex perspective on how film works as a commodity. We then looked into various techniques that capitalism uses to expand its markets, such as privatization, intellectual property control and trade liberalization. The ways in which the film industry has consolidated power and ownership through oligopolies, conglomeration and transnationalism were treated in the middle of the chapter. Here we focused mainly on Hollywood's history of vertical and horizontal integration in order to assess their bearing on movie production, distribution and consumption. Finally, we explored the methods through which governments, as well as international organizations such as the WTO, IMF, World Bank and UNESCO try to direct the flows of film trade. With this information, you are now equipped to situate cinema within the machinations of global trade and the politics that regulate it.

FURTHER READING

Cryan Dan, Shatil, Sharron and Piero. *Introducing Capitalism: A Graphic Guide*. London: Icon Books, 2009.

> While this book may not have film as its subject, it is one of the most approachable introductions to the workings of capitalism in print. Key concepts are defined with clarity and contextualized within a thorough history of capitalism's development.

De Vany, Arthur. *Hollywood Economics: How Extreme Uncertainty Shapes the Film Industry*. London: Routledge, 2004.

> De Vany fleshes out many of the economic determinants that have been introduced in this chapter, paying particular heed to the risk and unpredictability that shapes contemporary movie production. He also explores how factors like the star system might reduce financial uncertainty. Legal matters receive in-depth treatment, particularly anti-trust legislation.

Kindem, Gorham (ed.). *The International Movie Industry*. Carbondale and Edwardsville: Southern Illinois University Press, 2000.

> Another edited collection, but one that draws upon regional expertise to offer welcome snapshots of non-Hollywood national industries, from Senegal to Brazil. The timespan runs from film's invention to the moment of publication.

McDonald, Paul and Wasko, Janet (eds). *The Contemporary Hollywood Film Industry*. Oxford: Blackwell, 2008.

> Bolstered by a precise detailing of Hollywood history, this book describes the commodification of cinema across a number of different formats and ancillary markets. Each chapter has been put together by a leading researcher on its topic.

Miller, Toby, Govil, Nitin, McMurria, John, Maxwell, Richard and Wang, Ting. *Global Hollywood 2*. Berkeley: University of California Press, 2011.

> A wide-ranging and punchy book with a lot of statistical muscle behind it, *Global Hollywood* situates the American film industry squarely within its global economic contexts. Topics covered include marketing, cultural imperialism, co-production and runaways, making it a useful source-point for many of the debates that arise in later chapters of this volume.

FILMS REFERENCED IN CHAPTER FIVE

Battle Royale (Kinji Fukasaku, 1999)

Charlie's Angels (McG, 2000)

Country Strong (Shana Feste, 2010)

The Da Vinci Code (Ron Howard, 2006)

Doctor Dolittle (Richard Fleischer, 1967)

Fatal Attraction (Adrian Lyne, 1987)

Harry Potter and the Sorcerer's Stone (Chris Columbus, 2001)

Housefull (Sajid Khan, 2010)

Kambakkht Ishq (Sabbir Khan, 2009)

The King and I (Richard Rich, 1999)

The King's Speech (Tom Hooper, 2010)

Kung Fu Panda (Mark Osborne and John Stevenson, 2008)

The Land Before Time series (various directors, 1988–2007)

Lost Horizon (Charles Jarrott, 1973)

The Matrix (Andy and Larry/Lana Wachowski, 1999)

Oldboy (Park Chan-wook, 2003)

Performing the Border (Ursula Biemann, 1999)

Ring (Hideo Nakata, 1998)

Rush Hour (Brett Ratner, 1998)

The Simpsons Movie (David Silverman, 2007)

Star Wars (George Lucas, 1977)

NOTES

1 Robert Brauneis, "Copyright and the World's Most Popular Song," *Journal of the Copyright Society of the U.S.A.* 56 (2009), 335/ GWU Legal Studies Research Paper No. 392, http://papers.ssrn.com/sol3/papers.cfm?abstract_id=1111624, accessed 18 August 2013.

2 As revealed by the documentary film *The Corporation* (Mark Achbar and Jennifer Abbott, 2003).

3 Pang Laikwan, *Cultural Control and Globalization in Asia: Copyright, Piracy and Cinema* (London: Routledge, 2006), 109.

4 Thomas Schatz, *Boom and Bust: The American Cinema in the 1940s* (New York: Charles Scribner's Sons, 1998), 297.

5 Schatz, 291.

6 John Thornton Caldwell, *Production Culture: Industrial Reflexivity and Critical Practice in Film and Television* (Durham, NC: Duke University Press, 2008), 9.

7 From "Table for the World's Largest Media and Entertainment Corporations (2004)" in Terry Flew, *Understanding Global Media* (Basingstoke: Palgrave, 2007), 71.

8 As quoted in Anders Åslund, *Russia's Capitalist Revolution: Why Market Reform Succeeded and Democracy Failed* (Washington, DC: Peter G. Peterson Institute for International Economics, 2007), 90.

9 David Hancock, "Alternative Content in Cinemas," *Screen Digest*, 22 March 2011, http://www.screendigest.com/reports/2011222a/2011_03_alternative_content_in_cinemas/view.html, accessed 27 July 2013.

10 David Kinsella, Bruce Russett and Harvey Starr. *World Politics: The Menu for Choice* (Boston: Cengage Learning, 2010), 72.

11 Kie-Un Yu, "Global Division of Cultural Labor and Korean Animation Industry," in *Themes and Issues in Asian Cartooning: Cute, Cheap, Mad, and Sexy*, ed. John A. Lent (Bowling Green, OH: Bowling Green State University Popular Press, 1999), 37.

12 Referenced in John A. Lent, "Overseas Animation Production in Asia," in *Animation in Asia and the Pacific*, ed. John A. Lent (Eastleigh, UK: John Libbey Publishing, 2001), 240.

13 Med Hondo, "What Cinema Is for Us," in *African Experiences of Cinema*, ed. Imruh Bakari and Mbye Cham (London: BFI, 1996), 39–41: 40.

14 Sarah Dilorenzo, "France Threatens Veto of EU-US Trade Deal," *Huffington Post*, 11 June 2013, http://www.huffingtonpost.com/huff-wires/20130611/ap-eu-europe-us-free-trade/?utm_hp_ref=media&ir=media, accessed 8 August 2013.

15 "What We Do," Eurimages, http://www.coe.int/t/dg4/eurimages/about, accessed 17 August 2013.

16 See Janet Wasko, "Critiquing Hollywood: The Political Economy of Motion Pictures," in *A Concise Handbook of Movie Industry Economics*, ed. Charles C. Moul (Cambridge: Cambridge University Press, 2005), 14 for further details of these political dynamics.

17 Jack Valenti, "The 'Foreign Service' of the Motion Picture Association of America," *Journal of the Producers Guild of America* 10 (March 1968): 22.

SECTION II
HOW DO MOVIES GET MADE?

INTRODUCTION

You are now entering the second section of this book. The previous five chapters have all concentrated on the prevailing reasons why films get made: as entertainment; as a mode of self-expression; as a means of informing us; as politics; and as commodities aiming to make money. Clearly, each of these sustained and dominant motivations for turning out movies has had a deep impact on what cinema is and what we expect from it. Now prepare to explore how those films come into being.

It will be old news to you that the sorts of movies most people watch cost millions of dollars and hundreds of people's efforts to make. What you can look forward to next in this book is a thorough investigation of how all this is coordinated. Here, we certainly do not want simply to parade accountancy records before you to show you how the books are balanced. Instead, the emphasis lies on acknowledging how the making of films tallies with priorities we have already examined. Chapter 4 noted how crucial cinema has been to propaganda and political influence. In the upcoming chapters, you will learn how governments get involved in the actual nuts and bolts production of movies. Their influence is more subtle and far-reaching than many people at first imagine. Similarly, we have just appreciated, via Chapter 5, that cinema sits in a web of conglomeration and globalization. Now we can begin extending that knowledge into a deeper analysis of how the film industry physically puts together its wares. Conglomeration, for instance, can dictate a film's look (through product placement, say) or its narrative (if the plot is based on a novel to which the parent company owns the rights). Globalization, as the example of outsourced animation work to South Korea has already shown, bears enormous consequences for who gets to make movies and where that happens. It is practically impossible to watch a film that is the product of one country now. The ensuing chapters will plot out what that means, in practical terms, for the people involved. As a consequence, that knowledge will give those of us in front of the screen a more nuanced grasp of the material we are consuming.

The next chapter focuses on the early stages of getting a movie off the ground up until the moment when the cameras start rolling, which is usually called principal photography. Here we will be asking fundamental questions about why certain ideas are transformed into movies, who pays for them, and what their expectations might be. That first concern draws in everything the previous chapter unveiled about (intellectual) property. We can now supplement our understanding by looking into how ideas are sourced, traded, merged, profited from and rejected by the industry. Through this, we will come to notice the protracted interface between the commercial interests of ancillary markets and the look and feel of the movies that garner broad global distribution deals. Given their high costs, only very particular investors involve themselves in financing films and each has their own range of incentives. Banks, multinational corporations, major studios, agencies of nation-states, advertisers and crowd-fund donors all have very distinct views on what movies should look like. These can certainly clash and they most definitely shape, sometimes overrule, the aspirations of the creative personnel involved. Chapter 6, then, will afford you the opportunity to assess how the stakes of various types of contributor (both creative and financial) inflect the movies we know and love. If you have ever wanted to make your own films, the next few pages will also give you an inkling of the many hurdles you will have to jump in order to get those projects off the ground.

Chapter 7 picks up at this point and reveals what happens after a movie's concepts and funding are in place. Here we will be getting to grips with how production is organized. People commonly talk about "the film industry," but what, precisely, is an industry and how does this specific formation influence the end products we watch? This chapter works in dialogue with the upcoming Interlude section. There you can learn what the key jobs are in filmmaking, from pre- to post-production. Chapter 7 supplements those descriptions by thinking more broadly about various trends in managing these costly and labor-intensive endeavors. Through time, practices change, often in line with shifts in how transnational capitalism functions. Film fans like to attribute particular styles and preoccupations to, for instance, named directors, or even just plain common sense. However, it is equally crucial that we acknowledge how such decisions might be the result of larger trends in industrial planning. The way a movie is made, as a complex, controlled, collective effort, will, ultimately, bear enormous consequences for its aesthetics.

Last up in the current section is a focus on the types of work this industry demands. Many people study film with the hope of gaining a job in this sector, but few properly understand what that truly entails. To lessen this unfamiliarity, Chapter 8 will consider a number of different occupations, from runners and clapper loaders to talent agents and actors. More pointedly, though, it will present certain pervasive trends within cinematic labor: long hours, prolonged unemployment, scarce and unequal opportunities, a lack of job security and atomized working conditions, alongside the thrill of engrossing specialized work, team spirit and creative fulfilment. We will discern the problems film crews experience in a globalized employment market, as well as learn about the ways they have stood up for their rights as workers. As such, Chapter 8 logically leads on from the financial and industrial analyses that precede it. It will alert you to the consequences of all those more abstract managerial decisions for the real living people who make our movies.

Our strong contention within Section II is that having a command of cinema cannot stop short at merely valuing end results like masterful acting or editing. This is clearly an important dimension of film scholarship, but should go hand in hand with a critical eye to what is going on behind the scenes – the latter very much influencing the former. If you wish to understand cinema properly, inside and out, you will enjoy connecting these dots. If you are keen to find a job in the industry, knowing how it functions is all but essential.

CHAPTER SIX
STARTING POINTS

We have all heard stories about actors who turned down particular roles and puzzled over how a movie would have fared with them as the lead. Warren Beatty or Jack Nicholson as Michael Corleone, instead of Al Pacino, in *The Godfather* series (Francis Ford Coppola, 1972–1990), for instance. It can be an uninspiring incipient script, an inexperienced director or shaky financing that deters actors. Perhaps the budget will not stretch to their usual fee. Whatever the reason, parameters set during these early days of a film's life bear immense consequences for what the end product will look and sound like. The same, quite logically, goes for its special effects, location and so on, which can only ever be as lush as the budget permits. What we aim to do in this chapter is introduce you to how these decisions get made. Ultimately, how do a set of ideas get shaped into an actual movie?

Cinema gossip is rife with stories about how "the money" demands safer projects than the ones dreamt up by "the talent". Tragic endings are converted into happy ones for the sake of box office. Gay characters become straight. With *Live Free or Die Hard* (Len Wiseman, 2007), for instance, the producers were so desperate to reach the profitable PG-13 audience, that the franchise's hero, John McClane's, now-famous catch phrase "Yippee-ki-yay, motherfucker" had to be cut. What leads to these differences of opinion; what divergent incentives are at work here? Funding deals arranged well in advance of release can even mean that a film will not make it to many cinemas. No matter if it has won top awards and rave notices. It will still have to premiere on the small screen if its production company has brokered a contract beforehand with a TV network.

WHAT WE WILL DO IN CHAPTER 6

- Establish what the conventions for commercial movie financing and development are and why investment in and profit from cinema can be so unpredictable.
- Discern who the typical backers for film are – from banks to governments – and get to grips with their stakes in the industry.
- Assess what happens when a group of different countries collaborate in the manufacture of single movies.

BY THE END OF CHAPTER 6 YOU SHOULD BE ABLE TO

- Appreciate what a lottery making a movie usually is and therefore understand why certain formulae are relied upon more than others.
- Chart the stages through which a film travels before principal photography (or shooting) commences.
- Weigh up for yourself the pros and cons of the various financial resources upon which cinema can draw.

Whatever our views on the sorts of decisions "the money" can make, commercial films would not even come into existence without their injections of cash. In order to concentrate on as many aspects of this complex dynamic as possible, we will be concentrating here on the kinds of movies that stand a chance of reaching theatres around the world. For solid details on how amateur material comes to fruition, please refer back to Chapter 2's discussion of YouTube uploads and their relatives. Thinking about the middle ground, although shooting in digital and editing on home software has dramatically reduced the cost of putting a film together, paying for a successful international release is an entirely different matter. The numbers of people scrambling to make it in this sort of commercial cinema far outstrip the funds available to support them. Even a micro-budget film is classed as anything under $150,000, which is hardly an amount every aspiring young filmmaker has lying dormant in their bank accounts. The average Hollywood feature film weighs in at around $106 million, of which approximately $35.9 million is dedicated to the advertising that is believed needed to recoup costs and convert the movie into something that makes money.[1]

Profit is never guaranteed, rendering almost all cinematic production a massive gamble. Predicting a movie's success is notoriously tricky, despite the not insignificant cash and effort apportioned to trying to second-guess the capricious whims of audiences. This inexact science can run aground as the world changes during the lengthy time spans it takes to turn an embryonic idea into a finished product. As Arthur De Vany puts it in *Hollywood Economics: How Extreme Uncertainty Shapes the Film Industry*:

> motion pictures are complex products that are difficult to make well; no one knows they like a movie until they see it; movies are "one-off" unique products; their "shelf life" is only a few weeks; movies enter and exit the market on a continuing basis; movies compete against a changing cast of competitors as they play out their theatrical "runs"; most movies have but a week or two to capture the audience's imagination; a rare handful have "legs" and enjoy long runs.[2]

In fact, almost 70 per cent of films fail to make back their production costs during their time in cinemas. We are no longer in the age of classic vertical integration, when ready-made homes on the exhibition circuit welcomed the majors' releases. This truth has to be factored into how movies are financed. No wonder funding can be so mercurial, pulled at any moment up until the release date. It is not unknown for shooting to be canceled even the day before it is slated to commence, or for films to be frozen in post-production because of a lack of funds. It is a miracle that movies are ever finished, and a good number are not.

In sum, movies are expensive, high-risk ventures. At their very outset, they demand a substantial infusion of cash, a leap of faith while clinging to abstract ideas, all of which are susceptible to constant tinkering. Who on earth, then, are the people who propel movies into production? What impels them? As previous chapters have illustrated, profit, prestige and political persuasiveness run high on why investors are attracted to the medium. Anyone siphoning their money into cinema aims to gain something in return. There are all manner of incentives: from money laundering (as has been the case in Indian and Egyptian film history), to associated glamor, to, naturally, the high returns of a global smash hit.

And there are just as many ways to finance movies as there are reasons for doing so – as many methods as there are creative minds to think up new ways to take advantage of ever-changing economic conditions. This being the case, we cannot possibly hope to cover all bases with this chapter. Instead we have decided to converge on bigger budget undertakings, the type that most people imagine when you mention the words "the movie business" and that allow us to investigate a broader range of financing options than more modest endeavors would. The sections below run through the mechanics of development, pre-production and financing in that order, which is not to say that filmmaking adheres at all to this sequence. Development will certainly require financing, but money can only be won if some of the core ideas are already in place. A lot of these actions happen in parallel. However, for ease of comprehension, these three dimensions have been separated out in what follows.

PROPERTY DEVELOPMENT

Which potential film projects make it off the ground the most readily? When certain ideas are reckoned to be money-spinners, they then undergo a process that the industry calls **development**. Development encapsulates activities like securing and redrafting the script, as well as working out what elements of the film might prove lucrative in what are known as **ancillary markets** (non-theatrical spaces from home-viewing to airline screens). Logistical tasks such as casting and location scouting fall into what is known as the pre-production phase. This chapter stops short of what we call actual production – the shoot itself – which is more squarely the topic of the one after. We have just noted how hard it is to make good on investments in cinema, let alone turn a healthy profit. Yet this is the overriding objective driving the development stage of a film. Movie executives earn their dues – and sizeable salaries – by somehow having a sense of what will work and what will not. Such people are hired and fired on these abilities with noticeable regularity, which goes to show just how volatile audiences' tastes actually are. But there are certain staples upon which the industry has come to rely.

Having a star attached to a package often pays dividends and, as such, attracts investors to a project. A-listers like Bruce Willis and Johnny Depp land upwards of $20 million per movie precisely because their presence will more likely guarantee its widespread success. In industry lingo, such figures are "bankable" and can "open a movie" or, in other words, their performance is enough to tempt people into cinemas. Small wonder, then, that modest indie films – no matter how compelling their subject matter – do not appeal greatly to investors. Stars really are key to what makes people select one movie over another.

EXERCISE

Drawing on sources like industry gossip publications or biographies, compile a list of actors who have been considered for famous roles (such as the *Godfather* example above) but who were not ultimately cast.

- Try to think why, from a *producer's* perspective, this might have been the case.
- Consider how "bankable" these stars would have been at the time and why?

Next write a list of movies that have flopped because of what was regarded to be poor acting performance (your own judgements as well as film journalism may help build up this picture).

- Conjecture on why, once more from a financial point of view, these actors would have been cast regardless.
- Consider the breadth or narrowness of the demographic to which they might appeal.
- Imagining, again, that you are a producer, to whom would you have given the part instead?
- Weigh up their typical salaries and the box office success of their prior output to assess whether you have made a prudent decision.

Another clear way to entice backers is to argue that the film project will fare well with a wide spectrum of viewers. And that it will do well beyond its theatrical release. In fact, DVD, television and online provision net higher profits than cinematic release. The 70 per cent of movies mentioned above that do not do well during their first run hope to (and largely do) recoup their costs this way. As a consequence, a hefty portion of upfront funding is accrued by selling advance distribution rights for these markets.

For all these income streams to perform well, productions have to think globally. North America is by far the largest market in the world, followed by Europe (France, the UK, Germany, Italy and Spain in particular) and then Japan. Other countries have keen and populous film-going communities, but may not bring in weighty profits on account of their low ticket prices. India is a good example, and over the last few decades "Bollywood" has deliberately looked beyond its borders, appealing to the 30 million plus non-resident Indians (NRIs) and people of Indian origin (PIOs) living overseas, as well as to audiences who do not share a South Asian heritage. Triumphs like *My Name is Khan* (Karan Johar, 2010) and *Bodyguard* (Siddique, 2011) have sold well across the globe, in no small part because they incorporate western countries into their *mise-en-scène* and deliver a significant amount of dialogue in English. Similarly, countries like the UK capitalize on the fact they can easily produce English-language movies, often tailoring their output to North American fantasies of British life – be they contemporary

(*Four Weddings and a Funeral* (Mike Newell, 1994), which has grossed over $245 million worldwide[3]) or literary-historical (*Pride and Prejudice* (Joe Wright, 2005)) – or by incorporating an American protagonist (such as Julia Roberts in *Notting Hill* (Roger Michell, 1998)).

Another market that pays dividends is demographic in character: the adolescent audience. Teenagers seem happier than any other age group to leave the house to venture to the cinema. Furthermore, they spend a significant amount of their disposable incomes on the kinds of commodities that studios can license, like electronic games and fast food. Younger children are a similar catch in that they often watch movies repeatedly on home formats and are a core market for toys, which, again, can be film-related. When trips to the cinema are planned, at least one accompanying adult will have to buy a ticket too.

What these consumer trends tell us is that related non-film products are central to a movie's overall commercial success. Logically, then, merchandising features heavily in how films are green lit. Revenues can be acquired through, for example, product placement, which functions as a type of advertising within the narrative. It seems unlikely that Nokia phones would have been mentioned by name in the Korean movie *The Host* (Bong Joon-ho, 2006) had not that company been fighting a pitched battle with home-grown telecommunications giants Samsung and LG at the time. Films can even be sponsored by clusters of individual companies, as has been humorously pointed out by *The Greatest Movie Ever Sold* (Morgan Spurlock, 2011), a documentary whose actual diegesis involves the search for suitable business partners. Official merchandise, like the Darth Vader figure discussed in Chapter 5, is also added to the balance sheets.

Ancillary markets are now so important that they dominate the development phase of many a movie. This period takes at least half a year and frequently several. While development typically involves assembling a winning package of, for instance, a writer, director, script and some actors, tracking down a profitable "**property**" is similarly crucial. In the movie business, a property is anything on which a movie can be based, be that a concept, a story, or even a human life, if the narrative is biographical. We talked about property more generally in Chapter 5 and the same rules stand. Property implies possession and, as a result, its owners can charge money via copyright legislation for any reference or reproduction. A good property can spin out into all manner of profitable commodities, from TV programmes and soundtrack CDs to theme park rides. The principal business of mainstream cinema is licensing these rights, which, today, can amass around 80 per cent of a film's income. Understandably, then, the development stage is dominated not only by

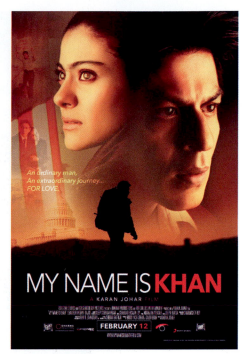

6.1 Note how the American flag features in this poster for *My Name is Khan* (Karan Johar, 2010). Courtesy of Dharma Productions/The Kobal Collection.

6.2 *Toy Story 3* PS3 game. Courtesy of CTRPhotos/iStock.

6.3, 6.4, and 6.5 Moments of direct, on-screen advertising in *The Greatest Movie Ever Sold* (Morgan Spurlock, 2011).

producers, creative personnel and financers, but also brand managers and lawyers specializing in intellectual property, copyrights, distribution rights, syndication and publication, not to mention litigation, if another company's property is mistakenly infringed.

Writing saleable commodities into movie narratives is where the big money is to be made. The development stage of larger movies therefore has to be conscious of knitting these possibilities into a workable cinematic narrative. A type of movie known as the **high concept** film aims to sell itself according to "the look, the hook and the book." Here "the look" is a direct and dynamic iconography for the production, something that works well on posters and related products, even in advance of the film. The *Batman* logo is one such image. "The book" refers to the plethora of extra commodities that the property can spin off. And "the hook," which metaphorically pulls in the audience, is a catchy storyline. The easier it is to grasp, so the logic goes, the quicker viewer affinity is established, the faster people will begin to start spending money on it. We would recommend Justin Wyatt's monograph *High Concept: Movies and Marketing in Hollywood* as an excellent starting point if you want to know more about how all this works, with its in-depth analyses of trailblazing examples like *Flashdance* (Adrian Lyne, 1983).

High concept films famously take only a sentence or two to "**pitch**": the process of summarizing a story theme swiftly and effectively to potential investors. Film festivals the world over hold "speed dating" events, where filmmakers bounce from funder to funder within a matter of minutes and try to persuade them to invest. This is not purely a time-saving exercise. If a movie idea is immediately computable, and can be grasped by almost anyone, it is believed to draw a broader range of consumers than a complex, nuanced scenario. The "high concept" is one of the many ways in which economic prerogatives are seen to mould the types of movies that fill our screens.

One means of circumventing audience unfamiliarity is to head straight to the heart of a property that is already known and loved. Best-selling novels or comic books are regularly optioned. **Optioning** is the practice of gaining exclusive rights to adapt something into a movie. Remakes (authorized and unauthorized) abound, as is witnessed by Turkey's *The Return of Superman* (Kunt Tulgar, 1979), or *Vanilla Sky* (Cameron Crowe, 2001), a Hollywood feature which re-versioned the successful Spanish property *Open Your Eyes* (Alejandro Amenábar, 1997) and even cast its original star, Penélope Cruz. If a formula already works, why not exploit it further? The same principles apply to sequels, cycles and genres, as this chapter's case study on Mexican *lucha libre* films exemplifies. Distributors are twice as likely to book a sequel and a sequel can build on a franchise's prior success to augment its capacity for commodification.

These trends in how films are developed, funded and, ultimately, made indisputably impact upon how scripts are commissioned and written within mainstream cinema. Because of the priority given to working up strong properties, studios and production companies tend to be cautious about whom they hire. Proven hands settle the minds of their insurers too (more of them in a minute). The agents that broker contracts for actors, directors and writers are sometimes concurrently involved in film financing and insist on particular "packages," which can dramatically shape who is hired. A "package" might demand a production employ whomever they suggest in return for a desirable A-list star. Creative Associates Agency (CAA), for example, manages film personnel, sports celebrities and musicians, while maintaining interests in investment banking, consulting and advertising. It is therefore usually keen to arrange packages that benefit a range of these concerns. The bulk of scripts work off the back of a

CASE STUDY: THE *LUCHA LIBRE* FILM CYCLE – HOW MEXICO "MEXPLOITED" A GAP IN THE MARKET

Mexico, right after World War II. The Americans had just curtailed their conflict-time investments in the Mexican film industry, preferring to target the recently re-opened and more lucrative European markets. As a result, production in Mexico slowed significantly. None of this is to say that Hollywood eased up on trying to flood Mexican cinemas with its own wares, despite protectionist attempts from Mexico. The competition was ferocious and Mexico needed to devise a formula that would attract the home audiences if its industry were to survive.

Thus was born the Mexican wrestling, or *lucha libre*, movie. The genre capitalized on the fact that the country was already deeply enthralled by the sport, a 1930s adaptation of Texan pro-wrestling. In the terms of this chapter, *lucha libre* was a strong "property" or "hook" because it could attract an already devoted consumer base. Today, we also know these films, and others in a similar vein, by the tag "Mexploitation." The *lucha libre* variants amount to around two hundred features, turned out between 1952 and 1983.

Why this time frame? Wrestling appeared on television for a brief two years between 1952 and 1954, after which it was banned from the airwaves. The film industry seized the opportunity censorship created to take advantage of an already established fan base. Aficionados of wrestling could continue to follow the feats of stars like Blue Demon and Mil Máscaras by going to the cinema instead. As we have already witnessed, a loyal, ready-made audience is one of the only sure-fire ways to secure a film's success.

Other bonuses included familiarity and cost effectiveness, both of which featured in the planning that buttressed the genre. Familiarity came in the form of melding wrestling with horror narratives. Mexico had been making its own popular versions of Hollywood classics, such as *Drácula* (George Melford, 1931), since the 1930s. Two (sometimes more) reliable concepts – neither effectively protected by copyright legislation then – added to Mexploitation's potential to succeed at the box office. These re-workings and amalgamations not only stuck to recognizable and well-loved plots and themes, they also enabled producers to recycle. Plots, sets, even footage were re-purposed to make new vehicles, while casts and crews repeated their roles quickly and comfortably, sometimes taking on more than one job on any given movie. In fact, fight sequences were often simply cut into the action, meaning that wrestlers (or *luchadores*) did not even have to learn to act because their contributions could be divorced from the main flow of the plot. Still, by even loosely positioning their fights within a storyline, the sport circumvented the censors' ire.

However hackneyed, the genre did, nevertheless, manage to concoct a pleasing "Mexican-ness" for its local viewers. The films were suitably melodramatic, which fitted in with the prevalent aesthetics of the day. They intertwined elements of comedy and action that broadened the audience base. And *lucha libre* in its original form takes up a moral struggle between combatants, a dimension that works well within cinema's narrative conventions.

Modernization, so topical for Mexicans at the time, figured prominently in plots. The battle between good and evil often played out as one between industrial and infrastructural development and an evil scientist or monster from bygone days trying to foil these initiatives. Although rarely overtly political, *lucrador* Misto did lend his support to the ruling PAN party in the drug war and Superbarrio was decidedly leftist. Hiding behind masks and fantastical stories enabled the wrestlers to express beliefs in ways that might not have been possible through more overt means.

The biggest star by far, though, was Santo (real name: Rodolfo Guzmán Huerta), who performed in around fifty such movies, including *Santo vs. The Vampire Women* (Alfonso Corona Blake, 1962) and *The Mummies of Guanajuato* (Federico Curiel, 1972). Santo was admired throughout Latin America, proving an earlier point: that shared language across nations can augment a movie's saleability. For a good three decades, Santo comic books flourished in these markets, exemplifying the importance of synergistic alliances to an effective property – even if the majority of *lucha libre* merchandise has been unofficial.

While the genre was on the wane in the 1970s, the real death knell sounded when Mexican television finally deigned to screen wrestling matches again. Cinema, at that point, lost its niche position in this particular market.

6.6 *Santo vs. The Zombies* (Benito Alazraki, 1961). Courtesy of Filmadora Panamericana/The Kobal Collection.

"property" – the makers buying or developing the property, and then hiring someone to convert it into a screenplay. What are known as "spec scripts" – scripts that have been speculatively sent off to studios, producers or agents – rarely make it into theatres. In fact, only around one in a hundred even passes beyond the vetting teams hired to assess their quality and onto the desks of more influential players.

By the point at which a workable script emerges, a movie has usually reached its **pre-production** phase. The upcoming Interlude section of this book lays out exactly what pre-production entails, tasks such as location scouting, casting, hiring crew, renting studios, leasing equipment, as well as finalizing budgets and additional funding. The work is overseen by a team of producers, whose roles are further defined in the Interlude. What concerns us here is how these jobs dovetail with other financial intricacies and possibilities. As you have already read, money can be pulled from a film or schedules delayed at a moment's notice. Assembling a cast and crew when nothing can be concretely assured, not to mention persuading them to decline other offers, can be quite some balancing act. So much so, in fact, that many top name actors and directors insist upon "pay or play" clauses in their contracts, a safety net which ensures they receive their salaries whether the film is made or not. One such example: Bob Hoskins was originally slated to play Al Capone in *The Untouchables* (Brian de Palma, 1987). When its director eventually managed to persuade his top choice for the role, Al Pacino, to appear, Hoskins was paid off with £20,000 without committing a day's work on set.[4]

Decisions reached by the pre-production team can also add to the film's coffers. Choosing where a film is shot, for instance, can bear positive consequences for its budget. As will be explored presently, film commissions exist to promote their locale as a prime spot for shooting. Film commissions help out with red tape, hiring skilled workers, securing locations and equipment and so on, all in return for the boost to the economy that a film production can stimulate. This chapter's penultimate section reveals that there are even tax rebates for shooting in particular areas.

The evidence suggests, then, that movies build up financial resources slowly and wherever they can along the way. The rest of the chapter testifies to the wide variety of different funding sources, including loans, pre-sales, distribution deals and public funds. Each of these comes with its own stipulations. 100 per cent upfront financing is rare, but it does happen occasionally, so it pays to examine at least one production that has succeeded in this. In his lively and informative book, *The Hollywood Economist*, Edward Jay Epstein pulls out *Lara Croft: Tomb Raider* (Simon West, 2001) as an example of a film that latched down all its necessary funding before shooting had even started. So much clever accounting had already been conducted in advance that the movie could only turn profit. Foundational here is how the movie benefited from co-production tax breaks within the UK and Germany. These were issued in return for shooting in the UK and temporarily handing over the film's copyright to Germany's Tele München Gruppe. Distribution rights for Britain, France, Germany, Italy, Spain and Japan were sold to Germany's Intermedia Films for $65 million, while the studio – Paramount – maintained free rein on distribution throughout the rest of the world.[5] Courtesy of this creative bookkeeping, the movie became an almost risk-free venture.

The strategies used to make *Lara Croft* and other movies will all be unraveled in the next three sections, but precise figures always remain vague. Ultimately, real budget breakdowns are tightly guarded secrets. No producers want to reveal a loophole they have discovered and benefited from in tax law. Similarly, product placement contracts are kept under wraps because their exposure would lower the

6.7 James Bond enjoys a certain brand of beer in *Skyfall* (Sam Mendes, 2012).

credibility of any given merchandise. If audiences knew that James Bond was driving an Aston Martin or drinking a Heineken beer merely because advertisers had paid exorbitant amounts for the privilege, they might be less inclined towards these goods than if they believed them somehow more intrinsic to Bond's lifestyle. Likewise, the personnel involved in placement deals have to be smart about choosing the sort of commodities that fit with particular characterizations.

Although many of these individual deals are conducted behind closed doors, we do know a lot about the types of manoeuvre that take place. The remaining sections of this chapter investigate them, starting with money input by private sources. After that, we shall move on to government provision. Then we will finish the chapter with an analysis of co-production: creative partnerships between two or more entities, which often amount to an amalgamation of private and public sponsorship.

PRIVATE SECTOR REVENUE STREAMS 1: STAKES, LOANS AND SHARES

All the money that is given or lent to the film industry comes with conditions. Appreciating what these are and how they influence the movies we end up watching gives us a more nuanced understanding of cinema. A raft of different financial resources exists for supporting filmmaking within the private sector. The size of the production and its potential for penetrating multiple markets dictates where it might appeal for support. A larger scale work, as we have discovered, should be able to attract merchandising and product placement deals. A less "high concept" movie will rely more on pre-sales to television companies. But what other sources are out there? In the *Industry Guide* published for the 2012 London Film Festival, the Film London Production Finance Market claimed that, in 2011, it "had attracted almost €245 million of production value through leading equity, hedge fund, tax, banking, and public and broadcaster financiers."[6] The next three sections of this chapter will introduce you to these resources.

There is one that has been left off this list, however: film studios themselves. Profitable studios, quite evidently, can afford to pay for their own productions, although they often choose not to. Back in the days of vertical integration, the studio moguls ran tight economic ships. Budgets were controlled from on high and largely fixed before production commenced. If a film was conceived as a cheap B-movie, it usually ended up as one. A studio knew, for the most part, what funds it had and distributed them among its many projects according to what it felt would draw in the crowds. As has already been explained, vertical integration guaranteed that studio movies would find their ways into cinemas. In effect, this made production less of a gamble, but also cheaper. Less money, proportionally, needs to be spent on advertising when a movie's distribution future is secure. The advantages of vertical integration have not altogether disappeared. Paramount is affiliated to the television network Showtime. 20th Century Fox has access to all the broadcast, satellite and cable TV outlets within the News Corporation portfolio. These range from the Star TV channels across Asia, to Fox Movies, which reaches more than thirty countries and mainly screens the studio's own back catalogue. Do not be surprised if this sounds very much like the vertical integration of old. Moreover, the bankrolling of studio films can be cushioned by the profits generated by the other wings of the larger corporation within which the studio sits.

Things have changed in other ways, however. Planning is less centralized within the studios now and films are green-lit individually, rather than as a coordinated group. A lot of the production is carried out by smaller, independent companies with financial input from the studios. In this scenario, much of the industry's characteristic risk is shouldered by the smaller company. The money is loaned according to certain provisos from the majors. The big studios still have, if not clear production identities (lush musicals for MGM, and so on), then at least strong ideas of what will and will not sell. They often intervene in a production company's work by insisting upon what many consider to be "safer" alternatives, ones they presume to be more audience friendly.

Despite all their monetary facility, studios have never entirely functioned as closed investment circuits. They hold long-standing relationships with **banks** that date back to the very first years of cinema and, today, large banks like JP Morgan typically comprise an entertainment division that specializes in these deals. What is the role of banks in film culture as we know it? While banks do not typically interfere with the content of movies, they have been known to act extremely restrictively, especially in a studio's darker hours. It is not just studios that deal with banks. In fact, ordinarily, the more modest the production, the more the banks are involved. The industry, across the board, relies on banks for its financing more than any other type of outside investor. Banks, on average, provide around 60 per cent of all the upfront money for film production that is not directly provided by a studio; significantly more for smaller operations. In total, these sums run into billions each year. Where would we be without the banks and what are film's main draws for them?

Banks have been responsible for building up the industry as we know it. The concentration of power in oligopolistic structures through both vertical and horizontal integration has been presided over and given blessing by the banks historically. Without their loans, the industry could not have grown in the way it did. In order to purchase expensive equipment, develop its technologies and buy real estate for studios and theatres, the movie business has been consistently indebted to banks. They played a formative role in the costly transition to sound in the late 1920s, and, as Janet Wasko points out, "The sound systems adopted by the major film corporations were owned by AT&T and RCA, which, in turn, were ultimately controlled by major banks and financial interests."[7] Recently, the return to a more commonplace use of 3D (discussed in further detail in Chapter 11 on Exhibition) has resulted in major borrowing by both film producers and exhibitors to obtain the requisite equipment for shooting and screening. Each of these technological developments has brought profit their way.

What sets a bank apart as an investor from a studio, or, ultimately, a large, well-heeled parent corporation? For starters, a corporation will input its own capital, while a bank is investing other people's money (its clients'). In this respect, many of us have actually been investors in cinema without even knowing it. Banks' earnings derive from such things as fees and interest, rather than any stakes they hold in films themselves, or the profits that unfurl from box office success. Like the multinational corporations that hold ruling interests in much film production, banks are, correspondingly, enormously powerful around the world – even more so, arguably, because they have their fingers in industrial, political and even military pies.

Yet, although they hold similar sway and share comparable tactics to the MNCs, banks exert this influence differently. They do so by setting themselves at a certain remove from primary ownership and manufacturing. To put it baldly, banks are not particularly interested in cinema itself. They drop film projects often, preferring to move their money around to where it can reap the best benefits. Banks are not as concerned with products as they are with assets. Or, more exactly, the uncertain potential of cinema is no way near as attractive to them as the property the industry already owns in more concrete terms. These are things like real estate, which can transfer into the hands of the banks if business goes badly. In turn, the fear of this possibility keeps filmmakers' minds on profit potential, which is not necessarily the case for state-funded cinema, a topic dealt with in our next section.

On the other hand, the banks' disinterest in meddling at the level of production choices is refreshing in comparison to intrusions from stakeholders from other arenas. Banks do not maintain shares, which would reap rewards proportional to the profits that are amassed. To this end, they do not really care if a film makes money – as long as their loans, interest and fees are paid. Banks typically ask to be reimbursed first and quickly. This, in turn, encourages the industry to open films "big" (across as many screens as possible), which comes with its own advertising and booking expenses. Here we witness one of the subtle ways in which banking affects how we access movies and also how much they end up costing. Banks garner considerable wealth from interest, which usually runs at around 20–22 per cent for film industry borrowing. The bigger the budget, the higher the bank's gains, so it is to their advantage to spike up borrowing. Interest rates, of course, all depend on how much collateral a company has to borrow against – what they can offer the bank in real terms if the project collapses. The less a company has to their name, the higher the rates of interest and the stiffer the bank's conditions. At the very least, this would amount to a distribution deal, other forms of pre-sales (see below) or maybe merchandising secured in advance.

It is also standard procedure for a bank to demand a **completion guarantee** or **bond**. This is an insurance contract that pays out if the company fails to finish a film, or deliver it on time and on budget. The fee charged for this runs at approximately 5–6 per cent of the total budget and, if the company cannot conclude production, the guarantor may well have the right to assume control over the process or recoup its investment before other investors. Supplementary types of insurance that may be required include safeguards for cast, directors, props, sets, equipment, the negative, as well as protection against legal actions like defamation claims or copyright infringements. These processes impact upon the industry in a variety of ways. Insurers simply will not take certain risks. Drug use amongst actors, for instance, is a serious concern, which, in turn, impinges upon who can be cast. For *The People vs Larry Flynt* (Miloš Foreman, 1996), the insurance for Courtney Love (scheduled to play Althea Flynt in the movie) was so high because of her previous history of addiction that the studio refused to pay it. Famously, the director, producer (Oliver Stone), lead actor (Woody Harrelson) and Love herself put forward the money instead, allowing Love to deliver a superlative and critically acclaimed performance that would not otherwise have reached our screens. This tale of exception proves how, ordinarily, the insurance industry increases its revenues without ever risking too much. During the studio era, drug users certainly proved liabilities for productivity and quality. But iconic actors such as Judy Garland and Marilyn Monroe could still work more easily than would be the case these days. The current situation allows two related sectors – banking and insurance – to profit purely through fees and interest in a way that was much less common in the past.

Other types of investors gather their returns differently. Around 40 per cent of the budget of any top- to middle-range movie (those not relying on more thorough studio backing) originates from what is called **direct investment**. The term implies that money is assigned in exchange for receiving a share of the profits, rather than a fee for arranging a loan or from interest rates. This is the point at which those somewhat unfamiliar terms of "equity" and "hedge funds" enter the scene.

Equity basically means ownership. In return for funding, the investor gets a share in the film and thus its earnings. The benefits for filmmakers include, firstly, capital that could not be raised elsewhere. In addition, the equity investor literally has a stake in the enterprise – they care what happens to it. There are pluses and minuses to this. In wanting the film to succeed, these investors may encourage the sorts of conservatism that are the bugbear of those struggling for a vibrant, challenging and innovative cinematic culture. But these investors also encourage an imaginative approach to finding other sources of what is called "**soft money**" (such as tax breaks and government grants). After all, the quicker the movie is out of the red on the balance sheets, the better for everyone. The sums infused by equity are astronomical and truly allow the industry to function in the manner to which it is now accustomed. To give some sense of this, in the first decade of this century, Goldman Sachs sealed a $490-million deal with The Weinstein Company and another contract worth $600 million between Relativity Media, Sony and Universal.[8] Overall, as with the banks, billions of US dollars are in circulation in this sector.

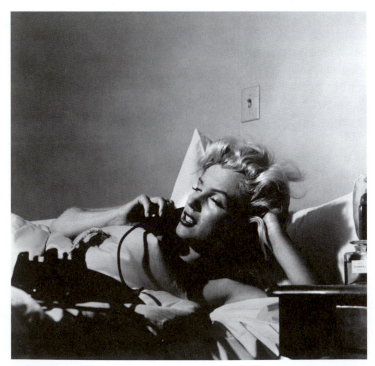

6.8 Marilyn Monroe. Courtesy of The Kobal Collection.

Hedge funds function similarly. In theory, they invest other people's money in safe bets that will always net a profit in return for a fee or percentage of income. Their entry-points into film production are identical. Hedge funds pick projects that seem reliable (thus bolstering conservatism, some argue), asking for a proportion of takings, which they then partially redistribute amongst their own investors.

Equity and hedge fund participation in the cinema fluctuates wildly, depending on how lucrative cinema is at any given moment. While their managers care about how well a film will fare, they are not moved by the medium per se and will have no qualms moving their business to other more rewarding sectors. They commonly lend support on a film-by-film basis, which can have a devastating effect on those working in the industry. Because the hedge fund managers are not part of the film community, they are less concerned about workers' rights than they are about profit and they have been known to pressure for longer hours, decreased pay and fewer overall employee benefits. When the studios held greater sway in the industry, money was more directly reinvested back into its development. Today, those profits are shared out beyond its confines. Conversely, the industry often chooses to bring hedge fund money on board because hedge fund managers have proven willing to accept less preferential rates, and therefore a slimmer proportion of profits, than the film industry actually collects.

Ultimately, private sector investors, history proves, are regularly willing to take the sorts of chances that characterize movie manufacture. In fact, such gambles, frequently rather perilous ones, are central to how the financial sector itself has thrived – and they are pivotal to the widespread criticism it has received since the beginning of the 2008 recession. Untrammeled risk-taking, beyond the capacities of capital and resources, is considered one of the major contributors to that economic crisis. And, moreover, their speculations have been conducted using the savings of their clients. Further problems ensue from their ethos. The financial sector is preoccupied with generating interest, rather than directly improving living standards (although, as Chapter 5 explained, liberal economic theory believes that the growth that such risks generate allows wealth to trickle down). In keeping with this rationale, there is currently more debt in the world, including in filmmaking, and, in this way, the financial sector generates considerable wealth servicing these debts.

PRIVATE SECTOR REVENUE STREAMS 2: SALES AND OTHER SOURCES

Pre-selling movie rights, be they connected to distribution or merchandising, is comparably hazardous, but unconnected to the accrual of interest. Instead of the shareholder model that equity and hedge funds assume, rights-based financiers basically buy entitlement to market the film property within their specialist arena. This might be overseas or online distribution. It could be a promotional tie-in with their own products, such as limited-edition soft drinks branded with the movie's imagery. It might be a licensing deal with a company like Entertainment Jewelry, who sell earrings, pendants and rings inspired by the *Twilight Saga* (Catherine Hardwicke, Chris Weitz, David Slade, Bill Condon, 2008–2012). Pre-selling is still a chancy business. A production company or studio hopes to gather up funds in advance of a release by selling off something unknown – their film's capacity to make money. One possible outcome could be them gaining amounts that will never be made back by the rights buyer. On the other hand, they might have sold a rewarding revenue stream for a pittance. Again, the high concept blockbuster triumphs here because it breeds many more properties than a small indie movie.

6.9 Licensed *Twilight Saga* tie-in merchandise at "Twilight at Midnight" DVD Launch Event, Los Angeles, California. Courtesy of Getty Images.

Sales agents are key to these transactions. They bear the responsibility for brokering such deals, maintaining strong connections with distributors and players in other compatible industries. At prominent movie markets, like the annual *marché du film* at the Cannes Festival, they will organize lavish, showy parties, fly out stars and invite other influential people, all with the hope of setting up contracts, for which they receive commission. They, along with the rest of the industry, must keep an eye on trends and fluctuations. For instance, they have had to adapt to the boom in internet-based access to cinema and to formulate ways for movies to earn well within these realms. They have also had to think creatively around the fact that overseas markets (in part because of piracy and how it overrides staggered global releasing) are less profitable than they once were.

All these games of prediction patently dominate cinema's private sector funding mechanisms. There are certainly a few opportunities which do not function according to these priorities; their influence, however, is considerably smaller. Every now and then, a rich individual will hand over some money to a film production purely on impulse. Stars have been known to invest in projects they believe in and thereby take a producer credit. **Crowdfunding** via online platforms like Kickstarter and Cinema Reloaded has proven successful in encouraging the general public to contribute production costs. Crowdfunding involves filmmakers making a public call for support, usually via a website that can handle payment. Members of the general public can then donate as they see fit. High-quality and profile projects are increasingly reaching out in this way. One such example is *Lynch Three* (Jason S., 2014), a documentary conceived through enduring and complex collaboration with its subject, the renowned director David Lynch.

6.10 *Lynch Three*'s Kickstarter page. Courtesy of the David Lynch Foundation.

Significant resources for pre-production, shooting and post-production can also be won in the competitions held by international festivals, such as those convened in Rotterdam and Busan. It must be noted that the battle for this type of support is fierce and the rewards relatively low. One of the most feted festival grants, the Sundance Documentary Fund, apportions a meagre one or two million dollars to around 45 to 55 filmmakers.[9] Sundance receives between 1,700 and 2,000 applications, meaning there is a one in forty chance of collecting a sum that is nowhere near sufficient to launch a movie of the scope we have been focusing on within this chapter. The gap between studio-backed teams and more independent productions is immense.

While nothing much is expected of the successful festival applicants, save the promise of a premiere, other benefits transpire. Prizes like these entice top talent to that particular festival, which simultaneously hosts film markets where financiers gather to strike production and co-production deals. If that particular festival becomes known as a gateway for high-quality films, then investors are more likely to travel there than to other similar markets. Their presence, in turn, feeds the local economy, from its movie theatres to its hotels and restaurants. Such thinking replicates the reasoning of local film commissions, which are treated in the next section. In fact, festivals are often underwritten by public money, rendering them a bridge between this portion of the chapter and what follows.

EXERCISE

Try and think of a "property" that has yet to be made into a film. It could be a novel, a game, even an historical event. Or a "high concept" all your own. Assume you have experienced no difficulty acquiring this property. How would you now go about raising money from the private sector to turn it into a film?

- Will you appeal to a major studio for support? Why do you feel they would be drawn to your property? What changes to your project do you envision them demanding?
- Would you borrow from a bank? If so, do you think there will be any knock-on effects for your casting, locations or other plans caused by their insurance requirements?
- Are you interested in pitching your idea to shareholders (via equity, hedge funds or crowdfunding)? What can you offer investors in return?
- Is there scope for arranging product placement deals? What sort of commodities would fit into your narrative comfortably?
- What is the merchandising potential offered by your film?
- Can you brainstorm any other ways of finding the cash you need?

PUBLIC FUNDING FOR CINEMA

To reiterate an important point from above: organizations do not readily hand over cash for film production without implicitly or explicitly expecting something in return. The previous two sections detailed how the private sector usually asks for financial rewards in the form of interest, arrangement fees or licensing rights. What public bodies typically want from their investments are pleasing images of the people and places over which they have authority, either for their own citizens or a foreign market; that, or a spur to the local economy.

The fourth chapter of this book laid out how crucial film can prove to establishing and propagating ideology. Governments are clearly wise to this and dole out funds accordingly. Nationalized cinemas (which we cover in several chapters) amount to the most thorough incarnation of this practice. Here a government pays for the bulk, if not the entirety, of film production and often does not expect a profit in return. Most former Communist countries, as well as more socialist-inclined states such as Algeria and Syria, have benefited from this structure. Other places, such as France, Brazil and Pakistan, institute strong **quota systems**, dictating that a proportion of all films screened in the country have to be domestic products. In effect, this is a government-sanctioned near-guarantee of exhibition which reduces the speculative risk holding sway elsewhere.

As you might imagine, critiques of nationalized cinemas abound. Why consent to film becoming a mouthpiece for those in power? For every dictatorial regime that closely monitors and restricts its cinema, though, there are examples of much more freewheeling nationalized output. Cuban state cinema from the 1960s onwards, as touched on in Chapter 2 and Chapter 3's investigations of Third Cinema, is a case in point. Its *Death of a Bureaucrat* (Tomás Gutiérrez Alea, 1966), for instance, is a wry, often slapstick appraisal of many aspects of life under Cuban socialism. *One Way or Another* (Sara Gómez, 1978) points out that, for all its supposed liberties, the Cuban revolution has yet to adequately tackle the problems of housing and machismo. In essence, these films epitomize one of the many agendas driving state provision for cinema: giving a voice to its citizens, particularly those who have been underrepresented historically.

These days, very few nation-states support their film industries so comprehensively. More typical is the provision of a set amount of money for which filmmakers compete, administered by a quasi-autonomous institution. One example would be Eurimages, a pan-European initiative, which donates €10.48 million of its member countries' contributions per year to film production amongst European Union participants. Eurimages communicates its objectives for doing so accordingly:

> Eurimages' first objective is **cultural**, in that it endeavours to support works which reflect the multiple facets of a European society whose common roots are evidence of a single culture. The second one is **economic**, in that the Fund invests in an industry which, while concerned with commercial success, is interested in demonstrating that cinema is one of the arts and should be treated as such.[10]

Political imperatives are made clear from the outset. The heterogeneity of the continent is deliberately underplayed and cultural protectionism dominates. At the end of the day, governments carry a moral responsibility not to waste their taxpayers' money supporting work that they cannot see to be in their interests, although these may also include entertainment and profit, rather than outright political grandstanding.

The film history of South Africa over the last thirty or so years offers a useful example of how public funding can operate. Before the fall of state-endorsed apartheid in 1994, the government maintained racial discrimination by allocating money only to movie production that supported the regime and outright censoring material that denounced it. Afrikaans-language films were preferred to those shot in other African languages or English. When the African National Congress (ANC) came to power in 1994, it quickly launched the Reconstruction and Development Programme. The Programme's remit was to introduce an all-encompassing redressal of economic inequality, including within cinema. One upshot was the National Film and Video Foundation Act, which, in 1997, set up an institution expressly to tackle these imbalances within cinematic production. Specific sums were subsequently allotted for up-and-coming directors, and for supporting international crews working in the country. Distribution and exhibition assistance also fall under the National Film and Video Foundation's umbrella. A keen supporter of Burkina Faso's Panafrican Film and Television Festival of Ouagadougou (FESPACO), the NFVF regularly arranges for South African material to play at international festivals and enter international competitions. One of its most prominent victories has been *Tsotsi* (Gavin Hood, 2005), which won the 2005 Academy Award for Best Foreign Language Film.

Dedicated national policies like these deliberately support previously oppressed social groups' expression and economic development. As we will observe presently, these imperatives also open up South Africa's borders to other film initiatives. Another nation-state similarly focuses on international collaboration: Canada. Its government pledges funds to subsidize foreign productions in return for their employment of Canadian crews. As a result, American movies are regularly shot in Canada with Toronto, say, standing in for other US metropolises.

Similarly, many governments also inaugurate **film commissions** at national, regional and city levels. State-supported film commissions are tasked with greasing the wheels of movie production in a given locale. This might take the form of helping out with legal particularities and bureaucracy, suggesting suitable locations, coordinating the sealing off of these sites, finding hotels and sourcing crew. In exchange, the area receives economic benefits in the form of increased employment, boosts to local businesses and even the promotion on screen of the area as a future tourist destination. The Palestinian feature *Amreeka* (Cherine Dabas, 2009), for instance, is set largely in Illinois, USA, but was actually shot in Winnipeg, in the Canadian province of Manitoba, because, as its director outlines, "the tax incentives combined with the fact that Manitoba offered us provincial equity for shooting the film … enabled us to close our financing and go into production sooner rather than later."[11] Many of the economic tensions and uncertainties addressed earlier in this chapter were thus abated by the province's support of their project.

As Dabas' statement attests, indirect sponsorship exists the world over in the form of tax breaks. In many countries, as was also exemplified by the *Tomb Raider* example, governments willingly forgo certain tax revenues in order to render cinematic production cheaper. Ultimately, this amounts to an indirect subsidy. A certain proportion of the tax breaks the movie industry exploits arrive in the form of loopholes in legislation, cleverly made the most of by the production's lawyers and accountants. But there are also deliberate tax benefits in place, designed to stimulate local economies. South Africa, for instance, offers them for national and international production and post-production. In Germany, as the *Tomb Raider* example has affirmed, a production company merely had to hail from the country and no principal photography needed to be undertaken there.

6.11 *Amreeka* or Canada? Courtesy of First Generation Films/The Kobal Collection.

CASE STUDY: "100% MIDDLE-EARTH" – WHY THE NEW ZEALAND STATE FUNDED *THE LORD OF THE RINGS*

Peter Jackson's *The Lord of the Rings* trilogy – *The Fellowship of the Ring* (2001), *The Two Towers* (2002) and *The Return of the King* (2003) – stands as one of the highest grossing series of all time. Costing $297,000,000 to make, box office returns alone total over $3 billion worldwide, as of 2014.[12] Jackson's three-part adaptation of *The Hobbit* has comfortably extended this successful franchise. J.R.R. Tolkein's "properties," after all, are gold dust and Jackson is now trusted to translate them appropriately for the screen.

Unsurprisingly, like *Lara Croft*, *The Lord of the Rings* pretty much paid for itself before principal shooting commenced, thanks to healthy pre-sales and state subsidies. This case study will home in on how and why the New Zealand government decided to get so heavily involved in these particular productions. What did it think New Zealand would gain from them?

As the South African model exemplifies, national film policy often concentrates on boosting locally made films. *The Lord of the Rings* is, instead, an intricate international hybrid. Although its director and much of its crew hail from New Zealand, Hollywood control and capital have loomed over these movies courtesy of "indie" giant New Line, which was then a subsidiary of Time Warner. Their direct investment was lowered by subcontracting various aspects of production to smaller local businesses, which then shouldered a certain amount of the risk. Overarching all these deals, though, was a financial partnering with the New Zealand government. The state threw its chips in with private investors, although, in this instance, using taxpayers' money.

The scene was set for the collaboration in 1999 when New Zealand's Labour Party won the election. Their agenda resolutely favored cultural production as a motor for the economy and was also keen to creatively promote "Brand NZ" via a number of platforms, including cinema.[13] While the opposing National Party have been in power since 2008, they have continued along the same path. Prime Minister John Key even embarked on a month-long tour of Hollywood, aiming to lure further projects to the country. Alongside *The Lord of the Rings* series, New Zealand has also netted NZ$350 million by hosting the *Avatar* (James Cameron, 2009) shoot.

The government and its Film Commission have remained cagey about the total amount of subsidies they offered *The Lord of the Rings*. Some estimates reckon that as much as NZ$217 million worth of potential taxation has been lost, beyond the fraction that was recouped from ticket receipts. Certain citizens have been disparaging of the way their state has confected further subsidies and special labor laws, which buckle compliantly to Hollywood's, rather than local, needs. But, broadly speaking, the majority of New Zealanders support these initiatives. Here is why. The combined revenues that *The Lord of the Rings* has brought New Zealand have been calculated at around NZ$700 million. The sectors benefiting most are tourism and, naturally, the film industry.

Principal photography for all three films, as well as *The Hobbit* series, has taken advantage of over 150 different locations throughout the country, as well as specially built sets and sound stages. Many of these are within national parks and conservation areas, which have since experienced a massive influx of visitors as a result. Over the 2000s tourist arrivals rose by nearly a million, a phenomenon that prompted Bruce Lahood of Tourism New Zealand to claim "*Lord of the Rings* was the best unpaid advertisement that New Zealand has ever had."[14] It is undoubtedly a moot point whether the plug was, in fact, free.

Affiliations between cinema and tourism are no new phenomenon. The Mexican global hit *Like Water for Chocolate* (Alfonso Arau, 1992) secured funding from the country's Secretariat of Tourism and regional airline Aviacsa. Films as dissimilar as *The Rainbow Troops* (Riri Riza, 2008) and *Eat, Pray, Love* (Ryan Murphy, 2010) have attracted people to Indonesia. In response to these possibilities, New Zealand has incorporated imagery familiar from *The Lord of the Rings* into its established "100% Pure New Zealand" campaign.

Certain incoming flights on the national carrier, Air New Zealand, screened the series exclusively, preceded by safety videos delivered by *Lord of the Rings*-inspired characters. Upon arrival, the official visa stamp comprises the message, "Welcome to New Zealand/Middle-earth" (the story's fictional setting). Once through customs, visitors can drop in on the Hobbiton Movie Set in Matamata (which received 367,135 visitors in 2004) or perhaps sign up for a more adventurous tour of the movies' locations. An average of 47,000 international tourists have been to one of these sites over the last ten years.[15] State-run New Zealand Tourism's website tempts fans by asking, "Are you a Halfling, an Elf or a Wizard? Embark on an adventure through New Zealand with a magical, Middle-earth inspired itinerary."[16]

Both the public and private sectors take advantage of the film's popularity through selling ancillary merchandise. Commemorative one New Zealand dollar coins retail at NZ$30, or $11,000 for a set of three NZ$10. As one would expect, trinkets and souvenirs abound in the shops. Peter Jackson has even launched his own video game company, Wingnut Interactive, to further cash in on the franchise.

The benefits of New Zealand's investment in the series have also paid off within the labor force. The screen industry now contributes almost NZ$3 billion a year to the national economy with the local industry growing sixteen-fold since *The Lord of the Rings* arrived. With its lengthy shoot of 438 days, comprising no less than seven different shooting units, local crews are now highly experienced technicians. Advantages to foreign production companies include English-speaking personnel who are cheaper to hire than, say, American employees (according to contemporary exchange rates anyhow), and who are not, historically, affiliated to protective bodies like labor unions, which would fight for higher wages. In justifying his trip to Hollywood, John Key continues, "in simple terms, this visit is about jobs for New Zealanders … we have made sure our law is flexible."[17]

Yet many New Zealanders are now concerned that these compromises aimed at attracting overseas film projects are a step too far. They feel that, as *The Lord of the Rings* boom subsides, their state will grow ever more compliant with the demands of the Hollywood studios, and often to the detriment of the local economy. Warner Bros. (now in charge of the franchise since it fully assimilated New Line) has already threatened to move production somewhere cheaper. This, in turn, prompted the government to slacken its labor laws in favor of Hollywood demands. Meantime, shooting and increased tourism has taken its toll on the environment of the national parks.

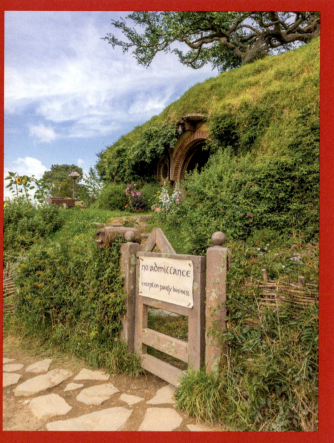

6.12 The Hobbiton movie set, Matamata, New Zealand. Courtesy of iStock.

These measures foster a transnational dimension within filmmaking, explored further in the next chapter. Before we reach that point in this book, we will take a brief look at exactly this in the form of co-production funding, largely from public reserves.

FINANCING THROUGH CO-PRODUCTION

Co-production is the name for any kind of official collaboration across borders in the making of a movie. Surf around the Internet Movie Database or wait for the end of a final credit sequence and you will certainly notice that a large proportion of films have been officially sponsored by more than one country. How do such endeavors drum up financial resources?

Co-production, to all intents and purposes, swells the benefits available from any one country to those of two or more. The nations involved treat the project as if it were (at least partially) home-grown, meaning that the film can take advantage of supplementary "soft money": each government's range of subsidies, tax breaks and film commission support. In addition, there are funds dedicated exclusively to co-production. Eurimages, who were mentioned above, only support co-productions. Skills and knowledge are exchanged across borders and, in a way, a sort of diplomatic encounter takes place. Hence the incentive for governments to contribute.

One such venture is *The Boda-Boda Thieves*, directed by Uganda's Donald Mugisha and still due for release, if it secures the necessary capital. With state support from South Africa's National Film and Video Foundation, the movie has also picked up backing from various international sources, like the Global Film Initiative and the World Cinema Fund, as well as the European festivals of Berlin and Rotterdam.[18] Piecemeal cross-border financing of this order is standard for more modest features and, in this instance, also mirrors the movie's cross-border eclecticism at the level of style, seeing as how the movie draws inspiration from the Italian classic *Bicycle Thieves* (Vittorio De Sica, 1948).

Yet there are also certain disadvantages to the co-production process. It can be a drag trying to make Manitoba look like Illinois. A number of key scenes in *Amreeka* required a White Castle fast food restaurant – a chain that does not exist in Winnipeg. Sets had to be built when the real thing would have sufficed in America. Adaptation to the multi-site funding can fragment or complicate the narrative with, for example, characters from particular countries showing up somewhat incongruously in the scenario because the funder has insisted on dialogue in a particular language. Often a large number of crew members will be replaced by another bunch when a shoot moves from location to location, which can be extremely disruptive. At times, then, it proves troublesome trying to fuse the needs of every provider into one single cinematic entity. In all these ways, a co-production functions like a border. It can be both a link and a division.

EXERCISE

Pick a film from your own country. Ascertain the public backing it has received. This is a relatively straightforward process as all such sponsors (whether funding bodies, film commissions or city authorities) are listed in the movie's credits and can be further researched via quick internet searches.

- Has the movie received substantial or minimal support from state institutions?
- Have these resources been supplied by just one country, or by more?
- What has been the impact of these provisions, do you think? For instance, has their assistance meant that the fictional setting has been transplanted to another actual location?
- Is there a way of telling where the crew come from, perhaps as a condition of national funding edits?
- Have concessions seemingly been made to cater for a particular audience – one that the funding body aims to provide for? To get a closer sense of this, look out for stars from that country or the languages that are used.

Then there is the perpetual accusation that co-production frequently acts in a paternalistic, even neo-colonial fashion. A quick zoom in on French support for African cinema will help clarify these claims and the arguments against them. In the 1960s, the French Ministry of Cooperation launched various initiatives to fund, technically support and train African filmmakers, enterprises that have continued to exist, in various incarnations, until today. Francophone Africa has since become justly famous the world over for its complex, challenging and aesthetically striking output, from Mali's *Yeelen* (Souleymane Cissé, 1987) to Burkina Faso's *Tilai* (Idrissa Ouedraogo, 1990). Films of quality have been released by these countries thanks, in part, to budgetary leg-ups from the French Ministry of Cooperation. And as we saw from the Cuban examples earlier, government funding does not necessarily buy, in this instance, a pro-French perspective.

Why, then, are criticisms leveled at these income streams? Detractors argue that they function in a fashion akin to other forms of aid, rendering African filmmakers dependent in uncomfortable ways. As Nigerian video-films have shown us (see Chapter 1), there might, in fact, be no real need of outside support. A cheaper, locally grown cinema could well flourish independently. And the stipulations these organizations enforce might not be exactly in the best interests of African cinema's autonomy and resilience. As with other types of governmental aid, it could be contended that this cash is actually buying more valuable rights and commodities. For one, French support has secured French distributors monopolies over African screens as a thank you from local governments. Co-production requires that French film workers are hired, people whose perspectives are often at odds with an African vision. Filmmakers can be asked to incorporate a certain percentage of French dialogue, which symboli-cally re-enacts a colonial presence in countries that might rather be rid of this legacy. In the 1980s, emphasis was placed on sponsoring films that would do well in French cinemas. As such, African directors complained that they were being asked to produce images of their homelands that fitted French fantasies of Africa, rather than their own perspectives. For fuller details of these manoeuvrings, it is well worth tracking down the documentaries *Caméra Afrique* and *Caméra Arabe* (Férid Boughedir, 1984) (collected together as *Twenty Years of African Cinema*), which interview many of the filmmakers affected, as well as incorporating a rich array of clips from their movies.

Co-productions have been afoot for quite some time in South Africa too, well before *The Boda-Boda Thieves* was conceived. *Tsotsi* profited from British input, but, despite its international success, it has been taken to task for concocting a stereotypical rendition of the country, rife with AIDS, carjacking and homelessness. Both *Drum* (Zola Maseko, 2004) and *Hotel Rwanda* (Terry George, 2004) were shot in South Africa, but star American actors – Taye Diggs and Don Cheadle, respectively. Their casting as Africans, many Africans argue, undermines the abundant talent to be found within the continent itself. Job opportunities for Africans in co-productions are, therefore, somewhat curtailed. At the same time, cast and crews can feel exploited in other ways. In budgetary terms, it is often markedly cheaper to shoot movies in Africa, in the main because salaries are lower.

These factors prove that decisions made at the funding stage reverberate in how a film is shot and what the end results might be. As such, the next two chapters will carry such concerns into these new terri-tories, thinking first about production processes (Chapter 7) and then about working conditions (Chapter 8). What we have learnt from this chapter is that no financier arrives at a potential movie project wanting nothing in return for their investment. The yields, as has been witnessed, may be economic, but also political or cultural.

177

CHAPTER SUMMARY

The opening section of this chapter explained why a movie's success is hard to predict, following on from this by detailing how the industry tries to short-circuit around financial loss by securing rewarding properties. We commenced our analysis of film funding by investigating the private sector opportunities that are open to the industry. This led to an identification of the primary investors in film production (such as studios, banks, hedge funds, advertisers, licensers, distributors, governments, and film commissions) and conjecture on their motivations for getting involved. After that, we examined how governments and publicly owned institutions involve themselves in financing cinema, rounding off with an evaluation of the incentives, mechanisms and results of international co-production.

 FURTHER READING

De Vany, Arthur. *Hollywood Economics: How Extreme Uncertainty Shapes the Film Industry.* New York: Routledge, 2004.

> We recommended this book in the previous chapter on commodities. It furthers ideas covered in this chapter too by offering a detailed breakdown of how money flows into and out of the film industry. Unsurprisingly, given its title, the emphasis rests on the instability and risky nature of the movie business bolstered by lots of illuminating graphs and statistics.

Epstein, Edward Jay. *The Hollywood Economist: The Hidden Financial Reality Behind the Movies.* New York: Melville House, 2010.

> A truly readable explanation of how moviemakers raise money, written by an investigative journalist and full of juicy details that few textbooks uncover.

Wasko, Janet. *Movies and Money: Financing the American Film Industry.* Norwood, NJ: Ablex Publishing Corporation, 1982.

> For a meticulous account of the long-standing relationship between the banks and the American film industry, look no further than this book. In a sea of "how to" texts about movie financing, this analysis stands out by properly outlining why the banks, in political terms, connect with cinema and thus consolidate their much broader global standing. *Movies and Money* will seem a little difficult, if not dry, at times, but it is well worth persevering.

Wasko, Janet. *How Hollywood Works.* London: Sage Publications, 2003.

> Janet Wasko delivers again. Here she lays out all the stages through which a US mainstream film progresses before it reaches us. The sections on pre-production will supplement what has been provided in this chapter, while her detailing of production, post-production, promotion and exhibition will prove useful for your later studies.

 **FILMS REFERENCED IN CHAPTER SIX**

Amreeka (Cherine Dabas, 2009)

Avatar (James Cameron, 2009)

Bicycle Thieves (Vittorio De Sica, 1948)

The Boda-Boda Thieves (Donald Mugisha, n.d.)

Bodyguard (Siddique, 2011)

Caméra Afrique and *Caméra Arabe* (Férid Boughedir, 1984)

Death of a Bureaucrat (Tomás Gutiérrez Alea, 1966)

Drácula (George Melford, 1931)

Drum (Zola Maseko, 2004)

Eat, Pray, Love (Ryan Murphy, 2010)

The Fellowship of the Ring (Peter Jackson, 2001)

Flashdance (Adrian Lyne, 1983)

Four Weddings and a Funeral (Mike Newell, 1994)

The Godfather series (Francis Ford Coppola, 1972–1990)

The Greatest Movie Ever Sold (Morgan Spurlock, 2011)

The Hobbit (Peter Jackson, 2012)

The Host (Bong Joon-ho, 2006)

Hotel Rwanda (Terry George, 2004)

Lara Croft: Tomb Raider (Simon West, 2001)

Like Water for Chocolate (Alfonso Arau, 1992)

Live Free or Die Hard (Len Wiseman, 2007)

Lynch Three (David Lynch, 2011)

The Mummies of Guanajuato (Federico Curiel, 1972)

My Name is Khan (Karan Johar, 2010)

Notting Hill (Roger Michell, 1998)

One Way or Another (Sara Gómez, 1978)

Open Your Eyes (Alejandro Amenábar, 1997)

The People vs Larry Flynt (Miloš Foreman, 1996)

Pride and Prejudice (Joe Wright, 2005)

Rainbow Troops (Riri Riza, 2008)

The Return of Superman (Kunt Tulgar, 1979)

The Return of the King (Peter Jackson, 2003)

Santo vs. The Vampire Women (Alfonso Corona Blake, 1962)

Tilai (Idrissa Ouedraogo, 1990)

Tsotsi (Gavin Hood, 2005)

Twilight Saga (Catherine Hardwicke, Chris Weitz, David Slade, Bill Condon, 2008–2012)

The Two Towers (Peter Jackson, 2002)

The Untouchables (Brian de Palma, 1987)

Vanilla Sky (Cameron Crowe, 2001)

Yeelen (Souleymane Cissé, 1987)

NOTES

1 See David Roos, "Why Do Movies Cost So Much to Make?," *How Stuff Works*, http://entertainment. howstuffworks.com/movie-cost1.htm for an analysis of these statistics as a list of primary industry sources from which this information was collated, accessed 5 August 2013.

2 Arthur De Vany, *Hollywood Economics: How Extreme Uncertainty Shapes the Film Industry* (New York: Routledge, 2004), 73–74.

3 *Box Office Mojo*, http://www.boxofficemojo.com/movies/?id=fourweddingsandafuneral.htm, accessed 5 August 2013.

4 "Bob Hoskins Paid Not to Play Al Capone," *Metro*, 19 March 2009, http://metro.co.uk/2009/03/19/ bob-hoskins-paid-not-to-play-capone-553319, accessed 18 August 2013.

5 Edward Jay Epstein, *The Hollywood Economist: The Hidden Financial Reality Behind the Movies* (New York: Melville House, 2010), 102–103.

6 Film London, "Industry Events: Production Finance Market," http:/filmlondon.org.uk/pfm, accessed 10 October 2014.

7 Janet Wasko, *Movies and Money: Financing the American Film Industry* (Norwood, NJ: Ablex Publishing Corporation, 1982), 60.

8 Alejandro Pardo, *The European-Hollywood Coopetition: Cooperation and Competition in the Global Film Industry* (Pamplona: Ediciones Universidad de Navarra, 2007), 101.

9 "Documentary Fund," Sundance Institute, http://www.sundance.org/programs/documentary-fund, accessed 23 December 2012.

10 Council of Europe, "EURIMAGES – European Cinema Support Fund," http://www.coe.int/t/dg4/eurimages/about/default_en.asp, accessed 24 December 2012.

11 Randall King, "Prejudice Close to Home for Amreeka Director," Winnipeg Free Press, 31 October 2009, http://www.winnipegfreepress.com/arts-and-life/entertainment/movies/prejudice-close-to-home-for-amreeka-director-67901492.html, accessed 24 December 2012.

12 "Box Office History for Peter Jackson's *The Lord of the Rings* Movies," *The Numbers: Where Data and the Movie Business Meet*, accessed 11 October 2014, http://www.the-numbers.com/movies/franchise/Peter-Jacksons-Lord-of-the-Rings.

13 Bridget Conor, "Hollywood, Wellywood or the Backwoods? A Political Economy Study of the New Zealand Film Industry," MA diss., AUT University, 2004.

14 Statistics New Zealand, *Tourism Satellite Account 2000–2003* (Wellington: Statistics New Zealand, 2004), 8; Statistics New Zealand, *International Visitor Arrivals to New Zealand February 2011* (Wellington: Statistics New Zealand, 2004), 8; Ethan Gilsdorf, "Cities Both Big and Small are Offering Tours of Film Locations," *USA Today,* 9 November 2006, accessed 24 December 2012, http://usatoday30.usatoday.com/travel/destinations/2006-11-09-movie-tourism_x.htm.

15 Tourism New Zealand, "Sector Marketing: Information on Key Tourism and Special Interest Sectors," accessed 11 October 2014, http://www.tourismnewzealand.com/sector-marketing/film-tourism/fast-facts.

16 "Home of Middle-earth," New Zealand Tourism, http://www.newzealand.com/int/feature/middle-earth-itineraries, accessed 24 December 2012.

17 Toby Manhire, "Hobbit Tourism Scatters More of Tolkein's Magic Across New Zealand," *Observer*, 13 October 2012, http://www.guardian.co.uk/world/2012/oct/13/hobbit-new-zealand-tourism, accessed 24 December 2012.

18 Christopher Vourlias, "'Bicycle Thief' Remake Steals Buzz: Producers High on Pan-African 'Boda-Boda'," *Variety*, 13 April 2012, http://www.variety.com/article/VR1118052630/?refcatid=19&printerfriendly=true, accessed 24 December 2012.

CHAPTER SEVEN
FILM PRODUCTION PRACTICES

Nazir Shaikh wants to make films. Regardless of his total absence of prior training or experience, the fervent adoration of cinema in his home town of Malegaon, India spurs him on to learn as he goes. Throughout *Supermen of Malegaon* (Faiza Ahmad Khan, 2008) – the documentary that charts his reworking of the Superman idea as a local, Urdu-language spoof – we too gain an insight into the processes of film production. Watching Nazir Shaikh at work, but also ruminating on his early moviemaking development from dubbing VHS cassettes together on domestic VHS players, we acquaint ourselves with the mechanics of the creative experience. His trials range from how to record musical scores and conjure green-screen special effects, to what happens when you fail to secure shooting permission or drop your only camera in a river. All on a miniscule amount of money, but with a lot of goodwill from his town's citizens. The sharp discrepancy between what Nazir Shaikh can achieve and the options available to a big budget franchise like *Superman* begs all manner of questions about how films are made, what facilities and human-power they require, and what can or cannot be achieved with certain funds.

What we cannot help but notice is that the sorts of features that fill our multiplexes require particular resources in order to arrive in the form they do. Section II of this book commenced by investigating what it takes to get a movie off the ground. With this chapter, the aim is to understand, as Nazir Shaikh has attempted to, how films are then actually put together. What are the nuts and bolts of organizing all those people on a credits list? Or managing such enormous amounts of money in the most resourceful fashion? Plainly, there are as many ways to make a movie as there are movies. However, certain approaches have proven more popular than others. In what follows, these dominant practices will be explored and critiqued. In order to do this, the

7.1 Rigging up a flying scene in *Supermen of Malegaon* (Faiza Ahmad Khan, 2008).

focus will fall less on what are, ultimately, the more pervasive types of movies being made, which are amateur, low/no-budget, experimental or small-scale documentary. We have already looked at these in Chapter 2. Here we shall be concentrating instead on the more profitable cinema that circulates extensively throughout our theatres. Why does it deploy certain techniques over others? Filmmaking often follows and adapts broader global trends in manufacturing, so here we are going to get to grips with why that is. How have these tactics shaped what we love about cinema culture? We often credit particular styles to, say, an actor or director, and Chapter 2 helped us understand such attributions. But the practical mechanics of managing these creative processes also deeply influence what finished films look and sound like. Perhaps what appeals to you about a particular cinematic movement or genre is more sharply defined by dimensions that do not often command the column inches of gossip magazines, fan blogs or even auteurist studies. It might just as well be that your attraction derives from the managerial structure of a film studio, or even the buildings in which shooting took place. This chapter endeavors to make apparent the connections between the movies we enjoy and the specific ways in which they are made. It will help you to expand your appreciation of cinema so that it can encompass these more hidden elements of the filmmaking process.

The analysis of production techniques outlined in this chapter will then be further honed in the next one. At that point, we will be thinking less about how modes of production impact upon movies and more about how they affect actual film industry employees. How do preferred filmmaking methods create particular roles for those who carry out this work? What does it mean to hold down such jobs? To answer these questions, we first need to appreciate the bigger picture of how moviemaking is plotted out.

WHAT WE WILL DO IN CHAPTER 7

- Position filmmaking as an industry.
- Assess its dominant modes of production from artisanship to Fordism and then post-Fordism.
- Conduct a comparison of two very different animation production regimes in order to evaluate how specific creative and managerial environments dramatically shape the nature of cinematic output.

BY THE END OF CHAPTER 7 YOU SHOULD BE ABLE TO

- Give clear definitions of the major film production processes.
- Understand why those processes evolved or declined in relation to their historical contexts.
- Make strong connections between the style of a movie and the way it was made.

In its early days, moviemaking was conducted in a fairly ad hoc manner. Take, for example, *Workers Leaving the Lumière Factory* (Louis Lumière, 1895), a short which was introduced in Chapter 3. We might loosely say it was directed by Lumière in that he pointed the camera and shot the film from one fixed position. Yet, along with his brother Auguste, he also invented the technology on which it was captured, processed the stock, owned the very photographic factory that appears on screen, and had a major hand in distributing the movie. When films revolved around such simple premises, there was no need for the expertise of screenwriters, set builders, make-up artists or sound mixers. Then the demand for the medium swelled and expectations grew. As filmmakers realized there was money to be made in cinema, they began to outdo each other, creating ever more sophisticated products. With these developments came an urgent need to coordinate and rationalize the multiplying elements that contributed to these movies. What lies below is not an exhaustive list of what happened, but it does paint a picture of the prevailing trends within moviemaking history.

7.2 *Workers Leaving the Lumière Factory* (Louis Lumière, 1895).

INTRODUCING FORDIST FILM PRODUCTION

When we talk about "the film industry," we are acknowledging that moviemaking has gone through a process of **industrialization**. Amongst other things, this means that there are mechanisms in place which standardize how movies are made (in other words, which make everything conform to strict criteria). The benefit of this is that no one starts from scratch when they try to coordinate a film project. It would be utter chaos if there was no agreement on the specific types of cameras, microphones or edit suites that are in current use. This single dimension of what we call industrialization allows people to train themselves in operating the right equipment. It creates an acceptable vocabulary for matters like lighting techniques or acting styles. These shared foundations enable people to get on with their jobs as quickly and effectively as possible without having to explain themselves. A snug compatibility between all the tools of the trade is achieved. We will think about the impact of all this more thoroughly in a minute.

The word "industrialization" also means that films can be easily replicated to order. Anyone who wants to generate the amount of movie copies required for mass distribution will need access to duplicating technologies such as film laboratories and DVD pressing plants. Evidently, not all parts of the world possess or can hire the services of these expensive assets. But when they do, they are said to have a film industry.

These two features have been eased into play by the innovations of one major trend in industrialization: **Fordism**. Historically, the growth of cinema traveled hand in hand with the development of Fordism, which took hold within film production in the 1920s. It is unthinkable to consider the rise in cinema's influence without acknowledging the role Fordism has played in it. Cinema as we know it – a cheap, widely available commodity – owes much of its character to the Fordist approach to large-scale manufacturing. So what exactly is this? Fordism is typically described as a comprehensive form of production management designed to achieve maximum output at minimum cost. One of its chief objectives is to make goods affordable to everyday people, which, not coincidently, also augments profits. This may sound obvious, but, without this principle to the fore, cinema might well have developed into a luxury commodity like fine art. Individuals could have paid for the right to own an exclusive movie print, rather than simply watch it, or buy a cheap copy that exists amongst perhaps millions of identical ones. The concept takes its name from Henry Ford (1863–1947), the American founder of the Ford Motor Company. Ford made his reputation and fortune by successfully implementing economies of scale, standardization, assembly line manufacturing and central planning, all of which will be described in detail below. Although these processes were designed to aid car manufacture, they have been widely adopted in the world's various film industries too. Conversely, there are also elements of Fordism that were not absorbed into filmmaking. These would include the development of specific, simple tasks that did not oblige those who carry them out to be particularly skilled, such as repeatedly placing a single component onto the body of an unfinished car as it moved down a factory conveyor belt. This does not really happen so much within filmmaking because all movies are qualitatively different. Such variations and how they impact upon what it means to work in the film industry will be discussed in greater detail in the chapter that follows this one.

As has already been pointed out, moviemaking was fairly small scale in its early days. This is often called **artisanal production**, an approach distinguished by the fact that it is not created in a factory-like environment or mass-produced. If you have ever made a movie, it is more than likely that it was conceived in this way. In fact, artisanal production still accounts for the bulk of filmmaking if we take into consideration home movies or material shot on technologies like mobile telephones.

In contradistinction, by the 1930s and onwards, *professional* cinema had rapidly matured into an intricate industrial form. The irony of *Workers Leaving the Lumière Factory* is that it was an artisanal film that detailed an industrial workplace, exactly foreshadowing what cinema itself was to become. The most obvious example of industrialization would be the Hollywood studio system, as defined in Chapter 5. Within it, vertical integration allowed for comprehensive control of most aspects of film production and distribution. This kind of power and influence also made it possible for the studios to instigate ever-grander schemes of overall management, which they borrowed from Fordism. Other national film industries may not have wielded the muscle or reach of Hollywood, but they still put many of the tenets of Fordism into operation. Although the appeal of Fordism waned from the middle of the twentieth century onwards, it has still been responsible for many of the movies we now consider to be classics, from *Casablanca* (Michael Curtiz, 1942) to *Alexander Nevsky* (Sergei Eisenstein, 1938) and *Mughal-e-Azam* (K. Asif, 1960). How exactly, then, were these films made?

THE CHARACTERISTICS OF FORDISM

One core principle that characterizes Fordism is attention to **economies of scale**, an idea we briefly touched on in Chapter 5. An economy of scale can be defined as a strategy that brings down the cost per unit of anything by making it in large numbers. In the context of car manufacturing, an economy of scale is achieved by turning out large numbers of identical vehicles through the recurrent use of the same machinery. This method lessens overhead costs because little new equipment needs to be purchased. You simply use the same kit again and again. In addition, workers become familiar with their tools without regular (and costly) specialist training or updating. Of course, this principle cannot be translated wholesale into all aspects of filmmaking. While we might be happy enough to own replica Blu-ray disks, MP4 downloads, posters or action figures, we want the actual movie texts to be distinct from one another. Ultimately, most of us will pay to see new films more regularly than we buy new cars, so the economies of scale are less far-reaching. However, there are ways of modifying the economies of scale approach so that it fits the need for the quick generation of varied film commodities. What we call the studio model, as it variously evolved around the globe, was adept at this.

Within studio production, filmmaking was, sometimes still is, undertaken, as much as possible, within one site. Unsurprisingly, this is the studio itself. Sticking to one location cuts down expenditure on transportation. It also eases the smooth movement of the movie through the various phases of production. From script development to primary non-location shooting, to print processing, editing, soundtrack recording and publicity – all these stages were conducted in close proximity. As with other forms of factory work, the same equipment, sets and personnel were used time and time again, making them highly cost effective. People were employed on fairly lengthy contracts, allowing the studio to benefit long term from the skills they had helped these workers to acquire. In order not to waste these attributes, multiple film projects were executed at once. If done right, this resulted in all of the studio's assets (technological, physical and human) being used to their maximum and most resourceful capacity. So, although the studios were not churning out exactly the same products (like a car factory would), they did learn from the lessons of economies of scale by reusing their facilities and minimizing downtime.

If you watch a number of films from one studio (wherever it is in the world), you are likely to notice a recycling of sets and costumes, not to mention actors. The same avoidance of wastefulness is evident in storylines and star performances too. As was noted in previous chapters, familiarity with popular actors or genres is an excellent way of guaranteeing a film's box office success. It is also a clever means of saving money. Studios like Japan's Toho or Brazil's Atlântida Cinematográfica became known for genre movies (*kaiju eiga*/monster movies and *chanchadas*/musical comedies respectively). This meant they did not have to regularly re-invest in new specialized equipment, sets or costumes, and that writers or actors could work in modes in which they already felt familiar. No one would need extra time or education to feel at home in these milieux.

Repetition as a means of saving money ties in with another central characteristic of Fordism: **standardization**. Standardization has already been referred to as a key quality of industrialization. As was previously stated, it entails making sure that particular human practices and technological applications are broadly accepted as the norm. This facilitates the effortless functioning of all levels of industrial production. Imagine you were one editor of many working on a feature film and you were all using different software. It would prove much harder later to stitch together the elements you had all been toiling over into a final cut. Standardization assists distribution too. For instance, the gauge of film stock has, for decades, most typically been 35mm. It is no accident that this width fits the projectors that the vast majority of the world's film auditoria have agreed to use. Over the years, there have been fraught battles about which format wins the prized position of becoming the standard. In the 1970s and 1980s, for instance, a "war" was waged between VHS and Betamax as to which video type would become the global norm. Without such standardization procedures, movies would not be as inexpensive or as globally mobile as they currently are. The industry would have had to spend considerable money providing material in a number of different formats. Varying equipment too wildly also makes it harder to find spare parts or qualified repairers if they break down.

7.3 *Godzilla: King of the Monsters!* (Terry O. Morse, Ishirō Honda, 1956), one of Toho's scores of such movies.

Standardization also leaves its mark on cinema aesthetics. It has just been pointed out that aspects like genres re-emerge across movie output from any given studio. The same is true of plots, character types, acting styles, customary camera set-ups and shot sequences, sets and costumes. All the elements of film style were effectively given the Fordist treatment, enabling moviemaking that was as quick and simple as it could be without compromising quality too much. Clearly, the end result is that certain styles become established. This is especially true in a studio set-up because the same group of people are consistently working together, sticking to what is tried and tested as a method, often, of saving time and money. In turn, we learn these patterns and come to accept them as "the way movies should be." The next time you watch a film, think about how it draws upon traditional and seemingly logical techniques. Then try and imagine why these styles have become dominant in light of the practicalities of economies of scale and standardization. This does not just happen in the case of the average full-length feature. Genres such as, for example, professional pornography, are particularly invested in relatively predictable narrative configurations, not to mention sequels. What better way to save money than not to waste time developing new ideas, performance repertoires or methods of capturing all this on film?

Repetition and standardization also allow for easier dissemination once movies are completed. "High concept" films, for instance, as Chapter 6 observed, benefit enormously from a known formula. Audiences often prefer a movie that they can understand according to past experiences of something similar. Standardization helps us to make informed choices about our cinema purchases, to know what to expect. In fact, standardization is often a direct response to audience needs. It can adapt to specific genres that are in vogue. And even film length is standardized. Most people do not have long periods of time to dedicate to cinema, so film lengths, as was detailed in Chapter 1, have standardized at under three hours in most countries.

The *order* of how a film is put together has also been standardized. Earlier we pointed out how, in a studio, employees and technologies are intricately arranged so they can function at their top capacity. They do so in a mainly linear fashion, which can be seen to mimic the assembly lines of industrial plants. It is no accident, then, that Hollywood has been nicknamed "the dream factory" – producing fantasies, rather than motor vehicles. The trajectory from pre-production to production to post-production maps directly onto the assembly line logic and still, by and large, runs according to this established sequence today. Have you ever wondered what a movie might be like if its soundtrack was written before its script? Certain hierarchies of power are upheld by this temporal arrangement of production and this is something we will be investigating in the following chapter and the Interlude section beyond that. Whatever our thoughts on the assembly line role call, the sheer amount of strategizing and organization involved in streamlining production in these ways is breathtaking. When Hollywood, Mumbai and Hong Kong borrowed these Fordist techniques they were capable of producing their highest ever yields, running at hundreds of films per year.

How, in practical terms, were all these techniques enforced? Within Fordism, this is largely down to what we might want to call **central planning**. The term is more commonly used in reference to how governments oversee their country's economies. In that particular context, central planning is alternatively referred to as a "command economy." In fact, cinema has frequently been subsumed under this style of leadership, as we will observe in this chapter's later discussion of Czechoslovak animation. However, implications that the principle of central planning carries can be useful for understanding more commercial and autonomous Fordist filmmaking too. In essence, central planning is a managerial perspective, a view from on high that comprehends the bigger picture and, from this position, dictates what goes on below. Just as studio production takes place as much as possible within one controllable space, so too is the administration of Fordist production limited to a few voices who strategize on the best possible harmonization of its disparate elements.

Adherence to tight planning is essential within Fordist doctrine and this is often aided by charismatic, authoritative, all-knowing leadership. There is a studio head, or a small bunch of executives, and then there are those below who must follow orders. Once a budget is instituted, those who are under contract to complete the film are heavily obliged to obey the rules that this budget and its advance planning dictate. At the same time, these employees are clearly highly creative and their imaginative input is what makes cinema so special. These people's vigor and insight frequently helped reformulate what this system could sustain and added to its coffers through their ingenuity. As a result, there is always a tension between individual expression (which can also contravene or slow down the even functioning of the assembly line) and the pragmatic need to conform to the "correct" or standardized mode of working. Cast and crew members are often compelled to make difficult sacrifices in order to fit the preordained rules of these standardizations. For instance, up-and-coming stars within the studio system were routinely asked to change the way their bodies looked in order to conform to these norms. This could include losing weight, dyeing their hair or even undertaking various types of cosmetic surgery. Top box office star of the 1940s, Rita Hayworth, for instance, endured electrolysis to heighten her brow-line, hair coloring (auburn instead of brown), skin lightening, and a name change away from

the "too ethnic-sounding" Margarita Carmen Cansino, all on the insistence of her studio, Columbia Pictures. Strict compliance with orthodox patterns of behavior was also encouraged by studio heads of the Fordist era (figures such as Walt Disney or Michael Balcon of Britain's Ealing Studios) according to highly paternalist values. Just as Henry Ford strived to create an atmosphere of company loyalty within his factories, the studios frequently projected themselves as a family. Job security and rewards were guaranteed for those who completed their duties effectively and without fuss. But rebels could easily find themselves on the outside of the studio gates, their contracts terminated. We will be thinking more about contracts in the following chapter, but, for the moment, it also pays to sympathize with why they were being asked to bend to these rules. The steady nature of the Fordist approach certainly granted those within it a high level of professional security, freeing them up to concentrate and nourish their talents in a stable environment. A seemingly supportive and enjoyable production process, like that of the animation company Pixar (as we will see later on in this chapter) emerges from a modified assembly line approach.

7.4 Rita Hayworth. Courtesy of Columbia/The Kobal Collection.

Whatever our thoughts on these methods or the movies that are their legacy, it is not hard to appreciate that they do not work for everyone. The Fordist ethos may not be possible or preferable in every instance of filmmaking. Because of this, Fordism has never been the pure or sole means by which movies come to life. In the next section, we will be examining some of the alternatives to this approach.

EXERCISE

Select one studio that has functioned according to the Fordist principles detailed above. It could be a Hollywood one, or one from any other country with an industrialized filmmaking capacity, like Japan's Studio Ghibli or Hong Kong's Shaw Brothers. Do some research into this studio's output.

- In what ways do their movies resemble each other? You might want to concentrate on style, genre or recurrent personnel like actors or directors here.
- Now think through these repeated characteristics in light of what you have just learnt about Fordist production.
- See if you can attribute their particular recurrent qualities to each of the following: economies of scale, standardization, assembly line manufacturing and central planning.

DEVELOPMENTS AWAY FROM CLASSIC FORDISM

The studio system, as Chapter 5 argued, lost its sure footing in the mid-twentieth century. Yet even when Fordism was still the dominant mode of movie manufacture, digressions from its methods were being successfully executed. Luis Buñuel and Salvador Dali's *Un chien andalou* (1929), familiar from Chapter 2, sits under this umbrella, as would many of the ground-breaking documentaries mentioned in Chapter 3, like the earlier work of Joris Ivens. What this fact makes unambiguous is just how mix and match filmmaking can be. As the majority of professional cinema is dedicated to generating as much revenue as possible, the industry will always do its best to forge the most cost-effective production route. At times, this has been Fordism; at others, something altogether different. Although this chapter is carried along by a certain sense of chronology, production styles can overlap. Cinematic Fordism bears the traces of other management strategies and, although less dominant now, has never entirely died out either. It is difficult to establish a distinct and abrupt transition between Fordism and what has now become known as post-Fordism. The aim of this current chapter section is to outline some of these fusions.

We shall be examining post-Fordism more closely in a minute. For the time being, it is sufficient to note that it favors smaller scale modes of production than the assembly line system. These are character-istics that can also be seen in what the industry calls **unit production**, a practice that was in operation as early as the mid-1920s. Unit production relies primarily on the more workshop-like principles that we can recognize from early cinema. In this sense, it bears both pre- and (as we will soon acknowledge) post-Fordist traits. A prime instance of a hybrid approach, unit production is well worth our consideration at this point.

Let us use Hollywood as an example. In contradistinction to the strict top-down control of Fordism, some of the studio heads began devolving their power to producers who were junior to them. Yes, the pecking order remained intact, but a certain rare sovereignty was bestowed upon these lower-ranking figures. What they were entrusted to achieve was the congregation of smaller production teams (units) that would specialize in particular corners of filmmaking. An illustration of this would be RKO boss Charles Koerner's facilitation of a unit controlled by producer Val Lewton. Although under the tight directive to make horror films for under $150,000 with titles supplied by management, the unit nevertheless flourished creatively. Comprising personnel like director Jacques Tourneur, actor Simone Simon, cinematographer Nicholas Musuraca, and scorer Roy Webb, the Lewton unit put out what have since become cult classics like *Cat People* (Jacques Tourneur, 1942) and *I Walked with a Zombie* (Jacques Tourneur, 1943), to name just two. Perhaps the most prestigious arrangement of this order was MGM's Freed unit. Its head, Arthur Freed, dwelt in a rare bubble of autonomy granted by the typically untrusting and all-controlling studio head, Louis B. Mayer. The rewards were some of the best-regarded musicals of the 1940s and 1950s, thanks to the help of contracted employees like choreographer-director Charles Walters, director Vincente Minnelli and performer Gene Kelly. Movies delivered by this unit include *Easter Parade* (Charles Walters, 1948), *An American in Paris* (Vincente Minnelli, 1951), *Singin' in the Rain* (Stanley Donen, 1952) and *Gigi* (Vincente Minnelli, 1958).

On the one hand, unit production might be interpreted as a deviation from the domineering administration strategies of the Fordist studio. Power was devolved in a manner atypical to the studios that funded these productions without studio heads lessening their grip over other work within their stable. On the other hand, perhaps unit production allowed for an even firmer handling. There was still a paternalistic (one might even say auteurist) figure in charge who masterminded how the movies were made, a trait familiar from Fordism. With a smaller group of films to manage, the unit producers could actually keep a closer eye on budget management than might have been feasible for a studio head. The philosophy of Fordist control was maintained, but also adapted to moviegoers' needs for specialized or niche products. As has already been pointed out, most people go to the cinema more often than they buy a new car. Concentrating on a balance of thriftiness, quality and diversity is therefore essential and something at which unit production can excel.

Unit production is one of the ways filmmaking sidesteps absolute Fordism, but it still functions broadly within that system. What of all those other movies that have not, by any stretch of the imagination, been able to take advantage of economies of scale? This would naturally include everything formulated outside the industrialized sectors, like the highly personal essay films explored in Chapter 2, or the activist documentaries described in Chapter 3. If we also bring amateur or aspirant cinematic production into our calculations, then the clear majority of the world's films are not Fordist. All of this output lacks the backing of large corporations and so cannot come close to affording the vast outlays necessary to build up a studio or an assembly line. As such, the artisanal mode of production is retained. A low-budget film, the kind that students make, say, can be the sporadic handiwork of a group of like-minded people. They almost always forgo any kind of wage, picking up the project whenever they have the spare time. This is a far cry from the salaried staff on studio contracts who would have to contribute to whatever they were given. Because economies of scale cannot be established with a one-off production (which is often what

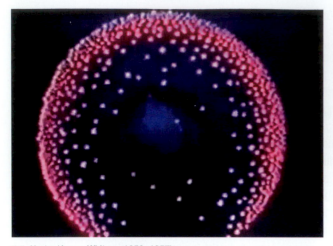

7.5 *Yantra* (James Whitney, 1950–1957).

these artisanal projects are), equipment may have to be hired or borrowed, rather than owned. Individuals might possibly possess cheap cameras, but it is highly unlikely that they have their own color laboratory. Subsequently, production will stop and start depending on uncertain funding flows, rather than run through the greased wheels of a constantly-in-motion assembly line. As this chapter will soon focus on animation, it makes sense to call upon an example from that genre. James Whitney's *Yantra* (released in 1957) is a mere seven minutes long, but took five years to make. You can watch it for free online easily enough. Whitney's short was put together entirely by hand through a process of punching holes in cards and painting through them to cards beneath. He worked alone for the most part. Therefore his movie exemplifies a production process that runs alongside Fordist history, but is almost its direct opposite. The same is true of many art or auteur films, even longer, successful ones, like some of Satyajit Ray's or Werner Herzog's.

Until the rise of sites like YouTube in the 2000s, movies of *Yantra*'s persuasion were harder to access than *Casablanca* or *Mughal-e-Azam*. As Chapter 5 witnessed, this unequal access can easily be attributed to specific, vertically integrated, oligarchical structures that, for a time, reigned within the film industry. However, we also relayed that these strangleholds momentarily weakened with the advent of the Paramount Decision. At that point, the studios lost their guaranteed markets and had to compete with smaller, independent film companies. It became harder and harder to successfully balance the massive overheads required for Fordist manufacturing. At the same time (the late 1940s, within the large domestic market of the United States), the rise in television's popularity, and the drift towards suburban dwelling with concomitantly more domestic lifestyles made cinema an even less stable investment. During the latter half of the twentieth century, movie production has increasingly functioned within a globalized economy. It has ultimately become cheaper to undertake filmmaking wherever the costs are lowest. That might mean that shooting takes place in Morocco and editing in France. Why maintain a multi-purpose factory-like space in any given location when it is easy enough to stitch together the different elements after the fact? *Lara Croft: Tomb Raider* (Simon West, 2001), the complex co-production examined in the previous chapter, surely looked so much the better for being shot on location in Cambodia, the UK, Hong Kong and Iceland, rather than on what are called **backlots** (large outdoor spaces attached to film studios which function as permanent sets with a basic theme that are then "dressed" to meet the specific requirements of any given movie's narrative).

All these historical twists and turns have taken their toll on the effectiveness of Fordism. The studios of the past have had to catch on to these developments in order to survive. Significant tactics have included selling off or renting out their studio space (often to television) and farming out movie production to smaller independent companies. The big studios as they once were (companies like Warner Bros. or Fox) are now primarily investors, rather than direct producers. They cushion their losses by diversifying and conglomerating. What is important to note here is that this has also brought into play significant shifts in how movies were made. These realignments are often collectively dubbed **post-Fordism**.

7.6 Paramount Studio's "New York City" backlot (actually in California). Photo by Kay Dickinson.

THE TURN TO POST-FORDISM: ITS CORE CHARACTERISTICS

Post-Fordism really became a force to be reckoned with during the 1960s and 1970s. Chances are, if you watch a contemporary movie from anywhere in the world, it will be a post-Fordist enterprise. In fact, we might want to think of cinema as one of the early testing grounds for post-Fordism. While most other industries weathered the bumpy journey out of Fordist domination in the second half of the twentieth century, post-Fordism kicked off in cinema in the 1950s. This production method is typified by: decentralization, flexibility, rapid adaptability, fragmentation, and increased access to technology. The precise meanings of all these will be explained in detail in this section of the chapter.

Let us start with **decentralization**. As we have noted, Fordism kept its costs low by concentrating as much of its manufacturing as possible in one small area. However, as has also become apparent, this is no longer the cheapest way of putting together a film. Chapter 2 discussed the practices of off-shoring and outsourcing and Chapter 6 co-production, which, by other names, are forms of decentralization. Here, portions of the filmmaking process are dispersed to whatever corner of the planet can promise to deliver finished components for the least money. One variant of this is the phenomenon of "**runaway production**," which you can read about in more detail in the case study below. These days, the globalization of capital has enticed filmmaking away from the centralized paradigm of the past. Whether we are talking about people traveling in airplanes or filmed data transmitted via satellite, infrastructural networks are now distinctly more reliable than they were in the decades of classic Fordism. And things change fast. A country that one year is a stable place in which overseas film companies could shoot may be troubled by a civil war the next. As such, long-term deals and assurances are no longer to be counted upon. We have already observed that American animators lost contracts to Korean counterparts who, in turn, are being undercut by Vietnamese and Chinese companies. This is how decentralization functions, restlessly searching out the best bargain, wherever in the world it is to be found.

CASE STUDY: "RUNAWAY PRODUCTION" – GLOBALIZING HOLLYWOOD VIA HUNGARY

"Runaway production" is one of the many ways in which the film industry economizes. The term refers to projects that are realized in countries where costs are lower than wherever the funder is seen to be based. The practice first took off in the 1950s and 1960s, when international air travel became more affordable. In effect, "runaway production" is geographical decentralization, an outsourcing of a certain proportion of principal photography. Now that studios own much less actual studio space, it is cheaper for them to rely on the flexibility of global labor. They are free to take their projects to wherever they can achieve them most efficiently. Examples of runaway productions that most people would think of as American are: *The Matrix* series (1999–2003; filmed in Australia), *Kill Bill* (Quentin Tarantino, 2003; the People's Republic of China) and *Hellboy* (Guillermo del Toro, 2004; the Czech Republic). Canada sees the majority of runaways from America because it is easy to reach from California and because most of their film industry also operates with English as a first language. For straight to video output (STV), Mexico also often stands in for the United States, or even further afield. Runaway productions typically save a backer around a million US dollars through a mixture of cheap labor and tax breaks that are offered by the host country. As Chapter 6 elaborated, a state will provide these loopholes in the hope that the production will stimulate growth in their own film industry. For instance, governments often stipulate that a certain percentage of local crew must be hired. There will also be spending within supporting sectors, such as hotel and transportation businesses.

We have framed "runaway" in scare quotes in the title to this section for a reason. The term seems to suggest that the film industry exists as some kind of stable hub from which production can escape. It harks back to the Fordist logic of a centralized studio where all but plot-essential production takes place in-house. In this way, the concept of "runaway production" denies the largely transnational disposition of most major movie corporations. "Hollywood," for instance, is perhaps better thought of as a brand, an ideology or a style than one actual place these days. It is globalized in its production processes as well as its distribution. Ever since its earliest days, Hollywood was always international in its make-up. As we turn our gaze towards runaway productions in Hungary, it is crucial to note that some of Hollywood's most famous folk, such as the actor Béla Lugosi, the directors George Cukor and Michael Curtiz, and the scorer Miklós Rózsa were all Hungarian.

But now the traffic moves in a decidedly more two-way fashion. *Underworld* (Len Wiseman, 2003), *Munich* (Steven Spielberg, 2005), *The Boy in the Striped Pyjamas* (Mark Herman, 2008),

Hellboy 2: The Golden Army (Guillermo del Toro, 2008), *Bel Ami* (Declan Donnellan and Nick Ormerod, 2010), and *Mission Impossible: Ghost Protocol* (Brad Bird, 2011) were all largely shot in Hungary. The country has made such a name for itself that the US company Raleigh Studios is now building a studio complex for shooting and post-production there.

Why has this happened? First and foremost, since the mid-2000s, Hungary has offered a 20 per cent tax break on total local production costs. The country can easily stand in for other European locations (or even Buenos Aires, as it did in *Evita* (Alan Parker, 1996)) and the summer weather is highly dependable, which is essential for outdoor shooting. A production completed in Hungary benefits from a highly developed film infrastructure, a legacy of past Communist backing similar to that of the former Czechoslovakia (as detailed elsewhere in this chapter). Hungary has a long-established film school (Budapest's University of Theatre and Film Arts), which has trained many professionals. The country boasts all the necessary technical facilities and has a history of co-production with countries such as France and Egypt dating back to the 1960s. And, just like the former Czechoslovakia (see below), it suffered near-devastating cuts once Communist support evaporated. Hence skilled labor is comparatively cheap and the government is eager to find work for its many film professionals not through protectionism, but by competing in a global marketplace.

So while the local economy will profit in certain direct ways, there is also a sense that such activity is complicit with the "race to the bottom" that was detailed in Chapter 5. There is also the impact on American film workers to consider when US companies farm out some of their

7.7 Turning Budapest into Buenos Aires: *The Making of Evita.*

jobs overseas in this post-Fordist fashion. Do these actions undermine the bargaining power of national trade unions? Do they drive down wages as a result of global competition? Those who campaign against runaway productions definitely believe so. At the same time, this set-up generates films that are largely shot in one country and then sold back to it as if they were overseas goods. The hired film laborers that have centrally contributed to them have had very little artistic say in what the finished product looks like. The main issue here is: do exercises like these make for a healthy, good-quality cinema culture, or one that we cannot forgive for exploiting those who craft it? Whatever our position is on this, it is very clear that governmental incentives and subsidies rarely breed the global film industry's loyalty to any given country. Canada was once the *bête noire* for "stealing" US movie jobs, then Australia and the Czech Republic. Romania is fast proving itself more cost-effective than Hungary and who knows where this decentralized version of "Hollywood" will travel next?

How else does decentralization affect day-to-day cinema production processes? For one thing, film production companies now consider it bad business to invest in long-term arrangements. Their sight-lines rarely extend beyond single movies because filmmaking opportunities can drastically mutate at any given moment. With reduced vertical integration, there are fewer guaranteed markets for any given film company. In this climate, it is hardly wise for them to relentlessly knock out movies. So, Fordism's economies of scale have been subsumed by what is frequently called **flexibility**. This is the facility to fragment all the elements of production so that any given portion can be rapidly replaced by another if a second one proves less expensive. We saw this in action through analyses of co-production models. Gone are the stabilities of old. It makes little sense, in a world of seemingly endless possibilities, to hunker down with a studio full of permanent staff and equipment. If you can scout the field for the cheapest and most qualified gaffer at any given time, why pay any particular one a monthly salary? Why not simply make a commitment for a shorter period (like the duration of principal photography)? You can then economize on wages by terminating the contract when no shooting is taking place. What is the point in investing money in developing studios in Australia, say, when it may be cheaper to rent them in Indonesia in years to come? In the post-Fordist era, film companies have shrugged off the obligation to maintain a permanent work force.

What does this mean for film professionals? Well, it is much more difficult to remain employable when you are up against similar people from practically anywhere in the world. Without a studio to support you, you have to become as flexible as the financiers in how you shape your career. You will probably have to train yourself, keep current with all the latest technological advances, and work without a steady, single-source salary. This is a far cry from the relative permanence of a studio existence. On the plus side, if you are employable, you could be posted to any number of exciting locations, getting to know new crews whose line-ups change with each different project. Life is much more varied than the daily studio grind. More disadvantageously, you do not have the security of a regular employer. This amounts to no assurance of a steady income stream and less of the typical permanent employee entitlements such as holiday or sick pay, medical benefits, funded training or pensions. Eschewing these outlays means that film production can be kept even more economical.

EXERCISE

Pick a narrative you know well. It could be a folk tale, a popular novel or a real-life news story.

- Now imagine you are a filmmaker in the early stages of conceptualizing it as a film.
- What would be the advantages and disadvantages of realizing your dream within the Fordist and then the post-Fordist systems?
- Be sure to consider the practical implications of things like: standardization, central planning, decentralization and flexibility. Detail who would be involved in the production: a large or a small crew, and from where? How might the look of the film be affected by any of these production method decisions?

THE STRUCTURAL IMPACT OF POST-FORDISM ON MOVIE PRODUCTION

How do post-Fordism's strategies shape the contemporary film industry? In essence, the big studios, as they now stand, are basically **subcontractors**. Subcontracting involves breaking down how something (such as a film) is made by drawing up separate, smaller contracts with others to complete a designated portion of the work. Major studios now rely on smaller independent production companies to bring projects to fruition. At the beginning of any contemporary film, you will have noticed the sequential presentation of at least two or three production company logos (idents). In the Fordist period, it would have more likely been just the one (Universal's revolving planet Earth, for instance). This change goes to show how much subcontracting is going on. The industry calls this the **package unit system**, an approach that mainstream cinema has increasingly preferred since the 1950s. The package unit system is the manifestation of all the post-Fordist practices detailed above translated into movie business lingo. As mass production dwindled, the way was paved for entrepreneurial independent producers to pitch "packages" to the studio financiers. So of all those logos at the beginning of a film, it is actually the smaller companies that have devised the movie concept, not the multinational conglomerates like Sony. A package will comprise the various saleable draws that the previous chapter detailed: a compelling script or the guarantee of involvement from a star actor or director.

After the independent production companies garner some big business backing, they will then hire even smaller units of workers to carry out the filmmaking, some of whom may, in fact, be individual freelancers. This fits the pattern outlined above: the package system is the progenitor and result of a decentralized, fragmented workforce. Even California, the one-time bastion of centralized studio production, has experienced the shift. Three-quarters of the state's registered film companies (be they catering services or special effects providers) now consist of four or fewer employees. We will be considering the bearing this has on film industry personnel in the next chapter. In the meantime, let us continue to focus upon how the turn to post-Fordism has changed cash flow within the industry.

Unlike in the studio system, profits are not immediately fed back into one single business. As we have noticed, production companies function according to the principles of flexibility and thus need to keep their assets mobile. They will rarely have either the capital or the inclination to invest in or keep up the spaces or technologies required for production. Few modern production companies reserve backlots, sound recording studios or camera cranes for their own streamlined use in the way that the big studios once did. Largely these facilities must be rented now, with the payment usually coming from studio loans or advance sales to distribution companies. Balancing these books can be tricky and it is not unknown, as we have already seen, for a movie to lose crucial financing the day before shooting commences. Evidently, there is a lot more risk involved in this mode of production.

CASE STUDY: HISTORICAL SHIFTS IN PRODUCTION PRACTICES WITHIN THE EGYPTIAN FILM INDUSTRY

Certainly, Hollywood seems the obvious place to start when mapping out the historical journey from artisanal filmmaking to studio-based Fordism to post-Fordism. However, it is not, by any stretch, the only regional cinema that has ridden out these changes. More than three thousand movies have been made in Egypt over the last ninety years. They are distributed around the Arabic-speaking world (often beyond) and are extremely popular. That said, Egypt's industry developed after America's. It is both influenced by it and a response to the trade competition US movies provoke.

Egypt's first films of any significant length were made by curious entrepreneurial figures with no access to centralized studio facilities. Key names here would include Mohammad Bayoumi (*In the Land of Tutankhamen*, 1923), Aziza Amir (*Layla*, 1927) and Ibrahim and Badr Lama (*A Kiss in the Desert*, 1927). There was a distinctly international flavor to this scene, with contributors hailing from Hungary, Germany, Palestine and Turkey, as well as Egypt itself. Filmmakers also frequently traveled overseas to train, as is still the case today. Women assumed important positions in production from the 1920s onwards. As early as 1935, the beginnings of a studio system were firing up in the country. This was partially supported by the government as a means of providing educational and news material to hard-to-reach areas.

Once sound technologies were invented, Egypt was quick to dominate film production in the Arab region, taking advantage of the shared language over a number of countries and the fact that few audience members were literate and therefore could not read the subtitles on non-Arabic movies. Soon cinema became Egypt's second most profitable export commodity (after cotton). In fact, there were moments in the 1940s and 1950s when demand outstripped supply. All this despite the fact that the studios were, by then, fully integrated environments, comprising sound stages, edit suites and laboratories. The Fordist mechanisms of private companies like Studio Galal can be spotted in the films themselves. Costumes and sets reoccur throughout various movies. Rationalization is evident in the stock roles that many of the actors assumed: Ismail Yassin as the slapstick goon, Layla Murad as the innocent heroine, and so on. Just as in India, there was a sustained horizontal integration with the music industry, meaning that box office success could be assured by the use of well-established singing icons like Oum Kalthoum and Abdulhalim Hafez.

Egypt gained its independence in 1952 after Gamal Abdul Nasser led the Officers' Revolt and assumed the position of president. Throughout the 1960s, the film studios were largely expropriated by the state and nationalized, as were a third of the movie theatres. A private cinema sector was allowed to run alongside the state one throughout much of this period. In the years that followed, most aspects of movie production were planned from within government agencies. During this era, the insecurities of package unit production did not threaten the Egyptian film industry. The overarching philosophy of the mid-1960s was one of maintaining the market dominance of Egyptian fare by producing material that would be widely popular across the region. Later on, policies shifted somewhat to favoring cinema that showed off Egypt's cultural sophistication.

Film workers within the public sector were kept on permanent salaries. Many who lived through this period testify that productions overran and budgets were overshot. Unfortunately, there was a general feeling that it was okay to splash government cash around in a somewhat reckless fashion. Millions were lost through mismanagement. This all came to a head in 1971 under the leadership of the new president, Anwar Sadat. As an advocate of trade liberalization, he re-privatized the industry.

7.8 Flats on the "Alexandria" backlot at the Egyptian Media Production City. Photo by Kay Dickinson.

However, this did not stop the government's construction of Film City in the Cairo suburb of Giza in 1973. The site has since been re-named the Egyptian Media Production City and has grown to comprise fourteen studios, various permanent sets (such as a beach, an Alexandrian street, the pyramids, and a traditional desert village), workshops of all descriptions, color laboratories, post-production suites and a training college, as well as hotels and a sports club. The government has stimulated production here by making Media Production City a free zone. This means that anyone, whatever their nationality, can hire the facilities whilst enjoying exemption from every kind of tax and custom duty. In its desire to attract offshore international production, Egypt has appealed to the rhetoric of globalization. It does so safe in the knowledge that labor is cheap in the country. The costly protectionism of bygone years no longer exists.

Egyptian films themselves, however, are struggling to survive at the moment. Although they are cheap to make (less than a couple of million US dollars per production), the returns are small and private investment is scant. Television has grown ever more popular in the Arab world and frequently relies on formats that are less costly than films. Illegal copying is also rife, meaning that official distributors will even sell DVDs outside first-run theatres in the hope of gaining some of the profits lost to pirates. It remains to be seen what will happen to the increasingly post-Fordist Egyptian film industry in years to come. For the meantime, many workers are trying their luck in television and music videos instead.

On the positive side, the flexibility of post-Fordism means that cinema can swiftly and deftly adapt to audience needs. Each movie is carefully tailored to what is believed to be a saleable idea. All the benefits of standardization are maintained (like accepted machinery) with, so the argument goes, none of the lumbering same-ness. Think back to Nigerian video-films, which we looked at in Chapter 1. They stand as one of the many post-Fordist success stories within world cinema, demonstrating that post-Fordism does not always favor the movie industry's big fish. Nigerian video-films come together on a project-by-project basis. Their rapid-fire manufacturing techniques mean that a new movie can be on the streets within a week of conception. The principles of post-Fordism allow Nigerian video-films to deal with relevant, up-to-the-minute audience concerns and desires. They therefore directly address the popular African audience (as well as others) in ways that had not previously been thought possible.

Nigerian video-films, we pointed out, erupted out of the rising availability of cheap filmmaking hard- and software. Increased access to new technologies is deemed a fundamental feature of post-Fordism. Globalized mass production systems have made these technologies significantly cheaper than in the past. They are affordable not just to large, rich corporations these days. This has prompted a so-called **democratization of technology**, ensuring that many more filmmakers can bypass the standard entry points into the industry or its distribution networks. People can teach themselves editing on pirated software or upload their own movies straight to the web, for instance. Even thirty years ago, a film industry aspirant could not have dreamt of launching a movie into general circulation with anything like this ease. However, for every keen new filmmaker who is now able to hone a film on their laptop, there are just as many "digital sweatshop" workers around the world. These are the kind of people we introduced in Chapter 5 when we investigated the outsourcing of animation to East and South-East Asia.

The expanded availability of technology has ushered in benefits and disadvantages, depending on where one stands. A trained animator in the Netherlands might be priced out of the market by cheaper labor from another country. Perhaps for that second person, post-Fordism affords them a lucky break that would have been unthinkable had they been born into an earlier generation. The worry for all those who care about workers' rights is how these components of post-Fordism are to be managed ethically. The extent to which financers and producers exploit or squeeze these fragmented and globally dispersed workers is something that concerns the following chapter.

Before that, however, what we really need to do is ground some of these more theoretical ideas about production processes with the help of concrete examples. As you will soon find out, no manufacturing methods unfold in socio-political isolation.

EXERCISE

Imagine you are trying to attract film production to your local area. What would it be possible to shoot there?

- Consider the environment: the scenery, buildings and weather, for instance.
- Does where you live offer any kinds of tax breaks (an internet search can help unearth these opportunities)?
- What sorts of facilities are on offer by way of studios, a density of trained filmmaking personnel, post-production companies and such like? What could be subcontracted out to the local population?
- What kinds of work would have to be outsourced?

Developing a picture of this order will help you to understand why movies are made in certain locations over others. From that, you can hypothesize on where your locality sits in relation to the global divisions within film production.

LOCATING AND HISTORICIZING PRODUCTION PRACTICES: CLOSE-UP ON CZECHOSLOVAK ANIMATION

This final portion of the chapter compares organizational processes from two very different centers of animation production: Czechoslovakia in the Communist period (1948–1989) and, in the next section, the renowned US studio, Pixar. When we take a closer look at actual examples of filmmaking like these, we find that their management also tallies with the political and economic prerogatives outlined in this book's Section I. For instance, whether funding comes from a state or a private source clearly shapes the final results. Manufacturing models, it will be argued, are often implemented, modified and innovated according to broader systems of social governance.

Animation is one of the most labor-intensive forms of filmmaking. Animators also remain a largely anonymous bunch. It is safe to say few of us are capable of naming any pioneer directors or character inventors. Who, then, are these people? How do they work on large joint projects when, in the case of Pixar, it can easily take several days to generate less than a second's worth of on-screen action? Chapter 5 detailed how expensive animation can be, a fact that has led to off-shoring. Whether or not animation is geographically dispersed in this way, it usually involves large groups who then break off into smaller or individual units in order to complete minute tasks. What sort of management is best suited to this situation? Answering that question with any kind of precision demands a closer look at the worlds into which each of these types of animation was born.

Czechoslovakia no longer exists as a nation-state. It did, however, from 1918 until its untroubled schism into Slovakia and the Czech Republic in 1993. For more than half of this period, the country was Communist. But even before that, in 1945, there were moves afoot to transform the film industry into public property. What developed was a complex mix of artisanal and Fordist practice that was financially supported by the state. Key names amongst Czechoslovak animators include Jiří Trnka, Karel Zeman, Hermína Týrlová, Jiří Barta and Jan Švankmajer. Their oeuvre is characterized by an intriguing mix of puppetry (a well-established popular art form in the region), stop-frame animation (which involves taking an individual photograph of a model, adjusting this model slightly, and then re-photographing to create the illusion of movement), amalgamating cut-outs from various different sources, and live action (filmed sequences of real things). During its heyday, this material regularly won international prizes at events like the Cannes Film Festival. Czechoslovakia had suffered Nazi occupation during World War II. As small compensation, it emerged from this difficult period with a highly modernized film industry, which the Nazis had developed for their own propagandistic ends. The ensuing governments wasted no time in taking advantage of and building up these facilities. Under the Communists, animation was seen as an ideal way to educate and entertain children. It was also considered a means of successfully positioning Czechoslovak culture, in this most fantastical and creative of forms, amidst the global market.

COMPARING CZECHOSLOVAK ANIMATION TO THAT OF PIXAR

The delightful inventiveness of Czechoslovak animation is equaled by the popular innovations of Pixar's collective output, from *Toy Story* (John Lasseter, 1995) to more recent ventures, such as *WALL-E* (Andrew Stanton, 2008) and *Monsters University* (Dan Scanlon, 2013). Pixar was launched by two men,

John Lasseter and Brad Bird, who had been fired from Disney for pushing too hard for computer-generated imagery during its early days. Although they have been "the bosses" throughout Pixar's history, Pixar attributes its success to having few executives in its structure. It thus leaves many of its core decisions to its thousand or so employees. How markedly different their management style is from that of the studio heads of the classical Fordist era, including Walt Disney.

However, Pixar is not an entirely autonomous unit either. From the outset, it struck a deal with Disney who swallowed up half of Pixar's profits in return

7.9 John Lasseter in his toy-filled office at Pixar Studios: *John Lasseter: A Day in a Life* (Pixar, 2011).

for marketing and distributing its movies. Pixar is now fully owned by the Disney Corporation. This dependency grows out of Pixar's vulnerability to the whims of market forces. At the other end of the economic spectrum, Czechoslovak animation was protected by the state and did not have to worry too much about turning a profit. Not that this stopped Czechoslovak animators signing outsource contracts for work on American cartoons like *Popeye* and *Tom and Jerry* in the 1960s.

The fact remains, however, that the Czechoslovak government was highly supportive of its animators and its film industry in general. Animation functioned within a highly centralized mode of production that was a small cog in a much larger planned economy. Like theatre, music and other cultural forms, cinema was meticulously organized. A film school (FAMU, the Filmová a televizní fakulta Akademie múzických umění v Praze, or the Film and TV School of the Academy of Performing Arts in Prague) was established and its students were rewarded with permanent state-salaried posts within the industry upon graduation. Even actors were retained on monthly wages, something we may find hard to imagine today. Budgets were managed according to designs that were laid out in advance. These detailed not just the amount of films that would be shot in any given year, but also the numbers of cinemas, new labs, regional studios or film workers' homes that would be built.

The nationalized film studios employed thousands of regular staff and, to a certain degree, cel animation (drawn by hand on transparent sheets) was completed in somewhat factory-like conditions. The artists, for example, would sit in rows at identical desks. However, animators were more likely to operate in small breakaway teams in their own workshops (such as the famous Trick Brothers Studio). In this sense, they carried out something similar to unit production. Each group was headed up by an experienced worker of some description – a producer, director or whoever. Within these collectives, there was a fairly flexible approach to who undertook what, everyone pulling together to realize the project.

As the Czechoslovak industry was, essentially, vertically integrated, there was no need to worry about whether these films would secure distribution deals. Any given animation would automatically be shown in Czechoslovakia, across the allied Communist countries and, as it later turned out, around much of the world. Without any of the post-Fordist worries about where the next payment was coming from and very little outside intervention, animators in Czechoslovakia were at liberty to experiment more than many of their contemporaries elsewhere. State policy decreed that television production would cater to popular tastes, while filmmakers were given a freer rein to pursue their own goals. Consequently, a wide variety of styles, many of them fairly abstract, quirky and even avant-garde, can be seen in this material. *Inspiration* (Karel Zeman, 1948) uses blown glass as its primary material; *The Pied Piper* (Jiří Barta, 1986) brings together two-dimensional animation and puppetry. Such films typically drew on the talents of all those trained within the state academies and working across the different horizontally integrated arts, involving actors, painters, puppeteers, composers and cinematographers. A Communist ethos of collaboration was fostered, supported by the fact that all of these artists essentially worked for the same employer: the state. There were even joint ventures between Czechoslovak artists and those from (then Communist) East Germany and Yugoslavia.

Pixar, too, steers clear of the post-Fordist model of manufacture. It prefers to conduct as much of its creative process as possible in-house, leaving it in the hands of permanently salaried workers. There is a production line that runs as follows: pitching; treatment; story-boarding; voice recording; the computer modeling of characters; set dressing (which, again, is a computer-based process); laying out shots; the

7.10 An animator working on a model for *The Pied Piper* in the studio of Jiří Barta: *The Making of Krysař*.

animation of the modeled characters (a process more like puppeteering than frame drawing); shading; lighting; rendering (compiling all of this and adding motion blur); and then post-production, such as sound and visual effects, along with the musical score. The making of any given film involves large numbers of employees. Just watch the lengthy credits after a Pixar film to get a sense of this. But, as with Czechoslovak animation, these people are grouped into smaller teams of five to eight members for any given section or specialization within a movie. In this sense, the working patterns mimic those of package production, except that Pixar's staff is all permanent and belongs to the same studio, rather than individual companies contributing on a freelance basis.

Pixar strives to banish any of the estrangement that one might attribute to working on such a small fraction of something much larger. Each day begins with an hour-long session where teams share their work, free to discuss its strengths and weaknesses. This is vastly different from the Fordist assembly line, where employees are rarely afforded the chance to influence or publicly critique any of the links in the production chain, not even their own. This sense of collaboration has been central to Pixar's success and was fostered during the company's inception. Unlike other organizations, where "creatives" are kept at a distance from managers and technologists, Pixar aims to treat all its employees as imaginative. This has meant that it has been able to develop its own highly powerful computer, Renderfarm, in-house, rather than having to buy such expertise from other companies. Computer specialists on Pixar's payroll are central to its structure. Therefore such services are not contracted and blossom organically through close association with the needs of the animators (who similarly adapt to programmers' requirements). So while Pixar maintains its heavily post-Fordist inventiveness with new technologies, it does so within a more centrally planned framework.

This level of strategic, overall administration can even be witnessed in the design of the Pixar building. The company understands that family-focused fare requires animators both to concentrate deeply and indulge an almost childish sense of eccentricity and exuberance. With this in mind, the studio is laid out in bold colors with any number of secret nooks and crannies. Scooters are available for employees to travel around the building and frequent races are held. Sociability and teambuilding are encouraged by locating mailboxes in the middle of the complex. Here staff have the chance to mingle and enjoy chance encounters with people from every one of the company's departments. A necessary artistic individuality is accomplished by allowing employees to modify their own workspaces. Each is given a "shed" which they then decorate and furnish according to their own whims. That might involve transforming it into a tiki hut, a Wild West saloon or a circus tent.

There is also great attention paid to employee welfare. One in three staff members suffered repetitive strain injury during the completion of *Toy Story 2* (John Lasseter et al, 1999), prompting a complete ergonomic revamping of the building. Overtime is strictly monitored and workers have free access to a gym, a swimming pool and tai chi or yoga classes. These sessions are offered by the "Pixar University," which also runs courses on new animation techniques and a number of other topics that are not strictly related to the task in hand. The logic behind the university is that it allows people from across the company to learn, share skills and make mistakes in front of each other in a relaxed fashion. In all these ways, Pixar bucks the post-Fordist trend of breaking teams apart once a project has come to fruition. The end result, the company claims, is a palpable loyalty that echoes Fordist principles, but which, just like Fordism, comes at quite a financial cost if economies of scale cannot be maintained.

Is the sort of care that the Czechoslovak state and Pixar have lavished upon their animators ultimately viable in today's globalized economy? In 1989, the Communist regime was dismantled in Czechoslovakia and, soon after, the film industry was privatized. This was driven by a massive push from, amongst others, USAID (the United States Agency for International Development, which distributes American overseas aid), who favored the industry's purchase by American, rather than local buyers. Studios were sold off at rock-bottom prices. In order to remain competitive in market terms without state support, many of their staff were laid off. Barrandov Studios now has 300 employees when once there were over 6,000. These days, Czech animators frequently perform as cheap freelancers on overseas projects, particularly in advertising.

Pixar has likewise experienced a takeover. In 2006, it was bought out by Disney. Not much later, John Lasseter was awarded the position of Chief Creative Officer at Disney in the hope that his approach would reinvigorate Disney's flagging success. Always wary of Disney's more autocratic treatment of its employees, a delicate battle is constantly being waged to guarantee Pixar workers' rights. Pixar has insisted that this is one of the main reasons for their global acclaim.

In both of these examples, the removal from or need for profit generation has shaped artistic creativity right down to the buildings in which animators work. Animation is an expensive, time-consuming business. Considerable planning and smart management is required to keep it afloat. By looking at the precise ways in which this is or is not achieved, this chapter has been able to flesh out the more abstract principles of Fordist and post-Fordist production.

DIFFERENCES BETWEEN FORDISM AND POST-FORDISM

Fordism	Post-Fordism
Central planning	Decentralization
Standardization	Rapid adaptability
Economies of scale	Flexibility
Assembly lines	Fragmentation
	Increased access to technology

Ways of making films never exist in a vacuum. What you have just read elucidates why particular methods have come to the fore or faded away. This chapter has also detailed the connection between production processes, national politics and the changes in the global economy more generally.

CHAPTER SUMMARY

This chapter commenced by differentiating artisanal and industrial production. While the former predominates in early and amateur filmmaking, the latter shapes the majority of the professional movies that reach us from around the world. Within industrial production, the influence of Fordism has dominated. Vital to the development of the studio system, Fordism inspired the centralization of film manufacturing, creating a factory-like working environment and, with that, profitable economies of scale. Fordism has ebbed away somewhat, particularly with the dissolution of vertical integration and, as such, alternative strategies like unit production emerged. Broadly speaking, these trends are termed post-Fordism, which is characterized by a rise in decentralization, flexibility and fragmentation. In the post-Fordist age, the movie business has also been able to benefit from a so-called democratization of technology. The close-up attention to animation towards this chapter's end relays the importance of examining wider political and economic conditions whenever one undertakes an analysis of any given production practice.

 **FURTHER READING**

Bordwell, David, Staiger, Janet and Thompson, Kristin. *The Classical Hollywood Cinema: Film Style and Mode of Production to 1960*. London: Routledge, 2006.

> Janet Staiger's contributions to this book are particularly valuable. She historicizes all the principles of Fordism that the Hollywood studios assumed. Strong links are formed between these management conventions and the style of classical Hollywood movies.

Christopherson, Susan and Storper, Michael. "The City as Studio; The World as Back Lot: The Impact of Vertical Disintegration on the Location of the Motion Picture Industry," *Environment and Planning D: Society and Space* 4(3) (1986): 305–320.

> With a focus on urban and economic geography, this article explores the impact of post-Fordism on where movie manufacturing takes place.

Piore, Michael J. and Sabel, Charles F. *The Second Industrial Divide: Possibilities for Prosperity.* New York: Basic Books, 1984.

> Although this book is not a film studies text, it is one of the fundamental works detailing the turn from Fordism to post-Fordism. This is a must for anyone seeking more detail on processes like flexible specialization.

 FILMS REFERENCED IN CHAPTER SEVEN

Alexander Nevsky (Sergei Eisenstein, 1938)

An American in Paris (Vincente Minnelli, 1951

Bel Ami (Declan Donnellan and Nick Ormerod, 2010)

The Boy in the Striped Pyjamas (Mark Herman, 2008)

Casablanca (Michael Curtiz, 1942)

Cat People (Jacques Tourneur, 1942)

Un chien andalou (Luis Buñuel and Salvador Dali, 1929)

Easter Parade (Charles Walters, 1948)

Evita (Alan Parker, 1996)

Gigi (Vincente Minnelli, 1958)

Hellboy (Guillermo del Toro, 2004)

Hellboy 2: The Golden Army (Guillermo del Toro, 2008)

I Walked with a Zombie (Jacques Tourneur, 1943)

In the Land of Tutankhamen (Mohammad Bayoumi, 1923)

Inspiration (Karel Zeman, 1948)

Kill Bill (Quentin Tarantino, 2003)

A Kiss in the Desert (Ibrahim and Badr Lama, 1927)

Lara Croft: Tomb Raider (Simon West, 2001)

Layla (Aziza Amir, 1927)

The Matrix (Andy and Lana Wachowski, 1999)

Mission Impossible: Ghost Protocol (Brad Bird, 2011)

Monsters University (Dan Scanlon, 2013)

Mughal-e-Azam (K. Asif, 1960)

Munich (Steven Spielberg, 2005)

The Pied Piper (Jiří Barta, 1986)

Singin' in the Rain (Stanley Donen, 1952)

Supermen of Malegaon (Faiza Ahmad Khan, 2008)

Toy Story (John Lasseter, 1995)

Toy Story 2 (John Lasseter et al, 1999)

Underworld (Len Wiseman, 2003)

WALL-E (Andrew Stanton, 2008)

Workers Leaving the Lumière Factory (Louis Lumière, 1895)

Yantra (James Whitney, 1957)

CHAPTER EIGHT

FILM LABOR

Since you are reading this book, chances are you would not mind a job connected to some aspect of cinema. You and millions of others. The allure might be the glamor, the opportunity to encounter famous, talented people. Perhaps you dream of spending your waking hours pushing your creative reserves to the limit. But how, exactly, do people land these positions? When they get their break, what are they actually doing on a daily basis? Conditions are challenging and unreliable – that much can be learnt from the previous chapter. Now we will penetrate further into film industry work and, later on, examine how its employees have tried to exact change for the better. Fleshing out Chapter 7's focus on prevalent modes of production, what follows is an analysis of how people train to enter these professions, what that work environment is like, and how film workers have protested its more unbearable dimensions.

Naturally, certain specificities will have to be bracketed out. Cinematic labor practices have altered substantially over time; they vary according to place of production, budget and suchlike. Only major influential trends can be dealt with here. At the same time, where does one start or stop when grouping movie-related careers? This chapter abides by a conservative definition of "film industry labor," concentrating in what follows mainly on the production and post-production phases (as detailed in this book's upcoming Interlude section). Many more jobs exist in film – marketing, PR, distribution, programming, exhibition, criticism and archiving (the topics of this book's next section) – and perhaps it is these that attract you most. A fuller picture of employment would also integrate, for example, the teams who write our editing and visual effects programs, who manufacture our hardware, or who sift through the dumps of our discarded TV sets and computers to find the often highly toxic elements within them that can be recycled into our new gadgets.

WHAT WE WILL DO IN CHAPTER 8

- Examine the propensities, initiations, and trainings that are hailed as helpful for getting a foot in the door of the film industry.
- Appreciate the rhythms of film work – its busy periods and the inevitable unemployment – positing some reasons as to why the industry structures its labor in this way.
- Assess what is intolerable about such work and the ways in which individuals, collectives and unions have gone about asking for better conditions.

BY THE END OF CHAPTER 8 YOU SHOULD BE ABLE TO

- Make connections between the ways in which film production is structured and rationalized and the impact it has on the people who work in the industry.
- Conjecture on whether movie workers are justified in taking issue with their working conditions, while assessing the efficacy of their means of doing so.

OPPORTUNITIES AND TRAINING: HOW PEOPLE FIND JOBS IN THE INDUSTRY

The question on so many lips is: "how do I get a job in film?" Answering this eager inquiry not with personalized insider tips, but with an acknowledgement of the genuine difficulties of such an endeavor provides us with a revealing picture.

Firstly, it is not what you know, but who you know that matters in the majority of cases. Most of you will be aware of that, but what does this actually tell us about the politics of work in this sector? Sad to say, the industry is anything but an equal opportunities employer. Jobs are rarely advertised. Agents negotiate interviews with producers for actors, directors and writers, a process that is seldom open to outside applicants. The US Bureau of Labor Statistics estimates that the annual mean salary of talent agents in 2010 was $178,340 per year, winning them a greater per capita income than any other worker operating in the movie business, and thus proving agents' clout as gate-keepers.[1] Earning proportional to their clients (at least 10 per cent), it is in their interests to manage employment, rather than make opportunities more accessible. For more technically oriented openings, producers tend to rely on word of mouth, prior experience and informal recommendations, rather than public call-outs. Collectively, these methods trigger certain deleterious consequences. Of all the directors of 2012's top 250 grossing Hollywood movies, just 9 per cent were women.[2] You have only to watch the parade of white male figures walking up the steps to collect Academy Awards (save for the female actors' prizes) to realize that the groups of people who make most mainstream films fail to represent the diversity of the world's population. Unlike other sectors, the movie business sets up few safeguards to outlaw hiring practices that discriminate against women and people of color. So, clearly the routes to success are not always transparent or meritocratic. But there still remain favored means of gaining many of the requisite skills.

In days gone by, and particularly within studio systems, experience could be acquired through on-the-job **apprenticeships**. Apprenticeships do still exist, but more so in craft-slanted enclaves like carpentry.

While such placements will lead to accreditation, final qualification can prove a protracted affair. As Susan Christopherson extrapolates,

> The vertical disintegration of the film industry altered the skill acquisition process in a variety of ways. Because workers were hired on fixed time or project contracts rather than employed continuously, the craft apprenticeship process was extended dramatically. To accumulate sufficient hours for certification as a grip or script supervisor [sic], union apprentices had to spend years working on intermittent productions.[3]

The rare apprenticeships within the niches of directing, writing or producing are highly competitive. Schemes favor entrants with at least a university degree and no small amount of prior experience. All these details build towards a picture of an industry that can afford to pick and choose its employee base whichever way it pleases and without demonstrable fear of dwindling rates of application.

Such popularity prompts a hunger for experience that makes way for our next tried and tested means of attempting to enter the film industry. Each year, thousands of people volunteer as **runners**. Something of a dogsbody role, the idea is that you gain experience, meet useful contacts and pay your dues. All for free, or minimal remuneration. A runner might carry out any number of tasks that are seen to help a production flow more smoothly: from fetching coffee and photocopying scripts to chauffeuring actors or showing guests around a studio. What is so telling about this post is how solidly it establishes a particular working identity. In film, running teaches us, one must be enterprising and ready to do anything with low odds of moving up the ladder. Running also establishes some of the exclusivity that was just mentioned. There are only certain segments of society, it must be stressed, who can afford to work for free in this capacity. Those requiring a wage to stay afloat or who need to juggle other commitments around more flexible or part-time hours are already at a disadvantage, which is mirrored by the demographics at the top end of the industry's payrolls. The case study on interns contributing to *Black Swan* (Darren Aronofsky, 2010), which features later on in this chapter, unfurls some of this discrimination in greater detail.

How else might one get recognized? Many hopefuls enhance their employability by enrolling in film school, as will be the case for many runners. Film school offers no clear guarantee of a job in the industry. In fact top-name directors such as Quentin Tarantino, Peter Jackson and James Cameron all bypassed this stage entirely. Notwithstanding, there are considerable advantages to the training on offer, including how it can lead onwards into a career.

As the previous chapter laid out, standardization is an important gel binding the film industry. Crews need to be familiar with whatever equipment is currently the norm; creative personnel should be aware of and adept with the most popular and typical aesthetics and story structures. A good film school education will cover these bases while encouraging students to push movie culture forward, creating a fresh new oeuvre that can expand the horizons of cinema. To this end, film school prepares a graduate to slip into a complicated job without the need for basic workplace training. In fact, some schools act as "feeders" for particular companies, such as CalArts (the California Institute for the Arts), set up by Walt Disney's brother Roy and originally staffed by retired Disney animators. A good film school will also nurture students' imaginations so that they have something unique to offer a very competitive sphere.

We stressed earlier how film industry employment relies heavily on contacts. Film school is one place to establish these. The top institutions have strong connections with their alumni. For instance, *Star Wars* director George Lucas graduated from the highly lauded School of Cinematic Arts at the University of Southern California and is still an active community member and benefactor. Note here the connections key players strive to maintain with their place of learning. A good school will arrange master classes with such names, ask them to judge end-of-year competitions, or arrange for trial placements on their shoots. Just as importantly, peers, the talent of the future, form a useful network. Students who help out on each other's graduation films might vividly come to mind for a more lavish production later on in life.

Opportunities may well abound, but they do not easily fall into anyone's laps. These difficulties in "breaking in" build towards a certain work culture that will occupy us later. The elite Beijing Film Academy, to take one example, accepts only 500 entrants from the 100,000 who apply. Furthermore, this sort of education can be prohibitively expensive. In 2011, New York University's Tisch School of Fine Arts, where Martin Scorsese and Oliver Stone learnt their craft, cost $45,674 per year in tuition fees alone. While the establishment awards a $200,000 prize to the top graduate to help finance their first feature, this is a rare concession by film schools, which often require that their students pay for the entirety of their graduation movies. Certain countries subsidize this education (such as France's La Femis, which only charges $517 a year for home students, yet $15,334 for internationals).[4] But, for the most part, the pathway is something of an exclusive one, especially given the costs. It is a far cry from an apprenticeship where one is paid as one learns.

These days, the expense of training is more regularly shouldered not by the government or the industry itself but by those dreaming of one day making a living through cinema. This has not always been the case, as the VGIK case study highlights. With the tendency to land the bill on the individual's own doorstep comes a host of attendant problems and restrictions. The first, quite obviously, is the answer to the question: who, exactly, can afford this type of education? In the most basic of terms, people from rich families or others who are willing to rack up a sizeable debt. The predominance of the first cohort alerts us to the narrow demographics succeeding in cinema. The second group highlights a worrying trend within the industry and in society at large. When students pay so dearly for their education, they leave with heavy loans hanging over their heads. In the US context, this can amount to a quarter of a million dollars when other expenses beyond tuition fees are factored in. A film graduate is nowhere near guaranteed steady employment in the industry, and yet will be expected to clear these accounts, as well as pay significant interest on them. It is all the more difficult to earn a living within a sector as unpredictable as cinema if one is simultaneously paying off what it cost to train. Financial situations of this order can severely restrict the type of work graduates might take on, which, in turn, begs a question. Will they truly be able to follow their dreams, to fulfil their creative potential in the ways they envisioned when they signed up for their course?

Such sobering realities make many wonder whether a film school education really does "pay off". Certainly, lots of would-be filmmakers explore other routes: teaching themselves skills on pirated software and cheap amateur equipment; uploading their work to online distribution sites such as Vimeo and YouTube with the hope that they will get discovered that way; avidly watching the same films and reading the same books as those enrolled in the elite academies. People "make it" in the industry through any number of means. Nothing is ever a guarantee of future success. But the point of this chapter is not so much to despair at this situation or to gird ourselves into believing that we will be the lucky few. Instead, let us attend to how these circumstances fashion a particular economy of labor within the movie business.

CASE STUDY: VGIK

The world's oldest film school opened its doors in Moscow (then in the Soviet Union) nearly a hundred years ago and still welcomes students today. Established in 1919, just two years after the Russian Revolution, it has gone by several names, but for the lengthiest period of its history it was known as Vsesoiuznyi gosudarstevennyi institute kinematografii (the All-Union State Institute of

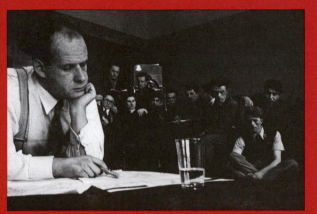

8.1 Sergei Eisenstein reading a lecture to students of the cinematography institute, VGIK. Courtesy of RIA Novosti/Alamy.

Cinematography), for which VGIK is an acronym. Almost every luminary of Soviet-era cinema trained here and many top directors served as professors: Lev Kuleshov, Sergei Eisenstein, Vsevolod Pudovkin and Oleksandr Dovzhenko, to name just four. Other teachers came from further afield, such as the highly respected Hungarian-German theorist Béla Balász.

The institute, like many others of that time and place, dedicated its energies to furthering the Communist ideals of the USSR. Cinema was to contribute to the texture of everyday revolutionary life and to help educate the population (see Chapter 4 on cinema as politics for further details). Of the 1,500 or so students lucky enough to be accepted each year, a rigorous education was provided entirely for free, including the costs of producing their graduate films. Students specialized in appropriate fields, such as acting, production economics, screenwriting or film criticism. Contrary to common stereotypes of Communist regimes, their schooling was far from dogmatic; experimentation, imagination and breadth of knowledge were encouraged. Budding directors, for instance, not only learnt their own craft, but were obliged to take classes in around thirty other subjects, including philosophy, political economy, psychology, writing, acting, sociology and the history of world cinema, art and theatre. This was no mere skills-based training. Students had access to a fine library of international books and movies. And professors such as Eisenstein fostered a praxis-led approach (the melding of theory and practice), giving their students concrete filmmaking exercises, but asking them to draw extensively on ideas garnered from other non-film classes. Students were often rewarded with the opportunity of contributing to their teachers' movies and discussing aesthetic decisions with them. VGIK also served as a testing ground for Eisenstein and others' theories of cinema and movie production. Many of the faculty not only made well-regarded films, they also wrote textbooks and political treatises on cinema while working at VGIK. The famous Kuleshov effect, wherein editing creates a build-up of interpretative associations for the viewer, was first developed by Kuleshov in his classrooms here.

The VGIK education owes many of its defining characteristics to broader social planning initiatives of the era, including centralization and standardization endeavors (the kind elucidated in Chapter 7). Anathema to the Communist ideal was a marketization of education that would make schooling affordable only to the rich or intellectually privileged. To offset this possibility, quotas were fixed so that the bulk of students would come from poorer backgrounds (75 per cent in the 1930s), from the smaller republics in the Soviet Union (like Turkmenistan), and from less economically stable countries around the world. The aim was to train up enough workers to sustain the newly industrialized cinema sector. In theory, the school was to graduate the right amount of students for the jobs available, as well as offer an unrivaled education for talented citizens of the Third World and other socialist nations. Some of the finest non-Soviet directors of the twentieth century, such as Ousmane Sembene (from Senegal), Souleymane Cisse (Mali), Abderrahmane Sissako (Mauritania/Mali) and Sjumandjaja (Indonesia), passed through VGIK's doors. One clear trademark of all their work, as with the Soviet-born filmmakers, is a pedagogical bent imbued with sensitivity to the needs of less wealthy populations. We might read VGIK's largesse towards African and Asian students as the USSR trying to widen its sphere of influence globally, including within its own multicultural communities. Nonetheless, the diverse assembly of students at VGIK encouraged genuine international dialogue. It would be worth considering these manoeuvres in relation to how co-production similarly spends money to create cross-border cultural rapport (see Chapter 6).

As exciting as this course of study was, there were inevitable disadvantages to the free education model. For starters, VGIK's buildings were, for many years, inadequate. Teaching rooms lacked basic equipment, from chairs to functioning cameras, and the dormitories were squalid and prone to parasite infestations throughout the 1930s. There were times in the 1920s when the institute suffered from a complete absence of stock, prompting Kuleshov to "shoot" "films without film" with his students, asking them to *imagine* what their practice work would look like rather than to actually produce a portfolio of material. During certain more conservative periods, the VGIK administration has also been accused of favoritism in their selection processes, despite the Communist pressure for equality of access. Not all teachers upheld the open-minded approaches of illustrious faculty members like Eisenstein.

During the period of *glasnost* (openness) and *perestroika* (restructuring) in the late 1980s, when state-sponsored Communism was on the wane, VGIK was generally considered to be a somewhat stagnant learning environment, although still rigorous and world-leading. With the collapse of Communism in the Eastern Bloc, the school, which is now known as the Gerasimov Institute of Cinematography, slipped more into line with equivalents around the planet. It currently charges non-Russians admission fees of up to $10,000 per year, or $5,000 for a summer school. Sadly, students no longer receive financial assistance for their graduation projects. VGIK's hallmark feature, its extensive, inter-disciplinary curriculum, lives on, meaning students spend between four and six years there in order to graduate. This does not include the extra time it might take non-natives to acquire the appropriate level of Russian to understand classes. In order to keep up to date with modern industry needs, the Institute now houses departments of multimedia and special effects.

EXERCISE

What are the most prestigious film schools in your country?

Go online and research:

- How much they cost.
- What they promise to teach their students.
- What their rates of admission are in relation to application numbers.
- Whether they offer opportunities for direct experience in the industry or exposure to influential players within it.

Once you have sketched out this portrait, use it to conjecture what type of future film workers are being trained. What sort of movies will they likely make and why? Who might be left out by the selection procedures they exact?

SOME FEATURES OF FILM WORK: THE EMPLOYERS' MARKET

Each of the preparatory phases just detailed builds towards a familiarity with what life will be like in the profession. Following logically onwards, actual daily work is the topic of the next few pages. While the upcoming Interlude section delineates specific industry roles, the emphasis here falls on broad trends characterizing this type of employment.

To aid our analyses, it pays to think expansively about how work is shaped, labeled and controlled, as well as what we can expect from it. Media scholar Matt Stahl offers a usefully attuned definition of "working conditions," a designation that does not simply encompass

> the degree of comfort or satisfaction one experiences at film and television work (is it too cold or too hot, can I go to the bathroom when I choose, are the rules and expectations clear, are my co-workers and supervisors kind or cruel, do I exercise my creative capacities in my work, and so on). The term also refers to political and economic aspects of work including remuneration, control of the work process, ownership of the products of labor, the rights and obligations of employers and workers, and workers' access to health and pension benefits.[5]

Naturally, the two dimensions are connected. Policy and legislation are meted and fleshed out in the more microcosmic qualities with which Stahl commences his description. Yet workers can only really expect or bargain for such conditions from a particular position of employment. Cinema, it must be recognized, does not function like many other industries. As a consequence, those involved have a different access to the benefits of labor.

The first truth to acknowledge here – and we have been leading in this direction for some time – is that very few actually make a living through movie work. Or, as Lois Gray and Ronald Seeber put it, "The average employee in the industry is attached to his or her craft more in spirit than in measurable employment."[6] There are many more people who consider themselves filmmakers than there are those who actually make ends meet that way. To lay this out in bald figures, the average member of America's Screen Actors Guild (SAG) in 2012 made a paltry $5,000 a year from their trade or, broken down, an hourly wage of $10.69. Only this much, despite the fact that film actors register as some of the richest individuals in the world. Given these statistics, the profession is what sometimes gets termed a "lottery economy." Many "pay in" (with free or lowly paid labor), but very few are lucky enough to "win." Of the 100,000 or so registered members of SAG, only around fifty could be classified as high-earning stars. In 2008, the median income of all non-supervisory film industry workers in the United States amounted to a mere $19 more than the average of what everyone else in the country combined (skilled and unskilled) earned.[7]

To sum up all these findings, this is an employment landscape marked by heavy competition for the available jobs. Let us take it for granted that there is good reason for this; that people want to get involved because the work is exciting and fulfilling. With that as a given, we can instead focus on how the industry takes advantage of our enthusiasm.

Most hopefuls barely get a look in. Out of eagerness to join the game, they take on unpaid labor (from amateur and student productions to internships) in the hope that fuller employment will result. Accordingly, countless hours of contribution do not need to be budgeted for. On a wider, structural scale, this renders the film industry an **employers' market**: lots of people looking for work, but not many jobs. The upper hand goes to whoever is looking to hire; bosses are pretty much spoilt for choice. The willingness to work, to do whatever it takes, means employers can get away with being extremely demanding. Hence the prevalence of "paying one's dues" through intensive free labor. Let us not forget other corruptions of power, such as the infamous "casting couch": people will agree to have sex with an executive or similarly influential figure in the hope that it will lead to employment. These sorts of abuse are possible in an employers' market.

The climate is one where people are glad to have any work at all. Subsequently, under these circumstances, it might seem awkward to ask for improved rights or pay. Bosses can always elect to hire someone else rather than a "whiner" or "troublemaker". You might instead choose to lie low about grievances in the hope of getting hired again in the future. Sadly, the film industry turns a blind eye to all manner of mistreatment that would not be permissible in other jobs. Who is willing to take a petulant, bullying director or star to an industrial tribunal? More often than not, their behavior is tolerated as a symptom of their superlative creativity. Yet, as the latter part of this chapter will attest, workers do very definitely take issue with their managers as well.

SO NEAR AND YET SO FAR: SPECIALIZATION AND ALIENATION

The strict hierarchy within filmmaking is not solely the outcome of an employers' market. Undoubtedly, this particular state of play has bred complicity and discipline within the industry. But it was primarily developed as an effective means of manufacturing movies on a grand industrial scale. Film does not "just happen" to function in these ways. Purposeful design played a role and has shaped a large number of people's lives, including those on the outside hoping to get in. If we refuse to take the dynamics of the industry as a given and instead look at how they were planned out, we come to a picture that might also allow us to change for the better the way work is carried out within cinema.

CASE STUDY: *BLACK SWAN* INTERNS FIGHT FOR PAYBACK

Black Swan (Darren Aronofsky, 2010): a tale of intense, destructive competition, of people driving themselves beyond their limits to secure their dream jobs. You would be right to think we are talking about the movie's plot here, but in fact it is also a fair description of how many interns working on it experienced the shoot. So much so that two of them – Alex Footman and Eric Glatt – felt justified in filing a class-action suit against its producers, Fox Entertainment Group. Of the more than $300 million the picture has made in a few years, none of the profits trickled down as wages for these interns. The plaintiffs argue this is not only unfair, but also illegal. Their battle has since become a test case for how free labor in film (and beyond) should be legislated for and carried out.

How did Footman and Glatt find themselves grafting for free and what did they see as wrong with their situation? As this chapter contends throughout, meeting the right people and building experience is everything in film. Add to that the excitement of actually gaining admission to a high-profile set, and it is not hard to understand why people apply in their droves for long periods of unpaid work in the industry. In comparison to the low-wage jobs in retail or services that many young people take to pay their way (but which do not reflect their career aspirations), an internship is often presumed to be a "foot in the door." In both instances, you might be making coffee – in one case for a salary, the other possibly not. Yet what few realize is that many of the things interns are asked to do are barely, if at all, legal under lots of countries' employment legislation.

In his meticulously researched book on the topic, *Intern Nation*, Ross Perlin points out that internships are, in fact, rather a new phenomenon. In the mid twentieth century, hardly anyone would have dreamt of working for free. Now an internship is a practically *de rigueur* rite of passage. Vast efforts are expended on finding the perfect internship. So much so that promotional businesses like the entertainmentcareers.net website exist. However, because internships have only really risen to prominence in the last two decades, their definition is still extremely vague and can hide a multitude of sins. Internships are very much the upshot of a post-Fordist world, where work is decentralized and hours easily unregulated. We live in the era of an internet economy, where an estimated 40 per cent of online content has been generated for free. When you think about it, many of us already contribute unpaid labor to the media industries, whether through publishing online reviews, uploading clips to YouTube or sending out promotional tweets about a movie we have seen. Given all this, where should we draw the line with our labor?

Those agitating against the ubiquity of internships argue that their presence decreases the amount of paid positions on offer. Moreover, in a weak economy, employers are taking advantage of a desperate workforce with few opportunities. Although an internship is presumed to be a mere stepping-stone on the route to success, many young people now move from one internship to another for years at a stretch, saving the industry millions. Film producers are certainly benefiting, but how about the interns? Given this context, were Glatt and Footman justified in speaking out?

Under the US Fair Labor Standards Act, an intern cannot replace work that would ordinarily be carried out by a paid employee, or would stop a company having to recruit extra staff. The key distinction between an intern and employee is that it is only legal not to remunerate someone if what they are doing can be constituted as training. Here universities, which often allow students to undertake internships for credit, might be read as complicit in the rise of free labor (or labor students themselves pay for, if we take their fees into account). As a production intern on *Black Swan*, Footman claims that the training he received amounted to exactly what any new employee would obtain in order to learn the ropes. His lawyers could not countenance his labor as especially educational. Footman's twenty-five to fifty hours per week were spent taking lunch orders, booking accommodation for cast and crew, photocopying, even taking out the trash. In sum, duties that were scarcely enriching or instructive. Likewise, Glatt devoted around fifty hours a week to such activities as tracking purchase orders and creating spreadsheets, receiving neither formal training nor university credit for his troubles. The plaintiffs contend that Fox Searchlight were the only people to truly benefit here. In their defence, Fox Searchlight claimed they were not even actually Footman and Glatt's "employer." True to post-Fordist management trends, they had outsourced the hiring of the interns to another company. Regardless of the outcome of such pleas, Footman and Glatt's protest brings to light basic rights of which very few interns are aware. At core, the case has publicized what interns can legitimately be asked to do and what they should receive in return.

Broader issues of fairness in the workplace emerge too. It is a sad fact that only certain sectors of the population can afford to take on unpaid work. If an intern is not independently wealthy, they may have to take out loans (further, perhaps, to their student debts) or rely heavily on financial support from relatives. Not everyone is in a position to do this. Running counter to the twentieth century's advances in equal opportunity hiring practices, the increase in internships is closing doors in the faces of people who cannot afford, effectively, to pay to build their curricula vitae in these ways. We should also acknowledge these inequalities not only from within our own countries, but also in terms of an international division of labor. Other repercussions prove similarly worrisome. An intern, unlike a contracted employee, rarely has recourse to the law for grievances such as sexual harassment. With these troubling vulnerabilities to the fore, it is about time we cast a critical eye on the systemic damage the intern economy wreaks, as well as the way it impacts upon interns on an individual basis.

8.2 The Fox logo reworded. Courtesy © Intern Labor Rights.

The pecking order we have observed is one legacy of a honed and dominant managerial strategy known as **Taylorism**. We should pause for a minute and get to grips with this approach. Taylorism was spearheaded by a mechanical engineer, Frederick Winslow Taylor, in the latter part of the nineteenth century. Although its popularity waned in the 1930s, its core principles still held great sway on how Fordism – and even post-Fordism (see Chapter 7) – would operate, including within cinema.

One of the basic rules of Taylorism is that you amass a group of workers who are highly specialized according to particular, tightly ordained skills. We shall see how this establishes a hierarchy in a minute, but first we need to understand the obvious benefits of the Taylorist system. The film industry houses plenty of Taylorized professions; for example, the clapper loader. A clapper loader's responsibilities, historically, have been confined almost entirely to looking after film stock: delivering it to set, making sure it is of the correct type, loading it into the cameras properly, insuring that it is catalogued accurately, and transferring it onwards to the lab for developing. On a larger production, this role might even be shared by two people: a clapper loader (or second assistant camera) and a film loader. Their tasks may seem narrow to an outsider, but a mishandling of stock could prove disastrous. With a day's shooting costing an enormous amount of money, lost or double-exposed stock would bear significant consequences.

The particularity of this example opens us out to the logic of Taylorist specialization. The aim is to build a team who are so focused that there is little scope for mistakes or wastage. A crew can achieve successful results by working as a well-integrated network in which everyone understands their specific niche and how it connects with those of others. These objectives fit snugly with Fordism, allowing the factory line to flow smoothly. A stunt performer will be hired exclusively to carry out dangerous physical actions on screen so an actor will not get injured and thus disrupt the shoot, or augment the insurance fees. Continuity personnel function on behalf of the editors during principal photography. Their job is to guarantee that shots cohere with one another, that costume or props, for instance, do not change between takes in a manner that would prove disruptive when the film is later stitched together. A clock cannot read 1pm in a shot that leads straight into one where we would see it displaying 3pm. Ultimately, the aim is to break film work down into manageable units where employees can truly concentrate on what they are doing and thus avoid costly errors. Many such employees love the focus, the feeling that they are contributing expert attention to a much larger group endeavor.

In addition, these stratifications of labor are never entirely set in stone; they vary according to broader labor trends. A smaller-scale crew, for instance, will often double up on duties. Nick Broomfield, the multi award-winning director of *Aileen Wuornos: The Selling of a Serial Killer* (1992) and *Ghosts* (2006), to take one such person, normally records his own sound, the reduced team proving more suited to his investigative documentary style. A downside of this digression from Taylorism emerges, however, in his film *Kurt and Courtney* (1998). Finally, some paparazzi they have temporarily recruited into the crew manage to illicitly sneak up on their antagonist, Courtney Love. It is at precisely this moment that the screen snaps to blue and we hear Broomfield intone, "unfortunately, the battery ran out." Techniques like Taylorism make a lot of sense for keeping tasks manageable and hence avoiding such blunders. They also streamline the production process. But how do they impact upon the actual workers who take up these circumscribed roles? We have noted that many relish concentrating their efforts, functioning as a single, but crucial jigsaw piece in an intricate and impressive puzzle. However, there are also downsides to consider.

One deep concern for a Taylorized workforce is that of de-skilling. As new technologies or working methods emerge, others are wiped off the roster altogether. Any pure distillation of abilities leaves an employee vulnerable if their expert knowledge is superseded. The job of the film loader was just detailed, but, with movies increasingly shot on digital, these folks are being replaced by digital imaging technicians. Not everyone is able to make a successful switch between areas of competence. While Taylorism creates a highly specialized crew, it can also invalidate their skills when there is a shift in manufacturing trends away from their trained comfort zones.

In his *Economic and Philosophic Manuscripts of 1844*, Karl Marx discerns four types of **alienation** prompted by capitalist labor conditions. These categorizations have proven useful for the analysis of work generally, including within the sectors treated in this book. The impact of alienation is central to the few scholarly studies to have been written on film labor, from classics like Leo Rosten's *Hollywood: The Movie Colony, The Movie Makers* and Hortense Powdermaker's *Hollywood the Dream Factory* to perceptive new texts like the anthology *Production Studies* (details below). It makes sense, then, to run through Marx's understandings of alienation one by one, each threatening any work we might do (in film and elsewhere), something we are sure you will pick up as you read on. For now, we will concentrate more on the causes and effects of alienation. If you are keen to learn more about the systems, ultimately revolutions, that Marx proposes as a way of extinguishing alienation, there is a wealth of further literature on this key political thinker upon which to draw.

The first classification we shall attend to is the propensity to alienate a worker *from the very act of producing*. Marx homes in on how reducing tasks to isolated, abstract, even machinic actions makes it difficult for anyone to gain a sense of real achievement. Let us cast this observation back over Taylorism's methods. For Marx, worker satisfaction remains significantly diminished if, say, a clapper loader has no input into how a movie's narrative is crafted or how its overall look is achieved. Their role of service (taking care of film stock) is plugged into an organism over which they have very little influence.

8.3 Nick Broomfield appears on screen in *Kurt and Courtney* (1998), his headphones and microphone clearly visible.

Counter to Marx's intuition, Taylorism works best when everyone acknowledges their role in a larger picture and is sympathetic to it. Film at its best will foster this kind of team spirit and the subsequent buzz is something that is a real draw and benefit to the people involved. Yet territorial impulses do definitely emerge. A director of photography, say, might make an impromptu aesthetic decision about the color of the film, which would step on the toes of the production designer or the post-production colorists. Their jobs complicate significantly as a result of this whim. Likewise, if picture editors overshoot their deadlines, they leave less time for a scorer to compose the soundtrack. In a competitive sector, where everyone is vying to do their best – to *impress* – jostling for primacy can easily slide into a disregard for others. Here we encounter another of Marx's categories of alienation: the type that exists *between workers*. At its most extreme, the doctrine of specialization renders it near impossible for members of a team to truly understand what the others are doing. Think how few moviegoers know what all those job titles listed on a closing credit roll actually involve. For Marx, the world would be a better place if we had a more holistic approach to labor and were not pitted against each other; if we cooperated to work towards common goals on an equal footing.

While certain productions have experimented with this sort of arrangement, moviemaking as a whole is instead steeply hierarchical. Nowhere is this more marked than in the perpetuation of what is known as "the line" – and whether one is placed above or below it. "The line," in industry parlance, acts to distinguish creative from technical labor. Creative work bequeaths greater rights, bargaining potential and claims to intellectual property.

ABOVE AND BELOW THE LINE

The following division of film labor places all the job titles mentioned in the Interlude section where they sit with regard to "the line." This is not an exhaustive list, but will give you some idea of how the industry values certain workers over others:

Above the line
Directors
Actors
Screenwriters
Executive and associate producers

Below the line
Location scouts
Line producers
Casting directors
Art department
Visual effects
Special effects
Art directors
Costume designers
Props masters
Make-up artists
Hair designers

Animal trainers
Grips
Transportation coordinators
Directors of photography
Camera assistants and loaders
Sound recordists
Production managers, coordinators and assistants

Unit managers
Assistant directors
Pyrotechnics coordinators
Editors
Compositors
Foley teams
Dialogue editors

Bill Nichols' book *Engaging Cinema: An Introduction to Film Studies* expertly catalogues how budgets are apportioned according to each of these departments, allowing a little insight into where salaries are set too.[8]

Above the line live the likes of scriptwriters, directors, producers, and actors. Below it, many indisputably imaginative people, including storyboarders and costume designers. The demarcation perpetuates a class system of sorts (or an estrangement of workers from each other, according to Marx), most notably in how prestige, autonomy and salaries are awarded. For instance, costume, hair and make-up departments contribute enormously to the success of a film's look. Yet they are notoriously badly paid, despite the fact these jobs demand some of the longest hours on set – all because they fall "below the line." Traditionally the domain of female employees, it is worth once more casting a critical eye on how creativity might be prejudicially measured within cinema.

On the upper side of the line, a privileged few (writers, directors, actors …) can earn what are known as **residuals** on the intellectual property they help create. These are extra payments, delivered when work is reissued, replayed, or sold to a new region or media platform. Why only these lucky recipients (as well as their agents, who glean a percentage fee)? The line, clearly, is a divisive entity. Although Marx's proposals about how workers are alienated from each other holds good here, the real discrepancies in pay accord with who holds the copyright. This is typically the studio or its multinational parent company, rather than any of the creative personnel. Historically, the studio's claims can be shockingly invasive. In *Contested Culture: The Image, the Voice, and the Law*, Jane Gaines details how Bette Davis' 1943 contract with Warner Bros. endowed them with "all rights to the Davis name, voice, and

likeness … the studio can claim 'Bette Davis' as its own corporate trademark for seven years."[9] We now confront one of the great ironies of the profession. Is it not the appeal of this job that it is billed as one of the most artistic and expressive vocations possible? It certainly can be, but, at the same time, actors are frequently treated as image and property, rather than as autonomous beings. Richard Dyer astutely comments that film stars are "both labour and the thing that labour produces."[10] For sure, they concoct their persona (in collaboration with others), but they are also the product on sale, a balancing act that will be further investigated in the following section of this book's examinations of stardom.

Marx's remaining two categories of alienation jibe well here. They are: (1) estrangement *from what one produces*, and (2) the disabling feeling that work *distances one from one's very self*. The first condition is a common one. How many of us earn our livings believing we are in utter control of what we make or do? In the world of acting, this could come in the form of casting decisions. During the studio era, performers were rarely allowed a say in the roles they were given. If

8.4 Bette Davis playing "herself" in *Hollywood Canteen* (1944). Source: Warner Bros./ The Kobal Collection.

they rejected a part, they could be docked months' worth of salary as punishment. While typecasting serves a particular function within Fordist replication (it is standardized, knowable, quick to recreate), it can certainly prove alienating to the person who has to conjure "the dumb blonde" or the "villainous foreigner" time and time again on demand.

The remaining form of isolation that Marx addresses is the loss of one's sense of self. Most people cherish the possibility of carrying out work that is connected to how they understand themselves, that carries personal integrity, and that contributes something they see as meaningful. If we do not feel independently rooted in our vocations, these opportunities shrink, Marx argues; likewise, if our sense of individuality, particularly our private matters, are infringed upon. Take the actor's situation again. They might be asked to make a radical change to the way they look, say, through cosmetic surgery (remember Rita Hayworth from the previous chapter). They may be obliged to submit to "morality clauses," which govern their behavior well beyond the hours they give up for the camera. All of these stipulations, these encroachments on autonomy, register as alienation from oneself within Marx's schema.

Such details reveal just how disciplinary working relations are – how a contract is not simply an economic arrangement, but also a pact that extends social control. While this section has laid out how a long-term employee within Fordist means of filmmaking might have felt encaged, post-Fordist working practices inculcate particular regimes and subjectivities too. It is to those that we turn next.

8.5 and 8.6 Even versatile actors get typecast. Both James Mason (here in *North By Northwest*, 1959) and Peter Lorre (with Humphrey Bogart in *The Maltese Falcon*, 1941) were regularly asked to play the "villainous foreigner." Courtesy of MGM/The Kobal Collection and Warner Bros./First National/The Kobal Collection/Mack Elliott.

EXERCISE

Select a DVD or Blu-ray of a film with which you are familiar – one that offers commentaries by several of the people who have worked on it in its "extras" package.

- Who has been chosen to discuss their work as part of these extras?
- Who has not, and why do you think this is the case?
- How does the commentator relate their experience of working on this movie?
- What claims to its intellectual property are they making, and do you feel they are justified?
- Do they relate back to the rhetoric you encountered in Chapter 2 on self-expression?
- What obstacles has the commentator encountered? Now that you have a better understanding of how the movie industry is structured, how would you account for these difficulties in terms of the financial culture that subsumes cinema?
- Can you spot any signs of alienation (from other workers, from the speaker's sense of their own rights or from their bosses) in what they are saying?

WORKING CONDITIONS WITHIN POST-FORDIST GLOBALIZED FILM PRODUCTION

Taylorism, as has been argued, is well suited to Fordism. Post-Fordism encourages a different set of strategies, which are logically referred to as **post-Taylorist**. Post-Taylorism takes into consideration the fragmentation of production across different companies and geographies. With the dissolution of centralization and the factory-line ideal, the static, targeted skill sets nurtured through Taylorism grow less and less apposite. They do not die away, they are supplemented.

Today, in order to find work, a job candidate must be adequately trained in order to get down to business in a new environment with the minimum fuss. This has always been the case within cinema, as has been shown. It is perhaps the *speed of movement from project to project* and the adaptability this demands that define post-Taylorism. There are no longer the same number of long-term studio era-style contracts. In this climate, it pays to adopt what goes by the name of **flexible specialization**: the ability to step into a number of different job roles, rather than cover one deeply concentrated area of vocational expertise.

Given the dispersal of filmmaking amongst a greater number of smaller subcontractors, the post-Taylorist worker also benefits if they can *network* well. To repeat the old adage, it is whom you know that matters. Thanks to decentralization and deregulation, the right people will not always be where we would expect them. It makes sense to explore as many avenues as possible. A successful post-Taylorist worker will likely have a facility, for example, for integrating her social life (on and offline) into her job-seeking. She will draw on a broad range of contacts to look for openings in unlikely places, including through the increasing number of voluntary posts. Marx's categories of alienation are challenged here. If anything, this restless search for openings, this bleed-through between on and off duty, can feel swamping and overwhelming, rather than distancing.

The temporalities of labor have also shifted of late, courtesy of the decrease in permanent contracts. Susan Christopherson puts it succinctly when, after significant empirical work in the industry, she summarizes: "Even the most successful entertainment industry worker has multiple employers during the course of the year, spells of intense work, and spells of unemployment."[11] Evidently, this movement from contract to contract inscribes a different working rhythm from those experienced under Fordism.

We must pay attention here to the tendency of larger studios and financers to subcontract production to small units in order to shrug off the economic risks associated with making cinematic commodities. In this equation, the latter company functions under certain restraints. The first of these is that the small unit must use all the tricks in the book to drive down costs in order to turn profit. One obvious way to do this is to save on labor expenditure. It is less legally incumbent upon smaller operations to abide by trade union rates of pay. Because their employees are treated as casual – purely with them for the duration of a single shoot – these enterprises are often not obliged to provide benefits such as holiday and sick pay or pensions. Such responsibilities then fall on the shoulders of the worker, rather than their employer.

Certainly, there are clear advantages to this state of affairs. The situation offers much greater flexibility and freedom than a studio contract like Bette Davis' ever did. A one-off agreement brokered by a director or actor (or, rather, their agent) may well accrue that person a much larger salary than they would have gained if signed as an unknown to a major studio sixty years ago. However, the disadvantages, especially if one does not land a lucky break, are also clear: no dependable income, few (if any) benefits, and increased periods of unemployment. The same is true of many other film-related professions, such as movie journalism, where reviewers might write for free (for the experience, for the love of the medium) or are typically paid per word and are seldom on the full-time staff of any given publication. Even film educators are increasingly casualized these days, working for hourly rates that do not compensate them during vacations. This mode of existence is now so prevalent that social theorists have assigned it a name: the **precarious class**. Their status is outlined in greater detail in books such as Guy Standing's *The Precariat: The Dangerous New Class* and Franco Berardi's *The Soul at Work: From Alienation to Autonomy*. Mark Deuze's *Media Work* (referenced at the end of this chapter) extends these arguments into the media sector. All three are well worth reading to garner a more precise picture of what life is like under such parameters, whether as a filmmaker or a contract cleaner. Here we will sketch out some basic tendencies.

One of the characteristics of what gets called "precarity," as has been illustrated, is the need to stand out in order to appear worthy of re-employment. This bind gives managers the scope to push their workers to the limit, all under the auspices of allowing them to prove themselves. In an employers' market and with production companies themselves desperate to cut costs, there is little reluctance about impelling freelancers to graft harder. Concurrently, when a worker cannot solidly rely on being hired again, any conditions seem better than none at all.

The "periods of intense work" that Christopherson observes arise from these circumstances. Project-by-project filmmaking differs from studio-manufactured fare in that it cannot spread out its costs and labor across a longer timeframe. A smaller decentralized production will be renting facilities, for instance, and will therefore need to maximize available usage. Financers demand speedy repayment, which urges companies to hurry along. All this is very understandable, but it certainly takes its toll on a film's cast and crew. In the UK, for instance, the average working week in paid filmmaking is seventy-two hours, often longer.[12] As a consequence, film workers are prone to damaging fatigue. Editors often suffer repetitive strain injury from spending long hours clicking a mouse. Handling heavy machinery such as cranes, rigs and cameras becomes positively dangerous if those in charge have completed a long late shift one day, and then been asked to return for a 6 o'clock start the following morning.

As Christopherson has indicated, these periods of intense activity are often counterweighed by prolonged unemployment. To be more precise, Christopherson calculates that only 33 per cent of American film workers (employees within one of the healthiest industries in the world) can only find enough work to occupy themselves 75 per cent of the time.[13] Most stay afloat earning money in other sectors, therefore intensifying the need for flexible specialization. Others willingly contribute the free labor discussed above in the hope that it will lead to something more remunerative in the future.

A host of factors contribute here. The reluctance of companies, large and small, to hire people permanently and full-time is certainly a reality. So too is the global division of labor outlined in earlier chapters. The American filmmakers to whom Christopherson alludes are regularly losing out to competitive "runaway" production, outsourcing, cheaper labor and attractive tax breaks in other countries. This leads, again, to the sort of animosity and alienation between workers that are familiar from the drawing of a "line" between different types of labor.

One particularly heinous example of this manifests itself in the slur "white Mexicans," used by certain American crews to describe British filmmakers who will submit to lower pay scales than they would. What is invoked here is a cruel stereotype of the global division of labor, buoyed by the alienation workers can feel from each other, as identified by Marx. Drawing on the assumption that economically desperate Mexicans undercut American citizens and thus devalue their worth, the term of abuse is protective of American rights to the point of exclusion. The tag stops short of trying to forge solidarities between all (film) workers, so that everyone is treated fairly, whether American, British or Mexican, whether "white" or not (all three countries comprising mixed demographics anyway). While there is a knee-jerk tendency to blame others for one's own unemployment, strong international attempts have

EXERCISE

Pick any film and watch its final credit sequence. Time it and make a list of any of the job titles you do not recognize.

- How long does the credit sequence last and what does this tell you about the types of work that are conducted?
- Look up any of the professions with which you are unfamiliar in the upcoming Interlude section of this book. Some you will have to find through online research. Would you call these Taylorist or post-Taylorist roles?
- Pay attention to the names and locations mentioned. What can you glean about the production's practices of outsourcing and off-shoring or the international division of labor from this mixture?

long been afoot to band workers together to fight injustices over working conditions and pay. This chapter's final pages will spend some time among these campaigns.

ESTABLISHING COLLECTIVE RIGHTS FOR FILM WORKERS

We have repeatedly asserted that movies are commodities. In order to turn profit, they must cost less to make than the money they accrue from sales. As long as there have been workers losing out to these profits, there have been struggles to assert their claims to a greater share of the spoils. Although it is rarely their capital that gets these movies off the ground, it is always their labor. Thus it is in their interests to try to raise the value of what they contribute in the eyes of their employers. These campaigns can be pursued on the individual contractual level, or by mobilizing unified groups, perhaps local, perhaps international.

One standard way to build collectivity is through **unionization** (also known as **organized labor**). A trade union is an institution that fights for the rights of its membership, people who broadly share the same interests and job. To keep itself afloat and pay full-time staff to initiate and coordinate its endeavors, a union funds itself through regular subscriptions from its members. Examples of this within film would include Australia's Media, Entertainment and Arts Alliance (MEAA), whose members hail from all manner of leisure-related professions. Other unions around the world look after more specific groups, such as screenwriters or actors. Film workers might also affiliate with practitioners of their trade who are not necessarily concerned with cinema, such as movie scorers seeking the protection of the Musicians' Union.

A trade union strives to ensure that a workplace is safe and equitable. Recalling Matt Stahl's inclusive definition of working conditions from earlier, a union especially aims to implement and expand employee rights through interventions in policy-making at national, even global, levels. Its core objective is to gather people together, believing that a combined voice is more powerful than a lone one. This practice generally goes by the term **collective bargaining**. And the ultimate bargaining chip a union holds is that it can threaten or enact work cessation on a large scale. The efficacy of any given union is, naturally, entirely reliant on the demand for its members' skills and an employer's desire that work should continue uninterrupted. If a particular film industry profession is dying out, it will have a hard time fighting for recognition, let alone protection or improved wages.

Organized labor within the American film industry first evolved in the 1910s and 1920s. Efforts were dedicated, for the most part, to leveraging fair working conditions and rates of pay in exchange for the service of its members. These trade associations (or "**guilds**," as they can be known) expounded strict definitions of the work appropriate to each job they supported. In so doing, they followed and were invigorated by the specialization tendencies preferred by Taylorization. By the 1940s, union and guild influence had spread, offering representation for almost all workers in the industry. The guilds encouraged standardization of equipment and practices between companies so that workers could move around. They also established codes of ethics and pay scales. Later on, the 1950s saw the consolidation of the **roster system**. With this, the studios and independent producers arranged contracts directly with the unions, who then helped determine fair wages for their members. In return, the unions placed workers with employers according to experience. The companies could therefore take advantage of a built-in screening process, while the workers benefited from fixed, well-negotiated salaries. A job opportunity would be assigned without them having to tout for it (as is more the case nowadays). Some employer–union associations were so tight as to be exclusive. The Screen Actors Guild, for example, demands membership before one can take up the majority of Hollywood acting jobs. And once he or she is a member, a performer is barred from working for non-signatory clients. In return, the actor is assured a comfortable minimum wage, overtime pay and residuals. In its most extreme incarnation, these restrictions amount to **closed shop unionization**, which means that specific jobs can *only* be given to union members. The argument running counter to this practice exposes how a closed shop ultimately reinforces narrow, unequal access to employment. Unions frequently – and justifiably – weather critiques of internal corruption. Pervading Hollywood in particular there is a general sentiment that the guilds and unions are predominantly a conservative force. They look after their current membership like an exclusive club, rather than pushing forward to exact changes for the good of all.

INDUSTRIAL ACTION

The closed shop is an incredibly commanding entity in any battle to increase privileges. If work can *only* legally be carried out by designated members, and they then elect to make certain demands, a boss will find it very tricky to refuse. Understandably, many governments around the world legislate against this extent of union authority, coming down in favor of the owners of the means of production, rather than the workers. Instead, unions usually have to take more of a gamble.

Their primary tactic in fighting for better working conditions is a disruption or withdrawal of labor, often in the form of a **strike**. A strike's efficacy depends upon other workers on principle refusing to step in to fill these voids. Anyone who does so is labeled a strike-breaker or **scab**. All manner of grievances prompt strikes, from low pay or over-work to redundancies or the introduction of a new technology. Here are a couple of famous examples that exemplify how disgruntled film personnel have challenged their managers.

The previous chapter showed how studio heads often instituted a patrician control over their workers, creating a "family" ambience. None more so perhaps than Walt Disney. We can read this two ways. A strong sense of identification can indubitably alleviate alienation; workers feel like they *belong*. But frequently this happens at a cost. Across the Disney empire, employees must abide by strict rules of behavior, language and dress. There is a "Disney University," where the company ethos is drummed into employees across the many branches in which Disney is invested.

The groundwork for these initiatives was dug early. Although popular beforehand, Disney established its primacy on the success of its spectacular 1937 feature animation *Snow White and the Seven Dwarfs* (William Cottrell et al.). In order to reach the lucrative winter holiday market that year, animators, painters and inkers were all urged to "pull together". Many clocked in an exhausting eighty-five-hour working week, which saw them sleeping at the studio, rather than taking the time off to travel home to bed. They were even forbidden from talking on the job. Disney was operating within, and exploiting, an employers' market. The Great Depression of the 1930s meant people were desperate for work, allowing Disney to recruit cheaply. Under these conditions, the company felt that a sizeable quota of the overtime hours required to complete *Snow White* could go unremunerated. Instead, only a portion of those whom Disney believed to be deserving received salary adjustments. Unfortunately, this then placed said employees on a pay scale on which they were no longer eligible for overtime pay. To add insult to injury, Disney himself took credit for much of their work (very few of the main progenitors of the characters were named on the movie's credits), and women were paid significantly less than men. The workers' loyalty under tough circumstances, they felt, had gone unrewarded and dissatisfaction fomented.

By 1941, many employees, with the backing of the Screen Cartoonists' Guild, decided to strike to improve their fortunes. Disney was outraged by what was to become a five-week action. He felt betrayed by his team (alienated, we might say), labeling the agitators ingrates and Bolsheviks. Federal negotiators stepped in in return for some goodwill ambassadorial work from Disney in Latin America. They eventually ruled in favor of the strikers, instigating union pay scales and other more uniform conditions.

8.7 Striking cartoonists at Disney Studios, 1941. Courtesy of the Delmar T. Oviatt Library. Urban Archives Center, California State University, Northridge.

More recently, 2007–2008 saw a well-publicized strike led by the Writers Guild of America (WGA). Their action was against the Alliance of Motion Picture and Television Producers (AMPTP), which represents giants such as Paramount, Sony and the Weinstein Company. The strikers' complaints were manifold, but converged predominantly around what they felt to be injustices in compensation for creating intellectual property. Writers were still receiving residuals for home viewing formats appropriate to the mid 1980s, when videocassettes were expensive and meagre proportional compensation seemed satisfactory. Their main battle focused on percentage payment for digital distribution. The writers had correctly foreseen that the future for sales would be electronic (downloads and streaming) and here the AMPTP refused to relinquish ground. Thus 12,000 professional entertainment writers refused to work for 100 days. The protest was resolved in their favor with an extension of reuse payments to cover work screened for profit online as well. What this union realized was that in a climate of precarious employment, the rolled-out arrival of residuals from a number of sources would be all but necessary for its members' economic survival.

CONTEMPORARY CHALLENGES FOR COLLECTIVE STRUGGLE

The WGA strike demonstrates how unions must now confront the specific contemporary problems incubated by post-Fordism and the worker subjectivities it fashions. Union power has certainly diminished within this period. The deregulation of the industry from the 1970s onwards dispersed employees in such a way as to make organized labor's control less tenable. Film workers are now scattered around the four corners of the globe, rather than coming to work in a fixed studio space each day. How can people come together to organize under these circumstances? Horizontal integration also means that a broad tranche of unions would now cover one single corporation. Concerns like Disney employ everyone from garment workers to toy store clerks. Their brand is much more dominant and unifying than any guild within it could ever be.

The problems that beset Disney during early 1941 have, in part, been offset by the possibilities transnationalism affords. Since the 1960s, the corporation has decentralized, sharing its animation contracts

8.8 Disney employees giving princess makeovers at the Bibbidi Bobbidi Boutique, Disneyland. Photo by Kay Dickinson.

8.9 Low-paid Disney garment workers interviewed anonymously about their lack of rights in the documentary *Mickey Mouse Goes to Haiti* (National Labor Committee, 1996).

across Japan, Australia and Canada, as well as America. Workers in each of these zones are now in competition and therefore less likely to strike. This much is familiar from the phenomena of "runaway" productions, international tax breaks or the "race to the bottom," all of which serve to undermine the power of locally or nationally bound unions. It is highly challenging to unionize over borders, especially when rates of pay and standards of living differ so dramatically. There are even spaces tailoring specifically to the off-shoring market. The Media and Studio "Cities" in Dubai, for example, are situated in what are called **free zones**, where earnings go untaxed and unionization is outlawed altogether.

The division of production between more modestly sized independent contractors has also taken its toll on union membership. It is hard to reach out to a now fairly atomized workforce who only come together on ever-varying single projects if they work on location, and possibly not at all if they do not. This being the case, employees might these days prove keener to comply with working conditions, not wanting to rock the boat or jeopardize being hired on a future project. The smaller a company, the less obliged it is to unionize or to hire union members. Such enterprises, combined, make up the bulk of the movie business at present. The employers' market gives them the liberty to request non-union workers (who are significantly cheaper).

For their part, the multi-skilled workers created by the post-Fordist, post-Taylorist employment landscape can find unions disaffecting. The strict job descriptions upon which unions rely do not speak to the actual labor they carry out. Union support is lost to other sectors too. For "above the line" vacancies, talent agents scooch into union territory. However, the type of negotiations over rights and salary they conduct are highly individualized in distinction to a union's collective ideals. All the same, certain unions still remain powerful in centers like Hollywood. Frequently, these are ones that stretch beyond the industry's parameters and command a strong base within trades such as construction or transportation. It is instructive to note associated differences in rates of pay between strongly and tenuously unionized professions. A construction manager on a movie, who supervisors the set builders, carpenters, painters and so on, will earn considerably more – sometimes tens of thousands of dollars per year more – than a director of photography. The former has the backing of a strong union.

But is this simply a union-aligned reinstitution of a "line"? There is no simple solution to workplace inequality, especially when jobs within film are so specific and so in need of unique talents. One thing is certain, however: that a clear understanding of how these situations have evolved and what the industry's objectives are will stand all of us in better stead if we hope either to work in cinema, or simply to fully appreciate the labor that goes into it.

CHAPTER SUMMARY

This chapter took on various widely held presumptions about work in the film industry: that jobs are hard to get and difficult to string together long term. We have examined the various entry points into the industry, from film school enrolment to apprenticeships and running, always with a sensitivity towards how the sector takes advantage of its employers' market. The central portion of the chapter considered why movie production is structured in the way it is, often according to the principles of Taylorism and post-Taylorism. The benefits of these employment philosophies were outlined, as were the hardships they entail for workers, which can include alienation, class subordination, unemployment and precarity. To round off, the chapter focused on some of the ways people have fought for their rights within the film industry. Here we also analyzed the difficulties the current global economy presents for these campaigns.

FURTHER READING

Caldwell, John Thornton. *Production Culture: Industrial Reflexivity and Critical Practice in Film and Television*. Durham, NC: Duke University Press, 2008.

> Using the stories film workers tell about their jobs as his launch pad, Caldwell offers up a nuanced and rigorous understanding of the industry. The analysis is far-reaching, delving into areas such as studio design and trade alliances that typically go unexplored within Film Studies as a discipline.

Deuze, Mark. *Media Work*. Oxford: Polity, 2007.

> Deuze presents up-to-date overviews of various media industries, including a strong chapter on film production, all contextualized within the contemporary precarious conditions of post-Fordist, largely digital employment.

Gray, Lois S. and Seeber, Ronald L. (eds). *Under the Stars: Essays on Labor Relations in Arts and Entertainment*. Ithaca, NY: ILR/Cornell Paperbacks, 1996.

> Although slightly old now and concentrated largely on American examples, this is still one of the few books to lay out how unions operate within the changing climate of the movie business. The authors in this anthology predominantly hail from industrial relations departments, so they deliver a much-needed perspective that evades everyday film scholars.

Mayer, Vicki, Banks, Miranda J., and Caldwell, John T. (eds). *Production Studies: Cultural Studies of Media Industries*. New York: Routledge, 2009.

> This volume premises its investigations on the idea that work is a culture: not simply a job, but a way of living and thinking about the world. Its authors add smart theoretical conjecture to their empirical studies and, as such, *Production Studies* has proven highly influential in the writing of the current chapter.

FILMS REFERENCED IN CHAPTER EIGHT

Aileen Wuornos: The Selling of a Serial Killer (Nick Broomfield, 1992)

Black Swan (Darren Aronofsky, 2010)

Ghosts (Nick Broomfield, 2006)

Kurt and Courtney (Nick Broomfield, 1998)

Snow White and the Seven Dwarfs (William Cottrell et al., 1937)

NOTES

1 David Roos, "10 Highest Paying Jobs in the Film Industry," *How Stuff Works*, http://www.howstuff-works.com/highest-paying-jobs-film-industry.htm, accessed 6 July 2013.

2 Martha M. Lauzen, "Behind the Scenes Employment of Women on the Top 250 Films of 2012," http://womenintvfilm.sdsu.edu/files/2012_Celluloid_Ceiling_Exec_Summ.pdf, 20, accessed 6 July 2013.

3 Susan Christopherson, "Flexibility and Adaptation in Industrial Relations: The Exceptional Case of the U.S. Media Entertainment Industry," in (eds), *Under the Stars: Essays on Labor Relations in Arts and Entertainment* (Ithaca, NY: ILR/Cornell Paperbacks, 1996), 107.

4 The details of these tuition fees were acquired from: Tim Appelo, "The 25 Best Film Schools Ranking," *The Hollywood Reporter*, 27 July 2011, http://www.hollywoodreporter.com/news/25-best-film-schools-rankings-215714, accessed 6 July 2013.

5 Matt Stahl, "Privilege and Distinction in Production Worlds: Copyright, Collective Bargaining, and Working Conditions in Media Making," in Vicki Mayer, Miranda J. Banks and John T. Caldwell (eds), *Production Studies: Cultural Studies of Media Industries* (New York: Routledge, 2009), 54.

6 Lois S. Gray and Ronald L. Seeber, "The Industry and the Unions: An Overview," in Lois S. Gray and Ronald L. Seeber (eds), *Under the Stars: Essays on Labor Relations in Arts and Entertainment* (Ithaca, NY: ILR/Cornell Paperbacks, 1996), 34.

7 Roos.

8 Bill Nichols, *Engaging Cinema: An Introduction to Film Studies* (New York: W. W. Norton, 2010), 215.

9 Jane Gaines, *Contested Culture: The Image, the Voice, and the Law* (London: BFI Publishing, 1992), 161. The following book is also extremely useful for documenting actors' relationships to their labor: Danae Clark, *Negotiating Hollywood: The Cultural Politics of Actors' Labor* (Minneapolis: University of Minnesota Press, 1995). Both monographs concentrate, with good reason, on the Hollywood studio system, elaborating on the strictures that kept performers in line, treating them often as products, rather than as workers.

10 Richard Dyer, *Heavenly Bodies: Film Stars and Society* (New York: Routledge, 2004), 5.

11 Susan Christopherson, "Labor: The Effects of Media Concentration on the Film and Television Workforce," in Paul McDonald and Janet Wasko (eds), *The Contemporary Hollywood Film Industry* (Oxford: Blackwell Publishing, 2008), 157.

12 "How Many Hours Are You Doing Today?," BECTU, http://www.bectu.org.uk/news/gen/ng0217.html, accessed 28 December 2010. This situation demands that those involved sign away their rights to protection under European labor law.

13 Christopherson, 157.

INTERLUDE ON FILM FORM

A YouTube video features Alexander Kluge, a magnificent German director and thinker about cinema, explaining "film in 1 minute". Here's what he says (but you should watch him saying it):

> The camera has an optical unconscious. As opposed to the human gaze, which we use daily, the camera shoots a subject and makes you wonder how unconventional and fantastic the recorded image looks. That's film. Now the second thing is framing, the capturing of one moment. When you edit those moments together, as contradictory as they may seem, at the point two images create contrast, even clash with one another, a third image appears, the epiphany. That is film. Film is an invisible image, that either manifests out of frame, or right on the cut.

It's an enigmatic and wonderful thing to think about film as an "invisible image," beyond the frame or in the interstices of the cut, but it's also helpful to be able to describe what it is that we *do* see and hear in ways that make sense to others and allow us to speak with precision about images and sound. Maintaining a sense of film's *difference* from everyday sight – that is, remaining alert to its magnificent possibilities – while mastering its conventions and grammar: this is the goal of this chapter. This Interlude assumes, in other words, that the language of formal analysis neither detracts from the thrill of watching movies nor serves as an end in itself. Giving you the vocabulary to make clear and consistent observations about film style, this Interlude empowers you, above all, to notice *choices* made by directors and other personnel that influence how we respond to what we see and hear. You may act upon those observations by using them in films you make yourself, or you may test those observations through further watching and writing. Whatever your own ends, this vocabulary will serve you well for specifying *how films work*. It does so in two parts. The first section treats the four key categories of film analysis: *mise-en-scène*, cinematography, editing and sound. The second section treats film labor: the personnel and roles involved in moviemaking, from large-scale industrial production to artisanal, experimental, or no-budget filmmaking. In each section, we provide you with the language specific to cinema that will enable you to enter into its worlds.

FILM ANALYSIS

There is no single or universal model for film analysis. Usually, however, we talk about "breaking down" a film into its component elements of composition, or "taking apart" a film the way you might "take apart" a tractor in order to reassemble it once you've learned the names and functions of its parts. In a comparison to literary analysis, the analysis of film form might involve the parsing of a sequence of shots, much as you might parse the grammar of a particularly dense sentence, or of a poem's lines. In any case, what we hope to accomplish is an understanding of the *how* of a film: *how* films astonish, delight, terrify, enlighten, convince, madden and so on *through* formal technique. By convention, scholars generally distinguish among four areas for the analysis of technique: *mise-en-scène* (everything involved in "staging the action" or what is placed before the camera), cinematography (everything to do with the camera, its placement, its focus, and its movement), editing (how shots are joined together and according to what rules or logic), and sound (everything from spoken dialogue to ambient sound to noise). We take each in turn here.

Mise-en-scène

Italicized because it's a French phrase meaning "put into the scene," *mise-en-scène* is itself parsed into different aspects. Some scholars see them as relatively static, on the model of the framing of the theatrical proscenium. We, by contrast, see them as dynamic, setting into motion relationships that are more akin to choreographies than to static framings. While it is helpful to isolate these elements for reasons of clarity, they will need to be put into action in relation to cinematography, which is the art through which these aspects are galvanized and put into motion.

Generally, we begin with **props** and **setting** (sometimes described together as "*décor*"), both fairly straightforward categories but ones that can have an enormous impact when enlisted for particular sensorial, cinematic purposes. Take the rotting meat prop in the "Men and Maggots" section of

I.1 Maggots in *Battleship Potemkin* (Sergei Eisenstein, 1925). Courtesy of Goskino/The Kobal Collection.

Sergei Eisenstein's *Battleship Potemkin* (1925): crawling with maggots that we, the spectators clearly see for ourselves through deliberate framing and editing, the meat is nonetheless pronounced fit for consumption by the ship's doctor. Shocked by the visceral image of rot through this **montage of attractions** (Eisenstein's term for such moments of embodied response), we are also enlisted quickly on the side of the sailors against the powerful officers. Setting, too, can do much more than simply set the mood of a sequence or of an entire film. Many cite the futuristic furniture and simple interior color palette in Stanley Kubrick's *2001: A Space Odyssey* (1968) as suggesting the space station's sterile and impersonal ambiance. But think of the role that the city of Rome plays in Rossellini's *Rome, Open City* (1945), a film that was shot **on location** as World War II was ending and the Allied forces were approaching Rome and bombing its outskirts: the city becomes as much a character in the film's story of resistance, collaboration, and survival as the young children who inhabit its streets. Shot secretly without the luxury of studios, the production crew could not even rely on a steady supply of electrical power for shooting interior scenes.

Another major component of *mise-en-scène*, then, is **lighting**, something that can appear to be simply "natural" but rarely is. Even films shot outdoors rely upon supplemental lighting, and lighting is always carefully calibrated to the film stock's speed (or digital exposure index), the camera's aperture and the camera's shutter speed. In this dance between lights and camera, either can take the lead: cameras can adjust to available light, and lighting can adjust to the demands the shot makes upon the camera (discussed in the next section below on cinematography). In all cases, however, we can discuss lighting in terms of its **quality**, **direction**, **source**, and **color**. Quality essentially describes the relative **intensity** of illumination. "Hard" lighting creates strong contrast and sharp shadows, whereas "soft" lighting creates more diffuse illumination, blurring textures and blunting contrast. **Direction** refers to the path light takes from its source toward its object, and control over lighting direction helps spectators to understand the space of a scene, the shape and texture of objects in a scene, and the overall feel or composition of a given shot. Some directions include **frontal** lighting, **backlighting**, **sidelighting**, **underlighting**, and **top lighting**, creating different effects, particularly on faces.

Lighting **source** refers to two different things. Especially in commercial narrative films, visible sources of light such as lamps and fireplaces and even spotlights rarely supply the actual sources of illumination for filming. Instead, filmmakers place at least two lights, sometimes more, for each shot; every time the camera moves, the lights move, too. (Again, we want to stress here the dynamism and interplay between light, objects, actors, and camera: the very setting into motion of space and time that is the cinema.) These lights can also be differentiated by their sources. For instance, the **key** light, as the name suggests, is the dominant or principal light in a given shot, while the **fill** light provides less intensity, softening shadows cast by the key light. Sometimes, a filmmaker will add a **backlight** to these two, in the system Hollywood developed called **three-point lighting**, still the industry standard in narrative filmmaking. We can further distinguish, therefore, between **high-key** lighting, which raises the fill light to the same intensity as the key light, creating even, bright light with few shadows, and **low-key** lighting, which uses little fill, creating strong contrasts, with the dark and shadowy moods of thrillers or detective films.

I.2 Futuristic furniture in *2001: A Space Odyssey* (Stanley Kubrick, 1968). Courtesy of MGM/The Kobal Collection.

I.3 *Rome, Open City* (Roberto Rossellini, 1945). Courtesy of Excelsa/Mayer-Burstyn/The Kobal Collection.

I.4 An example of sidelighting from *Gaslight* (Charles Boyer, 1944). Courtesy of MGM/The Kobal Collection.

EXERCISE

In a relatively dark space, experiment with lighting direction with a flashlight. Notice how sidelights highlight facial features, and how backlighting differentiates figure from background. Now think about how lighting, in relation to its object, can create an intensity or flow from one position to another. How does the interplay of light and shadow enlist your attention and embodied response?

I.5 An example of three-point lighting on the set of *Grand Hotel* (Edmund Goulding, 1932). Courtesy of MGM/The Kobal Collection.

Finally, lighting can be described in terms of its color, manipulated through filters but also manipulated digitally through processes of **color grading**. Developments in digital technologies, in fact, have created endless possibilities for color correction, "painting" the images captured with cameras. Primary **color correction** can adjust intensities across the color **spectrum** (red, green, blue, gamma, shadows, and highlights), creating consistency across a film, while secondary color correction can alter **lightness**, **saturation** and **hue** in a particular range or even within a particular area of the frame, creating a shift in **luminance** (the *perceived* brightness of color). As with other elements of *mise-en-scène*, color's characteristics supply aesthetic variables that can develop thematically, contribute to mood, and form patterns in characterization.

I.6 Film portrait of the thirteen dwarves in *The Hobbit: An Unexpected Journey* (Peter Jackson, 2012). Courtesy of New Line Cinema/The Kobal Collection.

Characterization, whether in narrative film or non-narrative forms such as documentary, is also articulated through **costume**, **make-up**, and **hair styling**. For Peter Jackson's film, *The Hobbit: An Unexpected Journey* (2012) UK-based costume designer Ann Mackrey had to develop distinctive looks for each of the thirteen dwarves. As she describes it:

> It was quite a challenge really, simply because there are 13 of them, and Peter Jackson wanted them to have such a distinct, separate look from each other. He really was very keen on them having a different silhouette even before we started talking about the different colors they would all have. And then beyond that, he wanted distinct characteristics, and also distinct hierarchy, because some of the dwarves are more noble than others. So I had to emphasize all of that in just the choice of fabrics and the level of decoration, and by the time you get to dwarf No. 7 of 13, you're thinking, "How are we going to make the next one look different?" It's difficult, but great fun, actually too. I did learn an awful lot as I went along.[1]

This attention to detail in costume and make-up is not limited to fantasy or science fiction genres, nor is it driven entirely by technologies such as shooting in 3D or at 48 frames per second, as *The Hobbit* was. Directors routinely enlist the perceptions of audiences based upon appearance. Soviet directors in the 1920s famously relied upon "typage," casting actors to portray often stereotypical representatives of a social class, historical movement, or social actor (the priest with crazy hair in *Battleship Potemkin* is a good example, as is the overall casting in Pudovkin's *Storm Over Asia* (1928)).

I.7 *Storm Over Asia* (Vsevolod Pudovkin, 1928). Courtesy of Mezhrabpom-Film/The Kobal Collection.

239

Typage also leads us to the final aspect of *mise-en-scène*, **figure behavior** (also sometimes divided into **figure expression and movement**) of which **acting** is a major component (but since "figures" may be non-human animals, droids, or objects, "acting" does not apply to all the behavior of figures in a scene). While there is considerable historical and cultural variation in styles of film acting (think of early Hollywood melodrama, slapstick comedy, Japanese *kyu-geki*, or the continuing role of non-professional actors), there are a number of elements that remain consistently important to address. First is the role of **facial expression**, or what philosopher Gilles Deleuze calls **faciality** (the face is a map, or a landscape). The ability of the camera to frame actors at any distance means that, unlike our fixed position in the theatre, spectators encounter actors in **extreme close-up** and as little specks in **long shots** (terms we will discuss with greater precision in the next section). Camera distance and **framing** determine the expressive possibilities of a given actor's role in a shot. As a window onto characters' emotion, then, faces in close-up are enormously important communicative tools in the cinema, as are figure movements that are socially codified bodily **gestures**. But the face also looks out: it does not simply emit signs of its meaning or depths but instead enlists us in the dynamics of recognition, psychic engagement, opacity and thwarted connection that are crucial to cinema.

I.8 An extreme close-up from *The Curse of the Werewolf* (Terence Fisher, 1961). Courtesy of Hammer/The Kobal Collection.

I.9 An extreme long shot from *Triumph of the Will* (Leni Riefenstahl, 1934). Courtesy of NSDAP/The Kobal Collection.

I.10 Director Mike Leigh with actress Sally Hawkins (2008). Courtesy of Film 4/Ingenious Film Partners/Potboiler Productions. Film 4/The Kobal Collection.

Actors do different types of work in cinema, some with major roles filled by **stars** (commanding larger salaries than other actors and receiving top billing); others, such as **supporting actors** are often cast in the same types of roles from film to film, as are **character actors** who develop a persona over time across roles. From Soviet films of the 1920s to Italian neo-realist film to the ensemble improvisations of British director Mike Leigh, **non-professional actors** have played important screen roles. There are also different methods of training professional actors, from the dominant **naturalism** of commercial narrative (portraying recognizable aspects of human life) to **method** acting (a technique of drawing upon one's own memories and experiences as a reservoir for a character's portrayal). Although not all roles involve speech, vocal training and voice acting, particularly for animated film, are elements of acting we would do well to study carefully. Finally, digital technologies such as **motion capture** (also known as **performance capture**), through which humans become the basis for digital characters, have introduced controversy into the valuation of craft in acting; actor Andy Serkis (Gollum in the *Lord of the Rings* trilogy (Peter Jackson, 2001, 2002, 2003)) was denied an Oscar nomination, signaling some skepticism about this form of acting as worthy of recognition.

I.11 Marlon Brando in *Apocalypse Now* (Francis Ford Coppola, 1979). Courtesy of Zoetrope/United Artists/The Kobal Collection.

Cinematography

Think about all of the things that now are already interacting before the camera as part of *mise-en-scène* and of all the variables encompassed therein. A whole new set of variables confront the **cinematographer** (or **Director of Photography** or **DP**), the person responsible for deciding which camera and which lenses to use, how to frame each shot compositionally, where to put the camera, how to focus the camera, at what angle (level, height, and distance) to approach the action, where the camera might move and using what equipment, and how long each shot should last within the overall logic or ambition of the film. He or she will obviously work closely with the chief electrician or **gaffer**, responsible for the lighting plan; with the gaffer's assistant, the **best boy**; and with the crew members or **grips** who handle the equipment, including the **Dolly** on which the camera often travels. As we did with *mise-en-scène*, we treat each aspect of cinematography as a separate set of decisions, each of which can influence a film's look, appeal, effectiveness, and meaning, but we stress their interplay and performative, evolving aspects, too. Starting with the **shot** and its variables, we then

I.12 DP James Wong Howe (1927). Courtesy of MGM/The Kobal Collection.

explore camera **placement**, **framing** and **composition**; **camera movement**; and finally the **duration** of the shot, forming a bridge to our next section on editing. Throughout, we discuss film and digital cinematography as involving similar fundamental elements. As ASC cinematographer Vilnos Zsigmond puts it, "The things we do with film still apply to digital. Composition, light, and shadow – that's still what cinematography is all about."[2]

Let's define the shot this way: as a continuously exposed length of film obtained in continuous time. We turn the camera on, record, and turn it off, whether it records on film or digitally. How long is a shot, then? Well, as long as we want to make it, given our goals and our equipment. If we rely upon a film **magazine**, a light-tight chamber holding both the unexposed film and then the film as it is exposed and taken up (that's what the big rabbit ears are on film cameras), we limit ourselves to the standard magazine capacities of 1,000 or 400 feet, where 90 feet equal one minute of film. That's for a film **gauge** (width) of 35mm, which means we could record a shot of just under ten minutes with the largest magazine for a 35mm camera. Most shots are much, much shorter in duration.

I.13 Director François Ozon on a tracking shot (2010). Courtesy of Music Box Films/The Kobal Collection.

I.14 Panavision magazine. Courtesy of Polygram/Egg/The Kobal Collection.

EXERCISE

Play any film on any device. Each time you see an **edit** (joining one shot to another by means of a **cut** or other type of edit, discussed at further length in the next section), a new shot begins. Watch for five minutes and tap your pen or pencil at each new shot. You'll start to get a feel for the **tempo** (changes per minute) of the editing, and you'll also start to understand the grammar of shot duration. What is the average length of the shots you just watched? Why are some shots shorter/longer than others? What role do shorter shots play in a sequence? Longer shots? How do you engage them differently in terms of your attention and emotion?

Digital cameras record as much as their memory will allow, depending upon the type of files saved in the process of recording, the compression rate, and the capacity of memory cards for storage. The film *People's Park/Renmin Gongyuan* (J.P. Sniadecki and Libbie D. Cohn, 2012), for example, is a single 75-minute continuous shot of a tour of People's Park in Chengdu, Sichuan Province. It takes in the activity of Chinese public space in a masterfully orchestrated, organic piece of filmmaking that involved many, many practice **takes** (or repetitions in recording a single shot in order to get it just right).

Every shot requires its own **set-up**, or configuration, of elements of *mise-en-scène*, camera, lights, crew (and sound recording equipment, about which also more soon). Even if you are using your smartphone to shoot the antics of your cat as it chases a toy, you'll need to know how to coerce the kitty into an evenly lit room, how to follow the action without creating a blur, how to generate interest and excitement in the image rather than bored dismissal, and so on. In planning each shot of a film carefully in advance, often with the use of a **storyboard** (illustrated sketch of each shot in a **sequence** of shots), a director can seize control over the many variables that contribute to a film's overall style and tone. Alfred Hitchcock is one director whose storyboards are historically famous for their level of detail; Alexander Witt, a Chilean-born director of photography working in Hollywood (*Skyfall*, *Casino Royale*, *The Bourne Identity*), is known for his reliance upon storyboards in the world of contemporary filmmaking.

Some properties of the shot are photographic, involving those processes minimally necessary to produce patterns of light and dark. The **speed** of film **stock** (the ISO rating of the film or the ISO setting on a digital camera) varies in how much light is required by the camera to create an image, from slow speed (lots of light) to fast speed. **Exposure**, the length of time the **aperture** of the camera remains open to light, is the second factor, a calculation simply of **shutter** speed. And the size of the aperture, determined by the lens's f-stop setting, determines how much light strikes the film or light sensor.

The laws of photographic vision place other constraints upon the camera before we even choose what to frame within our shot. Lenses see the way most of our eyes see, transforming a three-dimensional world onto two dimensions while translating relations of depth, scale, and spatiality, but different lenses – lenses with different **focal lengths** – register different perspectival relations in different ways. Cinematographers use **prime** lenses, of fixed focal length, and **zoom** lenses, of varying focal lengths, the latter particularly when focus changes (or **racks**) during a single shot. Focal length, simply defined,

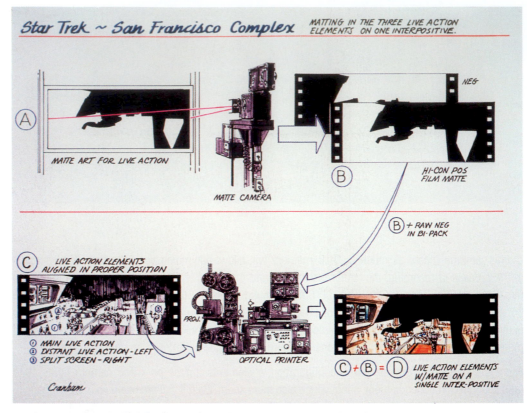

I.15 Storyboards from *Star Trek* (Robert Wise, 1979). Courtesy of Paramount/The Kobal Collection.

I.16 Director Alexander Witt (2004). Courtesy of Davis Films/Jasin Boland/The Kobal Collection.

I.17 Double exposure from *Hiroshima, Mon Amour* (Alain Resnais, 1959). Courtesy of Argos/Como/Pathé/Daiei/The Kobal Collection.

is the distance from the lens (focused on a subject in infinite space) to the film or sensor, measured in millimeters. More important, focal length determines not only the magnification of the subject, but also perspectival relations of depth and scale. We usually group lenses into three categories based upon focal length: short or wide-angle lenses, "normal" lenses, and long or telephoto lenses. Short focal length lenses, less than 35mm, intensify depth and often distort the edges of the frame (the "fisheye" effect); "normal" focal length lenses, up to 50mm, reproduce those perspectival relations we perceive with

the naked eye; and long focal length lenses, from 75mm and up, tend to flatten space. One way, therefore, to distinguish the use of a zoom lens from that of a moving camera is to watch perspectival relations – rather than simply the distance to the filmed object – change over the course of a shot.

I.18 An example of "fisheye effect" framing from *Man on a Ledge* (Asger Leth, 2012). Courtesy of Summit Entertainment/The Kobal Collection.

Framing provides us with the next set of choices: what is the optimum place for the camera to record the shot, in terms of aesthetic values and composition, conveying information, assuming a point of view, and orienting (or disorienting) the spectator? As with lighting, framing can often appear to be simply

I.19 Western horizon line in *The Searchers* (John Ford, 1956). Courtesy of Warner Bros./The Kobal Collection.

obvious or logical, but the camera's placement is crucially important for a number of different reasons. First, it divides space into **onscreen** and **offscreen** space, suggesting worlds far beyond those contained by the four edges of the frame. In **offscreen space**, filmmakers can imply actions and settings, while in **onscreen space**, filmmakers isolate the key pieces of action and information essential for a shot. Compositional patterns can develop over the course of a film or genre, such as the importance of the horizon line in the Western, or the use of offscreen space (and darkness) to generate fear and suspense in the horror film. The **angle**, **level**, **distance**, and **height** of framing are also important, especially when the shot is a **point-of-view** shot, one attributed to the vision of a character (whose exact parameters of vision the shot must mimic or assume). **Distance** is measured anthropomorphically, that is, according to the scale of the human body, in these terms (using the abbreviations filmmakers use to denote distance):

ELS: **extreme long shot**, in which the human is not or is barely distinguishable.

LS: **long shot**, in which the ground dominates the human body.

PA: *plan américain* (or "American shot"), in which the human is framed from about the knees up.

MLS: **medium long shot**, which is the same distance of framing as the *plan américain* but for non-human objects.

MS: **medium shot**, in which the human is framed from the waist up.

MCU: **medium close-up**, in which the human is framed from the chest up.

CU: **close-up**, in which the human face occupies the frame.

ECU: **extreme close-up**, in which only a portion of the human face, such as the eye, occupies the entire frame.

Framing can also involve choices of **aspect ratio**, the ratio of the width to the height of the recorded and projected image, a ratio that can be fixed by using **masks** that block borders or that can vary, such as digital cameras allow by recording in 1.1, 3.2, 4.3 or 16.9 ratios. In any case, the **aspect ratio** and other elements of presentation can change the look of a film dramatically, as historical shifts in technology have allowed for **widescreen** cinema, IMAX recording and projection, and 3D cinema.

When we add the element of movement to framing and discuss **mobile framing**, it is helpful to imagine movement along different axes. If the camera rotates around a vertical axis, the movement is known as **panning**, the most common example of which is "panning a crowd," or scanning faces simply by swiveling the camera around a stable vertical axis. If the camera rotates around a stable horizontal axis, however, that movement is called **tilting**, so that the camera tilts up, or down, toward the object or action. A tilt up to the cruel desert sun in the early minutes of the spaghetti Western *The Ruthless Four* (Giorgio Capitini, 1968) signals Sam Cooper's dizziness and imminent collapse. If the camera moves forwards or backwards across the floor, mounted on a **Dolly** or moving along trackings, it is referred to variously as a **tracking** shot, a **Dolly** shot or, less commonly, **Dollying**. If the mobile camera is lifted above ground, it is called a **crane** shot, and if the camera is moved by the human body rather than a piece of equipment, it is called **handheld** (sometimes aided by a stabilizing system such as the **Steadicam**). Stanley Kubrick devoted his career to exploring the evolving possibilities of the tracking shot and Steadicam motion. As technologies allow, the camera can be moved by anything to which it can be attached, as the GoPro HD camera can ride on skiers, hangliders, bicyclists, surfers, motorcyclist, skateboarders, and hockey players, just to name a few.

The final decision the director makes regarding a shot is its length, a matter of the film's aesthetics and also a matter of considerable debate among scholars. (By "length" we mean the shot's overall **duration** and not

I.20 *Plan américain* framing of Tim Curry from *The Rocky Horror Picture Show* (Jim Sharman, 1975). Courtesy of 20th Century Fox/The Kobal Collection.

I.21 3D film *It Came From Outer Space* (Jack Arnold, 1953). Courtesy of Universal/The Kobal Collection.

simply the length of each recorded **take**, which requires a bit of film at its beginning and end for the purposes of editing, our next section.) As we have indicated, while shots can be of relatively short or long duration, a preference for unusually long shots (not, again, a measure of camera distance but of duration), referred to as **long takes**, developed among filmmakers in order to achieve various effects; these effects include forcing something upon the viewer for contemplation, or trying a formal experiment such as our example of *People's Park* meant to suggest, or as Hitchcock managed in his film *Rope*, a film built out of only eight shots, each the precise length of a reel of film in the camera's magazine. The film theorist André Bazin put special emphasis on the long take as a technique to enlist the spectator's active interest and curiosity in the image, rather than allowing him or her to be carried along by the filmmaker's **montage**. Immersed in the long take, a spectator may discover something of the invisible image that Alexander Kluge refers to in this Interlude's opening paragraph.

I.22 Crane production still from *All Quiet on the Western Front* (Lewis Milestone, 1930). Courtesy of Universal/The Kobal Collection.

I.23 Production still from *Rope* (Alfred Hitchcock, 1948). Courtesy of Warner Bros./The Kobal Collection.

Editing

The mention of **montage**, the French term for editing and a term that refers also, and confusingly, to Soviet filmmaking of the 1920s, brings us now to editing, the joining together of shots into larger assemblages. If the shot is the smallest and most basic unit of film, the **sequence** is the next step, as a word is to a sentence. And just as we asked after a shot's duration, we can ask after a sequence's length: how long is a sequence? Usually, the answer depends upon film's coordinates of time and space: a sequence, by common definition, is a series of shots unified by time and space. Such unification is, of course, often dependent upon narrative convention and the system of **continuity editing** for narrative cinema, a system whose rules above all keep the spectator oriented in time and space. Before turning to that system, its rules (and some reasons for breaking them), it is important to learn the different types of **edits** that join one shot to another. (To translate these terms into some versions of digital editing language, the shot is the "clip," and the edit is the "transition," but most of the nomenclature and certainly the principles remain consistent across **media platforms**.)

The first and most common type of edit is the cut, which used to be made simply by splicing two lengths of film together with cement or tape: where one shot ends, the next begins. At the beginning of a film, you will often see a **fade-in**, lightening the screen progressively and from black, and at a film's end, a **fade-out**, gradually darkening the screen to black. A **dissolve** similarly takes place over time, usually a few seconds, during which the second shot is gradually superimposed over the first shot, eventually occupying the screen alone. In classical editing, a **wipe** is a means of the second shot displacing the first by pushing it out of the frame with a vertical line, while an **iris** either opens from black by means of a gradually expanding circle (like an aperture), or closes from an image to black (the classic example here is, of course, Looney Tunes' "That's all folks!"). Digital editing has made it easier to exploit the range of transitions within types (the dip dissolve, the cross dissolve, the ripple dissolve, and so on), but such transitions can just as readily reveal the amateurism of some digital filmmakers. Choices about types of transitions can come from their conventional uses – a fade to black signals time passing, a dissolve indicating a shorter period of time passing, a cut transitioning between spaces in a unified sequence, and so on – but there are no hard and fast rules as to their uses.

Editing, in other words, functions to establish *relations* between shots in four areas: (1) **graphic** relations, (2) **rhythmic** relations, (3) **spatial** relations, and (4) **temporal** relations. We have already discussed some graphic elements of the shot that emerge from choices in *mise-en-scène* and cinematography, particularly framing. Compositional care yields stunning results in the cinema of Yasujiro Ozu, for example, where patterning reveals layers of depth and complexity in the films' meaning. The repetition of a shot of a fishing boat in his film *Tokyo Story* (1953) suggests the cycle of life: where its first appearance introduced us to grief and mourning, its reappearance in the film's final shot helps us recognize the presence of death within ongoing life, timeless and cyclical. Between shots, graphic patterns can facilitate transitions: Pedro Almodóvar cuts from the circle of a stoplight to the circle of the sun in *Women on the Verge of a Nervous Breakdown* (1988). Similarly, as we have already noticed, by varying shot duration, editing creates rhythmic patterns that are sensed and felt by spectators; most notably, by decreasing shot length (fast cutting) over the course of a sequence, editors can intensify a feeling of suspense and excitement. In our discussion of screen space, we observed the creation of offscreen space via framing, and we now add to editing's function its crucial role in constructing a film's

I.24 *Good Morning* (Yasujiro Ozu, 1959). Courtesy of Shochiku Films Ltd/The Kobal Collection.

space. In a pattern called **establishment–breakdown–re-establishment**, shot A might introduce a space to us by way of an **establishing shot**: an exterior of a building, or the grounds of a university. Subsequent shots break down that space for us so that we understand further its spatial relations: the hallway leads to the meeting room, or the alley leads to the *hutong*, or the campus student center sits next to the library. Conversely, a series of shots may construct a space for us where no actual contiguity exists. Called the "**Kuleshov effect**," after a series of film experiments by the Soviet filmmaker Lev Kuleshov in the 1920s, in the *absence* of an establishing shot, audiences infer spatial contiguity (or the sense of a spatial whole) merely on the basis of two shots' juxtaposition. Finally, editing can manipulate a film's sense of time: its temporal order (for example, by including some information in **flashback**) and its temporal duration (by constructing **temporal ellipses**, or condensing the duration of actions, as almost all films do). All of these areas of editing contribute to the system of **continuity** editing, which is the dominant system for **narrative** editing.

Continuity editing

In essence, the goal of continuity editing is *to keep the spectator oriented in time and space*. As a system, it assumes that the spectator should not become confused, challenged, jarred, surprised, or

I.25 (a, b, c, d, e, and f) Kuleshov effect.

irritated *by the editing*; that is, editing, in this system, is not a tool for provocation but a system whose purpose is to maintain narrative continuity. Violating it can therefore be a powerful thing.

Let us begin with temporal continuity, then. In order to understand narrative film construction, an essential distinction between **plot** and **story** obtains. Plot defines all of those elements, including their causal relations, we actually, directly see and hear in the course of a film. In John Ford's Western, *The Searchers* (1956), for example, we meet 15-year-old Debbie (Natalie Wood), a white woman abducted by Indians whose rescue drives the narrative, in a dramatic encounter at the Comanche camp. The **story** is the entire world we *infer* from what we see and hear: we imagine Debbie's abduction by Chief Scar and her years spent as a hostage, but we don't see them onscreen. The plot, then, leads us to build **backstories** and much greater worldviews, including, in this case, a generalized fear of Indians that is a feature of many such racist captivity narratives. Plot can rearrange the temporal order of story elements, with, as we've said, some actions appearing in **flashback**. Very few elements of story time are presented in the same duration of **screen time**, however. **Characters**, those mainstays of narrative

I.26 Natalie Wood as Debbie in *The Searchers* (John Ford, 1956). Courtesy of Warner Bros./The Kobal Collection.

I.27 Part of a montage sequence from *Citizen Kane* (Orson Welles, 1941). Courtesy of RKO/The Kobal Collection.

film, rarely take baths that last for twenty minutes on screen: instead, story elements are presented, also as we've said, through narrative ellipses (entering the bathroom, steam filling the shot, and exiting with a towel). Continuity editing simply means to tell us when temporal order has changed, or when we are encountering a foreshortened time frame. A cut that simply matches the action in one shot to its extension in the next, called a **match on action**, lets us know that the hand on the door handle in shot A and the door swinging open in shot B happen in temporal succession. Editing cues help us understand: a dissolve or fade will let us know that a flashback has begun. A **montage sequence** (to be distinguished carefully from Soviet montage) is a compression of a longer period of time (a decade of marriage, a war, the first century of a nation's growth) into a short sequence, for example of newspaper headlines spanning the period, or, in Alan Parker's Irish film *The Commitments* (1991), a series of hopefuls turning up at the door for auditions for the soul band.

Spatial continuity is slighter harder to control, and so the system of continuity editing to ensure spatial orientation is a bit more complicated. If a match on action suggests temporal continuity, it also suggests spatial contiguity: same hand, same door, same space. Two other editing tactics for ensuring spatial continuity are the patterns of **shot/reverse shot** and the **eyeline match**, which we explain after explaining the broader system of spatial orientation upon which all three of these tactics rely.

The **180-degree system** is that overall system. At its heart is a line that runs directly through the (real or imaginary) space the film wishes to construct for each sequence: the central gathering space in a village, an office, a parade or an apartment room. That line is called the **180-degree line** or the **axis of action** (or sometimes simply the **center line**). The line functions in two key ways: maintaining common space from shot to shot and maintaining consistent screen direction. And the key to both is this: for each shot in a given sequence, the camera must remain on the same side of the axis of action; this is called the **180-degree rule**.

In order to think about maintaining common space from shot to shot, imagine shooting a conversation in shot/reverse shot sequence. Shot/reverse shot is such a common pattern of editing in narrative film that you may observe it in almost any film you choose (and it has been extended to television and other media). Used to establish spatial continuity between characters, it involves in its most limited grammar a pattern of shots A, B, C, and D:

> Shot A: a **twoshot** or shot of two characters, let us call them Xavier and Magneto, occupying the same space (playing chess, let us say), across from one another – we see only their hands on the chess pieces.

> Shot B: a medium close-up shot of Xavier taken from the shoulder of Magneto, such that we see the torso of Xavier as he makes his move.

> Shot C: a medium close-up shot of Magneto taken from the shoulder of Xavier and therefore from the reverse perspective of Xavier, looking at Magneto.

> Shot D: a twoshot of the characters from roughly the same position as shot A.

In this shot/reverse shot sequence, actually taken from the film of the *X-Men* (Bryan Singer, 2000), the wonderful actors Patrick Stewart (as Xavier) and Ian McKellen (as Magneto) remain on one side of the axis of action, so that we see one wall of the glass cube behind each of them in shot and reverse shot. We can make further sense of the space's continuity because it carries over from shot to shot: a bit of the chessboard, a bit of the segmented wall. In the sense of establishing the two characters as inhabiting a common space and then showing us each character's position within it, such a shot/reverse shot sequence also partakes of the pattern of establishment/breakdown/re-establishment we have discussed. An eyeline match likewise helps to maintain orientation in space. Shot A shows us a character looking at something or someone offscreen. Shot B shows us what the character in shot A was looking at. From such an edit, the spectator is able to discern directionality and narrative focus at the same time.

Sometimes, breaking rules of the continuity system introduces new stylistic possibilities that become themselves identified with movements or cycles of filmmaking. In France in the 1960s, filmmakers identified as the "New Wave" broke a rule we haven't discussed yet: the **30-degree rule**. In order for shots to be recognizably distinct from one another for a shot/reverse shot sequence, the change in

I.28 *X-Men* (Bryan Singer, 2000). Courtesy of 20th Century Fox/Marvel Ent Group/Attila Dory/The Kobal Collection.

camera angle from one shot to the next must be greater than 30 degrees. Otherwise, if the change in angle is smaller, characters will simply appear to "jump" from one position in the frame to another. Exploiting that effect, filmmakers such as Jean-Luc Godard employed smaller-than-required variations deliberately to produce the "**jump cut**." His film *À Bout de Souffle* (*Breathless*) (1960) provides classic illustrations of the technique, used to call attention to the fact that the world of the film is a constructed, rather than naturalized, one.

Godard continues a tradition of ideological and aesthetic provocation begun with the Soviet practices of **montage**, now understood as a way of thinking about the collision of images to produce new realities and politics. In the work of Dziga Vertov, in his film *Man with a Movie Camera* (1929), cinematic vision becomes the vision of a new revolutionary society, capable of harnessing the energy of modernity (of which cinema is but one technological representative). (You can contribute to an internet based, worldwide, shot-for-shot remake of Vertov's film through **Man with a Movie Camera: The Global Remake**, a creative digital project by Perry Bard that continually updates an archive of submitted images to remake the film, at dziga.perrybard.net.) In the work of Sergei Eisenstein, we have already observed the montage of attractions (in the example of the rotting meat from *Battleship Potemkin*). Eisenstein, however, developed an elaborate conception of montage that more properly emerges from composition and editing over the course of a sequence; **intellectual montage** describes the near-total calibration of images as they clash into one another to agitate the sensual responses of audiences and ultimately awaken them to revolutionary consciousness. Like another master of cinematic calibration, Alfred Hitchcock, Eisenstein believed in the power of images to stir deep emotions that could lead to revolutionary action.

Experimental films that break with narrative conventions rarely adhere to the system of continuity editing, or they allude to it in order to play with our expectations. Maya Deren's films, such as *Meshes of the Afternoon* (1943) and *At Land* (1944), famously fracture spatial continuity in order to explore interior consciousness, in order to produce, as she would write, "a reality in its own terms." Experimental studies of light and motion, such as Ralph Steiner's dazzling study of water in *H2O* (1929) or Austrian filmmaker Peter Kubelka's patterns of positive and negative images of dancers in a bar in *Adebar* (1957), dispense with continuity editing because they are not particularly interested in narrative, characters, or temporal order. Instead, they rely almost entirely upon graphic and rhythmic editing, sometimes under self-imposed systems or rules of **structural** filmmaking, especially popular in the 1960s and 1970s in Europe and the United States. Likewise, while some documentary films forsake continuity editing in favor of more experimental or radical ends, many rely upon its rules in order to make their arguments. Michael Moore's controversial documentary *Roger and Me* (1989) played with the temporal order of sequences involving his quest for Roger Smith, the CEO of General Motors, whom Moore accuses of causing the destruction of Flint, Michigan. **Cross-cutting** (a form of **parallel editing** that creates the illusion of simultaneous action) the footage of the GM Shareholders meeting with an eviction, Moore creates a causal argument: the greed of GM caused the family's downfall. Although Moore was criticized for suggesting simultaneity when it did not in fact exist, such is the power of cinema to create arguments and fodder for political debate.

Sound

Meshes of the Afternoon serves as a useful bridge to our final category of film form, sound. Shot initially as a silent film, *Meshes* became a sound film with the later addition, in 1956, of a sound track by Deren's third husband, composer Teiji Ito. The track combines two elements of film sound: **music** and **sound effects**, in this case fused together into a single chain of sound that both responds to and retreats from the images onscreen in a complex dance. In order to think further about the relationship between sounds within the world of the film and those imposed from without, we distinguish initially between **diegetic** and **non-diegetic** sound. Essentially, diegetic sound belongs to the story world inhabited by characters in the film: if Toto the dog barks in *The Wizard of Oz* (1939), Dorothy hears him. Non-diegetic sound, such as music, often serves as a cue for the spectator but is not heard by the characters: when the violins swell in a melodramatic moment, we don't assume that the characters are listening to them! Sound is thus composed of both diegetic and non-diegetic elements in three areas: music, sound effects (sometimes called **noise**), and **speech**. All three must be selected, mixed and calibrated in relation to the edited images to which they will be matched.

Just as filmmakers shape every dimension of the sequence through mise-en-scène, cinematography, and editing, so too do they actively shape sound for different sorts of film. Some of the questions proposed by film sound scholar James Lastra to address the shape and materiality of sound include the following:

> How do we create sound continuity? How do we enhance or support narration? How can we create the impression of subjectivity? Why is it important to understand that sound is manipulated if we cannot readily perceive these manipulations? How is film sound related to radio, phonography, and popular music recording? Are there different forms of listening?[3]

We can apply further criteria for analysis to do with broader dimensions of film sound to the three categories of sound we have discussed. In considering the editing of visual materials, we have already alluded to the first dimension, **rhythm**. The second dimension is **fidelity**, a term with at least two meanings. The first meaning belongs to the measurement of the accuracy of a copy to its original: a worn-out vinyl record will be of lower fidelity to the master recording than a remastered compact disc. The second meaning, however, is what concerns us more readily in describing film sound: fidelity here denotes the sound's faithfulness to its source. Comedy often exploits sonic infidelity: an exaggeratedly high voice emanates from an angry and threatening dog in Pixar's *Up* (Pete Docter and Bob Peterson, 2009). Sources and sounds aren't simply "there" in some unmediated fashion, however. Sounds are produced through different distances from the microphone ("**miking**"), producing different degrees of clarity and focus, and creating spatial relationships in the process. The third dimension, then, is this **spatial dimension** of sound. A sound source can be onscreen or offscreen, and indeed offscreen sound sources help us map space and understand aspects of narrative. Finally, sound has a **temporal dimension**. We usually expect **synchronous** sound in which sound pairs with image during projection; **asynchronous** mismatches between sound and image are often a source of frustration or of comedy. But there are many instances in which recorded sound is necessarily "out of sync" with the image. In processes of shooting without resources for recorded sound, the sound track, including dialogue, might be added to the film after editing; such was the case for many spaghetti Westerns, for which many supporting actors did not speak the English lines that were later **dubbed** or inserted into the sound track (this is an example of **postsynchronization**). Another distinction that obtains in the temporal dimension is that between diegetic **simultaneous** (sound taking place at the same time as the story event) and diegetic **non-simultaneous** sound (sound occurring earlier or later than the story event). Hearing the voice of a dead character is a common example of the latter.

Film soundtracks are composed of layers of carefully recorded sound, with the primary sound element at any given time being that which is most important for the filmmaker's purpose. If it's crucial that we hear something in the scene's dialogue, speech takes prominence; if the sequence is meant to tug at our heart strings, music may prevail.

Any element may therefore serve different functions. Music, for example, can do all of the following:

- establish mood;
- help to identify genre and location (the time and place of the film's story);
- identify people, objects and themes through motifs or leitmotifs;
- offer ideological critique;
- connect to other commodities (sound tracks, songs);
- serve as an onscreen event (as in musical performers and performances);
- connect to sub- and counter-cultures;
- provide a window onto other social contradictions and tensions;
- and even suggest utopias (which are always grounded in material histories). As Richard Dyer points out, while people were hungry and deprived during the Great Depression, they especially enjoyed the lavish spectacle and opulence of Busby Berkeley musicals.[4]

Since the development of classical narrative norms for sound, the layered sound track has consisted of a background that provides consistency (often using sound to link two shots together, through the use of a **sound bridge**) and a foreground that works in relation to the image (not always to reinforce it): they create a **soundscape** that is appropriate to the film's world. Modern sound recording introduces two further changes in the nature of that soundscape. First, recording technologies (including noise reduction technologies) have allowed for greatly expanded dynamic and frequency ranges: lower lows, higher highs, denser sound. Second, the ability to sculpt sound in space through multichannel **surround sound** has allowed for both a greater focus on place (location and ambience) and a more immersive sonic experience for the spectator. As you find yourself increasingly plunged into sonic worlds of cinema, try to describe them as carefully as you can, and to ask over and again: "What is this sound *doing*?"

MAKERS OF CINEMA

In his book *How Movies Work*, Bruce Kawin observes the work of a film shoot in a wonderful description we cite in its two opening paragraphs here:

> It is 1978, and we are on the set of *Prophecy* (1979), a generously budgeted horror film about the environmental effects of mercury poisoning. It is 11 a.m. The crew has been setting up a shot since early morning. The floor of the sound stage is covered with cables and is marked with pieces of tape. A cabin has been constructed in the center of the sound stage: it has three walls and a roof. Where the fourth wall ought to be, there is an array of cameras and personnel. Director John Frankenheimer is talking with the cinematographer about the framing of the shot.

He has already discussed the shot with the performers, Robert Foxworth and Talia Shire, who are off in their dressing rooms for final makeup. Up on the cabin's roof, two crew members are rigging a stick of dynamite. Now Frankenheimer goes over to a tall youth in a basketball uniform and explains what he wants him to do. The youth smiles affably and climbs into a huge bear suit. Shire appears, attended by a makeup artist who is spraying water into her hair to make her look as if she has just struggled out of a lake. The lake, which is supposed to be just outside the cabin, is actually in the Northwest [of the United States], and this studio shot must be made to match the details of the previously-shot location material. Foxworth looks all business, and even Shire looks like a businesslike drowned rat.

The sound track in this scene will consist entirely of effects: the sounds of feet, a door, and a smashed roof. The production mixer (head of the sound crew) sits behind a blocky console; on a pad, he notes that this shot will be MOS, that is, silent. **MOS** stands for "mit-out sound" and is a continuing industry joke on the German directors who came to Hollywood in the late 1920s and early 1930s and preferred to add sound to their shots in post-production. The production mixer leans over to a colleague and whispers, "I hope his next film is a talkie."[5]

While Kawin's account of working on set is one of the best in the film studies literature, there are proliferating additional sources for learning the collaborative dynamics of the **production** phase of filmmaking, including the "making of" bonus features on DVDs and other behind the scenes videos, press coverage, YouTube material, and studio publicity. Few individual stories provide the big picture, from pre-production to distribution, so in what follows we use the making of a successful small budget film, *Beasts of the Southern Wild* (Zeitlin, 2012), as an anchor for identifying the roles of individuals and also exploring the ethos of collaborative artmaking. We chose *Beasts* in part because it is provocative (at the level of its environmentalism, its fantasy elements, its racial and gender politics, and its relation to place), in part because it is a film in which many strands of work converge beautifully (art direction, special effects, location shooting, community participation), and in part because it was made by young people whose passions about storytelling were fueled in high school and college, people, in other words, like you.

Filmmaking personnel

Beasts began as a one-act play, *Juicy and Delicious*, by Lucy Alibar, telling the story of Hushpuppy, a young boy who confronts the illness and death of his father. Alibar reworked that **source** material with her friend Benh Zeitlin, whom Alibar had met as a teenager at Young Playwrights Inc., a New York theatre for young people founded by Stephen Sondheim. Zeitlin would become the film's **director**. The two developed a **screenplay** over the course of more than a year's work and receive joint **screenwriting** credit for the script, which remakes the main character into an African-American girl rather than a white boy and relocates the action from the play's setting in Georgia to rural Louisiana. **Location scouts** sought out communities steeped in the bayou waters and isolated by levees and found Terrebone Parish, Louisiana, where the film was ultimately shot. Zeitlin belongs to a group of family and friends he co-founded called Court 13: artists who call themselves a "grassroots, independent filmmaking army" (www.court13.com) and who collaborate on projects, of which *Beast* is the first feature-length film. Based upon the screenplay's promise, Zeitlin received funding for the film from sources including Sundance, a non-profit group called Cinereach, the San Francisco Film Society, and the Japanese broadcaster NHK. The funding then comes under the control of the

I.29 Court 13 Headquarters.

I.30 Casting flyers for *Beasts of the Southern Wild* (Benh Zeitlin, 2012).

I.31 Quvenzhané Wallis.

I.32 Dwight Henry.

films' team of producers: the **producers**, who enable the assemblage of money, talent, and personnel; the **executive producers**, who play some special key contributing role to bringing the film to fruition; and those **co-producers**, **producers** and **associate producers** who work with them. The **line producer** is the person on set day to day who keeps the production on track and reports to the studio. Traveling to rural Louisiana for **pre-production** for *Beasts*, then, a group of about thirty amateurs and young professionals set up the Court 13 shop in an old gas station.

While the director and production team worked with storyboards and other resources to begin to imagine bringing the screenplay to life, **location scouts** and the **production designer** began to identify places and means to build the film's worlds, to bring the community of the Bathtub to the screen. In place of a **casting director** (who would invite professional actors to read for major roles), members of the Court 13 group conducted auditions in the community for **non-professional actors**, eventually identifying the then-five year-old Quvenzhané Wallis for the role of Hushpuppy and a baker across the street from Court 13's New Orleans office, Dwight Henry, for the role of Wink. From a year spent after college in Prague, Zeitlin had known Ben Richardson, whom Zeitlin brought from England to serve as **cinematographer**.

In this particular production, large teams contributed to the **art department**, the **visual effects** team, and the **special effects** team. Zeitlin's sister Eliza contributed her own art, and many other amateurs and professionals invented the detailed world of Beasts. Through a DIY (do-it-yourself) aesthetic and ethos, the teams (including the production designer, the **art director**, the **costume designer**, the **props master**, the **make up artist**, the **hair designer**, and many others) started to ponder the challenges of the relation between the more realist action and the film's fantasy components, primarily the melting ice fields and the migration of the ten-foot tall "aurochs," the extinct species of wild cattle who haunt the film (and are just one of the "beasts" of the title).

I.33 Art direction on the set of *Beasts of the Southern Wild* (Benh Zeitlin, 2012).

In and around the Court 13's gas station headquarters, the crew began finding and building sets on location, creating the details of *mise-en-scène* crucial to the story's places: Lady Jo's store, the Elysian Fields floating barge, the School Boat and Ark, and the houses for the main characters. A sunken school bus became Wink's house, while a pair of oil drums provided a foundation for Hushpuppy's short-lived house. When Zeitlin's pickup truck inexplicably exploded on set, part of its chassis provided the infrastructure for the Horse Beast ridden by Wink in the town parade, while the truck's bed became Wink's boat, The Turck (Hushpuppy's spelling of "truck").

Meanwhile, wanting to work with real animals for the aurochs (in addition to the **miniatures** and **puppets** used in the film), the film's **animal trainer** decided to raise and train a litter of Vietnamese pot-bellied pigs, little animals who, with some modifications, would appear to Hushpuppy as larger-than-life compatriots of the Earth. (There is also a credited **pig adoption services** person, who may in fact be the sister of the animal trainer!) Under the supervision of Ray Tintori, the **Aurochs and Special Effects Unit Director**, five of the pigs were taught to wear costumes, do tricks, and run on treadmills to film **green-screen** shots that would later contribute to **matte** or **composite** shots of the aurochs in the world of the Bathtub. Tintori painstakingly added fur and tusks to the pigs to create the effect of the otherworldly creatures and worked through the duration of the film's **production** to bring these images to fruition. Since the film fuses the human and animal worlds so insistently, the animal crew had responsibility for many animals beyond the aurochs (goats, dogs, chickens …).

I.34 Aurochs in *Beasts of the Southern Wild* (Benh Zeitlin, 2012).

I.35 Zeitlin's pickup truck explodes on the set of *Beasts of the Southern Wild* (Benh Zeitlin, 2012).

I.36 An animal trainer with a pot-bellied pig on the set of *Beasts of the Southern Wild* (Benh Zeitlin, 2012).

I.37 A greenscreen shot from *Beasts of the Southern Wild* (Benh Zeitlin, 2012).

I.38 Fur and tusks on a pot-bellied pig.

I.39 Grips and the director of *Beasts of the Southern Wild* (Benh Zeitlin, 2012).

I.40 Pyrotechnics on the set of *Beasts of the Southern Wild* (Benh Zeitlin, 2012).

I.41 Screening of the weekly dailies with the cast and crew of *Beasts of the Southern Wild* (Benh Zeitlin, 2012).

Shooting the film involved a whole new set of workers, the **crew**, who handled the cinematography, lighting, stunts, special effects, and miscellaneous labors, from creating hurricanes to handling a crocodile. **Grips** work with cameras and with lighting: the **key grip** handles camera movement and works closely with the DP and the gaffer (who, you'll remember, is the chief lighting technician). The **Dolly grip** handles the camera moving on a Dolly or a track. For the many shots in *Beasts* that take place on the water, however, grips had to set up camera equipment and lighting from boats, under the auspices of the **transportation coordinator**. The **best boy grip** is the chief assistant to the **key grip**, that is, the second in charge of the grips, while the **best boy electric** is the second in charge of the electric. Others who work with the camera equipment include a **first assistant camera** and a **film loader**. During production, the director relies heavily on the **production manager**, who works under the line producer on all of the physical/technical aspects of production, including the daily budget and shooting schedule; a **production coordinator**, in turn, handles all of the logistics for the production manager. Additional **units**, such as the special effects unit, report to a **unit manager**. Helping the director are also the **first assistant director**, who oversees the working context for the shoot – such as making clear the motivation and action for actors and extras in a given shot – and who makes sure that the film comes in on schedule, while the **second assistant director** is responsible for creating **call sheets** for daily shooting.

The credits for *Beasts* reveal a whole range of other jobs and tasks on set or off: childcare, tutoring for child actors, chefs and caterers, medics, acting coaches, legal consultants, lifeguards and swim instructors, demolition workers, and stunt coordinator. A **pyrotechnics coordinator** managed to conduct the many explosions that take place in *Beasts* safely, controlling those fires and rockets and smoke that all contribute to the film's fantastic feel. In an unusual practice, the entire cast and crew gathered for weekly parties to screen the week's **dailies**, the footage they've collectively produced each day. To a high degree, the production stage of *Beasts* was an inclusive and collaborative process, unlike even many independent productions that reproduce Hollywood hierarchies.

I.42 The cast and crew of *Beasts of the Southern Wild* (Benh Zeitlin, 2012).

Post-production joins the footage shot during the production stage, and the sound recorded during it as well, to the digital production process and editing stage. Although the aurochs in *Beasts* were developed while shooting of the film, post-production editing (by **editors** Crockett Doob and Affonso Gonçalves) and work by the team in visual effects allowed them to join the world of Hushpuppy. A group of **compositors**, responsible for those composite shots we discussed earlier, made it possible for Hushpuppy to look into the eyes of an aurochs (a process discussed helpfully at length in the documentary *Making of …*). Editors determine the rhythms of the story: everything from Wink's furious chase of Hushpuppy while her house burns to the frenzied escape from the rescue shelter, both set against the slower rhythms of the floodwaters and the mournful time next to Wink's deathbed.

Visual rhythms are accompanied by sounds: first, the sound effects created by the **Foley artist**, recorded by the **Foley mixer**, and edited by the **Foley editor**. Named after Jack Foley, who created the art of post-production sound for Universal Studios when it made the transition to sound film (in the late 1920s), Foley artists generally recreate what are thought to be the "realistic" sounds that the props and sets were unable to generate. When the storm comes to Bathtub, and Hushpuppy and Wink hear its havoc, those were Foley sounds added to footage recorded MOS. With regard to speech, Hushpuppy's voice in **voice-over** is also added in post-production, as are some elements of dialogue through the **automatic dialogue replacement** (or **ADR**) process, all supervised by the **dialogue editor**.

What is perhaps most compelling about the use of sound in *Beasts* is its score, also a collaborative effort by director Zeitlin and Dan Bromer. Few directors compose their own scores, among them horror specialists Dario Argento and John Carpenter (as well as Indian director of the parallel cinema, Satyajit Ray), but Zeitlin's ability to tell stories through both images and music seems clear from *Beasts*. With its memorable melodies and pop hooks, the score is almost entirely of their making; snippets from two Louisiana artists – Leroy "Happy Fats"" LeBlanc and the Balfa Brothers – also find their way into scenes in the Bathtub. Composed over a two-week period of twenty-hour work days, the score emphasizes strings (particularly the sounds of the fiddle), a trumpet, and the celesta (a keyboard instrument popular in film scores and featured in John Williams' score for two of the *Harry Potter* films). If you listen carefully to the *Beasts* score, you can distinguish themes used in the sequences in the Bathtub from those used in scenes outside the tightly knit community.

Although we haven't listed everyone, we'll end with those **production assistants** who do much of what we haven't covered: move that, hold this, stand over there, tape that down. As much as filmmaking has become a process involving computers and digital imagery, it remains the magic of electricity, light, bodies, and spaces. And lots of work.

NOTES

1 Noelene Clark, "'Hobbit' Costume Designer Ann Mackrey's Favorite Look? Radagast," *The Los Angeles Times*, http://herocomplex.latimes.com/2012/12/02/hobbit-costume-designer-ann-maskreys-favorite-look-radagast/, accessed 19 January 2015.

2 Jon D. Winter, "Neorealism in Downtown L.A.," *American Cinematographer* (November 2012), http://www.theasc.com/ac_magazine/November2012/ShortTakes/page1.php, accessed 19 January 2015.

3 James F. Lastra, "Teaching Film Sound," in Lucy Fischer and Patrice Petro (eds), *Teaching Film* (New York: MLA, 2012), 289.

4 Richard Dyer, "Entertainment and Utopia," in Rick Altman, *Genre: The Musical* (London and Boston: Routledge and Kegan Paul, 1981), 175–189.

5 Bruce Kawin, *How Movies Work* (Berkeley: University of California Press, 1992), 288.

WHERE DO MOVIES GO?

INTRODUCTION

Film production involves a series of collaborations among the personnel who participate in the creation of films – from gaffers to costume designers, from stunt performers to directors – and among the institutions that finance films – from banks to studios to international co-production partnerships. The previous section introduced you to the obstacles and opportunities that shape film production from the initial moments of securing financing for a film during the pre-production phase to the final moments of editing a film during the post-production phase.

This section maps where films go. It traces a new network of global pathways, following films after they are produced as they travel to reach distributors, audiences, critics and archives. It introduces you to industrial and cultural practices that are often overlooked in the analysis of film: marketing, distribution, exhibition, criticism and preservation. Our overview of these sectors of the film industry traverses poster design, piracy, film festivals, online film criticism and film archives, among a range of other topics.

Chapter 9, "Marketing," examines how markets for films are framed, profiling the forms of market research that studios conduct to determine which films to make and how to sell them to their target audiences. This chapter (like the chapter on distribution that follows it) situates a focused analysis of contemporary industrial practices within a discussion of foundational moments in film history and important alternative models. Film marketing involves the identification and analysis of target audiences, the development of hooks to feature in advertising campaigns, and the production of promotional materials. Many discussions of marketing (of films and of other products) define these practices as manipulative. While this book acknowledges the presence of deceptive tactics in film marketing, we focus on the interpretive force of film marketing. Posters, trailers and other marketing texts offer not only previews of the films they advertise but also interpretations of the films. Many of these texts (for example, film posters) are works of art in their own right and invite both industrial and aesthetic analysis.

Marketing efforts are often coordinated with distribution strategies. Chapter 10, "Distribution," outlines the dominant distribution models for contemporary commercial cinema, explaining the role of distributors, the available timelines for releasing commercial films and the destinations for film (a topic discussed at much greater length in the subsequent chapter on film exhibition). Chapter 10 emphasizes the importance of distribution for both the profitability of individual films, studios and national film industries and the vitality and diversity of regional film cultures. Most films will never enjoy the global distribution of the limited number of Hollywood blockbusters that reach audiences in many countries within a very short period of time, but some of these films reach audiences through alternative distribution networks. We profile several of these networks, from an online indigenous media platform to a corporate pornography distributor, to signal the many ways that films travel outside studio-controlled circuits.

Chapter 11, "Exhibition," then follows films to the destinations mentioned in our discussion of distribution. Spaces of exhibition involve more than just a screen. This chapter invites you to consider the material and social conditions that define different exhibition venues. From outdoor screenings to home exhibition, this chapter explores the many different forms that "cinema" may take. The location of the theatre (or other viewing environment), the size of the screen and the number of people in the room are only a few of the elements of film exhibition that might transform your viewing experience. This chapter presents both historical and theoretical accounts of these spaces and practices to give you a clearer understanding of the ways that exhibition impacts the film industry and our experiences of watching films.

Chapter 12, "Evaluative contexts," focuses on the reception of film within spheres of critical authority, including film criticism, film festivals and film awards. These discussions enable an analysis of the formation of film canons – collectively produced lists of the "best" films. Canon formation involves shifting definitions of the value of cinema, and different participants in the formation of a film canon (including critics, scholars and curators) may have conflicting values and approaches. This chapter (like the book as a whole) does not insist on a specific canon of global cinema, but it acknowledges the role of canon formation in generating revenue for filmmakers, studios and distributors, and in creating interest in specific films as works of art.

Canon formation is linked to practices of film preservation. Often resources for film preservation are devoted to films that are widely recognized to be of critical importance. Chapter 13, "The longevity of films," introduces the work of film preservation, explaining the logistics and politics of film archives, the different practices involved in the preservation of celluloid film and digital cinema, and the issues of access and authenticity that animate discussions of preservation. Introducing the material decay of film and the (alleged) death of cinema as industrial and critical preoccupations, this chapter draws your attention to the afterlives of films in private and public archives.

The first three chapters of this section trace the path a film follows from production to exhibition: marketing–distribution–exhibition. In fact, the activities of marketing, distribution and exhibition often overlap. Distributors, for example, work very closely with marketing teams and may produce or commission their own marketing materials. So, while it is logical to see marketing–distribution–exhibition as a series of sequential steps, these practices are at the very least dependent on each other and in some cases intertwined. Chapter 12 and Chapter 13 complicate our understanding of the routes that films travel by underscoring the fact that most films remain difficult to find through major distribution channels. The corporate structures that favor the global distribution and exhibition of a small number of films (as outlined in Chapters 9, 10 and 11) limit the number of films that most people can access in theatres, and to a lesser extent in home exhibition. The cultural institutions profiled in Chapters 12 and 13 may expand the number of films that we watch by advocating for the value of films that are not promoted by major studios. However, these institutions (and the individuals whose tastes define them) may also limit our access even further by isolating only a small selection of films for their praise and preservation. The chapters that follow in this section will give you the tools to recognize where films go and why they circulate (or fail to circulate) in certain patterns.

CHAPTER NINE
MARKETING

After the Sony Pictures Classics logo flashes on the screen, the trailer cuts to a series of lush landscape shots as the familiar male voice-over begins:

> In a land of eternal beauty and infinite mystery, a legend was born. The story of a warrior, the woman he loved, a daring outlaw, and a princess destined to become a warrior. Sony Pictures Classics proudly presents: Chow Yun-Fat, Michelle Yeoh, and Ziyi Zhang in an extraordinary romantic adventure. From Ang Lee, the director of *Sense and Sensibility* ... *Crouching Tiger, Hidden Dragon*.

Don LaFontaine narrates this trailer. A ubiquitous aural presence in American film culture until his death in 2008, he introduced many audiences to the films that were coming soon to their local theatres. In over 5,000 trailer voice-overs, he made dramatic pronouncements about what audiences might see "in a world" where a new cinematic experience was about to unfold. The clichéd nature of these voice-overs points to the predictable structure of film trailers. LaFontaine's voice-overs elide the differences among the many films he helped to market, temporarily transforming all of those films into "extraordinary" Hollywood "adventures."

The trailer for *Crouching Tiger, Hidden Dragon* (*Wo hu cang long*, Ang Lee, 2000) packages the film as a familiar Hollywood epic. The editing of the selected shots and the accompanying voice-over use a series of rhetorical appeals, or marketing hooks, to attract as large an audience as possible to the theatre. A brief review of these rhetorical appeals demonstrates the complex series of marketing strategies packed into the two-minute trailer. First, the trailer introduces the film's three popular stars – Chow Yun-Fat, Michelle Yeoh, and Ziyi Zhang – showing a series of close-up shots of the three actors as LaFontaine recites their names. Once they are introduced, most of the subsequent shots feature one or more of these actors. Shots from the film's many action sequences follow, defining the film as an action film (or a *wuxia* martial arts film, to be more precise). The final shots of the trailer reveal glimpses of the "romantic adventure" announced by the voice-over, repositioning the film as a romantic drama. Finally, the closing lines of the voice-over brand the film as a product of its director, Ang Lee, linking the film to his other prestige productions, particularly *Sense and Sensibility* (1995). This short trailer efficiently and clearly markets the film's main stars, its genres, and its director, simultaneously soliciting the interest of multiple (perhaps overlapping) segments of the trailer's audience. This chapter will examine trailers as part of a broad spectrum of film marketing in order to reveal how films are sold to particular audiences.

WHAT WE WILL DO IN CHAPTER 9

- Review the key demographic factors – nationality, gender, age, and media usage – that studios consider when addressing film markets.
- Analyze the elements of film – including genres, stars, and directors – that marketing campaigns foreground.
- Investigate the individual components of a marketing campaign, including posters, trailers, and social media marketing.

BY THE END OF CHAPTER 9 YOU SHOULD BE ABLE TO

- Describe the strategies used to market films domestically and internationally.
- Explain the connections between film marketing and film production, distribution, and reception.
- Analyze film posters, trailers and other marketing paratexts.

FRAMING FILM MARKETS

In 1910, Carl Laemmle, head of the Independent Motion Pictures Company, intentionally circulated the false story that Florence Lawrence, the actress who was starring in his upcoming film *The Broken Oath*, had been killed in a car accident. He then promptly released a full-page announcement in the paper *Moving Picture World* denouncing the story as a lie. Laemmle transformed the public shock in response to Lawrence's death and their subsequent confusion and curiosity in response to the revelation that she was still alive into buzz for *The Broken Oath*. A publicity stunt produced an excited film audience. This anecdote is often cited as the foundational moment of the Hollywood star system. It may also be recognized as one of the foundational moments of film marketing.

Film marketing includes promotion and publicity. The official **promotion** for a film and the official and unofficial **publicity** for a film often overlap in ways that are difficult to untangle. Promotion includes official advertisements (posters, trailers, and social media campaigns), official events (for example, the film's stars being interviewed on a television talk show or in a magazine), and cross-promotional initiatives (including synergistic branding strategies). Publicity includes these promotional efforts along with reviews (by critics and fans), gossip (including features in tabloid magazines and on television shows), and leaks (which, as the Carl Laemmle example illustrates, may or may not be true and may or may not originate from an official source). This chapter will focus on film promotion, with the emphasis on the domestic and global marketing of contemporary Hollywood film. The introduction to contemporary film marketing strategies, from market research to social media marketing, focuses on the marketing campaigns launched by major Hollywood studios in support of films in wide theatrical release, but many of the practices discussed are also used by other film industries around the world.

Film marketing campaigns unfold over a long period of time, with new marketing elements introduced at set intervals. Sometimes teaser trailers or unofficial "leaked" footage may circulate online over a year before a film's release. The official trailer may surface in theatres several months before the film's release. Then, several weeks before the film's release, short trailers will appear on television, and print and multimedia advertisements will surface (from newspaper and magazine ads to websites to interactive games to billboards). Studios may invest tens of millions of US dollars on a single marketing campaign. During the era of studio conglomeration, studios spent the bulk of their marketing budgets on television advertising, but the growth of the audience for new media advertising has started to shift marketing priorities towards internet advertising and other new media venues. The timeline for rolling out a marketing campaign and the nature of that campaign will be adjusted based on the audience that a studio has in mind.

9.1 Director Quentin Tarantino promoting *Kill Bill: Vol. 1* on the talk show *Jimmy Kimmel Live* (2003). Courtesy of ABC-TV/The Kobal Collection.

When marketing a film, producers and distributors define the potential audiences for it according to several factors – geographic location (nationally and regionally), demographic identities (focusing primarily on age and gender but also considering race, religion, and other aspects of identity for the marketing of specific films), and media usage (what audiences read, write, watch, and play and where). This section will review the ways that marketing teams pitch films to audiences based on these market segmentations. It is important to note at the outset of this discussion that these divisions are necessarily very reductive. A studio's assumptions about the films that will appeal to people in particular demographic groups will not reflect the tastes of everyone in those groups. While these market speculations are generalizations (and often reinforce stereotypes), they exert significant influence on the decisions by studios to greenlight films for production and on their subsequent decisions about how to market those films.

Marketing research

Market research has been a part of the film industry since its inception. Film scholar Finola Kerrigan notes that even before the introduction of the "sneak preview" screenings in the 1930s, film producers and exhibitors conducted informal market research. In the 1920s, theatre ushers waited in the restrooms after screenings to ask audience members for their reactions to the films they had just seen.[1]

Market research has become increasingly important since the **conglomeration** of Hollywood studios. The large media conglomerates that bought Hollywood studios in the 1960s applied market research methods from their other corporate holdings (for example, businesses in the energy and publishing industries) to the film industry in order to reduce the financial risk of each production. The need for expanded marketing budgets (and extensive market research to direct the spending of these budgets) has been produced by the growing popularity of **saturation release** distribution. When a studio slates a film for saturation release, it releases the film in hundreds or thousands of theatres simultaneously. This strategy limits the impact of **word-of-mouth marketing**; studios and exhibitors don't have time to allow films to build interest among audiences over time. Films in saturation release need to make money very quickly, and marketing campaigns for saturation release films aim to drive as many people to the theatre on the opening weekend as possible. Studios thus need to invest much more money in pre-release marketing, and they need to identify and locate the target audience for each film in order to spend that money as efficiently as possible. The high cost of advertising, particularly television advertising, makes advance market research a necessity for films with large marketing budgets.

In his analysis of high concept cinema (discussed in relation to film production in Chapter 6, "Starting points"), Justin Wyatt outlines three forms of pre-production market research: **concept testing**, **casting tests**, and **title tests**:

> Concept testing involves breaking down a script into a short concept, which is then read to respondents so that the attractive (read "marketable") elements might be identified. Similarly, casting tests are designed to identify marketable stars and the match between a star and a particular concept, while title tests gauge the connotations suggested by a particular title.[2]

Most market research, however, takes place after a film has been made. Pre-selected audiences are invited to advance screenings. After the film, audience members complete written surveys, and they may also be asked to become part of a **focus group** to discuss their reactions to the film in more detail.

Wyatt notes that pre-production market research favors **high concept** film ideas. Audiences are more likely to understand a familiar story idea or respond favorably to a familiar star. Innovative concepts and casting choices are more likely to be rejected by audiences during the pre-production phase. Post-production marketing offers audiences a complete cut of the film to evaluate, so it is inherently more reliable. However, the reactions of the audience after the screening represent a very small audience sample. It is difficult to build a profile of the overall potential audience for a film based on the small sample audiences involved in market research.

Domestic and international markets

One of the primary factors a marketing team considers is the geographical location of the audience. Different national and regional film cultures enjoy different film genres and film styles. Marketing teams study these cultural expectations through market research and tailor their marketing campaigns to individual global regions to satisfy those tastes. Film marketing across national borders must first address the issue of translation. International **distributors** will make arrangements for the film to be translated through **subtitling** or **dubbing** depending on the cultural preferences of each national market. The marketing for the film also involves translation. Local translators will produce subtitles and voice-

overs for trailers. Local artists will design billboards, posters and other print advertisements in a regional style. Marketing teams must also consider the genres, stars, and styles that appeal to viewers in particular markets. These decisions are often made at the local level by firms hired by regional distributors.

The US *Crouching Tiger, Hidden Dragon* trailer is particularly interesting in this regard because it successfully concealed the fact that the film dialogue is in Mandarin. The film was released in the US with English subtitles. LaFontaine's English language voice-over frames the film as a Hollywood film. (It was co-produced and distributed by Sony Pictures Classics in the United States.) American audiences are notoriously resistant to watching films with subtitles, and very few films screened in theatres in the United States are in languages other than English. Despite this resistance, *Crouching Tiger, Hidden Dragon* became the highest grossing foreign language film in US history. As of this writing, it has not yet been surpassed. Produced for a budget of only $17 million,[3] it earned $128 million in the United States (and another $85 million in other markets). There are many reasons for the film's success. It was nominated for ten Academy Awards and won four, capping off a year of rave reviews. Critics have speculated, however, that the film's success can be attributed in part to Sony's deceptive marketing campaign. By concealing the fact that the film is in Mandarin, Sony may have secured a much larger theatrical audience for the film in its critical opening weeks.

9.2 *Crouching Tiger, Hidden Dragon* poster. Courtesy of Columbia/Sony/The Kobal Collection.

This success was not repeated overseas. *Crouching Tiger, Hidden Dragon* underperformed in Asian markets. Its box office performance in Korea, Japan, and Hong Kong was particularly weak. One disappointed viewer explained the unenthusiastic reception of the film by comparing its slow pacing to "grandma telling stories."[4] Hong Kong audiences expect more complicated and dynamic fight sequences from martial arts films, and they expect their favorite Cantonese-speaking stars to speak in fluent Cantonese rather than strained Mandarin. *Crouching Tiger, Hidden Dragon* was thus only a modest success in Asian markets while it became an international blockbuster.

Market quadrants

Marketing a film is more complicated than separating film audiences into a domestic audience and an international one. Marketing campaigns further divide film audiences according to several demographic criteria. One common industrial framework for segmenting a film audience is the model of **market quadrants**. An article in *The New Yorker* on contemporary film marketing and the career of Tim Palen, the Chief Marketing Officer for Lionsgate (the Hollywood studio now widely recognized in the industry as the "seventh major studio"), offers the following summary of the four quadrants:

Marketers segment the audience in a variety of ways, but the most common form of partition is the four quadrants: men under twenty-five; older men; women under twenty-five; older women. A studio rarely makes a film that it doesn't expect will succeed with at least two quadrants, and a film's budget is usually directly related to the number of quadrants it is anticipated to reach. The most expensive tent-pole movies, such as the "Pirates of the Caribbean" franchise, are aimed at all four quadrants.

The collective wisdom is that young males like explosions, blood, cars flying through the air, pratfalls, poop jokes, "you're so gay" banter, and sex—but not romance. Young women like friendship, pop music, fashion, sarcasm, sensitive boys who think with their hearts, and romance—but not sex (though they like to hear the naughty girl telling her friends about it). They go to horror films as much as young men, but they hate gore; you lure them by having the ingénue take her time walking down the dark hall.

Older women like feel-good films and Nicholas Sparks-style weepies: they are the core audience for stories of doomed love and triumphs of the human spirit. They enjoy seeing an older woman having her pick of men; they hate seeing a child in danger. Particularly once they reach thirty, these women are the most "review-sensitive": a chorus of critical praise for a movie aimed at older women can increase the opening weekend's gross by five million dollars. In other words, older women are discriminating, which is why so few films are made for them.

Older men like darker films, classic genres such as Westerns and war movies, men protecting their homes, and men behaving like idiots. Older men are easy to please, particularly if a film stars Clint Eastwood and is about guys just like them, but they're hard to motivate. "Guys only get off their couches twice a year, to go to 'Wild Hogs' or '3:10 to Yuma,'" the marketing consultant Terry Press says. "If all you have is older males, it's time to take a pill."[5]

This account reveals the generalizations that studios make about film audiences based on their age and gender. If this model fails to capture your film preferences, you now understand the limitations of market research. Mainstream film production marginalizes many film audiences in order to appeal to as many market quadrants as possible and maximize profits.

The market quadrants model also ignores the other demographic factors that might bind film audiences together. For example, this framework does not address race. Most Hollywood films feature white stars, with non-white actors consigned to supporting roles. These films are marketed to all audiences rather than only to white audiences. The few films produced each year featuring multiple black actors in starring roles are often marketed as "black films." Studios market the films directly to black audiences through commercials and print advertisements placed in media outlets with predominantly black audiences, following the model of successful niche marketing on television networks like Telemundo, a Spanish-language television network owned by NBC Universal that programs content specifically for Spanish-speaking audiences in the United States (and in many other countries). George Lucas publicly shared his frustration as a producer with his struggle to find studio support for the film *Red Tails* (Anthony Hemingway, 2012). The film profiles the "Tuskegee Airmen," a group of African American pilots who fought for the US during World War II while facing racial discrimination at home. The film stars Terrence Howard and Cuba Gooding, Jr., among an ensemble cast of primarily black actors. Lucas shopped the film to various studios over a period of twenty years before finding backing from 20th Century Fox. Lucas has lamented in interviews the difficulty he had convincing studio heads to see the film as an action film or a war film with broad marketing potential to all four marketing quadrants as opposed to a "black film" marketable only to black audiences.

Media usage profiles

Media usage models define audiences according to their habits as media consumers. Tracking how particular audience segments engage with different media allows studios to customize multi-media marketing campaigns, concentrating their marketing investments in specific media. Placing a print advertisement in the Japanese daily newspaper *Yomiuri Shimbun* to advertise the upcoming release of the latest *Pokémon* movie will be a much less effective way of reaching its target youth audience than a marketing campaign that features in-game advertising in

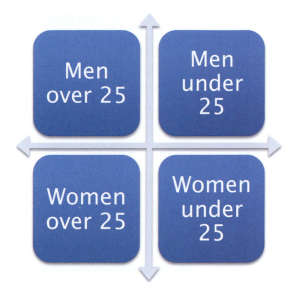

9.3 The market quadrant model used by Hollywood studios. Created by the author.

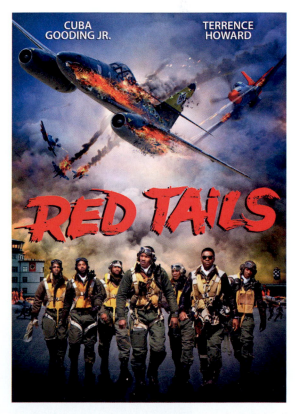

9.4 *Red Tails* poster. Courtesy of 20th Century Fox/Lucasfilm Ltd/Partnership Pictures/The Kobal Collection.

popular video games or television commercials screened during popular anime shows. In order to make sure that their advertising dollars are being efficiently used to reach their target audience, studios rely on market research that profiles the media habits of consumers. Before they pay for costly television advertising, producers need to guarantee that their target audience watches television. Then they need to determine which shows they watch and where they watch them.

Consumer surveys administered by media research corporations yield statistical information about how people in each market segment divide their time across various media. Film studios rely both on information from these sources and on more precise data that they collect through in-house marketing research teams. Information about how people in various demographic groups learn about movies (for example, from television, word-of-mouth, theatrical trailers, online, or in print media) helps studios to plan marketing campaigns for specific films. The data produced by media research corporations may offer a snapshot of industrial or cultural trends, but these profiles are based on small population samples. The small percentage of people sampled through this research is only one concern raised by critics of this form of research. The methods used to select people to poll, to design the questions they are asked, to collect information, and to analyze information influence the results. The media research corporations who generate this information and the studios and other companies that purchase it often focus on the headline rather than the fine print, ignoring the factors that may undermine the value of the data. To get a glimpse of one problem with this form of media research – the small size of the sample – ask as many people as you can if they have ever been polled by a media research corporation. Then calculate the percentage of people you polled who have been polled. If you find that the percentage is close to zero, you will have a sense of why many people (and organizations) question the merits of this research. In spite of these concerns, however, studios continue to use quantitative research as the basis for production and marketing decisions.

EXERCISE

Choose three films currently in production, and propose a marketing plan for each film. You may find lists of films in production at the websites for BBC Films (http://www.bbc.co.uk/bbcfilms) or Screen Australia (http://www.screenaustralia.gov.au/productions/upr.aspx), for example. Determine the percentage of the film's total marketing budget that you would spend for each of the following marketing expenses:

- print advertising (newspapers and magazines)
- posters
- billboards
- theatrical trailers
- television trailers
- website development
- web advertising
- social media.

Draw a simple pie chart like the sample in figure 9.5 to visualize the allocations you have made.

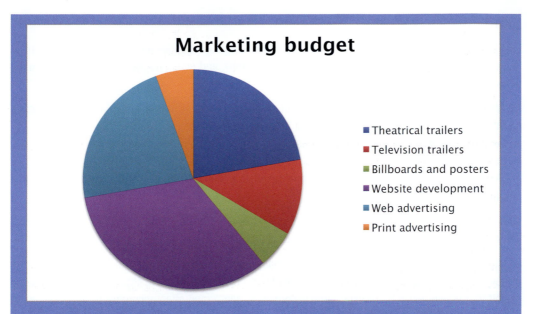

9.5 Sample marketing budget allocations. Created by the author.

Which market quadrants would you target with each form of marketing? Are considerations of the age or gender of your target audience crucial to your decisions, or were other factors more relevant? Were your allocations consistent for each film, or did each film require a different marketing strategy? Why?

THE LANGUAGES OF MARKETING

Market research and market profiles inform the design of marketing materials. In her discussion of film trailers in *Coming Attractions: Reading American Movie Trailers*, film librarian Lisa Kernan explains the link between demographic research and marketing rhetoric:

> Demographics has an impact on trailer rhetoric as quantified by market research and/or as imagined by trailer makers. Different markets are made visible in trailers by textual evidence of "targeting" or appeals to specific genders, age groups, or other categories of subjectivity.[6]

Kernan outlines the three primary **rhetorical appeals** or hooks that trailers use to advertise films: genres, stories, and stars. Trailers and other marketing tools feature these familiar elements in order to engage the interest of specific market segments. Different advertisements frame a film in different ways, but each example will involve one or more rhetorical appeals. In this section, we will consider an expanded list of rhetorical appeals used in international film marketing. These include: genres, stars, directors, properties, studios, awards, technology, and national cinemas.

Genres

Film **genres** link together films that share **genre codes**, common narrative and stylistic elements. These genre codes may include characters, settings, iconography, and cinematography. For example, many films associated with the horror genre include:

- Characters: a monster (which may or may not be human) and a victim (or multiple victims, including "the final girl" featured as the last survivor in many slasher films).
- Settings: poorly lit and/or abandoned houses, graveyards, and forests (always at night, of course).
- Iconography: blood, knives and full moons.
- Cinematography: point-of-view shots, long takes that build suspense, and chiaroscuro lighting patterns.

While this list is by no means exhaustive, it offers a glimpse of the common features many horror films share, linking them together as a coherent set of films.

Genres are important marketing tools because many audiences define their own film tastes in terms of genre. Filmgoers who like one horror film will often enjoy other horror films. Marketing campaigns exploit that phenomenon by labeling films according to genre (and often according to multiple genres in order to engage several audience sectors). Online distributors have even created algorithms to track the genre preferences of consumers. A pop-up message from a distributor's website claiming that "If you liked *Suspiria*, you'll love *Kill, Baby ... Kill!*" has used the viewer's interest in the Italian horror film *Suspiria* (Dario Argento, 1977) to market *Kill, Baby ... Kill!* (*Operazione Paura,* Mario Bava, 1966) – another Italian horror film.

Stars

Stars are one of the main rhetorical appeals featured in film marketing. A **bankable star** can command a very high salary (and often a percentage of box office returns and profits from ancillary markets) because of the industrial emphasis on a star's ability to "sell" a film. The theory of **superstar economics** justifies the exorbitant salaries of certain film stars by linking box office performance to the marketing of **star images**. Superstar economics explains the frequency with which the presence of stars such as Jackie Chan and Will Smith in a film will generate robust box office returns even if the films in which they star receive poor reviews from critics and fans alike. There is now a large body of box office evidence to debunk the industry's faith in superstar economics. For example, the box office failures of the Jennifer Aniston star vehicles *The Switch* (Josh Gordon and Will Speck, 2010) and *Love Happens* (Brandon Camp, 2009), along with many other Hollywood romantic comedies starring Aniston, suggest that studios should rethink the lavish sums she has been paid to headline these films. Meanwhile, *Paranormal Activity* (Oren Peli, 2007) became a surprise international box office hit and spawned several successful sequels without featuring any stars (and with a production budget of only $15,000). *The Switch* and *Love Happens* logged theatrical grosses of less than $28 million and $23 million respectively, while *Paranormal Activity* earned over $107 million.

In spite of examples like these, the top stars continue to command top salaries, and star images continue to feature prominently in film marketing. A review of film posters for films starring Brad Pitt showcases the importance of stars as primary rhetorical appeals. It is logical to see a still image of

9.6 (a and b) Posters for *Inglourious Basterds* and *The Curious Case of Benjamin Button* featuring Brad Pitt. Courtesy of Universal Pictures/The Kobal Collection, and Paramount Pictures/Warner Bros. Pictures/The Kobal Collection.

Brad Pitt dominating the posters for the films *Moneyball* (Bennett Miller, 2011) and *The Curious Case of Benjamin Button* (David Fincher, 2008) since Pitt is arguably the star of both films based on the amount of time he spends on screen. It is less logical to see Pitt's image similarly dominating film posters for *Inglourious Basterds* (Quentin Tarantino, 2009) and *Babel* (Alejandro González Iñárritu, 2006). In these films, Pitt shares screen time with a large ensemble of other actors. These films, however, showcase Pitt's star image in order to compensate for elements that would be difficult to market: complex narratives, international casts, and multiple languages. The box office power of Pitt's star image helped both films to overcome these marketing obstacles. (*Babel* earned $135 million, and *Inglourious Basterds* earned $321 million).

The foregrounding of a star image as a rhetorical appeal reaches a point of spectacular excess in the trailer for the Bollywood film *Om Shanti Om* (Farah Khan, 2007). Available on the website for the film's distributor, Eros Entertainment (www.erosentertainment.com), the trailer focuses on the film's superstar, Shah Rukh Khan. The film features several dozen beloved Bollywood stars who appear together in a song-and-dance sequence at the end of the film, but the trailer focuses instead solely on Khan. Almost every shot in the trailer features either Khan alone or Khan in focus in the foreground. These shots present Khan in over twenty different costumes, and in several of these Khan is shirtless. The plot of the film, its popular song-and-dance sequences, and its remarkably long roster of Bollywood film stars are all overshadowed by Khan's star image.

Directors

The analysis of stardom focuses on actors, but many film **directors** are stars in their own right. Some directors helm their own production companies, and act as writer, producer and director for each of their projects. The more creative and industrial control that a director exerts over his films (and as we saw in Chapter 2's exploration of self-expression, it is almost always a he), the more likely it is that his star image as a director will be used to market his films. Spike Lee's 40 Acres and a Mule Filmworks produces all of Lee's films, and Lee is usually the writer, director, and producer of his films. At the end of their credit sequences the logo "A Spike Lee Joint" appears, branding the film as a product of Lee's artistic imagination and industrial authority (see figure 9.7). Audiences for Lee's films may remark that they like "Spike Lee movies" in the same way that other audiences may express a preference for horror films.

The advent of DVD distribution has arguably reinvigorated the critical status of the director. The practice of releasing a **director's cut** of a film on DVD as a special edition presents the director's original vision for the film (the version that existed before a studio's editorial interference) as artistically superior to the studio-approved theatrical version. Director's cuts elevate the director's prestige. Similarly, the bonus features included with DVDs often include the director's voice-over commentary, an interview with the director, production notes, or other archival information that emphasizes the importance of the director's role in film production. These DVD editions often frame the director as an **auteur**, a concept that was introduced in Chapter 2.

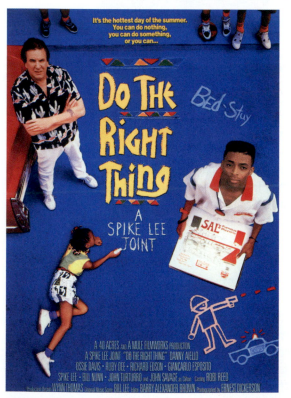

9.7 Poster for *Do the Right Thing* – "A Spike Lee Joint." Courtesy of Universal/The Kobal Collection.

The Criterion Collection is a US-based DVD and Blu-ray distributor that markets "important classic and contemporary films" to North American audiences. The Criterion Collection focuses on directors as a key rhetorical element in the marketing of films across international borders, particularly for films made outside Hollywood. The directors of international art films gain visibility through the festival circuit, and their names become marketing tools for the distribution of their films in other regions. For example, the Criterion Collection has issued two films by the Hong Kong director Wong Kar-Wai on Blu-Ray. The covers of *In the Mood for Love* (*Fa Yeung Nin Wa*, 2000) and *Chungking Express* (*Chung Hing sam lam*, 1994) display the films' titles in large text as *Wong Kar-Wai's In the Mood for Love* and *Chungking Express A Film by Wong Kar-Wai*. The combination of the director's name with each film's title under-scores the importance of the director as a rhetorical appeal. The Criterion Collection markets the films as products of their director. The bonus features for *In the Mood for Love* include Wong's documentary about the making of the film, an interview with Wong, and a director's commentary. These special features build on the critical acclaim Wong has received through festival awards, including the Best Director award for *Happy Together* (*Chun gwong cha sit*, 1997) at the Cannes Film Festival.

CASE STUDY: ABBAS KIAROSTAMI

Abbas Kiarostami is a contemporary Iranian director who has achieved critical recognition as an international *auteur*. Kiarostami is associated with the Iranian New Wave, a filmmaking style that began in the 1960s in Iran. Kiarostami and other directors (including Jafar Panahi, Mohsen Makhmalbaf, and Majid Majidi) have produced films that combine poetic dialogue and imagery with political and philosophical meditations. Iranian New Wave films share some features with other cinematic "waves," including Italian neo-realism. Kiarostami's films in particular share the Italian neo-realist investment in featuring children as central protagonists, making dramatic use of location shooting, and exploring current political crises through intimate stories.

Kiarostami began his career in the film industry by helping to found a film production studio at the Institute for Intellectual Development of Children and Young Adults in Tehran in 1969. The studio became an important center for Iranian filmmaking and has produced many of Kiarostami's films (along with the work of other Iranian New Wave directors). Kiarostami worked on the films of other directors (often as a screenwriter or editor) and directed his own short films before making his first feature film, *Report* (*Gozaresh*), in 1977. Since then he has directed dozens of shorts and feature films, including several documentaries. *ABC Africa* (2001), produced in collaboration with the UN's International Fund for Agricultural Development, profiles the Ugandan children who have been orphaned by the AIDS epidemic. *10 on Ten* (2004) tours film locations from his other films as part of a series of reflections on filmmaking.

Kiarostami's films feature several key aesthetic elements. The Koker trilogy films – *Where is the Friend's Home?* (*Khane-ye doust kodjast?*, 1987), *Life, and Nothing More* (*Zendegi va digar hich*, 1992) and *Through the Olive Trees* (*Zire darakhatan zeyton*, 1994) – take place in the Koker village in northern Iran and use the landscape as a central tool in the exploration of the relationship between the land and the experiences of the people who live there. *Ten* (2002) adopts a very different formal strategy. The film was shot entirely through a digital camera mounted on the dashboard of a car, confining the cinematic space in the film to the interior of the car and the fragments of the city that can be seen through the car windows. The use of windows to frame space and the focus on long automobile journeys are signature elements of many of Kiarostami's films, but these elements are used in a particularly intense way in *Ten*. Kiarostami's films also involve blurred boundaries between fiction and reality. *Close-up* (*Nema-ye Nazdik*, 1990), for example, presents the story of a con artist who impersonates the Iranian director Mohsen Makhmalbaf. Based on real events, the film combines documentary footage with re-enactments of key events. While some Kiarostami films are labeled as documentaries, many of his "fiction" films include documentary elements, challenging the audience's understanding of cinematic reality.

The film *Certified Copy* (*Copia Conforme*, 2010) was shot in Tuscany and includes French, Italian, and English dialogue. This film marked a departure for Kiarostami whose previous work had featured Farsi dialogue and had been shot on location in Iran (with notable exceptions like the Uganda-based *ABC Africa*). While *Certified Copy* is Kiarostami's first experience with international

9.8 The interior of the car in *Ten* (Abbas Kiarostami). Courtesy of MK2/Abbas Kiarostami Prod/The Kobal Collection.

co-production, he has been a leading figure on the international art cinema scene since the success of his 1997 film *Taste of Cherry* (*Ta'm e guilass*), winner of the Palme D'Or at the Cannes Film Festival that year. Kiarostami's status as a celebrated international "auteur" has been used to market his films. For many audiences, Kiarostami is synonymous with Iranian cinema.

Kiarostami functions as an international brand, and his name has been used successfully to market Iranian cinema to international audiences. However, Kiarostami's work has polarized both international critics and Iranian film audiences. Skeptics argue that his rejection of conventional cinematic storytelling and genre modes alienates many viewers and that the international celebration of his work overshadows the films made by other Iranian directors. In his review of Kiarostami's *Ten*, the film critic Roger Ebert laments the international critical acclaim for Kiarostami's work:

> Part of Kiarostami's appeal is that he is Iranian, a country whose films it is somewhat daring to praise. Partly, too, he has a lot of critics invested in his cause, and they do the heavy lifting. The fatal flaw in his approach is that no ordinary moviegoer, whether Iranian or American, can be expected to relate to his films. They exist for film festivals, film critics and film classes. The shame is that more accessible Iranian directors are being neglected in the overpraise of Kiarostami.[7]

Ebert suggests that international audiences should instead turn to more popular Iranian films like *Two Women* (Tahmineh Milani, 1999), a drama about two female architecture students during the early years of the Islamic Republic. The reception of Kiarostami's work in Iran must be understood within the contexts of the censorship of his films by the Iranian government and the difficulty of reconciling art cinema with popular tastes. Ebert's resistance to Kiarostami's films, however, points out that the marketing of directors to international audiences may overlook (or strategically ignore) the reception of their work in their home countries.

Properties

Some films are able to build on an audience's **pre-awareness** or prior knowledge of another media property associated with the film. (Properties were discussed in detail in Chapter 6, "Starting points".) **Sequels**, **prequels**, **remakes**, and **adaptations** develop a story that was introduced to audiences in another film, book, or media object. Film studios treasure these films because the existence of a built-in audience minimizes the financial risk of producing and marketing the film. *Howard's End* (James Ivory, 1992) adapts the E.M. Forster novel of the same name for the screen. *Transformers* (Michael Bay, 2007) is also an adaptation – based not on a novel but on the Transformers toy line by Hasbro – and has, in turn, generated several sequels.

A remake is a film based on an earlier film. Remakes may reimagine a film for a new filmgoing generation. In 2010, Joel and Ethan Coen released *True Grit*, a remake of the classic John Wayne Western *True Grit* (Henry Hathaway, 1969). Some remakes rebrand a film for a different global region. In an unusual example, the Austrian director Michael Haneke remade one of his own films. The original *Funny Games* was released in German in 1997. Haneke remade the film in English ten years later. The remade *Funny Games* (2007) stars Naomi Watts and Michael Pitt in a nearly identical story.

The relationships between and among transnational film remakes can be difficult to identify. For example, the Bollywood

9.9 A poster for Haneke's remake of *Funny Games*. Courtesy of Dreamachine/The Kobal Collection.

film *Kaante* (Sanjay Gupta, 2002) was marketed as a remake of the Hollywood film *Reservoir Dogs* (Quentin Tarantino, 1992). Set in Los Angeles and featuring a South Asian cast, *Kaante* preserves many elements of the original film's heist plot. The comparison of these two films by critics and fans largely ignored the fact that *Reservoir Dogs* itself is heavily indebted to the Hong Kong film *City on Fire* (*Lung fu fong wan*, Ringo Lam, 1987) starring Chow Yun-Fat. The relative invisibility of *City on Fire* within this transnational trilogy points to the ease with which many Hollywood studios remake films from other countries without foregrounding the importance (or even the existence) of the original films.

Studios

During the classical Hollywood period, the major **studios** were often associated with particular film genres. MGM was known for its musicals, and Warner Bros. was briefly known for its gangster films. As we saw in Chapter 5, film production is no longer managed in a factory-style system, and studios typically produce films in one-off arrangements. As a result of these changes in production practices, studios are no longer associated with particular genres or styles.

There are several exceptions to this rule. For example, the Pixar Studios brand is indelibly linked with innovative animated films like *Toy Story* (John Lasseter, 1995), *Up* (Peter Docter and Bob Peterson, 2009), and *WALL-E* (Andrew Stanton, 2008). Zentropa Entertainments, a Danish production company co-founded by the director Lars von Trier in 1992, not only produces von Trier's films, including *Breaking the Waves* (1996), *Dancer in the Dark* (2000), and *Melancholia* (2011) but also many of the other films associated with the Dogme 95 filmmaking movement, including Lone Scherfig's *Italian for Beginners* (2000). Dogme 95 is an avant-garde filmmaking style launched in 1995 with a manifesto co-written by von Trier. Dogme 95 values minimalist productions without large budgets or special effects. The films made under this banner focus instead on intense performances. While Zentropa is primarily known as the studio home for Dogme films, it also produces hardcore pornography.

There are relatively few studios that exclusively produce a particular kind of film, but there are instances when a studio's reputation will be featured in the marketing of a film. Sometimes this marketing strategy is a red flag that the film being advertised has little else to recommend it. For example, posters for the Hollywood romantic comedy *When in Rome* (Mark Steven Johnson, 2010) cheered "From the studio that brought you *The Proposal*." *The Proposal* (Anne Fletcher, 2009) was a lucrative release for Touchstone Pictures, and the studio was likely very eager for another over-performing romantic comedy. In this case, however, the marketing strategy barely concealed the lack of other rhetorical appeals at the marketing team's disposal.

In other cases, using a studio as a marketing tool can successfully bolster the public profile of a strong film that might otherwise be overlooked. Print advertisements for *The Town* (Ben Affleck, 2010) urged viewers to see the new film from "the studio that brought you *The Departed*." In this case, the two films share a location (contemporary Boston), a genre (the neo-gangster film), and a studio (Warner Bros.). Warner Bros. is no longer the "gangster studio" it was in the 1930s, but its affiliation with both films was used to generate higher-than-expected box office returns for *The Town*, a film that might otherwise have had a difficult time reaching potential viewers in spite of the celebrity of its director and star, Ben Affleck.

Awards

When a star or director wins (or is nominated for) an Academy Award, they can expect that every film they star in after that will introduce them with the title "Academy Award® Winner." Awards are an important part of film marketing. The use of previous Academy Awards earned by the director or actors to market a new film attempts to trade on their prestige in order to draw audiences. Of course, there is no guarantee that the new film (or the performances in it) will be worthy of the Oscar® label, but foregrounding these past accolades can be an effective marketing technique.

For many Academy Award winning films (or winners of the many other film awards across the globe), the awards are announced after the primary theatrical run of the film has ended. Sometimes films will launch a second theatrical run to take advantage of the public interest generated by their critical success. More often the awards will be used instead to generate revenue for the film in video, DVD and internet markets. Distributors will adorn DVD covers with lists of awards, print advertisements in trade periodicals will congratulate the individual winners (or the winners may place advertisements to congratulate themselves!), and new trailers and teasers will foreground the awards through celebratory voice-overs.

Awards are particularly important for the international marketing of films. Few international genre films cross national borders, and very few reach the lucrative US market. Generally the films that receive the broadest distribution to the United States, the UK, and other English-language markets are **international art films**. These films secure distribution deals through the international film festival circuit, and the awards they receive at those festivals become a central part of their marketing. Audiences associate the Cannes Film Festival with cinematic prestige, so a film's announcement that its director has won the coveted Palme d'Or for directing the "best feature film entered in official competition" at the festival may attract international audiences during its theatrical and post-theatrical releases. Winners of the Palme d'Or include: Abbas Kiarostami (Iran) for *Taste of Cherry* (*Ta'm e guilass,* 1997), Cristian Mungiu (Romania) for *4 Months, 3 Weeks, and 2 Days* (*4 luni, 3 saptamâni si 2 zile*, 2007), and Apitchatpong Weerasethakul (Thailand) for *Uncle Boonmee Who Can Recall His Past Lives* (*Loong Boonmee raleuk chat,* 2010).

Technology

Some marketing campaigns focus on the technological innovations that distinguish the film from other films in theatrical release. Beginning with the marketing of the cinema of attractions in the early years of film exhibition, film marketing has focused on technology as a lure to draw audiences to theatres. This strategy reached one commercial peak in response to television and other postwar challenges to cinema's dominant grasp on the public's entertainment dollars (as discussed in Chapter 11, "Exhibition"). For example, the trailer for *This is Cinerama* (Merian Cooper, 1952), the film that showcased the new Cinerama widescreen exhibition format, promised, "Cinerama will put you in the picture and into a Technicolor wonderland!"

The proliferation of media content and media exhibition platforms has presented a new challenge to theatrical exhibition. Film marketing must compete not only with television but also with DVD and Blu-ray, mobile phones, online streaming, and social media. The contemporary media landscape has scattered the attention of consumers across multiple screens. In order to draw audiences to theatres, producers and exhibitors have returned to spectacle-focused marketing strategies.

The marketing campaign for the film *Avatar* (James Cameron, 2009) is a helpful case to analyze. *Avatar* is a science fiction film helmed by a very successful Hollywood director, so its marketing campaign could foreground its genre or its director. To a limited extent, it did both, releasing film posters that featured enigmatic close-ups of an unrecognizable Zoe Saldana as the blue-skinned Neytiri, introducing the fictional Na'vi people to science fiction fans. These posters included only two textual elements – the film's title and the phrase "From the director of *Titanic*," building on the success of Cameron's previous effects-laden international blockbuster. These posters were only one element of a multi-pronged marketing campaign that included pre-released scenes, behind-the-scenes demonstrations of the camera built for the performance-capture process, and interviews with Cameron and other creative personnel.

Each of these elements dwelled on the technological innovations developed for the film. The film's marketing invites viewers to marvel at how the film was made. In this case, knowing how the magician pulled off the trick makes us enjoy the trick even more. Central to this focus on technology as a rhetorical appeal is the endless speculation about the film's budget. Estimates of $500 million (including up to $150 million in international marketing costs) frequently appeared in various periodicals without any official confirmation (or any official correction). For *Avatar*, the budget itself became an element of the film's marketing. Audiences were curious to see the film for many reasons: because James Cameron had not released a film in over a decade and interest in his next project had been building for a long time, because 3D and performance capture technology commanded the public's interest as dramatic alternatives to the miniaturized images circulating on mobile phone and laptop screens, and because audiences wanted to see a $500 million film.

National cinemas

During the heyday of video stores, most stores in the United States collected all of their non-Hollywood films in a section called "foreign films." *Rashomon* (Akira Kurosawa, 1950) would sit on the shelf next to *Red Desert* (*Il deserto rosso,* Michelangelo Antonioni, 1964), sharing little in common other than the first letter of the English translations of their titles. "Foreign film" is not a genre. First, a film is only foreign from the point of view of a particular audience. For other people, the film is a central part of their local film culture. Second, the category of foreign films includes films from a large number of film-producing regions and a long list of genres. As the example above demonstrates, these films often have little in common apart from their perceived foreignness from the point of view of particular audiences.

For some cinephiles, "foreign film" as a category is a powerful cultural lure. Some film audiences are drawn to films from particular national cinemas, flocking to French films or to Bollywood films. There are many reasons for these attachments to national cinemas, including a shared language or an interest in a particular director, star, or genre. Someone who goes to see every French film that reaches their local theatre may not have a passion for film at all but may instead be a native or novice French speaker who longs to hear the French language spoken on screen. In spite of this appeal, national cinemas are used infrequently as labels in major marketing campaigns. Studios are reluctant to alienate audiences who may be worried about their inability to understand a foreign language and thus decide to skip the film (as the discussion of the trailer campaign for *Crouching Tiger, Hidden Dragon* at the beginning of this chapter illustrates). A national cinema may, however, appear as a marketing tool in the wake of an international box office success. For example, the French film *Amélie* (Jean-Pierre Jeunet, 2001) sparked an interest in other French films among international audiences.

MARKETING PARATEXTS

In some places, the local cinema is still an important cultural destination for the community. Moviegoers will head to the theatre each weekend regardless of what film is being shown. They are interested in the experience of going to the theatre itself. For many audiences, however, going to the theatre is one of many options that compete for their leisure time and money. Whether a trip to the cinema is a regular event or a rare occurrence, viewers make decisions in advance about which films they feel are worth seeing in the theatre. Some moviegoers may actively research the films at their local theatre in order to decide which film to see. They might read film reviews online, ask friends or family members to share what they have heard about recent releases, or search for trailers online. Many moviegoers, however, will rely on impressions they have made based on the many film **paratexts** they have (often passively) encountered for each film. Paratexts are elements of a film or of film marketing that either shape our expectations about the film before we have seen it (for example, trailers and posters) or extend our engagement with the film after we have seen it (for example, toys and DVD bonus features). This section examines these paratexts and the ways in which they inform the public's understanding of individual films and film cultures.

In his book *Show Sold Separately: Promos, Spoilers, and Other Media Paratexts*, film and television scholar Jonathan Gray points to the ubiquity of paratexts in the everyday lives of people in media-saturated environments. He uses the term **speculative consumption** to describe the reception of these paratexts:

> When faced with a multiplex full of unwatched movies, or an extended cable television package full of unwatched shows, one must engage in speculative consumption, creating an idea of what pleasures any one text will provide, what information it will offer, what "effect" it will have on us, and so forth. As such, with all the hype that surrounds us, announcing texts from subway cars, website margins, or highway roadsides, we can spend a surprisingly large portion of our everyday life speculatively consuming new texts.[8]

Going to the movies entails a certain level of consumer risk because, as Gray notes, "If we do not like the film, we cannot get our money back, since we paid for the *chance* of entertainment, not necessarily for actual entertainment."[9] Paratexts offer consumers the ability to make more informed moviegoing decisions (although many paratexts offer only a glimpse of the film and some are actually misleading).

Paratexts shape the audience's expectations about the film and provide frameworks for the audience's reception of the film. In other words, a paratext may determine not only whether or not you choose to see a film but also *how* you see the film. Gray argues persuasively that the study of paratexts is important because audiences consume many more paratexts than texts. He points out that "when at a multiplex we choose to watch one of the ten films on offer, we not only create an interpretive construction of the film that we saw; we have often also speculatively consumed many of the other nine."[10] (Check the current line-up of films playing at a theatre near you and consider how much you already know about the films on this list based on the paratexts you have encountered.) This section will analyze some of the paratexts that are central to Gray's discussion and central to the marketing of film: titles, trailers, posters, tie-ins, bonus features, and new media and social media campaigns.

Titles

One of the most significant marketing decisions for a film is its title. A title can signal the genre or theme of a film, as in *American Gangster* (Ridley Scott, 2007), the premise of the film, as in *Home Alone* (Chris Columbus, 1990), or the setting of the film, as in *Seven Years in Tibet* (Jean-Jacques Annaud, 1997). Many film titles are more enigmatic. For example, the title for the film *Chronicle* (Josh Trank, 2012) does not hint that the film will be about a group of teenagers who acquire superpowers. Without other paratexts to frame their expectations about the film, audiences would have no way to guess what the film might be about. Film titles featuring the names of characters may be similarly vague. For instance, the title for the Russian film *Elena* (Andrey Zvyagintsev, 2011) refers to its main character, but the title does not give away any other information. These cases are relatively rare. If you review the list of movies currently playing at your local theatre, you may notice several titles that directly reference the film's genre, setting, or plot.

Titles like *American Gangster* and *Seven Years in Tibet* are effective marketing tools because they provide prospective audiences with accurate (albeit minimal) information about the films. In some cases, a film title can become the centerpiece of a film's marketing campaign. One example is the film *Snakes on a Plane* (David Ellis, 2006). Originally titled *Venom*, this film about – you guessed it – venomous snakes unleashed on a plane generated valuable pre-release publicity from its title. Early fan communities emerged online to speculate about how the film would unfold. The producers even incorporated suggestions from fans during the film's production, shooting additional scenes and adding additional lines of dialogue. The film's star, Samuel Jackson, reportedly convinced the producers not to change the film's title to the far less amusing *Pacific Air Flight 121*. He claimed that he had agreed to star in the film *because* of its title.

Trailers

Some people will rush to the theatre in order to arrive in time to see the long suite of **trailers** that precedes a feature film. In some theatres, the program of trailers may last as long as twenty minutes. Other people deliberately wait until the last possible moment to arrive at the theatre in order to miss them. Film trailers are commercials for films, and some people prefer to skip the commercials.

Trailers may include shots from the film, carefully edited to give viewers an impression of the film without giving away so much information that viewers will lose their incentive to see it. Many trailers are produced while films are still in **production** or **post-production**, so it is not uncommon for a trailer to include shots that later end up on the cutting room floor. As the earlier analysis of the trailer for *Crouching Tiger, Hidden Dragon* demonstrated, trailers have a predictable narrative structure and typically engage multiple rhetorical appeals. Trailers may include some or all of the following elements: a voice-over that provides information about the film's story and its production, music from the film, the names of the director and stars, a memorable line of dialogue and a **tagline**. Producers will create multiple trailers – with two-to-four-minute trailers designed for theatrical release and fifteen-to-thirty-second trailers designed as television commercials. These trailers will circulate online on websites for the film and the studio, in trailer archives, on YouTube, and on media-centered "magazine" websites such as Entertainment Weekly (www.ew.com), the A.V. Club (www.avclub.com), and the Guardian (www.theguardian.com). Trailers have generated intense interest among critics and fans, with trailer archives like Trailer Addict (www.traileraddict.com) making trailers more accessible, and prizes like the Golden Trailer Awards recognizing artistic achievement in trailer design.

Posters

Film posters often mobilize fewer rhetorical appeals than trailers do, but they provide key information about how marketers want audiences to understand a film. Posters are only one element in the print advertising campaigns for films. They receive more critical attention than billboards and newspaper and magazine advertisements because film posters are also revered as popular art objects. Fans and collectors buy posters as permanent décor for their homes, and many international poster designers are celebrated as graphic artists.

As Gray notes, audiences encounter more paratexts than texts. The creative work of Palestinian artists and filmmakers Tarzan and Arab is an unusual example of this phenomenon. The artists, whose real names are Ahmed and Mohamed Abu Nasser, are twin brothers who live in Gaza where they have no access to film theatres. Although they eventually made a short film, *Colourful Journey* (2011), which has been exhibited in the UK and US, Tarzan and Arab's signature artistic production is a series of film posters they designed for non-existent films. Inspired by the tattered film posters they saw hanging on an abandoned Gaza theatre and by their own desire to become filmmakers, they created a series of film posters that feature themselves as stars. Using the names of military operations as fictional film titles – *Summer Rain*, *Autumn Clouds*, *Defensive Shield* – the posters transform these operations into cinematic fantasies. "For us the names were like war films," Arab remarked.[11] The posters invite viewers to imagine films that do not exist.

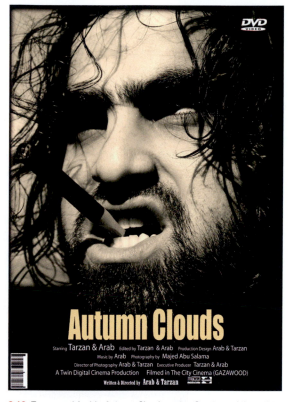

9.10 Tarzan and Arab's *Autumn Clouds* poster. Courtesy of the artists, Ahmed and Mohamed Abu Nasser.

CASE STUDY: INTERNATIONAL FILM POSTERS

One of the most exciting (and often overlooked) elements of regional film cultures is poster design. Post-World War II poster design followed different industrial and aesthetic paths in different parts of the globe. In the United States, National Screen Service, an independent company, created almost all of the posters for the major and minor Hollywood studios until it closed in 2000. Some of the US posters were produced outside the National Screen Service monopoly. Posters for exploitation films released by independent studios such as American International Pictures featured sensational taglines, towering figures, and explicit representations of sex and violence. With titles like *Runaway Daughters* (Edward L. Cahn, 1956), *Dragstrip Girl* (Edward L. Cahn, 1957), and *Hot Car Girl* (Bernard L. Kowalski, 1958), these films promised cheap thrills. Exploitation films (which we will return to in Chapter 10) showcased sex, violence, and tabloid-based spectacles – monsters, aliens, and natural disasters. The films were made with shoestring budgets, sometimes shooting an entire film in a single day. The posters for these films captured the "exploitation aesthetic."

At the same time in the United States, several "poster auteurs" emerged, including Saul Bass and Bob Peak. These designers developed a signature style over the course of prolific design careers. Saul Bass designed iconic posters for *Vertigo* (Alfred Hitchcock, 1958), *The Man with the Golden Arm* (Otto Preminger, 1956), and *West Side Story* (Robert Wise and Jerome Robbins, 1961). Bass worked in many areas of commercial design, creating title sequences and logos in addition to film posters. His designs are known for their elegance and their incorporation of mid-century modern design principles into film marketing. He often foregrounded a single object positioned against a bright background in his designs.

Analyzing poster design within a specific national film industry can reveal valuable insights into the relationships between national film cultures and international film distribution (discussed at length in Chapter 10, "Distribution"). During the postwar period in Poland, films were censored in order to fit the agenda of the ruling Communist Party. Poster designers reported to Film Polski, the state production agency, but they enjoyed more artistic freedom than film directors:

> [P]oster art enjoyed a surprising degree of freedom from the demands of Stalinist social realism, perhaps because the authorities saw in poster art a healthy outlet for avant-garde impulses that was still rooted in a popular and pragmatic tradition. The simple, abstract designs could also be printed quickly and cheaply, seldom requiring more than two or three colors.[12]

Film Polski emphasized design training in graphic arts schools that enabled the development of a recognizable national style. Posters by Tadeusz Trepkowski, Roman Cieślewicz, and

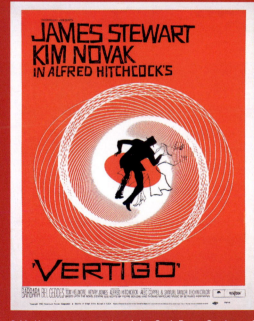

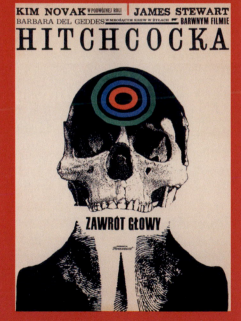

9.11 *Vertigo* poster designed by Saul Bass. Courtesy of Paramount/The Kobal Collection.

9.12 *Vertigo* poster designed by Roman Cieślewicz. Courtesy of Paramount/The Kobal Collection.

Franciszek Starowieyski marketed Hollywood thrillers, Italian neo-realist dramas, and French art films to Polish audiences. Freed from the marketing directives that drove design strategies in other countries, these designers drew from diverse avant-garde art movements to produce innovative posters that were often very abstract. Because of bureaucratic restrictions in Polish film culture, in some cases poster artists did not have access to the films they were illustrating, tying their poster designs even more closely to artistic movements and traditions other than film. Many of these designers shared Bass's interest in identifying a single visual element as the focus of the poster, but their work is less influenced by commercial design. In an interview, Cieślewicz remarked, "I dislike the image for its own sake. I am always attracted by the icons of the street and the present moment."[13] His poster designs mix images and text in surprising arrangements.

In Argentina, poster designers often based their designs on the original versions. Osvaldo Venturi is known for watercolor poster designs that reimagined American, British, and Italian films for Argentinian audiences. His posters for *I Vitelloni* (Federico Fellini, 1953), *Belissima* (Luchino Visconti, 1951), and other films use warm color palettes and present the films' stars during moments of heightened emotion. These common design elements framed many films from other countries as melodramas, a popular genre among Argentinian audiences. Looking at examples of Argentinian film posters provides an important archive of information about how films were marketed to audiences in a specific global region and how films from other global regions were made local through the art and business of poster design.

9.13 Osvaldo Venturi's poster for *Los Inutiles* (*I Vitelloni*, Federico Fellini, 1953). Courtesy of Peg Film/Cite Film/The Kobal Collection.

Tie-ins

Tie-ins include toys, video games, clothing, soundtracks, and other merchandise associated with a film. Many tie-ins are designed to develop ancillary revenue streams. Studios and their corporate stake-holders look for opportunities to transfer an audience's emotional investment in a film into a financial investment in merchandise associated with it. Often these texts are designed for consumers to purchase after they have seen the movie. Gray observes that consumers engage many of these paratexts before they see the film itself. For some consumers, the paratext exists independently of the movie. A child can enjoy playing with *Star Wars* action figures without having seen any of the *Star Wars* films. A teenager might play the Xbox 360 game *The Godfather* without any knowledge of the film on which the game is based. These paratexts can then create new generations of viewers.

Bonus features

Not all paratexts are keyed to a film's theatrical release. DVD's digital storage capabilities have made possible the inclusion of multiple **bonus features** on each disc. These bonus features package (and in many cases repackage) the film for audiences. In *Production Culture: Industrial Reflexivity and Critical Practice in Film and Television*,[14] film and television scholar John Caldwell provides a framework for analyzing bonus features in terms of their industrial and cultural significance. He identifies the rhetorical strategies that DVD bonus features use to appeal to audiences:

- Resuscitation: rebranding box office failures.
- Cross-promotion: marketing other related media properties.
- Virtual filmmaking: inviting fans to participate in the production process through interactive editing workshops and other features.
- Authorial control: highlighting the creative impact of the director on the film.
- Intelligence/virtuosity: foregrounding the expertise involved in the production.

- Cultural influence: explaining the historical significance of the film.
- Legacy/authenticity: establishing the credibility and relevance of the film.
- Against all odds: documenting the obstacles that had to be overcome in order to produce the film.
- Rebuttal: defending the film against critics.
- Fan barter: providing fans with extensive insider information about the making of the film.

Many DVD and Blu-ray editions will include a set of features that combine several of the rhetorical strategies listed above. Caldwell's taxonomy for analyzing bonus features demythologizes them. His framework exposes the marketing objectives of the extras that are sold to audiences – often for a higher price than DVD editions that do not include bonus features. In fact, there are many films with multiple DVD versions. Each version promises more features than the one before, enticing those fans that already own the film on DVD to purchase the latest version.

EXERCISE

Choose a DVD or Blu-ray disc from your collection or borrow a DVD or Blu-ray disc from a friend, a library, or a video store. Then analyze the disc's marketing features.

- Begin with the disc's cover, noting each element of the design, including images and text. How does each element contribute to the cover's presentation of the film?
- What information appears on the back cover? Are there quotes from critics and stars or additional stills from the film? How do these elements influence the disc's presentation of the film?
- Opening the cover, are there any inserts included with the disc? If there is a booklet, review the information it contains. You may find essays by critics, scholars, and industry personnel; photographs taken on set; and production trivia. How does this information frame your understanding of the film? If there is not a booklet, are there any print advertisements or other inserts included with the disc? If so, what do these advertisements suggest about the cross-promotional efforts of the producers?
- Review the menu of bonus features (if one exists). What features does the disc include? Watch a few of the features. Which of the strategies of bonus features that John Caldwell discusses does each feature adopt?
- What audience do you imagine that the producers of this disc have in mind?

New media and social media

Before Facebook and Twitter were central components of media marketing, *The Blair Witch Project* (Daniel Myrick and Eduardo Sanchez, 1999) harnessed the power of **new media** to market their low budget film. An inexpensively produced website for the film (http://www.blairwitch.com/legacy.html) circulated the misinformation that the film was composed of authentic "found footage." Some people in the early audiences for the film believed that they were watching recovered footage from a handheld video camera documenting a terrifying supernatural encounter. At the time, audiences were far less savvy about the packaging of "reality" in film and television and the power of new media marketing. Now new media marketing is a thriving segment of the film industry, including the design of websites, apps, and games. Social media campaigns are one of the most vital new media strategies for marketing contemporary films. **Social media marketing** has the potential to lead millions of viewers to marketing content (and then to the film) for a minimal investment (relative to the cost of traditional marketing tools like television commercials). Social media marketing agencies specialize in these campaigns.

Jetset Studios was responsible for the successful social media campaign supporting *Ted* (Seth MacFarlane, 2012). According to their website (http://www.jetsetstudios.com/yes-we-did-ted/), Jetset Studios is "a social media agency that specializes in capturing brand voice. We are storytellers who write, direct, produce, and create original content that builds audiences and drives conversations that move the needle for the world's biggest brands." Their social media marketing campaign for *Ted* helped it to earn almost $480 million for Universal Studios, making it the highest grossing original R-rated comedy to date. Their campaign included: the @WhatTedSaid Twitter account (written from the point of view of Ted, the foul-mouthed stuffed bear who stars in the film), a Facebook page, Ted e-cards, and a "My Wild Night with Ted" app that allowed users to insert themselves into photos with Ted. The campaign generated over 500,000 Twitter followers and over six million Facebook "likes." The Jetset social media strategy was complemented by other new media initiatives, including the release of a **red band trailer** on the online comedy site Funny or Die (www.funnyordie.com). The *Ted* marketing campaign successfully branded the film as an adult comedy and focused its advertising in the new media venues where its target audience (men under 25) spends most of its time.

Social media can propel very obscure independent films or major studio releases to more robust box office returns. The structure of social media – for example, the ability to "re-tweet" a message with the click of a button – has revitalized the importance of word-of-mouth marketing in the film industry. "Viral marketing" compounds the reach of social media marketing. It remains to be seen how more traditional marketing tools will fare as social media becomes a more central part of film marketing. With limited budgets for film marketing, both independent distributors and major studios have started to devote more resources to social media.

CHAPTER SUMMARY

Film marketing is a vital part of the film industry. Marketing budgets account for a significant percentage of the total budget for a film, occasionally matching the production budget for a film. Studios invest money in film marketing because the success (or failure) of a film in its opening weekend often determines the long-term financial future of the film. Few films are given the time to build commercial success through word-of-mouth support. In order to maximize their returns on their marketing investments, studios conduct market research to learn about the geographic, demographic, and media usage profiles of their target audiences. They design marketing campaigns to reach those audiences in as many venues as possible. Film marketing may feature genres, stars, directors, properties, studios, awards, technology, and national cinemas in order to capture the interest of potential viewers. Marketing campaigns generate a series of paratexts, including titles, trailers, posters, tie-ins, DVD bonus features, and new media and social media campaigns. These paratexts frame the film for potential audiences and can be analyzed as artistic and industrial objects in their own right. As new media and social media continue to transform the contemporary media landscape, marketing strategies are gradually shifting to meet audiences where they spend most of their time.

FURTHER READING

Gray, Jonathan. *Show Sold Separately: Promos, Spoilers, and Other Media Paratexts*. New York and London: New York University Press, 2010.

> Gray's analysis of media paratexts devotes chapters to trailers, bonus features, viewer-created paratexts, and games. Discussing both film and television paratexts, Gray introduces many contemporary examples to demonstrate the cultural and industrial importance of paratexts as texts that frame our understanding of not only the films we have seen but also the films we have not seen. The opening chapters explain the connection between paratexts and related concepts such as synergy and convergence.

Kernan, Lisa. *Coming Attractions: Reading American Movie Trailers*. Austin: University of Texas Press, 2004.

> Kernan approaches film trailers as a distinct film genre and carefully unpacks their structure and style. She analyzes examples from American film history to trace how film trailers have combined elements of cinema and advertising to attract audiences. While she focuses exclusively on Hollywood films, the critical framework she offers for evaluating a trailer's rhetorical appeals to an audience may be productively applied to film trailers for non-Hollywood films as well.

Salewitz, Judith, Drate, Spencer, Sarowitz, Sam, and Kehr, Dave. *Art of the Modern Movie Poster: International Poster Style and Design*. San Francisco: Chronicle, 2008.

> *Art of the Modern Movie Poster* is filled with images rather than text. Organized like a museum exhibition catalog rather than a scholarly book, it includes over 1,500 images of film posters from over fifteen countries, including Poland, Italy, Belgium, Argentina, Japan and Turkey. A key feature is that the book presents the film posters produced for a single film in as many as a dozen different countries, providing an opportunity to compare national marketing strategies and styles.

FILMS REFERENCED IN CHAPTER NINE

4 Months, 3 Weeks, and 2 Days (*4 luni, 3 saptamâni si 2 zile*, Cristian Mungiu 2007)

10 on Ten (Abbas Kiarostami, 2004)

ABC Africa (Abbas Kiarostami, 2001)

American Gangster (Ridley Scott, 2007)

Avatar (James Cameron, 2009)

Babel (Alejandro González Iñárritu, 2006)

Belissima (Luchino Visconti, 1951)

The Blair Witch Project (Daniel Myrick and Eduardo Sanchez, 1999)

Breaking the Waves (Lars Von Trier, 1996)

The Broken Oath (Harry Solter, 1910)

Certified Copy (*Copia Conforme*, Abbas Kiarostami, 2010)

Chronicle (Josh Trank, 2012)

Chungking Express (*Chung Hing sam lam*, Wong Kar-Wai, 1994)

City on Fire (*Lung fu fong wan*, Ringo Lam, 1987)

Close-up (*Nema-ye Nazdik*, Abbas Kiarostami, 1990)

Colourful Journey (Ahmed and Mohamed Abu Nasser, 2011)

Crouching Tiger, Hidden Dragon (*Wo hu cang long,* Ang Lee, 2000)

The Curious Case of Benjamin Button (David Fincher, 2008)

Dancer in the Dark (Lars Von Trier, 2000)

Do the Right Thing (Spike Lee, 1989)

Dragstrip Girl (Edward L. Cahn, 1957)

Elena (Andrey Zvyagintsev, 2011)

Funny Games (Michael Haneke, 1997)

Funny Games (Michael Haneke, 2007)

Happy Together (*Chun gwong cha sit*, Wong Kar-Wai, 1997)

Home Alone (Chris Columbus, 1990)

Hot Car Girl (Bernard L. Kowalski, 1958),

Howard's End (James Ivory, 1992)

I Vitelloni (Federico Fellini, 1953)

In the Mood for Love (*Fa Yeung Nin Wa*, Wong Kar-Wai, 2000)

Inglourious Basterds (Quentin Tarantino 2009)

Italian for Beginners (Lone Scherfig, 2000)

Kaante (Sanjay Gupta, 2002)

Kill, Baby … Kill! (*Operazione Paura,* Mario Bava, 1966)

Life, and Nothing More (*Zendegi va digar hich*, Abbas Kiarostami, 1992)

Love Happens (Brandon Camp, 2009)

The Man with the Golden Arm (Otto Preminger, 1956)

Melancholia (Lars Von Trier, 2011)

Moneyball (Bennett Miller, 2011)

Om Shanti Om (Farah Khan, 2007)

Paranormal Activity (Oren Peli, 2007)

The Proposal (Anne Fletcher, 2009)

Rashomon (Akira Kurosawa, 1950)

Red Desert (*Il deserto rosso,* Michelangelo Antonioni, 1964)

Red Tails (Anthony Hemingway, 2012)

Report (*Gozaresh,* Abbas Kiarostami, 1977)

Reservoir Dogs (Quentin Tarantino, 1992)

Runaway Daughters (Edward L. Cahn, 1956)

Sense and Sensibility (Ang Lee, 1995)

Seven Years in Tibet (Jean-Jacques Annaud, 1997)

Snakes on a Plane (David Ellis, 2006)

Suspiria (Dario Argento, 1977)

The Switch (Josh Gordon and Will Speck, 2010)

Taste of Cherry (*Ta'm e guilass*, Abbas Kiarostami, 1997)

Ted (Seth MacFarlane, 2012)

Ten (Abbas Kiarostami, 2002)

This is Cinerama (Merian Cooper, 1952)

Through the Olive Trees (*Zire darakhatan zeyton*, Abbas Kiarostami, 1994)

The Town (Ben Affleck, 2010)

Toy Story (John Lasseter, 1995)

Transformers (Michael Bay, 2007)

True Grit (Henry Hathaway, 1969)

True Grit (Ethan Coen and Joel Coen, 2010)

Two Women (Tahmineh Milani, 1999)

Uncle Boonmee Who Can Recall His Past Lives (*Loong Boonmee raleuk chat,* Apitchatpong Weerasethakul, 2010)

Up (Peter Docter and Bob Peterson, 2009)

Vertigo (Alfred Hitchcock, 1958)

WALL-E (Andrew Stanton, 2008)

West Side Story (Robert Wise and Jerome Robbins, 1961)

When in Rome (Mark Steven Johnson, 2010)

NOTES

1 Finola Kerrigan, *Film Marketing* (London: Routledge, 2009), 42–43.

2 Justin Wyatt, *High Concept: Movies and Marketing in Hollywood* (Austin: University of Texas Press, 1994), 158.

3 All budget and revenue figures in this chapter are listed in US dollars and sourced from www.boxofficemojo.com. All figures are rounded to the nearest million. All revenues represent gross worldwide box office returns unless otherwise noted.

4 Steve Rose, "'The film is so slow – it's like grandma telling stories'," the *Guardian*, 13 February 2001.

5 Tad Friend, "The Cobra: Inside a Movie Marketer's Playbook," *New Yorker*, 29 January 2009.

6 Lisa Kernan, *Coming Attractions: Reading American Movie Trailers* (Austin: University of Texas Press, 2004), 14–15.

7 Source: http://rogerebert.suntimes.com/apps/pbcs.dll/article?AID=/20030411/REVIEWS/304110305/1023, accessed 24 September 2014.

8 Jonathan Gray, *Show Sold Separately: Promos, Spoilers, and Other Media Paratexts* (New York: New York University Press, 2010), 24.

9 Gray, 24.

10 Gray, 26.

11 Harriet Sherwood. "Tarzan and Arab: The Gaza Artists Determined to Make it against All Odds." The *Guardian*, 15 August 2011, http://www.theguardian.com/world/2011/aug/15/tarzan-arab-gaza-artists, accessed 24 September 2014.

12 Dave Kehr, *Art of the Modern Movie Poster: International Postwar Style and Design* (San Francisco: Chronicle Books, 2008), 12.

13 Kehr, 36.

14 John Thornton Caldwell, *Production Culture: Industrial Reflexivity and Critical Practice in Film and Television* (Durham, NC: Duke University Press, 2008).

CHAPTER TEN
DISTRIBUTION

Oscilloscope Laboratories. Wanda Vision. Midas Filmes. Cinema Prestige. Mares Films. Each of these companies owns the rights to distribute the film *Reality* (Matteo Garrone, 2012). After its successful debut at the 2012 Cannes International Film Festival, *Reality* secured nine different distribution deals. An article in *The Hollywood Reporter* listed its distribution partners:

> U.S. rights to the film were already acquired by Oscilloscope, which said it would probably release it Stateside in 2013. In the latest round of sales, rights were picked up in Spain by Wanda Vision, by Curious in Australia, in Portugal by Midas Filmes, in Russia by Cinema Prestige, by Demiurg in the former Yugoslavia, in Brazil by Mares Film, in Greece by Seven Films, by the Film Point Group in Poland, and by Suez in Hungary. Co-producer Fandango will distribute the film in Italy starting in September.[1]

During its march through the international film festival circuit, *Reality* landed another important distribution deal at the Toronto International Film Festival. The British companies Independent Distribution and Fandango Portobello announced plans to co-distribute the film in the UK.

An Italian–French co-production (produced by Archimede-Fandango and Le Pacte-Garance Capital with RAI Cinema), *Reality* presents the story of an Italian fishmonger obsessed with joining the cast of *Big Brother*, the local version of the hit reality television show. The film chronicles his obsession with the show and the paranoia that results from that obsession. The film's success in securing international distribution may be attributed to several elements that distributors could showcase when marketing the film to exhibitors. First, the film followed Garrone's previous feature film *Gomorrah* (*Gomorra*, 2008), a critical and commercial success. Second, the film's focus on reality television could appeal to international audiences who otherwise might not be drawn to Italian films. Finally, like *Gomorrah* before it, *Reality* won the prestigious Grand Prix award at Cannes.

For some distribution companies, *Reality* also complemented their company profile. Oscilloscope Laboratories, founded by Adam Yauch of Beastie Boys fame, specializes in "unique, independently produced films" according to their company website (www.oscilloscope.net). *Reality* fits well within an eclectic film catalog that includes *Meek's Cutoff* (Kelly Reichardt, 2011), *Samsara* (Ron Fricke, 2012), and *Exit Through the Gift Shop* (Banksy, 2010). Oscilloscope's experience distributing independent and international films to arthouse theatres and other medium-sized venues positioned it as an ideal company to distribute *Reality* to potential exhibitors and audiences.

Contemporary audiences are accustomed to seeing a long list of companies introduced during a film's opening credits: "Studio X presents ... a Studio Y film ... in partnership with Studio Z ... and Independent Distributor A." Some of these companies contributed financing for the production of the film, and others contributed resources for its distribution. For *Reality*, the festival circuit was crucial to landing international distribution deals. Other films secure distribution from major Hollywood studios before production begins. Some films – in fact most films – never find a theatrical distributor. For these, online distribution will be the primary method for reaching audiences. Even for those films that enjoy a wide global release, online distribution is a vital revenue source. This chapter will review global film distribution strategies in the contemporary marketplace, focusing first on commercial theatrical distribution and then discussing other distribution markets and models.

WHAT WE WILL DO IN CHAPTER 10

- Examine the dominant distribution models for contemporary feature films.
- Trace the release patterns for feature films across different platforms and global regions.
- Compare these distribution models to alternative distribution practices linked to niche audiences and local audiences.

BY THE END OF CHAPTER 10 YOU SHOULD BE ABLE TO

- Identify the major global distribution networks for commercial film.
- Explain the path that a feature film takes from production to multiple sites of exhibition.
- Describe other models of film distribution, including the distribution of indigenous media, exploitation cinema, experimental cinema, pornography, and amateur film.

MAPPING GLOBAL DISTRIBUTION

Distribution is a vital element of the international film industry. The accessibility of digital equipment and the success of independent models of film production have made it much easier to produce a feature film with limited financial and industrial resources. Once an independent film is made, however, it is nearly impossible to show it in theatres without the support of a major distributor. A very small group of international film distributors controls what audiences see on screens around the world. These distributors have the resources to support the **P and A cost**, or prints and advertising cost, associated with distributing a film. According to the Motion Picture Association of America (MPAA) Theatrical Market Statistics Report for 2007 (the last year, at the time of writing, for which the MPAA released market data), the average cost to produce and distribute a film by an MPAA member studio was $106.6 million. This sum includes a **negative cost** (the cost of producing the film) of $70.8 million and a prints and advertising cost of $35.9 million. The P and A cost is a significant part of a film's overall budget. Distributors must produce thousands of copies of the film, ship the copies to theatres across the world, and market the film to exhibitors and audiences.

The conversion to digital projection in theatres worldwide has reduced the cost of producing prints. A 2013 study published by Screen Digest reported that almost 90 per cent of screens worldwide were digitized. According to the report, the percentage of digitized screens varies widely, with almost 100 per cent of screens digitized in South Korea and Singapore but only 20.2 per cent of screens converted in Venezuela as of 2013.[2] Digitization may alter the economics of distribution, but wide theatrical releases require advertising budgets that only large studios can shoulder. While producers can find ways to minimize the negative cost of a film (for example, shooting with digital cameras and hiring non-professional actors), finding innovative ways to infiltrate theatrical distribution networks without the support of a major studio is very difficult.

Distributors

Today the **Big Six** Hollywood studios dominate the distribution of Hollywood films worldwide, and Hollywood films dominate the box office in many global regions. The Big Six continue to produce films through their primary studios and their subsidiary studios, but distribution is the core of their business. Paramount Pictures, Columbia Pictures, Warner Bros. Pictures, Walt Disney Pictures, Universal Pictures, and 20th Century Fox control the distribution of Hollywood films both in the United States and in international markets. Large conglomerates with diverse media holdings own each of these studios:

Conglomerate	Film studio
Viacom	Paramount Pictures
Sony	Columbia Pictures
Time Warner	Warner Bros. Pictures
Disney Company	Walt Disney Pictures
Comcast/General Electric	Universal Pictures
News Corporation	20th Century Fox

Conglomeration, which we introduced in Chapter 5, is key to the success of Hollywood distribution. Few films are profitable based on their theatrical release in the US market alone. Many films do not turn a profit either until after their global theatrical release or until after their release in ancillary markets, as discussed in Chapter 6. For example, *Resident Evil: Afterlife* (Paul W.S. Anderson, 2010) earned $60 million in its domestic box office release in the United States. With a production budget of $60 million, the film broke even after its domestic release. Then it earned an additional $236 million from its global theatrical release. Its first week of DVD sales in the United States generated an additional $9 million.[3] Large conglomerates have the resources to distribute the films they own across international theatrical and ancillary markets and to wait for films to make a profit. Successful film distribution requires a lot of money and a lot of patience.

The heads of the individual studios report to **parent divisions** within the larger conglomerates. For example, the parent division for Columbia Pictures is Sony Pictures Entertainment. As the parent division for the studio, Sony Pictures manages the distribution of films produced by: Columbia Pictures, Sony Pictures Classics (their "indie" or "art house" division), several other subsidiary studios (including TriStar Pictures and Sony Pictures Animation), and independent studios or producers who have negotiated distribution deals with Sony. In addition to distributing the films produced by these studios for domestic and international theatrical exhibition, Sony Pictures Entertainment also manages the distribution of television shows to networks, the distribution of film and television shows on DVD and Blu-ray and online, and the distribution of apps (tied to their film and television properties) for mobile devices. Their corporate website (www.sonypictures.com) lists the films that are currently in DVD and Blu-ray distribution.

If you browse the catalog of Sony's films on DVD and Blu-ray, you may recognize only a small percentage of the titles. Sony owns the rights to distribute many more films than they will ever release in theatres. This practice is called **overstocking** and relates to the practice of **differential promotion**. In *Understanding Media Industries*, media scholars Timothy Havens and Amanda D. Lotz explain:

> Differential promotion refers to the fact that distributors tend to shower praise, attention, and money on only a small fraction of the products they acquire, specifically, those songs, artists, films, and television series that they believe have the greatest potential to become hits. These products benefit from large promotional budgets and strong-arm promotional efforts designed to cajole exhibitors, retailers, and even critics to give those products privileged treatment.[4]

The other films receive much less attention. Some of these become "straight to DVD" releases that never see the inside of a theatre. The Sony Pictures DVD catalog includes several types of straight to DVD films: Christian films such as *The Moment After* (Wes Llewellyn, 1999); classic films from Columbia's film library such as *Once More, With Feeling!* (Stanley Donen, 1960); and imported films such as the British *Tonight, You're Mine* (David McKenzie, 2011).

Most independent films also go straight to ancillary markets if they are unable to secure distribution from a major studio. To prevent this fate, independent production companies or independent producers often negotiate distribution rights for their films with the large studios as early as possible. Some films will not secure distribution until the post-production stage, after the film has been screened on the festival circuit, where both large and small distributors shop for films. Other films will presell their distribution rights either before production begins or while production is ongoing, in effect inviting the distributor to co-produce the film. In this case, the major studios function as banks for the independent studios. They provide larger production budgets and access to broad distribution networks in exchange for the majority of theatrical and ancillary revenues. The major studios can afford to take risks on independent productions. When these films perform well at the box office, the studios earn significant profits. The studios also benefit by expanding their **libraries** of films for distribution in ancillary markets, particularly on television, where studios continue to furnish networks with many of the films they broadcast.

Studio investment in independent film has declined since its height in the 1990s. Important "indie" studio divisions such as Warner Independent Pictures and Paramount Vantage have been closed in response to declining DVD sales and shrinking global markets. Filmmakers who cannot access the distribution resources of the major studios may elect to self-distribute their films. **Self-distribution** or **DIY distribution** may involve several small distribution companies that specialize in DVD, video-on-demand, or local theatrical distribution. Filmmakers may also hire consultants who specialize in distribution to specific audiences or through specific channels.

The marketing and exhibition of self-distributed films often relies on new media and social media. YouTube, Facebook and Twitter are important sites for the promotion of self-distributed films. Self-distribution enables filmmakers to connect more directly with their audiences through these sites. Self-distribution also brings creative advantages. Studios often require filmmakers to make changes to their scripts (or to the final cut of the film, depending on when the studio enters the picture) in order to expand the potential audience for the film. Self-distribution allows filmmakers to maintain creative control over their work. In spite of these opportunities and advantages, however, it is a difficult path.

One of the earliest examples of self-distribution is the career of the African-American director Oscar Micheaux, who famously carried prints of his films from theatre to theatre in a practice referred to as **bicycling**. In *Black Films/White Money*, film scholar Jesse Algeron Rhines explains Micheaux's distribution practices:

> His solution to the problem of how to distribute his films was to "bicycle" or hand carry individual prints from theatre to theatre across the nation in early spring. He would show his movie to a house manager, along with the script for the next feature to be made. Sometimes his star actors and actresses would accompany him. Micheaux would then begin to haggle with the manager for rental fees and length of play in the theatre in an attempt to secure an advance against the film's return. By late spring Micheaux would be back in New York to film the script as its producer, director, and even cameraman. He would edit during the summer, and by fall he would be on the road again bicycling his film from theatre to theatre and promoting it as he went along.[5]

With this method, Micheaux successfully distributed over twenty films from 1919 to 1948, including *Within Our Gates* (1920), *Body and Soul* (1925), and *The Girl From Chicago* (1932). While new media have made self-distribution easier in many ways for contemporary filmmakers than it was for Micheaux, it remains very difficult to generate profits through self-distribution.

Films from outside the United States may also rely on the major Hollywood studios for international distribution. However, as the earlier discussion of the distribution arrangements for *Reality* demonstrates, an international network of smaller, regionally based distribution companies also supports the distribution of non-Hollywood films. Some of these companies have close ties to the major studios (or function as studio subsidiaries), but many operate as independent distributors in specific international territories. For example, Cinema Prestige in Russia specializes in the distribution of art films and television series. Their catalog includes films and television shows produced in France, Italy, Poland, and Japan. Whether films made outside the United States acquire distribution through a Hollywood studio or other regional distributors, the international film festival circuit is an important marketplace for films with global distribution ambitions, particularly international art films. Genre films made outside the United States are often distributed only nationally or within a set network of countries where a particular genre (or national cinema) is popular among local audiences.

EXERCISE

Research the distribution deals made during a recent international film festival. The Cannes Film Festival, the Sundance Film Festival, the Toronto International Film Festival, and the Busan International Film Festival are several of the most prominent international film festivals, serving as important venues where film producers secure domestic and international distribution deals. Choose one of these festivals (or one of the many other festivals known for generating distribution agreements) and search online for information about the distribution deals that were negotiated there. You will find valuable information on the festival's own website, in trade periodicals like *Variety* and *The Hollywood Reporter*, on industry blogs, and in the online English-language editions of local newspapers.

- How many films negotiated distribution deals at the festival?
- Identify the distributors for each film. Did films negotiate multiple distribution deals for different global regions?
- Do the films with international distribution deals share any features (for example, a common language or genre)?
- How does the festival describe its mission on its website? Do you see any connections between its mission and the films that reached distribution agreements at the festival?

Destinations

The major distributors supply films to theatre chains and independent theatres throughout the world. The term "global Hollywood" captures the extraordinary distribution reach of the Big Six studios.[6] They place their products in theatres around the world, using their financial resources to corner international markets and thus limit opportunities for the distribution and exhibition of films from other countries. Sony Pictures Global, for example, has local offices in over sixty countries, from Latvia to Lebanon, from Sweden to Serbia. (A complete list of their global offices is available at www.sonypictures.net.) These studio arms arrange the distribution of the studio's products in local theatres, supervise local marketing campaigns, and organize translations for the films if necessary. The MPAA reported that in 2011, $22.48 billion of the $32.6 billion in total box office revenues for Hollywood films were generated in international markets.[7]

10.1 Global top twenty feature films 2009.

2009

Rank	Top 20 feature films	Origin	Type	Language	Weighted scores	Sequel/ franchise*
1	Ice Age: Dawn of the Dinosaurs	USA	Animation – Family	English	450	Yes
2	Harry Potter and the Half-Blood Prince	GBR INC/ USA	Fiction – Action/ Adventure	English	334	Yes
3	2012	USA	Fiction – Action/ Adventure	English (*Tibetan, Mandarin*)	304	No
4	Avatar	USA/GBR	Fiction – Action/ Adventure	English	302	Yes
5	The Twilight Saga: New Moon	USA	Fiction – Drama	English	197	Yes
6	Up	USA	Animation – Family	English	188	No
7	Angels & Demons	USA	Fiction – Action/ Adventure	English (*Italian*)	173	Yes
8	Transformers: Revenge of the Fallen	USA	Fiction – Action/ Adventure	English	154	Yes
9	Slumdog Millionaire	GBR	Fiction – Drama	English (*Hindi*)	64	No
10	The Hangover	USA/DEU	Fiction – Comedy	English	57	Yes
11	Fast & Furious	USA	Fiction – Action/ Adventure	English	43	Yes
12	Inglourious Basterds	USA/DEU	Fiction – Action/ Adventure	English	36	No
13	The Proposal	USA	Fiction – Comedy	English	32	No
14	Terminator Salvation	USA	Fiction – Action/ Adventure	English	31	Yes
15	Bolt	USA	Animation – Family	English	28	No
16	Millennium 1 – The Girl with the Dragon Tattoo	SWE/DNK/ DEU	Fiction – Drama	Swedish	28	Yes
17	Millennium 2 – The Girl who Played with Fire	SWE/DNK/ DEU	Fiction – Drama	Swedish	24	Yes
18	Michael Jackson's This Is It	USA	Documentary	English	23	No
19	Night at the Museum: Battle of the Smithsonian	USA	Fiction – Family	English	23	Yes
20	Madagascar: Escape 2 Africa	USA	Animation – Family	English	18	Yes

Notes: CZE: Czech Republic DEU: Germany
DNK: Denmark ESP: Spain
FRA: France ITA: Italia
GBR: United Kingdom HUN: Hungary
NZL: New Zealand RUS: Russian Federation
SVK: Slovakia SWE: Sweden
USA: United States

*: For franchises, while many films have connections to merchandise or other media (books, comics, etc.), only the titles that are part of extended film or television properties are recorded here.

Source: UNESCO Institute for Statistics, January 2012, http://www.uis.unesco.org/datacentre; http://www.uis.unesco.org/culture/Documents/ib8-analysis-cinema-production-2012-en2.pdf, 5.

10.2a Total admissions for the top ten countries and percentage of the world total, 2005–2009.

Rank	2005		2006		2007		2008		2009	
1	India	3,770,000,000*	India	3,997,000,000*	India	3,290,000,000	India	3,251,000,000*	India	2,917,000,000*
2	United States	1,403,000,000	United States	1,449,000,000	United States	1,399,316,912	United States	1,341,346,867	United States	1,415,238,501
3	France	175,520,898	China	188,772,263	China	195,800,000	China	209,800,000	China	263,800,000
4	China	164,700,000	France	176,200,000	France	178,168,096	France	190,081,537	France	201,142,290
5	Japan	160,452,000	Mexico	164,584,000	Mexico	175,000,000	Mexico	182,000,000	Mexico	178,000,000
6	United Kingdom	157,200,000	Japan	156,560,402	United Kingdom	163,190,000	United Kingdom	164,200,000	United Kingdom	173,500,000
7	Mexico	153,997,284	United Kingdom	154,283,256	Japan	162,400,000	Japan	160,490,000	Japan	169,300,000
8	Rep. of Korea	145,600,000	Rep. of Korea	153,400,000	Rep. of Korea	158,770,000	Rep. of Korea	150,830,000	Rep. of Korea	156,960,000
9	Germany	127,640,000	Germany	134,613,450	Russia	116,930,692	Germany	118,000,000	Germany	135,600,000
10	Spain	126,234,617	Spain	121,650,000	Germany	111,400,000	Russia	115,100,000	Russia	132,000,000
World admissions		7,369,925,156		7,757,508,474		7,043,068,559		7,006,527,010		6,948,916,820
Total for Top 10		6,384,344,799		6,696,063,371		5,950,975,700		5,882,848,404		5,742,540,791
Share of the Top 10		86.6%		86.3%		84.5%		84.0%		82.6%
Countries covered		72		73		72		74		72

Note: (*) Estimations from Focus World Film Market Trends, European Audiovisual Observatory 2011.

Source: UNESCO Institute for Statistics, January 2012, http://www.uis.unesco.org/datacentre; http://www.uis.unesco.org/culture/Documents/ib8-analysis-cinema-production-2012-en2.pdf, 17.

10.2b Growth rate of admissions, 2005–2009.

	2005–2006	2006–2007	2007–2008	2008–2009	2005–2009	Average
Growth rate of world admissions	5.3%	−9.2%	−0.5%	−0.8%	−5.7%	−1.3%
Growth rate of Top 10	4.9%	−11.1%	−1.1%	-2.4%	−10.1%	−2.4%
Growth rate of world admissions (without India)	4.5%	−0.2%	0.1%	7.4%	12.0%	2.9%
Growth rate of Top 10 (without India)	3.2%	−1.4%	−1.1%	7.4%	8.1%	2.0%

Source: UNESCO Institute for Statistics, January 2012, http://www.uis.unesco.org/datacentre; http://www.uis.unesco.org/culture/Documents/ib8-analysis-cinema-production-2012-en2.pdf, 17.

The statistics in tables 10.1 and 10.2 compiled by UNESCO document the top-grossing films and the top performing countries. They capture the dominance of global Hollywood distribution. Of the twenty top-grossing films internationally in 2009, only three were produced primarily outside of the United States – *Slumdog Millionaire* (Danny Boyle), *The Girl with the Dragon Tattoo* (*Män som hatar kvinnor*, Niels Arden Oplev), and *The Girl who Played with Fire* (*Flickan som lekte med elden*, Daniel Alfredson). With Hollywood films occupying most international screens, there is little room for the distribution of locally and regionally produced films. Some countries combat Hollywood's distribution monopoly with quotas that limit the percentage of films from other countries on domestic screens (as discussed in Chapter 5, "Film as a commodity").

Not all countries have film industries that can support quotas. For example, Romania has approximately eighty theatres for a population of approximately 22 million people (compared to approximately 40,000 theatres in the United States). The limited scale of film exhibition in Romania reduces the domestic box office foundation for Romanian films. Some Romanian films released during the 2000s – often referred to as the "Romanian New Wave" – have earned critical acclaim through the international film festival circuit. *The Death of Mr. Lazarescu* (*Moartea domnului Lazarescu*, Cristi Puiu, 2005), *12:08 East of Bucharest* (*A fost sau n-a fost?*, Corneliu Porumboiu, 2006), and *4 months, 3 weeks, and 2 days* (*4 luni, 3 saptamâni si 2 zile*, Cristian Mungiu, 2007) are among the Romanian releases to have won key prizes at the Cannes International Film Festival. Critics associate these films with a "New Wave" because they share a minimalist style, an interest in cinematic realism, and a spirit of dark humor. While these films have been celebrated on the international art house circuit (screening at festivals, independent theatres, and universities), they are less popular in Romania, where Hollywood films dominate theatrical exhibition.

CASE STUDY: EROS ENTERTAINMENT

The UNESCO charts reveal that India has led all other countries in total box office admissions every year, with more than double the total admissions recorded in the United States. India has a thriving film scene and a prolific film industry. While there are no Indian titles on the list of the top twenty global feature films, Indian films are an important global export. Eros Entertainment is a Mumbai-based Bollywood production and distribution company with a library of over 1,500 films. Eros distributes approximately 70 films each year for theatrical release through its Eros International unit, including both regional-language films and big-budget films featuring well-known stars. In addition to its international distribution offices in the UK, United States, and Canada, Eros distributes films in South Africa, Singapore, Thailand, Malaysia, Australia, New Zealand, Sri Lanka, Burma, Kenya, Uganda, Indonesia, and dozens of other countries. Eros describes their distribution and marketing strategy for potential partners, emphasizing the effects of the digital conversion mentioned earlier:

> The Indian theatrical market has seen growth in both multiplex and single screen theatres with the number of digital screens overtaking physical print distribution thereby creating high margin revenue increases. The increased availability of screens has seen a trend towards wide releases and therefore a greater skew towards opening box office weekend. The revenue model in India continues to be revenue share from multiplexes based on a pre-agreed share and minimum guarantee advances from single screen chains. The main theatrical markets outside India are the UK, USA/Canada, Dubai, South Africa, Australia, Fiji and Singapore and are serviced through our local distribution offices in these places. This also allows us to leverage our marketing strength globally, which is an integral part of our distribution strategy as we believe that while markets are global, audiences are local. We tailor campaigns to the market and to the film, utilizing brand-tie-ups, outdoor, television, print, in-cinema, radio, mobile and online mediums to promote and generate momentum building up to the theatrical release of the film, which we believe gives Eros a big competitive edge.[8]

Eros considers the rhetorical appeals associated with each film (as discussed in Chapter 9, "Marketing") before designing a distribution strategy. Films with a marketable star and an international storyline (with characters living in or traveling to countries outside India) have the broadest appeal. For example, *Devdas* (Sanjay Bhangali, 2002) stars Shah Rukh Khan and Madhuri Dixit in a story that brings its characters to London. The film was very successful in its theatrical release in the UK and was nominated for a BAFTA (British Academy of Film and Television Arts) Award for Best Foreign Language Film. Eros has the resources to translate its films into over twenty-five languages for international distribution, and all of its films are available with English subtitles.

Like many other distribution companies, ancillary markets provide a significant percentage of Eros Entertainment's revenue. Eros distributes films for Indian television and for international television markets, including the BBC and Channel 4 in the UK. The satellite channel B4U or

Bollywood for You was modeled on HBO as a provider of "premium" content for Bollywood audiences across five continents. Available in the United States, the UK, Spain, Russia, Greece, Egypt, and Yemen, to name only a few of its television distribution zones, B4U makes Bollywood cinema accessible to audiences who may not have the opportunity to see Bollywood films in theatres. Eros also distributes films to cable and broadcast networks. Eros "bundles" new releases with older films from its library (a version of block booking), using the demand for popular new films to place older films on television. Eros has also partnered with HBO Asia (jointly owned by Time Warner and Paramount) to create two new premium networks that air both Hollywood and Bollywood films and HBO original series. The advertising-free "premium" channels have dual-language screening options in English and Hindi for some films and television shows. This partnership is one of many co-production and co-distribution agreements at the core of the Eros operation. Eros is both a regional and a global company, partnering with other global companies who want to invest in the Indian media market. The global distribution of Bollywood cinema remains Eros's chief venture, but the company continues to explore new products and markets.

One of the distinguishing features of Bollywood cinema is the importance of film music. Song-and-dance sequences have a life of their own outside the films. Songs are released in advance of the films to build anticipation among audiences, music videos are released on television and online, and distributors like Eros release compilation DVDs and CDs of popular songs. These DVDs may focus on songs performed by a particular film star, songs sung by a particular playback singer (the musical stars who sing many beloved Bollywood film songs but who never appear on screen), or songs associated with a particular film genre or theme. The Eros Channel on YouTube (http://www.youtube.com/user/erosentertainment) features many music videos and clips in its programming line-up. The site boasts over one billion views – an impressive number for a channel that specializes in promotional material (including music videos, trailers, and interviews). Eros also owns its own music label so that it can produce and distribute music in tandem with its films. For example, Eros Music partnered with Sony Music Entertainment to produce and distribute the soundtrack for the Bollywood "zombie comedy" *Go Goa Gone* (Krishna D.K. and Rak Nidimoru, 2013), a film Eros produced. Eros and Sony combined their distribution resources to expand the market for physical and digital copies of the soundtrack and individual songs. With this global partnership, Eros maximizes the profits from a single film through both multiple products and multiple distribution territories.

Platforms

The primary market for films distributed by Hollywood studios is the large theatre chain. When the Hollywood studios had tight control of theatrical exhibition in the United States (before the breakup of their vertically integrated monopolies through the 1948 Paramount Consent Decree), studios could force theatres to rent their films through two coercive practices. **Blind bidding** requires exhibitors to rent films they have never seen. **Block booking** packages highly anticipated films (produced by famous directors or featuring beloved stars) with less exciting fare. While these practices no longer shape film distribution in the United States, distributors still exert control over film exhibition, leaving many exhibitors with little room to make innovative or independent programming decisions. Contracts with exhibitors often specify that distributors will recover the majority of **grosses** (total box office receipts) during the opening weekend and a slightly smaller percentage of grosses with each passing week. In effect, distributors take the highest percentage of profits during the most lucrative weekend. To provide some balance in this arrangement, exhibitors charge distributors for their operational costs and keep 100 per cent of the profits generated by concessions. The distributors, however, still earn the bulk of the revenue generated by film exhibition. They then pay the directors, stars, writers and producers who have been contractually guaranteed a percentage of the box office profits through **back-end deals**. The distributors pay these parties only after they have paid themselves a fee, recovered their marketing costs, and repaid any investments they made in the film's production.

Ancillary markets often generate more revenue for a studio than theatrical distribution, as we saw in Chapter 6. A typical release pattern for a Hollywood film is: first-run theatres, airplane and hotel exhibition, DVD and Blu-ray, video-on-demand or pay-per-view, premium cable television, internet, second-run theatres, and cable and broadcast television. This sequence is not fixed or applicable to every film. Video-on-demand services frequently advertise that they are offering new releases before they are available on DVD. Some small distributors release their films through video-on-demand before releasing them theatrically in order to generate early buzz for them. **Piracy** complicates this sequence further, since pirated copies of a film can be released at any point in a film's run in theatrical and ancillary markets.

Ancillary markets generate a significant percentage of the total revenue for films released by the major studios. The Big Six studios also generate profits from the *mode* of exhibition rather than solely from the products being exhibited. The following account of Sony's ownership of multiple points of a film's distribution chain illustrates the many revenue streams that lead back to the conglomerates:

> In the case of the Sony Corporation, which owns Columbia Pictures, MGM, and United Artists, it is possible for a consumer to purchase or rent a film produced by one of the company's subsidiaries and distributed by Columbia-TriStar Home Video for playing on a Sony DVD or VHS player for viewing on a Sony television monitor. Another option is for the consumer to download a movie from Movielink, of which Sony is part owner, for viewing on a Sony personal computer. Additionally, a consumer might purchase a video game based on one of the company's films for playing on a Sony Playstation unit.[9]

It is important to emphasize again that theatrical distribution is available only to a limited number of films. Most films will only be distributed in ancillary markets. For these films, DVD, video-on-demand, and internet distribution are the primary rather than the ancillary markets.

DVD distributors divide international territories into six distinct numbered regions. For example, Region 1 includes the United States and Canada; Region 2 includes Europe, the Middle East and Japan; and Region 3 includes Southeast Asia, South Korea, Taiwan, and Hong Kong. The discs produced in one region are not compatible with the DVD players produced in another region, establishing distribution walls between the zones. Large DVD distributors have the resources to release films on DVD in every region simultaneously, but independent distributors will often only release their films within one global region. Devoted cinephiles can navigate these DVD borders by purchasing multi-region DVD players or using various online programs to neutralize a DVD region code when screening a film on a computer. Many consumers, however, only purchase the DVDs that are distributed for sale in their region, thus limiting their access to the vast catalog of world cinema available for home exhibition. Blu-ray has concentrated distribution into three region codes. While this system, like the DVD system, allows distributors to adjust release dates and prices for each region, many studios release region-free Blu-ray discs that can be played on any Blu-ray player.

DVD piracy has provided one solution to incompatible DVD regions, with DVD distributors selling previously unavailable titles to local cinephiles. For example, the "Quiapo cinémathèque" in Manila is a bustling local market that provides both local and international tourists with a diverse library of pirated DVDs. Film scholar Jasmine Nadua Trice explains the importance of the Quiapo markets to film culture in the Philippines:

> As one might expect, the availability of more obscure works is limited, with films such as the low-budget Irish movie, *Once*, or works of classical Hollywood cinema never being shown in Manila's theatres, but eventually making their way to the bins in Quiapo. In these instances, Quiapo is a solution to cinema-going problems for movie fans existing at the margins of legalized world cinema distribution, overcoming difficulties with regard to accessibility and low incomes.[10]

DVD piracy in Manila remains an important distribution channel for local cinephiles and curious tourists in spite of several successful raids by the local Optical Media Board.

DVD revenues, which had been the focus of distribution efforts for home exhibition for over a decade, have begun to decline. A 2010 report announced:

> wholesale revenue from DVDs in 2010 was $4.47 billion, down from $7.97 billion in 2009 and a high of $10.13 billion in 2007. The drop comes despite an 18 per cent increase in the number of titles released by studios, to 415. However, the average number of units sold per title dropped by more than half, to 545,000, from 1.14 million in 2009.[11]

For the major studios, revenues from Blu-ray and legal digital downloads offset some of these losses. Whether or not DVD continues to be a relevant format for film distribution, earlier models of distribution for home exhibition are already nearing extinction. Many communities no longer have video stores. Consumers may purchase DVDs through brick-and-mortar chain stores, buy DVDs from online retailers, or rent DVDs from online distributors. Many viewers with high-speed internet connections and internet-enabled home theatre systems opt to access films online, eliminating the need for DVDs altogether.

Online exhibition promises more immediate and less cumbersome access to films from other international regions. However, obstacles to a truly global online distribution system persist. Hulu, for example, is a US-based online exhibition platform that distributes films and television shows from hundreds of **content providers**, including Big Six studios like Universal and 20th Century Fox (http://www.hulu.com/partners). Their service allows viewers to stream some content for free and to access other "premium" content by paying a minimal subscription fee for their "Hulu Plus" service. Hulu has featured its growing library of films and television shows in its marketing campaigns, but the Hulu platform is available only to viewers who are accessing the internet in the United States. In 2012, Hulu launched Hulu Japan, its first major online exhibition portal in a market outside the United States. Not all of Hulu's content providers, however, made their films and television shows available to Hulu Japan. In 2014, Hulu announced the sale of Hulu Japan to the Japanese television network Nippon TV.[12] The slow and uneven distribution of legal content online and the dizzying proliferation of illegal content online suggest that barriers to the legal online exhibition of films from around the world will stay in place for some time.

Release patterns

There are two primary models for the distribution of Hollywood films worldwide: **platforming** and **wide release**. Distributors select a distribution strategy for a film based on its marketing potential. Platforming depends on the gradual development of word-of-mouth buzz for a film. A studio will release a film in the United States in New York City and Los Angeles on its opening weekend, after placing the film in several festivals where early critical praise can be generated. After the film has begun to generate interest among audiences (often based on positive reviews by professional film critics or nominations for prestigious awards), the distributor will gradually broaden its release. If you live in a small town, it may take several weeks or even several months before a platform release will reach your local theatre. Films released via platforming often share one or more of the following characteristics: a modest marketing budget, an older target audience (men and women over 25), an absence of special effects or other spectacular elements, an original story that is difficult to frame through high concept marketing, and awards potential.

Films that open in wide release may reach theatres in small towns on the same day that they open in large cities. Only films with the support of the major distributors enjoy wide release because it requires extensive resources to invest in a marketing campaign that will successfully lead audiences to the opening weekend in large numbers. Films that underperform on their opening weekend may be pulled from theatres by the end of the week to make room for other titles, so distributors time the release of their films so that they are not placing promising films in direct competition for opening weekend grosses with films from other studios. To avoid these face-offs, studios may delay the release of a **tentpole film** for several weeks. Tentpole films – supported by large production and marketing budgets – are expected to prop up the revenues of the major studios, offsetting losses from lower-budget films or unexpected flops.

In local theatres, the effects of wide release strategies are evident. A successful tentpole film may remain in a local theatre for several months if, in spite of predictably diminishing profits each week, it continues to generate sizable revenues for the distributor and exhibitor. A film that opened at a local multiplex on multiple screens with a show starting every hour may only be playing on one screen at that theatre several weeks later, perhaps sharing the screen with another film in a rotating screening schedule. If you go to the movies every weekend, you will notice that the line-up of films usually doesn't change dramatically from week to week. One or two immediate flops may disappear from the marquee and a long-running blockbuster may finally retire, leaving room for only a few new releases each week. Because studios overstock their slate of new films, they can easily replace underperforming films with new titles.

The **theatrical window** refers to the length of time between a film's initial release in theatres and its release in various ancillary markets. The theatrical window has been shrinking gradually each year. According to reports published by the National Association of Theatre Owners, the average theatrical release window for films distributed by the Big Six studios and two mini-major studios (Lionsgate and New Line) has decreased from four months and twelve days in 2010 to three months and twenty-seven days in 2014.[13] Theatre owners have protested this shrinking window because they make most of their money from box office receipts during the end of a film's run. Shorter theatrical runs translate into smaller revenues for exhibitors. Studios defend their reduction of the theatrical window by citing the need to curtail piracy. Distributing a legal version of the film on DVD and online as early as possible may cut into box office revenues, but it limits the losses to the distributor from the sale of illegal DVDs.

Day-and-date releasing is a distribution strategy designed to combat film piracy. It used to be common to release Hollywood films in the US and then delay the release in international markets for several weeks (or longer in some cases) in order to concentrate initial advertising costs in the domestic market. With the advent of DVD piracy and online piracy, audiences in other markets now have many opportunities to see illegal copies of the film before its theatrical release. Day-and-date releasing synchronizes the worldwide release of Hollywood films in order to undermine piracy efforts. Piracy, however, continues to pose a formidable challenge to film studios. Some studios opt to release films in theatres in other international markets before the domestic release in order to generate critical buzz for the films before the critical opening weekend.

Some critics and analysts predict that the studios will eventually move to a model of the **instantaneous worldwide release.** In a frequently cited example, *The Matrix Revolutions* (Andy and Lana Wachowski, 2003) premiered theatrically in 100 countries at 1400 Greenwich Mean Time. Warner Bros. featured this release strategy in its marketing campaign leading up to the film's opening night. While this unusual release was not necessarily designed to usher in a new industry-wide release pattern, it serves as an example of how an instantaneous worldwide release model could function in the future. In this model, studios would simultaneously release their films in theatres worldwide and on DVD, Blu-ray, and video-on-demand. This strategy would require the widespread adoption of digital projection in theatres to enable fast and efficient simultaneous distribution.[14] The current emphasis on wide release distribution and concentrated marketing campaigns leading to the opening weekend has already established the distribution and marketing framework for the instantaneous worldwide release. By harnessing the potential of digital exhibition, studios can perfect an already successful distribution formula.

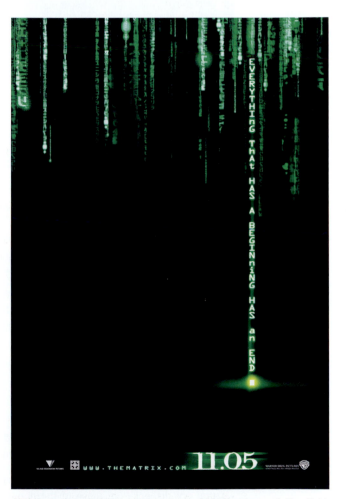

10.3 Poster advertising the instantaneous worldwide release of *The Matrix Revolutions.* Courtesy of Warner Bros./The Kobal Collection.

EXERCISE

Using Box Office Mojo (http://boxofficemojo.com/intl/) as a resource, analyze the current box office statistics in five different countries. For each country, note the top ten box office releases, the studios that are distributing those films, the number of screens on which each film is currently being shown, and the total revenue each film has earned.

- What percentage of the top-grossing films in each country are Hollywood films? Are the same Hollywood films playing in each country? Based on your research, which Hollywood films currently have the broadest global distribution? Drawing on what you have learned in this chapter, how would you account for the global reach of those films?
- How many locally produced films are currently in theatres in each country? If you notice a robust line-up of local films in a particular country, search online for information about trade policies, quotas, taxes, or other governmental or institutional measures that might support national production and exhibition.
- How many non-Hollywood films from other countries are in theatres in each country? How would you account for the distribution of one country's films in another? Do the countries share a language, a co-production agreement, or a geographic border?

Select one of the Hollywood films you discovered and one of the non-Hollywood films you discovered, and click on each title to see the number of different countries in which each film is being screened. How many regions has each film reached?

ALTERNATIVE DISTRIBUTION MODELS

The distribution strategies outlined in the previous section target a mass audience. As the discussion of the global Hollywood distribution model demonstrates, Hollywood studios seek a large global audience for their films. Independent feature films and films produced within other national and regional film industries access as large a segment of Hollywood's global audience as possible. Many films, however, are made with a much smaller and more specific audience in mind. These films target **niche audiences**, smaller groups who share an interest in a film genre, style, or format, or who have other personal, cultural, or political ties. This section will profile some industrially and culturally significant niche audiences and the distribution practices for circulating films to niche markets.

Indigenous media

Indigenous media involve the production and distribution practices of indigenous peoples. According to the United Nations, there are over 370 million indigenous peoples living in over seventy countries:

Practicing unique traditions, they retain social, cultural, economic and political characteristics that are distinct from those of the dominant societies in which they live. Spread across the world from the Arctic to the South Pacific, they are the descendants – according to a common

CASE STUDY: WOMEN MAKE MOVIES

The Center for the Study of Women in Television & Film at San Diego State University reports:

> In 2011, women comprised 18% of all directors, executive producers, producers, writers, cinematographers, and editors working on the top 250 domestic grossing films. This represents an increase of 2 percentage points from 2010 and an increase of 1 percentage point from 1998. Women accounted for 5% of directors, a decrease of 2 percentage points from 2010 and approximately half the percentage of women directors working in 1998. 38% of films employed 0 or 1 woman in the roles considered, 23% employed 2 women, 30% employed 3 to 5 women, and 7% employed 6 to 9 women.[15]

Women make movies, but they do not have many opportunities to do so within the mainstream commercial film industry.

The distribution company Women Make Movies (WMM) was founded in the United States in 1972 to provide more film production opportunities for women. In the 1970s, WMM sponsored various programs to train women to become filmmakers. During the late 1970s and early 1980s, WMM gradually shifted its focus to the distribution of films made "by and about women," maintaining a Production Assistance Program to preserve its original goal. This shift strengthened WMM's industrial influence. The WMM mission statement explains their distribution model:

> The Women Make Movies Distribution Service is our primary program. As the leading distributor of women's films and videotapes in North America, Women Make Movies works with organizations and institutions that utilize non-commercial, educational media in their programs. This includes media arts centers, museums, galleries, colleges and universities, as well as other non-profit organizations and agencies, ranging from hospitals to prisons to labor unions to the U.S. Army. Our collection of more than 500 titles includes documentary, experimental, animation, dramatic and mixed-genre work. The films and videotapes represent a diversity of styles, subjects and perspectives in women's lives. More than half of the works in the collection were produced by women of diverse cultures, and the collection includes a variety of works by and about lesbians, older women and women with disabilities. In the last three years, WMM has returned more than $1.5 million to women producers in royalty payments.[16]

A few examples of WMM releases offer a sense of the diverse catalog that WMM maintains. *Jasad & The Queen of Contradiction* (Amanda Homsi-Ottosson, 2011) is a documentary about *Jasad*, the Arabic-language magazine founded by Lebanese poet and writer Jouman Haddad. The documentary examines the magazine's artistic and scientific exploration of the body and sexuality and the controversies it has generated in the Arab world. *Say My Name* (Nirit Peled, 2009) interviews female MCs who discuss their confrontations with misogyny in the male-dominated world of hip hop. Erykah Badu, MC Lyte, Estelle, and over a dozen other artists share their experiences in the music industry. *Water Children* (Aliona van der Horst, 2011) profiles the

Japanese pianist Tomoko Mukaiyama, who created a multimedia art installation in a Japanese village out of 12,000 silk dresses in order to explore the life cycle of female fertility. WMM distributes films produced by women from around the world who engage with issues that concern women locally, regionally, and globally.

Many of the films distributed by WMM emphasize self-expression. The work of several of the feminist filmmakers discussed in detail in Chapter 2, "Film as self-expression," features prominently in the WMM catalog, including Mona Hatoum's *Measures of Distance* (1988); Barbara Hammer's *The Female Closet* (1998), *Out in South Africa* (1995), and *Tender Fictions* (1995); and Pratibha Parmar's *Emergence* (1986), *Jodie: An Icon* (1996), and *Warrior Marks* (1993), among many other titles. The catalog (available in both print and online versions) functions as a reference guide to women's cinema, with basic information about each film supplemented by critical annotations that not only summarize the films but also situate them in relation to film history and feminist theory. WMM operates as a distributor and as an archive, as promoter and historian.

Most WMM films are distributed on DVD. Costs vary by title, but many films in the WMM catalog are available for sale for $295 (US) and for rental for $90 (US). WMM defends the high cost of the films (relative to films available in mass market DVD distribution) by including the following explanation from film scholar Patricia R. Zimmermann on their website:

> Women Make Movies offers work that is more like a quality reference book for a public library. That's why none of these films cost $19.99 or can be found in the remainder pile at K-mart: they cost more because they are harder to produce, attract a smaller market, and present a unique vision that the media behemoths can't produce. These higher prices subsidize WMM's sliding scale policy, guaranteeing that women's film and video will get to prisons, Native American tribes, battered women's shelters, self-help groups, high schools and even the Girl Scouts. They also allow Women Make Movies to pay higher royalties that fuels new work by women media artists.

Women Make Movies does not set its prices with individual consumers as a target audience the way major retailers do. Instead WMM designs its pricing structure to guarantee the largest possible returns to the women who produce their films and to reach the broadest possible audience through alternative exhibition venues like universities, libraries and community organizations.

definition – of those who inhabited a country or a geographical region at the time when people of different cultures or ethnic origins arrived. The new arrivals later became dominant through conquest, occupation, settlement or other means.[17]

Media produced by indigenous peoples document and preserve customs and traditions, challenge state policies and narratives, and solicit international intervention and support for local causes. Indigenous media forms include film and video, television, radio, digital archiving, and print and digital journalism. Indigenous media are often circulated only within indigenous communities.

10.4 *Atanarjuat: The Fast Runner* (Zacharias Kunuk, 2001). Courtesy of Igloolik Isuma/CTV/Kobal Collection.

Isuma.tv (www.isuma.tv) is a web archive designed as an online portal for indigenous media. Zacharias Kunuk and Norman Cohn, the directing and producing team behind the breakout Inuit feature film *Atanarjuat: The Fast Runner* (*Atanarjuat*, 2001), created the site to provide an alternative to YouTube and Facebook for indigenous mediamakers. The easy broadcasting format and social networking features on the site allow indigenous peoples to distribute their work to an unlimited global audience. The site, first launched in 2008, already features over 2,600 films in over forty-six languages. Each filmmaker uploads films to a unique channel devoted to their work. Isuma values the preservation of aboriginal languages, but some films are available with English, Spanish, or French subtitles. The site allows users to harness the power of online distribution networks to reach a global audience with locally produced work. Isuma also functions as an indigenous networking platform, bringing indigenous mediamakers into dialogue with one another to share their ideas and concerns about the challenges of developing media cultures outside of dominant distribution channels.

Exploitation cinema

Exploitation cinema describes a set of films and film production practices that transform low budgets into a distinct filmmaking style. Continuity errors, unsuccessful special effects, and bad performances (characterized by flubbed lines, wooden delivery, and miscast actors) enhance the viewing experience for the **cult audiences** who enjoy exploitation films. Exploitation films include films from dozens of genres – from the mainstream (horror films, war films, and science fiction films) to the obscure (women in prison films, cannibal films, and biker films). These films bypass traditional distribution circuits, thus avoiding many local censorship regulations. In their heyday in the 1960s and the 1970s in the United States, exploitation films were screened in independent theatres and in drive-in cinemas rather than in the theatres owned by the major chains.

American International Pictures was the largest producer and distributor of exploitation films in the United States during this period. Exploitation films focus on sensational elements to lure largely young audiences. Samuel Arkoff, the executive producer of AIP, promoted the "ARKOFF formula" for attracting audiences: Action, Revolution, Killing, Oratory, Fantasy, and Fornication. AIP used this formula to build a devoted fanbase of teenage boys. AIP is known primarily for the films produced by the legendary producer and director Roger Corman, including *The Wasp Woman* (1959), *House of Usher* (1960), and *A Bucket of Blood* (1959). They were also the central distributor in the United States for international exploitation films, which they often dubbed and re-edited. The titles they distributed include: Japan's *Godzilla* (*Gojira*, Ishirô Honda, 1954), South Korea's *Yongary, Monster from the Deep* (*Taekoesu Yonggary*, Ki-duk Kim, 1967), and Italy's *The Girl Who Knew Too Much* (*La Ragazza Che Sapeva Troppo*, Mario Bava, 1963). The Italian *giallo* genre, slasher films named for the "yellow" pulp novels that supplied their stories, was one of the primary international products that AIP distributed for American audiences. AIP worked closely with the network of independent theatres in which their films were shown to build focused marketing strategies. Often AIP posters were completed before the films, demonstrating the importance of distribution and marketing considerations to their production process.

10.5 Poster for Roger Corman's *The Wasp Woman* (1959). Courtesy of Santa Cruz/The Kobal Collection.

By the early 1980s, AIP had stopped producing and distributing films, and most of the independent and drive-in theatres where their films had been exhibited had closed. Exploitation films are still made, but they are now almost exclusively distributed for DVD or online exhibition. There are dozens of online distributors (for example, www.blue-underground.com, www.boulevardmovies.com, www.diabolikdvd.com) who specialize in exploitation cinema in general or in specific exploitation genres. Many of these distributors require visitors to their sites to be aged 18 or older because of the explicit content featured in their films. Some still sell films on VHS because of the popularity of the format among exploitation enthusiasts who savor its pre-digital aesthetic. These sites comprise an alternative DVD distribution universe, making accessible rare (and occasionally out-of-print) titles that are unavailable through large retailers. The distributors define themselves and their consumers as collectors rather than consumers.

Some distribution networks for exploitation cinema are more local. **Narco cinema** is a prolific independent industry in Mexico. Growing in popularity since the 1980s, narco cinema describes a genre of action films that center on illegal drug trafficking in Mexico, particularly in the city of Tijuana. Made for very small budgets and often shot and distributed within two weeks, films made in the narco cinema tradition feature drug dealers, prostitutes, and corrupt government officials in violent scenarios that explore the drug trade. The stories are fictional, but they are often based on real events. Given the very short time frame for production and distribution, these films may depict events that took place in Mexico only a few weeks before the distribution of the film. Narco cinema has produced its own stable of stars, including Mario Almado, the "John Wayne of narco cinema," who has acted in over a thousand films. These films are released only on DVD for immediate distribution in the Mexican "videohome" market. Narco cinema often features "narcocorridos," drug ballads performed by bands like Los Tigres del Norte. An episode of the American television show *Breaking Bad* featured the band Los Cuates de Sinaloa singing "Negro y Azul," a drug ballad commissioned for the show, demonstrating a significant link between television and film and between Mexican and American media cultures.

Experimental cinema

Experimental cinema has been exhibited in independent theatres, underground theatres, film archives, galleries, museums, and universities. Distribution practices for experimental film are as varied as the different films collected under this umbrella term. One of the major distributors for experimental film is the museum-based archive. For example, the Museum of Modern Art Circulating Film and Video Library in New York City circulates films from its collection of over 1,200 titles, including silent film, avant-garde film, and video art, to institutions, organizations, and individuals. MOMA distributes films for sale and for rental on 16mm film, DVD, and VHS. Exhibitors must insure the films that they rent and must make special arrangements for public screenings of films in the collection. Because the collections held by MOMA and other distributors of experimental cinema in film and video formats are inaccessible to consumers who lack the institutional and financial resources to rent their titles, online archives such as Ubu (profiled in detail in Chapter 13, "The longevity of films") are increasingly important for the distribution and exhibition of experimental cinema.

Some national film industries also support the production and distribution of experimental film. The National Film Board of Canada funds documentary, experimental, and animated films "that take a stand on issues of global importance that matter to Canadians—stories about the environment, human rights, international conflict, the arts and more."[18] While NFB supports diverse filmmaking practices in a variety of styles and genres, one of its most famous products is the experimental animated work of Norman McLaren. McLaren's film *Neighbors* (1952) showcases two of his innovations – the use of the stop-motion technique of pixilation and the production of a soundtrack by scratching the edge of the filmstrip. McLaren's films were made through Studio A, the NFB animation studio he founded.

The National Film Board's (NFB) distribution strategy focuses on their mission to make available their entire library of films. The Department of Canadian Heritage provided NFB with the initial funds to digitize the over 13,000 films in their collection. The ongoing project, now financed internally by NFB, has made available 2,000 films, clips, trailers, and interactive works on the NFB website (http://www.nfb.ca). Many of these films are also available via various apps for exhibition on internet-connected televisions, tablets, and smartphones. This ambitious digital distribution strategy has helped Canadians and international cinephiles to access an important archive of experimental film.

Pornography

The international **pornography** industry is difficult to document. Pornography remains illegal in many countries and its legal status is murky in others. Even in countries where the production and distribution of pornography is legal, unofficial distribution networks make it impossible to account fully for the volume of pornographic films circulating in a particular region. Statistics citing industry revenues are usually erratically sourced and widely contested.

There are, however, several large global distributors of pornography. Their corporate profiles offer a rare snapshot of an otherwise invisible distribution network. The Private Media Group is a distributor of pornography based in Barcelona, Spain. They distribute content from their library of over a thousand films to forty different countries in multiple languages. Their corporate website features content in English, Spanish, French and German. They distribute pornographic films for the following platforms: television, DVD, hotel pay-per-view channels, mobile phones, and the internet. They also license their content to over fifty video-on-demand providers.

In spite of Private's claim to be "Europe's leading producer and distributor of premium quality adult content" with a "global content distribution network,"[19] the profits for porn distribution have declined sharply in the internet era. Production and distribution companies have reported losses of 30–50 per cent since 2007.[20] Industry executives cite the easy accessibility of free online pornography as the central factor undermining their profits. Some internet sites offer pirated pornographic content, and others feature amateur films. At first, online distribution boosted revenues for the porn industry, but the expansion of illegal and amateur content online has eroded the market for commercially produced pornography.

Amateur film

As discussed in Chapter 2, in an era when anyone with access to a cellphone camera and an internet connection can upload a whimsical video of their cat for anyone to watch, it is difficult to imagine a time when **amateur film** occupied an unexamined, marginal place in film culture. Film scholar Patricia Zimmermann's *Reel Families: A Social History of Amateur Film* traces the long history of amateur film during its confinement to the old medium of film. She excavates amateur film from the "unsightly sprawling underside of more traditional commercial-film histories"[21] dominating film studies. The **home movies** profiled in *Reel Families* were not widely distributed, but their social history provides insights into the importance of filmmaking in the private sphere.

Amateur film has now entered the public sphere with overwhelming force. YouTube is the largest of a set of massive online archives where users can upload and view videos. Some users post their original videos in an effort to generate one of the rare feats of YouTube distribution – a virally distributed video that will generate a large audience and significant publicity both within and beyond the site. While these global distribution ambitions motivate some YouTube submissions, many more videos are posted with small audiences in mind. Anthropologist Patricia Lange isolates a subset of originally produced videos on YouTube that are designed to forge "feelings of connection" with people who identify with the same "hobbies, institutions or ideologies that are the overt content of a video."[22] These **videos of affinity** transform home movies into elements of social networking within a small community. The potential audience for these videos is not anyone or everyone but a relatively small number of viewers with whom the user imagines a social connection. Videos of affinity connect amateur film distributed online to early amateur film. These forms of amateur filmmaking engage a small audience with common interests, values, or experiences. Most amateur films circulate in a much more limited orbit than the viral sensations that dominate discussions of online film distribution in the mainstream media.

Informal distribution

The strategies for distributing film to niche audiences do not present a significant challenge to the dominant distribution model associated with global Hollywood. These alternative models operate on a much smaller financial scale and target much smaller audiences. The biggest challenge to the distribution of commercial narrative cinema by Hollywood studios is piracy (discussed at length in Chapter 5, "Film as a commodity"). The anti-piracy initiatives spearheaded by the MPAA and other governments and organizations have attempted to identify and shut down the major global centers of DVD and online piracy in places such as Mexico, Hong Kong and the Philippines. Despite some high-profile successes, new international networks for illegal film content continue to emerge. Online distribution channels present both the possibility of robust new revenue streams for the major film distributors and one of the greatest threats to their income.

10.6 Pirated DVDs. Courtesy of The Kobal Collection.

EXERCISE

Research the anti-piracy laws currently in effect where you are living. (These may include national and international laws.) Note the criminal penalties for violating these laws. With this information in hand, interview several other students about their awareness of and attitudes towards anti-piracy laws. You may ask some or all of the following questions:

- Have you ever watched an illegal copy of a movie (in any format)?
- Do illegal copies account for all, most, some, or none of your movie viewing?
- Are you aware of the current criminal penalties for watching pirated content?
- Are you concerned about your criminal liability for watching pirated content? If so, does that concern influence your decisions about whether or not to watch pirated content?
- Do you believe that anti-piracy legislation should be strictly enforced? Why or why not?

Review the answers that you received from each person you interviewed. How would you characterize the awareness of anti-piracy legislation and the attitudes toward anti-piracy legislation among the people that you interviewed? What surprised you about the answers each person gave?

Film scholar Ramon Lobato situates piracy within a broader network of distribution practices he terms **informal distribution**. Films distributed through informal means are difficult to track because they usually escape the measurement tools deployed by the MPAA, UNESCO, and other institutions that track media production and distribution. The data circulated by these institutions focuses on films in wide theatrical distribution, overlooking not only illegally distributed films but also films distributed through small independent theatres, independent DVD distributors, and local and regional networks. Lobato notes that informal distribution has always been an element of film culture, from the unofficial copies of *Trip to the Moon* (*Le voyage dans la lune*, Georges Méliès, 1902) that circulated in the United States, leaving the director unable to earn any money from his film, to the pornographic films that traveling exhibitors in the 1910s screened at "stag parties" they hosted.[23] Lobato's account of informal distribution counters the narrative of Hollywood's global distribution dominance, drawing attention to the endurance of unofficial forms of film exchange. Lobato notes:

> Stressing the largely informal nature of global distribution reminds us that movie business happens not only in corporate boardrooms, at festival soirées or industry conventions, but also in street markets, bazaars, illegal rental businesses, places of worship and grocery stores. Distribution is the province of enthusiasts, small-time traders, fly-by-night entrepreneurs, gangsters, preachers and a whole host of other non-professional agents.[24]

Lobato's analysis of informal film distribution investigates straight-to-video films, Nigerian video films (discussed in detail in Chapter 1, "Cinema as Entertainment"), and internet piracy, among other examples. His discussion of the distribution history of the Brazilian film *Tropa de Elite* (*Elite Squad*,

10.7 *Tropa de Elite* (Jose Padilha, 2007). Courtesy of Zazen Producoes/The Kobal Collection.

Jose Padilha, 2007) demonstrates the unpredictability of the relationship between informal and formal distribution practices. *Tropa de Elite* is a blockbuster action film set in Rio de Janeiro, dramatizing corruption in the police force in the face of a thriving drug trade (while a visit from the Pope looms). Lobato recounts that a stolen copy of the film was leaked online before the film was released, citing a statistic from a Brazilian polling company that as many as ten to twelve million people watched one of the many pirated versions of the film that flooded the informal market before the film's theatrical release.[25] While many industry analysts would have predicted that the massive scale of this piracy would doom the film to box office oblivion, *Tropa de Elite* became a box office hit, outperforming Hollywood blockbusters in exhibition in Brazil. The pirated copies generated word-of-mouth buzz for the film. Even those people who had already seen the film before its official release went to the theatre to see it again for the experience of seeing a locally produced action film (with recognizable locations and stories) on the big screen. This case study and the complicated exchanges between informal and formal distribution and between local and global film cultures underscore the importance of recognizing the uneven, unpredictable, and at times invisible distribution of film. Informal film distribution, in its legal and illegal forms, at times undermines and at times bolsters formal film distribution.

CHAPTER SUMMARY

"Global Hollywood" dominates international film distribution. Hollywood studios distribute their films – often via local distributors – in most global territories. Many Hollywood films make significantly more money overseas than they do in the United States, so negotiating global distribution rights is an important part of the film industry. Most films made outside of Hollywood (either by independent producers in the United States or by producers in other countries) have a difficult time securing distribution for their films in the US market. Instead, they distribute their films locally or regionally, or they rely on other distribution channels (including DVD and internet distribution). For many films, DVD and internet distribution represent a larger percentage of their profits than theatrical distribution. Many films are distributed outside the theatres and other venues that comprise the global Hollywood distribution circuit. Indigenous media, exploitation cinema, experimental cinema, pornography, and amateur film circulate through different distribution channels in an effort to reach very specific audiences. The primary challenge to the successful international distribution of Hollywood films comes not from these alternative distribution practices or from other national film industries but from commercial and independent piracy. The film industry, in collaboration with trade organizations and national governments, has been fighting to stop (or at least limit) piracy, but DVD and online piracy continue to flourish.

FURTHER READING

Havens, Timothy and Lotz, Amanda. *Understanding Media Industries*. Oxford: Oxford University Press, 2012.

> This book situates an analysis of film production and distribution within the broader framework of media industry analysis. Since the distribution of film relies extensively on corporations with multiple media holdings and on multiple media platforms, the expanded focus of this book provides a helpful framework for understanding how films circulate in the contemporary media landscape. A chapter devoted to distribution and exhibition maps the paths that contemporary films follow to reach global audiences.

King, Geoff. *Indiewood, USA: Where Hollywood Meets Independent Cinema*. London: I.B. Tauris, 2009.

> The case studies in this volume draw attention to the differences between independent film as a style and as a distribution model. Individual chapters profile the production and distribution histories of independent films within major studios or by mini-majors, challenging the value of "independent" as a descriptive term. *Indiewood, USA* captures the dominance of Hollywood distribution within the United States while tracing a history for contemporary American independent film.

Wilson, Pamela and Stewart, Michelle (eds). *Global Indigenous Media: Cultures, Poetics, and Politics*. Durham, NC: Duke University Press, 2008.

> *Global Indigenous Media* introduces readers to over a dozen examples of contemporary indigenous media practices. These indigenous media producers forge distribution channels outside the dominant channels discussed in this chapter (and in other books recommended in this

section). The book includes several examples of film and video production and distribution within a broader selection of media practices (including television, radio, and new media). Case studies include Maori cinema in New Zealand, Zapatista videomaking, and Inuit video collectives.

4 months, 3 weeks, and 2 days (*4 luni, 3 saptamâni si 2 zile*, Cristian Mungiu, 2007)

12:08 East of Bucharest (*A fost sau n-a fost?*, Corneliu Porumboiu, 2006)

Atanarjuat: The Fast Runner (*Atanarjuat*, Zacharias Kunuk, 2001)

Body and Soul (Oscar Micheaux, 1925)

A Bucket of Blood (Roger Corman, 1959)

The Death of Mr. Lazarescu (*Moartea domnului Lazarescu*, Cristi Puiu, 2005)

Devdas (Sanjay Bhangali, 2002)

Elite Squad (*Tropa de Elite*, Jose Padilha, 2007)

Emergence (Pratibha Parmar, 1986)

Exit Through the Gift Shop (Banksy, 2010)

The Female Closet (Barbara Hammer, 1998)

The Girl From Chicago (Oscar Micheaux, 1932)

The Girl Who Knew Too Much (*La Ragazza Che Sapeva Troppo*, Mario Bava, 1963)

The Girl who Played with Fire (*Flickan som lekte med elden*, Daniel Alfredson, 2009)

The Girl with the Dragon Tattoo (*Män som hatar kvinnor*, Niels Arden Oplev, 2009)

The Girl with the Dragon Tattoo (David Fincher, 2011)

Go Goa Gone (Krishna D.K. and Rak Nidimoru, 2013)

House of Usher (Roger Corman, 1960)

Japan's Godzilla (*Gojira*, Ishirô Honda, 1954)

Jasad & The Queen of Contradiction (Amanda Homsi-Ottosson, 2011)

Jodie: An Icon (Pratibha Parmar, 1996)

The Matrix Revolutions (Andy and Lana Wachowski, 2003)

Measures of Distance (Mona Hatoum, 1988)

Meek's Cutoff (Kelly Reichardt, 2011)

The Moment After (Wes Llewellyn, 1999)

Neighbors (Norman McLaren, 1952)

Once More, With Feeling! (Stanley Donen, 1960)

Out in South Africa (Barbara Hammer, 1995)

Reality (Matteo Garrone, 2012)

Resident Evil: Afterlife (Paul W.S. Anderson, 2010)

Samsara (Ron Fricke, 2012)

Say My Name (Nirit Peled, 2009)

Slumdog Millionaire (Danny Boyle, 2008)

Tender Fictions (Barbara Hammer, 1995)

Tonight, You're Mine (David McKenzie, 2011)

Trip to the Moon (Georges Méliès, 1902)

Warrior Marks (Pratibha Parmar, 1993)

The Wasp Woman (Roger Corman, 1959)

Water Children (Aliona van der Horst, 2011)

Within Our Gates (Oscar Micheaux, 1920)

Yongary, Monster from the Deep (*Taekoesu Yonggary*, Ki-duk Kim, 1967)

NOTES

1 Eric J. Lyman, "'Reality' Inks Distribution Deals," *The Hollywood Reporter*, 4 June 2012.

2 Source: http://variety.com/2013/film/news/digital-cinema-conversion-nears-end-game-12005009 75/, accessed 24 September 2014.

3 Sources: www.boxofficemojo.com and www.the-numbers.com, accessed 24 September 2014.

4 Timothy Havens and Amanda Lotz, *Understanding Media Industries* (Oxford: Oxford University Press, 2011), 155.

5 Jesse Rhines, *Black Films/White Money* (New Brunswick: Rutgers University Press, 1996), 23–24.

6 See Toby Miller, Nitin Govil, John McMurria, Ting Wang and Richard Maxwell, *Global Hollywood 2*. (London: British Film Institute, 2008).

7 Source: www.mpaa.org, accessed 24 September 2014.

8 Source: http://www.erosplc.com/Theatrical.aspx.

9 Robert E. Davis, "The Instantaneous Worldwide Release," in Elizabeth Ezra and Terry Rowden (eds), *Transnational Cinema: The Film Reader* (London: Routledge, 2006), 78.

10 Jasmine Nadua Trice, "The Quiapo Cinémathèque: Transnational DVDs and Alternative Modernities in the Heart of Manila," *International Journal of Cultural Studies* 13(5) (2010), 542.

11 Source: http://latimesblogs.latimes.com/entertainmentnewsbuzz/2011/05/dvd-revenue-plummets-44-in-2010-study-says.html, accessed 24 September 2014.

12 http://blog.hulu.com/2014/02/27/an-international-update-from-hulu-in-japan/, accessed 24 September 2014.

13 Source: http://natoonline.org/data/windows/, accessed 24 September 2014.

14 Davis.

15 Source: "The Celluloid Ceiling: Behind-the-Scenes Employment of Women in the Top 250 Films of 2011" (http://womenintvfilm.sdsu.edu/research.html, accessed 24 September 2014).

16 Source: http://www.wmm.com, accessed 24 September 2014.

17 Source: http://www.un.org/esa/socdev/unpfii/documents/5session_factsheet1.pdf, accessed 24 September 2014.

18 Source: http://www.nfb.ca/about/, accessed 24 September 2014.

19 Source: http://www.prvt.com, accessed 24 September 2014.

20 Source: http://articles.latimes.com/2009/aug/10/business/fi-ct-porn10, accessed 24 September 2014.

21 Patricia R. Zimmermann, *Reel Families: A Social History of Amateur Film* (Indianapolis: Indiana University Press, 1995), x.

22 Patricia Lange. "Videos of Affinity on YouTube," in Patrick Vonderau, Pelle Snickars and Jean Burgess (eds), *The YouTube Reader* (Stockholm: National Library of Sweden, 2010), 71. This book is available for free online at http://www.youtubereader.com.

23 Ramon Lobato, *Shadow Economies of Cinema: Mapping Informal Film Distribution* (London: Palgrave Macmillan, 2012), 14.

24 Lobato, 19.

25 Lobato, 51.

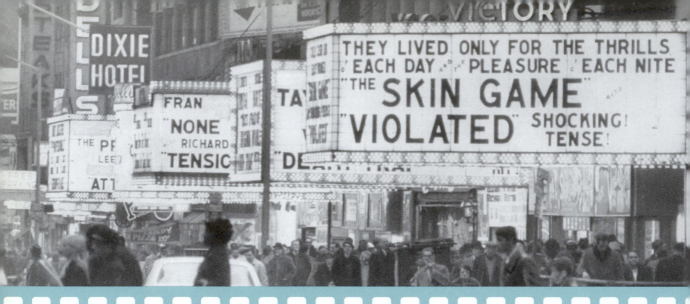

CHAPTER ELEVEN

EXHIBITION

It has never been easier to get access to films to watch. Whether legally or illegally, viewing can now take place in a diverse array of locations: at the cinema, on television, on computers, tablets and phones, on airplanes, and so on. Your regular film viewing patterns are likely to include experiences that run from watching a DVD or Blu-ray to catching an extract of a movie through a streaming or file-sharing website, from seeing the latest blockbuster at a multiplex to flicking the television into a film part-way through its running time. In all of these cases, the film gets to you through the mechanics and technologies of exhibition.

Film exhibition is the crucial third component in the linear chain that connects filmmakers and their audiences. Following production, movies pass through various distribution systems and methods (discussed in Chapter 10), and are finally exhibited to viewers in a multitude of ways and places. Exhibition is a large subject area, covering a range of interlocking fields. These fields include: economics (how those behind film production eventually make some of their money back); architecture and geography (the actual buildings and spaces in which we watch films, from homes to galleries, hotels to multiplexes); work and labor (the jobs specifically associated with exhibition); local and national history (the significance of particular exhibition sites and practices for specific places); and legal matters (who is allowed to show films to the public, whether for profit or otherwise). While touching on all of these subjects, this chapter primarily examines the breadth of technologies and places via which movies have been watched in order to highlight the extraordinary flexibility of exhibition practices across cinema's history.

WHAT WE WILL DO IN THIS CHAPTER

- In the first section of this chapter, we identify the extent to which the history of film exhibition is also a history of technological developments. Innovations in the realm of exhibition, and shifts in consumer behavior patterns, are usually connected to the introduction of new methods of looking at and listening to movies.

- Wherever film is exhibited, it relies on a technical apparatus. A number of theorists have written about the key components of the apparatus – projector, screen, speakers, and seating – and the ways in which they shape our relationship to the movies. These exhibition components, they suggest, help to construct how we watch, and how we understand what we watch. Collectively, these writings are usually referred to as "apparatus theory." The second section of this chapter introduces this body of theory.

- The history of exhibition can also be understood as a survey of the spaces in which films have been exhibited: purpose-built locations such as cinemas, from palaces to flea-pits; locations temporarily fitted out for a screening; domestic locations; exhibition on the move; and so on. The third and final section of this chapter considers a selection of this array of spaces in detail.

BY THE END OF THIS CHAPTER YOU SHOULD BE ABLE TO

- Identify key technological components and innovations associated with exhibition, and why these are of significance.
- Outline key arguments associated with "apparatus theory."
- Discuss a range of spaces and locations that have been used for cinema exhibition, and how these differ from each other.

EXHIBITION AND TECHNOLOGY

Film exhibition is a pragmatic and practical topic: what means can be used to see a specific film? It is also centrally technological: what bits of machinery can enable and enhance the viewing of a certain movie? In this section, we introduce some key developments in the history of film exhibition through specific technological innovations. All of these developments altered audiences' relationships to cinema, as well as the ways in which films were made, and the types of stories that filmmakers could tell. Each subject considered in brief here has its own lengthy and complex history. This list is by no means exhaustive, but provides some sense of the significance of exhibition in the global story of film.

Projection equipment

At the end of the nineteenth century, a number of innovators in different countries were experimenting with moving image technology, and attempting to identify how to enable audiences to view strips of images which had been photographed in quick succession. Initially, through devices such as W.K.L.

Dickson's Kinetoscope, first displayed in 1893, films were watched by individual viewers in isolation. For a small fee, film strips were projected through standalone machinery that had a viewing slot, and the solitary spectator watched the short movie unfold. Quite swiftly, however, the viewing booths largely disappeared. Projection equipment was developed that enabled communal viewing in spaces that had a similar layout to theatres and music halls, with chairs facing a stage and screen. Indeed, following the introduction of such projection machinery, some of the first places in which films were shown were theatres, as part of a menu of entertainment that might include music, comedy, dramatic sketches and scenes, and magic. In France, Louis and Auguste Lumière created the Cinématographe, which recorded onto, printed and projected strips of film; they used this to project a screening for an audience in Paris in 1895 (often identified as the official birth of cinema). Other inventors, including Thomas Edison, designed their own projectors. Standards were established after a few years: Edison's 35mm film stock and the Lumières' sixteen frames per second projection speed were widely adopted. The projector has remained a vital component in many film exhibition scenarios, throwing moving images through a beam of light at a screen. Innovations in this equipment have occurred over the decades: it became available in smaller and lighter versions, which could be transported more easily; analog projectors were supplemented with (and later, largely replaced by) digital projectors.

11.1 Edison's Kinetoscope, c.1895. Courtesy of The Kobal Collection.

11.2 The Cinématographe Lumière, 1895. Courtesy of SSPL via Getty Images.

Sound

Experimentation with film sound technologies occurred throughout the era of silent cinema, attempting to overcome the problems of accurate synchronization and adequate amplification. Dozens of film sound systems were patented, such as the Chronomegaphone (1910) and the Polyscope (1914), but they were too flawed to launch. This is not to suggest that silent cinema was experienced by audiences as silent, of course: the exhibition of films in various countries during the first decades of the twentieth century was often accompanied by planned sound, whether the Japanese *benshi*, a live narrator of the story, or an orchestra pit containing musicians playing a live score. In the late 1920s, following the development of techniques for recording sound directly onto film such as Warner Bros.' Vitaphone (1926), a shift towards sound film – or "talkies" – occurred swiftly. For those in the exhibition business, this was an enormously expensive transition: in order to project films successfully to audiences, sound equipment was also now needed. Technical concerns arose: which were the best speaker systems? Where should they ideally be placed in relation to the screen and the audience? How loud should the sound be played? What amplification systems were best at avoiding sound distortion?

Sound has remained a crucial factor in film exhibition. For many exhibitors, it is important to consider how the labor of a film's makers, who have worked to meld together voices, sound effects and music, can be best presented to audiences. When screening films with sound, exhibitors need to consider

ATTENTION!

This motion picture will be shown in the startling new multi- dimension of

SENSURROUND

Please be aware that you will <u>feel</u> as well as see and hear realistic effects such as might be experienced in an actual earthquake.

The Management assume no responsibility for the physical or emotional reactions of the individual viewer.

11.3 Sensurround: this lobby card was used as part of the promotional campaign for *Earthquake* (Mark Robson, 1974). Courtesy of Universal/Kobal Collection.

such factors as clarity, fidelity, volume, balance, and the most effective ways to promote audience immersion. Of the numerous innovations that have occurred in the realm of film sound exhibition over the decades (including Quadrophonic sound, 1970, and Sensurround, 1977), arguably the most significant was the development of **Dolby**. Ray Dolby (1933–2013) established Dolby Labs in 1965; his company has created a series of noise reduction systems, which help to eliminate unwanted background noise, as well as audio encoding and compression technologies. Dolby Stereo was launched in 1975, cleaning up and enhancing the sound of films which employed it; the first version of Dolby Digital appeared in 1992. Dolby technology has affected the quality of film exhibition beyond the cinema: DVD and Blu-ray home viewing formats adopted Dolby as part of their specification.

Widescreen

Some experiments with widescreen filming and exhibition took place in the first half of the twentieth century, but they were scarce. Perhaps the best-known example is Abel Gance's film *Napoleon* (1927), which was planned for and exhibited on three screens joined together horizontally. Aside from such rare instances, for decades the standard recording and screening **aspect ratio** – that is, the width:height of the film frame – remained fairly stable. Silent films were shot in 1.33:1. With the introduction of recording sound directly onto film, which affected the size of the frame by lodging an audio channel into the stock in a stripe, slight moderations to aspect ratio were required. In 1932 in the United States, 1.37:1 was proposed by the Academy of Motion Picture Arts and Sciences as the new standard; this screen shape is also known as the **academy ratio**. Following the widespread uptake of television as a domestic entertainment technology in the 1950s and 1960s, filmmakers and producers in numerous countries recognized that they needed to offer an experience that could lure audiences out of their homes and back into the cinema auditorium. Widescreen was identified as one spectacular element of movies that might tempt viewers, and so was experimented with by directors and cinematographers. A range of aspect ratios began to proliferate (see figure 11.4 below). Some forms of widescreen cinema were shot on standard 35mm film stock, but projected using aperture plates to give the illusion of widescreen – this is known as **masked** or **flat** widescreen. In other cases, for what is termed **anamorphic** widescreen, camera lenses were used to squeeze a wider image onto 35mm stock, which would then be stretched in projection by another lens. It was also possible to shoot on 70mm stock for **large gauge** widescreen, but this required cinemas to own 70mm projectors. Indeed, experiments with widescreen posed particular challenges for exhibitors, who needed screens wide enough to accommodate new formats – and a variety of image shapes and sizes.

11.4 Film aspect ratios. Source: http://ccnmtl.columbia.edu/projects/filmglossary/web/pics/aspectratio.jpg. Image courtesy of the Columbia Center for New Media Teaching and Learning. © 2014 by the Trustees of Columbia University in the City of New York. For additional information, visit: ccnmtl.columbia.edu/projects/filmglossary/.

Whilst widescreen projection enabled cinema to distinguish itself from television, making the most of the former's large screens, the later exhibition of these films on television presented some technological challenges. Early television screens had a 4:3 ratio, not too different from the Academy aspect ratio. In order for widescreen images to fit into the 4:3 screen, films would need to be **letterboxed** (presented in the correct ratio, but with black bars across the top and bottom of the TV screen) or **pan-and-scanned** (presented full-height, edges cropped, and with artificial "pans" following the action within the frame). Over the course of the last decade or so, larger and wider-screened televisions (usually of a 16:9 ratio) have become the market norm, and the amount of pan-and-scanning has significantly decreased.

3D

Three-dimensional cinema, which enhances the illusion of depth perception, has experienced two boom periods: the 1950s, and the 1990s through today. However, experiments with the format have occurred throughout cinema history: Edwin Porter screened some test stereoscopic reels to an audience in New York in 1915. Particular technological systems and devices are required for recording, exhibiting and watching 3D films. Imagery needs to be recorded simultaneously from two perspectives that mimic the minor distance between human eyes; alternatively, CGI can be used to produce these perspectives in post-production. In the screening space, projection equipment must be able to handle this complex, layered imagery, and audiences are required to wear special eyewear. The expenses associated with using and installing these technologies – and fluctuations in audience interests in 3D – largely kept 3D cinema as a niche interest throughout the twentieth century. Only with the recent widespread adoption of the system, and box office successes such as *Avatar* (James Cameron, 2009), *Life of Pi* (Ang Lee,

2012), and *Gravity* (Alfonso Cuarón, 2013), has 3D cinema established a slightly more stable foothold as an exhibition experience.

Although various technological experiments with 3D cinema have occurred throughout the last century, two main exhibition formats have predominated. **Anaglyph 3D** superimposes the two visual perspectives through colored filters, one red, the other cyan. The glasses worn by the spectator have different colored lenses which cancel out the projection filter hues. In contrast, **polarization 3D** projects two images superimposed through polarizing filters. The viewer's spectacles contain filters that only let through light which is similarly polarized, so that each eye perceives a different image. Polarization 3D has been the standard exhibition method since the early 1950s, although anaglyph has remained in use in some circumstances.

As with widescreen, 3D cinema first experienced a boom in the 1950s as a technology that might draw spectators away from television, out of the home and back into the theatre. It is possible that the success of widescreen was one of the reasons that 3D failed to take off adequately as a regular exhibition experience at this time: it was much less expensive for filmmakers and exhibitors to employ, and did not require any gizmos such as special spectacles. The return of 3D in the 1980s began with IMAX (see the case study in Chapter 1), and with theme park rides. Its reappearance in standard cinemas only began to manifest in force in the twenty-first century. It is notable that this period of time – the 1980s to the present day – coincides exactly with the proliferation of home and mobile viewing formats from VHS to Blu-ray, from laptops to tablets. In other words, more recent uses of 3D need to be seen as another attempt by filmmakers and exhibitors to entice audiences into cinemas. The lure of the spectacle – one which cannot be replicated anywhere outside particular screening contexts – has remained a constant throughout cinema exhibition history.

11.5 Poster for *House of Wax* (André de Toth, 1953), which claims 3D to be "the most realistic film process ever developed." Courtesy of Warner Bros./ The Kobal Collection.

Seating

The history of cinema exhibition necessarily incorporates a history of chair design. Manuals on cinema interior design fittings throughout much of the medium's history, for instance, have advised exhibitors on the latest developments in "entertainment seating," and the ways in which these should be installed to best enhance the consumer experience. Of course, some contemporary film screening experiences – such as in a gallery environment, or watching saved or streaming content on a handheld device whilst on public transport – might occur with the spectator standing. However, on the whole, movie consumption usually takes place with the viewer seated. For cinema exhibitors, this raises such crucial issues as the arrangement of seating, type of seats, and the angle of floor raking.

EXERCISE

Think about your own preferred film viewing locations.

- If you like one cinema – or one screen in a cinema – over others, to what extent is this influenced by the seats that they have installed?
- Do you prefer to sit in a particular place in a given auditorium – and if so, why?
- If a seat is hard, are you more likely to watch intently, or to be distracted from the movie?
- If you watch a lot of movies at home, what particular items of seating furniture (chairs, sofas, beanbags, cushions, and so on) enhance or contribute to the viewing experience?

Consider a simple distinction in cinema architecture: **low pitch viewing floors** versus **stadium seating**. In low pitch viewing auditoria, the floor may be flat or subtly raked, with back rows marginally higher up than those at the front. Seats are normally staggered, so that (except for those in the front row) any one chair's view of the screen lies between the two seats in the row in front. Stadium seating, in contrast, is more steeply raked, with stairs for ascending the auditorium. Each row is notably higher than that below, enabling each spectator to see the screen equally effectively. This has architectural ramifications: for an average auditorium containing 250 seats, stadium seating adds nine to ten meters to the height of the space.

Seat comfort is of crucial concern for cinema exhibitors. How large and how comfortable should a cinema seat be? If the seat is too comfortable, might spectators fall asleep? What fabric should seats be covered in? (Given the volume of refreshments consumed in cinemas, fabric choice may be motivated by such factors as stain resistance and absorbency.) Multiplex seats tend to feature drinks holders – in part, to prevent spectators from having to pick refreshments up off the floor, and thus divert their gaze from the screen. Home cinema systems can be accessorized with "home cinema chairs," which mimic the form of multiplex seating: wide, plush, and equipped with drinks holders, sometimes featuring additional components such as reclining backs and foot supports.

CINEMA APPARATUS

The exhibition technology and hardware that the first section of this chapter has introduced and discussed requires a little more interrogation. Irrespective of the type of screening venue, there are fundamental elements of the cinema auditorium that are constant: a large blank screen or wall; a projector, via whose light beam images are thrown; seats arranged to face the screen; sound speakers, often hidden behind the screen and/or around the seating area. Such is their persistence that a number

CASE STUDY: TAKING A BREAK

What impact does it have on a viewer's experience of a film if it is broken into parts? Although many filmmakers may prefer for their completed works to be seen uninterrupted, from start to finish, this may not be the way that they are exhibited or consumed. Throughout film history, exhibition practice has often inserted breaks into film screenings. These may have been factored into a film's content – as with the formal "intermission" title that appears midway through *Gone With the Wind* (Victor Fleming, 1939) – or they may be inserted

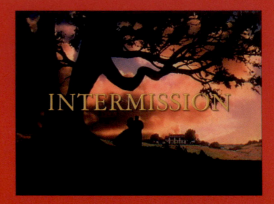

11.6 The "intermission" in *Gone with the Wind* (Victor Fleming, 1939).

by exhibition venues. With the advent of film viewing opportunities outside cinemas, breaks in a film's running time became even more widespread. Television screenings of movies by commercial channels normally insert regular advertising breaks, each several minutes in length. Home and mobile viewing formats, from VHS to streaming, allow viewers to be fully in control of the intermissions in a film's running time. These can be inserted wherever and whenever the spectator desires, breaking the movie into an infinite variety of small chunks.

Breaks in a cinema film screening could occur for a number of reasons. Pragmatically, especially during cinema's early years, intermissions might be required in order to allow reel changes to occur. The intermission is an exhibition tactic indebted to theatre: a play's acts may be separated by breaks in which the house lights come up, the audience moves around, and the stage design might be reset. This echo of theatrical practice may serve to confer on cinema viewing a sense of occasion, perhaps even an increment of theatre's standing as a worthy and valuable cultural form. Indeed, in the United States in the 1950s and 1960s, large budget studio movies were often exhibited as "road show" releases. As film scholar Peter Kramer notes, this would entail a film being "presented with all the trappings of a night out at the 'legitimate' theatre: separate performances (instead of the normal practice of running films continuously throughout the day), advance bookings, an orchestral overture and an intermission."[1] The film intermission might also be included in line with ideas relating to how long audiences can feasibly concentrate, and the length of time that they can endure physical immobility in a cinema seat. Can an audience feasibly take in all 219 minutes of *Heaven's Gate* (Michael Cimino, 1980) in one sitting, or is an intermission necessary to prevent them from losing focus?

The cinema intermission serves further purposes. It allows for a "comfort break" – that is, for customers to use the bathroom without missing any of the film. And it provides the opportunity for viewers to purchase refreshments (and thus for the cinema to boost its revenue). However, the psychological ramifications of the intermission require consideration: inserting a break into a film's running time can interrupt immersion, pulling the viewer back to the real world. If a film is watched in pieces – with, perhaps, significant time elapsing between each morsel – then the viewer may struggle even to remember key plot details; they may evaluate the film differently if they have not experienced it as a whole. Intermissions in cinema exhibition are now increasingly rare: removing the break allows for more film screenings to be scheduled into the calendar; digital film projection has removed the need for reel changes; cinemas may be concerned that intermissions allow spectators to move between different auditoria without being detected. (In the absence of the comfort break, websites and apps can now advise viewers of the best time to scoot out of a film to visit the facilities, and not miss too much plot or action.)

In India, however, the intermission remains a significant component of the cinemagoing experience. Bollywood films regularly run to around three hours in length, with directors anticipating a structural break in the film. The start of the second half may be marked by a clear tonal shift. When films from other countries are screened in Indian cinemas, they almost always have an intermission inserted; international distributors may advise Indian exhibitors on where to place this break. According to journalist Garima Sharma, the persistence of the Indian intermission is largely related to food sales:

> An intermission may not help a film as much as it does cineplexes – after all, their main revenue comes in from people getting up to buy refreshments during the break. Statistically, a multiplex earns only about 25–30 rupees per customer for a film, as the major share goes to the government and film distributors. Hence, they have to bank on food and beverage sales, which constitute 30–40% of a multiplex's income. Pricewise, one movie show on an average earns 15,000–20,000 rupees on food and beverage sales alone.[2]

Throughout cinema exhibition history, in locations around the world, the intermission has often been intimately connected to the sale of refreshments. With the removal of the intermission in most countries, alternative methods need to be adopted to promote food and drink sales: selling tickets and refreshments at the same tills; positioning concession stands in places where they are difficult to avoid; using environmental prompts such as sweet smells and warmth to encourage consumption; heavily salting popcorn, which can produce dehydration, and thus enhance the volume of drinks sold; reminding patrons in the auditorium that there is "still time to purchase."

of film theorists have explored the ramifications of this apparatus, and how it impacts on the viewing experience. These writings, known collectively as "apparatus theory," were largely produced in the 1970s, but remain influential. The theorists who produced these writings were particularly inspired by a mixture of Marxist politics, psychoanalysis and semiotics.

Perhaps the most important "apparatus theory" essay was French theorist Jean-Louis Baudry's "The Ideological Effects of the Basic Cinematographic Apparatus," first published in 1970 in the journal *Cinéthique*. As the title identifies, Baudry explores key elements of the cinema apparatus and their relation to the operations of ideology (a subject which we examined in some detail in Chapter 4). In addition to discussing the workings of particular components of the apparatus, Baudry argued that the cinema apparatus as a whole is ideological because it disguises how the "reality" of the film that unfolds on the screen is put together. The technology that reproduces the film for the spectator (projector and screen), and the space in which the film is watched (seats, auditorium), furnishes a context in which the movie's "reality" seems to unfold naturally. The film viewer, then, is somewhat duped: we are distracted from the labor and trickery that was used to construct the film's world and story, and seduced into its flow. Critical distance is removed or prevented, and we float along with the film's narrative and characters, unaware that we have been coerced into adopting this viewing position. As Baudry puts it:

> Projection and reflection take place in a closed place, and those who remain there, whether they know it or not (but they do not), find themselves chained, captured, or captivated [...] The paradoxical nature of the cinematic mirror-screen is without doubt that it reflects *images* but not "*reality*" ... In any case this "reality" comes from behind the spectator's head and if he looked at it directly he would see nothing except the moving beams from an already veiled light source.[3]

Crucially, then, the powerful illusionism of cinema is located not only in the content of the films themselves, but also in the instruments and institutions which create and screen them.

In addition to this broader argument, Baudry also claimed that specific aspects of the cinema apparatus have particular effects on spectators, all of which contribute to the overall impact. The darkened theatre heightens our reliance on vision. Our seating location in close relation to the screen and projector places us centrally in front of the image, in a Renaissance perspective position of mastery and power. The comfortable seating in a cinema reduces our motor capacity, and can contribute to the experience of a state of regression. The mechanics of exhibition serve to evoke in the audience the conditions of dreaming. Watching a film can be a transcendental experience, in part because the mobility of the camera lifts us out of our bodies, giving us perspectives on the story being told that are powerful, commanding, and artificial. As Baudry writes:

> And if the eye which moves is no longer fettered by a body, by the laws of matter and time, if there are no more assignable limits to its displacement – conditions fulfilled by the possibilities of shooting and of film – the world will be constituted not only by this eye but for it. The mobility of the camera seems to fulfil the most favourable conditions for the manifestation of the "transcendental subject."[4]

The crane shot, for instance, can provide audiences with a sense of perspective over a landscape or scene that the small, relatively immobile human body can never attain.

Although Baudry did not discuss sound in great detail – his writings argue for the primacy of vision in the cinema exhibition space – other writers have explored this aspect of the apparatus. Pascal Bonitzer and Mary Ann Doane have both explored the role of the voice in cinema, and the relationship of this to the apparatus.[5] Claudia Gorbman, in her book *Unheard Melodies*, discusses the apparatus and the workings of musical scores.[6] These writers all address the dominant ways in which sound and image

EXERCISE

- Do Baudry's comments fit with your own experiences of watching films?
- Does the relationship between seat position, screen and filmed space provide a sense of control or power on your part? If so, how exactly does this work? It may help here to think of concrete examples.
- What connections can you identify between film viewing and the experience of dreaming? Again, try anchoring this in particular movies that you have seen.
- Are you ever aware of aspects of the apparatus (screen, projector beam, speakers) during a film screening? If so, how does this affect your relationship to the movie's content?

operate neatly together, sealing audiences into the film's depicted worlds. However, they also identify those moments when image and sound do not seamlessly connect up, potentially exposing the audience to a critical awareness of the apparatus.

A number of authors have taken issue with the arguments put forward by Baudry and other apparatus theorists. On the whole, criticisms of this model of the machinery of cinema center on its reliance on one, limited type of exhibition practice. As film theorist Vance Kepley, Jr. puts it, apparatus theory "treats a particular type of film exhibition – one that may have been prominent in certain industrialized societies for a period of years in the early to mid-twentieth century – as though it were a universal."[7] Apparatus theorists seem to assume that audiences sit quietly in cinemas, isolated socially from one another – and yet filmgoing is often a social experience, one form of entertainment amongst many that a group of friends or peers might enjoy. The model posited by Baudry and elaborated upon by others is also culturally and historically specific. It attempts to posit a general model from the perspective of a French intellectual in the 1970s, yet cannot feasibly take into account all prior (and subsequent) variations in exhibition practices and experiences around the world. Apparatus theory is centered on one circumscribed and delimited type of exhibition space, but there are many other locations in which film has been exhibited and consumed throughout cinema history. It is this variety of spaces to which our discussion now turns.

EXHIBITION AND SPACE

With the development of mobile viewing technologies such as laptops, tablets and phones, it is now possible to screen films almost anywhere, irrespective of geography: should you want to watch, say, *Solaris* (Andrei Tarkovsky, 1972) whilst in Antarctica or Zimbabwe, you could. However, over cinema's history, there has been a certain consistency in the types of place in which films are exhibited and experienced. As with the discussion of technology in the first section of this chapter, the list that we present here is not exhaustive. Rather, it identifies key examples, and highlights the broad variety of ways in which film exhibition has occurred.

The picture palace

In its earliest years, cinema was exhibited in a range of locations, including vaudeville theatres, circuses, penny arcades, nickelodeons, and stores. At the start of the twentieth century, a new type of exhibition space devoted to screening cinema emerged: the movie palace or picture palace. These were big, elaborately decorated spaces which attempted to confer to cinema a certain status as "culture." Their architecture borrowed components from vaudeville theatres and European opera houses. Décor would mix together Renaissance, Classical, Egyptian, Chinese, Gothic styles and more. The picture palaces would often be given exotic-sounding or extravagant names that signified escape, opulence and indulgence. As historian Charlotte Herzog notes,

> Much of the ambience of the palace was the safety, comfort and luxury of its interior. There were numerous appointments and several auxiliary spaces such as foyers, lounges, corridors, and promenades, extra services (ushers) and lobby entertainment (trios and pianists). The exterior and interior of the theatre were lavishly decorated in a romantic but highly eclectic historic mode to distinguish it from the other buildings around it and to give it the stamp of legitimacy. With the help of materials like terra cotta and plaster, architects combined their own improvisations with exact reproductions of entire renowned buildings or parts of buildings to achieve their effects.[8]

11.7 Omnia Cinéma Pathé, Paris, 1908. Courtesy of Roger Viollet/Getty Images.

Although the movie palace is largely discussed by historians as a phenomenon of the United States, picture palaces appeared in many other countries, including France, the UK, India, and the Netherlands. The Omnia Cinéma Pathé was opened in Paris in 1906. The following year, the Elphinstone Picture Palace launched in Calcutta. In the United States, the first movie palace opened in 1914 in New York: Samuel "Roxy" Rothapfel's 3000-seat Strand cinema. In 1917, Balaban and Katz's New York Central Park Theatre admitted its first audiences. They went on to build three picture palaces in Chicago, on the fringes of the city, strategically located near the middle-class suburbs.

In the picture palace, cinema was only part of the entertainment on the menu. Features would be screened along with shorts and newsreels; musical entertainment and live dramatic sketches would also be presented. The location itself was part of the entertainment experience. This was particularly notable with what were known as "atmospheric" picture palaces, which often attempted to convey the experience of sitting in an outdoor courtyard. In these spaces, the interiors were decorated with images of exotic flora and fauna, and projections of clouds and stars onto the ceiling would continue even whilst films were screening. Movie palaces, in other words, were highly distracting environments for watching films, in which multiple environmental enticements competed with the screened materials.

The movie palace screening is now largely lost to history as an exhibition experience, although some of the buildings still operate as locations for theatrical and operatic performances, and some, such as the Art Deco Theatre Tuschinski in Amsterdam which opened in 1921, continue to screen movies. Film scholar Stephen Barber in his book *Abandoned Images* surveys the twelve picture palaces on Broadway Avenue in downtown Los Angeles. Built between 1910 and 1931, all of these cinemas are now closed down and destitute. Some are used for storage of goods, while others have run to ruin. As Barber's book highlights, remnants of cinema exhibition history can often be spotted in cities around the world. Formerly grand venues are repurposed for alternative means, turned into bowling alleys, apartments, restaurants; fragments of hoardings or location names survive, affixed to or engraved into exteriors. Although the picture palace experience fell out of favor with audiences, the locations themselves still haunt numerous urban centers.

The grindhouse

The grindhouse cinema offered a markedly different exhibition experience from the picture palace. Although the grindhouse is normally discussed in relation to the United States, the spaces and exhibition policies associated with the term have manifested in many countries around the world. The origin of the term "grindhouse" to refer to particular cinemas has been traced to the 1920s, when it was used to designate those spaces that employed sensationalist promotion techniques to lure viewers in for screenings, such as lurid advertising displays and "barkers" (staff attempting to drum up custom from the pavement in front of the venue). But the "grind" in "grindhouse" also refers to a "grind policy" of screening, in which films are shown continuously throughout the day and night, with the cinema sometimes barely closing, and audiences paying cut-rate admission prices. Of course, this tactic of repeatedly "grinding" a film had a material impact: the stock would become battered, scuffed and worn, and the projector could overheat or break down. As film theorist David Church notes:

> The grind business model assumed that higher audience turnover at cheaper ticket prices would be more profitable than the dominant, non-grind practice of offering less than half a dozen shows per day; this business model was especially different from the staggering of select seating prices at first-run picture palaces.[9]

The grindhouse, then, was a cinema with a notably less grand design than the elegant movie houses. Films were shown without the support of other types of entertainment, in a "no frills" loop. The film being exhibited might not be screened in the best condition. However, especially during periods of economic instability, a variety of audiences frequented the grindhouse, happy to pay the lower entrance fee.

The types of films shown in grindhouses were often distinct from those in more up-scale venues. Although larger budget feature films might eventually screen in the grindhouse after they had been shown in classier cinemas, the grindhouse became associated with genre films: horror, crime, Westerns,

11.8 A grindhouse cinema in Times Square, New York, 1967. Courtesy of NY Daily News via Getty Images.

science fiction. Exploitation films (which we introduced in the previous chapter) and titles imported from abroad might also be shown. Grindhouses were usually located in less safe, "skid row" parts of cities; they were often close to burlesque and strip joints, and (in later decades) to cinemas exclusively showing pornography. Due to this geographical placement, and the sorts of film that they regularly screened, grindhouses became increasingly associated with a mainly male clientele. Over the course of the twentieth century, grindhouses were regularly criticized by the press, people working in the film industry, and some patrons, for their scruffiness and seediness; their reputation became steadily more tarnished. Ultimately, as David Church highlights, the types of film that a notable percentage of these cinemas often relied on – low-budget features and exploitation titles, many of which were violent and/or salacious in content – became conflated with the venues themselves, leading to the term "grindhouse" designating not only particular spaces, but also certain forms of cinema.

The multiplex

Although the multiplex – or multiple-screen cinema exhibition venue – is now a recognizable enter-tainment space in many cities and suburbs around the world, the idea of screening more than one film in different rooms in the same building has a relatively short history. The Elgin Theatre in Ottawa, Canada, was altered in 1957 to incorporate two screens that could show different films simultaneously; it is often identified as the starting point of any history of the multiplex. Prior to this, for more than sixty years, cinemas only had one screening space. From the 1950s onwards, the number of screens in individual cinemas began to multiply. The design of the spaces also altered. As film scholar Jocelyn Szczepaniak-Gillece has highlighted, from the mid twentieth century in the United States, the "neutralized theatre" became popular as an exhibition space concept:

> Neutralization broke with the elaborate and enormous movie palaces of the 1910s and 1920s by shrinking auditorium size and seating, reducing or eliminating vestiges of live theatre such as proscenia, darkening the lights, removing extraneous decoration, and designing an auditorium that directed visual attention at the screen. Most importantly, the notion of neutralization implies an importance of an invisible style that, in the very act of effacing itself, privileges the screen, thereby bringing it closer to the audience's contemplative gaze. Gaudy palace architecture was simply too *visible*; neutralization tended instead in the direction of stylistic erasure. This functional approach would eventually shape mall, multiplex, and most standardized moviegoing and lead to current theatres' darkened and minimalist auditorium centred on an ever-enlarging screen.[10]

This is not to suggest, however, that building a multiplex is a simple affair. The "invisible" design and architecture of many multiplexes requires careful planning and consideration of such factors as acoustics, seating, insulation, air conditioning, exit and escape routes, and so on.

Multiplexes can now be found all over the world, from the sixteen-screen Mayajaal multiplex in Chennai, India to the twenty-five-screen Kinepolis Madrid in Spain, from the fifteen-screen Arena in Sofia, Bulgaria to the eighteen-screen Cineworld in Glasgow, Scotland. Larger multiplexes are sometimes referred to in trade lingo as "megaplexes". Multiplexes are often carefully positioned geographically. As cost consultants Davis, Langdon and Everest point out, many multiplexes

> have been located on large edge-of-town sites, often alongside mixed leisure schemes featuring bowling, nightclubs, restaurants and so on. Cinemas have also become an integral part of most recent shopping centre projects. Multiplexes have been particularly successful in attracting the public into the "dead areas" of shopping centres such as upper levels or the dead-ends of malls. Multiplexes have been used to anchor and re-image unsuccessful shopping centres as part of refurbishment schemes. The co-location of cinema and shopping centre is mutually beneficial, with research showing

11.9 Cineworld multiplex cinema in Glasgow, Scotland, 2013. Courtesy of Alan Oliver/Alamy.

that multiplexes contribute to an increase in footfall and sales. For example, three-quarters of the cinema audience will use other amenities such as bars and restaurants before their cinema visit.[11]

The multiplex, in other words, may be carefully situated within a network of other entertainment and shopping options, whose proximity promotes sustained consumption.

Mobile cinemas

The history of cinema exhibition is not solely concerned with the fixed spaces which are designed for screening films, or which can accommodate cinema as one component of the entertainment programme that they offer. It is important to identify the existence of a parallel history of mobile cinema exhibition. Although the term "mobility" has been deployed as a key criterion in attempts to market hand-held devices such as tablets and smartphones to consumers, suggesting that screen mobility is a recent innovation, the mobility of film exhibition has long been a possibility. If all that is needed to exhibit a film is a screen, speakers, a projector, maybe somewhere to sit, and the movie itself, then "pop-up" cinemas can be easily constructed in both indoor and outdoor locations. In the late 1910s, for instance, "agit trains" or "kine trains" traveled around the Soviet Union, disseminating propaganda. The trains operated as movie studios on wheels, containing the technology needed to record, process, and exhibit films. To give another example, Charles Acland has highlighted how important mobile cinemas have been for educational provision throughout the last century, used in schools (and elsewhere) "for instructional, scientific, promotional, community and religious purposes."[12]

Mobile screening equipment may supplement existing cinemas in cities, proliferating exhibition opportunities. Beyond cities and their suburbs, as the number of cinemas begins to dwindle, the mobility of screening technology may enable diverse audiences to enjoy and encounter the moving image. Village and town halls, which host a range of forms of entertainment, can employ mobile cinema elements to screen films as part of their programme of events. Alternatively, screenings could be held outdoors after dark. Such forms of mobile cinema operate across the globe. Many countries – from Australia to Russia – contain large geographical stretches with very few inhabitants. Mobile cinemas can be used to take cinema to such audiences. When the Shaw brothers – the focus of a case study below – were establishing their cinema chain in Singapore and Malaya in the 1920s and 1930s, they took a mobile cinema unit on the road. Wherever they encountered significant interest in their screenings, they recognized that such places might be able to accommodate a cinema. Brian Larkin, in his book *Signal and Noise*, has identified the role that mobile film units played in Nigeria, beginning in the 1930s:

> These were educational teams created by the government to show a mix of documentaries, newsreels, and pedagogical dramas intended to instruct audiences about the achievements of the state and educate them in modes of health, farming, and civic participation … Traveling all over the nation, mobile cinema vans would arrive in rural and urban areas, set up a screen and, once the sun had set, project programmes of short films, usually accompanied by a short lecture. The address of the films was political, aimed at educating a mutable, developmentalist citizen, yet its practice created a highly popular event, and its influence far exceeded the intentions of its organizers.[13]

11.10 Mobile cinema in Barbados, 1952. Courtesy of The National Archives.

Mobile forms of cinema, then, can provide diverse audiences with cinematic pleasures – even when these might counteract the aims and goals of those operating the screening.

The domestic

As we identified in our discussion of film as a commodity (Chapter 5), less than 15 per cent of box office revenue comes from screening movies in cinemas. That is, the majority of movies are now consumed outside cinema spaces – on television, online, on the go and elsewhere. One of the main spaces in which films have been watched, ever since the widespread uptake of television after World War II, is the domestic. The benefits of domestic consumption of cinema are transparent: the viewer does not have to leave the comfort of their home; the cost of consumption (beyond initial shelling out for the requisite technology) is minor; the proliferation of VHS, DVD, Blu-ray, TiVo and other digital recording and playback devices enables the viewer to be in full control of when something is watched, and whether or not it is viewed in total in one sitting.

As we have already identified, developments in cinema exhibition over the last fifty years have often directly attempted to seduce audiences away from their homes and back into auditoria. Television and other domestic viewing technologies have developed a similar line of competition enticing viewers to stay at home: cathode ray tubes replaced by digital flat screens; widescreen televisions with better sound and image resolution replacing previous limited formats; the introduction and refinement of "home cinema" systems. Portable and mobile devices only broaden the range of home entertainment possibilities, enabling several family members in the same home to watch different material simultaneously, streamed or downloaded as desired.

Crucially, however, viewing in the domestic space is fundamentally different from viewing in the cinema. It has the potential to be more interactive and less reverential, with group viewing including discussion and commentary. Image and sound quality will never equal that of the best cinema exhibition, and the image/sound balance may be notably different. Although domestic spaces can be darkened, most home viewing occurs in rooms that are at least partially illuminated, altering viewer perception of screen content. As we noted in our case study on "taking a break," above, domestic viewing is more likely to be interrupted, fracturing a movie into multiple parts (possibly against the intentions of the filmmakers). And domestic viewing is also often distracted, less immersive, with eyes and ears repeatedly diverted away from a film's content.

The non-place

Mobile devices such as laptops, tablets and phones allow films to be watched on the move, and in almost any location. Is there any consistency to the places in which viewers use this exhibition technology, however? They can be employed to help pass the time in transit, or when away from the ready availability of domestic viewing technologies. The spaces in which they are predominantly used, we could suggest, are what the French philosopher Marc Augé has called "non-places." These sorts of locations have proliferated in recent decades, and many of us spend a great deal of time in them, or passing through them. As Augé writes:

> non-places are the real measure of our time; one that could be quantified … by totalling all the air, rail and motorway routes, the mobile cabins called "means of transport" (aircraft, trains and road vehicles), the airports and railway stations, hotel chains, leisure parks, large retail outlets, and finally the complex skein of cable and wireless networks that mobilize extraterrestrial space for the purposes of a communication so peculiar that it often puts the individual in contact only with another image of himself.[14]

For Augé, excessive information and excessive space connect in the era of "super modernity." Another way of putting this is that "non-places" of transit and pause, from airports to trains, from hotels to retail parks, have spread in recent decades. Mobile devices that enable cinema viewing opportunities have manifested and proliferated in line with this shifting and developing geography. It could be argued that the growth and spread of laptops and other such viewing technologies have occurred precisely because humans now spend so much of their time in "non-places." This exhibition "location," due to its flexibility and variability, is one of the most complex to comprehend and theorize. However, it now accounts for a considerable percentage of film viewing experiences, and thus deserves sustained thought.

CASE STUDY: SHAW THEATRES

A significant percentage of cinemas around the world are linked in exhibition chains. Such linking enables a brand identity to be created, disseminated and sustained. It also allows running costs to be trimmed through a centralization of management. Examples of cinema chains can be found on every continent. The Finnkino chain in Finland operates over a dozen cinemas spread across a number of cities, including Helsinki, Turku, and Vantaa. In Vietnam, the Megastar Cineplex chain runs ten cinemas, including five in Ho Chi Minh City. The Belgian company Kinepolis runs twenty-three multiplexes in five countries across Europe: Belgium, France, Poland, Spain, and Switzerland. Hoyts Exhibition, part of the Australian Hoyts Group of companies, operates forty cinemas in Australia and ten in New Zealand.

Shaw Theatres is a chain of seven cinemas in Singapore, operated by the Shaw Organisation. The history of the chain and its creators provides valuable insight into shifting practices of film exhibition, and reveals the complex interrelationships that operate between production, distribution, and exhibition. The Shaw Organisation's cinema business began with production and distribution. In 1925, identifying the financial opportunities available in the relatively new field of cinema, four brothers from Zhejiang Province in China – Runje, Runde, Runme, and Run Run – formed the Tianyi (Number One) Film Company in Shanghai, and started to make silent films. Wanting to expand their market beyond the domestic, Runme and Run Run moved to Singapore in 1928, and established Shaw Brothers Ltd. In 1934, Tianyi relocated to Hong Kong, in order to expand the number of films they were producing in Cantonese. The production company was renamed as the Nanyang (South Sea) Studio. By the end of the 1930s, through forging partnerships with diasporic Chinese business figures, Runme and Run Run had built a distribution network across the Singapore–Malaya region. They distributed not only films made by Nanyang, but other titles made in Hong Kong and Shanghai. In essence, the Shaw brothers had assembled a vertically integrated company: cinemas owned and operated by Run Run and Runme would screen the films made by the family's production studio in Hong Kong. As Poshek Fu identifies, the building of these connections was facilitated by existing international trade and business links:

> Throughout the 1930s and 1940s, the relationship between Nanyang in Hong Kong and the Shaw Brothers Ltd in Singapore-Malaya was markedly transnational. Taking advantage of the British colonial network (e.g., the Hong Kong and Shanghai Banking Corporation and shipping routes in the region), the territorial boundaries between both cities were continuously transgressed. Although Nanyang's operation depended on the steady cash flow and distribution network of Singapore, the Shaw Brothers Studio could not accumulate its capital and continuously expand without the constant supply of commodities, skills, and equipment from Hong Kong, Shanghai, and Guangdong.[15]

World War II was a difficult time for the Shaw Organisation. During the Japanese Occupation, many of the company's properties in Singapore–Malaya and Hong Kong were destroyed.

However, after the end of the conflict, the organization once again boomed, with the Shaw brothers expanding their interests into amusement parks, dance halls, and commercial property development (including apartment complexes, hotels and office blocks). Their distribution network was expanded, importing films from Europe, India, and the United States. Their exhibition business also grew; at one peak, they operated more than 130 cinemas across Southeast Asia.

The "Shaw Brothers" name remains primarily associated with production. Nanyang was renamed as the Shaw Brothers Studio in 1957, when Run Run moved to Hong Kong to take over the running of the business. In 1965, the Shaw Brothers launched Movietown, an enormous modern film studio located in Hong Kong's Clear Water Bay which had on offer color film development facilities, fifteen stages, two permanent sets, and an array of cutting-edge film equipment imported from North America and Europe. Films produced by this studio were made in Eastmancolor and "Shawscope" widescreen. Run Run Shaw operated Movietown – which had around 1,300 members of staff – according to Taylorist and Fordist models of business: assembly-line production, cost efficiency, rational management. (For more on how these models of business work, please refer back to our discussion of production processes in Chapter 8.) Shaw Brothers Studios attempted to expand their business beyond China and Southeast Asia, to a more global market. They did so by entering their films in international film festivals, and forging co-production projects with film studios in the United States and Europe. For many audiences around the world, the Shaw Brothers Studio remains associated with the genre of kung fu: the company broke into the mainstream market in the United States with *Five Fingers of Death* (Cheng Chang Ho, 1965). The popularity of dubbed martial arts movies in the 1970s with African American audiences in the United States, as well as cinemagoers in Africa and Latin America, extended the global reach of the Shaw Brothers name.

From the 1970s onwards, the Shaw Brothers Studio's film output began to dwindle, and the company started investing in television. However, the Shaw name continues to be associated with cinema. In Singapore, this is most notable in relation to exhibition. The Shaw Organisation, which runs the seven Shaw cinemas in the region, plans to open two additional multiplexes by the end of 2015. Although many of the audiences attending these cinemas may not realize it, the cinemas serve as a visible trace of one of the most significant and ambitious cinema businesses in Chinese history.

11.11 The title card announcing productions shot in Shawscope widescreen.

CHAPTER SUMMARY

This chapter has provided an overview of a range of topics related to the subject of exhibition. In the first section, we outlined the associations between exhibition and technology, by considering a number of key aspects of film exhibition history: projectors, sound, widescreen, 3D and seating. Expanding this consideration of exhibition technology, we turned our attention to the body of writing known as "apparatus theory," and noted that particular exhibition experiences and strategies might complicate its central tenets. Finally, in our third section, cinema exhibition's relation to space and geography was explored through specific types of screening space: the picture palace; the grindhouse; the multiplex; the mobile cinema; the domestic; the non-place.

FURTHER READING

Belton, John, Hall, Sheldon, and Neale, Steve (eds). *Widescreen Worldwide*. London: John Libbey, 2010.

A wide-ranging collection of essays on one particular aspect of exhibition: widescreen cinema. Though many of the essays are focused on the US context, there are also valuable examinations of technological experiments in other countries, including Italy, Japan, and Hong Kong.

Hark, Ina Rae (ed.). *Exhibition: The Film Reader*. London and New York: Routledge, 2001.

An excellent collection of historical texts and theoretical articles, prefaced by a wide-ranging and perceptive introduction. The focus of the book is on examples and perspectives from the United States.

Jancovich, Mark and Faire, Lucy with Stubbings, Sarah. *The Place of the Audience: Cultural Geographies of Film Consumption*. London: BFI, 2003.

This book provides a survey of different types of exhibition spaces in which films are shown. The strength of this book is that it maps these spaces through the history of one particular city, Nottingham in the UK, and frames this history through theoretical approaches to exhibition.

Rosen, Philip (ed.). *Narrative, Apparatus, Ideology: A Film Theory Reader*. New York: Columbia University Press, 1986.

This collection contains a section devoted to apparatus theory, which includes the key essays by Jean-Louis Baudry, "Ideological Effects of the Basic Cinematographic Apparatus" and "The Apparatus: Metapsychological Approaches to the Impression of Reality in Cinema." Rosen's introduction to the section also provides invaluable contextualization.

FILMS REFERENCED IN CHAPTER ELEVEN

Avatar (James Cameron, 2009)

Five Fingers of Death (Cheng Chang Ho, 1965)

Gone With the Wind (Victor Fleming, 1939)

Gravity (Alfonso Cuarón, 2013)

Heaven's Gate (Michael Cimino, 1980)

Life of Pi (Ang Lee, 2012)

Napoleon (Abel Gance, 1927)

Solaris (Andrei Tarkovsky, 1972)

NOTES

1 Peter Kramer, *2001: A Space Odyssey* (London: BFI), 37.

2 Garima Sharma, "Do We Need the Intermission?," *Times of India*, 21 January 2011, http://articles. timesofindia.indiatimes.com/2011-01-21/news-interviews/28369961_1_interval-bollywood-movies-hindi-movies, accessed 23 October 2013.

3 Jean-Louis Baudry, "The Ideological Effects of the Basic Cinematographic Apparatus," in Philip Rosen (ed.), *Narrative, Apparatus, Ideology: A Film Theory Reader* (New York: Columbia University Press, 1986), 294.

4 Baudry, 292.

5 Pascal Bonitzer, "The Silences of the Voice"; Mary Ann Doane, "The Voice in the Cinema: The Articulation of Body and Space"; both in Rosen.

6 Claudia Gorbman, *Unheard Melodies: Narrative Film Music* (Bloomington and Indianapolis: Indiana University Press, 1987).

7 Vance Kepley, Jr., "Whose Apparatus? Problems of Film Exhibition and History," in David Bordwell and Noël Carroll (eds), *Post-Theory: Reconstructing Film Studies* (Madison, WI: University of Wisconsin Press, 1996), 536.

8 Charlotte Herzog, "The Movie Palace and the Theatrical Sources of its Architectural Style," in Ina Rae Hark (ed.), *Exhibition: The Film Reader* (London and New York: Routledge, 2001), 52.

9 David Church, "From Exhibition to Genre: The Case of Grind-House Films," *Cinema Journal* 50(4) (2011), 4.

10 Jocelyn Szczepaniak-Gillece, "In the House, In the Picture: Distance and Proximity in the American Mid-Century Neutralized Theatre," *World Picture* 7, Autumn 2012, http://www.worldpicturejournal. com/WP_7/Szczepaniak-Gillece.html#_edn5, accessed 23 October 2013.

11 Davis, Langdon and Everest, "Cost Model: Multiplex Cinemas," *Building* 18 (2000), http://www. building.co.uk/data/cost-model-multiplex-cinemas/1779.article, accessed 23 October 2013.

12 Charles R. Acland, "Curtains, Carts, and the Mobile Screen," *Screen*, 50(1) (2009), 152.

13 Brian Larkin, *Signal and Noise: Media, Infrastructure, and Urban Culture in Nigeria* (Durham, NC and London: Duke University Press, 2008), 77–78.

14 Marc Augé, *Non-Places: Introduction to an Anthropology of Supermodernity*, trans. John Howe (London: Verso, 1995), 79.

15 Poshek Fu, "Introduction: The Shaw Brothers' Diasporic Cinema," in Poshek Fu, *China Forever: The Shaw Brothers and Diasporic Cinema* (Urbana and Chicago: University of Illinois Press, 2008), 2.

CHAPTER TWELVE
EVALUATIVE CONTEXTS

Public opinion of a given movie generally grows out of a general "buzz" that circulates around it, and publicists, reviewers, and audiences – usually in that order – all contribute to that drone and influence each other in the process. The buzz usually starts well before the picture's release and grows (or dies) over many weeks afterward, and the cacophonous overlaps that compose it often make it hard to determine which voices are the most dominant or influential.

Jonathan Rosenbaum[1]

In the last three chapters, we have provided an overview of the various ways in which completed films are marketed, distributed and exhibited to audiences. Films are always in competition with each other for a viewer's attention, and marketing, distribution and exhibition tactics attempt to make sure that audiences are aware of which films are being released, and that those films are made as widely available for viewing as possible. This chapter deals with a seemingly simple concern: how are films judged, and by whom? Of course, all films are judged by their audiences – as your own post-viewing conversations with friends and relatives will easily demonstrate. But films usually arrive with audiences already trailing some sort of evaluation – such as praise from a festival's jury, or comment and critique from a film journalist. What are these different forms of evaluation? And what impact do they have on where movies go?

WHAT WE WILL DO IN THIS CHAPTER

This chapter will introduce you to a number of particular evaluative contexts within which a film's quality and success are judged. All of these contexts have an impact on where the film goes in the future: does it have shelf life, a reputation and status, or will it swiftly disappear from view? The following topics are explored:

- The field of film criticism in newspapers, magazines, and online.
- What distinguishes the professional film critic from the lay one, what might characterize distinctive film criticism, and the reach and influence that film critics can exert.
- The role of film festivals in adjudicating cinematic "worth" and "quality."
- The ways in which box office takings may be used to judge a film's success.
- What it means for a film to be "popular": if a film manages to attract a large audience, does this mean that it is of a high standard?
- The construction of a "canon" of "the greatest films of all time," including who contributes to this canon, and how films become part of it.

BY THE END OF THIS CHAPTER YOU SHOULD BE ABLE TO

- Identify some of the main differences between print and online film criticism.
- Discuss how film festivals contribute to the evaluation of movies.
- Outline the relationships between box office receipts, "popularity," and "quality".
- Critically discuss how the cinematic canon has been formed, and assess the value of artistic canons.

FILM CRITICISM

Film criticism is published in hard form in a large number of places: daily newspapers, weekly and monthly magazines (whether "life style," centered on news/politics, or devoted specifically to cinema), and magazines and journals of criticism and opinion. Almost every country around the world has its own periodicals devoted solely to cinema, from Argentina's *El Amante Cine* to Finland's *Filmihullu*, from Italy's *CineForum* to Serbia and Montenegro's (formerly Yugoslavia's) *Ekran*. A great deal of film criticism is also published online, on blogs and websites – some of which are the digital versions of print sources. Retrospectively, some film critics have their reviews and articles collected in books: there are volumes, for instance, by Jean-Luc Godard, Pauline Kael, and Jonathan Romney, amongst many others. Film criticism also appears on television and on the radio, as streaming audio or video clips online, as podcasts and so on. In the first sections of this chapter, we will provide an overview of the field of film criticism, discuss the ways in which blogging and online film criticism are altering the practice of movie critique, and outline how film criticism can affect where films travel and which audiences they reach. We will focus mainly on written forms of film criticism, though many of the points that we raise can be applied to the field as a whole. We return to the subject of film criticism in the coda to this book, in which it is discussed as one of several types of "Writing about Cinema."

12.1 The cover of *Hooked: Film Writings 1985–1988* by Pauline Kael. Courtesy of Marion Boyars Publishers Ltd.

What does a film critic do, and how do they manage to get this job? Film critics often have a background in journalism; the best have access to a comprehensive memory and broad knowledge of the history of the medium (their own, rather than one sourced online). For those professionally employed as film critics for the press, there may be networking or unionizing organizations which support their endeavors, such as the Argentine Film Critics Association, the Kerala Film Critics Association, or the Australian Film Critics Association. Some of these organizations also give out annual awards for the best achievements in cinema. Although the job of film critic may seem glamorous and entertaining – watching movies for a living, attending events alongside film industry personnel – critics have to sit through screening after screening of films of variable quality, which many in the general audience would never choose to endure, and they have to find things to say about the blandest of output. To give an example, in the space of one week the film critics from the print edition of the UK newspaper the *Guardian* reviewed eleven films: *Blue is the Warmest Colour* (Abdellatif Kechiche, 2013), *Breakfast with Jonny Wilkinson* (Simon Sprackling, 2013), *Computer Chess* (Andrew Bujalski, 2013), *The Family* (Luc Besson, 2013), *Flu* (Sung-su Kim, 2013), a re-release of *Gone with the Wind* (Victor Fleming, 1939), *The Hunger Games: Catching Fire* (Francis Lawrence, 2013), *Killing Oswald* (Shane O'Sullivan, 2013), *Parkland* (Peter Landesman, 2013), *Vendetta* (Stephen Reynolds, 2013), and *¡Vivan las Antipodas!* (Victor Kossakovsky, 2011).

Film critics usually have access to films before the public, through advance press screenings and film festivals they attend (more on the latter subject below). They offer opinion on the quality of individual films before their appearance in cinemas, and thus critics can have an impact on the commercial success of individual titles. Consider here that posters and hoardings advertising a film often carry quotes from film journalists recommending it. Opinions aired by critics at festivals may even affect distribution, and whether or not a film reaches audiences at all. Alternatively, negative critical responses may help with a film's reach. Two hundred and fifty people walked out of a screening of Gasper Noé's *Irréversible* at Cannes in 2002. The film contains a great deal of violent and sexual content, including a lengthy rape sequence. However, due to Noé's status as a recognized auteur, and because controversy can be used to sell a film, *Irréversible* was widely distributed internationally.

What is film criticism for? How does it differ from the general audience giving a film a personal score out of ten when they exit the cinema? Useful definitions have been offered by particular writers of the value and distinctive character of film criticism. For Alex Clayton and Andrew Klevan,

> We find the best criticism *deepens* our interest in individual films, *reveals* new meanings and perspectives, *expands* our sense of the medium, *confronts* our assumptions about value, and *sharpens* our capacity to discriminate. Moreover, it strives to find expression for what is seen and heard, bringing a realm of sounds, images, actions and objects to meet a realm of words and concepts.[2]

That is, film criticism should offer the reader an alternative angle on particular films, challenge the reader's own tastes and values, and offer a way, in words, to think through and about an audio-visual medium. Clayton and Klevan challenge the objection sometimes leveled against film criticism that it is too personal in comparison to academic film writing, arguing that this is a false dichotomy. They also defend the critic's right to make value judgements:

> one might argue that most, if not all, films are made to be good and this objective is an integral part of their presentation and address. For film criticism, the tension between a film's aspiration or potential and its actual achievement is as palpable to a viewer as that generated by plot or character or composition. The viewer monitors the success with which the film handles its elements; and this is not of supplementary interest, but of pressing importance every step of the way.[3]

Indeed, film criticism may engage directly with whether or not a film will provide its audience with pleasure (a complex topic that we return to at length in Chapter 14). It could also be added that film criticism should be entertaining, engaging, and provocative – for surely the best film criticism hooks in readers.

12.2 Poster for *Her* (Spike Jonze, 2013). Courtesy of Allstar Images.

EXERCISE

The websites metacritic.com and rottentomatoes.com aggregate reviews from a large number of publications.

- Look up three reviews, using one of these websites, of a film that you have seen recently. You should choose a positive review, a middling review, and a poor review. Read all three reviews thoroughly.
- How does the content of the reviews differ? Do they concentrate on different aspects of the film (story, performances, visual style, and so on)?
- Whose reviewing style do you like, and why?
- Are the three reviews pitched at different readers – and if so, how can you tell?
- Which reviewer do you agree with, and why?
- Did any of the reviews offer you an alternative perspective on the film that you had not considered? Did this enhance the pleasure that you got from the review, or its usefulness?

Of course, it is crucial to ask here: how many people in the cinema audience read the opinions and reviews of film critics? Even for those who do, how much do they glean? Most reviews in newspapers and magazines are capsules, brief and pointed, and often little more than a few sentences in length: they cannot reveal a great deal. There is also the possibility that the film industry – especially the major studios – puts pressure on film reviewers to frame their releases positively. Many press screenings provide film critics with **press kits**, including plot summaries and production information that can be recycled into reviews, thus saving some critics from needing to spend too much time on formulating these parts of their writing. Further, most movie reviews are published in the press on the day that films are released into cinemas. Sitting alongside advertisements for those same movies, the reviews can sometimes seem like little more than product endorsement. And yet, the opinions of film critics provide a crucial evaluative context that influences many viewers in making their cinemagoing choices. And given that most viewers will only see a small sample of the films released into cinemas every year, and that a trip to the cinema may be an expensive outlay, they require guidance.

It is debatable whether readers follow the criticism of particular writers in the print press, or whether it is the publication itself that is favored. Do readers of the *Hindu* newspaper's film reviews trust Y. Sunita Chowdhary, their main film reviewer, or do they trust the newspaper and its hiring policies? The devoted reader of the UK's *Empire* magazine may go to see a film because "*Empire* gave it four stars," not because they are aware of who wrote the movie's review. As the director Samuel Fuller allegedly once stated about a famous critic:

> If Vincent Canby got fired from the *Times* today, and he went to a bar and started talking about a movie he'd just seen, nobody there would give a fuck what he thought. They'd probably just tell him to shut up.[4]

When a film viewer *does* follow the reviews of a particular critic, how has that trust been earned? The newspaper or magazine film critic will most likely be reviewing something that you have not yet seen, their review telling you to see something or warning you away: if their opinion turns out to be bogus, then the status of the critic as informed and perceptive will be damaged.

BLOGGING AND ONLINE CRITICISM

In 2008, a number of articles appeared in US newspapers claiming that film criticism in print media (newspapers, in particular) was under threat. A number of high profile publications – such as the *Village Voice* and *Newsweek* – had recently paid off, laid off or reassigned film critics on their staff. In defence of these critics, David Carr in the *New York Times* wrote that, "for a certain kind of movie, critical accolades can mean the difference between relevance and obscurity, not to mention box office success or failure."[5] He quoted creative personnel involved in the making of smaller budget and independent films, who acknowledged that without press coverage for their films, those movies could struggle to find an audience. However, is it not enough for those accolades to appear online? Does film criticism in newspapers and magazines have a higher status than that on blogs and other websites?

There are now thousands of blogs devoted to cinema. Some are primarily oriented around news and gossip, informing audiences of upcoming releases; some are devoted to specific genres or stars; some are centered solely on "art house" cinema. Certainly, with the number of critical, high-quality film-related blogs and websites growing every year, and access to these online sources being free for anyone with internet access, traditional print film criticism seems to be under threat. This is merely one aspect of a larger cultural shift, in which "hard" media are being challenged by digital or "virtual" media forms. Any such shift inevitably causes concern for those working in the medium that is being undermined or eroded. However, it is worth pausing to consider the main differences between print and online film criticism, in order to evaluate the distinctive contributions that they make to the evaluation of cinema.

Quality

Perhaps the main criticism that is leveled against the expansion of online film criticism is related to quality. For those with internet access, assembling a blog is free and easy to do. Once that step has been taken, the blogger interested in cinema can begin to post their opinions about specific movies, directors, and so on. Many of these bloggers may lack a grounding in film history, or a sense of cinema beyond what their local multiplex shows. Their opinions may be fatuous, or poorly expressed. Lacking an editor, their writing may be factually inaccurate and riddled with spelling errors. Blogging allows for a widespread expression of critical opinion that, at its worst, is akin to simplistic evaluative grading. However, there is also some lazy and clumsily written criticism about cinema in the printed press.

Timing

Much print criticism of cinema is centered on contemporary releases: it is necessarily in thrall to the weekly timetable that connects distributors and exhibitors. Indeed, the life of the press reviewer is largely ordered by industrial forces: scheduled press screenings, anticipated release dates in cinemas, and publication deadlines. Even when press film criticism offers commentary and reviews from film festivals, these events are similarly locked into calendars, and many films screen at festivals only a short time before they appear in theatres. The press journalist will likely be offering comment on films that the audience has not seen, giving guidance on the quality of individual films; the interaction with the reader is thus essentially one-way, with the critic operating as an authority.

For the blogger or online film critic, the pressure of publishing deadlines that afflicts the press writer is less of a concern. Of course, the online writer may want to project a sense of professionalism and trust-worthiness, and to appear diligent in their attention to current and up-to-date films and topics. However, posting can be done as often or irregularly as suits the critic. Perhaps most importantly, the blogger or online writer does not have to be in thrall to the contemporary release slate – they are free to write about whichever films they choose. For Paul Brunick, writing in *Film Comment*, this is one of the major strengths of film criticism online: it can be used for "proselytizing on behalf of the creatively triumphant but commercially marginal; trawling through cinema's back catalogues in search of unappreciated masterpieces; placing movies within the broader narratives of intellectual history."[6]

Word count

For film critics writing for print media, word counts are normally established in advance. A lead film review is accorded a certain amount of space; an essay or argumentative piece (normally also on a contemporary release or re-release) may be given a little more room; capsule reviews are often less

CASE STUDY: THE "CRITIC-PROOF" MOVIE

At times, reviews by critics and box office receipts align. The British farce remake *Run for Your Wife* (Ray Cooney and John Luton, 2012) was roundly drubbed by film journalists, and ticket sales amounted to less than £750. *The Lone Ranger* (Gore Verbinski, 2013) was derided by critics and fared poorly at cinemas. Disney, the studio behind the film, swiftly claimed that its failure would cause them to be somewhere between $160 and $190 million out of pocket. At other times, critical opinion and audience interest diverge. Excellent reviews for innovative and interesting movies do not always translate into "bums on seats." Conversely, films that are poorly reviewed may still fare well in cinemas.

Sex and the City 2, written and directed by Michael Patrick King, was released into cinemas around the world in May and June of 2010. It cost approximately $100 million to make, and took $288 million at the global box office. It was thus less financially successful than the first *Sex and the City* film, released in 2008 and also written and directed by King, which had a budget of $65 million and took $415 million worldwide. What is worth exploring about *Sex and the City 2* in relation to the topics discussed in this chapter is that it was critically derided, yet a box office success. Reviews aggregator metacritic.com, calculating the average of thirty-nine reviews, gave the film a score of 27 out of 100. More dramatically, rottentomatoes.com, aggregating 195 reviews, scored the film 15 out of 100. "Even in the context of that lumpy, overpriced Birkin bag of stuff we call Hollywood product, *Sex and the City 2* hits a new low of idiocy and crassness," wrote Stephanie Zacharek of *Movieline*.[7] Andrew O'Hehir at salon.com called it a "bloated mess of a movie," a "ghastly, gassy, undead franchise-extender."[8] The novelist Andrew O'Hagan, writing in London's *Evening Standard*, claimed that *Sex and the City 2* "could be the most stupid, the most racist, the most polluting and women-hating film of the year."[9]

And yet in the wake of the cinema release of *Sex and the City 2*, some journalists wondered whether the film was "critic-proof"; that is, if critics' opinions would have little or any influence over the box office success of the film. The two *Sex and the City* films were spin-offs from the popular television series of the same name which ran on HBO from 1998 to 2004. The TV show was especially successful with women viewers; it is feasible that, no matter how poorly it was reviewed, many women would use *Sex and the City 2* as the focus for a social event. Word of mouth, the critical opinion of friends and acquaintances, may have been a significant factor at play in the film's box office success – even if that word of mouth suggested that "it isn't as bad as some people have said." Of course, it is difficult (if not impossible) to identify to what extent negative reviews may have hit the movie's final box office tally. As the O'Hagan quote above reveals, one of the recurrent criticisms of *Sex and the City 2* was the allegation of racism: a sequence of the film set in Abu Dhabi was repeatedly singled out as offensively stereotyped, with the four lead female characters (and thus the film itself) taking part in a crass and exploitative form of cultural tourism. Did this serious allegation hurt the movie's takings? It is difficult to gauge whether those viewers who went to the cinema to see *Sex and the City 2* enjoyed it, agreed with (parts of) any reviews they had read, were offended by it, or even walked out.

12.3 *Sex and the City 2* (Michael Patrick King, 2010). Courtesy of New Line Cinema/Kobal Collection.

Sex and the City 2 was merely the latest "critic-proof" Hollywood blockbuster. *The Flintstones* (Brian Levant, 1994), *Lara Croft: Tomb Raider* (Simon West, 2001), *The Da Vinci Code* (Ron Howard, 2006), *Transformers: Revenge of the Fallen* (Michael Bay, 2009), *Alvin and the Chipmunks: The Squeakquel* (Betty Thomas, 2009) – all scored pitifully with critics, and yet fared well at the box office. However, these films all have something in common: they were based on already existing and highly popular cultural properties, whether a cartoon, toy, computer game, or novel. *Sex and the City 2* and *Transformers: Revenge of the Fallen* were sequels to hugely financially successful movies, and thus could expect to attract (at least a percentage of) viewers who had enjoyed the first entries in the series. Further, many of these "critic-proof" movies were marketed using blanket and saturation strategies so that their release was difficult to ignore.

In many cases, public opinion of the quality of individual films differs from that of critics. And there will inevitably be many more "critic-proof" films released in the future. What these chasms between critical opinion and global box office takings can reveal, however, is of substantial significance in relation to how films are evaluated. Are these films successful because audiences are influenced by marketing and distribution tactics, or because they genuinely disagree with the opinions of critics regarding a movie's quality? With "critic-proof" films, are reviews merely one element of the "noise" that surrounds a movie's release, and which may have an effect on a viewer deciding to see the film?

than a hundred words long. Word counts are determined not only by how much text can be squeezed onto an individual page, but also on the cost to the newspaper of paying journalists for particular lengths of writing. Online, these concerns are not relevant: postings can be of any length. Short think pieces can flirt with particular ideas. Lengthier essays can explore ideas in significant detail – though these may not appeal to all readers, simply due to the time they take to work through.

Irrespective of whether film viewers read reviews in the press or online, film criticism is a crucial evaluative context which impacts on how audiences receive and understand films. Criticism assists audiences in determining how to tell a good-quality film from a poor one; identifies the valuable parts of weaker films and highlights weaknesses in better-quality titles; and proffers guidance in the different ways that particular kinds of film can be judged.

FILM FESTIVALS

Film festivals occur all over the world, throughout the calendar year; most take place on an annual basis. Some festivals have been running for decades – Venice, for instance, the oldest film festival in the world, launched in 1932 – although new festivals start up every year. Some are devoted to specialist subjects, such as Kashish, the Mumbai Queer Film Festival, or Giffoni, the Italian festival of films for children. There is even an International Film Festival for Mountains that has been held in the ski resort of Bansko in Bulgaria every year since its launch in 1998. Many film festivals, however, have a broader scope, screening films in a range of genres and formats, perhaps with themed strands, and featuring both contemporary and archival movies. Due to the large number of film festivals that take place around the world, there is competition between them in relation to the attractiveness of the location, convenience for international access, and the exclusivity of the movies that are screened. Film festivals also compete over their placement in the schedule on the annual calendar.

In her book *Film Festivals*, Marijke de Valck outlines a history of film festivals in three stages. Stage One lasted from 1932 to 1968, when political turmoil and unrest caused the Cannes film festival to close down. During these decades there were only a limited number of film festivals, but many of those which continue to have cultural and financial significance (Cannes, Berlin, and so on) were launched. Stage Two ran from 1968 to the 1980s, as smaller and more independent film festivals flourished, and a global cinema market was established. Stage Three, which runs from the 1980s to the present day, is characterized by a global boom in film festivals, but also by the institutionalization of the film festival circuit. Certainly, many contemporary film festivals not only serve as a space in which to screen new films for critics and movie fans, but also append events such as film markets (to connect makers with distributors), networking symposia and other opportunities.

Film festivals are a crucial context in which the evaluation of movies takes place. They will screen new films before they go on general release, with the first festival showing being sold to audiences as the film's national or international premiere. The audience for these advance screenings is therefore able to judge the film – and possibly tell others their opinion of it, through written reviews or word of mouth – before a wider audience has access to it. Simply being selected for screening in a particular festival may provide a film with kudos. Retrospective and archival screenings allow for revaluation of the work of individual creative personnel: screenwriters, producers, directors, costume designers, and so on. Many festivals also give out awards, and these can then be used by publicists to demonstrate to audiences

12.4 Poster for the 2014 Giffoni Film Festival. Courtesy of the Giffoni Film Festival.

the quality of their films – a topic that was discussed in our exploration of Marketing in Chapter 9. For instance, the Iranian film *A Separation*, written and directed by Asghar Fahardi, won the Golden Bear at the Berlin Film Festival in 2011, as well as Silver Bear awards for best actor and best actress. Marketing materials used to sell the film internationally, such as advertisements and posters, drew attention to these awards (see figure 12.5). However, the winning of awards at a film festival does not always translate into significant international distribution or wider critical recognition. For example, Ira Sachs' *Forty Shades of Blue* won the Grand Jury Prize at the Sundance Film Festival in 2005; Christopher Zalla's *Padre Nuestro* was given the same award in 2007. And yet the former was only distributed in Austria, France, and the UK; the latter only in Colombia, France, India, Mexico, Poland, and Spain.

A "buzz" may begin to develop around certain new movies screened at film festivals, especially if they are well received by audiences and critics. Of course, they may also attain publicity if poorly or controversially received, as with the Cannes screening of Vincent Gallo's *The Brown Bunny* in 2003, a film that contains explicit and unsimulated sexual content. Film critic Roger Ebert reported on this reception:

> In May of 2003 I walked out of the press screening of Vincent Gallo's *The Brown Bunny* at the Cannes Film Festival and was asked by a camera crew what I thought of the film. I said I thought it was the worst film in the history of the festival … The audience was loud and scornful in its dislike for the movie; hundreds walked out, and many of those who remained only stayed because they wanted to boo. Imagine, I wrote, a film so unendurably boring that when the hero changes into a clean shirt, there is applause. The panel of critics convened by *Screen International*, the British trade paper, gave the movie the lowest rating in the history of their annual voting.[10]

12.5 Poster for *A Separation* (Asghar Farhadi, 2011). Courtesy of Allstar Images.

For filmmakers, especially those working with small marketing budgets, festival "buzz" may provide significant free publicity. Major film festivals such as Cannes, Venice or Toronto may be covered in depth by certain publications (broadsheet newspapers, film-related magazines, and websites). For journalists and newspaper editors, the festivals bring together film industry glamor and premieres in an enticing (and "newsworthy") combination, along with the potential to spot high-quality movies and "break" this information to readers. For producers, film festivals operate as a business networking opportunity at which international distribution partners and finances are located: positive festival buzz about a film can lead to swift financial deals being made.

Film festivals are important economically. As already noted, major industry players congregate socially, some with considerable amounts of money to play with. In addition, festivals may boost the cultural status of a city and enhance its tourism. More broadly, they can contribute to a nation's cultural standing, as many film festivals support indigenous production as well as exhibiting films from around the world. The best-known film festivals enhance a country's reputation as a hub of creative activity and of "taste."

CASE STUDY: BUSAN INTERNATIONAL FILM FESTIVAL (BIFF)

South Korea has a population of just under fifty million people, and a significant number of annual film festivals. In addition to international film festivals in the major urban centers – Gwangju, Jeonju, Seoul – there are also specialist festivals devoted to short films, animation, human rights and other subjects. Formerly known as Pusan, Busan is a port city with a population of around 3.6 million inhabitants. Pusan International Film Festival was launched in September of 1996. The idea for the festival originated with Kim Ji-seok, a film studies teacher, who worked with colleagues and friends (including staff of the magazine *Film Language*) to try to make it happen. However, it was only when Kim Dong-ho, former head of the government's film office, was invited to take on the role of the festival's director that an official launch became possible. The main focus of the festival is on screening new films and work by first-time directors, particularly those from Asia.

The first year of the festival was small in scale: around 170 films were shown, in less than salubrious screening venues. However, it was instantly successful. This has been attributed in large part to students traveling from all over South Korea and packing out every screening. Kim Dong-ho held unexpected and impromptu street parties every night of the event, which made the festival memorable for filmmakers and other visitors. The festival has subsequently grown in size and stature. The ninth BIFF, in 2004, was chosen by *Time* magazine as the best film festival in Asia. BIFF is particularly popular with a younger audience demographic. The screening programme now shows over 300 films every year, and incorporates a number of themed strands, including "Wide Angle" (shorts, animation and experimental work) and "Midnight Passion" (for late-night screenings). Several awards are given out at each year's event, including the New Currents Award, for best feature film by an Asian director, the BIFF Mecenat Award, for the best Asian documentary, and the KNN Foundation's Audience Award.

Part of the festival's expansion has seen the main screening programme augmented by a variety of workshops, funding opportunities, and networking events. These include the Asian Film Market, a marketplace at which industry personnel can connect; the Asian Project Market, which attempts to introduce potential funders to filmmakers with ideas requiring fiscal support; the Asian Cinema Fund, Script Development Fund, and Post-Production Fund, each of which awards monies to help filmmakers who are at different points in the completion of their projects; the Asian Documentary Network; and the Asian Film Academy, which supports the educational provision of film education throughout Asia and debates the potential futures of Asian cinema.

The growth of BIFF had a significant impact on the city's cultural status as well as its physical form. Busan rebuilt its infrastructure to meet the needs and requirements of the festival: a new subway line was assembled, and a new bridge built that spanned Gwangan Bay. In 2011, the festival moved to a new location, Centum City's Busan Cinema Centre. The building cost around $150 million, and incorporates several screening spaces, an archive, and conference rooms. Commentators have noted that, as the festival has grown, the city has swiftly become more sophisticated and cosmopolitan. Although it is unlikely that BIFF will ever rival the status and profile of Cannes and other world-renowned festivals, it provides a useful model of how a film festival can boost a city's cultural and economic standing. It also demonstrates how, within the space of fifteen years, a festival can move from a small-scale experiment to a huge and respected event embedded in the Asian film industry's calendar.

12.6 The Busan Cinema Centre. Courtesy of AFP/Getty Images.

BOX OFFICE TAKINGS AND POPULARITY

One of the main evaluative contexts in which new films are judged is the baldly financial: how much has it taken at the box office? In many countries around the world, the money a film has made from cinema admissions is measured daily, with weekly aggregates compiled. The opening weekend of a film is scrutinized closely by industry and press commentators, as is the weekly performance of the film while it remains in cinemas. How much does the audience for the film drop off from one week to the next? How many weeks does the film remain in cinemas, due to the fact that there are new (or returning) audiences still willing to see it? Using box office takings as an evaluative criterion – a monetary value that clearly demonstrates cinema's status as a capitalist product, a topic we discussed at length in

Chapter 5 – the most "successful" films are those that take the most money, and those which see the smallest declines in attendance week on week.

Charts can then be compiled of the films which are the most successful financially at the box office. According to the website boxofficemojo.com, the ten most successful films at the global box office up to June 2014 are as shown in table 12.1. However, this chart is worth unpacking. Rising ticket costs at cinemas mean that box office takings are tied to inflation. Indeed, if US box office takings across film history are adjusted for inflation, then the film that took the most money is not *Avatar* (James Cameron, 2009), but *Gone with the Wind* (Victor Fleming, 1939). Further, many *Avatar* ticket prices were higher than standard entry, due to the film being released in 3D and IMAX versions; a significant number of viewers went to see *Titanic* (James Cameron, 1997) more than once. In other words, box office financial figures somewhat obscure the actual number of tickets sold (and it may be impossible to measure return viewings).

Film	Worldwide box office	US box office	Non-US box office
Avatar	$2.782 billion	27.3%	72.7%
Titanic	$2.187 billion	30.1%	69.9%
Marvel's The Avengers/Avengers Assemble	$1.519 billion	41.0%	59.0%
Harry Potter and the Deathly Hallows Part 2	$1.342 billion	28.4%	71.6%
Frozen	$1.245 billion	32.3%	67.8%
Iron Man 3	$1.215 billion	33.7%	66.3%
Transformers: Dark of the Moon	$1.124 billion	31.4%	68.6%
The Lord of the Rings: The Return of the King	$1.120 billion	33.7%	66.3%
Skyfall	$1.109 billion	27.5%	72.5%
The Dark Knight Rises	$1.084 billion	41.3%	58.7%

Table 12.1

EXERCISE

Note down the titles of three films that you have seen recently. Using boxofficemojo.com and imdb.com, find out the budget and box office takings for the three movies.

- Do these figures help you to evaluate the film's success? Do you think the figures are reliable? (Where, for instance, do you think information about a film's budget comes from?)
- Look up each film's box office takings for the weeks in which it screened in cinemas, and the ways in which these change. Which are instant "smashes," with box office swiftly declining, and which are "sleepers," spending longer in cinemas with more consistent takings? Do these financial patterns tell us anything about a film's "quality"?
- For each film's worldwide box office takings, find out how much it took in different countries. Why might each of your films have been especially successful in certain locations? Might critics and audiences in particular countries have evaluated "quality" differently?

More problematically, these figures do not calculate return-on-investment. How much did a film cost to make, and how much of this did it recoup at the box office? Using this type of calculation, the most successful films become those which cost very little to make, and which took significantly larger sums at the cinema. According to the-numbers.com, the ten films shown in table 12.2 are the most profitable in terms of their return on investment.

Film	Production Budget	Approximate Profit
Paranormal Activity	$450,000	$89,779,401
The Devil Inside	$1,000,000	$36,950,440
Peter Pan	$4,000,000	$141,800,207
Grease	$6,000,000	$189,543,325
Paranormal Activity 2	$3,000,000	$77,218,935
Insidious	$1,500,000	$32,718,935
Jaws	$12,000,000	$219,668,909
Reservoir Dogs	$1,200,000	$20,799,036
The King's Speech	$15,000,000	$188,067,714
Beauty and the Beast	$20,000,000	$250,747,209

Table 12.2

Similar tables can also be assembled of the least successful films at the box office: those in which a film's budget was significantly higher than its box office takings, whether measured as a gross sum, or as a return-on-investment ratio.

Perhaps the main concern with all of these league tables, however, is that they fail to interrogate the connection between box office takings and a film's quality. One assumption underlying the monitoring of box office figures by industry analysts is that the "best" films will be the most financially successful; similarly, at the other end of the scale, it could be assumed that the biggest financial flops are those of a low quality. If a sizeable audience goes to see a film, then this may suggest it is of a particular quality. This brings us to an additional evaluative context, closely related to financial success: popularity. By "popularity," we mean that a film is not only successful with a large audience, but that a significant percentage of its viewers enjoy it, like it, take pleasure from it. Knowing of a movie's popularity might spur audiences into seeing it, and take a movie from limited release to wider distribution. Viewers may want to catch such a film so that they can discuss its merits or failings with their friends, and not feel left out. Some films open in a small number of cinemas and, when they prove popular, increase the scope and scale of their exhibition in order to meet demand. The movie *Paranormal Activity* (made by Oren Peli in 2007 but released in 2009), for instance, initially had a limited release in thirteen college towns in the United States. As the film's popularity grew, so did the level of distribution and exhibition: within three weeks it was playing much more broadly across the country and was the envy of the Hollywood studios, a cheap film grossing huge sums at the box office.

As we discussed at length in Chapter 1's consideration of film as entertainment, popular culture is often conceptualized in relation to the culture of the elite: "mass culture" is contrasted with "high culture." Popular culture attains the widest distribution, and is consumed by a very large number of people:

12.7 *Paranormal Activity* (Oren Peli, 2007). Courtesy of Blumhouse Productions/The Kobal Collection.

Avatar, rather than the films of Hungarian director Béla Tarr. "High culture" arguably appeals to a smaller section of the public, and is sometimes seen as more "refined," requiring a "sophisticated" level of appreciation. The notion of a "popular" film, then, is a complex one, and raises a host of concerns regarding social stratification, power and control, commercialization and commodification, and the politics of pleasure. Of course, it is possible for film critics and cultural commentators to praise popular films; "popular" is not the opposite of "quality." And yet the assumption often remains that popular films are lower status commodities, rarely to be identified by cultural guardians as amongst the best films ever made. The "popular," in other words, is a very different evaluative criterion from "the best."

THE FILM CANON

Which brings us to a crucial question: which are the best movies ever made? Who decides that these are the greatest films, and how are they selected? Although it is open to debate and discussion, and would be constructed differently depending on the source consulted, there does exist some agreement about the canon of the best films in the world. This canon has taken shape over the decades of the medium's existence. As David Bordwell has identified, it began to form early in cinema's history:

> Periodicals played a key role. National film industries had their catalogues and trade journals, which during the 1900s and 1910s often discussed the emerging canon and tested out aesthetic ideas as well. Publicity and trade journalism often helped a film achieve classic status … The canonical works were celebrated time and again in the small film magazines that proliferated during the 1920s. France's *Cinea* (founded in 1921) was followed by Germany's *Filmwoche* (1923), Austria's *Filmtechnik* (1925), Belgium's *Camera* (1932), Scotland's *Cinema Quarterly* (1932), and England's *Sight and Sound* (1932) and *Film Art* (1933) … Aware of only a dozen or

so years of film production, writers in the mid- to late 1920s incessantly returned to the same films and directors.[11]

The canon of great films, however, is continually under interrogation and reappraisal. In this regard, the film canon is somewhat like that of the best novels ever written, or the greatest works of painting and sculpture, or the finest pieces of classical music. That is to say, whilst the inclusion of each and every entry in the canon could be debated, discussing the canon as a whole enables an exploration and interrogation of how artistic quality and worth is judged.

The word "canon" is derived from the Greek term for a measuring stick; it refers to the standard against which something may be evaluated. As Gill Perry comments, writing about painting:

> When people speak of "the canon of art", they usually mean a body of works that have passed a (rather ambiguous) test of value. Despite its inherent ambiguity, the idea of a canon has assumed the air of spurious precision: it has come to mean a body of works deemed to be of indisputable quality within a particular culture or influential subculture. Only a few of those works classed as "art" within a society are generally perceived to make up a revered canon.[12]

Similarly, only a very small number of the vast quantity of films in existence are generally considered to be "canonical," worth including in a "greatest films" list. These are the films which are widely believed to have contributed most to the development of the medium and its cultural status. They may also be the films which challenge and provoke, which offer to audiences the possibility of intellectual – or perhaps even spiritual – enlightenment of some sort. Or it may be that they are the films seen to be most innovative, or as making best use of the distinctive characteristics of cinema. Film critic Mark Cousins, for example, in his book and television series *The Story of Film*, presents a chronological account of cinema's history that frequently connects formal, stylistic or technological innovation with canonical status.

Let us consider a concrete, well-known example of a canonical list. *Sight and Sound* is a monthly magazine published by the British Film Institute that began its life in 1932. Its coverage is largely devoted to auteurist "art house" cinema, though it is also a journal of record, reviewing every single film released into UK theatres. Every ten years since 1952, the magazine has conducted a poll of film professionals, asking them to vote for "the greatest film of all time." This poll is highly respected internationally. From 1962 to 2002, in five consecutive polls, the film judged to be the "best" was *Citizen Kane* (Orson Welles, 1942). In 2012, the "top ten" results of the vote were as follows:

Vertigo (Alfred Hitchcock, 1958)

Citizen Kane (Orson Welles, 1941)

Tokyo Story (Ozu Yasujiro, 1953)

La Regle du Jeu (Jean Renoir, 1939)

Sunrise: A Song of Two Humans (F.W. Murnau, 1927)

2001: A Space Odyssey (Stanley Kubrick, 1968)

The Searchers (John Ford, 1956)

Man with a Movie Camera (Dziga Vertov, 1929)

The Passion of Joan of Arc (Carl Theodor Dreyer, 1927)

8½ (Federico Fellini, 1963)

The replacement of *Citizen Kane* by *Vertigo* led to a significant amount of debate and discussion. After all, it wasn't as though *Vertigo* had become a better film between 2002 and 2012. Film historian Ian Christie offered the following comments on alterations to *Sight and Sound*'s canon, and possible reasons for changing evaluations of quality:

> So what does it mean? Given that *Kane* actually clocked over three times as many votes this year as it did last time, it hasn't exactly been snubbed … But it does mean that Hitchcock, who only entered the top ten in 1982 (two years after his death), has risen steadily in esteem over the course of 30 years, with *Vertigo* climbing from seventh place, to fourth in 1992, second in 2002 and now first, to make him *the* Old Master. Welles, uniquely, had two films (*The Magnificent Ambersons* as well as *Kane*) in the list in 1972 and 1982, but now *Ambersons* has slipped to 81st place in the top 100. So does 2012 – the first poll to be conducted since the internet became almost certainly the main channel of communication about films – mark a revolution in taste, such as happened in 1962?[13]

A similar poll of critics has been conducted by other film publications, including the *Village Voice* and Asian magazine *Cinemaya*. In fact, such lists proliferate: the American Film Institute, for instance, has

12.8 *Vertigo* (Alfred Hitchcock, 1958). Courtesy of Paramount/The Kobal Collection.

since 1996 produced a poll of the "100 Greatest American Movies" once a decade. Annual surveys are also conducted: *Sight and Sound* runs a "best of the year" survey of critics and filmmakers, for example, as does *Lumen*. Although the films listed in these annual surveys may not trouble the next incarnation of the "greatest films ever" poll, they provide an adjudication on the continuing development of cinema as an art form, and a short-term snapshot that allows for consideration of how the film canon may be reformed in future.

From the discussion of canon formation presented so far, it is clear that critics are key players in the formation of the canon of "film greats." But who else contributes to building the canon? Academics – not always easily distinguished from critics – may be amongst those polled, or contributing their own perspectives and arguments. Curators and archivists also play a significant role in influencing which films are seen as worthy of attention. Curators assemble programmes of films, selecting those they determine are worth screening in a cinema (and bypassing others); similarly, archivists select the films they deem to be of enough value for preservation or restoration. How many films have been lost to history simply because, at some point, a decision has been made regarding which titles were of a quality worth keeping? We will examine the place and operations of film archives in more detail in the next chapter.

EXERCISE

In his book *Why Read The Classics?*, first published in 1991, the Italian author Italo Calvino provides fourteen statements that he believes characterize "classic" works of fiction. He then assesses case studies, putting his propositions to the test. Among Calvino's statements are the following:

The classics are books which exercise a particular influence, both when they imprint themselves on our imagination as unforgettable, and when they hide in the layers of memory disguised as the individual's or the collective unconscious.

A classic is a book which with each rereading offers as much of a sense of discovery as the first reading.

A classic is a book which has never exhausted all it has to say to its readers.

Classics are books which, the more we think we know them through hearsay, the more original, unexpected, and innovative we find them when we actually read them.[14]

- Bearing in mind that Calvino is talking about literature, rather than cinema, do you think that his arguments can be applied to film? For instance, is a "great" film one that you can watch repeatedly, and always find something new and interesting?
- What do you think makes a film a "classic"? Is this the same thing as what makes a film "high quality"? Does a film have to be of a certain vintage before it can be considered a classic?

The canon is also affected by filmmakers themselves, who in interviews or other publicity materials may acknowledge their debt to ancestor or contemporary filmmakers, and to particular films by those individuals; sometimes that debt is blatantly on display in the content or style of the film itself. To take just one example: the DVD release of Max Ophüls' *The Reckless Moment* (1949) contains an introduction to the film by director Todd Haynes, in which he raves about Ophüls' film and concedes that he stole a shot from *The Reckless Moment* for use in his own film, *Far from Heaven* (2002).

Perhaps most importantly, the knowledgeable and committed film student and connoisseur can contribute to the canon. Film students should interrogate, as part of their studies, what they think makes a film "great," and discuss this with their peers (as one of the exercises in this chapter asks you to do). This can then lead into a more considered dissection of the standard canon. Connoisseurs, in contrast, are those fans of cinema whose tastes may align closely with those of the sort of critics polled by film-related magazines and websites. Avid filmgoers, and perhaps also collectors, they will be immersed in their passion, committed to the cinema as an art form. (They are, perhaps, a category of consumers comparable to the opera buff.) DVD/Blu-ray labels such as the Criterion Collection and Eureka/Masters of Cinema produce their carefully selected output with the connoisseur in mind: lavish packaging, plentiful extras, highest quality transfers of image and sound.

Just as the list of the "biggest successes at the global box office" is a problematic evaluative context in relation to film quality, so the film canon of the "greatest movies ever made" is debatable and open to interrogation. Certainly, having a list of films that are seen, by a notable number of commentators, as having significantly contributed to the cultural standing of film as an art form is a valuable context against which to measure any new film. What makes those films great? How does this new film compare to those? Critic Jonathan Rosenbaum has argued that canons of great films are now, in the twenty-first century, even more necessary than ever, especially as film culture becomes dominated by advertisers, capsule film reviewers with snappy star ratings, and industry players who champion banal product over innovative and challenging movies.[15]

And yet the formation of artistic canons is always an exclusionary process. If these films are being included, what is being missed out? Can generic films such as horror movies and thrillers ever be "amongst the greatest"? Why are all of the top ten *Sight and Sound* films directed by men, only one of whom is Asian? The film canon of the "greatest movies ever made" is blighted by similar problems as the canon of "great art." Griselda Pollock suggests two ways out of this conundrum:

> The canon is selective in its inclusions and is revealed as political in its patterns of exclusion. We might, therefore, approach the problem of the canon as critical outsiders with one of two projects in mind. The first is to expand the Western canon so that it will include what it hitherto refused – women, for instance, and minority cultures. The other is to abolish canons altogether and argue that all cultural artifacts have significance.[16]

Whilst this second proposal may seem extreme, even impossible to effect, it is worth pausing to consider: how would our relationship to cinema change, and how would we evaluate it, if canons of "the greatest films" were abolished?

CHAPTER SUMMARY

This chapter has considered a number of different evaluative contexts by which films are rated, judged and compared. All of these contexts have an influence on where movies go – and how long they stay there, once they arrive. Critics in print and online can have a significant effect on how broadly films are distributed, and whether or not audiences take the time to watch them. Film festivals operate as a first screening window for many movies, and an initial venue for judging their quality; filmmakers screen their movies at festivals in hopes of their work winning awards and being picked up for distribution in countries around the globe. Due to film's nature as a commodity, box office takings are a significant yardstick by which success is evaluated. Similarly, if a film is popular, seen by sizeable audiences, then it attains some sort of widespread success; however, as was noted, the politics of popular culture are far from simple. Finally, this chapter examined the nature of the canon, lists of "the greatest films ever made" and how these are constituted. In different ways, if to differing degrees at distinct times, all of these evaluative contexts influence the ways in which we access movies, as well as what we choose to watch.

FURTHER READING

Clayton, Alex and Klevan, Andrew (eds). *The Language and Style of Film Criticism*. London and New York: Routledge, 2011.

> An approachable and readable collection of essays that reflects on the topic of film criticism. Following a valuable introduction on the value of film criticism and the different forms that it may take, individual chapters pay attention to specific topics, such as the ways in which criticism can handle performance.

Hing-Yuk Wong, Cindy. *Film Festivals: Culture, People and Power on the Global Screen*. New York: Rutgers University Press, 2011.

> A comprehensive introduction to the operations of film festivals across the world, including their significance for Hollywood and independent cinema. Chapter 3 of the book is particularly useful in relation to our discussion of "evaluative contexts," as it explores the role of film festivals in the constitution of cinematic canons. The book features, as its final chapter, a valuable detailed case study of the Hong Kong International Film Festival.

Rosenbaum, Jonathan. *Essential Cinema: On the Necessity of Film Canons*. Baltimore and London: Johns Hopkins University Press, 2004.

> A collection of Rosenbaum's reviews and journalism, which repeatedly returns to the notion of the film canon and the worth of forming such a selection. Sections of the book revisit "classics," interrogate "special problems" which challenge the constitution of a canon, and explore "other canons, other canonizers." The introduction to the book is especially valuable, as it makes a spirited defence of the film canon. The book ends with a list of "1000 Favourites (A Personal Canon)."

FILMS REFERENCED IN CHAPTER TWELVE

8½ (Federico Fellini, 1963)

2001: A Space Odyssey (Stanley Kubrick, 1968)

Alvin and the Chipmunks: The Squeakquel (Betty Thomas, 2009)

Avatar (James Cameron, 2009)

Beauty and the Beast (Gary Trousdale/Kirk Wise, 1991)

Blue is the Warmest Colour (Abdellatif Kechiche, 2013)

Breakfast with Jonny Wilkinson (Simon Sprackling, 2013)

The Brown Bunny (Vincent Gallo, 2003)

Citizen Kane (Orson Welles, 1941)

Computer Chess (Andrew Bujalski, 2013)

The Da Vinci Code (Ron Howard, 2006)

The Dark Knight Rises (Christopher Nolan, 2012)

The Devil Inside (William Brent Bell, 2012)

The Family (Luc Besson, 2013)

Far from Heaven (Todd Haynes, 2002)

The Flintstones (Brian Levant, 1994)

Flu (Sung-su Kim, 2013)

Forty Shades of Blue (Ira Sachs, 2005)

Frozen (Chris Buck/Jennifer Lee, 2013)

Gone with the Wind (Victor Fleming, 1939)

Grease (Randal Kleiser, 2010)

Harry Potter and the Deathly Hallows Part 2 (David Yates, 2011)

The Hunger Games: Catching Fire (Francis Lawrence, 2013)

Insidious (James Wan, 2010)

Iron Man 3 (Shane Black, 2013)

Irréversible (Gasper Noé, 2002)

Jaws (Steven Spielberg, 1975)

Killing Oswald (Shane O'Sullivan, 2013)

The King's Speech (Tom Hooper, 2010)

Lara Croft: Tomb Raider (Simon West, 2001)

The Lone Ranger (Gore Verbinski, 2013)

The Lord of the Rings: The Return of the King (Peter Jackson, 2003)

The Magnificent Ambersons (Orson Welles, 1942)

Man with a Movie Camera (Dziga Vertov, 1929)

Marvel's The Avengers/Avengers Assemble (Joss Whedon, 2012)

Padre Nuestro (Christopher Zalla, 2007)

Paranormal Activity (Oren Peli, 2007)

Paranormal Activity 2 (Tod Williams, 2010)

Parkland (Peter Landesman, 2013)

The Passion of Joan of Arc (Carl Theodor Dreyer, 1927)

Peter Pan (Clyde Geronimi/Wilfred Jackson/Hamilton Luske/Jack Kinney, 1953)

The Reckless Moment (Max Ophüls, 1949)

La Regle du Jeu (Jean Renoir, 1939)

Reservoir Dogs (Quentin Tarantino, 1992)

Run for Your Wife (Ray Cooney and John Luton, 2012)

The Searchers (John Ford, 1956)

A Separation (Asghar Fahardi, 2011)

Sex and the City (Michael Patrick King, 2008)

Sex and the City 2 (Michael Patrick King, 2010)

Skyfall (Sam Mendes, 2012)

Sunrise: A Song of Two Humans (F.W. Murnau, 1927)

Titanic (James Cameron, 1997)

Tokyo Story (Ozu Yasujiro, 1953)

Transformers: Dark of the Moon (Michael Bay, 2011)

Transformers: Revenge of the Fallen (Michael Bay, 2009)

Vendetta (Stephen Reynolds, 2013)

Vertigo (Alfred Hitchcock, 1958)

¡Vivan las Antipodas! (Victor Kossakovsky, 2011)

NOTES

1 Jonathan Rosenbaum, "Introduction," in *Placing Movies: The Practice of Film Criticism* (Berkeley, CA: University of California Press, 1995), 15.

2 Alex Clayton and Andrew Klevan, "Introduction: The Language and Style of Film Criticism," in *The Language and Style of Film Criticism* (London and New York: Routledge, 2011), 1.

3 Clayton and Klevan, 5.

4 Samuel Fuller quoted in Rosenbaum, *Placing Movies*, 14–15.

5 David Carr, "Now on the Endangered Species List: Movie Critics in Print," *New York Times*, 1 April 2008, http://www.nytimes.com/2008/04/01/movies/01crit.html?_r=0, accessed 6 October 2013.

6 Paul Brunick, "Online Film Criticism Part One: The Living and the Dead," *Film Comment*, July/August 2010, http://www.filmcomment.com/article/online-film-criticism-part-one-the-living-and-the-dead, accessed 6 October 2013.

7 Stephanie Zacharek, "Yes, Sex and the City 2 Really is as Horrific as You've Heard," *Movieline*, 27 May 2010, http://movieline.com/2010/05/27/review-sex-and-the-city-2-is-just-as-horrific-as-youve-heard/, accessed 9 October 2013.

8 Andrew O'Hehir, "Sex and the City 2's Utter Badness," *Salon*, 27 May 2010, http://www.salon.com/2010/05/27/satc2/, accessed 9 October 2013.

9 Andrew O'Hagan, "Sex and the City 2 is Ugly on the Inside," *Evening Standard*, 28 May 2010, http://www.standard.co.uk/goingout/film/sex-and-the-city-2-is-ugly-on-the-inside-7420066.html, accessed 9 October 2013.

10 Roger Ebert, "The Brown Bunny," http://www.rogerebert.com/reviews/the-brown-bunny-2004, 3 September 2004, accessed 29 November 2013.

11 David Bordwell, *On the History of Film Style* (New York: Harvard University Press, 1998), 22.

12 Gill Perry, "Preface," in Gill Perry and Colin Cunningham (eds), *Academies, Museums and Canons of Art* (New Haven and London: Yale University Press, 1999), 12.

13 Ian Christie, "Chronicle of a Fall Foretold," *Sight and Sound* 22(9) (2012), 57.

14 Italo Calvino, *Why Read the Classics?* (London: Vintage, 2000), 4–6.

15 Jonathan Rosenbaum, *Essential Cinema: On the Necessity of Film Canons* (Baltimore and London: Johns Hopkins University Press, 2004).

16 Griselda Pollock, *Differencing the Canon: Feminist Desire and the Writing of Art's Histories* (London: Routledge, 1999), 6.

CHAPTER THIRTEEN
THE LONGEVITY OF FILMS

In 1926, the *New York Times* reported a call by Will Hays, the then-president of the Hollywood film industry's Motion Picture Producers and Distributors of America (MPPDA), to store films in a low temperature, low humidity vault so that "schoolboys in the year 3,000 and 4,000 A.D. may learn about us."[1] In another century, what will schoolboys, and schoolgirls, find of our world's film industries? Will they be watching *Star Wars* (George Lucas, 1977) and *E.T. the Extra-Terrestrial* (Steven Spielberg, 1982) (both films that have been restored with special effects)? *Vertigo* (1958) and *Rear Window* (1954), the Hitchcock flicks chosen for posterity? Maybe Akira Kurosawa's *Yojimbo* (1961) and Fritz Lang's *Metropolis* (1927)? Or will they rely on the vast storehouse of YouTube and Ubuweb for their education in twentieth- and twenty-first-century image culture, a partial record of a receding past?

The earliest films were recorded on a plastic substance called "celluloid," invented in England in the mid-nineteenth century. This cellulose nitrate film base turned out to be not only spectacularly flammable but also given to wildly unpredictable decomposition. A more unreliable substrate for the medium of cinema, in other words, one cannot imagine. But it was the best thing around for many decades, and its very instability means that our own archives of the silent film era are a mere fraction of what the early decades of cinema actually produced. Film historians guess that fully 90 per cent of films made in the United States during the silent era are now entirely lost to us. (Fifty per cent of sound films made before 1950 also are lost.) In this chapter, we explore the longevity of film, including issues of the availability of various cinemas (which have survived and why); the techniques and debates in preservation (which films ought to be preserved and how);

the process of decay and its implications (including the aesthetic appreciation of fragments and decomposition); the politics of various forms of archiving (including the digital archives mentioned above); and what it means to work in film archives.

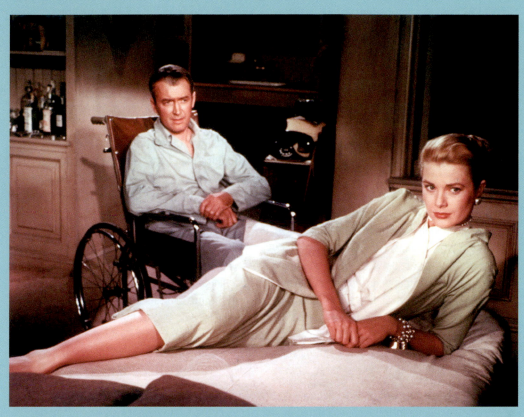

13.1 Grace Kelly and James Stewart in *Rear Window* (Alfred Hitchcock, 1954). Courtesy of Paramount/The Kobal Collection.

WHAT WE WILL DO IN CHAPTER 13

- Encounter fundamental questions about the *value* of films.
- Understand the differences between film restoration and preservation.
- Learn how to use and navigate film archives.

BY THE END OF CHAPTER 13 YOU SHOULD BE ABLE TO

- Defend the value of a film.
- Write about films only accessible through archives.
- Define a film's provenance through archival research.

At the heart of the chapter is an extended exploration of film **archives** and **preservation**, since both are vital areas. Archives are not just inert repositories for cultural objects; instead, they shape what we know of our past and condition what we value. The proliferation of media on a range of **digital platforms** raises insistent questions about the very limits of archives: is it possible, let alone valuable, to keep a record of what the entire internet looked like on a given day, such as today? Is it important to store original film negatives (which require precise temperature and climate control) when they can be easily digitized? What systems are necessary and useful to organize and access the vast quantities and types of data that constitute our film archives (not only moving images themselves but photographic stills, production notes, original sets and costumes, budgets, scripts, props, and so on)?

Similar questions arise concerning preservation. Many, many of the world's films are dying. They are improperly stored. Or the prints have run through projectors so many times that they are worn, scratched and torn. Or long sequences have exploded into flames during projection. Color frequently fades, including trademarked processes such as **Eastmancolor**. Often films were cut due to censorship in different exhibition contexts, creating so many multiple versions that it becomes impossible to define the "original" or "definitive" version. Many films exist only as fragments: pieces of documentary or ethnographic footage, for example, that remain unidentified, glimpses of some other time and place. If some films can indeed be restored – through expensive and painstaking work – which ones should be chosen? For what reasons? Which films, in other words, should live? These questions lodge themselves within a broader debate between **restoration** and preservation, a debate that is not merely theoretical – with its roots in arguments about architecture in the nineteenth century, as we shall see – but has implications for our relation to our cinematic past and future. One of the most vocal and active supporters of film preservation is the director Martin Scorsese, who began the Film Foundation with fellow directors George Lucas, Steven Spielberg, Stanley Kubrick, and Clint Eastwood (and has now expanded what was largely an American movement into the World Cinema Foundation). For Scorsese, the need for preservation is central to rediscovery. He says:

> Someone born today will see the picture with completely different eyes and a whole other frame of reference, different values, uninhibited by the biases of the time when it was made. You see the world through your own time – which means that some values disappear, and some values come into closer focus. Same film, same images, but in the case of a great film the power – a timeless power that really can't be articulated – is there even when the context has completely changed.

> But in order to experience something and find new values in it, the work has to be there in the first place – you have to preserve it. All of it.[2]

These "celebrity preservationists" have enabled large-scale preservation efforts, as have institutions such as the British Film Institute and the University of California at Los Angeles, and so this chapter considers both particular projects and the growing field of professional archive and preservation studies and training.

While archivists and preservationists largely worry about reversing decay and restoring fragments to better if still imperfect wholes, others have embraced decomposition, fragmentariness, and imprecise reproduction as intrinsic to the making and circulation of moving images. A whole community of experimental filmmakers work with "**found" footage**, pieces of film discovered at flea markets or in rubbish bins, assembling them into new stories and sci-fi worlds. Other makers explore the aesthetics of decay, re-photographing the effects of cellulose nitrate degeneration for their unique beauty and revelation. Entire film festivals and symposia are devoted to "orphan" films, films outside the commercial mainstream. Finally, digital archives make fragments of film culture available for all, without too much worry about the fidelity of the image you may now see on your computer screen or cell phone to its filmic original. All of these examples of where movies go, or where they *don't* go, help us to understand the relationships among commodity, copyright, value, normative expectations (say of films having a beginning, middle and end), and access.

EARLY ARCHIVES

No one thought to save early films for their own sake, or, to be fair to the pioneers, very few did. In the rush to embrace the new medium and to contribute films to new markets, speed and volume were the buzzwords of the late nineteenth century (much as they are today with digital platforms voracious for new content). The record we do have today of the first ten or fifteen years of cinema we owe, in fact, to the emergence of the new medium *as* a market, that is, as a realm of commodity

13.2 Eastmancolor poster. Courtesy of Europix/The Kobal Collection.

13.3 Martin Scorsese with Robert De Niro on the set of *Goodfellas* (Martin Scorsese, 1990). Courtesy of Warner Bros./The Kobal Collection.

exchange, for it was for the purposes of securing copyright that many film producers filed some version of their films as a record of a unique and bounded product. In the United States, copyright law did not recognize motion pictures until 1912; as a result, some early producers (including Thomas Edison and his cameraman, William K. Dickson) filed paper contact prints at the US Copyright Office in the Library of Congress. These were photographic reproductions of films on paper the same size and width of the film itself, meant to serve merely as a record of a film, frame by frame. (Others, however, filed only what they considered illustrative sequences.)

While nitrate photographic prints (discussed above) exploded or otherwise self-destructed, these paper prints survived and awaited discovery by film historians. The paper print collection, with over 3,000 entries, constitutes one of the most significant archives of early films from the United States, France, the UK, and Denmark. In many cases, this is the only glimpse we have of cinema from the turn of the century and early part of the twentieth century. In order to make this collection available, the staff in the Library of Congress is re-photographing every single film, frame by frame, for the *second* time: a first go-round, on 16mm film, was undertaken in 1955, but a much-improved process on 35mm film is currently being undertaken. Digitization makes these paper prints available to students and scholars throughout the world, and one can simply log in to see works from fascinating collections including the New York, President McKinley, the Pan-American Exposition, Westinghouse Works, 18 San Francisco, Variety Stage, Spanish-American War, and Edison collections.

13.4 Thomas Edison. Courtesy of Edison/The Kobal Collection.

Another effort, one combining photography and cinema, sought more pointedly to record and preserve glimpses of life across the globe in this period. In 1909, the wealthy French banker and philanthropist Albert Kahn dispatched a team of cameramen to record images of the peoples of the world in a project he called *Archives of the Planet*. His preferred medium was the autochrome process, an early true-color photographic process, and his preferred method was simply to cover as many cultures as possible as war threatened worldwide change and destruction. Kahn's project was, in other words, ethnographic: he sought to document peoples and their cultures through still and motion picture photography, often with the exoticist and orientalist baggage such recording reproduced. With images from countries from Dahomey (now Benin) to Iraq, Vietnam to India, Brazil to Canada, these archives of the planet offer rare insight as much into the lives of those photographed and filmed as into the assumptions of what constituted a spectacle sufficiently exotic to record. Among potential themes, films of dances and the hunt predominate. Until recently, the Khan archives remained relatively unknown, but with a BBC series and publication of companion media, *The Wonderful World of Albert Khan*, the Musée Albert-Kahn's treasures have been discovered and can be accessed without a trip to Paris.

13.5 A reel from one of the Library of Congress's paper prints. Courtesy of Frank Wylie.

13.6 The cover of *The Wonderful World of Albert Khan*, featuring photographs from *The Archives of the Planet*. Courtesy of The Random House Group.

379

NATIONAL MEMORY

The location of an archive, however, matters. Archives, that is, have important roles to play in the production and maintenance of national and historical memory, and it is this aspect of film archives that enriches our understanding of the relationships among cinema, politics, and the nation. Your own past is deposited in that archive: the sights and sounds of your town, your university, your family perhaps.

Albert Kahn's dreams of a global archive, in other words, have largely come true: there are national archives from New Zealand to Brazil to Ireland to South Africa. Many exist as self-conscious repositories of national culture, in which a print of every single current film, television program, radio program, or music recording is deposited for posterity. As the Federal Republic of Germany's film archive mission statement puts it, "It is the concern of every cultured nation to maintain, care for, make accessible to the public and continually supplement its stock of moving pictures."[3] What constitutes a "British" or an "Australian" film is governed by a combination of copyright (what corporate entity owns the film), licensing (what government body passed and/or rated the film for audiences), and sometimes shooting location (where was the film actually shot or made via post-production). These archives also collect media from the past, whether from corporate collections (film studio libraries, for example), public libraries, schools, or other sources. In striving to collect diverse forms of cultural expression, archives sometimes reach back to performance traditions from antiquity (Irish solo fireside singing, for example) and include today's global multimedia phenomena (such as *Riverdance*). Entrusted with the care of a culture, archives as "cultural heritage" institutions also strive, then, to create living conversations among makers and spectators, or the triumvirate of "creators, consumers, and curators" of cultural identity.

In promoting cultural identity, many archives explicitly seek to address or redress power relations established through colonial or imperial cultural formations, promoting traditional music, for example, or developing Aboriginal cinema, or highlighting indigenous radio broadcasting. In fact, archives have become crucial to preserving traces of indigenous cultures and to stimulating new cultural production, as archives become linked to institutions that promote film production (in Australia, for example). Some archives are devoted to ethnic projects, too: the Archivio Nazionale del Film di Famiglia collects home movies from Italian-American families that highlight and therefore track important lifecycle moments, family and community celebrations, and provide a window onto immigrant and ethnic traditions. Archives are therefore participants in, and not simply the results of, a struggle over voice, power, and national definition. In some cases, and increasingly as digital communications erode physical borders that separate makers and audiences by language, nation, region, and ethnicity, archives redefine our understanding of connections among previously separated and distinct traditions. An online initiative, the African Film Library, for example, collects works by more than eighty makers across the continent and offers their work to new audiences and to young scholars for whom access had previously been prohibitively expensive or difficult. Post-colonial archives help in the rearrangement of imagination and education that post-coloniality itself demands: that is, a reconfigured relation to the former colonial power, in which indigenous national culture, language, and art come to the fore.

As our examples of these and the early archives above are meant to indicate, then, collections of cultural documents emerge under specific conditions and for specific reasons beyond the mere collection of cultural heritage. Some of these are economic: to preserve films because their prints or digital versions can continue to circulate and generate profit, for example. Some are legal *and* economic: to preserve

13.7 Film director Ousmane Sembene, whose film *Camp at Thiaroye* is in the African Film Library. Courtesy of Les Films Terre Africaine/The Kobal Collection.

films or records of them for the purposes of declaring ownership over the images and thereby to profit from their circulation and exhibition. Some are ethical: to bear witness to an event and thereby to testify to its atrocity. Think here about the records of devastation following the bombings of Hiroshima and Nagasaki, or about the iconic footage of concentration camp survivors taken by liberators at Bergen Belsen.

The latter images, however, begin to alert us to some archival questions. To what degree does this image of the camp's liberation suggest the experience and fate, not of these particular people, but of Jews in general under the Nazi regime? Writers have in fact debated the force of these images and their capacity to serve as documentary testimony. Writer Anne Applebaum says:

> These pictures, which show starving, emaciated people, walking skeletons in striped uniforms, stacks of corpses piled up like wood, have become the most enduring images of the Holocaust. Yet the people in these photographs were mostly not Jews: they were forced laborers who had been kept alive because the German war machine needed them to produce weapons and uniforms.

She adds that "The vast majority of Hitler's victims, Jewish and otherwise, never saw a concentration camp."[4] Most of them were simply shot in the killing fields of Eastern Europe.

This fragment of film belongs to a broader archive of images of the Third Reich, and it raises a set of questions we must ask of any film and any archive in working with them critically:

- What is the **provenance** of the image? In other words, where does it come from? How do we know?
- Has it been **authenticated**? Has a curator or programmer or librarian verified its provenance? Is it archived alongside any authenticating documents (names, dates, sources, notes, etc.)?
- Does it belong to a larger **collection** or family of images with the same provenance? Is it representative, or is it anomalous? What can it say about the collection, and what can some knowledge of the collection say about it?
- What, finally, does archival knowledge contribute to what the film means? How does knowledge of its archival context help you to read the film or clip? What conclusions are you able to draw about its stylistic or aesthetic innovations in light of the archive?

EXERCISE

Ask these questions of a film or clip in an online archive. What distinctions can you claim with respect to:

- Knowledge of aesthetic norms?
- Balance of documentary and dramatic forms?
- Relevance, or the provocative nature of the subjects?
- Stylistic conventions such as camera placement and distance?

(A potential exercise would be for a group of however many of you to watch all 341 films in the Edison Collection (earning extra credit of course), while another group of similar number watched only those under the subject headings beginning with "E," and yet another group watched only those with titles to which they were for whatever reason attracted.)

USING ARCHIVES

As you have seen from the exercise, it is possible to access an archive online, explore its riches, and work closely with its objects. Indeed, digital media are radically transforming archival access, practices, data, and organization, as we discuss below. Catastrophic degradation of film formats only hastens these processes, which will need to be carried out in the next several decades in order to preserve vast quantities of damaged material. Here, however, we pause to consider further how we as researchers and film scholars can use archives to pose and to begin to answer fundamental research questions.

One of the reasons to test an object with questions of provenance, authentication, collection, and context is to *legitimate* it as an object for scholarly research. Within a media universe with multiple versions, bootlegs, copies or fragments of digital "texts," it is at least important initially to identify to what object you refer. When you write a paper, say if you are in Mauritius, on *Citizen Kane*, it is largely to one version that you will refer, and it is likely the same version that one of us taught last week in a class in New York, or that the BFI screened in its South London theatre. That film was widely distributed in a single version on film, and when it was transferred to a digital platform was in clean and singular shape. Not so with

13.8 Shahrukh Khan in *My Name is Khan* (Karan Johar, 2010). Courtesy of Dharma Productions/The Kobal Collection.

the version of *My Name is Khan*, the Shahrukh Khan blockbuster circulating on DVD in Canada, with hand-wrought subtitles despite the claims to "authentic DVD" on its cover. Whether national (such as the Bundesarchiv of film in Berlin), historical (such as the aforementioned Kahn archive), or commercial (such as the Criterion Collection DVD list), archives imprint texts, allow for common referents, set boundaries of reference, and facilitate scholarly comparisons.

Archives do not only collect texts, however. Some of the most important research questions in the area of film studies have been around questions of *circulation*, *distribution*, and *exhibition*, as the following case study illustrates. Finally, as we use online archives and tools, and as curators and archivists hone the systems and infrastructure that allow us to do so, we have to reckon with the issue of *access*. Does the availability of certain online content dissuade us from asking questions that require brick and mortar research? Do we tend towards conducting only partial research online, sampling and browsing rather than exhausting a collection, and with what results?

TECHNIQUES OF ARCHIVES: FILM CAN WAIT

We mention above that moving image archives face an imperative to preserve vast quantities of film before it degrades in the coming decades. Member archives of the International Federation of Film Archives (FIAF) have rescued over two million films in the past seventy years, and the obvious trend will be to digitize as much as possible in order to stabilize these archives and make them available to the

CASE STUDY: INDIAN FILM CENSORSHIP

Indian cinema provides a helpful case study for using archives to explore questions of censorship and certification. Of course, "Indian cinema" is not just one thing: it is an aggregation of many cinemas, in many languages, and for audiences including diasporic Indian communities beyond the subcontinent. Here we draw on the work of Indian film scholar Monika Mehta, who has used the film archives in Pune to build a fascinating argument about the nature of Indian film censorship.

Many previous scholars not only of Indian cinema but of films around the world have thought about censorship as an activity primarily of prohibition, saying "no" to a scene, a line, a word, a gesture or a narrative element on the basis of its perceived immorality or violation of received mores. This is prohibition through cutting, but it can also involve censorship through ratings, by prohibiting certain sectors of the populace, such as children under 17, from seeing material deemed "offensive." A similar understanding of censorship as prohibition obtains in examining changes to shooting scripts as resulting from such understandings. A funny version of the latter can be seen in the perhaps apocryphal story about the legendary film producer Samuel Goldwyn, the "G" in "MGM": when told that his studio had acquired a script that included lesbians, he replied "Well, we can always call them Bulgarians."

In Mehta's view, drawing upon a line of thinking inaugurated by French philosopher Michel Foucault, censorship should instead be understood as a *productive* activity, one in which the nation-state (in the form of its censorship board), the film industry (writers, producers, and directors), and its publics and audiences together *produce* sexuality as much as they call for its control. Her own case study is not an entire film but a song-and-dance number from the 1993 film *Khalnayak/The Villain* (Subhash Ghai).[5] *Khalnayak* belongs to that tradition of popular Hindi cinema made in Bombay/Mumbai, often exported under the name "Bollywood" and also importantly addressed to the large Indian diaspora (numbering over twenty-five million) abroad. *Khalnayak* is not unusual in including a soundtrack that is essential to the evolving industry's intermedial world; that is, products such as CDs circulate along with other ancillary tie-ins and are crucial to building fandom for the film itself.

Mehta's particular focus is on the "song" part of "song-and-dance," particularly the release of a recorded version of a song on audiocassette (now CD) while the film itself is still in production (that is, being made). This is a common practice in the Bombay film industry, and such releases are meant to stimulate interest in the film and to ensure a ready audience on its release. One of *Khalnayak*'s songs, "Choli ke peeche kya hai," is at the center of her research with respect to this film, for its allegedly "vulgar" effects and defamatory content, particularly in its offences to women. The song, which contains a *double entendre* in its lyrics ("What is behind the blouse? What is blah blah the veil?"), was understood to be offensive insofar as it challenged three related assumptions endemic to patriarchal discourse in India: first, that sexuality is obscene; second, that sexual references dishonor women; and third, that sexuality's entry into public space disrupts social boundaries.

THE LONGEVITY OF FILMS

Things get increasingly interesting, archivally speaking, in this case. Those who filed objections were largely members of the Hindu right wing, the Bhartiya Janata Party (BJP), and they objected not only to the song's lyrics but also to its very circulation, it "being sung through cassettes at public places, annoying the people at large, the undersigned specially." While debates about Indian cinematic morality are waged frequently through newspapers and other sites of public protest and focus on the screening of films themselves (such as Deepa Mehta's film *Fire* (1996)), these were notably lodged in the courts and therefore constitute a different archive of public sentiment over cinematic representation. In addition, the complaints were lodged about a song (an audio recording), and not a film, creating questions about legal jurisdiction and control.

Monika Mehta therefore reads the archival file regarding the film's movement through the cycle from production to exhibition in terms of its *production* of a discourse around female sexual agency, a discourse that is, crucially, not available in the text of the film per se. To the contrary, the archival record of debates around this single song and its moral implications provides Mehta with ample material to argue (in our view successfully) that censorship actively promoted public debate about the representation of sex in cinema, and that this public debate in turn prompted the classification of the film as "UA" (unrestricted access but with parental guidance for children under the age of 12). Censorship, in other words, both responds to and catalyzes public discourse around sexuality, women, Indian culture and tradition, and children's morality. It does not only say "no." As Mehta shows in her book-length study from which this case is drawn, *Censorship and Sexuality in Bombay Cinema*, studying state censorship sheds new light on the how relations among the industry, the state, and the public *produce* forms of sexual life.[6]

public. For the occasion of its seventieth anniversary, however, the organization coined a new slogan: "Film can wait (if you don't throw it away)." FIAF and its members, in other words, are committed not only to transferring film images to digital platforms but to acquiring and preserving *film as film*. Why? As they put it in their anniversary manifesto:

- A film is either created under the direct supervision of a filmmaker or is the record of an historical moment captured by a cameraman. Both types are potentially important artifacts and part of the world's cultural heritage. Film is a tangible and "human-eye readable" entity which needs to be treated with great care, like other museum or historic objects.
- All digital information carriers are vulnerable to physical and chemical deterioration and all hardware and software to obsolescence; and digital information has value only if it can be interpreted. Although film can be physically and chemically fragile, it is a stable material that can survive for more than a century, as long as it is stored under the recommended conditions of temperature and humidity and receives regular visual inspections. Its life expectancy has already proved much longer than moving image carriers like videotape that were developed after films. (At 35 degrees Fahrenheit, films might live for as long as several hundred years.)

- Film is currently the optimal archival storage medium for moving images. It is one of the most standardized and international products available and it remains a medium with high resolution potential. The data it contains does not need regular migration nor does its operating system require frequent updating.
- The film elements held in archive vaults are the original materials from which all copies are derived. One can determine from them whether a copy is complete or not. The more digital technology is developed, the easier it will be to change or even arbitrarily alter content. Unjustified alteration or unfair distortion, however, can always be detected by comparison with the original film provided it has been properly stored.[7]

Even the storage of film in archive vaults is complicated and requires evolving expertise. Housing black and white film prints in stacks (in cans, on cores) is possible at higher temperatures than storing color prints or negatives, since color fades by emitting gases that can hasten decomposition; these prints and negatives therefore require storage at temperatures around 35 degrees Fahrenheit, on individual shelves surrounded by as much air circulation as possible. Archiving film is, in other words, a science as much as an art, and it requires talented scientists who are passionate about the medium and its possibilities.

Despite this push to acquire and store actual films, archivists are at the same time overwhelmed with the **digitization** of content (audio, visual, broadcast) and its management. Digitization entails questions at every stage or moment in the lifecycle of media, from the use of various master files (AVI Uncompressed, QuickTime Uncompressed, MXF wrappers with JPEG 2000, for example) for digitizing analog video, to distinguishing among types of metadata (descriptive, structural and administrative, for example), to dealing with encoding specifications (time standards such as SIMPTE). Making sense of this alphabet soup requires lengthy training and frequently an advanced engineering degree. Essentially, however, digital files without appropriate metadata cannot be understood, managed or interpreted. Some metadata standards have been developed specifically for media (such as PBCore), and archivists work with the software developers to refine its use in collections. As digitization becomes a (if not the) key area of archivists' work with media objects, training programs and seminars increasingly focus on these issues.

FRAGMENTARY CINEMA

We have spoken up to this point a great deal about "lost" cinema, that which has disappeared from our grasp forever. Among archivists and cinephiles, this disappearance is accompanied by intense *feelings* of loss, the pain of loss called "nostalgia" we experience imagining that which is irretrievably gone and/ or idealizing it. We have also spoken at some length about material that is housed in archives, protected against loss, preserved for future generations. Here we want to mention, if only briefly, a different response to the evanescence, partiality and fragility of the medium of cinema: that is, an often irreverent and always political-aesthetic interest in making new things out of old and decaying images.

From its beginnings, cinema has exploited the capacity to join different worlds together through the cut, assembling realities that exist only for the spectator and her seemingly irrepressible need to make coherence. Remember the experiments of Lev Kuleshov that we discussed in the Interlude. He famously stimulated spectators to attribute feelings to his actor's blank face when juxtaposed with different objects to which the face was thought to be reacting. Similar experiments on even grander scales characterize the work of "found cinema" makers, who assemble together bits of film footage from disparate sources into new wholes.

Like much experimental cinema, this work tends to be *reflexive*, meditating on the very capacities of cinema as a medium to create worldviews out of fragments. Bruce Conner's *A MOVIE* (1958) is an example of the reflexive capacities of this mode of filmmaking. Beyond the title, which references something generic ("a movie," any movie at all, all movies in one), Conner plays with temporality, authorship, genre, vision and the gaze, fetishism, causality, and ultimately death and apocalypse with found footage, combining the gruesome and the playful, the vertiginous and the ordinary, the comic and the tragic in a short film that leaves some audiences breathless. The film opens, for example, with the director's name, which Conner leaves on the screen for more than thirty seconds (watch it online: it seems interminable). Quickly, "A" "MOVIE" "BY" flashes by, and we return to "BRUCE CONNER," seeming to bask in the narcissism of his status as the film's director. Several seconds of leader (countdown) give way to a pornographic image of a nude woman with stockings, startling the audience into some reflection on its own voyeurism or pleasure in degradation, this degradation being social and not the physical degradation of film. A title card, "THE END" follows, one minute and twenty

13.9 *A MOVIE* (Bruce Conner, 1958). © DACS © Centre Pompidou, MNAM-CCI, Dist. RMN-Grand Palais/Hervé Véronèse.

seconds into a twelve-minute film. Of course Conner is playing with conventions and expectations, but "the end" is also an apocalyptic description and a philosophical question about directions, or goals. And "THE END" is just the beginning: the rest of the film is as complicated, generative, and provocative.

Other examples of makers who followed in Conner's footsteps include Craig Baldwin and Jack Walsh, both San Francisco artists and Conner students very much indebted to, but building from, Conner's experiments. Baldwin's *Spectres of the Spectrum* (1999), for example, paints a science fiction picture of a world gone mad by retelling the history of media from the perspective of an anti-corporate, participatory point of view. Combining live action footage he shot himself with found footage, Baldwin engages in what have been described as media mash-ups, collage narratives, and remixed forms of cinema, all in the service of imagining new forms of media that are shared and active. Baldwin has taken a strong stance against copyright laws that forbid the kind of borrowing that collage demands, challenging ideas of ownership in the context of a world of fragmented and recombined images. Like other queer filmmakers who have been pushed to explore the relationship between the sayable and the unsayable, between what can be shown and what cannot, Walsh creates political parables, a different gloss on film reflexivity. In his film *Dear Rock* (1993), Walsh, like Mark Rappaport with his *Rock Hudson's Home Movies* (1992), which we discuss in a case study later, comments on the cinematic relation between the private and the public, between sequestered and closeted worldviews and those built by the fantasies of the commercial cinema. Here, too, we witness a commentary on who controls images and what flourishes beneath their public display.

A very different example of the use of found footage comes in the work of Peter Forgács, a Hungarian filmmaker whose work might better be described as documentary, or, maybe better, as working with the raw material of home or amateur movies to create moving re-combinations of history. His tour de force film (1997), to take but one example, features the home movies recorded by a teenage member of the Peereboom family, a Dutch Jewish family experiencing the pre-World War II and then wartime years in Amsterdam. Our knowledge of the fate of this family – knowledge they did not have, or might have come to know dimly as the women sewed and packed for "work camp" in the last images we have of them – structures our encounter with the film images recorded by Max Peereboom, one of

13.10 Experimental filmmaker Craig Baldwin. Photograph by Alice Patterson, courtesy of Craig Baldwin.

the family's sons. Forgács delights in this family's joys, bodies, smiles, and rituals: their marriages and children, their holidays and games, their ever-shrinking world (made smaller by the anti-Semitic laws increasingly implemented in the Netherlands) and the domestic life they share together. He asks us to be open to them, too, while also seeking some understanding beyond the Peerbooms' specific experiences of the wider trauma of the Holocaust. This understanding comes in another set of home movies, intercut with those of Max Peereboom: movies of the Arthur Seyss-Inquart family, the Reich Commissioner for Holland, who arrived in 1940 to implement the very Nazi genocide that murdered the Peerebooms. Shown outside, in natural light, the Seyss-Inquarts play tennis (with Heinrich Himmler, the leader of the Nazi SS), ride horses, and play with babies (as we have seen the Peerebooms do with Max and his wife Annie's two children, born over the course of Max's "career" as a filmmaker). Superimposed over the footage from the Seyss-Inquart family, however, is an ominous voice-over reading of the text of those laws affecting Jews, a powerful use of sound that demonstrates the devastating consequences of bureaucratic-legal powers controlled by Seyss-Inquart. Using period sound (radio broadcasts and the like, other "found"

13.11 Studio portrait of Rock Hudson, 1954. Courtesy of Universal/The Kobal Collection.

materials) and a score by Forgács' frequent collaborator Tibor Szemzo, Forgács creates a one-hour meditation on the power of images to preserve life and record loss, to brood over human devastation and to celebrate the power of aesthetic responses to that very destruction.

13.12 *The Maelstrom: A Family Chronicle* (1997) by Hungarian filmmaker Peter Forgács. Copyright Lumen Film.

Finally in this context we mention Bill Morrison's film *Decasia* (2002), one of the most aesthetic reckonings with cinematic decay. At once a luminous engagement with the surfaces of cinema and their waning, and with the existential fact of film's attempt to preserve what appeared before the camera, *Decasia* gives us a glimpse of how to *do* film theory: how to get to the essence of cinema through its cycle of animation (giving life) and death (decay, the still).

13.13 Decaying nitrate film. Courtesy of The Kobal Collection.

CASE STUDY: ORPHANS, PRELINGER AND UBU

Exchanges between "old" forms of cinema and new media, including varieties of digital cinema, encourage further thought about mixing: about mash-ups and remixes, about recombination and parametric modification, about amateur play and high art. As we mentioned previously, "orphan" cinema has become, since the early 1990s, a term that organizes festivals and symposia devoted to cinema of unknown provenance, abandoned by its owner or copyright holder. It encompasses all types of film outside the commercial mainstream, including public domain materials, home movies, out-takes, unreleased films, industrial and educational movies, independent documentaries, ethnographic films, newsreels, censored material, underground works, experimental pieces, silent-era productions, stock footage, found footage, medical films, kinescopes, small- and unusual-gauge films, amateur productions, surveillance footage, test reels, government films, advertisements, sponsored films, student works, and sundry other ephemeral pieces of celluloid (or paper or glass or tape or …). Here would be some subgenres of orphan cinema that have been important in the history of cinematic argument and persuasion: political campaign ads, advertising films, television commercials, newsreels, newsfilm, religious pictures, sponsored and sales films, promos, public service announcements, electronic press kits, military productions, clandestine or subversive work, trailers, snipes, documentaries, essay films, public affairs and public access programs, activist and advocacy pieces, propaganda, issue ads, culture jamming, stereotypes and counter-stereotypes, intelligence work, censored footage, indoctrination and training films, triggers,

13.14 Newsreel cameramen. Courtesy of The Kobal Collection.

guidance and educational films, and amateur samizdat. We mean to suggest by these lists the enormity of "cinema" that exists outside the boundaries of the commercial narrative feature film, a treasure trove of image culture that can be mined and excavated.

Much of that excavation can now take place online with archives such as the Prelinger Archives and Ubuweb. The Prelinger collection, founded by Rick Prelinger in 1983, grew to over 60,000 "ephemeral" films (educational, industrial, amateur, and advertising films) and was transferred to the Library of Congress in 2002. With still images, videotape collections, and the original film collection, it represents as a whole more than 10 per cent of the *total* films made in the sixty-year period between 1927 and 1987 in these genres. Among the highlights of the collection are films about the cities of San Francisco and Detroit, as well as often-downloaded, hilarious instructional films such as *Good Table Manners* (Ted Peshak, 1951).

Another web resource for non-commercial film is Ubuweb, a portal for avant-garde content of all sorts, from poetry to recorded sound to cinema. Ubuweb hacks: it does not request or receive permission for anything that it posts, and it has, as a result, come under a good deal of scrutiny for its practices. It is worthwhile to think about whether this kind of use differs from

13.15 *Panorama Ephemera* (Rick Prelinger, 2004), accessible from an online archive. Courtesy of Rick Prelinger/The Prelinger Archive.

the kind of piracy we discuss elsewhere. In response to questions about its legality and tactics, Ubuweb's founder Kenneth Goldsmith, himself an artist whose work troubles the boundaries of artistic originality and authenticity, penned a lengthy supplement to its FAQ, which reads in part:

> We know that UbuWeb is not very good. In terms of films, the selection is random and the quality is often poor. The accompanying text to the films can be crummy, mostly poached from whatever is available around the net. So are the films: they are mostly grabbed from private closed file-sharing communities and made available for the public, hence the often lousy quality of the films. It could be done much better.

> Yet, in terms of how we've gone about building the archive, if we had to ask for permission, we wouldn't exist. Because we have no money, we don't ask permission. Asking permission always involves paperwork and negotiations, lawyers, and bank accounts. Yuk. But by doing things the wrong way, we've been able to pretty much overnight build an archive that's made publically accessible for free of charge to anyone. And that in turn has attracted a great number of film and video makers to want to contribute their works to the archive legitimately. The fastest growing part of Ubu's film section is by younger and living artists who want to be a part of Ubu.[8]

Ubuweb thus posts films and videos from artists as well-known as Andy Warhol and Jean-Luc Godard, as well as pieces from young and emerging artists who want a public platform for their work.

EXERCISE

Access and view an orphan, ephemeral, or avant-garde film from an online archive, such as the Prelinger archive or Ubuweb. What are its defining features when compared to a commercial narrative feature film? (It's probably shorter, in black and white ….) What is it trying to do: make an argument? Grab your attention? Play with your perception? Teach you? How does the context of its viewing shape your experience of it? Finally, in what ways did it surprise you, in terms of its form or its content or both?

COLLECTING, COLLATING, ARCHIVING ACTIVITIES (THE PRESERVATION VERSUS RESTORATION DEBATE)

> The images and sounds of film, television, radio and recording are a reflection of our creativity
> – a window onto our life and times, our dreams and stories, our place in the world.
>
> (National Film & Sound Archive, Australia)[9]

We turn now to an issue that arises from the drive to archive, the impulse to save old film and audio recording for posterity. This is a conceptual debate that we inherit from discussions about architecture in the nineteenth century, between preservation and restoration. Because its history is important to how we understand these terms today, we review it briefly in what follows in order to see how it applies to the world of cinema.

In the early part of the nineteenth century, architects were faced with the question of what to do with crumbling buildings, such as cathedrals dating from the Middle Ages that had been added to, continued, demolished, rebuilt, and otherwise modified so as to result in buildings that were stylistically unrecognizable. What should be the standards for restoring these buildings? The theorist Eugène Viollet-Le-Duc proposed an answer in the form of a theory of *restoration*: a precise and learned knowledge of architectural history and its periodization could yield a probable if not definitive sense of the style in which the *original* construction was undertaken. Under the credo of *l'unité de style* (unity of style), he proposed that architects could approach buildings with a sense of aesthetic unity derived from that periodization of architectural history. What this meant in practice was a diverse and perverse set of undertakings: it argued for destroying newer parts of buildings in order to restore older parts, even when the "newer" parts were stunning architectural elements often centuries old. Taking place in the era of the Gothic Revival, when medieval styles were aesthetically privileged, the discussion sometimes led restorationists to restore buildings in a style in which they had actually never been built; and new materials and modern methods replaced original construction without concern for the integrity or intrinsic importance of original materials. In vastly simplified terms, this is *restorationism*.

By the latter half of the nineteenth century, resistance to this position started to be articulated in Britain, by two figures who have become associated with the other pole of the debate, *preservation*. English textile designer and author William Morris and Victorian art critic John Ruskin argued that restoration was essentially destruction: by destroying what succeeding generations had added to a building, by peeling off layers of historical intervention in order to discover an ostensibly "original" core, restoration destroyed history itself. Morris and Ruskin argued to the contrary: that the proper response to the decay of old buildings was to keep them alive, to prolong their survival into the future, to preserve them. Ruskin in particular articulated a sense of a duty of the present towards the past, a respect for the age worn on the wall of a building and an appreciation for "the sweetness in the gentle lines which rain and sun had wrought."[10] Preservations displayed a high degree of tolerance for aesthetic disunity, in favor of a respect for the continuity buildings proposed between the past and the present, as though the wear on a building's wall serves as an index of lives lived in it, human traces of history.

This debate was in practice never as clear as it was in theory, but you can begin to appreciate its ramifications for film, which inherits some of the tensions between these two positions. For some time, "film preservation" meant only the process of *duplication*, of creating a stable, durable, and accurate copy of an original film (assuming an original existed). It certainly involves repair. But restoration, as in the architectural debates from previous centuries, involves returning a film to a version most faithful to its original release, often by combining many different sources or fragments. This process of recombination is expensive, painstaking, and difficult work.

CASE STUDY: *METROPOLIS*

The case of the restoration of Fritz Lang's *Metropolis*, originally released in Berlin in 1927, has all of the intrigue of a detective novel like *The Da Vinci Code*. On its premiere screening on 10 January that year, the film ran 153 minutes; by the time its distributors (Ufa in Germany and Paramount in the US) prepared its wider release, it had been cut to ninety minutes' running time. In the summer of 2008, archivists in Buenos Aires, Argentina, discovered a negative that contained about twenty-five minutes of material that had not been seen since the film's Berlin debut eighty years earlier. A practical puzzle presented itself to a team of preservationists who had completed a landmark restoration of the *same film* just ten years earlier.

In this case, it is significant that *Metropolis* is often recognized as one of the world's most important films. A glimpse of a future in which the rich enjoy pleasure gardens, an Olympian stadium, and all of the benefits of a splendid city, while the workers live in a dark underground, *Metropolis* established the iconic terms through which cinema would imagine the future tension between plutocracy and laborers for decades to come. It is the foundational film in the genre of science fiction. As film critic Roger Ebert describes it:

> From this film, in various ways, descended not only *Dark City* but *Blade Runner*, *The Fifth Element*, *Alphaville*, *Escape From L.A.*, *Gattaca* and *Batman*'s Gotham City. The laboratory of its evil genius, Rotwang, created the visual look of mad scientists for decades to come, especially after it was so closely mirrored in *Bride of Frankenstein* (1935).[11]

13.16 *Metropolis* (Fritz Lang, 1927). Courtesy of UFA/The Kobal Collection.

13.17 *Blade Runner* (Ridley Scott, 1982). Courtesy of The Ladd Company/Warner Bros./The Kobal Collection.

On the back cover of the restored version issued on DVD in the United States, *New York Times* film critic A.O. Scott calls it "the movie every would-be cinematic visionary has been trying to make since 1927." Its fantastic sets, including the workers' clock that measures ten-hour days, and its obsessive attention to visual style render it one of the most richly detailed films of the silent era, if not that era's signature achievement.

Here is the story of it twice restored. Before the film's Berlin debut, Paramount Studios sought to cut the film for what it considered a "normal" American feature-length running time of around 100 minutes. (National cinemas have their own norms for length: compare Nigeria's films to Bollywood's lengths, often over 200 minutes.) The studio commissioned playwright Channing Pollock to make the changes, which involved large pieces of the central plotlines (the conflict between Joh Fredersen the industrialist and Rotwang the scientist-inventor, the pursuit of Fredersen's son Freder, and the majority of scenes in "Yoshiwara," the red light district). In order to make the film somewhat comprehensible in light of these major changes, he altered the inter-titles. Pollock's changes were significant enough that he claimed to have given the film coherence and meaning:

> As it stood when I began my job of structural editing, *Metropolis* had no restraint or logic. It was symbolism run such riot that people who saw it couldn't tell what the picture was all about. I have given it my meaning.[12]

To condense a very long story, after the Berlin debut, the German studio Ufa decided to cut the film along the lines of the American version, presenting a shortened version to the censors. This shortened German version is the only version that was exported and shown outside Berlin. The original version stood at 4,189 meters; the second, shortened German version stood at 2,589 meters. A duplicate (or "dupe") negative of this second, shortened version serves as the basis for most circulating copies of *Metropolis* in western countries: a version that came to the Museum of Modern Art (MoMA) in New York in 1936, made into a dupe negative in 1937. In 1986, that dupe negative went back to Germany to the Munich Filmmuseum. But the dupe negative evidences even more missing footage: it stands at 2,532 meters, having lost an additional 57 meters somewhere along the way. Paramount, for their part, seem to have sent their original negative back to Germany in the 1930s, and it found its way to the Reichsfilmarchiv, which collection was inherited by the Bundesarchiv-Filmarchiv in 1990. There was a third negative that has never been found, a negative given to the Ufa export department, but prints from that negative are in Britain, the United States and Italy.

Using new source materials from censorship records, the screenplay, and the musical score, archivists sought to build a version of *Metropolis* based upon the best available technology and the best available source materials (using the Paramount negative supplemented by material primarily from existing nitrate copies for the quality of the photography). That version was declared "definitive" and released in 2001/2002 as the "75th Anniversary Restoration" by the F.W. Murnau Foundation/Transit Films.

And then: in a little, temporarily closed museum in Buenos Aires, the Museo del Cine, turns up a version of *Metropolis* twenty-five minutes longer than any version since the film's Berlin premiere. It turns out that an Argentinian distributor did not agree that the Berlin version was too long, and he brought that original version to Argentina, where it was housed in his collection. Eventually, he sold that collection to the Argentinian state, which made a 16mm copy of the film and destroyed the nitrate negative. It is that copy that made its way to the Museo, and which was "discovered" by a historian and collector named Fernando Peña. When that print was cleaned, restored, and blown up to 35mm, audiences saw *Metropolis* again, for the first time.

WORKING IN ARCHIVES

Many students study films in order to make them, but there are other careers in cinema and media that offer different combinations of skills and challenges, mastery of technical aspects of the medium, and steadier employment! Film preservation is one such field, and there are now postgraduate (in UK usage) programs that train students in all aspects of film preservation. Students learn museum practice and collection management, curatorial theory and practice, techniques and procedures for preservation and restoration, archive management, and so on. As archives grow, so too will the need for professional archivists, ready to preserve the future of film for those schoolboys and schoolgirls with whom we opened this chapter.

CHAPTER SUMMARY

From the earliest moments of the medium, cinema was archived as a matter of money-making and as a dream of a total record of our planet. We explored the role of archives in managing national memory and culture, and of cinema as a kind of historian of the twentieth century and beyond. Archives are not inert depositories, however, and so we devoted some time to discussing how they may be used, both in scholarly and artistic ways. These uses are furthermore debated in theoretical terms, particularly in the long-standing debates between preservation and restoration, which we introduced from their nineteenth-century origins into contemporary instances. Finally, we note the emergence of schools for training archivists, offering professional pathways for working with the material of film.

 FURTHER READING

Amad, Paula. *Counter-Archive: Film, The Everyday, and Albert Kahn's Archives de la Planète*. New York: Columbia University Press, 2010.

> Paula Amad examines the political and intellectual forces that shaped Albert Kahn's ambitions for the Archives of the Planet and situates that collection more broadly in its historical context.

Frick, Carolyn. *Saving Cinema: The Politics of Preservation*. Oxford: Oxford University Press, 2011.

> Brings the preservation versus restoration debates squarely into the politics of film archiving, discussing the role of public debate and the financing of film preservation.

Magliozzi, Ronald S. "Film Archiving as a Profession: An Interview with Eileen Bowser." *The Moving Image* 3(1) (2003), 132–146.

> An interview with one of the most influential archivists of the twentieth century: Bowser helped to reformulate film studies with her work at the Museum of Modern Art in New York.

Usai, Paolo Cherchi. *The Death of Cinema: History, Cultural Memory, and the Digital Dark Age*. London: British Film Institute Publishing, 2008.

> A passionate argument for saving film, written by a key figure in film archives, the senior curator of the George Eastman House.

FILMS REFERENCED IN CHAPTER THIRTEEN

Alphaville (Jean-Luc Godard, 1965)

Batman (Tim Burton, 1989)

Blade Runner (Ridley Scott, 1982)

Bride of Frankenstein (James Whale, 1935)

Citizen Kane (Orson Welles, 1941)

Dark City (Alex Proyas, 1998)

Decasia (Bill Morrison, 2002)

Escape from L.A. (John Carpenter, 1996)

E.T. the Extra-Terrestrial (Steven Spielberg, 1982)

The Fifth Element (Luc Besson, 1997)

Gattaca (Andrew Niccol, 1997)

Good Table Manners (1951)

Khalnayak/The Villain (Subhash Ghai, 1993)

The Maelstrom: A Family Chronicle (Peter Forgács, 1997)

Metropolis (Fritz Lang, 1927)

A MOVIE (Bruce Conner, 1958)

My Name is Khan (Karan Johar, 2010)

Rear Window (Alfred Hitchcock, 1954)

Riverdance (performance originated 1994)

Rock Hudson's Home Movies (Mark Rappaport, 1992)

Specters of the Spectrum (Craig Baldwin, 1999)

Star Wars (George Lucas, 1977)

Vertigo (Alfred Hitchcock, 1958)

Yojimbo (Akira Kurosawa, 1961)

NOTES

1   Johnston, Alva, "Films Put on Ice for Fans yet Unborn," the *New York Times*, 24 October 1926.

2   Martin Scorsese, "The Persisting Vision: Reading the Language of Cinema," *New York Review of Books*, 15 August 2013, http://www.nybooks.com/articles/archives/2013/aug/15/persisting-vision-reading-language-cinema/?page=2, accessed 30 November 2013.

3   Das Bundesarchiv, http://www.bundesarchiv.de/bundesarchiv/organisation/abteilung_fa/, accessed 1 December 2013.

4   Anne Applebaum, "The Worst of the Madness," *New York Review of Books* 57(7), 11 November 2010, 10.

5   Monika Mehta, "What is Behind Film Censorship? The *Khalnayak* Debates," *Jouvert* 5(3), http://english.chass.ncsu.edu/jouvert/v5i3/mehta.htm, accessed 24 September 2014.

6   Monika Mehta, *Censorship and Sexuality in Bombay Cinema* (Austin: University of Texas Press, 2011).

7   FIAF 70th Anniversary Manifesto, "Don't Throw Film Away," http://blog.unl.edu/dixon/2012/11/20/don%E2%80%99t-throw-film-away-the-the-international-federation-of-film-archives-fiaf-70th-anniversary-manifesto/, accessed 2 December 2013.

8   UbuWeb, http://www.ubuweb.com/.

9   National Film and Sound Archive, http://www.nfsa.gov.au/about/, accessed 2 December 2013.

10 John Ruskin, "The Lamp of Memory," in John D. Rosenberg (ed.), *The Genius of John Ruskin: Selections from his Writings* (Charlottesville, VA: University of Virginia Press, 1998), 135.

11 http://www.rogerebert.com/reviews/great-movie-metropolis-2010-restoration-1927, accessed 2 December 2013.

12 "Channing Pollock Gives his Impressions of *Metropolis*," in the press release of Paramount Pictures' *Metropolis*, Bundesarchiv Filmarchiv File on the Reconstruction of *Metropolis*.

INTRODUCTION

In the fourth and final section of this book, we turn our attention to the raft of issues that surround the consumption of movies. This section is centrally concerned with the arrival of the completed film with the viewer, and the subsequent variety of complex relationships that individual spectators may have with cinema. Where our first three sections have traced the journey of a film from idea to screen – why it might be made, how it gets made, and the complex and sometimes tortuous barriers and routes that it could pass through after filming has completed – this part of the book, finally, discusses you, and what you do with movies.

This is not to suggest, of course, that the audience has not been of any significance up until this stage. Many films would never get made without some anticipated audience in sight. For most commercial films, which aim to be successful as commodities (a topic we discussed at length in Chapter 5), the potential audience for the product is key. During the planning stages of these films, the target audience is identified and content altered according to perceived understandings of them. Focus group screenings of films serve as testing grounds with potential audiences, and may result in particular elements of films being reworked, reshot or excised entirely before their official release. Marketing, distribution, and exhibition strategies – all examined at length in Section III – take shape around ideas of the audience: what they might want to see, where and how they will want to watch. The audience is also shaped by these strategies: audiences for particular films are carefully built and solicited, seduced and delighted (or, perhaps, disappointed). This section extends these previous discussions of how audiences are imagined, turning to the complexities of our experiences watching movies.

The first chapter in this section focuses on cinematic pleasure, examining the ways that cinema both responds to the desires of film viewers and produces those desires. The chapter starts with a discussion of cinephilia, or the passionate love of cinema. Cinephilia has been associated with a very elite form of engaging with cinema, tied both to the theatrical exhibition of art cinema and other critically acclaimed films, and to the cultural influence of film festivals, film criticism, and film societies. This chapter examines the forms of cinephilia that have emerged in response to the changes in film distribution and exhibition outlined in Chapters 10 and 11, and the pleasures available through technologies that enable us to watch movies on laptops, tablets, phones, and other small screens, at home or on the go. The remaining sections of the chapter focus on several of the many pleasures that viewers may (or may not) enjoy in relation to cinema. The first section discusses film genres and the pleasures generated both by the viewer's recognition of familiar narrative structures in a film and by a film's introduction of a new element to a genre formula in order to combine repetition and difference. The second section examines the phenomenon of stardom, analyzing the pleasures of watching film stars both on and off screen. The final section introduces three specific objects of pleasure that challenge our understanding of a film as a stable textual object: fashion, technology, and locations. Individual costumes in a film may overwhelm our visual connection to the film, emerging from the film as the primary focus of our attention. Technology – either in the form of special effects within the film or in the form of the projection of the film itself – may become the focus of a viewer's pleasure (or anxiety) in relation to individual films or to cinema in general. Film locations may endure as tourist destinations long after a movie leaves the theatres, allowing viewers to extend their pleasure beyond viewing a film. Not all viewers will experience the cinematic pleasures profiled in this chapter, and not all of the pleasures generated by cinema are discussed within the space of the chapter.

Chapter 15 explores the topic of identification and identity, interrogating the mechanics of how exactly spectators might relate to depicted content on screen. Where the previous chapter discussed aspects of cinema that attempt to produce pleasure and inspire devotion, Chapter 15 examines in depth the bond that is forged between spectators as individuals with distinct identities, and the actors onscreen playing roles. The chapter begins from a "folk model" of identification which presumes that spectators identify with characters with whom they share key identity characteristics, or whom they aspire to be. However, as a number of film theorists have explored in detail, identification is much more complicated than this model suggests. Pleasure remains a key concern in this chapter: is it possible to enjoy a film without identifying with its characters? Can viewer pleasure be obtained even if characters are suffering (as, for instance, in many horror films)? Our discussion follows an outline of several key theoretical positions on identification with an examination of how identification might actually work in practice, rooted in ethnographic data drawn from viewers. We also consider cases where identification between viewer and film might be blocked or stymied – but argue that, in such cases, it may be possible to employ particular strategies to facilitate such a relationship. Alternatively, identification may be less concerned with the relationship between audience and film than with that between individual spectators in the audience. Chapter 15 considers in some detail how cinema texts may promote, or be used as the basis for, group identification. Identification, we summarize, is a fragile, slippery and malleable experience – but this squares neatly with many conceptual understandings of identity itself. If identification is rarely stable, neither are our own identities – and audiences' complicated relationships with cinema expose this clearly.

The final chapter in this section investigates the many ways in which films are transformed. Acts of transformation take place at every stage along the paths that films travel from production to distribution to exhibition to reception. Chapter 16 thus serves as a conclusion to this book, considering how transformative practices may impact films at different moments along the linear trajectory that the previous sections have traced. Whether these transformations are introduced during the early stages of production or after a film has been released, they impact the experiences of audiences. By examining several prominent forms of cinematic transformation, this chapter draws attention to the textual instability of film. One person's experience of a film may differ radically from another person's, not only because of the different ways in which people identify with films (as discussed in Chapter 15) but also because of the textual differences between different versions of a film. The first section of Chapter 16 discusses censorship. While often associated with a repressive institutional practice that deletes explicit scenes of sex and violence or stifles expressions of political opposition, censorship also encompasses many more quotidian practices. This part of the chapter thus discusses not only the censorship of potentially offensive content but also mundane practices like the cutting of films to meet standard running times. Subsequently the chapter focuses on the translation of film dialogue, exploring the traditions of subtitling and dubbing and the aesthetic, industrial, and social consequences of both translation strategies. The final part of the chapter examines the reception of films by fans, profiling practices such as the production of remix videos. Remix culture engages many of the concerns that have been outlined in this book – the nature of film authorship, the politics of film production and distribution, and the pleasures of film reception, to name only a few of the critical issues you will encounter again in this final chapter.

CHAPTER FOURTEEN
PLEASURE AND DESIRE

You may have been asked (maybe even multiple times) to list the five films that you would bring with you if you were going to spend the rest of your life on a desert island without access to any other media. Film critics and fans share their "desert island films" online and elsewhere, and these lists spark lively dialogues and debates.

This exercise differs from the construction of lists like the *Sight and Sound* list of the "Greatest Films of All Time" (discussed in detail in Chapter 12, "Evaluative contexts"). The *Sight and Sound* list reflects evaluations by professional film critics and directors of the historical importance of specific films and their aesthetic and narrative innovations and achievements. These lists generate their own fierce debates, with critics and fans battling over the films that were omitted from the lists and the biases and blind spots those omissions expose. Lists of "desert island films" provoke different discussions. You may agree that Carl Dreyer's *The Passion of Joan of Arc* (1927) deserves to be recognized as #9 on the 2012 *Sight and Sound* list, but you may or may not want to watch it on a weekly basis for the rest of your life. Building a desert island list invites us to shift the way that we value films, prioritizing the pleasure that we take in watching a film rather than its critical value. A desert island list may include films that appear on the *Sight and Sound* list, but desert island lists more often reflect idiosyncratic personal tastes.

The Australian Centre for the Moving Image (ACMI) features on its website a series of video interviews with well-known figures in the film industry who share their desert island film lists. Australian film critic Margaret Pomeranz selects: *Nashville* (Robert Altman, 1975), *The Flower of My Secret* (Pedro Almodóvar, 1995), *The Women* (George Cukor, 1939), *In the Cut* (Jane Campion,

2003), and *Magnolia* (Paul Thomas Anderson, 1999); while her fellow critic David Stratton selects: *Duel in the Sun* (King Vidor, 1946), *Smiles of a Summer Night* (Ingmar Bergman, 1955), *Loves of a Blonde* (Milos Forman, 1965), *Singin' in the Rain* (Stanley Donen, 1952), and *The Last Wave* (Peter Weir, 1977). Hollywood director Tim Burton chooses *The Omega Man* (Boris Sagal, 1971), *War of the Gargantuas* (Ishirô Honda, 1966), *The Golden Voyage of Sinbad* (Gordon Hessler, 1973), *The Wicker Man* (Robin Hardy, 1973), and *Dracula A.D. 1972* (Alan Gibson, 1972). A review of these interviews reveals two important observations about the ACMI project. First, no two people choose the same five films. Second, the rationales that people provide for their choices capture the many different pleasures that cinema generates. In his discussion of *The Omega Man*, Tim Burton explains that he enjoys the film's "rough edges," citing its "cheesy one-liners" and the use of obvious stunt doubles as examples of the film's appeal. He describes the pleasure of watching the film as a form of "masochism" since he lets the film, with all of its flaws, "wash over [him] again and again" as a source of inspiration for his own filmmaking.[1] The elements of *The Omega Man* that might lead other viewers to dismiss it are the very features that Burton values.

This chapter moves beyond the cliché that no two people will see a film in the same way, examining cinematic pleasure from the vantage points of producers and audiences. Pleasure may be engineered into the structure of a film as is the case with genre films, but these textual structures cannot anticipate or control the reception of films by individual viewers who bring their own tastes, experiences, and desires to each film they see. This chapter thus explores cinematic pleasures at the intersection of the desires of producers and viewers. This study of cinematic pleasure is by no means exhaustive; rather it provides an introduction to the importance of pleasure as a film moves from production to distribution to exhibition, the same path traced by this book.

WHAT WE WILL DO IN CHAPTER 14

- Examine the status of cinephilia as a specific form of pleasure in contemporary film cultures and its distinction from earlier experiences of cinephilia.

- Explore the structure and mobility of film genres and the pleasures that viewers experience through their encounters with familiar narrative forms.

- Investigate film stardom, focusing on the global circulation of star images and the ways that viewers engage with star texts.

- Survey the ways that viewers extend cinematic pleasure through their investments in fashion, technology, and tourism.

BY THE END OF CHAPTER 14 YOU SHOULD BE ABLE TO

- Describe the three forms of contemporary cinephilia.
- Identify the ways that film genres generate pleasure for viewers.
- Explain the ways in which stardom, fashion, technology, and tourism produce pleasure both within and beyond individual films.

CINEPHILIA

In her 1996 essay "The Decay of Cinema," the writer Susan Sontag declared:

> Until the advent of television emptied the movie theaters, it was from a weekly visit to the cinema that you learned (or tried to learn) how to walk, to smoke, to kiss, to fight, to grieve. Movies gave you tips about how to be attractive. Example: It looks good to wear a raincoat even when it isn't raining. But whatever you took home was only a part of the larger experience of submerging yourself in lives that were not yours. The desire to lose yourself in other people's lives … faces. This is a larger, more inclusive form of desire embodied in the movie experience. Even more than what you appropriated for yourself was the experience of surrender to, of being transported by, what was on the screen. You wanted to be kidnapped by the movie – and to be kidnapped was to be overwhelmed by the physical presence of the image. The experience of "going to the movies" was part of it. To see a great film only on television isn't to have really seen that film. It's not only a question of the dimensions of the image: the disparity between a larger-than-you image in the theater and the little image on the box at home. The conditions of paying attention in a domestic space are radically disrespectful of film. Now that a film no longer has a standard size, home screens can be as big as living room or bedroom walls. But you are still in a living room or a bedroom. To be kidnapped, you have to be in a movie theater, seated in the dark among anonymous strangers.[2]

While her essay is called "The Decay of Cinema," Sontag primarily laments the death of **cinephilia**, the passionate love of cinema. Sontag blames the alleged death of cinephilia on: (1) the "hyperindustrial" mode of contemporary filmmaking (particularly the Hollywood emphasis on producing blockbusters); (2) the exhibition of films on multiple screens and in multiple venues where the "wonder" of cinema is diluted; and (3) the encroachment of television, not only as a source of entertainment itself but as an exhibition platform for film. For Sontag, the desire to "lose yourself" in a film can only be realized when watching certain films in certain spaces. Other critics and scholars share Sontag's assessment of cinephilia's demise, linking the love of cinema both with a theatrical exhibition tradition that is less and less central to global film cultures and with cinematic "masterpieces," or film as art.

Sontag's claim has been influential (and may be shared by some readers), but cinephilia has flourished in many new forms and formats – for example, the online archive "Cinephilia and Beyond" (http://cinearchive.org). This section will trace three forms of cinephilia: theatrical cinephilia, domestic cinephilia, and mobile cinephilia. While these forms of cinephilia may be strongly associated with specific periods in film history, this framework is *not* a periodization of cinephilia. Contemporary film cultures involve all three forms of cinephilia. Theatrical, domestic, and mobile cinephilia define cinephilia in terms of the locations and practices of film exhibition and the forms of cine-love that those experiences inspire.

Theatrical cinephilia

Sontag identifies *Cahiers du cinéma* (discussed in detail in Chapter 2, "Cinema as self-expression") as a key locus of international cinephilia, beginning in the 1950s. *Cahiers* and other magazines and journals about film provided cinephiles with an evolving canon of films to see, a language for discussing those films, and a sense of urgency about the act of going to the movies. Sontag captures the excitement of the period of cinephilia provoked in large part by the writing in *Cahiers* and the critical and creative activities of its authors: "The 1960s and early 1970s was the feverish age of movie-going, with the full-time cinephile always hoping to find a seat as close as possible to the big screen, ideally the third row center."[3] For Sontag, this period marks the historical climax of cinephilia, a period when film journals, film societies, and independent theatres flourished.

Theatrical cinephilia, however, continues. In part, the new forms of theatrical cinephilia are tied to the conditions that Sontag blames for cinephilia's demise. For example, the recent popularity of 3D has given viewers renewed incentives to watch films in the theatre rather than at home or on the go. Viewers may revel in the richness and depth of the 3D images in *Hugo* (Martin Scorsese, 2011), itself an expression of its director's cinephilia, or Werner Herzog's *Cave of Forgotten Dreams* (2010). These films challenge the assumption that commercial filmmaking or the foregrounding of special effects necessarily undermine the artistic value of cinema.

14.1 Director Martin Scorsese on the set of *Hugo*. Courtesy of GK Films/The Kobal Collection.

Theatrical cinephilia also continues through the proliferation, visibility, and relevance of international film festivals. While relatively few film viewers have opportunities to view films at festivals (just as relatively few film viewers have opportunities to visit independent theatres), these exhibition venues continue to thrive and to influence cultures of cinephilia in other sites. In other words, while a self-described cinephile may not be able to attend the Toronto International Film Festival, she can read the reviews posted by critics during and after the festival and track the prizes that were awarded. Her exposure to the critical conversations that emerge from the festival (if not to the films themselves) may then shape her decisions to see (or skip) certain films that were screened at the festival when they reach her local theatre or when she can access them in other formats.

Domestic cinephilia

Film scholar Barbara Klinger explores the development of domestic cinephilia, the relocation of the pleasures of cinema to the domestic sphere. Domestic cinephilia involves the consumer's desire to collect both a personal archive of films and the hardware to play them. Klinger traces the links between the form of cinephilia described in the previous section, with its emphasis on the public screening environment of the theatre, and this new version of cinephilia, with its emphasis on the private screening environment of the home:

> The contemporary film collector's romance with various technological aspects of the films and machines that make up the experience of cinema in domestic space suggests that cinephilia has been broadened to encompass the "forbidden" territories of television and the home. Film's domestication has not obliterated cinephilia; rather the conditions fueling this kind of zealotry have been relocated and rearticulated within the complex interactions among media industries, commodity culture, and the private sphere.[4]

According to Klinger, the cinephile's pleasure derives from both "films and machines." The cinematic apparatus (discussed in Chapter 11, "Exhibition") has been reconfigured for the home and generates a new form of cinematic pleasure.

Klinger analyzes the relationship between cinephilia and collecting, focusing on the practice of collecting DVDs. Collectors devote themselves not only to collecting treasured films on DVD (and, more recently, on Blu-ray disc) but also to collecting the newest and most expensive hardware for screening those films at home. Some films, including action movies and science fiction films, fully exploit the technical possibilities of DVD presentation in a high-end home viewing environment. Domestic cinephilia revalues these films, emphasizing form over content and spectacle over story. Klinger calls the new tendency to "evaluate films through the lens of hardware priorities" the **hardware aesthetic**.[5] Through the hardware aesthetic, cinephilia is tied to **technophilia**. However, science fiction and action films with dazzling special effects are not the only films that cinephiles collect. The large and diverse markets for DVD distribution (as discussed in Chapter 10, "Distribution") provide collectors with an opportunity to find rare titles that may never have been released in theatres. In addition to searching for obscure or out-of-print films, collectors may also focus on buying discs that include bonus features and other collectible enticements.

For Klinger, the collector is both a cinephile and an archivist. A collector may focus on the size of the collection, the organization and presentation of the collection in the home, and the presence of rare titles in the collection. Some collectors present their collections in homemade videos and post them online for other collectors to view and discuss. A YouTube search for "my DVD collection" or "my Blu-ray collection" will yield hundreds of videos documenting private film collections. These videos often feature the collectors as tour guides to their collections. The cinephile thus becomes the director and the star in a new film genre. The film collection video is part of a larger genre of user-generated videos called **haul videos** in which collectors share either their entire collections or recent acquisitions of various commodities – from sneakers to Superman comics. Klinger identifies the ways in which film collections can provide the collector with a sense of creative mastery while obscuring the influence of media industries on the collection itself:

> [S]elf-referentiality is a key ingredient in the individual relationship to and pleasure in commodities. In the case of cinema, collected objects ultimately refer to the collector as a kind of auteur, a producer of an intelligible, meaningful, private cosmos – a dynamic that occludes the relations the collection has to the outside world, particularly to the social and material conditions of mass production. A chain of logic among property, passion, and self-referentiality helps to explain the collector's zeal and also the significant place films have attained in the home as personal possessions.[6]

The act of collecting DVDs for home exhibition is a powerful form of film reception that allows the collector to reframe film consumption as film production.

Mobile cinephilia

Digital and networked technologies have introduced multiple ways in which even the most reticent viewers can become more active participants in their viewing experiences. Many films and film studios now release not only websites for their films but also interactive apps, social networking campaigns, and games for mobile devices. Whether watching a film in a theatre or at home, viewers can engage with multiple screens simultaneously in order to enhance their viewing experience. **Connected viewing** disperses the viewer's attention across multiple screens while connecting the viewer to other members of the audience. Even the viewer who is watching a film at home alone becomes part of a viewing public.

In effect, the mobility of films across multiple screens, formats, and platforms encourages cinephilia. From an industrial perspective, encouraging the passionate love of cinema is a smart business practice. By generating new points of contact between viewers and film, studios generate new revenue streams. From a critical perspective, these industrial trends require a re-evaluation of what cinephilia means. A mobile cinephile may not value the third row center seat in the theatre that Sontag coveted, but she may anxiously refresh her browser every few minutes waiting for a new clip from an unreleased film to be posted on the film's website, or she might "follow" the progress of the film's production on Twitter. The experience of mobile cinephilia may begin months before a film is released and continue for years after its last theatrical showing. The wonder of seeing the film for the first time – the pleasure described with such love and conviction by Sontag – may be a key part of her experience as a cinephile. She may, in fact, watch the film multiple times in the theatre. However, her experience will likely also involve other media platforms and other media objects.

The rest of this chapter explores the textual and extra-textual pleasures available not only to film viewers who describe themselves as cinephiles but to all film viewers. **Textual pleasures** include the experiences generated by a viewer's contact with the film itself – the stories the film presents and the style the film employs to share those stories. **Extratextual pleasures** include the experiences that extend beyond the film itself, from reading tabloid magazines to visiting a film location. These divisions are not rigid. Stardom, for example, is a cultural phenomenon that moves from the text of the film to other locations. A viewer might focus her investment in a specific star on that star's filmography, watching all of his or her films but not devoting any attention to the star's extra-textual existence (for example, ignoring tabloid photos and articles, talk show interviews, and red carpet appearances). Another viewer might focus exclusively on these extra-textual points of contact, following the coverage of the star's personal life attentively while never watching any of his or her films. The distinction between textual and extra-textual pleasures is thus very fluid. Noting the differences between them is important only in order to drawn attention to the fact that cinematic pleasure does not end when the lights go on in the theatre (if you were watching a film in a theatre in the first place).

GENRES

One of the textual pleasures of cinema is the set of expectations that viewers have regarding **film genres**. As discussed in Chapter 9's exploration of marketing, many films belong (either explicitly or subtly) to a film genre. A genre is a type or kind of film that involves a set of common **genre codes**: characters, settings, iconography, cinematography, narrative situations, and themes. In *Genre and Hollywood*, film scholar Steve Neale lists the following major Hollywood genres: action-adventure, biopics, comedy, crime (including detective films, gangster films, and suspense thrillers), epics and spectacles, horror and science fiction, musicals, social problem films, war films, Westerns, film noir, and melodrama.[7] Expanding this list to include minor genres, we might add dance films, disaster films, and children's films. To include **subgenres** of the major genres, we might add screwball comedies, romantic comedies, and slapstick comedies (without exhausting the subgenres of a single genre). And, finally, since genres exceed Hollywood taxonomies, we might add Korean melodrama, *commedia all'italiana*, and Japanese Yakuza films, to name but a few genres cultivated elsewhere.

Genres serve the interests of producers and audiences. In both large-scale and small-scale production contexts, genre films take advantage of the efficiencies of mass production and reproduction. Films within a genre share both the same narrative structures and the same visual style. A studio can easily reproduce a generic style across a set of films by relying on the same personnel and equipment. This production strategy applies not only to film studios but also to independent producers. For audiences, genres promise the linked pleasures of familiarity and repetition. A film must deliver the genre pleasures that the audience expects while simultaneously introducing new elements to the genre formula. The mixing of genre elements by producers can generate new **hybrid genres**. For example, the 2004 film *Shaun of the Dead* (Edgar Wright) was described as a horror comedy.

Film scholar Linda Williams proposes a rubric for discussing three genres that are often dismissed as "low" genres. She links horror, melodrama, and pornography together as **body genres** and explains that "the success of these genres is often measured by the degree to which the audience sensation mimics what is seen on screen."[8] Horror films provoke fear in the audience, melodramas provoke sympathy, and pornography provokes arousal. In each case, the experience of the viewer mimics the experience of one or more characters on screen. Viewers may associate the pleasure of these genres with the bodily sensations they catalyze – for example, the cathartic experience of crying while watching a melodrama. Williams notes that this pleasure is also tied to "the spectacle of a body caught in the grip of intense sensation or emotion."[9] Body genres not only provide pleasure for the individual viewer but also serve a social function. By foregrounding sex, violence, and emotion, body genres grapple with cultural anxieties about gender, sexuality, and identity. For Williams, sex, violence, and emotion are not gratuitous; rather these core elements of body genres provide an experiential and critical outlet for complicated social problems.

14.2 *Shaun of the Dead* (Edgar Wright). Courtesy of Big Talk/WT 2/The Kobal Collection.

EXERCISE

Select a film genre mentioned in this section that you know little about and watch the trailers for at least ten different films in that genre. As you watch the trailers, note the elements of each film that are featured in the trailer. You might notice details about the trailer's presentation of the film's story, characters, stars, location, dialogue, and music, to name only a few elements. After you finish watching all of the trailers, review your notes and circle the consistent features in the marketing for each film in the genre. Based on these observations, what conclusions might you draw about the genre as a whole and the pleasures it might provide?

Genre films may generate pleasures that encourage viewers to watch a film again (and again) and to seek out related media products to intensify their engagement. For example, film musicals incorporate the performances of songs that may appear in additional media forms – as singles playing on the radio or available online, as part of a movie soundtrack, and as music videos, to name only a few of the ways in which musicals travel across media. Viewers can access these songs in order to deepen their involvement with the film.

CASE STUDY: BLAXPLOITATION'S FEMALE AUDIENCES

For a brief period in the 1970s, black action films flourished in independent urban American theatres. Films in this genre incorporated elements from several other popular genres – from crime to horror – but most were loosely described as action films. They were often screened as part of a double feature with a martial arts film, linking the two genres together in American film history. These black action films or "Blaxploitation films" featured a black cast and complex funk and soul soundtracks steeped in black American musical traditions. Many black audiences found the representation of black characters as dynamic heroes and anti-heroes to be exciting and empowering.

At this point in Hollywood history, the black experience was either absent from the screen or reflected through a racist white point of view. Black audiences had watched many Hollywood films with no black actors or with black actors cast only as criminals, extras, or maids. For example, the celebrated black American actress Hattie McDaniel won an Academy Award for Best Supporting Actress in 1939 for her performance as a servant in *Gone with the Wind* (Victor Fleming). Her extensive acting filmography, including approximately one hundred roles, is catalogued on the Internet Movie Database (www. imdb.com). If you review the list of roles she played both before and after she won her Oscar, you will notice that she

14.3 Hattie McDaniel posing with her Oscar. Courtesy of The Kobal Collection.

413

continued to play maids and cooks throughout her career despite the critical acclaim her *Gone with the Wind* performance had received.

The postwar period in American cinema offered a series of more progressive representations of black American characters. This movement may be best exemplified through the acting career of Sidney Poitier who starred in dozens of films, including a string of films in the 1960s that promoted Poitier as an intelligent, charismatic, and kind leading man. In films like *Lilies of the Field* (Ralph Nelson, 1963), *To Sir, With Love* (James Clavell, 1967), and *Guess Who's Coming To Dinner* (Stanley Kramer, 1967), Poitier emerged as a leading man with an impeccable star image, on screen and off screen. Some viewers and critics, however, saw Poitier's star image as overly idealized, leaving audiences unable to relate to Poitier. This legacy provides a context for understanding why the advent of black action cinema was greeted with such enthusiasm among many black audiences. Black action films brought black actors and characters to the center of the screen and the center of the action.

Black action cinema, however, was not universally praised by black audiences. These films were called "Blaxploitation" films in reference to their low-budget "exploitation" production practices. Like other exploitation films, blaxploitation films involved sex, violence, and crime, delivering entertaining genre thrills for a very low budget. The term "blaxploitation," however, also resonated with the exploitation of stereotypes of black Americans in the films, leading some audiences and critics to lament the fact that the starring roles offered to black actors in these films were often drug dealers, prostitutes, and corrupt policemen. Pioneering blaxploitation films like *Sweet Sweetback's Baadasssss Song* (Melvin Van Peebles, 1971), *Shaft* (Gordon Parks, 1971), and *Super Fly* (Gordon Parks, 1972) featured sensationalized representations of sex and violence. These films foreground black characters, but they don't realistically portray the diverse lived experiences of black American audiences. The reception of blaxploitation films was (and is) mixed, particularly among black female audiences.

14.4 *Guess Who's Coming to Dinner* poster. Courtesy of Columbia/ The Kobal Collection.

In her book *"Baad Bitches" and Sassy Supermamas: Black Power Action Cinema*, media scholar Stephane Dunn analyzes the reception of blaxploitation films among female viewers across generations. Dunn's work relies on both critical theory and ethnographic research to produce a layered analysis of the reception of black action cinema then and now. Dunn's ethnographic analysis involves both surveys of and interviews with female viewers. She distributed a survey to black American women between the ages of 22 and 60, asking them a series of questions about their experiences watching blaxploitation films. She then hosted a series of viewing parties for black women to watch *Coffy* (Jack Hill, 1973), featuring Pam Grier, and *Cleopatra Jones* (Jack Starrett, 1973), featuring Tamara Dobson. (Important ethnographic scholarship on film audiences will be discussed at greater length in relation to identification and stardom in the following chapter.) Grier and Dobson were two of the most prolific and beloved female stars of blaxploitation cinema, and the social and political value of their overtly sexualized star images has been one of the most debated topics in discussions of blaxploitation. Summarizing the results of her research, Dunn observes:

> While the younger generation viewers tended to demonstrate less antagonism toward the explicit relationship of sex and female power drawn in the films, black women across class and age were quite savvy about recognizing how the character representations of the superheroines were shaped by, as one sister wrote, a "white man's fantasy vision" that somewhat celebrated stereotypes of black female sexuality.[10]

One viewer described her reaction to Dobson as Cleopatra Jones: "I like her look, the way she carried herself; her whole vibe is sharp to me. And she was a dark-skinned, strong, beautiful woman."[11] Dunn finds that the women she surveyed were able to recognize the disturbing gender and racial politics circulating in blaxploitation films and simultaneously to enjoy the pleasures of watching empowered (and often outrageous) black female heroines on screen. For example, in one fight scene from *Coffy*, Grier pulls a razor blade out of her afro. The representation of Grier as *Coffy* in the film's poster captures the uneasy combination of female power and female objectification that both energized and troubled audiences. Grier starred in several other blaxploitation films in the 1970s, including *Black Mama, White Mama* (Eddie Romero, 1973), *Scream, Blacula Scream* (Bob Kelljan, 1973), and *Foxy Brown* (Jack Hill, 1974). These titles offer a hint of the pleasures and problems associated with these films and with Grier's star image. Her star image today is also tied to her role in the US television series *The L Word* (2004–2009), among other performances, but her association with blaxploitation films remains an important element of her stardom.

The pleasures of watching blaxploitation films were amplified for many viewers by the experience of watching these films in urban theatres largely populated by other black viewers. Dunn focuses on viewers' accounts of watching these films as part of an urban black audience. These viewing experiences often involved an active call-and-response engagement with the film, with audiences talking back to the screen. Dunn shares one woman's memory of sneaking into blaxploitation films with her friends against her parents' wishes: "There'd be a bunch of black people laughing and talking, both to each other and the people on screen. We hollered right along with them and had a good time."[12] These memories demonstrate the value of using ethnographic research to study audiences as a viewing public. The pleasures of many film experiences obtain from their exhibition contexts rather than merely from the film text. Dunn's insights about the complicated pleasures produced by blaxploitation films for female viewers rely on her engagement with viewers; a textual analysis of the films wouldn't yield the challenging conclusions she presents.

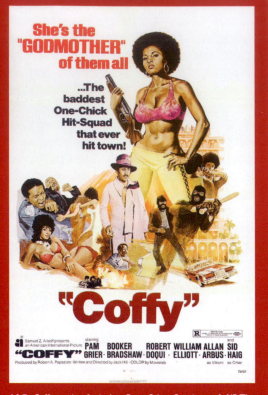

14.5 *Coffy* poster featuring Pam Grier. Courtesy of AIP/The Kobal Collection.

STARDOM

Stars are a key element in the economics of cinema, and they are also one of the main visual and cultural attractions for film audiences. Stars are thus positioned at the intersection of two related forms of investment: filmmakers invest in stars as capital assets that will help them to market their films and generate profits, and fans invest in stars as the objects of their desires. It might at first seem logical to describe the producer's investment in stars as financial and the fan's investment in stars as emotional, but this section will explain that filmmakers and fans invest both financially *and* emotionally in stars.

One of the most influential early analyses of stardom as an industrial and cultural phenomenon is Richard Dyer's book *Stars*, originally published in 1979. Dyer unpacks the production of star images by Hollywood and the reception of those star images by fans. One of the keys to Dyer's analysis is its insistence that stars are "representations of people. Thus they relate to ideas about what people are (or are supposed to be) like. However, unlike characters in stories, stars are also real people."[13] This observation may at first seem very obvious. We know that the actor Javier Bardem is not the painter Juan Antonio in *Vicky Cristina Barcelona* (Woody Allen, 2008) or the Cuban poet and novelist Reinaldo Arenas in *Before Night Falls* (Julian Schnabel, 2000) or the murderer Anton Chigurh in *No Country for Old Men* (Joel and Ethan Coen 2007). We recognize that these are characters (or, in the case of Reinaldo Arenas, a character based on a real person), and we do not conflate the actor with the character. However, when actors frequently play characters with similar qualities, we may begin to ascribe the qualities of the characters to the actors. One of the most famous examples of this phenomenon is the reception of the Hollywood actor John Wayne. Wayne appeared in dozens of Westerns and war films during his long career. Often playing sheriffs and military officers, Wayne developed a screen persona associated with traditional expressions of authority, morality and masculinity. Over time, audiences associated these qualities with Wayne himself. Bardem's more eclectic filmography does not lend itself to similarly consistent associations.

The pleasures associated with the performances of stars vary based on performance styles. Barry King describes the two different approaches to film performance represented by Bardem and Wayne respectively as **impersonation** and **personification**. Impersonation dictates that the "'real' personality of the actor should disappear into the part," while personification suggests that the "range of the actor is limited to parts consonant with his or her personality."[14] King cautions that these two different performance styles should not be linked to an assessment of a star's talent:

> [T]he process of character portrayal in film, whether angled towards impersonation or personification, takes on a quasi-automatic form in which the actor's performance in part originates in his or her behavior and in part the action of the filmic apparatus, including in the latter lighting and camera deployment. In other words, the projection of interiority becomes less and less the provenance of the actor and more and more a property emerging from directorial or editorial decision.[15]

14.6 Javier Bardem as Anton Chigurh in *No Country for Old Men*. Courtesy of Paramount/Miramax/The Kobal Collection.

King's assertion that all film performances rely in part on the interventions of directors, editors, and the technology of cinema acknowledges the ways that film performances and star images are constructed collaboratively.

King's model of stardom in relation to types of performance develops Dyer's claim that stars are "representations of people." Fans may associate Wayne with characters like Sheriff John Chance in *Rio Bravo* (Howard Hawks, 1959), but they do not believe that Wayne *is* Chance. The second part of Dyer's claim is more difficult to unpack: stars are "representations of people [...] and also real people." Of course, Javier Bardem is a real person. We can read about his life in magazine and newspaper articles, listen to him discuss his experiences on and off set during radio and television interviews, and watch him arrive at film premieres. No one disputes that Javier Bardem exists. The critical complication stems from the fact that viewers may confuse the **star image** of Javier Bardem with the real person. Dyer's detailed analysis of stardom dwells on the production of star images, a constellation of meanings and associations that may share many qualities and values with the real person on which the image is based, but may also incorporate aspects of the star's screen performance and other elements implanted for promotional purposes. The film industry invests considerable time and money in the production of popular star images, and fans generate a return on those investments by spending money on the films, magazines, and other commodities that prominently feature their favorite stars.

Dyer provides a helpful model for analyzing the pleasure that stardom provides for film viewers, beginning with the claim, "Stardom is an image of the way stars live."[16] This formulation stresses the status of stardom as a representation. Dyer's analysis focuses on five elements of stardom that drive our fascination with stars: consumption, success, ordinariness, decline, and love. According to Dyer, **conspicuous consumption** is central to the representation of stars' lifestyles. Conspicuous consumption is "the way by which the wealthy display the fact that they are wealthy."[17] Fashion (which will be discussed in detail in the following section) is a crucial element of conspicuous consumption. By wearing elaborate clothes that make it impossible to work, stars (particularly female stars) display the fact that they do not have to work (ignoring the fact that both acting and the other practices associated with stardom – including interviews, photo shoots, and preparation for performances – are forms of labor). Stardom has generated many **ancillary industries** that support conspicuous consumption. Stars commission **stylists** to choose their wardrobes, **agents** to negotiate their product endorsements, and **publicists** to plan flattering media coverage that protects their star images.

The second prong of stardom is success. Dyer notes that stardom involves the simultaneous maintenance of several contradictory myths of success: "that ordinariness is the hallmark of the star; that the system rewards talent and 'specialness;' that luck, 'breaks,' which may happen to anyone typify the career of the star; and that hard work and professionalism are necessary for stardom."[18] These myths of success intersect with the third dimension of stardom: ordinariness. Representations of stardom suggest that anyone can become a star *and* that stars are magical. In other words, we are asked to believe that stars are ordinary *and* that stars are extraordinary. The coverage of stars in tabloid magazines (and in other popular media) reinforces these contradictions. In the same tabloid issue, you might find a feature called "Stars: They're Just Like Us!" that includes photos of deglamorized stars: wearing casual clothes and no make-up, stars buy groceries, jog in the park, walk their dogs, and do many of the other things that non-stars do every day. A few pages later the same issue might feature photos of the same stars walking down a red carpet at a film premiere wearing tuxedos and gowns.

The pleasures circulated by tabloid magazines are even more complicated than the comparison of these two staple tabloid features suggests. While fans may revel in the celebratory coverage of a star's rags-to-riches rise to fame or their marriage to another star or their recent critical acclaim for a film role, fans also enjoy reading about stars' falls from grace. The fourth element of Dyer's model is decline. Dyer notes that the public fascination with the sordid side of stardom dates back to the 1930s when fan magazines published stories like "Tragic Mansions" with the subheading "the strange story of heartbreak houses in heartbreak town." Avant-garde filmmaker Kenneth Anger's 1965 book *Hollywood Babylon* compiles anecdotes and legends about Hollywood stars from the silent period through the 1960s, including Fatty Arbuckle, Lana Turner, Charlie Chaplin, and Marilyn Monroe. The book has been criticized for its factual inaccuracies and its inclusion of graphic images, but it captures the lurid fascination with the decadence, decline, and death of film stars.

The fifth and final dimension of stardom that Dyer discusses is love. Dyer observes that while the romantic relationships of stars (their courtships, their weddings, and their children) are a common focus in the public representation of stardom, the problems of love are discussed just as frequently. Like characters in television soap operas, stars appear to have no problems to face other than the problems of love. The representation of stardom thus serves as an occasion to explore "the problems posed by notions of romance and passion within the institution of compulsory heterosexual monogamy."[19]

EXERCISE

Buy a tabloid entertainment magazine (or browse one at a store). As you review the headlines, articles and photographs, note the elements of stardom from Dyer's framework that you recognize in the coverage of film stars. (Many tabloids will include features about other celebrities – for example, reality television stars, politicians, and musicians. For the purpose of this exercise, it is more valuable to focus on the representation of film stars.)

- How are individual star images presented?
- What differences do you notice between the presentation of female star images and the presentation of male star images?
- How is the experience of stardom presented?
- What pleasures does the tabloid promise its readers?
- What pleasures do you experience?

Dyer's analysis of stardom provides a useful model for understanding both the production and the consumption of stardom. Stars provide an outlet for the desires of fans, and the industrial and cultural production of stardom (and of individual star images) in turn produces those desires. While our analysis of stardom has focused on the circuit of images and ideas about stars that connect individual films with other cultural representations and experiences, one of the most important sites of cinematic pleasure is the cinematic image. The star system has been linked with the development of the close-up as an element of cinematic grammar. The close-up allows the viewer to contemplate and enjoy the beauty of a star's face. Consider this description by Roland Barthes of the face of Greta Garbo:

> Garbo still belongs to that moment in cinema when capturing the human face still plunged audiences into the deepest ecstasy, when one literally lost oneself in a human image as one would in a philtre [a love potion], when the face represented a kind of absolute state of flesh which could be neither reached nor renounced.[20]

You may recognize in this description of losing "oneself in a human image" a resonance with Sontag's description of being "physically overwhelmed by the image" of cinema. The presentation of a star's face through a close-up is an important site of cinephilia.

All of the stars mentioned above could be described as **transnational stars**. Garbo was a Swedish actress who received a contract from the Hollywood studio MGM and starred in a series of successful silent films before appearing in her first "talkie" *Anna Christie* (Clarence Brown, 1930) and revealing her signature accented English to adoring audiences throughout the world. Bardem is a Spanish actor who has appeared in both Spanish and Hollywood films, moving comfortably between Spanish, English, and multilingual films. Wayne was recognized as one of the most popular film stars in the world in the 1950s in spite of his association with American militarism. Film scholars Russell Meeuf and Raphael Raphael note that:

> since the early 1900s, with the emergence of film stars and the modern star system as we know it, the culture of celebrity has always been transnational, marked not simply by Hollywood stars crisscrossing the globe as part of the US industry's international dominance but by a variety of transnational flows as international film industries sought to market their films abroad and as performers followed their popularity into new markets and industries.[21]

Transnational stardom takes several forms: (1) the global popularity of stars such as Arnold Schwarzenegger and Jackie Chan whose star images can be used to market films in all global film regions; (2) the transnational migration of a star to another film industry such as the Japanese actor Sessue Hayakawa's successful career as a silent film actor in Hollywood; (3) and the cultivation of multilingual stardom such as the career of Penélope Cruz who performs in Spanish, English, and Italian. Hollywood star images have more global mobility than star images produced in other film industries because of the distribution resources of Hollywood studios, but star images circulate transnationally outside Hollywood networks. The patterns of new media distribution discussed in Chapter 10, "Distribution," have enabled the transnational distribution of star images and have opened new opportunities for the cinematic pleasures of stardom across borders.

EXTRA-TEXTUAL PLEASURES

Fashion and beauty

Richard Dyer describes stars as idols of consumption that everyone in society can emulate through their habits as consumers. Dyer explains, "They may spend more than the average person, but nonetheless they can be on a smaller scale, imitated."[22] Few people can afford to buy the homes, cars and other grand accoutrements of celebrity that the most successful film stars own. The marketing of fashion and

14.7 Maggie Cheung featured in an advertisement for Olay Regenerist face cream.

beauty products provides consumers with an opportunity to participate in the glamor of celebrity in a reduced form (and at a reduced price.) The one-of-a-kind couture dresses made for female stars to wear at high-profile events will be reproduced as ready-to-wear garments and marketed to the masses within months or even weeks. The beauty products endorsed by stars are usually even more affordable for film fans. The Olay advertisement above uses a close-up of Hong Kong film star Maggie Cheung to market a face cream. In this image, Cheung's flawless face glows. A reader may be inspired to buy the Olay product or may simply take pleasure in the perfection of the close-up. The pleasures of identification with stars through consumption will be discussed in the following chapter. Below we will review briefly the pleasures of fashion and beauty within the cinematic image.

Film scholar Stella Bruzzi argues that iconic clothes can "disrupt the normative reality" of a film.[23] These garments become the focus of our visual pleasure, overwhelming our attention and distracting us from our engagement with the film's narrative. Building on this critical recognition of the ability of a costume to emerge as a "visual exclamation point" in a film, film scholar Jane Gaines devotes an entire essay to the analysis of a single costume: the seductress dress designed by Gilbert Adrian for the actress Kay Johnson in Cecil B. DeMille's *Madam Satan* (1930). In *Madam Satan*, Johnson plays Angela Brooks, a woman who plots to seduce her own unfaithful husband at a masquerade party by wearing a bewitching dress. The dress (pictured in the figure below) seduces Mr Brooks and the film viewer. Gaines comments, "*Madam Satan* presents us with a costume that consumes our seeing. Within seduction scenes all vectors direct our attention toward what is transpiring on the body as defined by the dress that sculpts out the space on the screen."[24] The costume "consumes" our seeing, echoing the language of being "lost" in or "kidnapped" by the cinematic image introduced by Sontag and Barthes.

14.8 Gilbert Adrian's *Madam Satan* seductress dress. Courtesy of MGM/The Kobal Collection.

While classical set and costume design principles steered designers toward realistic designs that would not compete with the story or the stars' performances, Adrian's design in *Madam Satan* becomes the visual focal point of the film. Describing the dress, Gaines emphasizes that its design provokes the viewer's desire to analyze it:

> since this is a dress that has been literally sliced open up the front in such a way that the viewer is invited to see into it … to imagine it from the inside out (as worn) as well as from the outside in (as seen).[25]

The dress promotes two forms of cinematic pleasure – the pleasure of observing the dress and the pleasure of analyzing the dress.

Technophilia

Reports of cinema's death may have been greatly exaggerated, but the many mutations of cinema traced in this book suggest that we must acknowledge the replacement of the pleasures of third row center cinephilia with multiple versions of cinephilia. **Technophilia** is a subset of cinephilia that involves a passionate attachment to the technologies and technological artifacts of cinema, from Arriflex cameras to laser discs to home theatre installations. In contemporary film culture, multiple film technologies exist side by side, so technophiles may customize their cinematic pleasures, particularly in domestic viewing spaces.

The advent of digital cinema has produced a new matrix of technological pleasures. Film scholar Chuck Tryon outlines the pleasures associated with digital cinema. In *Reinventing Cinema: Movies in the Age of Media Convergence*, Tryon identifies several nodal points of digital cinema: DVD culture, digital effects, digital projection, digital distribution, blogging, and remix culture. Tryon investigates the ways in which media industries have framed technological innovations for consumers and the ways in which consumers use (and reframe) those technologies. The introduction of digital effects and digital projection has produced both excitement about the immersive possibilities of digital media and anxieties about the ways in which "digital technologies will transform the medium of film and the construction of identity."[26]

Tryon quotes from an interview in *Wired* magazine with director Steven Spielberg before the release of his film *Minority Report* (2002):

> Someday the entire motion picture may take place inside the mind, and it will be the most internal experience anyone can have: being told a story with your eyes closed but you see and smell and feel and interact with the story.[27]

Spielberg's futuristic vision may prompt dystopian fears or utopian fantasies, depending on the disposition of the reader. The unique aesthetic properties of film as a medium are an integral part of the cinephilia described by Sontag, Barthes, and many other critics, scholars, and fans. Digital cinema threatens not only the medium of film but also the collective experience of cinema; the cinematic experience that Spielberg envisions is completely, radically individualized, far beyond the individualization of watching a film on a mobile phone. Tryon's analysis captures the cultural ambivalence generated by technological innovations in film culture. The inventions of digital cinema – both fully realized inventions like digital projection and abstract speculations like Spielberg's internal projection – may provoke anxiety, but they are also a source of pleasure as commodities and fantasies.

Film tourism

The commodities that circulate to extend cinematic pleasure beyond the screen include not only products but also experiences. Film tourism has emerged as one of the experiences that filmgoers seek to deepen their connection with a film or a set of films. Film tourism markets film locations as tourist destinations. From organized tours of Hollywood film studios to casual visits to the "Rocky Steps" at the Philadelphia Museum of Art, featured in the original *Rocky* (John Avildsen, 1971), tourists may include film-related destinations in their travels. In recent years, film tourism has expanded beyond Los Angeles and scattered sites like the Rocky Steps to involve entire towns and even entire countries, as in the tourism encouraged by New Zealand in relation to the *Lord of the Rings* film franchise (discussed in detail in Chapter 6, "Starting points"). Organized film tourism on this scale leverages the popularity of locations featured in blockbuster films to promote film-themed vacations. Film tourism includes location tours, museum exhibitions, and ancillary tourist attractions (like local restaurants that feature film-related menu items and merchandise). Film tourism transforms the film audience into global tourists, promising fans intimate and immersive access to a film by visiting the locations where the film was shot. The case study on "Global film locations" provides a tour of some of the most successful sites of contemporary film tourism.

CASE STUDY: GLOBAL FILM LOCATIONS

Forks, Washington, USA

The real site for the fictional world of the *Twilight* franchise (the four books written by Stephenie Meyer and the films they have inspired), Forks, Washington is a very small town. With approximately 3,500 permanent residents, the self-described "rainiest town in the contiguous United States" has enjoyed a huge tourism boom since the release of the *Twilight* films: *Twilight* (Catherine Hardwicke, 2008), *The Twilight Saga: New Moon* (Chris Weitz, 2009), *The Twilight Saga: Eclipse* (David Slade, 2010), *The Twilight Saga: Breaking Dawn – Part I* (Bill Condon, 2011), and *The Twilight Saga: Breaking Dawn – Part II* (Bill Condon, 2012). The town's website (www.forkswa.com/twilight) estimates a 1000 per cent increase in hotel reservations. *Twilight* fans flock to rainy Forks to eat a "Bella Burger" at Sully's Drive-In (named for the franchise's heroine) and to stay in one of the black-and-red vampire-themed rooms at the Dew Drop Inn. Despite the fact that most of the filming for the *Twilight* movies was completed in other locations in the region, the sleepy lumber town of Forks seduces *Twilight* fans by promising to immerse them in the fictional world of the films. The *Twilight* audience includes both male and female viewers across generations. The town of Forks, however, imagines its film tourists as (young and old) women. Their website even includes a "Guy's List" of "manly" things for male tourists to do in Forks while their female companions explore the world of *Twilight*. Film tourism in Forks points to both the potential for location marketing and merchandising to film audiences and the flawed assumptions about audiences that often underlie those efforts.

Stockholm, Sweden

The city of Stockholm has tried to exploit the popularity of Stieg Larsson's Millennium Trilogy. The three novels inspired a set of Swedish films made for television and theatrical release in 2009 – *The Girl with the Dragon Tattoo* (Niels Arden Oplev), *The Girl who Played with Fire* (Daniel Alfredson), and *The Girl who Kicked the Hornet's Nest* (Daniel Alfredson) – and the Hollywood adaptation of *The Girl with the Dragon Tattoo* (2011) directed by David Fincher. Unlike the quaint charms of Forks, Washington, the Stockholm featured in the Millennium Trilogy is a dark, sordid place. In order to counter that depiction, Stockholm's film tourism centers its appeal to fans on the protagonist Lisbeth Salander's various haunts in the film. Fans can join a walking tour of Stockholm that ends at a special Millennium Exhibition at the Stockholm City Museum and stop along the way at the pubs and cafés Lisbeth frequents and the apartments where she lives. This instance of film tourism ties film locations to a specific character. The strategy allows Stockholm to take advantage of the popularity of the novels and films without risking a negative association between the city and the graphic crimes that preoccupy the trilogy.

Odessa, Ukraine

One of the most globally recognizable symbols of the city of Odessa is the "Odessa Steps." This enormous staircase presents two optical illusions for visitors. From the top, the steps are invisible, and viewers can only see the landings below; from the bottom, the landings are invisible, and viewers can only see the steps above. The steps were featured in a famous sequence from *The Battleship Potemkin* (Sergei Eisenstein, 1925), in which they are the site of the massacre of civilians by Tsarist soldiers. The sequence is one of the most celebrated and cited examples of Eisenstein's theory of montage. With homages to the scene appearing in several films, including Brian De Palma's *The Untouchables* (1982), viewers who have not seen *The Battleship Potemkin* may still recognize the suspenseful image of the baby carriage's perilous descent down the stairs in the middle of the massacre. The status of this sequence as a milestone in film history adds interest to the Primorsky Stairs, as they are officially called after having been referred to as the Potemkin Stairs until Ukraine gained independence from the Soviet Union. While the grandness of the stairs and the novelty of the optical illusions they generate would (and do) compel tourists to visit even without the connection to Eisenstein's film, the cinematic reference intensifies and expands their appeal.

14.9 Tourists at the Odessa Steps in Odessa, Ukraine. © Dean Conger/Corbis.

14.10 The Odessa Steps sequence in *The Battleship Potemkin*. Courtesy of Goskino/The Kobal Collection.

Transylvania County, North Carolina, USA

The release of the first film in the *Hunger Games* trilogy (based on the series of young adult novels by Suzanne Collins) prompted a wave of film tourism promotions in Asheville, North Carolina and the surrounding counties where the film was shot. The range of fan experiences available to *Hunger Games* film tourists is much more immersive than the examples discussed above. The "Movie Star Adventure and Survival Package" invites fans to stay at the Hotel Indigo in Asheville, where the actors in the first film stayed and to enjoy excursions to the local restaurants and cafés where the actors dined. These off-screen vicarious pleasures focus on the film's stars rather than on the locations depicted in the films. The *Hunger Games* "Adventure Weekend" takes a different approach. Fans tour the Dupont State Recreational Forest, where many scenes were shot, before plunging into a detailed simulation of the events depicted in the film. After participating in a lottery, the adventure tourists take a series of survival classes before competing in a mock Hunger Games event.

Tozeur, Tunisia

George Lucas chose the Tunisian Sahara desert as the location for the planet Tatooine, the childhood home of Anakin Skywalker or Darth Vader in the *Star Wars* films. In both *Star Wars: Episode I – The Phantom Menace* (1999) and *Star Wars: Episode II – Attack of the Clones*

(2002), the desert outside Tozeur, Tunisia serves as the backdrop for the construction of Skywalker's childhood village of Mos Espa, a series of small buildings. The set remains intact as a tourist destination, with an estimated 100,000 visitors traveling to Tunisia to tour the site each year. In 2013, however, news broke that a large sand dune is traveling towards the set at a rate of 4cm per day. Scientists speculate that if the set is not moved to a secure location, the dune will soon destroy it, mirroring the danger the desert posed to the inhabitants of Tatooine in the *Star Wars* films. Fans of the film franchise have been urged to travel to Tunisia as soon as possible so that they can see the site while it still exists.

14.11 The Tunisian desert in *Star Wars*. Courtesy of Lucasfilm/20th Century Fox/Kobal Collection.

EXERCISE

Select one of your favorite films, and plan a tour linked to the film. First, search online to see if there are already tourism packages linked to it. If so, analyze the opportunities that are available.

- Are they linked to the locations where the film was shot; the locations that the film represents; stars or characters featured in the film?
- What pleasures do the tours promise?
- If you had the time and the means, would you visit these locations? Why or why not?

If you can't find any existing tours affiliated with the film, plan one.

- What locations would you feature?

- How would you market the location to consumers?
- Would the tour be of interest only to devoted fans of the film or would your tour appeal to a broader population?
- Would you design experiences for visitors beyond providing them access to the location?

If it is difficult to imagine a film tour associated with the film you selected, consider the reasons for that difficulty. What makes some film locations more suitable for tourism than others?

SUMMARY

Cinema promises a range of pleasures to its viewers, from the pleasures derived from the familiarity of genre conventions to the pleasures derived from browsing a fashion magazine featuring a beloved star. Cinema's pleasures circulate both within the filmic text, through visual style and narrative structure, and beyond the text, through the circulation of commodities and experiences that extend the viewer's engagement with the film. The star system produces star images that allow viewers to enjoy interactions with their favorite stars both through their cinematic performances and in their extra-textual appearances in magazines, on red carpets, in television interviews, and in other venues. Extra-textual pleasures include fashion, technophilia, and film tourism. The cinematic pleasures discussed in this chapter are only a few of the pleasures generated by film; these examples serve as starting points for analyzing film's pleasures.

FURTHER READING

Dyer, Richard. *Stars*. London: British Film Institute, 1979.

Dyer's analysis of stardom provides a critical foundation for star studies as a field and for the close reading of star images in any scholarly context. Dyer examines the economic, social and ideological underpinnings of stardom. *Stars* explains the ways in which star images are produced and consumed, and the ways in which stars as signs are linked to characters and performance styles. Dyer limits his analysis to Hollywood stars, including Jane Fonda, Marlon Brando, and Marilyn Monroe, but many features of his analytical model may be applied to the analysis of star images in other industrial contexts.

Gaines, Jane and Herzog, Charlotte (eds). *Fabrications: Costume and the Female Body*. London: Routledge, 1990.

This important collection of essays about screen fashion provides an overview of the ways in which cultural studies, film studies and feminist theory converge in the analysis of clothing. Focusing on fashion in relation to stardom, set design, consumer culture and sexuality, among other topics, this book investigates the pleasures of film fashion with close readings that reproduce those pleasures. The essay by Gaylyn Studlar on costuming and the star image of Marlene Dietrich, and the essay by Jane Gaines on costume and narrative are particularly relevant to the discussion of cinematic pleasure in this chapter.

Tryon, Chuck. *Reinventing Cinema: Movies in the Age of Media Convergence*. New Brunswick: Rutgers University Press, 2009.

Reinventing Cinema surveys the forms of contemporary cinephilia that have been produced by media convergence. Tryon explores the consequences of the increased mobility of films (across multiple platforms and screens) and the increased participation of viewers in film culture (from blogging to trailer mash-ups). Tryon focuses on media convergence in the United States, but his analysis addresses the globalized context of the distribution and reception of film.

FILMS REFERENCED IN CHAPTER FOURTEEN

Anna Christie (Clarence Brown, 1930)

The Battleship Potemkin (Sergei Eisenstein, 1925)

Before Night Falls (Julian Schnabel, 2000)

Black Mama, White Mama (Eddie Romero, 1973)

Cave of Forgotten Dreams (Werner Herzog, 2010)

Cleopatra Jones (Jack Starrett, 1973)

Coffy (Jack Hill, 1973)

Dracula A.D. 1972 (Alan Gibson, 1972)

Duel in the Sun (King Vidor, 1946)

The Flower of My Secret (Pedro Almodóvar, 1995)

Foxy Brown (Jack Hill, 1974)

The Girl who Kicked the Hornet's Nest (Daniel Alfredson, 2009)

The Girl who Played with Fire (Daniel Alfredson, 2009)

The Girl with the Dragon Tattoo (Niels Arden Oplev, 2009)

The Girl with the Dragon Tattoo (David Fincher, 2011)

The Golden Voyage of Sinbad (Gordon Hessler, 1973)

Gone with the Wind (Victor Fleming, 1939)

Guess Who's Coming To Dinner (Stanley Kramer, 1967)

Hugo (Martin Scorsese, 2011)

In the Cut (Jane Campion, 2003)

The Last Wave (Peter Weir, 1977)

Lilies of the Field (Ralph Nelson, 1963)

Loves of a Blonde (Milos Forman, 1965)

Madam Satan (Cecil B. DeMille, 1930)

Magnolia (Paul Thomas Anderson, 1999)

Minority Report (Steven Spielberg, 2002)

Nashville (Robert Altman, 1975)

No Country for Old Men (Joel and Ethan Coen 2007)

The Omega Man (Boris Sagal, 1971)

The Passion of Joan of Arc (Carl Dreyer, 1927)

Rio Bravo (Howard Hawks, 1959)

Rocky (John Avildsen, 1971)

Scream, Blacula, Scream (Bob Kelljan, 1973)

Shaft (Gordon Parks, 1971)

Shaun of the Dead (Edgar Wright, 2004)

Singin' in the Rain (Stanley Donen, 1952)

Smiles of a Summer Night (Ingmar Bergman, 1955)

Star Wars: Episode I – The Phantom Menace (George Lucas, 1999)

Star Wars: Episode II – Attack of the Clones (George Lucas, 2002)

Super Fly (Gordon Parks, 1972)

Sweet Sweetback's Baadasssss Song (Melvin Van Peebles, 1971)

To Sir, With Love (James Clavell, 1967)

Twilight (Catherine Hardwicke, 2008)

The Twilight Saga: Breaking Dawn – Part I (Bill Condon, 2011)

The Twilight Saga: Breaking Dawn – Part II (Bill Condon, 2012)

The Twilight Saga: Eclipse (David Slade, 2010)

The Twilight Saga: New Moon (Chris Weitz, 2009)

The Untouchables (Brian De Palma,1982)

Vicky Cristina Barcelona (Woody Allen, 2008)

War of the Gargantuas (Ishirô Honda, 1966)

The Wicker Man (Robin Hardy, 1973)

The Women (George Cukor, 1939)

 NOTES

1 http://www.acmi.net.au/desert_island_flicks_revealed.htm, accessed 1 October 2013.

2 Susan Sontag, "The Decay of Cinema," the *New York Times*, 25 Februrary 1996, http://www.nytimes.com/books/00/03/12/specials/sontag-cinema.html, accessed 1 October 2013.

3 Sontag.

4 Barbara Klinger, *Beyond the Multiplex: Cinema, New Technologies, and the Home* (Berkeley: University of California Press, 2006), 55.

5 Klinger, 75.

6 Klinger, 89.

7 Steve Neale, *Genre and Hollywood* (London: Routledge, 2000).

8 Linda Williams, "Film Bodies: Gender, Genre, and Excess," *Film Quarterly* 44(4) (1991): 4.

9 Williams, 4.

10 Stephane Dunn, *"Baad Bitches" and Sassy Supermamas: Black Power Action Cinema* (Champaign: University of Illinois Press, 2008), 15.

11 Dunn, 13.

12 Dunn, 20.

13 Richard Dyer, *Stars* (London: British Film Institute, 1998), 20.

14 Barry King, "Articulating Stardom," in Christine Gledhill (ed.), *Stardom: Industry of Desire* (London: Routledge, 1991), 168.

15 King, 177.

16 Dyer, 35.

17 Dyer, 38.

18 Dyer, 42.

19 Dyer, 46.

20 Roland Barthes, "The Face of Garbo," in Gerald Mast and Marshall Cohen (eds), *Film Theory and Criticism* (New York: Oxford University Press, 1985), 650.

21 Russell Meeuf and Raphael Raphael (eds), *Transnational Stardom: International Celebrity in Film and Popular Culture* (New York: Palgrave Macmillan, 2013), 7.

22 Dyer, 39.

23 Stella Bruzzi, *Undressing Cinema: Clothing and Identity in the Movies* (London: Routledge, 1997), 17.

24 Jane Gaines, "On Wearing the Film: *Madam Satan* (1930)," in Stella Bruzzi and Pamela Church Gibson (eds), *Fashion Cultures: Theories, Explorations, and Analysis* (London: Routledge, 2000), 167.

25 Gaines, 173.

26 Chuck Tryon, *Reinventing Cinema: Movies in the Age of Media Convergence* (New Brunswick: Rutgers University Press, 2009), 42.

27 Quoted in Tryon, 43.

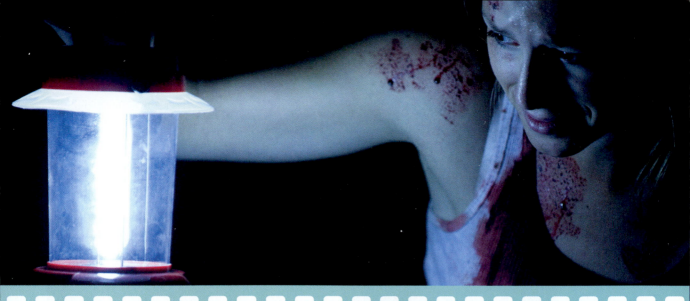

CHAPTER FIFTEEN
IDENTIFICATION AND IDENTITY

The Japanese horror film *Ringu* (Hideo Nakata, 1998) was adapted from Koji Suzuki's 1991 novel of the same name. In the movie, a young female journalist called Reiko Asakawa (played by Nanako Matsushima) explores a string of deaths which turn out to have been caused by supernatural forces. Each victim dies seven days after watching a cursed videotape. Reiko finds the tape and watches it; a day later, so does her ex-husband Ryuji (Hiroyuki Sanada). Near the film's end, after Reiko and Ryuji believe they have broken the curse, Ryuji is at home alone. His television switches itself on. A monstrous ghost crawls out of the TV, and advances across the floor towards him.

At this point, near the film's conclusion, it is safe to say that the people who made the film want audiences to be emotionally involved – specifically, to experience fear. Ryuji, seeing the ghost crawl through his TV screen, is so scared that he has a heart attack and dies. Whilst Hideo Nakata presumably did not want the audience of his film to die of fright, this scene should terrify viewers. But how exactly does this work? Watching this film, whether in a cinema, on a television, or by some other means, the audience member is most likely stationary, seated, and in a relatively safe environment, possibly accompanied by other people. The images on the screen are not real; they were fabricated in order to tell this distracting story. Does this mean that the experience of fear at a horror film is not "real" fear? Further, how might the viewer's emotional response be influenced by factors that could connect them to, or separate them from, what is portrayed on screen? For instance, would young Japanese men – those who are the same sex and a similar age to Ryuji – be more susceptible to the film's effects, especially the impact of this sequence? Might an older female viewer who is not from Japan and who does not speak

Japanese be scared to an equivalent degree, and in a similar manner, to a younger Japanese man watching the film? During the film's narrative, Reiko serves as the protagonist, and she is in danger from the curse. Are viewers scared for her – and then, later, also scared for Ryuji? Does the emotional reaction to the film in fact have nothing to do with the identity of specific characters, the identity of the viewer, and whether or not the latter identifies with the former?

15.1 *Ringu* (Hideo Nakata, 1998). Courtesy of Omega/Kadokawa/The Kobal Collection.

WHAT WE WILL DO IN THIS CHAPTER

This chapter explores the notion of identification, the ways in which this is related to identity, and how these affect our relationship to cinema. The chapter is divided into three main sections.

- In the first, we introduce a number of theoretical writings that propose models and taxonomies of identification. Beginning from a "folk model" understanding, we consider several alternative conceptions of how identification between spectators and cinema may operate.
- In the next section, we look at how the models of identification discussed in the first section might work in practice. We do this by examining accounts of film spectators and their

investments in particular actors and genres. Our discussion also takes into consideration how group identity formation may take shape around, and in relation to, cinema viewing through such practices as ritual film consumption and film club membership.

- In the third and final section of the chapter, we turn our attention to the notion of identity. We begin to problematize the two key concepts at the heart of this chapter, "identity" and "identification." We outline accounts of identification provided by feminist film theory, and the particular challenges that these pose. Our attention then turns to alternative forms of identification, in particular those experienced or constructed by minority and resistant audiences. Here, we outline the affective and mental labor involved in such tactics as "reading against the grain" – that is, imagining different ways into a film's content.

BY THE END OF CHAPTER 15 YOU SHOULD BE ABLE TO

- Outline theoretical understandings of how identification in the cinema works.
- Provide practical examples of identification in operation.
- Discuss the relationship between identity and identification.
- Identify audience tactics that may be employed to forge identification with a film's content.

THEORIZING IDENTIFICATION IN THE CINEMA

Identification, of course, is not solely something that happens in relation to cinema. But the concept is a crucial one for understanding audience engagement with individual films, stars, and genres. The concept of identification in relation to film audiences has been explored in depth by a number of different writers. In this first part of the chapter, we will look in detail at arguments made by four key authors: Christian Metz, Noël Carroll, Carol Clover, and Murray Smith. In their writing, each offers complex and challenging perspectives on this topic.

Before turning to the opinions of these writers in detail, it is worth drawing attention to what Smith calls the "folk model" of how spectators respond to films. This is the "common sense" understanding of how identification works. Smith expresses it as follows:

> We watch a film, and find ourselves becoming attached to a particular character or characters on the basis of values or qualities roughly congruent with those we possess, or those that we wish to possess, and experience vicariously the emotional experiences of the character: we identify with the character.[1]

This is a valuable starting point. Here, identification is rooted in one of two relations to characters on a screen: we identify with someone who is like us, or with someone whom we desire to be like. These are quite different relationships: one of equivalence, and one of aspiration. In the former, our identity matches, to some degree, that of the character on screen; in the latter, though there may also be some match, our identity is notably distinct from the character. In both cases, however, the emotional ups and downs of the character are experienced, by proxy, by the viewer — and it is this relationship that we think of as identification.

The distinction between relationships of "equivalence" and "aspiration" is found throughout the literature on cinema and identification. You may find it useful to pause here and think about your own experience. How are certain actors and/or stars constructed as more "ordinary," more "everyday," than others? How does this affect your relationship to them? Think of the last few films that you have seen. Which characters were positioned as ideals, figures of aspiration? Film stars (as opposed to film actors) are often perceived as set apart due to their physical beauty, their charisma, or other such factors. Can "stars" also play "ordinary people"? Do different sorts of cinema – commercial narrative features, lower-budgeted independent titles, documentaries, and so on – feature more or less of certain types of characters, affecting the ways in which audiences identify and engage?

Smith raises immediate concerns about the "folk model" of identification. It seems to suggest that, when we watch a film, we forge a singular and unbroken relationship with one character. The "folk model" does not account for how perceiving the existence of a character might develop into an affective or emotional relationship with that character. And it seems to suggest that "identification" is an "on/off" response, in which we either identify with a particular character or do not. Perhaps identification actually exists on a sliding scale, occurring with different levels of intensity. In summary, the model is too simplistic. More detailed and complex models are needed – and these are provided by Metz, Carroll, Clover, and Smith (amongst others).

A key figure in the history of film studies, the French theorist Christian Metz (1931–1993) used ideas from psychoanalysis and semiotics in order to try to understand cinema. Over several pages in his book *Psychoanalysis and Cinema: The Imaginary Signifer*, first published in French in 1977, Metz discusses various forms of identification that happen when a spectator watches a film. Metz noted that audience identification occurs with characters in narrative films, as well as with humans in other kinds of cinema. However, he was left with a major concern. As he wrote,

> [cinema] often presents us with long sequences that can (literally) be called "inhuman" … sequences in which only inanimate objects, landscapes, etc. appear and which for minutes at a time offer no human form for spectator identification: yet the latter must be supposed to remain intact in its deep structure, since at such moments the film *works* just as well as it does at others, and whole films (geographical documentaries, for example) unfold intelligibly in such conditions.[2]

This is a crucial point for any attempt to understand identification. In a fictional film, if the character – or characters – with whom a viewer identifies leave(s) the screen, what happens? Does identification stop when the narrative focus moves aside (even if only temporarily)?

For Metz, the answer to this conundrum is that identification with characters, or humans, on the screen is only a **secondary** form of identification. It is less important than **primary identification**, which he suggests is with the camera and projector. This may seem like a strange or perverse proposition. How can I identify with a machine? And why would this be more important, more significant, than identifying with a human being? (You may find it useful to think through Metz's arguments in relation to the tenets of "apparatus theory" that were introduced in Chapter 11, "Exhibition.") Metz argues that the point of view that is given to the spectator in the auditorium is one of power. Each sequence is presented to us for our benefit, with maximum visibility afforded. We can see and hear many things that the characters cannot – things that occur when their backs are turned, for example. Editing and camera movement usually ensures that we have as full a perspective on the world of the film as possible. The spectator is thus, says Metz, "a great eye and ear without which the perceived would have no one to perceive it, the instance, in other words, which *constitutes* the cinema signifier (it is I who make the film)."[3] This look, this omniscient and powerful perspective, is that of the recording camera, and is replicated in the viewing space by the projector. We are powerful, because the film is there for us, created for us, delivered to us; we are all-seeing in relation to what unfolds on the screen, equivalent to the camera. That the camera's movements – pans, tilts, tracking shots – are analogous to the ways in which our vision works only enhances and contributes to this identification.

Metz's statements about primary identification can be difficult to assimilate. One way in which his implications can be understood is to think of examples of films that do not feature humans. Take, for instance, the French documentary *Winged Migration/Le peuple migrateur* (Jacques Perrin, Jacques Cluzaud, and Michel Debats, 2001). The film follows several species of migratory birds, including terns and penguins, over the course of four years, observing their patterns of behavior and the rigors of their existence. A narrator delivers voice-over information regarding what we are seeing and hearing. Of course, identification may happen with some of the birds, especially as they experience specific difficulties: hunger, exhaustion, and so on. On the whole, however, the film does not have a "protagonist" or a "narrative" with which we engage. Instead, the pleasures of the film are related to the access the filmmakers provide to the life of birds. As we marvel at many of the shots – How exactly was this filmed? How did the filmmakers get access to this scene? – we are identifying with the filming process itself, with the camera. Perhaps this identification is in part with the filmmakers, the people behind the camera, who

15.2 *Winged Migration/Le peuple migrateur* (Jacques Perrin, Jacques Cluzaud, and Michel Debats, 2001). Courtesy of Sony Pictures/The Kobal Collection/Renan Marzin.

control and construct what the viewer gets to see. Certainly, this example helps us to understand Metz's sense of mastery over what unfolds before the camera's eye as it becomes ours.

Let us now turn to the opinions of Noël Carroll, an American philosopher who has written extensively about cinema. In his book *The Philosophy of Horror, or Paradoxes of the Heart* (1990), Carroll interrogates the ways in which viewers of horror films experience fear. Carroll suggests that the word "identification" may actually be an inappropriate term to use, as it implies that viewers imagine themselves into the narrative positions of characters within a film. He dismisses the possibility that there is a "fusion" or "mind-meld" between spectator and character. Carroll argues that we react emotionally (if, of course, we react at all) to the thought of a character in a particular situation, as distinct from the thought of actually *being* the character in that situation. So, for example, when a character in a horror film hears noises in the attic of her house, and decides to ascend the stairs (the lights have probably stopped working, too, so she carries a rather pathetic flashlight), we do not feel that *we* are ascending the stairs, but rather think – and possibly say or shout out loud – "Don't go into the attic!"

A distinction of fundamental importance here is that between **sympathy** and **empathy**. Empathy is the ability mutually to undergo the thoughts, emotions, and direct experience of others. It entails, in part, a collapse of the distinctions between self and other. Sympathy, in contrast, entails feelings of care and understanding for others, but always from a more distanced vantage point. Noël Carroll's arguments about horror films are valuable because they highlight how the spectator's relationships to characters on screen are predominantly sympathetic, rather than empathetic. This is not to suggest that empathy

15.3 Exploring dark and sinister spaces in *The Silent House* (Gustavo Hernandez, 2010). Courtesy of Tokio Films/The Kobal Collection.

15.4 *A Nightmare on Elm Street* (Wes Craven, 1984). Courtesy of New Line/The Kobal Collection.

does not happen – it is possible to experience both sympathy and empathy at the same time. However, what horror films help us to recognize is that sympathy is the dominant spectator–character relationship experienced when audiences are watching films.

Horror movies are a privileged example because they also enable us to understand how identification may shift over the course of a narrative. This topic is explored by Carol Clover in her book *Men, Women and Chainsaws: Gender in the Modern Horror Film* (1992), particularly in her analysis of "slasher" films. Clover states that audiences for this subgenre of horror movies are, on the whole, "groups of boys who cheer the killer on as he assaults his victims, then reverse their sympathies to cheer the survivor on as she assaults the killer."[4] The gendered terms in this sentence are of paramount significance. In the films that Clover discusses – which include *The Texas Chain Saw Massacre* (Tobe Hooper, 1974), *Halloween* (John Carpenter, 1978), *Friday the 13th* (Sean Cunningham, 1980), and *A Nightmare on Elm Street* (Wes Craven, 1984) – the monstrous killer that terrorizes a group of teenagers is nearly always male, and the final surviving teen is usually female. (Clover calls this latter character the "Final Girl.") Frequently during the unfurling of the narrative, as the killer attacks and murders, his point of view aligns with the camera's perspective, a link which may promote identification (even if the monster's identity is largely unknown). By the narrative's conclusion, however, the main point of view adopted by the camera is that of the Final Girl.

The viewing pleasures of these films are complex. (Admittedly, many people may fail to see how they provide any pleasure at all.) When the teenagers are in peril, we might feel sympathy for their plight, whilst also criticizing them for their foolish behavior; when the monster is vanquished, we may experience thrills of retribution and resolution. Simultaneously, the "slasher" film provides audiences with the spectacle of routine and inventive gory death. If you watch a movie such as *Friday the 13th* with an audience in a cinema, the murders (of the teenagers, and of the monster) are often celebrated with whoops and cheers. Perhaps slasher films (and other types of horror cinema) allow audiences a safe space in which taking pleasure in the killing of characters can be indulged. But in the instance of each death, how is identification operating? How is sympathy with a character's experience of peril combined with glee at the destruction of the same character? Clover highlights that these push–pull audience relationships with diverse characters are complicated yet further by the gendered dynamics of the slasher film. Not only do the men in the audience shift their sympathies across the run of the narrative from the male killer to the Final Girl, but the gender identity of these two characters is also often qualified: the monster is frequently feminized, and the Final Girl is usually a tomboy with an androgynous name. This means not only that viewers of slasher films shift their identificatory allegiances from killer to Final Girl, from male monster to female survivor, but also that their main sympathetic bonds whilst watching the film are with characters who are not straightforwardly or conventionally "male" or "female." We will return to these sorts of challenge to identification in more detail in the third part of this chapter.

EXERCISE

What is the relationship between a movie's soundtrack, and our experiences of identification? Anahid Kassabian, in her book *Hearing Film: Tracking Identifications in Contemporary Hollywood Film Music* (2001), explores the ways in which pop and classical music affect our reception of, and responses to, a film's content. Identification with characters in a narrative, she argues, operates in distinct ways, depending on whether scenes are accompanied by a composed (usually orchestral) score, or popular songs. Composed scores, Kassabian states, lead to **assimilating** identifications; they operate to "draw perceivers into socially and historically unfamiliar positions."[5] In contrast, scores compiled from popular songs induce **affiliating** identifications. As Kassabian writes, these affiliating bonds "depend on histories forged outside the film scene, and they allow for a fair bit of mobility within it. If offers of assimilating identifications try to narrow the psychic field, then offers of affiliating identifications open it wide."[6]

Compare and contrast two fictional feature films: the first with an orchestral score, and the second with a soundtrack made up of previously existing popular songs. Pay particular attention to the ways in which the score is intended to influence your relationship to the narrative and characters.

- In what ways is your identification with the characters in each film affected by the different types of music? To what extent does this support or challenge Kassabian's arguments about the two sorts of soundtrack?
- With the first film, how is identification affected if the classical score employed by a film is constructed from previously existing music, some of which may be well known?

- With the film featuring a popular music score, how is your relationship to the film's content shaped by knowing or not knowing the songs that are used?
- If a film soundtrack employs both orchestral or composed score and popular songs, how might this affect the movement of identification over the course of the narrative? In this case, do we drift between "affiliating" and "assimilating" forms of identification?

Finally, let us turn to Murray Smith, whose book *Engaging Characters: Fiction, Emotion, and the Cinema* (1995) provides a nuanced model for how audience identification operates. Like Noël Carroll, Smith suggests that the term "identification" is problematic. He proposes, instead, a model with separate and distinctive "levels of engagement" through which audiences relate to fictional characters. Taken together, these levels make up what Smith terms a "structure of sympathy." There are three different "levels of engagement": recognition, alignment and allegiance. Smith offers definitions of each:

- "*Recognition* describes the spectator's construction of character: the perception of a set of textual elements, in film typically cohering around the image of a body, as an individuated and continuous human agent."[7] This basic building block of the operations of identification is rarely identified or commented on. However, "recognition" is crucial in order for viewers to experience an affective relationship with a screen character.
- "The term *alignment* describes the process by which spectators are placed in relation to characters in terms of access to their actions, and to what they know and feel. [...] I propose two interlocking functions, *spatio-temporal attachment* and *subjective access* ... as the most precise means for analysing alignment."[8] In other words, identification or sympathy with a character is facilitated by the extent to which the filmmaker aligns us with them. Are we provided with access to their thoughts, perhaps through voice-over? Do we share their relationship to space, maybe through repeated use of point-of-view camerawork?
- "*Allegiance* pertains to the moral evaluation of characters by the spectator [...] Allegiance depends upon the spectator having what she takes to be reliable access to the character's state of mind, on understanding the context of the character's actions, and having morally evaluated the character on the basis of this knowledge."[9] Here, then, the viewer judges the character, and works out whether this is an individual with whom they can connect sympathetically.

Smith goes further: he argues (as we have already suggested) that aspects of sympathy and empathy may occur at the same time. Smith states that his "structure of sympathy" needs to be supplemented by concepts that help us to understand how spectators may also experience empathy, including emotional stimulation. The value of Smith's model is that it applies rigor to complex affective relationships between viewer and screen materials. It dissects the notion of sympathy into constituent components. Of course, when we are watching films and engaging with particular characters and their stories, we may not be able surgically to pull apart our relationship to them. Retrospectively, however, Smith's model enables us to interrogate the workings of our own psychology, and to begin to comprehend the difficult task that filmmakers have in creating believable characters with whom audiences might sympathize.

CASE STUDY: THE INTERNATIONAL APPEAL OF BRUCE LEE

Bruce Lee's martial arts films were popular in numerous countries around the world. How can we explain the appeal of this actor to such diverse audiences? Did viewers in North America relate to or identify with Lee in the same way as audiences in Hong Kong?

Bruce Lee was born in San Francisco's Chinatown in November 1940, to parents from Hong Kong. At the age of three months, his family returned to Hong Kong. Lee's father performed in the Cantonese opera, as well as acting in films; he introduced his son to the film industry. By the time he was 18, Bruce had already appeared in twenty films, and he returned to the United States to complete his education; he studied at the University of Washington, majoring in drama. During these years of study, Lee began teaching martial arts.

Spotted taking part in a martial arts exhibition, Lee was invited to audition for television. He was cast as sidekick Kato in the TV series *The Green Hornet*, which only ran for one season, from 1966 to 1967. Lee made guest appearances on several other television programmes, including *Ironside*. In 1971, Lee returned to Hong Kong, possibly because he was disappointed that he did not get the lead role in the TV series *Kung Fu* (the role went to David Carradine). In Hong Kong, Lee signed a deal with Raymond Chow and his Golden Harvest Productions; he starred in the films *The Big Boss* (Wei Lo, 1971) and *Fist of Fury* (Wei Lo, 1972), both significant box office successes. For his third film as lead actor, *Way of the Dragon* (1972), Lee was given full control as writer, director, star and fight choreographer. Lee began making a fourth film for Golden Harvest, *Game of Death*, but Warner Bros. offered him the chance to star in *Enter the Dragon* (Robert Clouse, 1973). Shortly after completing work on *Enter the Dragon*, Lee died of a cerebral oedema or swelling of the brain.

The release of *Enter the Dragon* in the United States coincided with, and contributed to, a brief kung fu craze. At one point in May 1973, the films *Fists of Fury*, *Deep Thrust – The Hand of Death/Tie zhang xuan feng tui* (Feng Huang, 1972), and *Five Fingers of Death/Tian xia di yi quan* (Chang-hwa Jeong, 1972) occupied the first, second and third slots, respectively, on *Variety*'s chart of the week's top movies at the box office. Lee's reputation, status and appeal persisted after his death: *Game of Death* (Robert Clouse, 1978) was completed and released posthumously, and he was the subject of a biopic, *Dragon: The Bruce Lee Story* (Rob Cohen, 1993).

Bruce Lee was popular as a figure of identification for Chinese audiences (for some, he remains so). Stephen Teo has suggested that this is related to Chinese nationalism; Lee's strength, agility and martial arts prowess enabled him to be embraced by Chinese spectators as a physical embodiment of national power and strength.[10] Beyond this, Lee also appealed to a broader Chinese audience around the world. These geographically dispersed spectators may have experienced sympathetic connections with Lee's characters in *The Big Boss* and *Way of the Dragon* for specific reasons: in these films, Lee not only plays immigrant figures, separated from his country of birth, but uses forms of knowledge and cultural skill that are identifiably Chinese in order to best or win over those around him. Chinese viewers around the world, then, might identify with various aspects of Bruce Lee demonstrated in his films: his attractiveness, his physical skills, the narratives of the films in which he starred, and his embodiment of a specifically Chinese national identity.

15.5 *Game of Death* (Robert Clouse, 1978). Courtesy of Golden Harvest/Paragon/ The Kobal Collection.

However, Lee did not appeal only to spectators of Chinese descent. His films were successful in North America with youthful audiences of various races and ethnicities, and with black viewers. Warner Bros. and other distributors would screen their films in downtown spaces attended by these particular demographic groups. Martial arts films would appear on double bills with blaxploitation films (a genre that we explored in the previous chapter). The content of the kung fu films, which included Lee's handful of martial arts movies, might have specifically fostered engagement and identification for black and youth viewers. As David Desser writes:

> The appeal of the genre for black audiences is not hard to gauge. Outside of the blaxploi- tation genre it largely replaced, kung fu films offered the only non-white heroes, men and women, to audiences alienated by mainstream film and often by mainstream culture. This was the genre of the underdog, the underdog of colour, often fighting against colonialist enemies, white culture, or the Japanese. The lone, often unarmed combatant fighting a foe with greater economic clout who represented the status quo provides an obvious but nonetheless real connection between kung fu films and black audiences. The same may be said, more generally, for young audiences, a characteristic of youth being alienated from the mainstream, seeking images of rebels with or without causes. Many kung fu films portrayed a rather anarchic world view, routinely a nihilistic one, with violent death a way of life and continued and continual trial-by-combat the typical narrative drive. Such filmic values and motifs clearly mirror the psychosociological states of young people.[11]

Bruce Lee's martial arts films, then, possibly appealed to black American audiences because of the centrality of a non-white underdog protagonist. As they identified with Lee across racial lines (African American/Chinese), pleasure was afforded in witnessing economically superior "villains" being taken down. And for youth viewers of various races and ethnicities, Lee's characters appealed as rebellious, anti-authoritarian figures.

IDENTIFICATION IN PRACTICE: AUDIENCE TACTICS

The theoretical models of identification and audience sympathy we outlined in the previous section of this chapter offer valuable concepts for thinking through the relationships between viewers and characters on screen. But how might these relationships work in practice, beyond the level of philosophical speculation? Ethnographic studies of audiences of particular actors, films, and genres can provide us with concrete evidence of the ways in which audiences relate to movies. When conducted, such studies are often of those who self-identify as fans. Film fandom entails a particular form of personal investment – one arguably more heightened, more extreme, than that experienced by the average spectator. Due to the heightened nature of the relationship between fan viewer and screen, the fan is often able to articulate in detail their sympathetic and empathetic bonds with particular actors, characters, movies, or genres.

In addition, valuable insight can be gained into the complex connections between identity and identification by examining the centrality of certain films, actors or genres – or even the act of cinema viewing per se – for particular social groups. For some people, specific aspects of cinema (such as individual films or stars) provide or strengthen a sense of identity, both singular and communal. Some films have ritual behaviors associated with their screenings, at which particular actions and activities are enacted and repeated by the audience; performing the communal actions with a like-minded group may be as important to the audience as the film itself, if not more so. Enthusiasm for particular forms of cinema may lead to social interaction with others who share the same passion; conversely, the interest may manifest as a result of such socialization. Here, then, identification begins to bleed off the cinema screen, and audiences may start to identify themselves with other spectators, with this identification impacting on the viewers' sense of their own identity.

Jackie Stacey, in an essay entitled "Feminine Fascinations," which was first published in 1991 and which served as the starting point for her 1994 book *Star Gazing: Hollywood Cinema and Female Spectatorship*, provided a taxonomic approach to the ways in which female spectators relate to stars on screen. She placed an advertisement in two weekly magazines for women, asking readers to write to her about their favorite Hollywood stars of the 1940s and 1950s. She then analyzed the letters that she received, and the sorts of behavior and beliefs described by her respondents. Stacey discovered a strikingly diverse set of processes of identification, which took place both in the cinema whilst watching films, but also outside the auditorium.

Stacey identified two main groups of identificatory processes occurring in the accounts provided by her respondents. Firstly, there were *cinematic identificatory fantasies*, which occurred while the viewer was watching a film. Here, the relationship between spectator and star took a number of forms, which are not necessarily mutually exclusive:

- *Devotion and worship*: for some viewers, the star is distant and unattainable, out of reach, in a different sphere of existence. With no chance of closing the gap between ordinary spectator and screen ideal, the viewer perceives the star as an idol to be revered.
- *The desire to become*: although an immutable difference might exist between the star and the spectator, some viewers acknowledged a desire to move across that gap.
- *Pleasure in feminine power*: for some of Stacey's respondents, female stars (and the characters that they play on screen) were read as images of power. The spectatorial appeal of these figures lay in their embodiment of a bold and confident femininity.

- *Identification and escapism*: finally, other respondents stated that the recognized difference between themselves and the star provided the possibility of leaving the ordinary, pedestrian world temporarily and becoming part of the star's world. Identification with the character in the fantasy world depicted allowed brief escape from the humdrum.

In addition to these processes of identification which took place in the cinema, Stacey also identified a group of *extra-cinematic identificatory practices*, which occurred after the screening, when the audience had returned to their daily lives. These practices are all closely linked, and again may not be mutually exclusive:

- *Pretending*: for some viewers, identification with a particular star was enhanced by pretending to be the star (usually in a playful manner). Differences between the spectator and the star would be ignored, temporarily imagined away.
- *Resembling*: the fan identifies something which forges a connection between the star and the self ("I am like this particular star, because we share this in common …"). The isolation of this resemblance does not necessarily involve any transformation of the viewer, merely a drawing of attention to the link.
- *Imitating*: beyond pretending and resembling, some viewers would attempt actual imitation of a star. This would involve some transformation of the self, and a partial taking on of aspects of a star's identity.
- *Copying*: most often, this took the form of copying of elements of a star's appearance (through, for example, hair style).
- *Copying and consumption*: here, copying involved the purchase of cultural products, in order to enhance the bond with the star. This might include items of clothing, or particular commodities that the star has advertised outside their acting work (such as specific beauty products).

Stacey thus provides a detailed mapping of the different processes of identification that may occur between audiences and actors, both in the cinema and outside of it. She also connects her findings to the distinction between identification-based-on-similarity and identification-based-on-aspiration-and-difference, which we noted earlier in this chapter. She writes:

> the processes of identification articulated most strongly in terms of difference seem to be those relating more directly to the cinematic context where the image of the star is still present on the screen. The processes, and practices, which involve reproducing similarity seem to be those extra-cinematic identifications which take place more in the spectator's familiar domestic context.[12]

In other words, different kinds of identification may occur in the dimmed space of the cinema, in contrast to those which take place once the screening has ended and the viewer has returned home.

Stacey is not the only academic author to have undertaken ethnographic study of a group of film spectators, but her writings on the subject of audience–star relations remain enormously influential. In the years since "Feminine Fascinations" was published, a plethora of focused studies of particular groups of fans and viewers has been carried out. Many of these directly engage with Stacey's findings. To give just one example, Rachel Moseley, in her book *Growing Up with Audrey Hepburn*, centers her arguments on evidence provided by fourteen detailed interviews that she conducted, seven with women who were particularly invested in the actor in the 1950s and 1960s, and seven with younger women who only came to know the actor's work in the 1980s and 1990s. Moseley's book explores the

15.6 Audrey Hepburn in *Sabrina* (Billy Wilder, 1954). Courtesy of Paramount/The Kobal Collection/Bud Fraker.

significance of class and gender as key factors in her interviewees' relationships with Audrey Hepburn. She also discusses Hepburn's popularity with female audiences in relation to successive waves of feminism. One of the main aims of Moseley's book is to interrogate whether "identification" is actually an appropriate term to describe the complicated relationships that occur between female spectators, actors, and films. As she writes in her conclusion, on the basis of her findings:

> the relationships between audience members and stars are more diverse and indeed nebulous than existing theories of identification … can suggest. Accordingly, I want to hold on to the notions of affect, resonance and recognition as useful starting points which enable an address to the specificity of personal history; questions of gender, class, race, sexuality, generation, education and national identity are key factors in determining the form and the nature of relationships between audience member and star-text.[13]

Both Stacey and Moseley, then, flesh out our understandings of how identification operates in practice, between actual spectators and films. Stacey provides a comprehensive model of different forms of identificatory activity. Moseley, on the other hand, suggests that theories of identification need to be expanded and reformulated in order to adequately accommodate the diverse array of audience relations to stars and movies.

EXERCISE

Interview someone that you know for fifteen minutes, about a star or actor in whom they have (or had) a particular investment. (If possible, record the conversation, so that you can then revisit your interviewee's comments at your leisure.)

- How does your interviewee characterize their relationship to the actor? Can they identify what first led to their interest in this figure? How do they relate their own life trajectory and experiences to those of the actor?
- Does your interviewee identify moments in their life when they have altered their own behavior, in ways directly or indirectly related to their relationship with the actor?
- Can you identify some of Stacey's patterns of identificatory behavior in operation in your interviewee's responses?

(It may be, of course, that your interviewee cannot identify an actor they are invested in, or moments when they have changed themselves in relation to any such person. If so, then unpack these responses with your interviewee, as they can also reveal a great deal about how actual audiences relate to actors and the characters they portray on screen.)

In addition to the ways in which identification with characters and stars operates for the individual spectator, it is valuable to think through the subject of *communal identification*. By this, we mean instances where specific stars or actors take on significance for particular groups of people, and where identification with those figures on screen may become part of a group's identity – even if the film viewing takes place mainly in isolation. More broadly, communal identification may operate amongst film spectators whose sense of their own identity includes collective experiences of cinema consumption – whether specific films, stars, or genres.

One example of communal identification is provided by the actress Judy Garland, who has been a significant figure for gay male culture in many countries for decades. Understanding Garland's importance for gay men is a challenge. Why would homosexuals identify across the lines of gender and sexuality with a heterosexual female star? Given that Garland had a difficult life – numerous failed marriages, financial woes, and troubles with drugs and alcohol that led to an early death at the age of 47 – how can she occupy the position of idol? (Should you want to pursue these questions further, Richard Dyer's detailed exploration of Garland's star persona in his book *Heavenly Bodies: Film Stars and Society* will provide some answers.[14]) A second example – which has almost solidified into a stereotype – is the appeal of the American comedian Jerry Lewis to French audiences. Although Lewis had a period of popularity in the United States, he continues to be idolized by a significant percentage of French film viewers. To some extent, this could be due to the identification of him as an auteur figure by the influential French film journal *Cahiers du Cinéma*. But as Rae Beth Gordon suggests in her book *Why the French Love Jerry Lewis*, it may also be because he embodies in his roles a particular and distinctive type of comic performance style – tics, movements, grimaces, gestures – that was especially popular and widespread in France between 1870 and 1910.[15]

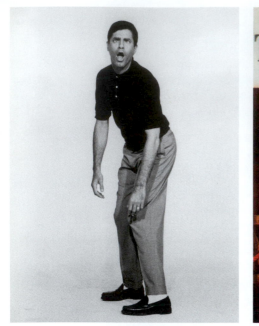

15.7 Jerry Lewis. Courtesy of The Kobal Collection.

15.8 *The Rocky Horror Picture Show* (Jim Sharman, 1975). Courtesy of 20th Century Fox/ The Kobal Collection.

In terms of cinema playing a significant role in an individual's sense of belonging to a social group, it is also valuable to highlight ritual viewings of cult films. Movies such as *The Rocky Horror Picture Show* (Jim Sharman, 1975), *Showgirls* (Paul Verhoeven, 1995), and *The Room* (Tommy Wiseau, 2003) have developed reputations for their raucous public screenings, at which spectators interact with the film and each other: they respond to specific lines of dialogue with shouted-out responses, throw items (rice for *Rocky Horror*, plastic spoons in *The Room*), recite dialogue along with the characters for key scenes, maybe even dress up. Audiences of all three of these examples have been the focus of ethnographic studies, which attempt to comprehend the sense of communal belonging that they provide – again, how identity, identification and cinema work together in practice.

COMPLICATING IDENTITY AND IDENTIFICATION

Up to this point, this chapter has mainly been exploring the notion of identification: what it is, how its constituent elements may operate, and how it might work for audiences watching films. At this juncture, it is necessary to interrogate the second key term in our chapter title: identity. We have largely been working from the position that identification for cinema viewers involves forging bonds between their own identities and those of characters on screen. But this presumes that a viewer has some sense of their own identity – and that it is relatively stable.

In fact, these presumptions are far from straightforward, and open to challenge. "Identity" is a complex concept to define, mainly because the ways in which we understand who we are are varied, complex,

CASE STUDY: TAMIL FILM FAN CLUBS

The Tamil film industry is based in Chennai, India, and produces feature-length films in the Tamil language. Most of the Tamil film studios are based in Kodambakkam, a residential neighborhood in Chennai which is also referred to as Kollywood. Film star fan clubs (or *rasikar manrams*) can be found throughout southern India. They are male-only groups, and almost all of them are devoted solely to male stars. Study of these clubs and their members provide insights into the ways in which cinema can operate as a focus for social groups and allegiances to form, becoming a central component of an individual's personal identity.

Members of the *rasikar manrams* tend to meet weekly or monthly, in the evenings and weekends, on street corners or at auto-rickshaw stands. Typically, fan clubs consist of around twenty members, friends and neighbors who are in their late teens and twenties. The clubs have a particular degree of visibility: signs for them can be spotted on the main thoroughfares of lower-class areas and in college buildings; announcements of events being run by specific clubs might be pasted up at bus stops and elsewhere. The clubs last for variable lengths of time: some have a very brief existence, whereas others keep going for years.

For members of clubs, this facet of their identity is often presented as of primary significance. This might be done through dress codes (for example, wearing a t-shirt featuring the star's image), styles of speech, or painting the star's picture on a tool or machine such as an auto-rickshaw. The reputation of film clubs within the wider public is not wholly positive: they are often perceived by outsiders as noisy, volatile, and rowdy. Most of the members of the fan clubs are from lower castes and classes, and are not particularly well educated. Typically, these men may work as tailors, drive auto-rickshaws, or sell tea or vegetables.

As well as fan club meetings, members engage in particular activities. They make and display film posters – portraits of particular stars. These are exhibited and related to by fan club members in ways that seem to have devotional significance. The fan groups also attend film screenings, at which they will throw confetti, cheer, and recite screen dialogue (interactive behavior not unlike that of *Rocky Horror* audiences, who we mentioned elsewhere in this chapter). If a particular film manages to stay in cinemas for one hundred days, a celebration will be held at the theatre. Fan clubs also organize functions, most of which are celebratory – for example, for a club's anniversary or for a star's birthday.

All fan clubs are part of a much larger organizational structure. Fan club membership is regulated by a centralized organization, which is run by the film star's agent. Networks of *rasikar manrams* are enormous; some of the most famous film stars will have up to 20,000 distinct but connected fan clubs. The networks of Tamil film fan clubs are hierarchically structured: operating below the main fan club administrator are branches; regional coordinators and organizers can be found in many villages and urban neighborhoods. The regional coordinators may have some social or community status: they might be business leaders, entrepreneurs, patrons, or elders. Within urban neighborhoods, a coordinator may be in charge of twenty or more *rasikar manrams*, each of which is based in a different spot. Due to the fact that many high-ranking members of Tamil Nadu government have previously been involved in the film industry, the film clubs themselves can also be of some political significance, however minor.

It is clear that being a member of a film fan club in southern India can provide an individual with a sense of social and cultural identity. Knowing more about a star and his films than other fans can enhance social standing within the clubs and be used as a marker of difference. Although the fan clubs are sometimes viewed pejoratively by outsiders, members seem to see themselves as performing worthwhile activities. In particular, they may see their club membership as providing them with some social mobility. As anthropologist Sara Dickey writes, "The young men who join fan clubs are sharply aware of their social and cultural distance from the upper class, and use their club membership to address and redress that distance."[16] Whether or not this is effective or successful is open to debate.

15.9 An Indian artist gives the finishing touches to a cinema hoarding featuring the actor Vijay. Courtesy of AFP/Getty Images.

relational, and endlessly shifting. Many of us are raised to believe that we are unique and distinctive individuals – that our identities are ours alone, and that we have a true "core" located somewhere inside us. This uniqueness, however, is open to challenge: as the sociologist Norbert Elias has pointed out in his 1936 book *The Civilising Process*, this understanding of identity only emerged around the time of the Renaissance, and has since became widespread and pervasive in the West.

Is it possible to argue that your identity is rooted in who you are, biologically? This is known as adopting an **essentialist** position. You could, for instance, define yourself as a woman, and as belonging to a certain ethnic or racial group. However, both of these facets of identity are not simply biological. They are also social and relational: if you identify yourself as a woman, or as Asian, then you are including yourself into (that is, *identifying with*) a substantial group of other people. Further, these identity categories are, in part, cultural. For example, although being male or female is in part about the anatomy of the body, it also involves types of behavior. Where and how did you learn to dress, talk and act appropriately for your sex (even if you do not)? We assimilate (and perhaps reject) this information from those around us as we mature: parents, peers, siblings, actors in movies, and so on. The same applies to ethnicity and race: although they have a basis in genetics, all ethnic and racial identities (including whiteness) have associated cultural elements involved in how they take shape and are expressed.

Our identities are not singular, but plural. No one individual has simply one identity – and certainly not a basic interior "core." You may be male, African-American, a teenager, middle-class and heterosexual (among other things). These facets of our identities are not cumulative, but work together in complex ways. This becomes apparent in relation to identification processes in the cinema. Which aspect of your identity becomes most significant when you are watching a particular film? Do you identify with the lead character because you have the same skin color, with the romantic interest because you are also Italian, or with the sidekick because they crack the best jokes, and you wish you were funnier than you are?

Identity is also not stable. Over the course of our lives, our identities change. They may change drastically – from one sex to the other, for instance. The ways in which we understand ourselves may also alter. The philosopher Paul Ricoeur has argued that our identities are in significant part constructed through the stories that we tell other people. As we narrate our lives to the people around us, we are actively constructing a sense for them (and for ourselves) of who we are. Cinema itself can be part of this process: as we let others know of our tastes and preferences, and tell them how we related to and understood particular films, they develop a deeper understanding of who we are.

At an extreme, some theorists have adopted a **non-** or **anti-essentialist** perspective on identity. From this point of view, identity is predominantly socially and culturally constructed, with biology having little to no impact on who we are. Feminist and queer theorist Judith Butler, for instance, in her 1990 book *Gender Trouble*, argues that our identities (in particular, our gender identities) are performed afresh all the time. Though repeat performances of the same identity serve to provide a sense of continuity, it is feasible that we could alter our identity by shifting our behavior patterns. Although this is a radical, destabilizing perspective to adopt, it is also liberating: if Butler is correct, then significant aspects of our identity can be altered at will over time.

The complex, multifaceted and performative nature of our identities clearly has ramifications for the experience of identification in the cinema. Think back here to Carol Clover's arguments about slasher films, and the ways in which men in the audience shift their allegiances from the monstrous murderer to the Final Girl, changing their sympathies from male to female. How might this process engage with different facets of the identities of these spectators? An alternative perspective to consider is that of Linda Williams, outlined in an essay on the film *Stella Dallas* (King Vidor, 1937) which was published in 1984. Although previous authors had suggested that women watching this film would identify with the protagonist and her suffering, Williams suggested that it was possible for female spectators to identify with several characters at the same time, and to take pleasure in this contradiction. Given the multiple-but-imbricated elements of all of our identities, this position could suggest that, when we watch any movie, our sympathies and identification are spread across and between several characters simultaneously.

Williams' essay on *Stella Dallas* contributed to a considerable body of writing produced by feminists in the 1970s and 1980s which interrogated the place of the female spectator, especially in relation to

15.10 *Stella Dallas* (King Vidor, 1937). Courtesy of United Artists/The Kobal Collection.

Hollywood cinema. The essay that is often identified as the origin of this mass of work is Laura Mulvey's 1975 essay "Visual Pleasure and Narrative Cinema." Mulvey's article is centrally concerned with identification and identity. She argues that Hollywood cinema connects together three looks: those of the camera, the viewer in the cinema auditorium, and the male protagonist. Together, these constitute the "male gaze." Women in the audience are required to look like men at the action depicted on the screen; in the narratives consumed, men are active and women largely reduced to objects to be contemplated for their beauty. For Mulvey, women watching Hollywood films are placed in an uncomfortable position, coerced into a type of cross-gender identification or shut out of the fiction – options that she finds politically problematic.

Mulvey's essay is significant for our discussion here because it raises an option that we have not considered so far: that sometimes identification may break down. As she suggests, identification in the cinema may be coerced, shaped and promoted by filmmakers in order to seduce viewers into alignment with a movie's point of view. It is possible, following her argument, that specific audiences (either individuals or groups) cannot forge bonds of identification with a significant percentage of movies, because they cannot find ways by which to connect with the content and narratives depicted. In both cases, disenfranchisement may be the outcome. This may be willed ("I refuse to be implicated in this film's content") or a matter of exclusion ("I am not addressed by this film in any way, and thus I am blocked out"). Although Mulvey writes about women and their relationship to Hollywood, this disenfranchisement could be experienced by a member of any group that feels it is not adequately represented, whose point of view is rarely adopted – whether this is centered on race, sexuality, disability, or some other aspect of identity.

If this is something a viewer experiences, then what can they do? Let us assume that identification is something that enhances the pleasure attained from consuming movies, and thus worth expending energy on building. A number of distinct strategies might be employed by spectators in order to cope.

- *Ignoring a film's messages.* The narrative trajectories of many characters conclude badly: they may end up unhappy, alone, punished, or dead. However, this does not mean that the film itself does not provide a range of pleasures during the remainder of its running time. Many films with independent and feisty women as the lead characters, for example, end with a heterosexual union that closes down the narrative, with marriage to an appropriate man supposedly providing "correct" closure. The message being reinforced is that all women will only find true happiness when they are paired off and married. But the audiences who reject this conclusion may still take pleasure from the remainder of the film, in which the protagonist's life before marriage is explored (and possibly celebrated).
- *Focus on key fragments.* Individual moments within particular films can take on significance beyond that afforded to them by the movie itself. They may provide a brief peek at what an alternative version of the film's world could have been like, and are thus affixed within the spectator's experience of (and memory of) the movie. These moments can enhance identification, or even merely enable it to take place.
- *Use extra-textual knowledge in the service of pleasure.* Let us use an example: for a member of the audience who has dyslexia, knowing that an actor also has experience of this learning disability might allow them to take pleasure in their films, even though dyslexia is unlikely to feature as part of their characterization. In such a scenario, identification with actors such as Abhichek Bachchan, Cher, and Keira Knightley can be enhanced by extra-textual knowledge. As an alternative example, knowing how a film was assembled, and what was happening on the set throughout the shooting, may also enhance a viewer's relationship to particular characters.
- *Reading against the grain.* It is possible, of course, for a film spectator simply to ignore some of a film's delivered content, and to impose their own reading on it – a process that has been called "reading against the grain." Peripheral characters may be interpreted as more significant than their screen time suggests. The negative connotations of certain characters can simply be ignored. Friendships between characters can be read as more romantic. Media theorist Alexander Doty suggests, in his book *Making Things Perfectly Queer*, that "reading against the grain" is not the imposition of a new meaning that is absent from the text, but an unearthing of one of many layers, many possibilities, that have always been there all along.[17]

EXERCISE

For a movie of your choice, try to read it against the grain:

- Make a list of the characters. What do you *know* and *not know* about their family ties, place of birth and upbringing, social connections, and so on? How might the gaps in your knowledge be used to forge new understandings of them, and their relationships with other characters?
- What extra-textual information – about the actors, scriptwriter, director, and so on – can you bring to the film, which might be used to cast its content in a different light?
- How does the film play out if you ignore the occurrence of certain scenes? If you did not see the final ten minutes, for instance, how are the film's meanings and messages affected?

CASE STUDY: *ROCK HUDSON'S HOME MOVIES*

When the American actor Rock Hudson died of an AIDS-related illness in 1983, sections of the US press expressed surprise. This was centered on his sexuality. How could Hudson have been gay? Throughout his career, he regularly played rugged and heterosexual characters. In fact, he could be said to have embodied a particular screen ideal of handsome, muscular masculinity. The films that Hudson made with the director Douglas Sirk, in particular, solidified this perception: in such films as *Magnificent Obsession* (1954), *All That Heaven Allows* (1955) and *Written on the Wind* (1956), Rock Hudson was cast as caring and thoughtful (but beefy) romantic lead. Studio publicity that circulated at the peak of his career concocted a heterosexual persona, and circulated rumors of relationships with a number of different women.

Embedded in the surprise of the press was the assumption that gay men and women actors cannot play straight characters. However, lesbians, gay men, and bisexuals have taken on roles as heterosexual characters throughout the history of cinema, and continue to do so. The actual sexual orientation of these actors is often hidden from the public, by the actors themselves and/or the industry in which they work, in order to keep their private lives private. In addition, due to the social and cultural pressures that gay men and women regularly experience, they often become adept at "passing" (or "acting") as straight. But once we discover that a particular actor or actress is not heterosexual – as happened with Rock Hudson – do we look differently at their previous screen appearances?

Mark Rappaport's documentary *Rock Hudson's Home Movies* (1992) retrospectively examined Hudson's films, looking for ways in which the actor's homosexuality manifested in his many roles. Rappaport's film was associated at the time of its release with the New Queer Cinema movement. New Queer Cinema was the title given to a body of films that appeared in the early 1990s, which offered fresh takes on the lives of lesbian, gay, and bisexual characters. These movies played with existing stereotypes associated with sexual minorities, and interrogated the notion of sexual identity as a stable basis for group belonging. Other films associated with the movement included Todd Haynes' *Poison* (1990), Gregg Araki's *The Living End* (1991), Tom Kalin's *Swoon* (1992), and Rose Troche's *Go Fish* (1994). Several New Queer Cinema films, including Rappaport's, examined the sexuality of famous stars, through suggestion, implication or overt fictionalization: *The Hours and Times* (Christopher Munch, 1991) hypothesized a sexual relationship between John Lennon and Brian Epstein; *The Meeting of Two Queens* (Cecilia Barriga, 1992) posited an erotic encounter between Greta Garbo and Marlene Dietrich.

In *Rock Hudson's Home Movies*, narrator Eric Farr speaks directly to the camera; behind him play selected fragments of Hudson's films. Through this assemblage, Rappaport highlights repetitive gestures, tics and movements used by Hudson. He also isolates recurrent themes in the actor's oeuvre. These include unresolved and fragile relationships with women, activities that seem like cruising (that is, seeking out sexual contact with other men), and the recurrence of characters with split personalities (into a "macho Rock" and a "homo Rock"). Across the short running time of Rappaport's film, audio-visual evidence is organized into a montage that seems to reveal that Hudson's identity as a gay man was often on display in his movies.

Does this mean that audiences of Hudson's films at the time they were made – when homosexuality had a less visible cultural presence, and was much less widely accepted (if at all) – did not see this "evidence" of his homosexuality? Was it hidden, or disguised, by the combination of the films' heterosexual plots and the image of Hudson generated by the studio publicity machine? Or is Rappaport's "proof" actually a trick of clever editing and juxtaposition? In relation to this chapter's discussion of audiences creating ways into movies, finding ways to identify, and attempting to connect up aspects of their own identity with what is depicted on screen, *Rock Hudson's Home Movies* provides a concrete example of how such tactics can work in practice. Whether Hudson's homosexuality was always on display in his films, or whether it has to be creatively conjured from their components, Rappaport's movie demonstrates how careful interpretation may enable a queer perspective to emerge.

15.11 *Rock Hudson's Home Movies* (Mark Rappaport, 1992).

SUMMARY

This chapter has provided an overview of various different conceptions of identification in the cinema, and how this relates to the identity of spectators. We have looked at the "folk model" of identification, Metz's model of primary and secondary identification, Murray Smith's nuanced model of "levels of engagement," and examined how horror films present particular challenges for thinking about identification. Through the writings of Jackie Stacey and others, and a consideration of communal identification, we have examined how identification works in practice. Finally, we have unpacked the notion of identity, and acknowledged the instability that lies at the core of both identity and identification. The chapter concluded with an examination of how identification can be creatively built by working with strategies such as "reading against the grain."

FURTHER READING

Lawler, Steph. *Identity: Sociological Perspectives.* Cambridge: Polity Press, 2008.

A short and readable introduction to many of the main perspectives on identity, this serves as an invaluable and perceptive primer. Individual chapters are devoted to such topics as genetics, memory, the unconscious, and storytelling.

Moseley, Rachel. *Growing Up with Audrey Hepburn.* Manchester: Manchester University Press, 2002.

Moseley's book is a thoughtful and engaging account of audience relationships to one specific star, centered on ethnographic study of two different generations of women. Particular attention is paid to personal styling – make-up, hair, dressmaking – and how these have been shaped for some female spectators by their bond with Hepburn.

Smith, Murray. *Engaging Characters: Fiction, Emotion, and the Cinema.* Oxford: Clarendon Press, 1995.

Smith's book offers a sustained interrogation of the notion of identification as it relates to cinema. Although *Engaging Characters* contains some challenging theoretical material, it also provides one complex and detailed model of the psychological and emotional processes involved when audiences watch movies.

Stacey, Jackie. "Feminine Fascinations: Forms of Identification in Star–Audience Relations," in Christine Gledhill (ed.), *Stardom: Industry of Desire.* New York and London: Routledge, 1991, 145–168.

Stacey's essay – summarized in some detail in this chapter – remains a crucial text for those wanting to explore how identification may work in practice. Her taxonomic breakdown of audience behaviors is clear, thoughtful and directly related to the theoretical writings on the subject.

FILMS REFERENCED IN CHAPTER FIFTEEN

All That Heaven Allows (Douglas Sirk, 1955)

The Big Boss (Wei Lo, 1971)

Deep Thrust – The Hand of Death/Tie zhang xuan feng tui (Feng Huang, 1972)

Dragon: The Bruce Lee Story (Rob Cohen, 1993)

Enter the Dragon (Robert Clouse, 1973)

Fist of Fury (Wei Lo, 1972)

Five Fingers of Death/Tian xia di yi quan (Chang-hwa Jeong, 1972)

Friday the 13th (Sean Cunningham, 1980)

Game of Death (Robert Clouse, 1978)

Go Fish (Rose Troche, 1994)

Halloween (John Carpenter, 1978)

The Hours and Times (Christopher Munch, 1991)

The Living End (Gregg Araki, 1991)

Magnificent Obsession (Douglas Sirk, 1954)

The Meeting of Two Queens (Cecilia Barriga, 1992)

A Nightmare on Elm Street (Wes Craven, 1984)

Poison (Todd Haynes, 1990)

Ringu (Hideo Nakata, 1998)

Rock Hudson's Home Movies (Mark Rappaport, 1992)

The Rocky Horror Picture Show (Jim Sharman, 1975)

The Room (Tommy Wiseau, 2003)

Showgirls (Paul Verhoeven, 1995)

Stella Dallas (King Vidor, 1937)

Swoon (Tom Kalin, 1992)

The Texas Chain Saw Massacre (Tobe Hooper, 1974)

Way of the Dragon (Bruce Lee, 1972)

Winged Migration/Le peuple migrateur (Jacques Perrin, Jacques Cluzaud, and Michel Debats, 2001)

Written on the Wind (Douglas Sirk, 1956)

NOTES

1 Murray Smith, *Engaging Characters: Fiction, Emotion, and the Cinema* (Oxford: Clarendon Press, 1995), 2.

2 Christian Metz, *Psychoanalysis and Cinema: The Imaginary Signifier*, trans. Celia Britton, Annwyl Williams, Ben Brewster and Alfred Guzzetti (London and Basingstoke: Macmillan, 1982), 47.

3 Metz, 48.

4 Carol Clover, *Men, Women and Chainsaws: Gender in the Modern Horror Film* (London: BFI, 1992), 23.

5 Anahid Kassabian, *Hearing Film: Tracking Identifications in Contemporary Hollywood Film Music* (New York and London: Routledge, 2001), 2.

6 Kassabian, 3.

7 Smith, 82.

8 Smith, 83.

9 Smith, 84.

10 Stephen Teo, *Hong Kong Cinema: The Extra Dimension* (London: BFI, 1997).

11 David Desser, "The Kung Fu Craze: Hong Kong Cinema's First American Reception," in Poshek Fu and David Desser (eds), *The Cinema of Hong Kong: History, Arts, Identity* (Cambridge: Cambridge University Press, 2000), 38.

12 Jackie Stacey, "Feminine Fascinations: Forms of Identification in Star–Audience Relations," in Christine Gledhill (ed.), *Stardom: Industry of Desire* (New York and London: Routledge, 1991), 160.

13 Rachel Moseley, *Growing Up with Audrey Hepburn* (Manchester and New York: Manchester University Press, 2002), 218.

14 Richard Dyer, *Heavenly Bodies: Film Stars and Society* (London: Macmillan, 1986).

15 Rae Beth Gordon, *Why the French Love Jerry Lewis: From Cabaret to Early Cinema* (New York: Stanford University Press, 2001).

16 Sara Dickey, "Opposing Faces: Film Star Fan Clubs and the Construction of Class Identities in South India," in Rachel Dwyer and Christopher Pinney (eds), *Pleasure and the Nation: The History, Politics and Consumption of Public Culture in India* (Delhi: Oxford University Press, 2001), 213.

17 Alexander Doty, *Making Things Perfectly Queer: Interpreting Mass Culture* (Minneapolis: University of Minnesota Press, 1993).

CHAPTER SIXTEEN
TRANSFORMATION

On 26 October 2013 at 9:00pm Greenwich Mean Time, thousands of dancers simultaneously performed the zombie dance sequence from Michael Jackson's music video *Thriller* (John Landis, 1982). Dancers in Australia, Austria, Brazil, Canada, China, England, Finland, Germany, Ireland, Japan, Mexico, the Netherlands, New Zealand, the Philippines, Rwanda, Scotland, Turkey and the United States practised the dance sequence using the instructional resources provided by Canadian dancer Ines Markeljevic who has organized the event since 2006 through the Thrill the World website (http://thrilltheworld.com). This global event is one iteration of the many transformations of Jackson's *Thriller*.

Jackson described *Thriller* as a short film rather than a music video. With a running time of thirteen minutes, *Thriller* was an ambitious project, situating the song "Thriller" within a layered set of horror movie vignettes. Over thirty years later, the film endures not only as a milestone in music video history (and an important contribution to the horror genre) but also as an evolving example of the ways in which films can be transformed. In addition to Thrill the World's annual global performance, the zombie dance sequence in the film has inspired several widely viewed "remakes" – from the performance by the inmates at the Cebu Provincial Detention and Rehabilitation Center in Cebu, Philippines to ones by wedding parties around the world. These re-enactments have been watched by millions of viewers on YouTube.

A brief overview of the history of the exhibition and reception of *Thriller* points to several of the most prominent ways in which films are transformed. First, the original music video was often aired on television in a truncated form, with networks cutting the thirteen-minute running time to two to three minutes in order to conform to a standard programming schedule (with the required

16.1 Michael Jackson's zombie dance sequence in *Thriller* (John Landis). Courtesy of Optimus Productions/The Kobal Collection.

number of commercial breaks for advertisers). A viewer might see the full version of the video on television and then see a shorter version on the same network later that day. *Thriller* was also sold on VHS as part of the "Making of Michael Jackson's *Thriller*" documentary. This chapter will incorporate such exhibition practices into a discussion of film censorship, one of the most influential transformations of film. Second, while the original song "Thriller" remained untranslated from English in the versions of the video that circulated globally, the dialogue in the short film was often subtitled in other languages. This chapter will explore subtitling, dubbing, and other forms of linguistic translation. Finally, the various fan-authored performances of the dance sequences from *Thriller* mentioned above capture the cultural significance and global reach of fan authorship, the form of transformation that is the focus of the final section of the chapter.

When scholars, critics, and fans discuss a film, they may be referring to different versions of the film. These variations may be a product of different exhibition conditions or of a material transformation of the film. Films may be copied, restored, colorized, miniaturized, damaged, censored, dubbed or appropriated. The chapter ahead investigates several practices that materially transform film – censorship, translation, and remixing – in an effort to remind you before the book ends that there are often many different versions of a film rather than a single film text.

WHAT WE WILL DO IN CHAPTER 16

- Survey the forms of censorship that transform film – from the governmental regulation of politically subversive content to the excision of scenes by exhibitors in order to trim a film's running time.

- Compare the forms of linguistic translation used in different national and industrial contexts, focusing on subtitling and dubbing practices.

- Explore fan authorship, particularly through the production of transformative works.

BY THE END OF CHAPTER 16 YOU SHOULD BE ABLE TO

- Identify a range of censorship practices that transform film.

- Understand the industrial and cultural significance of translation.

- Analyze the productive role that fans play in film cultures.

CENSORSHIP

Producers, distributors, and exhibitors may transform films in several ways and for several reasons. Scenes may be cut to reduce the running time of a film so that it will fit the schedule of a theatre or a network programming line-up. Scenes that contain violence, nudity, or profanity may be cut from films for exhibition on airplanes where a broad audience of adults and children may watch a film together. As we discussed in Chapter 10, films have been panned and scanned for distribution on home video or television, with actors and other elements of the cinematic image cut out of the frame. Producers have colorized some movies in order to attract a contemporary audience who might resist black-and-white images. Since the advent of DVD distribution, previously deleted scenes have been restored, producing "special editions" and "director's cuts" of the original films. Blockbusters have been re-released in theatres, sometimes in 3D versions. This long list of common industrial transformations indicates that film has never been a stable object – not only because of the material instability of the celluloid on which films were originally produced (as discussed at length in Chapter 13) but also because of the opportunities for producers, distributors, and exhibitors to transform film in order to serve different industrial goals. While each of these transformations merits further study, this section will focus on censorship and the industrial regulation of content.

One of the most familiar forms of film censorship is the use of ratings systems in different countries. The case study below explores the history of the ratings system in Hollywood where since 1990 films have been rated according to the following framework: G (general audiences), PG (parental guidance strongly suggested), PG-13 (parents strongly cautioned as material may be inappropriate for children under 13), R (restricted – persons under 17 not admitted without an adult), and NC-17 (no one 17 and under admitted). The British Board of Film Certification uses a different certification system. Their certificates include: U (universal or appropriate for all ages), PG (appropriate for all ages, but parental guidance is recommended), 12A (all children under 12 must be accompanied by an adult over 18 to see these films in a cinema), 12 (all children under 12 are ineligible to purchase or rent these films for home exhibition),

16.2 *Pan's Labyrinth* (Guillermo Del Toro). Courtesy of Tequila Gang/WB/The Kobal Collection.

15 (all audiences must be over 15), 18 (all audiences must be over 18), and R18 (films approved only for exhibition in licensed adult cinemas or for sale in adult stores). The British certification system makes distinctions between watching movies in the theatre and buying or renting them for viewing at home. The ages listed in the Hollywood and British systems are similar but not identical, and the standards they apply to movies vary.

Films that circulate globally may receive different ratings in each country. For example, *Pan's Labyrinth* (*El Laberinto del Fauno*, Guillermo Del Toro, 2006) received a 15 in Britain, an R in the US, a C in Mexico (restricting the audience to age 18 and above), an MA in Australia (under 15 must be accompanied by an adult), a 12 in France (unsuitable for children under 12), and an R21 in Singapore (no one under 21 is admitted). A critically acclaimed Mexican and Spanish co-production, *Pan's Labyrinth* presents the story of Ofelia, a young girl living in Spain in 1944, who explores a fantasy world populated by fauns, insects, and other creatures. The movie incorporates elements of the horror genre into its visual design and moves seamlessly between the fairy tale world that only Ofelia sees and the menacing reality of her new home with a sadistic stepfather. The brief sample of the various ratings the film received reveals very different assessments of the film, with the minimum age for audiences ranging from 12 in France to 21 in Singapore.

The rating or certificate a film receives in each country is based on a determination of whether or not the content of the film is appropriate for young audiences. These evaluations often focus on sex, violence, and profanity. In 2013, a different ratings system was introduced in Sweden. The Bechdel Test, named for Alison Bechdel who introduced the concept in her comic strip *Dykes to Watch Out For* in 1985, requires that a film include at least one scene in which two named female characters talk to each other about something other than a man. If a movie passes this test, it receives an A rating by the four independent Swedish theatres who adopted the policy. The Swedish Film Institute supports the Bechdel Test, but it is not an official regulation. The goal of the test is to draw attention to the lack of roles for women. Supporters of the measure argue that the rating brings public attention to the need to produce more films that feature women. The Bechdel Test seeks to transform film by influencing producers to develop stories and characters that involve women's perspectives and by educating audiences about the importance of considering gender representation when evaluating (and choosing) films.

In *This Film Is Not Yet Rated* (2006), director Kirby Dick exposes the lack of transparency and consistency that define the MPAA ratings board's decisions. In the film, Dick hires a private investigator to learn the identities of the members of the board. The investigator's findings reveal that the board members lack any relevant training. They do not even meet the MPAA's stated member selection criterion of being the

CASE STUDY: HOLLYWOOD FILM RATINGS

In *Hollywood v. Hard Core: How the Struggle over Censorship Saved the Modern Film Industry*, film scholar Jon Lewis recounts the development of the contemporary **MPAA ratings system**, the framework for the **content regulation** of Hollywood films for the US market. Lewis quotes a recollection by Jack Valenti, the longtime President of the MPAA who supervised the introduction of the ratings system in 1968, one of his first high-profile acts after assuming the helm of the MPAA in 1966. Valenti shares a conversation he had with studio executives about regulating potentially offensive dialogue in *Who's Afraid of Virginia Woolf* (Mike Nichols, 1966), a film that marked a turning point for film censorship in Hollywood. Valenti remembers:

> [F]or the first time on screen, the word "screw" and the phrase "hump the hostess" were heard. In company with the MPAA's general counsel, Louis Nizer, I met with Jack Warner, the legendary chieftain of Warner Bros., and his top aide, Ben Kalmenson. We talked for three hours, and the result was the deletion of the word "screw" and retention of "hump the hostess," but I was uneasy over the meeting. It seemed wrong that grown men should be sitting around discussing such matters.[1]

At the time of this meeting, the content of Hollywood films was self-regulated by the MPAA through the voluntary participation of the Hollywood studios who submitted their films for approval prior to release. The Production Code (or Hays Code, named for Will Hays, the President of the MPPDA or Motion Picture Production and Distribution Association, the precursor to the MPAA) was initially introduced in 1930 and was enforced beginning in 1934. The Code began with a general principle that "No picture shall be produced that will lower the moral standards of those who see it. Hence the sympathy of the audience should never be thrown to the side of crime, wrongdoing, evil, or sin." This broad pronouncement was followed by a series of specific applications including:

- Scenes of passion should not be introduced when not essential to the plot.
- Excessive and lustful kissing, lustful embraces, suggestive postures and gestures, are not to be shown.
- In general, passion should be treated in such a manner as not to stimulate the lower and baser element.
- Sex perversion or any inference to it is forbidden.
- Miscegenation (sex relationships between the white and black races) is forbidden.[2]

This list of prohibitions is a sample of the guidelines included in the Code under the heading "Sex." Other headings include: Crimes Against the Law, Vulgarity, Obscenity, Profanity, Costume, Dances, Religion, Locations, National Feelings, Titles, and Repellent Subjects. Concerns about the representation of sex and sexuality dominate the Code. Even the single prohibition under the neutral heading "Locations" addresses sex: "The treatment of bedrooms must be governed by good taste and delicacy."

16.3 *Who's Afraid of Virginia Woolf* (Mike Nichols). Courtesy of Warner Bros./The Kobal Collection.

The Production Code Administration's enforcement of the Code was a system of **prior restraint**: their interventions were aimed at film producers not consumers. The Code prevented films from being screened in theatres without the Production Code Seal of Approval (a seal visible in the opening frame of many classical Hollywood films). By designing a system of strict self-regulation, the MPAA insulated the industry from the outside interference of either the US government or organizations like the Catholic Church's Legion of Decency. Films that were not approved by the PCA were not banned or burned, and the directors of the films were not imprisoned or exiled. The Production Code, after all, was not a law. The economic and cultural consequences of the PCA's actions, however, were significant. Since the vertically integrated studios owned most of the theatres in the United States, only studio films that successfully navigated the approval process would have a theatrical release. The Code became a powerful tool for the studios as they sought to consolidate and maintain their control of film production, distribution, and exhibition. The Code also prompted a new cinematic grammar, as directors and writers tried to find ways to circumvent it. During the 1940s, for example, smoking cigarettes on screen developed into a visual shorthand for sex. From Bette Davis in *Now, Voyager* (Irving Rapper, 1942) to Humphrey Bogart in almost every film in which he starred, including *Casablanca* (Michael Curtiz, 1942), *The Maltese Falcon* (John Huston, 1941), and *The Big Sleep* (Howard Hawks, 1946), stars and the characters they played lit cigarettes on screen to signal both sexual seduction and consummation.

The influence of the Code had begun to wane by the time *Who's Afraid of Virginia Woolf* was released. Several factors contributed to the crisis in the late 1960s that led to the formation of a ratings system to replace the Code. First, by 1960 the major studios had sold the theatres they had owned, as a condition of the Paramount Consent Decree of 1948. Secondly, films from other countries had been screened more frequently at independent theatres in major US cities, generating enthusiasm among American audiences for more sophisticated representations of sex and other topics, threatening the relevance of the Code. *À Bout de Souffle* (*Breathless*) (Jean-Luc Godard, 1960), *L'Avventura* (Michelangelo Antonioni, 1960), and *La Dolce Vita* (Federico Fellini, 1960) arrived in the United States within a single year as part of a wave of "foreign films" that pressured Hollywood

16.4 Mae West in *Goin' To Town*. Courtesy of Paramount/The Kobal Collection.

to rethink its enforcement of the Code's morality. Thirdly, in 1952, the US Supreme Court ruled in the "Miracle Decision" that film was entitled to First Amendment protection as "free speech." The Court argued in favor of Joseph Burstyn, the distributor of the English subtitled version of the Italian-language film *The Miracle*, a segment of the anthology film *L'Amore* (Roberto Rossellini, 1948). The film was screened in 1950 in New York and was greeted with both critical praise (recognized as the best foreign language film of the year by the New York Film Critics Circle) and public outrage (deemed "sacrilegious" by the New York State Board of Regents). The Supreme Court's decision did not directly challenge the Code (since the Code was a system of industrial self-regulation rather than a law), but it undermined the Code's cultural influence.

The MPAA ratings system was officially introduced in 1968. Unlike the Code, the ratings system does not prevent films from being released theatrically by either granting or denying a seal of approval. Instead it assigns each submitted film a rating that indicates the appropriate audience for the film according to age. The original ratings were: G (general audiences), M (mature audiences), R (persons under 16 not admitted without an adult), and X (persons under 18 not admitted). The ratings have evolved over time, with M being replaced by PG (parental guidance strongly suggested) in 1972, PG-13 (parents strongly cautioned) being added in 1984, the age limit for R being raised to 17, and X being replaced by NC-17 (no one 17 or under admitted) in 1990.

16.5 *La Dolce Vita* (Federico Fellini). Courtesy of Riama-Pathé/The Kobal Collection/Pierluigi.

Lewis notes that the "MPAA's stated mission was to 'educate and inform,' not regulate."[3] The rating system, overseen by CARA (The Classification and Ratings Administration), invited parents to become more engaged in film culture in order to make informed choices about the films their children should and should not see. The new system became a marketing tool that allowed studios to produce films for specific audiences and to target those audiences more effectively through their promotions. Lewis explains:

> The system may well have been designed to educate and inform. But it was adopted by the MPAA, the National Association of Theater Owners (NATO), and the International Film Importers and Distributors of America (IFIDA) to get people back into the habit of going to the movies.[4]

The central motive behind the development of the ratings system was not education or regulation but profit. The involvement of exhibitors and distributors is crucial to the success and influence of the ratings system. While a film can be released theatrically without being submitted to the MPAA ratings board for an official rating, the major theatre chains will not exhibit unrated films or films with an NC-17 rating. Both unrated films and NC-17 films thus have a difficult time reaching audiences and earning money. The expansion of non-theatrical distribution platforms (as discussed in Chapters 10 and 11) has increased the opportunities for unrated and NC-17 films to generate revenue. Theatrical exhibition, however, remains an important source of income, at least for now.

parent of one or more children between the ages of 5 and 17. Dick also interviews filmmakers, including John Waters, Matt Stone, Kevin Smith, and Kimberly Peirce, to learn about their experiences submitting films to the board for review. These directors all produced films that were rated NC-17, and they argue that the rating is used to marginalize work identified as outside the cultural mainstream by the board's members. From these interviews, several decision-making patterns emerge. The board applies more restrictive ratings to: independent films (films made outside of the major studios), films containing explicit sex as opposed to explicit violence, and films depicting same-sex relationships as opposed to straight relationships. *This Film Is Not Yet Rated* captures both the ways that the ratings system protects the interests of the major studios and the seemingly arbitrary ways in which it exercises its authority. For example, director Matt Stone explains that he added several minutes of footage to a sex scene in his film *Team America: World Police* (Trey Parker and Matt Stone, 2004) so that he would have plenty of super-fluous material to cut when the ratings board inevitably asked him to reduce the length of the scene.

This Film Is Not Yet Rated focuses on the consequences of ratings decisions for independent filmmakers who are trying to secure an R rating for their films in order to access broad theatrical distribution. Film ratings also impact distribution on video and DVD. Film scholar Caetlin Benson-Allott analyzes the censorship of the film *Y Tu Mamá También* (Alfonso Cuarón, 2001) on DVD in the United States as an instance of the simultaneous censorship of gay sex, political critique and foreign language cinema. *Y Tu Mamá También* presents the story of two Mexican teenage boys, Julio and Tenoch, who embark on an impromptu road trip with an older woman named Lucia during the summer after they graduate from high school. Their road trip culminates in a climactic sex scene during which the boys turn their sexual attentions from Lucia to each other. In the final scene, the film's narrator explains in a voice-over that their friendship ended shortly after the road trip. The movie then closes with one final awkward conversation between the boys after a chance reunion. An unrated version was released in independent theatres in the United States. MGM had acquired the rights to distribute it on DVD, so they released two versions: the unrated version and an R-rated one with over five minutes of the film deleted, including the sex scene between the two main characters. The removal of this scene makes the film's conclusion – the rift between the two characters – confusing for viewers.

The consequences of the cut extend beyond this narrative gap. Benson-Allott explains that Cuarón develops the intimate friendship between the two boys, who occupy different class positions, as an allegorical critique of Mexican political and economic corruption. The deletion of the sex scene obscures that critique and points to a broader tendency in US domestic film distribution to censor films from other countries. Benson-Allott clarifies:

> [T]he censorship of Julio and Tenoch's love scene matters not only because it garbles Cuarón's movie but also because it exemplifies the latest challenge to foreign film distribution in the United States. The U.S. film industry has always sought to marginalize foreign sexuality, particularly foreign-language depictions of queer sexuality. However, today several economic factors directly related to the rise of home video have diminished foreign films' box office share to less than .5% and left it dependent on domestic distribution and thus prey to domestic censorship.[5]

Analyzing the censorship of *Y Tu Mamá También* for home video distribution in the United States reveals the centrality of market considerations to censorship policies and processes. As Lewis notes in his study of Hollywood censorship, "The motivation behind and function of content regulation reveal the truth in the old Hollywood adage 'When they tell you it's not about the money … it's about the money.'"[6]

While it is important to understand the factors that inform content regulation, it is equally important to recognize the material, cultural, and political consequences of content regulation. Censorship may take many forms in different industrial contexts – from criminalizing to cutting to classifying content. The agents of censorship may be governments, industries, or individuals. The scale of censorship may be global or local. In all of these cases, censorship transforms films. The unrated version of *Y Tu Mamá También* is a very different film from the R-rated version. Benson-Allott points out that while a DVD cover or a title screen may inform the viewer that the format of a film has been altered for domestic distribution (through panning and scanning, for example), viewers are rarely warned that the content has been altered. These transformations are significant, particularly because most viewers will remain unaware of them. Censorship may be not only a conventional or quotidian act but also a productive act, as the case study on censorship in India in Chapter 13 demonstrated. All instances of censorship, however, transform film, challenging our ability to identify a single filmic text.

EXERCISE

Research the censorship history of a film that you know well (or one mentioned in this book that you are eager to learn more about). Consult the Internet Movie Database (or another online source) to find a list of the film's certifications (or ratings) in the countries where it was released. Many of these certifications are organized by age – with the certification indicating the minimum age of viewers.

- Do you notice any inconsistencies in the list of certifications – in other words, is the certification more restrictive in one or two of the countries than it is in the others? If so, try to learn more about those certifications by conducting additional online research.
- What were the specific scenes in the film that provoked those strict certifications?
- Are the certifications consistent with those of other films in the same genre?
- Search for as many available versions of the film online as you can find, including legal and illegal copies of the film on DVD (or other home viewing formats) or available via streaming. In what ways does each version transform the film?
- Is the running time the same?
- Are there new scenes incorporated into the film or included as bonus features?
- What other alterations do you observe?

TRANSLATION

Before MGM's decision to cut scenes from *Y Tu Mamá También* so that the studio could release an R-rated DVD version in the US market, the film had already been transformed for its US theatrical release through the addition of English subtitles. Since the introduction of sound, language has been one of the primary barriers to both the global distribution of film and the regional distribution of film within multilingual communities. The translation of silent films was a much more straightforward process, with new inter-titles placed in the film for each new language market. The relative ease of this process certainly did not secure a wide global release for every silent film. As the earlier chapters on film as a commodity (Chapter 5) and on distribution (Chapter 10) have shown, global distribution involves a complicated and uneven set of negotiations and processes among studios, distributors, governments and consumers. Language, however, poses a special problem for sound cinema not only because distributors (or exhibitors) must arrange for the translation of films for distribution in global markets but also because the preferred translation methods vary from market to market. This section briefly profiles the challenges that translation poses and the most common solutions to that challenge.

The two most popular forms of film translation are **subtitling** and **dubbing**. Subtitling translates spoken dialogue through the appearance of written text, usually printed at the bottom of the film frame. Dubbing substitutes the original audio dialogue track with a new dialogue track featuring the primary language of the distribution region. Both processes translate dialogue from a **source language** into a **target language**. Preferences for subtitling or dubbing vary by region.

There are several considerations that inform translation formats: (1) cost, (2) literacy and (3) tradition. Dubbing is significantly more expensive than subtitling. Consider the costs of hiring dozens of voice actors, renting studio space for recording, and mixing the final recording as opposed to the cost of hiring a single translator to write subtitles and an editor to incorporate the titles into the film. This comparison oversimplifies the costs and considerations involved in each process, but the scope of resources required for dubbing is much more expensive than the cost of subtitling. Subtitles, of course, also require a literate audience. As the discussion of the marketing of *Crouching Tiger, Hidden Dragon* (Ang Lee, 2000) in Chapter 9 revealed, however, expectations about the nature of leisure time may be almost as significant an impediment to the acceptance of subtitling as literacy rates. In the United States in particular, many producers assume that audiences do not want to read subtitles, in spite of the presence of subtitles in blockbuster films such as *Star Wars* (George Lucas, 1977). Local traditions often outweigh concerns about cost or literacy. In Italy, for example, the dubbing industry thrives as a parallel film industry, and subtitled films have had a difficult time finding an audience (as explained in further detail in the case study later in this chapter).

In the contemporary film industry, subtitling a film may involve translators working on a freelance basis from remote locations. Subtitling is a form of media labor that workers can even complete from their homes, with minimal or no overhead investment from studios and distributors. With subtitling available for such a low cost, why would any distributor choose to dub films instead? Dubbing was established as a nationalized industry not only in Italy but also in Spain, Germany, and France, to name only a few examples. In each of these countries, the investment in the dubbing industry was linked to a desire to preserve national culture and to minimize the cultural and political impact of Hollywood films. In addition to imposing quotas to limit the number of films imported from other countries (as discussed in Chapter 5), national film industries can dub imported films into a national language in order to exert a sense of national ownership over them. Dubbing programs in France advanced the nation's interest in protecting the French language from the cultural incursions of English and other languages. In Spain, Germany and Italy, the national investments in an industrial infrastructure for dubbing began during the 1930s when fascist governments ruled in each country. In these cases, dubbing was an opportunity for the ideological expression of national pride. Film scholar Mark Betz notes, "The dictators of these countries were fully aware of how hearing one's language served to confirm its importance and reinforce a sense of national identity and autonomy."[7] This observation will be developed in the case study of dubbing in Italy.

The reception of dubbed and subtitled films has been mixed. Betz's analysis of subtitling and dubbing traditions within the context of European art cinema notes the disappointment that viewers experience when watching dubbed and subtitled films. Betz quotes film critic Richard Schickel's indictment of dubbing:

> You get fixed on those lips so obviously not speaking the lines you are hearing, you get to brooding about those radio station voices reading instead of acting their parts, and it becomes impossible to sustain identification with the figures on the screen. Subtitling is not a perfect solution to the language barrier, but it is relatively unobtrusive, does not deny the actors the use of their voices, the basic tools of their art, does not tamper with the intrinsic part of the film's design.[8]

Betz agrees with Schickel that subtitling involves the "least interference with the original film," but his long description of the ways that subtitles transform dialogue, mise-en-scène, and identification suggests that subtitled films may be as radically different from the original film as dubbed versions are:

> The primary issue for subtitling lies in the translation, which entails enormous cuts to the source dialogue – as much as half. While the ideal in subtitling is to translate each utterance in full, the limitation of screen space is a major obstacle. The average viewer's reading speed is 150 to 180 words per minute, with necessary intervals; this severely limits the duration and hence completeness of the subtitles, which means that source-language dialogue must often be translated in a condensed form. Subtitles also obstruct the integrity of composition and mise-en-scène by leading the viewer's look to the bottom of the frame. They focus audience attention on the translated words and the actors speaking them, excluding peripheral dialogue, sound, or characters. And they do not provide as full a translation as does dubbing. As well, audiences of subtitled films do not experience the words and the expressions of the performers simultaneously.[9]

Depending on the number of spoken languages in the film, the linguistic diversity of the target audience, and the visual form of the written languages presented in the translation (for example, letters or characters), a subtitled film may include subtitles in multiple languages positioned in different sections of the frame and presented in different graphic styles.

Some films will circulate in both dubbed and subtitled versions as a function of their distribution schedule. One prominent instance of this split translation strategy is the global distribution of the animated films of Japanese director Hayao Miyazaki. Miyazaki's films typically premiere in Japan featuring a Japanese cast of actors voicing all of the roles. Critically acclaimed for both their distinctive visual style and their sophisticated stories, films such as *Princess Mononoke* (1997), *Howl's Moving Castle* (2004), *Spirited Away* (2007), and *Ponyo* (2008) have been distributed globally in subtitled versions in order to accelerate their distribution. The process of dubbing takes much more time in the pre-production, production, and post-production phases, so arrangements for dubbed versions of the films usually begin while the subtitled versions are already in distribution (often in the international film festival circuit where Miyazaki's films have won many awards). This system gives distributors time to hire voice actors, record and mix their vocal tracks, and market the dubbed versions for both theatrical and home video distribution.

Miyazaki is the founder with Isao Takahata of Ghibli Films. His studio has a contract with Disney for the translation and distribution of the films Miyazaki directs to English-language markets. Disney has hired Hollywood stars to voice the main characters in the films. Matt Damon, Claire Danes, Betty White, Cate Blanchett, Liam Neeson, Christian Bale, Minnie Driver, and Lauren Bacall are among the stars who have voiced characters in Miyazaki's films. While the problems associated with dubbing still exist with dubbed versions of animated films (for example, imprecise lip synching), audiences have been much more open to dubbing in animated films.

The challenges presented by film translation are intensified in the case of multilingual films. One of the most famous examples of mistranslated multilingualism is Jean-Luc Godard's *Contempt* (*Le mépris*, 1963). The film brings together an international cast (including the German director Fritz Lang) to present the story of a troubled attempt to produce a film based on Homer's *Odyssey*. Only one character, the interpreter Francesca Vanini (played by Giorgia Moll) speaks all of the languages circulating in the film: French, German, Italian, and English. Her translations of dialogue within the film are a central source of Godard's critique of the compromises involved in international filmmaking. The dubbed Italian version transforms all of the dialogue into Italian, rendering the translator's role superfluous, even nonsensical. The dubbed English version released in the United States produces the same effect. Subtitled

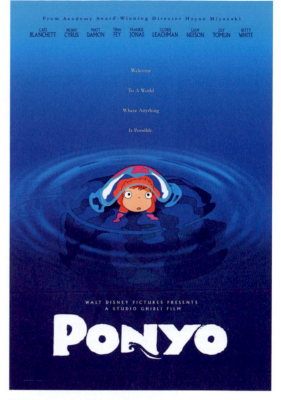

16.6 *Ponyo* poster featuring the names of Hollywood voice actors. Courtesy of Studio Ghibli/NTV/Dentsu/Toho/The Kobal Collection.

16.7 *Contempt* (Jean-Luc Godard). Courtesy of Rome-Paris-Films/The Kobal Collection.

versions at least preserve the sounds of the multiple original languages, allowing viewers who do not speak the languages but who might recognize acoustic differences between the languages to understand the context of the translator's interpretations (and deliberate misinterpretations).

Multilingual films have a long history. For a brief period after the introduction of sound, Hollywood studios recruited directors and casts from other countries to travel to Hollywood so that multiple versions of a single film could be shot at the same time, with each version featuring a different language. Paramount invested in the development of a satellite studio in Joinville, France (near Paris) to facilitate the production of these **MLV** (or **multiple language version**) films, as they were known. Sometimes over a dozen different versions of a single film would be shot within a period of one or two weeks. The Joinville studios would operate twenty-four hours a day, with each crew working in shifts. The French crew would pass their costumes and equipment to the Spanish crew, and then a few hours later the Spanish crew would pass their equipment to the English crew, and so on. This industrial solution to translation was short-lived, declining by the mid 1930s. Both the high costs of shooting multiple productions of the same film and the changing political climates in the European countries involved in MLV production made the Joinville experiment unsustainable. One of the most watched films from this period of MLV production is Universal's *Drácula* (George Melford), also known as "Spanish Dracula." Shot at night at Universal's studio in Hollywood after the shooting for Tod Browning's *Dracula* (1931) had wrapped for the day, *Drácula* has become a cult classic over the years. While many fans and critics treasure Bela Lugosi's performance as the title character in the English-language version, fans cite the improvisational performances, poor lighting, and continuity errors in the Spanish version as sources of pleasure. Shot on a budget of $55,000 (compared to the budget of $360,000 for the English-language version) *Drácula* not only translates the film into a different language but also shifts its visual style. *Drácula* looks more like an exploitation film than a Universal feature.

Multilingual films have become increasingly popular in the twenty-first century. *Slumdog Millionaire* (Danny Boyle, 2008), *Syriana* (Stephen Gaghan, 2005), *Inglourious Basterds* (Quentin Tarantino, 2009), *Monsoon Wedding* (Mira Nair, 2001) and *The Kite Runner* (Marc Forster, 2007) all feature dialogue in multiple languages, but they were all marketed as English-language films in anglophone countries. Film scholar Carol O'Sullivan explores the difficulties and opportunities that these films present for translators. She examines the use of different colors and fonts for the subtitles in the film *War* (Philip Atwell, 2007) to preserve linguistic differences. An action feature set in San Francisco, *War* foregrounds the conflict between rival gangs – the Chinese Triads and the Japanese Yakuza. O'Sullivan explains that the movie attempts to preserve multilingualism within its translation format, using different colors for each language and printing the subtitles in both the source language and the target language.[10] While this strategy is an improvement on subtitling practices that erase the differences between the spoken languages in a film, O'Sullivan notes that the strategy has not yet been perfected. The design codes Chinese characters as yellow and Japanese characters as red, reinforcing national and racial stereotypes. Furthermore, on some DVD versions of the film, the subtitles added for regional DVD audiences are printed over the subtitles incorporated into the original film, producing an illegible multilingual image.[11] While a perfect form of translation does not exist, digital technologies may generate new options for more precise translations through subtitling and dubbing. Many distributors release multiple linguistic versions of a film on the same disc and market "new and improved subtitles" for movies that have been distributed previously with poor translations.

16.8 *Drácula* (George Melford, 1931). Courtesy of Universal/The Kobal Collection.

EXERCISE

Choose a film that features a language that you do not speak. (Ideally you should choose a film in a language with which you have absolutely no familiarity.) Locate a copy of the film and watch the first fifteen minutes without any translation of the dialogue – in other words, without any dubbing or subtitling in the languages that you speak. Take notes, recording your impressions of the narrative and visual style. Then watch the film again with dubbing or subtitling in a language that you do speak. Take notes again, and then compare your observations from each screening.

- What did you notice during each screening?
- What did you enjoy most about the first screening?
- What were your biggest frustrations during the first screening?
- How did the second screening transform your understanding and experience of the film?
- Which screening did you enjoy more?
- Does language impact your experience of identification?

CASE STUDY: ITALIAN VOICE ACTORS AND THEIR FANS

The Italian dubbing industry and the forms of film reception it has generated both nationally and globally offer an opportunity to consider the impact of translation practices on film style and film culture. In the 1930s, Benito Mussolini, the Prime Minister of Italy and one of the architects of Italian Fascism, identified the Italian film industry as a potentially rich site for building national pride. Italy was a notoriously fractured country, with many Italians feeling a much deeper kinship with their local communities than with Italy as a whole. These local attachments were driven in part by the fact that many Italians spoke a regional dialect rather than the national version of Italian. The dubbing of all films into an official version of Italian simultaneously taught the Italian people to speak standard Italian and united them through a national film culture. With all actors on Italian screens "speaking" Italian, every film became an Italian film. The dubbing industry quickly emerged as a key component of the Fascist cultural agenda.

Dubbing studios opened throughout Rome, assembling production teams of voice actors, translators, directors, and audio technicians. Most early voice actors were recruited from the world of professional theatre, and they dubbed the Italian dialogue in polished, sophisticated accents. The dubbing studios were opened in order to dub films in other languages into Italian, but the studios soon started to dub the performances of local Italian actors as well (usually to override strong regional accents). Today dubbing is predominantly focused on international films, but the Italian dubbing industry still dubs some Italian films and many Italian television shows.

Responses to the Italian dubbing tradition have been mixed. The Italian director Michelangelo Antonioni and other directors have attacked dubbing. They claim that the acoustic and visual distractions of dubbing – for example, inept lip synching – undermine the director's vision for the film. Other directors embraced dubbing. For example, Federico Fellini relied on dubbing as a key element of his editing process, sometimes cutting the dialogue that the actors had spoken on set and replacing it with new dialogue performed by voice actors.

Italian audiences have generally been very accepting of dubbing. Fan cultures have embraced "doppiaggese" – the unique words and phrases that developed through attempts to synchronize the dubbed track with both the original dialogue and the screen actors' lip movements. Italian fans celebrate the words coined during the dubbing process and often incorporate those words into their own everyday dialogue as a cinematic slang.

The stars of the Italian dubbing industry also enjoy devoted fan followings. Voice actors typically dub all of the parts played by particular screen actors. For example, Oreste Lionello dubbed almost all of Woody Allen's screen performances; his voice may be heard in *Io e Annie/Annie Hall* (1977), *Manhattan* (1979), and *Misterioso omicidio a Manhattan/Manhattan Murder Mystery* (1993), among other Allen films. Italian audiences associate Allen's humor with Lionello's vocal performances. Other dubbing stars have voiced performances for multiple screen actors. Ferruccio Amendola, for example, dubbed roles played by Sylvester Stallone,

Robert De Niro, and Al Pacino. Italian audiences recognize the similarities among these vocal performances and associate these screen actors with one another. While many cinephiles argue that dubbing dilutes the purity of a film, Italian audiences appreciate the pleasure that dubbing adds to films. Audiences can enjoy not only De Niro's screen performance but also Amendola's vocal performance as if the two performances form a duet. In recent years, the association between particular voice actors and their screen counterparts has been less consistent. Voice actors are now often cast based on their suitability for a particular role rather than their association with a particular screen actor.

Recently, Hollywood stars have begun to dub their own performances. For example, Danny DeVito dubbed his performance in *The Lorax* (Chris Renaud and Kyle Balda, 2012) into both Italian and German. DeVito speaks only limited Italian, so his dubbed performance required extensive collaboration. An Italian dubber recorded a guide track for DeVito to follow. Then Italian dubbing directors worked with DeVito in a Los Angeles studio to produce his dubbed track. DeVito's heavily accented Italian was promoted in Italy as an authentic character trait.

Despite the popularity of dubbing in Italy, there are many legitimate points of resistance registered by those audiences who prefer subtitles. Dubbing can effectively erase the resonance of accents used in the original performances. The dubbing director may attempt to translate those accents into an equivalent Italian accent. For example, a southern Italian accent might be substituted for a southern American accent. These translations generally fail to capture the narrative and cultural significance of the original accent. Similarly, dubbing a multilingual film into a single language conceals the differences between the languages in the original film, often rendering narrative conflicts incomprehensible to the audiences of the dubbed version. In spite of the disadvantages of dubbing, subtitled films remain rare in Italy, with only a few art cinema theatres, such as Cinema Farnese in Rome, devoted to screening subtitled films (and very few films are distributed with Italian subtitle tracks). Dubbing has supported the development of the Italian film industry and produced a devoted base of fans.

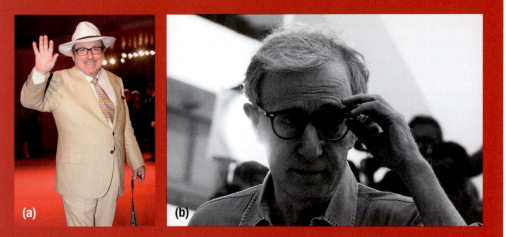

16.9 (a) Oreste Lionello and (b) Woody Allen. Courtesy of WireImage/Getty Images and AFP/Getty Images.

FAN AUTHORSHIP

This chapter has focused so far on the industrial transformation of film. From the MPAA's decision to assign an NC-17 rating to an independent film to the use of Italian voice actors to transform all films into Italian language films, we have profiled some of the most influential forms of film transformation initiated by studios, governments, producers and other film institutions and figures. In this final part of the chapter, we will focus on the transformation of film by fans. As the previous chapters on pleasure and identification revealed, fans have multiple opportunities for productive interactions with film culture, whether blogging about films as amateur critics, buying products associated with their favorite film stars, or visiting famous film locations, to name only a few examples of popular fan activities.

Fans differ from audiences in their attachment to specific films, genres, or stars (to name only a few of the media forms and figures that may energize fans). Unlike cinephilia, discussed at length in Chapter 14, **fandom** often involves the communal appreciation of movies and other cultural objects that are not valued by critics. Many analyses in the field of fan studies focus on popular (or obscure) television shows, magazines, graphic novels, and video games. Fandom is often understood as an experience that entails more than simply enjoying a film. Fans actively engage with the films (and other media texts) that they love, often participating in subcultural communities. The fans who attend conventions dressed in costumes from beloved science fiction films to buy and trade memorabilia, meet the stars who played their favorite characters, and interact with other fans fall into this version of fandom. Media theorist Henry Jenkins describes these fans as "active, critically engaged, and creative."[12] It is important to remember, however, that active forms of fandom are only one way in which viewers can engage with movies. Productive acts of fandom like the convention activities mentioned above are the most visible and organized opportunities for fans to demonstrate their excitement and commitment to a film, but many more fans will be content to maintain a more passive (and private) relationship to the media objects they love.

New media have impacted the activities of fans and their representation. While fan conventions still draw large crowds, online venues for fans have become a much more common and mainstream location for fan expression. Many of the activities that are associated with fan conventions – for example, **cosplay** or dressing in costumes to represent characters and often engage in role-playing activities and merchandise and memorabilia sales and trades – are now also conducted online. In addition to writing formal reviews of films and television shows through blogs, fans post **fan fiction** online, sometimes drafting scripts for new or revised scenes or entire films. In **slash fiction**, a subgenre within fan fiction, writers focus on the romantic relationships between characters, often developing relationships that were never explored in the film. Fans also participate in online discussion groups. Television producers have responded to the suggestions of fans by participating in these internet dialogues and even changing the scripts for future episodes, particularly when a dominant critique emerges. Fan communities often develop in response to film franchises because, like television shows, franchises invite audiences to sustain their attachment over a long time horizon. All of these activities involve transformation. Fans may transform films by reimagining and relocating their stories, characters and resolutions or even by exerting collective pressure on producers to change their creative decisions for upcoming films. The migration of fandom to online spaces has made the active forms of fandom profiled by Jenkins much more mainstream, allowing viewers to participate in fan culture without the investments of time and money associated with previous fan cultures.

CASE STUDY: REMIX VIDEOS

Fans have been producing homemade videos using footage from their favorite films for decades. When this involved working with VHS cassette tapes, the process was very cumbersome, and the videos that resulted were usually very roughly produced. The circulation of digital video (via DVD and online) and the proliferation of user-friendly video editing programs have made it much easier to produce a short video by editing original film footage, and the popularity of video-sharing sites like YouTube has made it much easier to distribute and view these videos. Remixing has thus become a much more common form of fan engagement than it was during the VHS era (and earlier periods of film history).

Remix videos often express a critical engagement with a film. For example, "Brokeback to the Future" combines excerpts from *Brokeback Mountain* (Ang Lee, 2005) and *Back to the Future* (Robert Zemeckis, 1985) in order to develop (or uncover) a romantic relationship between the two male lead characters in the latter film. Media theorist Virginia Kuhn asserts that remix videos should be understood as **digital arguments**:

> [A]lthough in common parlance the word *argument* connotes something like polemics, there are many forms of argument; the term is not limiting, and it can help break down the boundaries between fact and fiction. A poem can be an argument, as can a narrative, each deploying different rhetorical strategies.[13]

By identifying remix videos as digital arguments, Kuhn draws our attention to the rhetorical strategies that remix artists use and makes a place for the serious critical analysis of remix video. Kuhn's assessment of remix video as argument "resists the hierarchies that champion big media and make fannish efforts a second-class mode of discourse, the realm of the amateurish and the trivial."[14]

Remix videos offer fans an opportunity to produce an argument by interacting directly with a film. These videos generally do not circulate as commodities in the ways that commercially produced films do, but they circulate widely among fan communities and media scholars. There are many video genres and subgenres within the broader category of remix video, including recut trailers, fansubs, and **vids**. Below we will focus on vids both because vidding has received a considerable amount of recent scholarly attention and because **vidders** themselves are often active as media critics and theorists online, producing a rich body of creative and critical work as a resource for further study.

Vidding is a specific form of remix in which fans edit images from films or television shows into music videos, using a song (usually a pop song) to tell a new story about the found footage. These fanvids or vids are structured like commercial music videos. A vid usually features a single song and lasts for the duration of the song (with minimal editing of the audio track). The images are often edited into a montage sequence to tell a specific story about the featured characters, with the song providing a description or analysis of the story from the point of view of one of the characters or the vid's author. However, vids do not market songs in the way that music videos do. Instead, the songs used in vids enable the author to create an alternative narrative; the lyrics guide the viewer through the edited images, describing the actions and emotions of the characters on screen. The track thus becomes an expression of the author's desire.

A subset of fanvids called **shipper videos** captures fans' desires for a romantic relationship or "ship" to develop between two characters. This genre of fanvids dominates television vidding since many television narratives deliberately delay the romantic consummation of onscreen relationships in order to ensnare viewers in a shared experience of anticipation. The genre of shipper videos has become so established that other videos now operate as anti-shipper videos. For example, *Buffy v. Edward* (Jonathan McIntosh, 2009) rejects the celebration by fans of the character Edward Cullen from the *Twilight* film franchise by intercutting footage of Edward from *Twilight* with clips of the character Buffy from the American television show *Buffy the Vampire Slayer*. Using the convention of the eyeline match (discussed in this book's Interlude) to develop a visual rapport between the two characters, the video foregrounds Buffy's rejection of Edward's advances. Through the careful selection and organization of shots from the television show and the films, McIntosh exposes the misogyny underlying Edward's alleged romantic heroism and reasserts the feminist energies that surrounded the character of Buffy. The video has been viewed over three million times on YouTube.

While vidding has received a considerable amount of attention since the advent of the digital production and distribution of fan-created videos, vidding has a long history that predates the accessibility of digital editing and exhibition tools. Vidders, as the authors of vids are called, have been creating vids since the 1970s when they produced them by working with VHS tapes, sharing their work and their practices during fan conventions and by mail. Often working in grassroots collectives, a practice familiar from the discussion of collaborative filmmaking in Chapter 2, the majority of vidders are women. Media theorist Francesca Coppa explains the historical link between the labor of film editing and the development of remix culture as a form of fan authorship:

> Vidding is an art that happens through editing – a field historically open to women, as it was thought to be related to sewing. In the case of vidding, editing is not just about bringing images together; it is also about taking mass-media images apart. A vidder learns to watch television and movies fetishistically, for parts; to look for patterns against the flow of narrative structure; to slice desired images out of a larger whole.[15]

Vidders can stitch their own desires into the film's narrative, exposing the representational biases or gaps in commercial cinema and television and inserting new narrative preoccupations. This procedure can be particularly important for viewers whose desires are ignored or misrepresented on screen, serving as a strategy of resistant reading like those profiled in Chapter 15. Coppa explains:

> Entire characters and subplots can be eliminated or marginalized, so that the vid asserts the vidder's own narrative values. Foreground can become background and vice versa. Action sequences might be excised in favor of character development or relationships;

secondary characters might be moved into prominence. This customization of the visual text is particularly important for women and people of color, who often find their desires marginalized. In vidding, their priorities are central.[16]

One of the most prolific contemporary vidders is an artist who uses the alias Luminosity. Her YouTube channel includes over sixty original vids. Many of them focus on television shows, including *Buffy the Vampire Slayer*, *Angel*, and *Supernatural*. Television shows dominate vidding culture because they provide a large archive of found footage to reference. A vidder who wants to develop a relationship between two supporting characters in a television show may be able to draw from over one hundred hours of footage (in the case of a long-running show). When working with a feature film with an average running time of less than two hours, there is less material to transform. The length of a film in comparison to a television show is not only a practical constraint but also an emotional limitation; vidders often develop deeper attachments to television shows because they may be immersed in their stories for years rather than hours. Luminosity, however, has produced several important vids that engage with films. She has remixed *300* (Zach Snyder, 2006), *Death Proof* (Quentin Tarantino, 2007), *Night of the Hunter* (Charles Laughton, 1955), and *Last Year at Marienbad* (Alain Resnais, 1961), to name only a few examples.

A collaborative spirit defines the work of Luminosity and many other contemporary vidders. While digital production and distribution resources allow vidders to work very independently, they continue to showcase work at conventions ("Retrograde" premiered at the Vividcon convention in Chicago in August 2013) and to engage in lively dialogue with each other and their fans online. They also work together to archive their work online through efforts like the legal advocacy and archiving projects initiated by the Organization for Transformative Works (OTW). OTW hosts An Archive of Our Own, an online archive for vids and other remix videos. These efforts are vital for the preservation of transformative works because the copyright holders of the found footage remove many vids from public online exhibition spaces. Several of Luminosity's YouTube video links lead to messages reporting that the videos have been removed for copyright violations. In an interview, Luminosity commented on this form of censorship: "If anything, vids provide free advertising. I wish the industry would join us in the 21st century."[17]

Remix videos share many features with the genre of **found footage films** (or archival films) introduced in Chapter 13. Found footage filmmakers are usually grouped with experimental filmmakers because they work outside the industrial framework of commercial cinemas and produce films that challenge the formal and narrative expectations that most audiences bring to film. Filmmakers such as Tracey Moffatt, Les LeVeque, and Naomi Uman transform popular film footage into original short films. They use innovative editing techniques to bring characters and concepts from the periphery of the original film to the center of the new film. Tracey Moffatt's *Lip* (1999) presents scenes of female African-American servants in Hollywood films that through a word, a gesture, or a facial expression enjoy a fleeting opportunity to talk back to their employers. By editing these moments together into a condensed sequence, Moffatt allows the characters to generate a sustained critique of the social and political conditions their characters faced (and that many of the films in which the characters appeared reinforced). Les LeVeque's *Backwards Birth of a Nation* (2000) engages a single film: D.W. Griffith's *Birth of a Nation* (1915), a film both recognized for its achievement in the development of cinematic narrative structures and deplored for its overtly racist representation of the US Civil War and the postwar period of Reconstruction. By compressing the 187-minute film into thirteen minutes, screening it backwards from the final shot to the opening shot, and inverting the black and white images in each frame, LeVeque produces a haunting film that renders the racist imagery in the film both more visually abstract and even more emotionally unsettling. LeVeque's found footage films require precise digital manipulations, but found footage films also employ less technologically complicated strategies. For example, to make *Removed* (1999), Naomi Uman used nail polish remover to erase the female body from an old (and unnamed) porn film. By removing the female body from each frame, she produced a powerful critique of the ways that pornography invites viewers to gaze at women. *Rock Hudson's Home Movies*, discussed at length in a case study in the previous chapter, also uses found footage to produce a powerful argument; it differs from the films profiled here primarily through the scope of its engagement with Hudson's filmography, its longer running time, and its inclusion of the filmmaker as a central part of the film.

Fans who make remix videos employ many of the same editing techniques and rhetorical strategies used by experimental filmmakers. Amateur remix video makers, however, do not enjoy the same critical reception within media institutions (film archives, film festivals, and museums). Remix video circulates in different spaces: fan conventions, public and private online archives, and through word of mouth. Remix videos may express the intimate desires of individual artists, but remix culture is deeply social (and often anonymous, with vidders often adopting online aliases). In this sense, remix videos may be understood as one element of a broader social network in which fans form communities. The recent viral popularity of digital fanvids, however, has transformed vidders like Luminosity (profiled in the case study above) into media stars and sparked new scholarly projects like the journal *Transformative Works and Cultures*.

Some remix videos have also captured the attention of the media industries. Most vidders consider their videos to be **transformative works** that are protected under copyright law, but some fanvids have been subject to legal action. According to the "Code of Best Practices for Fair Use in Online Video" published by the Center for Social Media at American University in Washington, DC, the principle of **fair use** allows users to remix copyrighted film footage if "the nature of the use, the nature of the work used, the extent of the use, and its economic effect" are deemed appropriate.[18] Whether or not a remix video violates the principle of fair use is often a grey area for remix artists. Key to many legal discussions of fair use is the extent to which the original footage has been transformed. Often remix videos, especially vids, sufficiently transform the film footage that they use, but they use entire pop songs as the soundtrack for the video without permission from the artist. Many (though certainly not all) vids that are removed from online exhibition spaces by copyright holders are removed for music copyright violations. Many vidders and other remix artists discuss their work as an intimate form of self-expression (linked to the discourses of self-expression reviewed in Chapter 2), but their self-expression is not always legally protected.

OTW was founded in the United States to educate people about the limits and possibilities of the fair use of film footage, and to advocate for a dynamic and flexible understanding of fair use in order to preserve the products of fan cultures. Run "by fans and for fans," OTW is a politically active organization. In 2012, several of its members testified on behalf of OTW at the US Library of Congress's Digital Millennium

Copyright Act hearings in favor of renewing and expanding the exemption for "Noncommercial Remixers." Their collaborative efforts to promote and preserve transformative works include an online archive, a wiki, and an oral history project.

EXERCISE

Produce a storyboard for a video remix for one (or more) of your favorite films (one that you can easily access online or on DVD). As you design your remix video, keep in mind Kuhn's assertion that remix videos are *digital arguments*. Your video should present, should *be*, an argument, rather than merely an editing exercise. Select one of the following options for your video:

- Produce a trailer or music video that foregrounds your personal investment in the film (for example, your fascination with a particular star, a franchise, the film's dialogue, or the film's location).
- Create a "shipper" video, using editing strategies (for example, the eyeline match) to develop an imagined romantic relationship between two characters.
- Create a voice-over commentary for one scene from the film (or for an edited montage of clips from various scenes).
- Produce a set of alternate subtitles for one scene from the film.

Then write a short paragraph explaining the ways in which your video develops your relationship to the film as a fan (which may be adoring, critical, irreverent, resistant, or some combination of all of these positions).

Finally, if you have access to a video editing program (and time), create the video and upload your video to YouTube, Facebook or other online sites. Track the comments that are posted over the coming weeks (or months or years). (These videos may take weeks or more to produce, so creating a storyboard is a more manageable approach.)

You may find the Center for Social Media's overview of fair use for online video to be a helpful resource as you embark on this project: http://centerforsocialmedia.org/fair-use/related-materials/codes/code-best-practices-fair-use-online-video.

SUMMARY

Many analyses of cinema discuss a film as if it were a single, stable text. Film, however, is a reproducible medium, and the process of reproduction often involves significant, even radical, transformations. The discussion of the transformations of film covers very broad terrain – from the censorship of film to the translation of film to the remixing of film by fans in their own creative works. Censorship may entail the removal of entire films or segments of films from public circulation by governmental or industrial bodies for political and economic motives. In fact, many popular discussions of censorship imagine censorship as an inherently conservative and restrictive operation. While there are many examples in film history to support this view, censorship also takes place in less politically acute ways – from the decisions of exhibitors to cut scenes from a film in order to trim the film's running time to a studio's decision to include a happy ending in order to please audiences, leaving the original ending on the cutting room floor (only to be restored later as part of the "director's cut" of the film on DVD). The translation of dialogue also transforms films. Dubbing and subtitling processes transform film for different regional audiences, severing the films that different viewers watch from "the film" that much scholarship describes. Finally, films are transformed when fans assume the role of author and remix found footage from films for the production of new creative works. These fan productions are an increasingly vital part of film production because of their accessibility through online distribution networks.

FURTHER READING

Lewis, Jon. *Hollywood v. Hard Core: How the Struggle over Censorship Saved the Modern Film Industry*. New York and London: New York University Press, 2000.

> This study of Hollywood censorship traces the development of the current MPAA ratings system. Lewis reviews the shifting cultural values, economic considerations and individual films that sparked changes in the way that the MPAA approached censorship. *Hollywood v. Hard Core* includes both brief case studies of the censorship of individual films and broad analyses of the concerns that have shaped censorship policies. The book's appendix includes codes and standards that have served as frameworks for Hollywood censorship from 1927 to the present.

O'Sullivan, Carol. *Translating Popular Film*. London: Palgrave Macmillan, 2011.

> O'Sullivan discusses the ways that viewers encounter multiple languages in cinema and the forms of translation that overtly or covertly present those languages. Examining not only subtitling and dubbing but also the forms of visual translation that some films employ, O'Sullivan explores the role of language in cinematic storytelling. The book's filmography is both geographically and historically broad, but the bulk of her discussion focuses on Hollywood films.

Transformative Works and Cultures, http://journal.transformativeworks.org/index.php/twc/

> An online, peer-reviewed journal published by the Organization for Transformative Works. Media scholars, critics, and artists publish articles about transformative works, including fan fiction and fan vids. Many contributors take advantage of the online publication format to include links to the fan vids they analyze or other relevant online content. The journal thus serves as both an ongoing scholarly investigation of transformative works and an archive of transformative works.

FILMS REFERENCED IN CHAPTER SIXTEEN

300 (Zach Snyder, 2006)

L'Amore (Roberto Rossellini, 1948)

Annie Hall (Woody Allen, 1977)

L'Avventura (Michelangelo Antonioni, 1960)

Backwards Birth of a Nation (Les LeVeque, 2000)

Beasts of the Southern Wild (Benh Zeitlin, 2012)

The Big Sleep (Howard Hawks, 1946)

Birth of a Nation (D.W. Griffith, 1915)

À Bout de Souffle (*Breathless*) (Jean-Luc Godard, 1960)

Buffy v. Edward (Jonathan McIntosh, 2009)

Casablanca (Michael Curtiz, 1942)

Contempt (*Le mépris*) (Jean-Luc Godard, 1963)

Crouching Tiger, Hidden Dragon (Ang Lee, 2000)

Death Proof (Quentin Tarantino, 2007)

La Dolce Vita (Federico Fellini, 1960)

Dracula (Tod Browning, 1931)

Howl's Moving Castle (Hayao Miyazaki, 2004)

Inglourious Basterds (Quentin Tarantino, 2009)

The Kite Runner (Marc Forster, 2007)

Last Year at Marienbad (Alain Resnais, 1961)

Lip (Tracey Moffatt, 1999)

The Lorax (Chris Renaud and Kyle Balda, 2012)

The Maltese Falcon (John Huston, 1941)

Manhattan (Woody Allen, 1979)

Manhattan Murder Mystery (Woody Allen, 1993)

Monsoon Wedding (Mira Nair, 2001)

Night of the Hunter (Charles Laughton, 1955)

Now, Voyager (Irving Rapper, 1942)

Pan's Labyrinth (*El Laberinto del Fauno*, Guillermo Del Toro, 2006)

Ponyo (Hayao Miyazaki, 2008)

Princess Mononoke (Hayao Miyazaki, 1997)

Removed (Naomi Uman, 1999)

Rock Hudson's Home Movies (Mark Rapaport, 1992)

Slumdog Millionaire (Danny Boyle, 2008)

Spirited Away (Hayao Miyazaki, 2007)

Star Wars (George Lucas, 1977)

Syriana (Stephen Gaghan, 2005)

Team America: World Police (Trey Parker and Matt Stone, 2004)

This Film is Not Yet Rated (Kirby Dick, 2006)

Thriller (John Landis, 1982)

War (Philip Atwell, 2007)

Who's Afraid of Virginia Woolf (Mike Nichols, 1966)

Y Tu Mamá También (Alfonso Cuarón, 2001)

NOTES

1 Jon Lewis, *Hollywood v. Hard Core: How the Struggle over Censorship Saved the Modern Film Industry* (New York and London: New York University Press, 2000), 136.

2 Quoted in Lewis, 302–307.

3 Lewis, 141.

4 Lewis, 142.

5 Caetlin Benson-Allott, "Sex versus the Small Screen: Home Video Censorship and Alfonso Cuarón's *Y Tu Mam*á *También*," *Jump Cut* 51 (2009), accessed 1 October 2013.

6 Lewis, 7.

7 Mark Betz, *Beyond the Subtitle: Remapping European Art Cinema* (Minneapolis: University of Minnesota Press, 2009), 90.

8 Quoted in Betz, 49.

9 Betz, 91.

10 Carol O'Sullivan, *Translating Popular Film* (London: Palgrave Macmillan, 2011), 193.

11 O'Sullivan, 193–195.

12 Henry Jenkins, *Fans, Bloggers, and Gamers: Exploring Participatory Culture* (New York: New York University Press, 2006), 1.

13 Virginia Kuhn, "The Rhetoric of Remix," *Transformative Works and Cultures* 9 (2012), 3–2, accessed 1 October 2013.

14 Kuhn, 2–1.

15 Francesca Coppa, "An Editing Room of One's Own: Vidding as Women's Work," *Camera Obscura* 26(2) (2011), 124.

16 Coppa, 124.

17 Logan Hill, "The Vidder," *New York Magazine*, 12 November 2007.

18 http://www.cmsimpact.org/sites/default/files/online_best_practices_in_fair_use.pdf.

WRITING ABOUT CINEMA

Many students writing about cinema for the first time feel overwhelmed by the task. From hesitations about "overanalyzing" films that you love and thus destroying the pleasure you take in watching them to confusion about how to describe the filmic image, writing about cinema provokes a range of valid and important concerns. Fortunately, the best practices for writing in general also apply to writing about film. You may be relieved to learn that the writing skills that you have honed in other disciplines will serve you well as you approach the new task of writing about film. Like writing in other fields, the best writing about cinema presents original ideas in a clear and lively prose style with well-documented evidence. This chapter will introduce a set of strategies for writing about cinema that build on the knowledge you have already accumulated about good writing.

WHAT WE WILL DO IN "WRITING ABOUT CINEMA"

- Discuss the importance of reading for the development of writing skills.
- Outline the major critical frameworks for writing about cinema.
- Introduce research methods relevant to cinema studies.
- Present strategies for revising essays.

BY THE END OF "WRITING ABOUT CINEMA" YOU SHOULD BE ABLE TO

- Plan your essay by brainstorming and outlining ideas.
- Perform a close reading of key film scenes.
- Conduct research using a variety of print and online resources.
- Write and revise your essay.

READING ABOUT CINEMA

Good writers are usually good readers. In fact, many writers spend more time reading than they do writing. In the realm of literature, there is generally a much sharper awareness of the critical relationship between reading and writing. Acclaimed novelists are often asked to share lists of their favorite writers and books with prestigious journals, and some novelists also professionally review the novels published by their peers. These writers are embedded in discussions of good writing as an integral part of their profession. Scholars also review the books of other scholars, but these reviews generally focus on the academic intervention that the book makes (for example, introducing an archival discovery, presenting a new theoretical framework, or bringing together two fields of study) rather than the writer's style. In many academic fields, including cinema and media studies, scholars (and students) read many important books and articles that are poorly written. This chapter will focus not only on the mechanics of writing about cinema but also on the art of writing well.

The preparation for writing an essay will often (but not always) involve research, so reading is a key element of the early stages of the writing process. For all writers, however, reading should be an ongoing part of the development of good writing skills. In other words, writers should read as much and as often as possible, not only in the build-up to a particular writing assignment. Many writers who focus on cinema as a subject see reading about cinema as an extension of their love of film. Reading about the lives of film stars, the production histories of particular films, changes in film policy, gender politics in the film industry, or any of the many other topics that fall within the very broad field of cinema studies gives writers a richer understanding of film history, film theory, and individual films. Cultivating the practice of reading about cinema as a daily and ongoing form of engagement with film culture (as opposed to a targeted research project in preparation for a specific assignment) exposes writers to a variety of critical approaches and prose styles. Through extensive reading, writers develop an "eye" or "ear" for good prose, and this sensitivity then informs their own writing. Scholars are not the only people who write about film. This section will introduce writers from various professions and disciplines, the forms that their writing takes, and information about accessing their work.

Critics

The work of film critics reaches a broader audience than any other form of writing about cinema. As discussed at length in Chapter 12, "Evaluative contexts," film criticism is an influential part of film culture and the film industry. The internet has dramatically expanded the number of venues for film criticism (and the number of people who describe themselves as film critics). Once a coveted occupation held only by a small number of newspaper, magazine, and television journalists, "film critic" is now a job (albeit often an unpaid one) held by many people who actively publish film reviews on corporate, independent, and personal websites and blogs. While there are still high-profile reviewers who work for particular publications (for example, A.O. Scott or Manohla Dargis at the *New York Times*), the rise of amateur reviewing online has begun to chip away at the institution of professional film reviewing (and many reviewers have lost their jobs as a result). While that phenomenon may provoke disappointment and nostalgia, the internet has proven to be a valuable database and archive for film reviews both professional and amateur.

Sites like Metacritic (www.metacritic.com) catalog the film reviews published in a range of publications, including several online-only venues, and assign each review a score and then each film a composite score. While the scores serve as an interesting example of the effect of computational logic on film culture, Metacritic is most valuable as an archive. The site allows for both horizontal and vertical research – inviting readers to click links that lead to all of the reviews of a particular film or all of the reviews written by a particular reviewer. Following these links can provide a useful opportunity to learn about the critical reception of a film across an array of media outlets, encounter a range of different writing styles among the sample reviews, and trace the style of a reviewer across a number of reviews.

Metacritic should not be the only destination for writers who are interested in reading film reviews. The site limits its coverage to recent films released in the United States and reviewed by US media outlets. The book *American Movie Critics: An Anthology from the Silents until Now*, edited by Phillip Lopate, provides a broader historical survey of American film criticism. Turning to the online editions of newspapers and magazines in other countries will offer a glimpse of the international reception of particular films. Reading blogs will provide access to candid assessments of films, written without the (often welcome) constraints of major media outlets. For example, the film critic Baradwaj Rangan writes English-language reviews of international cinema for the periodical *The Hindu* (available online). Rangan also maintains an active personal blog where he reviews Hindu and Tamil films. A comparison of the reviews published in *The Hindu* with those published on the blog will indicate the stylistic differences associated with these publication contexts. The online edition of the British Film Institute journal *Sight and Sound* includes film reviews, interviews, and feature articles from the magazine. The site also provides links to other British Film Institute projects and resources, including publishing and programming activities. These links may provide valuable contexts for the *Sight and Sound* reviews. While most academic writing assignments require students to move beyond a film review to produce an essay with a scholarly argument, reviews are an important starting point and a key element of the practice of reading and writing about film.

Journalists

Film critics are not the only people who cover films and the film industry for newspapers, magazines and websites. Established **trade publications** like *The Hollywood Reporter* and *Variety* report on acquisitions by the major studios, production budgets, new trade policies, technological innovations and industry gossip. Their daily online editions keep readers up-to-date on industry trends and issues. Major newspapers such as the *New York Times* include special sections on the media, entertainment, technology, business, and style. Information about the film industry can be found in all of these sections on any given day. At the larger newspapers and magazines, each journalist will maintain a specific industrial focus in their work (for example, television or entertainment law), and some readers will follow the work of a single journalist with more devotion than the overall coverage of the film industry, especially if the journalist is a good writer. The media outlets with the most reliable coverage of the contemporary film industry will also often be useful archives for information about significant events in film history.

Programmers and curators

Programmers have produced revealing (and well-written) essays and books about cinema. Film programmers and curators work for independent theatres, museums, universities or film festivals. Their job in selecting films for exhibition is far more complicated and exciting than the work of exhibitors at the major theatre chains (who generally arrange to show the same limited slate of studio films that are in exhibition at all other multiplex theatres). Programmers and curators may select a set of films united by a shared director, composer, or star for a retrospective, or they may highlight an emerging national cinema in a film series, or they may invite a filmmaker to introduce an experimental film that is otherwise unavailable to audiences. Many programmers and curators write about the films that they select in essays for exhibition catalogues (a common practice at museums), in program notes (distributed at film festivals), or in newspapers and magazines. Their reflections on the historical and cultural importance of the films they have selected may be of great interest to readers who are investigating those films, and they often write in an engaging and accessible prose style.

Actors, directors, and other industry personnel

Books and articles published by directors, actors and other industry artists and insiders are among the most entertaining examples of writing about cinema. Many readers have encountered interviews with these figures in various publications, but reading memoirs and essays often provides an opportunity to learn much more not only about the author but also about the industrial and cultural context in which he or she worked or works. Some of the best examples focus on the industry itself. For example, journalist Lillian Ross examined the production of director John Huston's film *The Red Badge of Courage* (1951) in her book *Picture*, offering a behind-the-scenes account of Hollywood filmmaking. Others offer a broader account of the author's personal life within and beyond the industry. While these books may not at first glance seem relevant to cultivating the necessary skills for good writing about cinema, they accomplish two important things. Firstly, they provide details about the film industry and film history that readers may not encounter anywhere else (especially details about experiences on a film set). Secondly, they offer examples of lively and accessible writing styles. Some examples of this form of writing are found in the booklets that accompany DVDs and Blu-ray discs.

Scholars

Most of the books and essays referenced in this book are scholarly works. As discussed in the section below, different scholars approach the same film or set of films from very different points of view. Each approach will entail specific research and writing methods. When citing sources in a book or selecting books and articles to include on a syllabus, scholars usually pick the relevant examples that are the most historically significant (in other words, the canonical texts that have shaped or are shaping the field). While most or even all of these examples are models of good research skills and rigorous analytical thinking, not all of them are models of good writing. There is no reason that reading a memoir should be a pleasure but reading a scholarly book should be a chore. The best scholarly writing captures your interest from the opening paragraph and compels your curiosity until the conclusion.

EXERCISE

In your internet browser, open a new bookmark folder devoted to writing about cinema. As you discover trade periodicals, blogs, film journals, or individual articles you admire, bookmark those sites. They can become daily (or weekly) destinations for reading and browsing, sites that you will visit as frequently as your other favorite websites. To begin to make these reading practices a habit, establish some routines at the outset. For example, decide that every time you visit Facebook, you will next read an article in *Film Quarterly* online. Every time you check your e-mail, you will browse the front page of *Variety*. You can begin with only a few bookmarked sites and add to your folder gradually as you become more familiar with the world of writing about cinema online. Until then, you can use the recommendations in this chapter as a guide, and you can ask your instructors to recommend their favorite writers (stressing that you are asking them to recognize the best *writing* rather than the most important books).

CRITICAL FRAMEWORKS

Scholarly writing about cinema usually involves the establishment of a critical framework at the outset of the project. This book has introduced a selection of active critical frameworks for writing about cinema, offering an introduction to the ways in which scholars situate film as a political, industrial, cultural, and artistic object. These approaches to film analysis may frame film as a text, an event, or a set of practices (or some combination of these). When you encounter writing about cinema in any context, it is helpful to identify the writer's framework and the opportunities and limitations it entails. When you write about cinema, it is important to shape a critical framework that provides analytical opportunities that interest you (and to remain aware of the constraints of that framework).

Some writing assignments in cinema studies classes will specify a critical framework. For example, an assignment prompt may state: "Write an essay about the exhibition history of French cinema in New York City in the 1960s." The critical framework for this essay assignment – exhibition history – will involve specific research and writing methodologies. For example, the writer might search back issues of local newspapers and magazines for the screening schedules for local art house theatres, professional reviews, and interviews with French directors who traveled to New York to promote their films. In other words, the critical framework for the essay will shape its research agenda. This part of the chapter provides a brief (and by no means exhaustive) list of common critical frameworks for writing about cinema, and summaries of the defining concepts, questions and methodologies associated with each critical framework. This list is only a snapshot of some of the subfields within cinema studies, pointing to the diversity of scholarly approaches to analyzing cinema. Each approach presents opportunities and limitations for scholars.

Stardom

The analysis of national star systems or of individual star images can provide a critical foundation for an analysis of a single film or set of films. A scholar may isolate an individual star image as the basis for an analysis, discussing the ways in which that star image shapes or is shaped by the films. An analysis of stardom might involve the formal analysis of close-ups of the star, a review of tabloid images and articles featuring the star, a discussion of the use of the star's image in marketing campaigns, the close reading of interviews with the star or other documents with autobiographical information, a survey of film reviews that discuss the star's performances and a close reading of the star's performance style in key scenes.

Genres

Genres provide audiences with narrative codes that help them to anticipate and understand how a story will unfold, as discussed in Chapter 14, "Pleasure and desire." When a film is described with the genre labels of mystery, melodrama, action, comedy, horror, or romance (to name only a small sample of popular film genres), audiences enter the film with shared expectations about the film's characters, plot, and setting. The analysis of genres can be an important tool for scholars who want to understand how these genre codes shape both narrative structure and film reception. Genre analysis is particularly useful when comparing films transhistorically or transnationally, allowing scholars to track changes in genre codes over time and across national borders.

Global or transnational cinema

The terms "global cinema," "world cinema," and "transnational cinema" are sometimes used inter-changeably to describe the contemporary production and distribution of films across national borders. While patterns of economic globalization and the proliferation of new media have made global cinema a particularly relevant framework for understanding contemporary films, even early cinema involved international co-production agreements and the exporting of films across borders. Discussions of global cinema may address: co-production agreements, national film policies (including production subsidies and exhibition quotas), transnational adaptation and international stardom.

National cinemas

The transformed conditions of global film circulation have challenged the stability of national cinemas as both industrial formations and cultural institutions. In spite of the increasingly globalized circulation of films, national cinemas remain an important critical framework for understanding film history and film cultures, and important contributions to film scholarship continue to investigate national film industries. Many films circulate only within national or regional borders, and national film industries support the production and preservation of national film cultures. When analyzing a film through the perspective of a national film industry, scholars may situate the film with respect to: its conditions of production, including the involvement of privately owned studios, government institutions and subsidies, and local or regional organizations; its relationship to other films produced within the same production matrix; its reception within that national culture; its reception internationally; and regional and linguistic differences within national film industries.

Authorship

As discussed in Chapter 2, "Cinema as self-expression," authorship is an important framework for analyzing some films. Many scholars focus on authorship, identifying a single author for a film and investigating the creative agency of that author. Typically, the designated author is the director, but there are exceptions to this rule that focus instead on a screenwriter, an editor, a production designer, or even a star. Arguments about authorship, even those focused on a single film, usually involve a discussion of that author's entire filmography in order to establish stylistic patterns in evidence across the author's body of work. Discussions of authorship may analyze key scenes from the author's filmography, film reviews that cite the author's contributions to the films, interviews with the author and other documents where the author discusses his or her work, and production notes and other archival documents.

Exhibition and reception

Many of the critical approaches outlined above may limit their engagement with films to the film as a text (a relatively stable document that allows formal, narrative, and material modes of analysis). Some scholars move beyond these forms of textual analysis to engage with films as an event, analyzing conditions of exhibition and/or reception, as discussed in Chapter 11 "Exhibition" and Chapter 12 "Evaluative contexts". In other words, they investigate where, when and how particular films were exhibited to audiences and how those audiences responded to the films. These analyses may use archival and ethnographic methods to research theatres, film festivals, home exhibition technologies, box office statistics, and fan cultures. Studies of exhibition and reception can enliven our understanding of film history by capturing the historical, geographical, and cultural specificity of a particular instance of film exhibition and reception.

Marketing and distribution

The blossoming field of media industry studies has brought new attention to the importance of analyzing the business of film – from studio formations to governmental interventions, from distribution contracts to social media marketing strategies. Analyses of distribution and marketing often rely on primary documents, as examined in Chapter 9 "Marketing" and Chapter 10 "Distribution." Scholars may investigate distribution contracts, anti-piracy legislation, and film trailers and posters, among other documents. They also trace historical and emerging patterns of distribution – from the intrigues surrounding film patents and film reproduction during the early period of silent cinema to the informal distribution of film via digital piracy today. Analyses of distribution also involve the investigation of film festivals as distribution marketplaces and the shifting definitions of film as a commodity.

Ideology and representation

Some of the most urgent contributions to film studies explore the ideological underpinnings of films and examine the politics of the representation of race, gender, class, and sexuality in cinema. These analyses uncover the structures of identification that inform many screen representations, the social and political consequences of these representations, and opportunities for resistant reading. Discussions of representation often combine textual analysis (which may focus on visual style, genres, characters, or star images) with critical theory. Many discussions of film ideology involve inter-disciplinary research, bringing cinema studies into dialogue with the fields of literature, communications, gender and sexuality studies, anthropology, art history, and other fields. In fact, many important discussions of film ideology originate in other fields.

Technology

From the Kinetoscope to the mobile phone, technological innovations have impacted the presentation and reception of the filmic image. Investigations of film technology may focus on one of these devices, on one of the technological transformations of theatrical exhibition (for example, color film, sound, or widescreen cinema), or on the production of special effects (for example, CGI or 3D). The investigation of film technologies may involve an analysis of visual style, patents, special production units, exhibition history, and the reception of particular technological innovations and trends. Histories of film technology may dwell on the invention of cinema and its relationship to other technological and artistic forms, while investigations of contemporary issues in film technology often discuss the influence of media convergence and cinema's relationship to television and new media.

Aesthetics

Formal analysis may be a component of many of the critical approaches discussed above, or it may be the sole focus of a scholarly engagement with cinema. The analysis of cinematography, sound, editing, or *mise-en-scène* within a single film or across a set of films can yield important insights about film as an art form or about specific conditions of film production. This book's Interlude offers a detailed introduction to formal analysis and the language used to discuss film form.

While it will be helpful for you to identify the critical framework or frameworks that will anchor each essay you write and to familiarize yourself with the key works of scholarship in that field, it is also important to keep in mind that these frameworks are not fully independent from one another (or as internally coherent as the outlines above may suggest). Many of the examples of film scholarship that you will read (including many of those cited throughout this book) traverse several critical frameworks. The first essays that you write about film may have a less ambitious scope, but you will doubtless find that you will fuse several of the frameworks mentioned above in order to build your argument.

EXERCISE

Using a notebook or an online **concept-mapping** tool, brainstorm ideas for writing about a film that you have watched recently.

- Start by listing brief observations about the film.
- Then review these ideas and write a list of research questions in response.
- Then review those questions and draft a set of brief ideas or arguments.

As you build this web of possible points of entry into the film, you may start to notice that some of your initial observations have generated several different threads of ideas while others have not generated any. These long threads indicate the focus of your personal interest in the film and promising starting points for your research and analysis. Once you have identified these points, you can start a second concept map to focus on that set of ideas.

This **pre-writing** exercise should precede the formation of an argument. In fact, establishing a specific argument should not be an early goal for your writing process. When writers establish an argument prematurely, they often conduct their research and reading selectively, focusing only on those materials that support their argument and ignoring those materials that challenge it. If you are lucky enough to develop a working argument to guide your research during the concept mapping process, formulate that argument as a research question. This approach will allow you to preserve a degree of flexibility as you complete your research so that the argument you advance in your essay will be as comprehensive and as nuanced as possible.

Research

Once you have established a working research question for your essay, the next step is to begin (or if you have already gathered some preliminary information, to continue) your research. It is now a cliché to bemoan the impact of Wikipedia on academic research, particularly on academic research conducted by students. The crowdsourced online encyclopedia has been a source of both celebration and controversy. As a media artifact, Wikipedia can be a valuable location for information about how particular subjects are understood in the public imagination. It can also be a fine starting point for preliminary information about new and unfamiliar subjects. Wikipedia presents a problem for students and instructors alike when it is the sole destination for information about a particular topic rather than an opening maneuver. The best writing about cinema, like the best writing about any topic, usually draws from a rich bibliography of credible sources.

The best bibliographies involve both breadth and depth. In building a **bibliography** (a process that takes a lot of time), one should emphasize the development of a comprehensive array of sources from diverse locations. In this respect, Google can be a far more damaging site than Wikipedia. When writers rely on commercial search engines as their primary research tool, they limit their engagement with a subject to the sites selected by a capricious algorithm. Google – even Google Scholar – is not a scholar. The priority given to particular sites during searches all but guarantees that relevant and revealing materials about a particular topic will be buried so far down in the list of tens or hundreds or thousands of results that even the most determined writer will never find them.

Fortunately scholars have access to more precise and targeted **databases**. Many of these will be accessible via your university or college library. Students may have the privilege of being able to work with librarians to develop a research agenda for an essay, but many students do not exercise this privilege, preferring to rely instead on general online research. While it may be possible in some fields to avoid the library without compromising the quality of your scholarship, research in cinema studies benefits greatly from spending time in a library and taking advantage of the expertise of librarians. A library is both a place and a network of resources and practices, and librarians are the perfect guides to help you navigate these networks. The resources they introduce you to may include: subject-specific databases, library subscriptions to electronic journals and newspapers, and archives of print and digital materials.

Librarians may also help you to build a bibliography that includes a mix of print and digital sources, primary and secondary sources, and scholarly and popular materials. Your library may offer a long list of electronic databases and links to full-text online versions of book, articles and other resources. While the ease of conducting electronic research has made the research process more efficient for scholars in many fields, it is important to remember that there remain important resources that are only available in print versions. Many books are not available in electronic form; and many libraries have print editions of journals, newspapers, and magazines that have not been digitized. Enlisting a librarian's help to determine how your library's collection of print materials might enhance your research is a productive step to take at an early stage. A discovery you make in the print collection may become the focal point for your research.

Your research will likely include a mix of **primary** and **secondary sources**. The definitions of primary and secondary sources vary from discipline to discipline. Generally, primary sources include original documents or works, and secondary sources include interpretations and evaluations of primary sources. The classification of a source as primary or secondary is often a function of context. For the purposes of this brief overview, a series of examples of primary and secondary sources will clarify some of the differences between these two categories. Primary sources include: films, screenplays, interviews, patents, letters, photographs, works of art, and websites. Secondary sources include: scholarly books, journal articles, and newspaper and magazine articles. If you are writing about a single film, you may combine an analysis of primary sources (the film itself and the original screenplay) with an analysis of secondary sources (critical responses to the film by other scholars). The set of sources you review and the balance between primary and secondary sources will change based on the assignment.

Within the set of secondary sources you locate, you may find a mix of **scholarly** and **popular sources**. Scholarly sources, including books and peer-reviewed journals, provide an introduction to the information and conversations that have shaped research in a specific field and include citations that will lead you to other relevant sources for your research. Diana Hacker and Nancy Sommers highlight the central features that distinguish scholarly sources from popular sources:

> formal language and presentation, authors with academic or scientific credentials, footnotes or a bibliography documenting the works cited by the author in the source, original research and interpretation (rather than a summary of other people's work), quotations from and analysis of primary sources, and a description of research methods or a review of related research.[1]

Your research may also involve popular sources. Popular sources may feature a more accessible prose style. The popular sources you review for film research may include trade publications (periodicals like *Variety* that publish news and commentary about the film industry written by journalists and industry personnel), mass media publications (newspapers like the *International Herald Tribune*, where the film industry is covered as one of many topics discussed each day), or professional and amateur websites and blogs. While not all research about cinema requires both scholarly and popular sources, reading broadly will enrich your understanding of the research question you are exploring.

The types of sources that you include in your bibliography will be a function of the critical framework for your essay, but all bibliographies require the critical evaluation of sources. Not all of the sources that one discovers during the research process are relevant and reliable. You should frame your search to reduce the number of irrelevant and unreliable sources that you have to sort through to find the ones that are valuable to you. For example, using **Boolean operators** to narrow the results of an online search (either in a general search engine or in a specialized database) can make the research process much more efficient. Boolean operators are words or symbols that specify the relationships between your search terms. For example, using AND between two search terms narrows your search results to only those sources that include both terms. Directors may have a shoot to print ratio of 10:1, a pre-digital expression that compares the number of feet of film that a director shoots to the number of feet of film in the final cut. Writers may have a similar ratio for their research. You might read ten articles about a topic before you find one that introduces ideas or information that will help you to shape your argument. Making strategic decisions during the early stages of the research process may help you to shrink your ratio to a more Hitchcockian level. (Hitchcock was known for shooting exactly the amount of footage needed for the final cut of the film – leaving editors and studio executives with little editorial control!)

Once you have established a research agenda, the fun begins. While some of your research will likely include the print versions of books, scholarly journals, and newspapers and magazines, some of your research will be conducted online. The popularity of online research has changed some of the methods that scholars use to record information. In the past, many scholars embarked on their research projects armed with notebooks, index cards, pens, pencils, and highlighters. Many still do. Those scholars who love the physical interaction with the documents they are analyzing – for example, writing notes in the margins of books and highlighting key passages – have resisted the transition to online research. Over time, however, the methods for engaging in online research have mimicked many of these modes of material interaction. **Social bookmarking** sites enable scholars to bookmark online journal articles and other sites, to highlight passages, to write notes, and to share their research and their annotations with other scholars. One of the virtues of these sites is that they facilitate the gradual construction of research bibliographies over time. The research that a scholar conducts for one writing project may then become the foundation for a second writing project, with annotated versions of key articles cross-referenced in multiple folders, each devoted to a different research question or topic. This example of **remediation** combines useful elements of old media and new media in a user-friendly personal database that occupies much less shelf space than years of collected research notebooks.

No matter what method or tool you use, it is important to take notes during your research process. Research is not merely the collection of passages to quote in an essay. It is a series of interactions with various documents. The notes that you take during the research process will be the seeds of the essay you ultimately write. By taking notes that talk to the documents you are reading rather than about them, you will begin to develop the scholarly voice that will animate your essay.

EXERCISE

Conduct a week-long Google-free scavenger hunt for information about the film you used as the basis for the previous exercise. You will collect all of the items on the list below without using Google (or another general search engine). Instead you will use subject-specific databases and other library resources. To learn as much as possible about your film from as wide a variety of sources as possible, you should gather:

- a review from a major newspaper
- a review from a blog
- a scholarly article
- an article from a trade periodical
- a book
- an article from a tabloid
- a memoir
- a production still
- a print advertisement for the film
- an interview with the director or one of the film's stars
- the film's trailer
- an article about the film originally published in another language and translated into English
- a copy of the production budget.

FORMAL ANALYSIS

Many of the strategies for writing about cinema outlined above can be applied either directly or in a modified form to scholarly writing in other fields. Even students who feel confident about these research skills may remain overwhelmed by the prospect of writing about the filmic image. This book's Interlude introduces the vocabulary for describing film form and style. Practicing that vocabulary is one of the most important ways to prepare for writing a formal analysis of a film. Mastering these new terms cannot be accomplished through a simple program of memorization with index cards or other study tools (although that would certainly be a fine first step). It is also important to practice using these terms in context.

This part of the chapter discusses strategies for using the language introduced in the Interlude to produce original close readings of film form. It dwells solely on formal analysis because the other chapters in the book have modeled the other modes of analysis outlined in the set of critical frameworks above. For example, if you are interested in researching the preservation of amateur video, you might consult Chapter 2, "Cinema as self-expression" and Chapter 13, "The longevity of films" for discussions of amateur video production and film preservation respectively. Each chapter in this book investigates at least one critical framework for analyzing cinema and references and models the forms of analysis that define each framework. The section below complements the information introduced in the Interlude in order to add formal analysis to your stockpile of analytical strategies.

The key to formal analysis is multiple viewings. There is no quick substitute for the analytical discoveries enabled by watching a scene over and over again until you develop visual mastery of the scene. Fortunately for contemporary scholars, this process is far easier than it used to be. In his introduction to the second edition of his book *Film Hieroglyphs*, film scholar Tom Conley recalls the painstaking process that he used in order to produce the grainy film stills included in the book for its original publication in 1991:

> The pictures were shot from 16-millimeter copies of films of diverse provenance. Some were duplicates that had for some reason reached a public domain; others belonged to the Hennepin County public lending library; still others had come from distributors whose names (such as Kit Parker, Swank Pictures, and Blackhawk Films) have almost become history. Each and every one of the 16-millimeter prints had been run almost endlessly through the gates of three archaic projectors (a Kodak Pageant, found in a closet of the Department of French and Italian at the University of Minnesota; later, when the College of Liberal Arts made one available, a Kodak Athena; and, when all the other projectors failed, a portable Bell and Howell that could barely pull the film from one reel to the other). Each of the photograms was shot through a Duplikin lens, set on a bayonet mount of a 35-millimeter camera that reduced the scope of the original frame on the filmstrip. Daylight photography (mostly in the winter of Minnesota) required multiple takes of the same image at different shutter speeds and f-stops. The most adequate illustrations were chosen from a sizable number of photograms examined on contact sheets.[2]

Contrast this lengthy description of the process Conley used to produce still images from the films he was analyzing with the ease with which scholars today can create a screenshot from a film with a single click.

Technological innovations have expedited and streamlined not only the production of film stills but also the process of formal analysis. If you read an essay about a film written before the advent of VHS and its digital descendants and notice a factual error about the film – for example, an incorrect reference to a location, camera angle, or line of dialogue – keep in mind that the writer may have had only one opportunity to see the film – in a (possibly very crowded) theatre where they had no control over the viewing conditions (for example, a person talking in the row behind them throughout the film) and no opportunity to pause or rewind. Their analysis may have been based solely on this single, imperfect screening and any notes they may have taken. While there are some films, especially experimental films, that remain inaccessible to global audiences, the films that you will have an occasion to write about will likely be available in at least one new media format. You can buy or borrow a copy of the film and watch it as many times as you need to in order to analyze the frames and scenes that are central to your argument. It is vitally important to take advantage of this opportunity and to exploit all of the analytical possibilities of new media exhibition on the small screen.

Limiting your close reading of a scene to a single viewing (or even several viewings) will not produce a close reading at all. Formal analysis requires repetition. Rather than just watching the same scene over and over again without any variation, you should endeavor to schedule a series of viewings that focus on different elements of film form. By the end of this process, your screening notes will form a blueprint for a formal analysis. For a detailed set of guidelines for taking screening notes, see the boxed feature below.

GUIDELINES FOR TAKING SCREENING NOTES

Notetaking stages

- Divide your notetaking into three stages – pre-screening notes, screening notes, and post-screening notes.
- *Pre-screening notes*: Before the first screening, gather basic information about the film through online resources like the Internet Movie Database (www.imdb.com). Note the film's title, director, and year of release; the names of the central actors and the names of the characters they play; and basic information about the film's genre, setting, and plot. Recording this information in your notes before the screening will help you to get oriented more quickly when the film begins.
- *Screening notes*: Focus on a set of specific questions when you are watching the film – viewing questions you draft before the screening, observations or claims you encountered when reading a review of the film or one of the assigned readings for your class, or questions that emerged for you during another film screening that might be relevant. New questions and concerns may develop during the screening, but it will be helpful for you to approach the film with a set of questions defined in advance. In other words, you should have a clearly defined notetaking agenda when the film begins, but you should feel free to depart from that agenda if the film leads you in new directions.
- *Post-screening notes*: After the film screening (either immediately after the screening or the following day), you should review your notes. At this stage, some notetakers will transfer handwritten notes to their computers, fleshing out the skeletal framework of the original notes by reorganizing and developing the observations that were recorded. Other notetakers will keep the original handwritten notes and develop them by circling keywords, adding post-screening impressions of the film in the margins, and researching questions generated by the film. Many notetakers find it helpful to write a one-paragraph plot summary of the film or a one-paragraph review of the film to crystallize their impressions.

Formatting your notes

- *Use a notetaking format that fits your style as a viewer and a writer*: Some notetakers prepare lists in bullet point format. Others record their notes in outline form. Many notetakers use pre-screening viewing questions as an open, revisable document and record their answers to the questions within the document, generating lists or paragraph-length responses after some or all of the questions. Another approach involves dividing a notebook page into labeled quadrants and recording observations from the film in the appropriate quadrant. Any of these formats will generate a productive set of notes. Choose the format that corresponds to your style as a notetaker, and consider experimenting with different formats until you find one that works well for you.

Helpful hints

- *Screen the film in as many different exhibition contexts as possible*: It would be ideal for you to screen a film multiple times – with at least one screening in a theatrical setting with a large screen and several subsequent screenings. However, many students will watch the films from their classes only on small screens. When watching a film on a laptop or television screen, you can stop the film, rewind it and fast forward, and pause on a particular frame, allowing you to record precise information about the film and to isolate visual details that might escape the attention of other viewers. While it is vital to take advantage of the ways that small screen viewings enable close readings, you might consider screening a film first with a group of classmates and friends before beginning the work of close reading.
- *Choose your tools*: Find a system that works for you and outfit yourself with the right tools – an illuminated pen, a laptop, a small detective's notebook, index cards or another recording device. Do not assume that the tools that you use for taking notes in other classes will be the best tools for taking film notes.
- *Be yourself*: With rare exceptions, you are writing screening notes as a private resource, so write in a comfortable, informal style. Use arrows, diagrams, and even doodles. Develop a personal set of abbreviations for your notes (from cu=close-up to MB=Marlon Brando).
- *Do not record every detail of the film's action*: After the film ends, you will remember the action with more accuracy than you might imagine. In other words, you do not need to spend time writing down what happens in the film. Focus instead on recording your observations in response to a few key questions. Note the visual details, cinematographic strategies, or lines of dialogue that arrest your attention. Pay particular attention to the patterns that you notice.
- *Share your notes*: After you see a film in a theatre with friends, you will typically spend at least some time discussing your impressions of the movie and trading off-the-cuff reviews. For the scholarly analysis of film, it is equally important to share your impressions. While you will learn a lot by simply chatting with classmates after screenings, you should also consider exchanging film notes with a friend. You will discover details about the film from your friend's notes that escaped your attention, and your overall understanding of the film will almost always be enriched by these exchanges.

Given the fact that you will probably base your formal analysis of a film on a series of screenings on small screens, it is important to keep in mind that you are writing about one version of the film. Films are not stable texts. If you are writing about *Gravity* (Alfonso Cuarón, 2013) after watching it on your mobile phone, you will produce a very different formal analysis of the film than another writer who has watched the film multiple times in 3D in a crowded IMAX theatre. In general, particular exhibition contexts need not be overvalued, resulting in proclamations that you cannot analyze specific films unless you had the opportunity to see the film in its original exhibition format and context without any forms of interference.

The insistence on privileging some exhibition contexts over others has the (often intentional) effect of privileging the scholarship of people with access to museums, independent theatres, and festivals. It is important, however, to acknowledge the conditions of your access to a film either explicitly or implicitly when you write. If you are writing about *Gravity* after watching it on a miniature screen, your formal analysis should reflect on the ways that the miniaturization of the image impacts your experience of the film's unique spectacular appeals. All writers whose primary encounters with films are in new media formats must recognize that they are experiencing the films on a different scale and often with different visual qualities than the original version of the film (except, of course, for those films that are produced within new media formats). The pan-and-scan method of formatting films for VHS and television exhibition is one example of the ways that the film frame can be transformed as films move from venue to venue. While not all formal transformations are this obvious or egregious, it is to be expected that there will be at least minor differences as film migrates from format to format. Acknowledging these shifts within your writing will strengthen your analysis.

EXERCISE

Return to the film you researched in the previous exercise, and screen your favorite scene ten times in a row. Follow the guidelines below to shift the viewing conditions (and the analytical focus) of each screening. Take notes during each screening.

1 Watch the scene without any alterations.
2 Watch the scene with the volume muted.
3 Watch the scene with the director's commentary (if available).
4 Watch the scene with the volume muted again.
5 Watch the scene without any alterations.
6 Listen to the scene with the image covered or minimized on your screen.
7 Watch the scene without any alterations.
8 Watch the scene focusing only on one formal element – for example, costume design, lighting, or camera movement.
9 Watch the scene focusing again only on that formal element and with the volume muted.
10 Watch the scene without any alterations.

WRITING AS THINKING, WRITING AS CONVERSATION

Many writers enjoy everything about writing but the deadlines, and many writers respond to their anxiety about deadlines by procrastinating. For those writers who can become ensnared by procrastination, it is the act of writing the first sentence that is the most anxiety producing. Writers will describe their dread of staring at the blinking cursor on an empty screen. For some, they reason that they have more research and reading to do before they can begin writing their own essay. The research process thus becomes so ambitious and endless that the writing process never begins (or does not begin until the deadline is around the corner). For others, the research process has come to a close, but the pressure of finding the perfect opening has made it impossible to commit a sentence to the page or has led to an endless loop of writing and rewriting the introduction. The same piece of advice addresses both of these debilitating patterns: the best way to start writing is to start writing.

Too many writers conceptualize thinking and writing as two distinct processes, with thinking occupying their time during and immediately after the research process and writing beginning only after the process of thinking has been completed. The problem with this model is that it ignores two key facts. Firstly, one of the best ways to think through an analytical problem is to write. If you are having trouble grappling with a difficult passage in an essay or a confusing scene from a film or a complicated ideological argument, writing your way through your confusion may be the most productive approach. **Free writing** is a form of informal writing in which a writer will work through a tangle of ideas without any self-consciousness about form, style, or accuracy. Free writing is not a first draft. It is more preliminary and less binding than a first draft. Free writing is a form of thinking on the page. While you may generate prose during free writing that will ultimately find its way into the final draft of an essay, free writing may just as likely serve as little more than a way to move through an intellectual impasse. By waiting until after your thinking has crystallized into a well-honed argument before writing, many writers miss an opportunity to think *through* writing. Secondly, the separation of thinking and writing into two separate processes does not allow for the transformation of your ideas during the writing process. Good writing is a dynamic process that may involve multiple revisions to your initial ideas. Even the most experienced writers produce multiple drafts before they hone their ideas into clear and compelling prose. By bracketing off the process of thinking as something that ends when writing begins, writers may limit the potential of their own work.

EXERCISE

At an early stage in your writing process, set aside one hour for "free writing." Eliminate all possible interruptions: find a quiet and private place to write, turn the ringer on your phone off (not to vibrate – off!), log off all internet applications, and clear all possible distractions from your desk and your computer's desktop. Set an alarm for one hour from your start time and write for the entire hour. Do not pause to think, to compose sentences in your mind, or to read what you have written so far. Just write, write and keep writing until you hear the alarm. Write as if you are being paid by the word. When the alarm goes off, stop writing, take a break (check your messages and reconnect with the virtual world!), and then read what you have written and reflect on how the ideas you have recorded might inform your essay.

One important tool for uniting the processes of thinking and writing is a working **outline**. In order to be a manageable resource, an outline for an essay should be no more than one or two pages long. The work of drafting an outline can begin during the research process as you start to map the system of ideas that you will introduce in your essay. There are many formats for writing outlines, but the following features distinguish productive outlines:

1   A specific idea for the essay's introduction rather than simply the word "introduction."
2   The presentation of major ideas and arguments in the order in which they will appear in the essay.
3   The notation of key supporting evidence and details for each major idea listed in the order in which they will appear.
4   The notation of when special elements of the essay will be introduced – for example, an image or a chart.
5   A specific idea for the essay's conclusion rather than simply the word "conclusion."

A working outline is a flexible document. As your plans for your essay change, you should revise your working outline to reflect those changes. During the writing process, it is often easier to revise an outline than it is to revise the draft of an essay. Since an essay draft can be many pages long, it can be overwhelming to sift through those pages to identify the sections that need to be revised. The brevity and visual simplicity of a working outline make it easy to identify changes that need to be made. After you have revised the working outline, you can make the necessary changes to the essay draft. It will be much easier to make the essay revisions once you have revised the outline.

Revision is a crucial element of the writing process. Revisions should inform every stage of writing – from the revisions you make to your screening notes after the screening ends to the revisions that you make to your working outline to the revisions that you make to the late drafts of the essay before completing the final draft. Once you have a complete draft of your essay, you should use the following strategies to revise it.

Revise your essay by hand

Many writers are comfortable editing their work on the screen. Word processing tools that automatically check for grammatical and mechanical errors may make that process even easier (although they notoriously miss and generate important errors). It is, however, very productive to take the time to print a draft (ideally, every draft) of your essay and to make **hand revisions** as you read through your essay. When revising early drafts, focus more on big picture issues like the clarity of your argument, the organization of your ideas, and the introduction of evidence. Identify moments in the essay when you should cut a passage and move it to a different location, add textual evidence drawn from your screening notes, or clarify your use of a key term. When revising later drafts, sharpen your focus to close-up issues like spelling errors, missing details about cited films, and the proper formatting of quoted passages. It can be inefficient to focus on these issues when editing early drafts since you may labor over the perfect expression of sentences that ultimately end up on the cutting room floor, or you may resist cutting these sentences later because of the time you invested in crafting them even if they detract from your argument.

Revise as many successive drafts by hand as your writing timeline allows. Adopt a set of hand revision practices – a particular pen or a notation style – that works well for you. Consider shifting the work of hand revision to a different environment from the place where you typically write – for example, a café instead of the library. Sometimes a subtle shift of location will allow you to see your work with fresh eyes so that you can notice major and minor problems. In a similar spirit, it is ideal to take a break between writing and revising. If your schedule permits, wait until the day after you complete a draft before turning to the task of revision. That time off will have the same effect as the change of location – allowing you to see your own work from a critical distance. Like many of the practical strategies outlined in this chapter, this guideline is much easier to follow if you write your essay over a leisurely period of time rather than waiting until the last minute. Even if you are facing a deadline that is only hours away, however, set aside time to hand revise at least one draft of your essay before committing to a final draft.

Share your essay with other people

Even the writers who are the most devoted to careful revision over a number of drafts find the interventions of other readers to be invaluable. Everyone writes for a public, even if that public is only the individual who will read and grade your essay. It is productive to approach writing as a dialogue from the beginning of your writing process. Identify one or two students who are good readers and good writers and ask them to swap essay drafts with you. If you have particular concerns about your draft, let them know, and ask them for specific feedback about those concerns in addition to their feedback about other issues they may notice. Other readers will often catch problems that escaped your attention because you are too intimately tied to your prose. They may also propose efficient and elegant solutions to analytical and rhetorical problems that had not occurred to you and that will save you a lot of time as you enter the final phase of writing.

Serving as an editor for a friend or colleague's work often benefits your writing too. You may notice issues in their writing that also plague your own writing but that were less apparent to you when reviewing your own work. You may also be inspired by the strengths of their writing – a description of a scene from a film filled with finely detailed observations about visual style that leads you to want to rewatch the film or an exegesis of a complicated passage from a theoretical text that enhances your understanding of the theorist's argument. These moments of recognizing good prose will strengthen your writing, sometimes by suggesting stylistic or organizational strategies that you can emulate in your work, and sometimes simply by giving you renewed enthusiasm for writing about cinema.

Sharing your work with other people on a regular basis will also remind you that scholarly writing is at its best part of an ongoing set of conversations. When you write an essay about cinema, you are not reflecting on a film or a set of films in isolation but entering into a conversation with other scholars who are interested in the same ideas, problems and possibilities that have shaped your work. When you cite the work of these scholars, you are not only acknowledging the importance of their scholarship for the development of your ideas but also actively building on the intellectual foundations they have established. While few students have opportunities to publish their essays, it may be helpful to imagine a specific publication venue for each essay that you write. As you read more and more scholarly journals, you will begin to notice that each journal has a focus and style. Select a journal that seems like a good fit for your essay based on its critical framework and focus, and keep that journal's audience and style in mind as you write. Design your essay as a contribution to a conversation, responding to the work that preceded yours and inviting responses from the people who read your work.

EXERCISE

Write a proposal or pitch for an essay. Your proposal should be less than 300 words. Explain what the focus of your essay will be, the central argument that your essay will advance, the central texts that your essay will analyze, and the critical frameworks that you will use.

- Your proposal should answer three central questions: What? So what? How? What will your essay argue? Why is your argument important? How will your essay develop your argument?
- As you prepare your proposal, define a specific hypothetical publication venue for the article. Defining a publication context will help you to refine the focus, tone, and style of your essay and your proposal by linking your writing project to a specific audience and a distinct (and reviewable) set of writing practices and styles.
- Once you have finished your proposal, share it with another student and ask for their feedback. Enlisting outside readers at this early stage will encourage you to revise your work at every stage throughout the writing process and may help you to uncover weaknesses in your approach or discover new directions for your work before you commit too much time and energy to your initial plan.

SUMMARY

Writing about cinema may at first seem like a daunting task, but over time you will discover that writing about cinema can be a pleasure rather than a chore. Time is the key term in this assertion. Most of the strategies for learning to write about cinema involve a considerable investment of your time. Aspiring writers should first commit to reading about cinema, immersing themselves in film culture by reading reviews, memoirs, newspapers, and scholarly articles – as many different forms of writing about cinema as their schedules allow. Good writers are good readers. When preparing to write a specific essay, writers should first define a critical framework for their essay (often merging elements of two or more critical frameworks). With this framework in place, writers should begin the research process by making full use of available library resources. Every stage of the writing process should involve revision. Feedback from colleagues is a key element of revision, drawing attention to under-developed areas of an essay that might otherwise escape a writer's attention. Involving colleagues as editors and interlocutors also foregrounds the importance of both imagining a specific audience for each essay and framing each essay as part of an ongoing scholarly conversation.

FURTHER READING

Corrigan, Timothy. *A Short Guide to Writing about Film*. New York: Longman, 2010.

This brief reference book provides valuable overviews of the types of essay that students may have an opportunity to produce (the screening report, the movie review, the theoretical essay, and the critical essay), including sample student essays. It includes strategies for taking notes during film screenings, and a helpful list of print and online resources for film studies research. Corrigan's discussion demystifies the process of writing about cinema and offers concrete examples of writing about cinema for students to review.

Graff, Gerald and Birkenstein, Cathy. *They Say, I Say: The Moves that Matter in Academic Writing*. New York: W.W. Norton & Co, 2010.

This is a book that you can read in one day and then return to whenever you need guidance about how to situate yourself as a scholar in relation to your topic and to the other scholars who have written about it. *They Say, I Say* introduces practical strategies for entering into an academic conversation through essay writing. The authors explain how to summarize and quote the scholarly sources that you cite in your essays and how to develop your own critical voice as you discuss the contributions of those sources.

Hacker, Diana and Sommers, Nancy. *A Pocket Style Manual*. Boston: Bedford/St. Martin's, 2012.

While many details about the mechanics of writing may be found online in various style guides, many writers find a print version of a style manual to be an invaluable resource. This slim volume includes only the most relevant information, with sections devoted to clarity, grammar, punctuation and mechanics, research, and usage/grammatical terms. This well-organized, easily searchable and very portable book should accompany you wherever you decide to write, and you should consult it for guidance whenever you are in doubt about how to cite a blog, where to place a semicolon, or any of the other questions that might surface during the writing process.

FILMS REFERENCED IN "WRITING ABOUT CINEMA"

Gravity (Alfonso Cuarón, 2013)

The Red Badge of Courage (John Huston, 1951)

NOTES

1 Diana Hacker and Nancy Sommers, *A Pocket Style Manual* (Boston: Bedford/St. Martin's, 2012), 95.

2 Tom Conley, *Film Hieroglyphs* (Minneapolis: University of Minnesota Press, 2006), xvi.

INDEX

References in *italic* refer to illustrations

Transformers toy line 281
translation 460, 461, 468–75; costs 469
translators 271
transnationalism 138, 141, 148, 175, 229, 492
transportation coordinator 260
Transylvania County, North Carolina 426
Trepkowski, Tadeusz 288
Treut, Monika 43
Triads 472
Trice, Jasmine Nadua 309
Trick Brothers Studio 203
trickle-down effect 140
Tricontinental 111
Trier, Lars von 282
Trinh T. Minh Ha 48, 80
Trip to the Moon 320
TriStar Pictures 300
Triumph of the Will 61, 74, *75*, 76, 97, *240*
Trnka, Jiří 202
Troche, Rose 455
Tropa de Elite 320–1, *321*
True Grit (1969 and 2010 versions) 281
Truffaut, François 34, 36; "A Certain Tendency of the French Cinema" 32–4
"Truthers" 112
Tryon, Chuck, *Reinventing Cinema: Movies in the Age of Media Convergence* 423
Tsotsi 171, 177
Tunisia 22, 426–7, *427*
Turkey 159, 198
Turkmenistan 214
Turku 345
Turner, Lana 12, 419
"Tuskegee Airmen" 273
12.08 East of Budapest 305
20th Century Fox 78, 134, 164, 299, 309
Twenty Years of African Cinema 177
28 Days Later 21
Twenty-Year-Old Youth 109
Twilight Saga series 167, *168*, 424, 478
Twitter 53, 291, 292, 301, 410
Two Women 280
2 or 3 Things I Know About Her 47
2001: A Space Odyssey 236, *237*, 366
typage 239–40
typecasting 223, *223*
Týrlová, Hermína 202

Ubu 317
Ubuweb 374, 391–2, 393

Ucicky, Gustav 100
UFA 101, 394, 396
Uganda 176, 279, 306
Ullmann, Liv *35*
Ultimate New York Body Plan 90
Ultimate Risk 23, *23*
Uman, Naomi 479, 480
Uncle Boonmee Who Can Recall His Past Lives 283
underlighting 237
"Underneath the Arches" 76
Underworld 194
unemployment 225, 226, 231
UNESCO 145–6, 148, 320; distribution statistics 303–5, 306; General Conference 146
unionization 227–8, 231
unit manager 260
unit production 190–1
United Artists 132, 308
United Kingdom 66, 76, 81, 156, 162, 177, 192, 359; early films 378; as market 306, 307; periodicals 365
United Nations 145, 312; International Fund for Agricultural Development 279
United States of America 36–9, 43, 50, 61, 76, 81–3, 91, 95, 137; and China 129–30; Civil War 480; domestic market 192; dominance 141; Film Office 61; foreign films shown in 145; gay and lesbian life in 110–11; Library of Congress 391; Library of Congress Copyright Office 378, *379*; Library of Congress Digital Millennium Copyright Acts hearings 480–1; as market 306, 307; and Marshall Plan 145; Navy, Special Warfare Command 97; picture palaces 338; posters in 287–8; resistance to subtitling 271; Supreme Court 133, 465; trade policy 147; and UNESCO 146; and WTO 142–3; *see also* Hollywood
unity of style 393
Universal Pictures 137, 299
Universal Studios 21, 132, 166, 197, 261, 292, 309, 472; theme park, Florida *21*
universities 490
The Untouchables 425
Up 255, 282
USAID (United States Agency for International Development) 205
user-created content 60

Valenti, Jack 147, 463
Vallejo, Gerardo 112
value 377
The Vampire Women 161
Van Dyke, Willard 61, 66, 81, 82, 83
Van Gogh 49
Vanilla Sky 159
Vantaa 345
Varda, Agnès 42, 85–6, *86*
Variety 302, 442, 491, 497
Variety Stage collection 378
vaudeville theatres 338
Vendetta 352
Venezuela 299
Venice Film Festival 358, 360
Venturi, Osvaldo 289, *289*
vertical integration 133, 148, 155, 164, 186, 203, 206, 211, 307
Vertigo 288, *288*, 290, *357*, 366, 367, 374
Vertov, Dziga 70, 254
VGIK (All-Union State Institute of Cinematography, later Gerasimov Institute of Cinematography) (Russia) 212, 213–14, *213*
VHS 332, 477, 478, 499, 502
Viacom 299
Vicky Cristina Barcelona 416
video 66–7, 89–90, 112, 257, 282; analogue 386; stores 309
video clips 351
video games 137, 274, 290
video-films (VCDs) 16; *see also* Nigeria, video-films (VCDs)
video-on-demand 301, 311, 318
videohome market 317
videos of affinity 318–19
vids, vidding 477–9
Vietnam 80, 85, 143, 345, 379; cinema 48, 194
Vietnam War 41, 83
Vijay *450*
Village Voice 354, 367
Vimeo 112, 212
Vine 53
violence in movies 287, 352, 403, 412, 414, 461
Viollet-le-Duc, Eugène 393
viral video 59, 318
Virgin Machine 43
The Virgin Queen 106
Visconti, Luchino 30
visual effects 258
Vitaphone 329
I Vitelloni (*Los Inutiles*) 289, *289*
¡Vivan las Antipodas! 352